Magic, Witchcraft, and Religion

Magic, Witchcraft, and Religion

An Anthropological Study of the Supernatural

Fifth Edition

Arthur C. Lehmann and James E. Myers

California State University, Chico

Boston   Burr Ridge, IL   Dubuque, IA   Madison, WI   New York   San Francisco   St. Louis
Bangkok   Bogotá   Caracas   Kuala Lumpur   Lisbon   London   Madrid   Mexico City
Milan   Montreal   New Delhi   Santiago   Seoul   Singapore   Sydney   Taipei   Toronto

McGraw-Hill Higher Education ⚛

*A Division of The **McGraw-Hill** Companies*

MAGIC, WITCHCRAFT, AND RELIGION, FIFTH EDITION

Published by McGraw-Hill, a business unit of The McGraw-Hill Companies, Inc., 1221 Avenue of the Americas, New York, NY, 10020. Copyright © 2001, 1997, 1993, 1989, 1985 by The McGraw-Hill Companies, Inc. All rights reserved. No part of this publication may be reproduced or distributed in any form or by any means, or stored in a database or retrieval system, without the prior written consent of The McGraw-Hill Companies, Inc., including, but not limited to, in any network or other electronic storage or transmission, or broadcase for distance learning.
Some ancillaries, including electronic and print components, may not be available to customers outside the United States.

This book is printed on acid-free paper.

5 6 7 8 9 0   MAL/MAL   0 9 8 7 6 5 4 3

ISBN 0-7674-1692-9

Library of Congress Cataloging-in-Publication Data
Magic, witchcraft, and religion : an anthropological study of the supernatural / [compiled by] Arthur C. Lehmann and James E. Myers. — 5th ed.
    p. cm.
  Includes bibliographical references and index.
  ISBN 0-7674-1692-9
  1. Religion. 2. Occultism. I. Lehmann, Arthur C. II. Myers, James E. (James Edward).
BL50.M26 2000
291—dc21   00-026306

Cover: Waterhouse, John William. 1886. *The Magic Circle.* Tate Gallery, London/ Art Resource, NY

Sponsoring editor, Janet M. Beatty; production, Penmarin Books; manuscript editor, Jennifer Gordon; design manager, Glenda King; illustrator (masks), Betty Armstrong; cover designer, Diana Coe; print buyer, Danielle Javier. The text was set in 9/11 Palatino by TBH Typecast, Inc., and printed on 45# Highland Plus by Malloy Lithographing, Inc.

www.mhhe.com

In Memoriam

Arthur Lehmann, my dear friend and co-author of this book, died of lung cancer at his home in Chico, California, in September, 1999. Although dreadfully weakened by his disease, Art insisted on maintaining active involvement in the fifth edition of *Magic, Witchcraft, and Religion*. Indeed, just weeks prior to his death we worked several days at the university library agonizing over the final selection of articles to be either added or deleted in the new revision.

Throughout his long battle with cancer, Art was somehow able to keep his wonderful high spirits and *joie de vivre*. Art was revered on campus for his intellect, wit, and devotion to students and the discipline of anthropology. Blessed with a gift of blarney and love of people, he was also a favorite of the larger campus community. A short walk to the library from the anthropology building always turned into a time-consuming social trek, as Art found it necessary to hail every passing groundskeeper, maintenance person, or staff member—all of whom addressed him fondly as "Art"—and exchange bawdy jokes or the latest campus gossip.

Art's great sadness during the last months of his life was the realization that he would not be returning to Central African Republic to continue his longtime research with Pygmies.

Art is survived by his wife, Sharon, and his son, Jonathan. We all miss him terribly.

James E. Myers

Foreword

It has often been remarked that the challenge to anthropologists, as well as their opportunity, is to show the familiar in the strange and the strange in the familiar. Nowhere in anthropology are that challenge and opportunity more present than in the comparative study of religion. It is our task as anthropologists to encounter, study, record, understand, and interpret the social practices and cultural patterns of human groups, wherever and whenever they have gathered—from the Arctic to the tropics; from Neanderthal times to the present. We have thus brought together in our literature a vast collection of religious beliefs and practices, many of which may seem strange indeed to twentieth-century North Americans. Yet if we bring these beliefs and practices wisely under anthropological focus, as Professors Lehmann and Myers have done in this reader, they will be seen to be strangely familiar. They are beliefs, we discover, that under other circumstances we might have believed ourselves. They are ritual practices, we see, that we might have engaged in, as, often enough, did our own ancestors. In these beliefs and practices we come to recognize needs, desires, appetites, and satisfactions ultimately characteristic of all human experience.

It is not enough, then, to study strange practices unless that study somehow enables us to gain perspective on our own way of life—to understand better because we see as from a distance. That is what is meant by seeing the strange in the familiar. Anthropology, by taking us out to dwell, if only momentarily, among unfamiliar practices elsewhere, should by that act alone give us perspective on our own lifeways when we return. It is the particular virtue of this collection of readings, however, to give a convincing additional twist to the distancing we obtain from contemplating strange religious practices elsewhere in the world: The editors have included in each section studies of practices taking place in modern Western societies today, mostly in North America. They show us the "strange" not only in exotic circumstances but also in a society with which we are extremely familiar. Although we may not always be familiar with the specific behavior described—the health food movement or contemporary Satanism, for example—the fact that such beliefs and practices are active among us today underscores the continuing relevance and vitality of the anthropological study of religion, wherever it is conducted. The religious impulse, with all its variegated manifestations, remains at work even in the so-called secular societies of present-day North America.

Why, especially, should we want to make the strange familiar and the familiar strange? What can we gain from the added perspective achieved by seeing ourselves as from a distance? At least three answers may be given to this question: tolerance, diversity, and adaptability. We now live in an increasingly interdependent world in which we are constantly being brought into contact with the strange and with strangers. Order in such a world demands an increased tolerance for lifeways that are strange to us. Moreover, familiarity with the exotic not only creates respect for, but may also help preserve, an enlivening diversity in the world, rather than the homogenized, consumption-oriented, worldwide popular culture toward which we seem to be irrevocably moving. A homogenized world culture gives us a much less interesting world in which to live. Finally, an increased perspective on our own beliefs and practices (which is not incompatible with continuing satisfaction in them) helps us avoid inert or fanatical overcommitment to them. (This is particularly the case with religious practices, which have so often been attended by intolerance, if not fanaticism.) The hallmark of the human career as compared with that of other creatures has been our adaptability: our ability to change our lifeways to fit into many diverse environments and to respond quickly and effectively to the challenge of changing circumstances. The maintenance of a balanced perspective on our own beliefs and practices—the avoidance of overcommitment to them because we have come to see them as strange in their own way —is part and parcel of our adaptability, our readiness to meet and master changing circumstances.

Beyond these values of tolerance, diversity, and adaptability that can emerge from the study of comparative religion lies the fact of religion itself. Religion is a human universal: It is found in every culture known to anthropologists, in a great diversity and variety of forms of expression. No reader who embarks on an attentive reading of this rewarding selection of articles can fail to recognize the human creativity that lies in this diversity. Nor can he or she fail to recognize the particular power through which religion enables men and women to speak to and cope with the ultimate circumstances of human life: injustice, unpredictability, suffering, death. An attentive reading, then, will offer insight both into what makes us human and into some of the more effective ways we have of battling that frail humanity. Such insight and understanding are a main object of anthropological study of any aspect of culture, but the study of religion has been particularly rewarding in this respect. The anthropological study of comparative religion stretches out to embrace diversity, as does this collection of readings. It stretches out to diversity to try to show us not only what being human is but what it might be.

James W. Fernandez
University of Chicago

Preface

We designed this reader to reach a broad spectrum of students and to demonstrate a comparative approach to the major elements and categories of religion. The volume provides teachers and students with contemporary, provocative readings on both non-Western and Western subjects. These readings allow students not only to investigate their own religious belief systems but also to compare those systems with others outside their culture. We believe this text thus illustrates the importance of understanding religion in our own culture as well as in those of the non-Western world. Primarily designed to reach undergraduate students, it is appropriate as a supplemental reader for graduate students as well.

In preparing this volume, we carefully searched through the literature of comparative religion, sociology, psychology, and anthropology, intensively screening hundreds of articles on the basis of their readability, academic quality and level, topical interest, and subject matter (including geographical and cultural area). Our overall goal was to achieve a final collection that would introduce students to the main topics in the study of magic, witchcraft, and religion, while at the same time introducing them to the major ethnographic areas of the world. Although the book does center on the non-Western world, we placed in each chapter at least one article from contemporary Western culture, both to increase students' interest and to heighten their cross-cultural perspective.

Using the recommendations of students and the evaluations and suggestions of faculty from various universities who have taught a similar course over the years, we narrowed the field to the existing selections, which are organized topically into ten chapters: (1) the anthropological study of religion; (2) myth, ritual, symbolism, and taboo; (3) shamans, priests, and prophets; (4) the religious use of drugs; (5) ethnomedicine (religion and healing); (6) witchcraft and sorcery; (7) demons, exorcism, divination, and magic; (8) ghosts, souls, and ancestors (power of the dead); (9) old and new religions (the search for salvation); and (10) the occult (paths to the unknown).

Features

Based on responses from users of the past four editions, we have made some substantive changes in this edition, but we've retained the features that have been well received in the earlier editions:

• With the wealth of good classic and contemporary articles to choose from, and the proven usefulness of so many of the anthologized pieces, selecting the articles was no easy task, even with abundant good feedback in hand from users and reviewers. After making some hard choices, we've added ten selections and deleted ten, keeping the total number of readings at fifty-six.

• The content of the selections not only covers every major traditional topic in comparative religion, but also features separate chapters on the religious use of drugs, old and new religions, ethnomedicine, and the occult.

• Although the majority of the articles are contemporary pieces, classic readings by Victor

Turner, Claude Lévi-Strauss, Bronislaw Malinowski, Anthony F. C. Wallace, E. E. Evans-Pritchard, J. S. Slotkin, and Edmund Leach are also included.

• The selections were chosen specifically for students on the basis of compelling subject matter and readability.

• The readings represent a broad sample of the world's geographic areas and economic levels.

• To help readers get their geographic bearings, we've included a frontispiece map that pinpoints principal societies and locations cited in the articles.

• An introduction to each chapter presents a historical and theoretical overview of the major topics that follow, thus providing students with a framework for understanding the contemporary importance of the subject.

•Each selection is preceded by an introduction that draws out the main theoretical and substantive points in the work.

• A comprehensive glossary of terms, an extensive index of subjects, authors, and titles, and a complete bibliography offer students further help.

• To help busy instructors, we've prepared a test bank that contains short-answer and multiple-choice questions for all of the articles.

Acknowledgments

A number of people contributed significantly to the preparation and development of this volume. We acknowledge with thanks the comments and suggestions made by the following reviewers of the fifth edition: David Beriss, University of New Orleans; Anne Chambers, Southern Oregon University; Leslie G. Desmangles, Trinity College; Katherine Donahue, Plymouth State College; Douglas Hayward, Biola University; Winifred Mitchell, Minnesota State University—Mankato; and Phillips Stevens, Jr., SUNY Buffalo.

In addition, we thank Frank Graham for encouraging us to write the first edition, Jan Beatty for expertly guiding us through the subsequent editions, Hal Lockwood for bringing this edition smoothly through production, and Jennifer Gordon for a thoughtful editing of the final draft.

A.C.L.
J.E.M.

Contents

10

The Occult:
Paths to the
Unknown 381

This book is dedicated to Arthur.

Principal Societies and Locations
Featured in this Book

Eskimo

Nevada

Navajo

San Diego

Waco

New York City

West Virginia

Jamaica

Maya

Haiti

Jivaro

Aguaruna

Bolivia

Aka Pygmies and

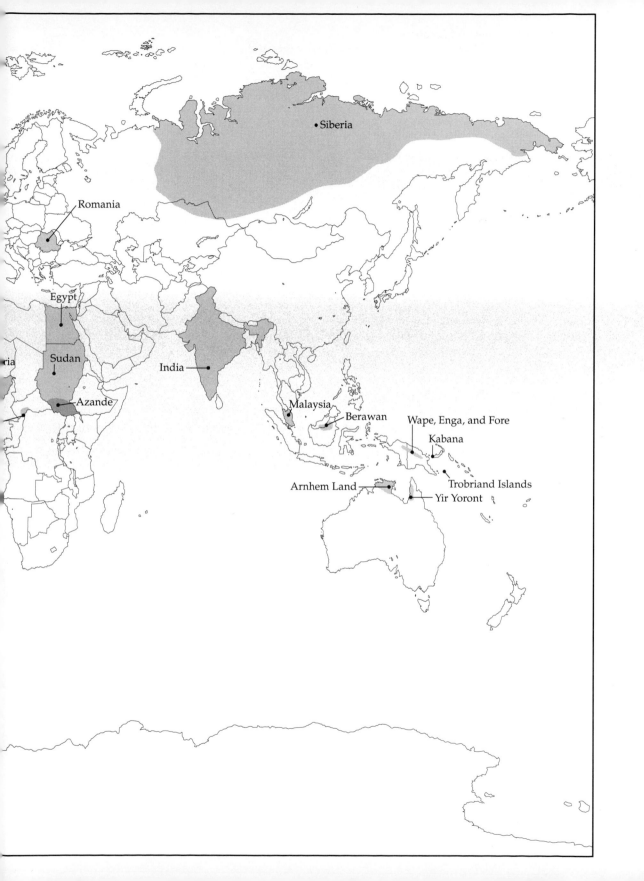

Magic, Witchcraft, and Religion

1

The Anthropological Study of Religion

Anthropologists have always been interested in the origins of religion, although the lack of both written records and archaeological evidence has made the subject speculative. It is reasonable to assume, however, that religion, like material culture, has a prehistory. Surely, uncertainty and change have always existed, exposing people in all ages to real and imagined threats and anxieties. The human animal alone senses a pattern behind the facts of existence and worries about life here and in the hereafter. We are born, we live, and we die. And although this is true of other animals, only humans are aware of the precariousness of life and the inevitability of death. As William Howells has observed, "Man's life is hard, very hard. And he knows it, poor soul; that is the vital thing. He knows that he is forever confronted with the Four Horsemen—death, famine, disease, and the malice of other men" (1962: 16).

The earliest surviving anthropological evidence of humans possibly expressing these concerns through religious practices dates from the era of *Homo sapiens neanderthalensis*, approximately a hundred thousand years ago. Because the Neanderthals buried their dead with tools, weapons, and other funerary objects, many

Buffalo mask of the Bobo, Upper Volta.

anthropologists have held that they were the first humans to believe in an afterlife of some sort. The era of *Homo sapiens sapiens* (modern man in the biological sense), approximately thirty thousand years ago, has yielded increasing evidence of religious beliefs—more elaborate burials, carved figurines ("Venuses"), and magnificent cave art. And during the Neolithic period, which began about ten thousand years ago, burials indicate a deep respect for the power of the dead. It is likely that during this period, which is marked by the cultivation of crops and the domestication of animals, cycles of nature became an important feature of magic and religious beliefs. Drought, storms, and other natural perils of the farmer could have created a growing dependence on supernatural powers.

The antiquity of religion indirectly testifies to its utility; however, the usefulness of supernaturalism to contemporary societies is a clearer, more provable demonstration of its functions. The many forms of adversity facing individuals and groups require explanation and action; we are unwilling to let challenges to health, safety, and salvation go unchecked. Just as adversity is universal, so too is the use of religion as an explanation for and solution to adversity. Although the form religion takes is as diverse as its practitioners, all religions seek to answer questions that cannot be explained in terms of objective knowledge—to permit people reasonable explanations for often unreasonable events and phenomena by demonstrating a cause-and-effect relationship between the supernatural and the human condition. This may be its most important function.

In his article "Religion: Problems of Definition and Explanation" (1966: 109–17), Melford E. Spiro has distinguished three sets of basic desires (cognitive, substantive, and expressive), each of which is satisfied by a corresponding function of religion (adjustive, adaptive, and integrative). Spiro's first and second functions are basically those of explanation and solution: the adjustive function of religion, as he defines it, is to satisfy the cognitive desires we experience as we attempt to understand what goes on around us (illness, natural phenomena); the adaptive function seeks to satisfy substantive desires (the desire for rain, or for victory in war). In his third category, however, Spiro moves to different territory: the often unconscious, expressive desires made up of what Spiro calls painful drives and painful motives.

According to Spiro, painful drives are anxieties concerning infantile and primitive fears (fears of destruction or of one's own destructiveness). Painful motives are culturally forbidden—for example, types of aggressive or sexual behavior that result in feelings of shame, inadequacy, and moral anxiety. Because of the pain they create in an individual, these drives and motives are usually relegated to the unconscious, where, "in the absence of other, or of more efficient means," religion becomes the vehicle "by which, symbolically, they can be handled and expressed." Thus, in what Spiro calls the integrative function of supernaturalism, "religious belief and ritual provide the content for culturally constituted projective mechanisms by which unconscious fears and anxieties may be reduced and repressed motives may be satisfied" (1966: 115).

Over the years, scholars have taken several approaches in their attempts to understand the reasons for the existence of religious behavior. The most prominent of these approaches are psychological, sociological, and anthropological. Spiro's belief that religious behavior serves to reduce unconscious fears typifies the psychological approach, which, briefly stated, sees religion as functioning to reduce anxiety. For example, the famous British social anthropologist Bronislaw Malinowski held that the proper use of religious rites reduced anxieties brought on by crisis. (Like all theorists who apply the psychological approach, Freud also believed that religion and ritual functioned to reduce anxieties, but, unlike others, he saw religion as a neurotic need that humans would eventually outgrow.) In contrast, the sociological viewpoint stresses the societal origins of religion. The French sociologist Emile Durkheim, for example, viewed religion as a manifestation of social solidarity and collective beliefs. According to Durkheim, members of society create religious objects, rituals, beliefs, and symbols in order to integrate their cultures. A. R. Radcliffe-Brown, a British social anthropologist, agreed with Durkheim that participation in annual religious rites functioned to increase social solidarity.

Although their functional analyses of religious behavior and phenomena do explain, in part, the universality of religion, neither the psychological nor the sociological theorists adequately provide answers to the origin of religion. Both approaches are too limited in focus, centered as they are on human emotions and social structure respectively;

neither explores the wide variety of cultural expressions of religion. Because religious experience, wherever it is observed, displays such great variation of cognitive and phenomenal expression, anything less than a wide-ranging holistic approach would not allow true comparisons; as a result, generalizations about the nature of religious systems would be incomplete as well as inaccurate.

The third, the anthropological approach to the study of religion, is by its very nature holistic, combining not only sociological and psychological, but historical, semantic, and evolutionary perspectives as well. Anthropologists today attempt to go beyond the observable to the analysis of symbolic forms. In order to make generalizations on pan-human religious behavior, symbology, and ideology, however, anthropologists must work from the common basis of a definition of religion. Without an acceptable and accurate definition, anthropologists would be unable to establish a common basis for comparison of religions cross-culturally.

Many definitions of religion have been generated by anthropologists. Edward B. Tylor, the father of modern anthropology, described religion as the belief in spiritual beings, what he called "animism," the most primitive form of religion. At the opposite extreme from Tylor's open-ended definition, which set no limits as to what the study of spiritual beings would embrace, are a majority of contemporary anthropologists who, like Spiro, define religion more narrowly as "an institution consisting of culturally postulated superhuman beings" (1966: 96). At first glance, Tylor's and Spiro's definitions appear similar, but Spiro's use of the term *superhuman,* unlike Tylor's *spiritual beings,* emphasizes an aura of omnipotence unknown to the living. Further, Spiro's position that religion is an institution places it in the realm of phenomena that can be empirically studied, as any other cultural institution can be. Still, similarities in Tylor's and Spiro's definitions are apparent: Both show, for example, that religion is the study of the nature of the unnatural. Spirits are not of this world, nor are superhumans; indeed, both are "supernatural," which has been defined by the anthropologist Edward Norbeck "to include all that is not natural, that which is regarded as extraordinary, not of the ordinary world, mysterious or unexplainable in ordinary terms" (1961: 11).

Expanding the definition of religion beyond spiritual and superhuman beings to include the extraor-

dinary, the mysterious, and unexplainable allows a more comprehensive view of religious behaviors among the peoples of the world and permits the anthropological investigation of phenomena such as magic, sorcery, curses, and other practices that hold meaning for both preliterate and literate societies. For this reason, this book focuses on the concept of the supernatural and incorporates a wide variety of contemporary examples of religious beliefs and practices that demonstrate the breadth of human ideology.

Through their comparative research anthropologists have shown that religious practices and beliefs vary in part as a result of the level of social structure in a given society. In *The Birth of the Gods* (1960), Guy Swanson applied a statistical approach to support the argument that religious forms are related to social development, and in *Religion: An Anthropological View* (1966: 84–101), Anthony F. C. Wallace presented a provocative typology of religious behavior based on the concept of the cult institution—"a set of rituals all having the same general goal, all explicitly rationalized by a set of similar or related beliefs, and all supported by the same social group" (p. 75). Ranging from the simplest to the most complex, Wallace describes individualistic, shamanic, communal, and ecclesiastical cult institutions. Each succeeding or more complex level contains all components of those preceding it. The ecclesiastical, for example, contains all the elements of the less complex individualistic, shamanistic, and communal cult institutions.

According to Wallace, in the simplest, *individualistic* cult institution, each person functions as his or her own specialist without need for such intermediaries as shamans or priests. Examples occur in both modern and primitive societies (the dream cult among the Iroquois, sealing magic among the Trobriand Islanders, and various cults among the Americans). The next level, the *shamanic,* also found in cultures around the world, marks the beginning of a religious division of labor. Individual part-time practitioners are designated by experience, birth, or training to help lay clients enlist the aid of the supernatural. The *communal* cult institution is even more complex, with laypeople handling important religious rituals for people in such special categories as secret societies, kinship groups, and age groups. (Examples include the ancestor ceremonies of the Chinese and some African tribal groups, Iroquois agricultural rituals, and Australian puberty rituals.) Although specialists such as shamans, skilled speakers, and dancers may participate, the lay group assumes the primary responsibility for conducting the sacred performance; an extensive religious hierarchy is still not in evidence. It is in the fourth, *ecclesiastical* cult institution that a professional religious clergy is formally elected or appointed and the division of labor is sharply drawn, with the laymen usually passive participants instead of active performers. Ecclesiastical cult institutions have characteristically worshiped either an Olympian pantheon of gods (as among the ancient Greeks and Romans) or a monotheistic deity (as among the Judeo-Christian and Muslim religions).

The differences between religious behavior and belief in so-called primitive and modern cultures has been of great interest to anthropologists over the years. Howells (1962: 5) observed several characteristics that he believed distinguished the major world religions from the belief systems of more primitive cultures. First, the "great faiths" are messianic, their origins stemming from such charismatic figures as Jesus, Buddha, and Muhammad. Second, they have a rigid ethical form. Third, each has a missionary, imperialistic aspect, seeing itself as the one and only religion. Finally, each displays an exclusiveness in its belief system to the degree of being intolerant of other faiths. Howells is quick to point out that he has been generalizing, reminding the reader that the varied nature and heterogeneity of native cults may make an understanding of their nature arduous, especially for anyone aware only of the differences among Christian sects (1962: 6). His concluding remark is important to an understanding of all the articles in this book; referring to the "perfect legitimacy" of native cults, he states that the

> primitive devotees are not people of another planet, but are essentially exactly like us, and are engaged with precisely the same kind of religious appetite as the civilized. And that appetite is fed and stilled by their own religions. This is very important; it is why we are taking those religions seriously. They are not toys. They are what we might be doing ourselves; and they are what most of our ancestors were indeed doing, two thouand years ago today. (1962: 7)

Tomes have been written on the universality and tenacity of religion, even when they were faced with harsh repression by governments, modernization, and economic globalization. Vernon Reynolds and Ralph Tanner maintain that

> there is more to life, it seems, than the secular state can encompass. People want religion and faith; many of them could hardly imagine life without these things. . . . Religions are also down to earth, and we believe that it is this contact with the material world that explains the continued existence of religions in all countries, why they have survived and multiplied during history, and why they are a real force in the world today. (1995: 4,9)

The four articles in this chapter have been selected to provide a basic understanding of the anthropological approach to the study of the supernatural. Each stresses the use of the comparative method, the very anchor for anthropological thought.

In the first article, Clifford Geertz demonstrates the importance of a historical, psychological, sociological, and semantic approach to the study of religion. Next, Marvin Harris discusses the fascinating possibility of religion among nonhuman species. In addition, he advances the notion that spiritual beings are found also in the religions of prestate societies.

In the third article, Dorothy Lee shows how religion is part and parcel of a preliterate people's total way of life. Lee tells us about preliterate societies in which ceremonies and their preparation occupy most of a year.

In the last selection, Lauriston Sharp provides the reader with a classic example of the cultural disruption that can occur when an outside group intervenes in the life of another group without careful consideration of the consequences.

References

Howells, William
   1962 *The Heathens: Primitive Man and His Religions.* Garden City, N.Y.: Doubleday.

Norbeck, Edward
   1961 *Religion in Primitive Society.* New York: Harper and Brothers.

Reynolds, Vernon, and Ralph Tanner
   1995 *The Social Ecology of Religion.* New York: Oxford University Press.

Spiro, Melford E.
  1966 "Religion: Problems of Definition and Explanation." In Michael Banton, ed., *Anthropological Approaches to the Study of Religion*, pp. 85–126. London: Tavistock Publications Limited for the Association of Social Anthropologists of the Commonwealth.

Swanson, Guy
  1960 *The Birth of the Gods: The Origin of Primitive Beliefs*. Ann Arbor: University of Michigan Press.

Wallace, A. F. C.
  1966 *Religion: An Anthropological View*. New York: Random House.

Religion

Clifford Geertz

In Clifford Geertz's classic work "Religion as a Cultural System" (1966), the author argued for a broadened analysis of religion. This argument, aimed primarily at the narrowness of the British sociological approach to the study of comparative religion, was accepted by American ethnologists and reflected in their contemporary research. In the following article, Geertz pursues his goal, demonstrating the importance of his historical, psychological, sociological, and semantic approaches to the study of religion and concluding that a mature theory of religion will integrate these approaches into a conceptual system whose exact form remains to be discovered. Geertz also explores the view of scholars who regard "primitive thought" as a distinctive mode of reasoning and/or a special body of knowledge, noting that their work persists as a minor but important theme in anthropological studies of religion. The article concludes with a discussion of the highly evocative work of Claude Lévi-Strauss, the leading exponent of the French structural school of anthropology. (An article by Lévi-Strauss appears in Chapter 5.) In addition to extensive fieldwork in Java, Geertz has also conducted research in Bali and Morocco.

THE ANTHROPOLOGICAL STUDY OF RELIGION HAS been highly sensitive to changes in the general intellectual and moral climate of the day; at the same time, it has been a powerful factor in the creation of that climate. Since the early discussion by Edward Tylor, interest in the beliefs and rituals of distant, ancient, or simpler peoples has been shaped by an awareness of contemporary issues. The questions that anthropologists have pursued among exotic religions have arisen from the workings—or the misworkings—of modern Western society, and particularly from its restless quest for self-discovery. In turn, their findings have profoundly affected the course that quest has taken and the perspective at which it has arrived.

Perhaps the chief reason for the rather special role of comparative religious studies is that issues which, when raised within the context of Western culture, led to extreme social resistance and personal turmoil could be freely and even comfortably handled in terms of bizarre, presumably primitive, and thus—also presumably—fanciful materials from long ago or far away. The study of "primitive religions" could pass as the study of superstition, supposedly unrelated to the serious religious and moral concerns of advanced civilization, at best either a sort of vague foreshadowing of them or a grotesque parody upon them. This made it possible to approach all sorts of touchy subjects, such as polytheism, value relativism, possession, and faith healing, from a frank and detached point of view. One could ask searching questions about the historicity of myth among Polynesians; when asked in relation to Christianity, these same questions were, until quite recently, deeply threatening. One could discuss the projection of erotic wishes found in the "totemic" rites of Australian aborigines, the social roots and functions of African "ancestor worship," or the protoscientific quality of Melanesian "magical thought," without involving oneself in polemical debate and emotional distress. The application of the comparative method—the essence of anthropological thought—to religion permitted the growth of a resolutely scientific approach to the spiritual dimensions of human life.

Through the thin disguise of comparative method the revolutionary implications of the work of such men as Tylor, Durkheim, Robertson Smith, Freud, Malinowski, and Radcliffe-Brown soon became apparent—at first mainly to philosophers, theologians, and literary figures, but eventually to the educated public in general. The meticulous descriptions of tribal curiosities such as soul loss, shamanism, circumcision, blood sacrifice, sorcery, tree burial, garden magic, symbolic cannibalism, and animal worship have been caught up in some of the grander intellectual battles of the last hundred years —from those over evolutionism and historicism in the late nineteenth century to those over positivism and existentialism today. Psychoanalysts and phenomenologists, Marxists and Kantians, racists and egalitarians, absolutists and relativists, empiricists and rationalists, believers and skeptics have all had recourse to the record—partial, inconsistent, and shot through with simple error as it is—of the spiritual life of tribal peoples to support their positions and belabor those of their opponents. If interest in "primitive religion" among savants of all sorts has been remarkably high, consensus concerning its nature and significance has not.

At least three major intellectual developments have exercised a critical influence on the anthropological study of religion: (1) the emergence, in the latter half of the nineteenth century, of history as the sovereign science of man; (2) the positivist reaction against this sovereignty in the first decades of the twentieth century and the radical split of the social sciences into resolutely psychological approaches, on the one hand, and resolutely sociological ones, on the other; and (3) the growth, in the interwar period, of a concern with the role of ideational factors in the regulation of social life. With the first of these came an emphasis on the nature of primitive reasoning and the stages of its evolution into civilized thought. With the second came an investigation of the emotional basis of religious ritual and belief and the separate examination of the role of ritual and belief in social integration. The concern with value systems and other features of the ideational realm led to an exploration of the philosophical dimensions of religious ideas, particularly the symbolic vehicles in terms of which those ideas are expressed.

Evolutionism and Its Enemies

Like so much else in anthropology, the study of the religious notions of primitive peoples arose within the context of evolutionary theory. In the nineteenth century, to think systematically about human affairs was to think historically—to seek out survivals of the most elementary forms and to trace the steps by which these forms subsequently developed. And though, in fact, Tylor, Morgan, Frazer, and the rest drew more on the synthetic social-stage theories of such men as Comte and Hegel than on the analytic random-variation and natural-selection ideas of Darwin, the grand concept of evolution was shared by both streams of thought: namely, that the complex, heterogeneous present has arisen, more or less gradually, out of a simpler, more uniform past. The relics of this past are still to be found scattered, like Galápagos turtles, in out-of-the-way places around us. Tylor, an armchair scholar, made no "voyage of the *Beagle*." But in combing and organizing the reports of missionaries, soldiers, and explorers, he proceeded from the same general premise as did Darwin, and indeed most of the leading minds of the day. For them a comprehensive, historically oriented comparison of all forms of a phenomenon, from the most primitive to the most advanced, was the royal road to understanding the nature of the phenomenon itself.

In Tylor's view, the elementary form out of which all else developed was spirit worship—*animism*. The minimal definition of religion was "a belief in spiritual beings." The understanding of religion thus came down to an understanding of the basis upon which such a belief arose at its most primitive level. Tylor's theory was intellectualistic. Belief in spirits began as an uncritical but nonetheless rational effort to explain such puzzling empirical phenomena as death, dreams, and possession. The notion of a separable soul rendered these phenomena intelligible in terms of soul departure, soul wandering, and soul invasion. Tylor believed that the idea of a soul was used to explain more and more remote and hitherto inexplicable natural occurrences, until virtually every tree and rock was haunted by some sort of gossamer presence. The higher, more developed forms of "belief in spiritual beings," first polytheism, ultimately monotheism, were founded upon this animistic basis, the urphilosophy of all mankind, and were refined through a process of critical questioning by more advanced thinkers. For this earnest Quaker the religious history of the world was a history of progressive, even inevitable, enlightenment.

This intellectualistic, "up from darkness" strain has run through most evolutionist thought about religion. For Frazer, a nineteenth-century figure who lived for forty years into the twentieth century without finding it necessary to alter either his views or his methods, the mental progress involved was from magic to religion to science. Magic was the primordial form of human thought; it consisted in mistaking either spatiotemporal connection ("sympathetic magic," as when drinking the blood of an ox transfers its strength to the drinker) or phenomenal similarity ("imitative magic," as when the sound of drumming induces thunderheads to form) for true scientific causality. For Durkheim, evolutionary advance consisted in the emergence of specific, analytic, *profane* ideas about "cause" or "category" or "relationship" from diffuse, global, *sacred* images. These "collective representations," as he called them, of the social order and its moral force included such sacra as "mana," "totem," and "god." For Max Weber, the process was one of "rationalization": the progressive organization of religious concern into certain more precisely defined, more specifically focused, and more systematically conceived cultural forms. The level of sophistication of such theories (and, hence, their present relevance) varies very widely. But, like Tylor's, they all conceive of the evolution of religion as a process of cultural differentiation: the diffuse, all-embracing, but rather unsystematic and uncritical religious practices of primitive peoples are transformed into the more specifically focused, more regularized, less comprehensively authoritative practices of the more advanced civilizations. Weber, in whom both intellectualism and optimism were rather severely tempered by a chronic apprehensiveness, called this transformation the "disenchantment *(Entzauberung)* of the world."

On the heels of evolutionism came, of course, anti-evolutionism. This took two quite different forms. On one side there was a defense, mainly by Roman Catholic scholars, of the so-called degradation theory. According to this theory, the original revelation of a high god to primitive peoples was later corrupted by human frailty into the idol worship of present-day tribal peoples. On the other side there was an attack, mainly by American scholars of

the Boas school, upon the "armchair speculation" of evolutionary thinkers and a call for its replacement by more phenomenological approaches to the study of tribal custom.

The first of these reactions led, logically enough, to a search among the most primitive of existing peoples for traces of belief in a supreme being. The resulting dispute, protracted, often bitter, and stubbornly inconclusive as to the existence of such "primitive monotheism," turned out to be unproductive—aside from some interesting discussions by Lang (1898) concerning culture heroes and by Eliade (1949) concerning sky gods—and both the issue and the theory that gave rise to it have now receded from the center of scholarly attention. The second reaction has had a longer life and great impact on ethnographic methodology, but it too is now in partial eclipse. Its main contributions—aside from some devastating empirical demolitions of evolutionist generalization—came in the field of cultural diffusion. Leslie Spier's study of the spread of the Sun Dance through the Great Plains and A. L. Kroeber's application of the age-area approach to aboriginal religion in California are good examples of productive diffusion studies. However, apart from their importance for culture history, the contribution of such distributional studies to our understanding of religious ideas, attitudes, and practices as such has not been great, and few students now pursue these studies. The call of the Boas school for thorough field research and disciplined inductive analysis has been heeded; but its fruits, insofar as religious studies are concerned, have been reaped by others less inhibited theoretically.

Psychological Approaches

The major reaction against the intellectual tradition of the cultural evolutionists took place not within anthropology, however, but in the general context of the positivist revolt against the domination of historicist modes of thought in the social sciences. In the years before World War I the rise of the systematic psychologism of psychoanalysis and of the equally systematic sociologism of the *Année sociologique* forced evolutionist theorizing into the background, even though the leaders of both movements —Freud and Durkheim—were themselves still very strongly influenced by it. Perhaps even more relevant, it introduced a sharp split into anthropological studies of religion which has resolved into the militantly psychodynamic and the militantly social-structural approaches.

Freud's major work in this field is, of course, *Totem and Taboo,* a book anthropologists in general have had great difficulty in evaluating—as Kroeber's two reviews of it, the first facilely negative, the second, two decades later, ambivalently positive, demonstrate. The source of the difficulty has been an inability or an unwillingness to disentangle Freud's basic thesis—that religious rituals and beliefs are homologous with neurotic symptoms—from the chimerical ethnology and obsolete biology within which he insisted upon setting it. Thus, the easy demolition of what Kroeber called Freud's "just so story" concerning primal incest, parricide, and guilt within some protohuman horde ("in the beginning was the deed") was all too often mistaken for total rejection of the rather more penetrating proposition that the obsessions, dreams, and fantasies of collective life spring from the same intrapsychic sources as do those of the isolated individual.

For those who read further in Freud's writings, however—especially in "Mourning and Melancholia" and "Obsessive Acts and Religious Practices"—it became apparent that what was at issue was the applicability of theories concerning the forms and causes of individual psychopathology to the explanation of the forms and causes of public myth and group ritual. Róheim (1950) analyzed Australian circumcision rites against the background of orthodox Freudian theories of psychosexual development, especially those clustered around the Oedipal predicament. However, he explicitly avoided recourse to speculations about buried memories of primordial occurrences. Bettelheim (1954) adopted a similar, though more systematic and less orthodox, approach to initiation practices generally, seeing them as socially instituted symbolic mechanisms for the definition and stabilization of sexual identity. Kardiner (1945), taking a neo-Freudian position, sought to demonstrate that the religious institutions of tribal peoples were projections of a "basic personality structure," formed not by the action of an unconsciously remembered historical trauma but by the more observable traumas produced by child-training practices, an approach later extended and cast into quantitative form by Whiting (Whiting and Child 1953). Erikson (1950), drawing upon developments in ego psychology which conceived the emer-gence of the adult personality to be a joint product of psychobiological maturation, cultural context, and historical experience, interpreted the religious notions of the Yurok and the Sioux in terms of certain basic modes of relating to the world. These relationships gradually developed during the whole course of childhood and adolescence. Others—notably Devereux (1951)—have attempted to use the auto-biographical, case-history approach to determine the relations between personality dynamics and religious orientation in particular individuals; still others—notably Hallowell (1937–1954)—have employed projective tests, questionnaires, reports of dreams, or systematic interviews toward similar ends.

In all such studies, even when individual authors have dissented from many of Freud's specific views, the basic premise has been Freudian: that religious practices can be usefully interpreted as expressions of unconscious psychological forces—and this has become, amid much polemic, an established tradition of inquiry. In recent years, however, responsible work of this type has come to question the degree to which one is justified in subjecting historically created and socially institutionalized cultural forms to a system of analysis founded on the treatment of the mental illnesses of individuals. For this reason, the future of this approach depends perhaps more upon developments within psychoanalysis, now in a somewhat uncertain state, than within anthropology. So far, perhaps only Kluckhohn's pioneering *Navaho Witchcraft* (1944) has attempted to systematically relate psychological factors to social and cultural aspects of primitive religion. The great majority of psychoanalytic studies of tribal beliefs and rites remain willfully parochial.

In any case, not all psychological approaches to religion have been Freudian. Jungian influences have had a certain impact, especially on studies of myth. Campbell (1949), for example, has stressed the continuity of certain themes both cross-culturally and temporally. These themes have been interpreted as expressions of transpersonal constancies in unconscious mental functioning which are at the same time expressions of fundamental cosmic realities.

Simple emotionalist theories have also been extremely popular. There have been two main varieties of these: awe theories and confidence theories. Awe theories have been based on some usually rather vague notion of "religious thrill" experienced by human beings when brought face to face with cosmic forces. A wide range of ethnologists, from Max Müller through Lang and Marett to Lowie and Goldenweiser, have accepted such theories in one form or another. However, awe theories remain mere notations of the obvious—that religious experience is, in the nature of the case, touched with intense feelings of the grandeur of the universe in relation to the self and of the vulnerability of the self in relation to the universe. This is not explanation, but circular reasoning.

Confidence theories also begin with a notion of man's inward sense of weakness, and especially of his fears—of disease, of death, of ill fortune of all kinds—and they see religious practices as designed to quiet such fears, either by explaining them away, as in doctrines of the afterlife, or by claiming to link the individual to external sources of strength, as in prayer. The best-known confidence theory was that set forth by Malinowski. He regarded magic as enabling man to pursue uncertain but essential endeavors by assuring him of their ultimate success. Confidence, or anxiety-reduction, theories, like awe theories, clearly have empirical foundation but do not adequately explore the complex relationship between fear and religious activity. They are not rooted in any systematic conceptualization of mental functioning and so merely point to matters desperately in need of clarification, without in fact clarifying them.

Sociological Approaches

The sociological approach to the analysis of the religions of nonliterate peoples proceeded independent of, and even at variance with, the psychoanalytic approach, but it shared a concern with the same phenomenon: the peculiar "otherness," the extraordinary, momentous, "set apart" quality of sacred (or "taboo") acts and objects, as contrasted with the profane. The intense aura of high seriousness was traced by Freud to the projection of unacceptable wishes repressed from consciousness onto external objects. The dramatic ambivalence of the sacred—its paradoxical unification of the commanded and the forbidden, the pure and the polluted, the salutary and the dangerous—was a symbolic expression of the underlying ambivalence of human desires. For Durkheim, too, the extraordinary atmosphere surrounding sacred acts and objects was symbolic of a hidden reality, but a social, not a psychological one: the moral force of the human community.

Durkheim believed that the integrity of the social order was the primary requisite for human survival, and the means by which that integrity superseded individual egocentricity was the primary problem of sociological analysis. He saw Australian totemism (which he, like Freud, made the empirical focus of his work) as a mechanism to this end. For example, the collective rituals involving the emblems of the totemic beings—the so-called bull roarers—aroused the heightened emotions of mass behavior and evoked a deep sense of moral identification among the participants. The creation of social solidarity was the result of the common public veneration, by specific groups of persons, of certain carefully designated symbolic objects. These objects had no intrinsic value except as perceptible representations of the social identity of the individuals. Collective worship of consecrated bits of painted wood or stone created a moral community, a "church," upon which rested the viability of the major social units. These sanctified objects thus represented the system of rights and obligations implicit in the social order and the individual's unformulated sense of its overriding significance in his life. All sacred objects, beliefs, and acts, and the extraordinary emotions attending them, were outward expressions of inward social necessities, and, in a famous phrase, God was the "symbol of society." Few anthropologists have been able to swallow Durkheim's thesis whole, when put this baldly. But the more moderate proposition that religious rituals and beliefs both reflect and act to support the moral framework underlying social arrangements (and are in turn animated by it) has given rise to what has become perhaps the most popular form of analysis in the anthropological study of religion. Usually called "functionalism"—or sometimes, to distinguish it from certain variants deemed objectionable, "structuralism"—this approach found its champion in Radcliffe-Brown and its major development in Great Britain, though its influence has now spread very much more widely.

Radcliffe-Brown (1952) agreed with Durkheim's postulate that the main role (or "function") of religion was to celebrate and sustain the norms upon which the integration of society depends. But unlike Durkheim (and like Freud), Radcliffe-Brown was concerned with the content of sacred symbols, and particularly with the reasons why one object rather than another was absorbed into rite or woven into myth. Why here stones, there water holes, here camp circles, there personified winds?

Durkheim had held this to be an arbitrary matter, contingent upon historical accident or psychological proclivity, beyond the reach of and irrelevant to sociological analysis. Radcliffe-Brown considered, however, that man's need for a concrete expression of social solidarity was not sufficient explanation of the structure of a people's religious system. Something was needed to tie the particular objects awarded sacred status (or, in his terminology, "ritual value") to the particular social interests they presumably served and reflected. Radcliffe-Brown, resolute empiricist that he was, chose a solution Durkheim had already magisterially demolished: the utilitarian. The objects selected for religious veneration by a given people were either directly or indirectly connected to factors critical to their collective well-being. Things that had real, that is, practical, "social value" were elevated to having spiritual, or symbolic, "ritual value," thus fusing the social and the natural into one overarching order. For primitives at least (and Radcliffe-Brown attempted to establish his theory with regard to the sanctified turtles and palm leaves of the pre-agricultural Andaman Islanders and, later on, with regard to Australian totemism), there is no discontinuity, no difference even, between moral and physical, spiritual and practical relationships and processes. These people regard both men and things as parts of a single normative system. Within that system those elements which are critical to its effective functioning (or, sometimes, phenomena empirically associated with such elements, such as the Andaman cicada cycle and the shifting monsoons) are made the objects of that special sort of respect and attention which we call religious but which the people themselves regard as merely prudential.

Radcliffe-Brown focused upon the content of sacred symbols and emphasized the relation between conceptions of the moral order of existence and conceptions of its natural order. However, the claim that the sanctity of religious objects derives from their practical social importance is one of those theories which works when it works and doesn't when it doesn't. Not only has it proved impossible to find even an indirect practical significance in most of the enormous variety of things tribal peoples have re-

garded as sacred (certain Australian tribes worship vomit), but the view that religious concerns are mere ritualizations of real-life concerns leaves the phenomenon of sacredness itself—its aura of mystery, power, fascination—totally unexplained.

More recent structuralist studies have tended to evade both these questions and to concentrate on the role played by religion in maintaining social equilibrium. They attempt to show how given sets of religious practices (ancestor worship, animal sacrifice, witchcraft and sorcery, regeneration rites) do in fact express and reinforce the moral values underlying crucial processes (lineage segmentation, marriage, conflict adjudication, political succession) in the particular society under investigation. Arnold van Gennep's study of crisis rites was perhaps the most important forerunner of the many analyses of this type. Although valuable in their own right as ethnography and as sociology, these structural formulations have been severely limited by their rigid avoidance on the one side, of the kind of psychological considerations that could account for the peculiar emotions which permeate religious belief and practice, and, on the other, of the philosophical considerations that could render their equally peculiar content intelligible.

The Analysis of Symbolic Forms

In contrast to other approaches—evolutionary psychological sociological—the field of what we may loosely call "semantic studies" of religion is extremely jumbled. There is, as yet, no well-established central trend to analysis, no central figure around whom to order debate, and no readily apparent system of interconnections relating the various competing trends to one another.

Perhaps the most straightforward strategy—certainly the most disarming—is merely to *accept* the myriad expressions of the sacred in primitive societies, to consider them as actual ingressions of the divine into the world, and to trace the forms these expressions have taken across the earth and through time. The result would be a sort of natural history of revelation, whose aim would be to isolate the major classes of religious phenomena considered as authentic manifestations of the sacred—what Eliade, the chief proponent of this approach, calls hierophanies—and to trace the rise, dominance, decline, and disappearance of these classes within the changing contexts of human life. The meaning of religious activity, the burden of its content, is discovered through a meticulous, wholly inductive investigation of the natural modalities of such behavior (sun worship, water symbolism, fertility cults, renewal myths, etc.) and of the vicissitudes these modalities undergo when projected, like the Son of God himself, into the flux of history.

Metaphysical questions (here uncommonly obtrusive) aside, the weaknesses of this approach derive from the same source as its strengths: a drastic limiting of the interpretations of religion to the sort that a resolutely Baconian methodology can produce. On the one hand, this approach has led, especially in the case of a scholar as erudite and indefatigable as Eliade, to the uncovering of some highly suggestive clusterings of certain religious patterns with particular historical conditions—for example, the frequent association of sun worship, activist conceptions of divine power, cultic veneration of deified heroes, elitist doctrines of political sovereignty, and imperialist ideologies of national expansion. But, on the other hand, it has placed beyond the range of scientific analysis everything but the history and morphology of the phenomenal forms of religious expression. The study of tribal beliefs and practices is reduced to a kind of cultural paleontology whose sole aim is the reconstruction, from scattered and corrupted fragments, of the "mental universe of archaic man."

Primitive Thought

Other scholars who are interested in the meaningful content of primitive religion but who are incapable of so thoroughgoing a suspension of disbelief as Eliade, or are repelled by the cultic overtones of this somewhat mystagogic line of thought, have directed their attention instead toward logical and epistemological considerations. This has produced a long series of studies that view "primitive thought" as a distinctive mode of reasoning and/or a special body of knowledge. From Lévy-Bruhl through Lévi-Strauss, and with important contributions from members of the evolutionary, psychoanalytic, and sociological schools as well, this line of exploration has persisted as a minor theme in anthropological studies of religion. With the recent advances in linguistics, information theory, the analysis of cogni-

tion, semantic philosophy, modern logic, and certain sorts of literary investigation, the systematic study of symbolic activity bids fair to become, in a rather thoroughly revised form, the major theme for investigation. The "new key" Susanne K. Langer heard being struck in philosophy in the early 1940s—"the concern with the concept of meaning in all its forms" —has, like the historicist and positivist "keys" before it, begun to have its echo in the anthropological study of religion. Anthropologists are increasingly interested in ideational expression, increasingly concerned with the vehicles, processes, and practical applications of human conceptualization.

The development of this approach has come in two fairly distinct phases, one before and one after World War II. In the first phase there was a concern with "the mind of primitive man" and in particular with its capacity for rational thought. In a sense, this concern represented the evolutionists' interest in primitive reasoning processes detached from the historicist context. In the second phase, which is still in process, there has been a move away from, and in part a reaction against, the subjectivist emphasis of the earlier work. Ideational expression is thought of as a public activity, rather like speech, and the structure of the symbolic materials, the "language," in whose terms the activity is conducted becomes the subject of investigation.

The first, subjectivist, phase was animated by a protracted wrangle between those who used the religious beliefs and practices of tribal peoples as evidence to prove that there was a qualitative difference between the thought processes of primitives and those of civilized men and the anthropologists who considered such religious activity as evidence for the lack of any such differences. The great protagonist of the first school was the French philosopher Lévy-Bruhl whose theories of "prelogical mentality" were as controversial within anthropology as they were popular outside it. According to Lévy-Bruhl, the thought of primitives, as reflected in their religious ideas, is not governed by the immanent laws of Aristotelian logical reasoning, but by affectivity—by the vagrant flow of emotion and the dialectical principles of "mystical participation" and "mystical exclusion."

The two most effective antagonists of Lévy-Bruhl's theories concerning primitive religion were Radin and Malinowski. Radin, influenced by Boas' more general attacks on theories of "primitive mentality," sought to demonstrate that primitive religious thought reaches, on occasion, very high levels of logical articulation and philosophical sophistication and that tribal society contains, alongside the common run of unreflective doers ("men of action"), contemplative intellectuals ("men of thought") of boldness, subtlety, and originality. Malinowski attacked the problem on an even broader front. Using his ethnographic knowledge of the Trobriand Islanders, Malinowski argued that alongside their religious and magical notions (which he, too, regarded as mainly emotionally determined) the "savages" also had a rather well-developed and, as far as it went, accurate empirical knowledge of gardening, navigation, housebuilding, canoe construction, and other useful arts. He further claimed that they were absolutely clear as to the distinction between these two sorts of reasoning, between mystical-magical and empirical-pragmatic thinking, and never confused them in actual practice. Of these two arguments, the former seems to be today nearly universally accepted and was perhaps never in fact really questioned. But with respect to the latter, serious doubts have arisen concerning whether the lines between "science," "magic," and "religion" are as simple and clear-cut in the minds of tribal peoples (or any peoples) as Malinowski, never one for shaded judgments, portrayed them. Nevertheless, between them, Radin and Malinowski rather definitively demolished the notion of a radical qualitative gap between the thought processes of primitive and civilized men. Indeed, toward the end of his life even Lévy-Bruhl admitted that his arguments had been badly cast and might better have been phrased in terms of different modes of thinking common to all men. (In fact, Freud, with his contrast between primary and secondary thinking processes, had already made this distinction.)

Thus, the debate about what does or does not go on in the heads of savages exhausted itself in generalities, and recent writers have turned to a concern with the symbolic forms, the conceptual resources, in terms of which primitives (and nonprimitives) think. The major figure in this work has been Claude Lévi-Strauss, although this line of attack dates back to Durkheim and Mauss's influential 1903 essay in sociological Kantianism, *Primitive Classification*. The writings of E. E. Evans-Pritchard on Zande witchcraft, Benjamin Whorf on Hopi semantics, and Gregory Bateson on Iatmul ritual and, among non-

anthropologists, works by Granet, Cassirer, and Piaget have directed attention to the study of symbolic formulation.

Symbolic Systems

Lévi-Strauss, whose rather highly wrought work is still very much in progress, is concerned with the systems of classification, the "homemade" taxonomies, employed by tribal peoples to order the objects and events of their world (see Lévi-Strauss 1958; 1962). In this, he follows in the footsteps of Durkheim and Mauss. But rather than looking, as they did, to social forms for the origins and explanations of such categorical systems, he looks to the symbolic structures in terms of which they are formulated, expressed, and applied. Myth and, in a slightly different way, rite are systems of signs that fix and organize abstract conceptual relationships in terms of concrete images and thus make speculative thought possible. They permit the construction of a "science of the concrete"—the intellectual comprehension of the sensible world in terms of sensible phenomena—which is no less rational, no less logical, no more affect-driven than the abstract science of the modern world. The objects rendered sacred are selected not because of their utilitarian qualities, nor because they are projections of repressed emotions, nor yet because they reflect the moral force of social organization ritualistically impressed upon the mind. Rather, they are selected because they permit the embodiment of general ideas in terms of the immediately perceptible realities—the turtles, trees, springs, and caves—of everyday experience; not, as Lévi-Strauss says, apropos of Radcliffe-Brown's view of totems, because they are "good to eat," but because they are "good to think."

This "goodness" exists inherently in sacred objects because they provide the raw materials for analogical reasoning. The relationships perceived among certain classes of natural objects or events can be analogized, taken as models of relationships—physical, social, psychological, or moral—obtaining between persons, groups, or other natural objects and events. Thus, for example, the natural distinctions perceived among totemic beings, their species differentiation, can serve as a conceptual framework for the comprehension, expression, and communication of social distinctions among exogamous clans—their structural differentiation. Thus, the sharp contrast between the wet and dry seasons (and the radical zoological and botanical changes associated with it) in certain regions of Australia is employed in the mythology of the native peoples. They have woven an elaborate origin myth around this natural phenomenon, one that involves a rainmaking python who drowned some incestuous sisters and their children because the women polluted his water hole with menstrual blood. This model expresses and economizes the contrasts between moral purity and impurity, maleness and femaleness, social superiority and inferiority, fertilizing agent (rain) and that which is fertilized (land), and even the distinction between "high" (initiate) and "low" (noninitiate) levels of cultural achievement.

Lévi-Strauss contends that primitive religious systems are, like all symbolic systems, fundamentally communications systems. They are carriers of information in the technical Shannon-Weaver sense, and as such, the theory of information can be applied to them with the same validity as when applied to any physical systems, mechanical or biological, in which the transfer of information plays a central regulative role. Primitives, as all men, are quintessentially multichanneled emitters and receivers of messages. It is merely in the nature of the code they employ—one resting on analogies between "natural" and "cultural" distinctions and relationships—that they differ from ourselves. Where there is a distinguishing difference, it lies in the technically specialized codes of modern abstract thought, in which semantic properties are radically and deliberately severed from physical ones. Religion, primitive or modern, can be understood only as an integrated system of thought, logically sound, epistemologically valid, and as flourishing in France as in Tahiti.

It is far too early to evaluate Lévi-Strauss's work with any assurance. It is frankly incomplete and explorative, and some parts of it (the celebration of information theory, for example) are wholly programmatic. But in focusing on symbol systems as conceptual models of social or other sorts of reality, he has clearly introduced into the anthropology of religion a line of inquiry which, having already become common in modern thought generally, can hardly fail to be productive when applied to tribal myth and ritual.

Whether his own particular formulation of this approach will prove to be the most enduring remains, however, rather more of a question. His rejection of emotional considerations and his neglect of normative or social factors in favor of an extreme intellectualism which cerebralizes religion and tends to reduce it yet again to a kind of undeveloped (or, as he puts it, "undomesticated") science are questionable. His nearly exclusive stress on those intellectual processes involved in classification, i.e., on taxonomic modes of thought (a reflex of his equally great reliance on totemic ideas as type cases of primitive beliefs), at the expense of other, perhaps more common, and certainly more powerful styles of reasoning, is also doubtful. His conception of the critical process of symbolic formulation itself remains almost entirely undeveloped—hardly more than a sort of associationism dressed up with some concepts from modern linguistics. Partly as a result of this weakness and partly as a result of a tendency to consider symbol systems as entities functioning independently of the contextual factor, many of his specific interpretations of particular myths and rites seem as strained, arbitrary, and oversystematized as those of the most undisciplined psychoanalyst.

But, for all this, Lévi-Strauss has without doubt opened a vast territory for research and begun to explore it with theoretical brilliance and profound scholarship. And he is not alone. As the recent work of such diverse students as Evans-Pritchard, R. G. Lienhardt, W. E. H. Stanner, Victor W. Turner, Germaine Dieterlen, Meyer Fortes, Edmund R. Leach, Charles O. Frake, Rodney Needham, and Susanne K. Langer demonstrates, the analysis of symbolic forms is becoming a major tradition in the study of primitive religion—in fact, of religion in general. Each of these writers has a somewhat different approach. But all seem to share the conviction that an attempt must be made to approach primitive religions for what they are: systems of ideas about the ultimate shape and substance of reality.

Whatever else religion does, it relates a view of the ultimate nature of reality to a set of ideas of how man is well advised, even obligated, to live. Religion tunes human actions to a view of the cosmic order and projects images of cosmic order onto the plane of human existence. In religious belief and practice a people's style of life, what Clyde Kluckhohn called their *design for living*, is rendered intellectually reasonable; it is shown to represent a way of life ideally adapted to the world "as it 'really' ('fundamentally,' 'ultimately') is." At the same time, the supposed basic structure of reality is rendered emotionally convincing because it is presented as an actual state of affairs uniquely accommodated to such a way of life and permitting it to flourish. Thus do received beliefs, essentially metaphysical, and established norms, essentially moral, confirm and support one another.

It is this mutual confirmation that religious symbols express and celebrate and that any scientific analysis of religion must somehow contrive to explain and clarify. In the development of such an analysis historical, psychological, sociological, and what has been called here semantic considerations are all necessary, but none is sufficient. A mature theory of religion will consist of an integration of them all into a conceptual system whose exact form remains to be discovered.

Why We Became Religious *and* The Evolution of the Spirit World

Marvin Harris

The following selection by anthropologist Marvin Harris originally appeared as two separate essays, one entitled "Why We Became Religious," the other, "The Evolution of the Spirit World." In the first essay Harris comments on the fascinating possibility of religion among nonhuman species. He also discusses the concept of mana *(an inherent force or power), noting that although the concepts of superstition, luck, and charisma in Western cultures closely resemble* mana, *they are not really religious concepts. Rather, according to Harris, the basis of all religious thought is animism, the universal belief that we humans share the world with various extracorporeal, mostly invisible beings. Harris closes the first essay with some thoughts on the concept of an inner being—a soul —pointing out that in many cultures people believe a person may have more than one.*

In "The Evolution of the Spirit World," Harris advances the notion that spiritual beings found in modern religions are also found in the religions of prestate societies. Thus, he briefly examines religious thought and behavior pertaining to ancestor worship at varying levels of societal complexity, starting with band-and-village level societies, the earliest of human cultures. Next, Harris notes the importance of recently deceased relatives in the religions of more complexly developed societies, such as those based on gardening and fishing. Chiefdoms represent an even higher level of development, one in which greater specialization arose, including a religious practitioner who paid special attention to the chief's ancestors. Finally, Harris observes that with the development of early states and empires, dead ancestors assumed a place of great prominence alongside the gods.

HUMAN SOCIAL LIFE CANNOT BE UNDERSTOOD apart from the deeply held beliefs and values that in the short run, at least, motivate and mobilize our transactions with each other and the world of nature. So let me . . . confront certain questions concerning our kind's religious beliefs and behavior.

First, are there any precedents for religion in nonhuman species? The answer is yes, only if one accepts a definition of religion broad enough to include "superstitious" responses. Behavioral psychologists have long been familiar with the fact that animals can acquire responses that are falsely associated with rewards. For example, a pigeon is placed in a cage into which food pellets are dropped by a mechanical feeder at irregular intervals. If the reward is delivered by chance while the bird is scratching, it begins to scratch faster. If the reward is delivered while a bird happens to be flapping its wings, it keeps flapping them as if wing-flapping controls the feeder. Among humans, one can find analogous superstitions in the little rituals that baseball players engage in as they come up to bat, such as touching their caps, spitting, or rubbing their hands. None of this has any real connection with getting a hit, although constant repetition assures that every time batters get hits, they have performed the ritual. Some minor phobic behavior among humans also might be attributed to associations based on coincidental rather than contingent circumstances. I know a heart surgeon who tolerates only popular music piped into his operating room ever since he lost a patient while classical compositions were being played.

Superstition raises the issue of causality. Just how do the activities and objects that are connected in superstitious beliefs influence one another? A reasonable, if evasive, answer is to say that the causal activity or object has an inherent force or power to achieve the observed effects. Abstracted and generalized, this inherent force or power can provide the explanation for many extraordinary events and for success or failure in life's endeavors. In Melanesia, people call it *mana*. Fishhooks that catch big fish, tools that make intricate carvings, canoes that sail safely through storm, or warriors who kill many enemies, all have mana in concentrated quantities. In Western cultures, the concepts of luck and charisma closely resemble the idea of mana. A horseshoe possesses a concentrated power that brings good luck. A charismatic leader is one who is suffused with great powers of persuasion.

But are superstitions, mana, luck, and charisma religious concepts? I think not. Because, if we define religion as a belief in any indwelling forces and powers, we shall soon find it difficult to separate religion from physics. After all, gravity and electricity are also unseen forces that are associated with observable effects. While it is true that physicists know much more about gravity than about mana, they cannot claim to have a complete understanding of how gravity achieves its results. At the same time, couldn't one argue that superstitions, mana, luck, and charisma are also merely theories of causality involving physical forces and powers about which we happen to have incomplete understanding as yet?

True, more scientific testing has gone into the study of gravity than into the study of mana, but the degree of scientific testing to which a theory has been subjected cannot make the difference between whether it is a religious or a scientific belief. If it did, then every untested or inadequately tested theory in science would be a religious belief (as well as every scientific theory that has been shown to be false during the time when scientists believed it to be true!). Some astronomers theorize that at the center of each galaxy there is a black hole. Shall we say that this is a religious belief because other astronomers reject such a theory or regard it as inadequately tested?

It is not the quality of belief that distinguishes religion from science. Rather, as Sir Edward Tylor was the first to propose, the basis of all that is distinctly religious in human thought is animism, the belief that humans share the world with a population of extraordinary, extracorporeal, and mostly invisible beings, ranging from souls and ghosts to saints and fairies, angels and cherubim, demons, jinni, devils, and gods.

Wherever people believe in the existence of one or more of these beings, that is where religion exists. Tylor claimed that animistic beliefs were to be found in every society, and a century of ethnological research has yet to turn up a single exception. The most problematic case is that of Buddhism, which Tylor's critics portrayed as a world religion that lacked belief in gods or souls. But ordinary believers outside of Buddhist monasteries never accepted the atheistic implications of Gautama's teachings. Mainstream Buddhism, even in the monasteries, quickly envisioned the Buddha as a supreme deity who had been successively reincarnated and who held sway over a pantheon of lower gods and demons. And it was as fully animistic creeds that the several varieties of Buddhism spread from India to Tibet, Southeast Asia, China, and Japan.

Why is animism universal? Tylor pondered the question at length. He reasoned that if a belief recurred again and again in virtually all times and places, it could not be a product of mere fantasy. Rather, it must have grounding in evidence and in experiences that were equally recurrent and universal. What were these experiences? Tylor pointed to dreams, trances, visions, shadows, reflections, and death. During dreams, the body stays in bed; yet another part of us gets up, talks to people, and travels to distant lands. Trances and drug-induced visions also bring vivid evidence of another self, distinct and separate from one's body. Shadows and mirror images reflected in still water point to the same conclusion, even in the full light of normal wakefulness. The concept of an inner being—a soul—makes sense of all this. It is the soul that wanders off when we sleep, that lies in the shadows, and that peers back at us from the surface of the pond. Most of all, the soul explains the mystery of death: a lifeless body is a body permanently deprived of its soul.

Incidentally, there is nothing in the concept of soul per se that constrains us to believe each person has only one. The ancient Egyptians had two, and so do many West African societies in which both patrilineal and matrilineal ancestors determine an individual's identity. The Jívaro of Ecuador have three souls. The first soul—the *mekas*—gives life to the body. The second soul—the *arutam*—has to be captured through a drug-induced visionary experience at a sacred waterfall. It confers bravery and immunity in battle to the possessor. The third soul—the *musiak*—forms inside the head of a dying warrior and attempts to avenge his death. The Dahomey say that women have three souls; men have four. Both sexes have an ancestor soul, a personal soul, and a mawn soul. The ancestor soul gives protection during life, the personal soul is accountable for what people do with their lives, the mawn soul is a bit of the creator god, Mawn, that supplies divine guidance. The exclusively male fourth soul guides men to positions of leadership in their households and lineages. But the record for plural souls seems to belong to the Fang of Gabon. They have seven: a sound inside the brain, a heart soul, a name soul, a life force soul, a body soul, a shadow soul, and a ghost soul.

Why do Westerners have only one soul? I cannot answer that. Perhaps the question is unanswerable. I accept the possibility that many details of religious beliefs and practices may arise from historically specific events and individual choices made only once and only in one culture and that have no discernible cost-benefit advantages or disadvantages. While a belief in souls does conform to the general principles of cultural selection, belief in one rather than two or more souls may not be comprehensible in terms of such principles. But let us not be too eager to declare any puzzling feature of human life forever beyond the pale of practical reason. For has it not been our experience that more research often leads to answers that were once thought unattainable?

The Evolution of the Spirit World

All varieties of spirit beings found in modern religions have their analogues or exact prototypes in the religions of prestate societies. Changes in animistic beliefs since Neolithic times involve matters of emphasis and elaboration. For example, band-and-village people widely believed in gods who lived on top of mountains or in the sky itself and who served as the models for later notions of supreme beings as well as other powerful sky gods. In Aboriginal Australia, the sky god created the earth and its natural features, showed humans how to hunt and make fire, gave people their social laws, and showed them how to make adults out of children by performing rites of initiation. The names of their quasi-supreme beings—Baiame, Daramulum, Nurunderi—could not be uttered by the uninitiated. Similarly, the Selk'-nam of Tierra del Fuego believed in "the one who is up there." The Yaruro of Venezuela spoke of a "great

mother" who created the world. The Maidu of California believed in a great "slayer in the sky." Among the Semang of Malaysia, Kedah created everything, including the god who created the earth and humankind. The Andaman Islanders had Puluga whose house is the sky, and the Winnebago had "earthmaker."

Although prestate peoples occasionally prayed to these great spirits or even visited them during trances, the focus of animistic beliefs generally lay elsewhere. In fact, most of the early creator gods abstained from contact with human beings. Having created the universe, they withdraw from worldly affairs and let other lesser deities, animistic beings, and humans work out their own destinies. Ritually, the most important category of animistic beings was the ancestors of the band, village, and clan or other kinship groups whose members believed they were bonded by common descent.

People in band-and-village societies tend to have short memories concerning specific individuals who have died. Rather than honor the recent dead, or seek favors from them, egalitarian cultures often place a ban on the use of the dead person's name and try to banish or evade his or her ghost. Among the Washo, a native American foraging people who lived along the border of California and Nevada, souls of the dead were angry about being deprived of their bodies. They were dangerous and had to be avoided. So the Washo burned the dead person's hut, clothing, and other personal property and stealthily moved their camp to a place where they hoped the dead person's soul could not find them. The Dusun of North Borneo curse a dead person's soul and warn it to stay away from the village. Reluctantly, the soul gathers up belongings left at its grave site and sets off for the land of the dead.

But this distrust of the recent dead does not extend to the most ancient dead, not to the generality of ancestor spirits. In keeping with the ideology of descent, band-and-village people often memorialize and propitiate their communal ancestral spirits. Much of what is known as totemism is a form of diffuse ancestor worship. Taking the name of an animal such as kangaroo or beaver or a natural phenomenon such as clouds or rain in conformity with prevailing rules of descent, people express a communal obligation to the founders of their kinship group. Often this obligation includes rituals intended to nourish, protect, or assure the increase of the animal and natural totems and with it the health and well-being of their human counterparts. Aboriginal Australians, for example, believed that they were descended from animal ancestors who traveled around the country during the dream-time at the beginning of the world, leaving mementos of their journey strewn about before turning into people. Annually, the descendants of a particular totemic ancestor retraced the dream-time journey. As they walked from spot to spot, they sang, danced, and examined sacred stones, stored in secret hiding places along the path taken by the first kangaroo or the first witchetty grub. Returning to camp, they decorated themselves in the likeness of their totem and imitated its behavior. The Arunta witchetty-grub men, for instance, decorated themselves with strings, nose bones, rattails, and feathers, painted their bodies with the sacred design of the witchetty grub, and constructed a brush hut in the shape of the witchetty-grub chrysalis. They entered the hut and sang of the journey they had made. Then the head men came shuffling and gliding out, followed by all the rest, in imitation of adult witchetty grubs emerging from a chrysalis.

In most village societies an undifferentiated community of ancestral spirits keep a close watch on their descendants, ready to punish them if they commit incest or if they break the taboos against eating certain foods. Important endeavors—hunting, gardening, pregnancy, warfare—need the blessings of a group's ancestors to be successful, and such blessings are usually obtained by holding feasts in the ancestors' honor according to the principle that a well-fed ancestor is a well-intentioned ancestor. Throughout highland New Guinea, for example, people believe that the ancestral spirits enjoy eating pork as much as living persons enjoy eating it. To please the ancestors, people slaughter whole herds of pigs before going to war or when celebrating important events in an individual's life such as marriage

and death. But in keeping with a big-man redistributive level of political organization, no one claims that his or her ancestors merit special treatment.

Under conditions of increasing population, greater wealth to be inherited, and intrasocietal competition between different kin groups, people tend to pay more attention to specific and recently deceased relatives in order to validate claims to the inheritance of land and other resources. The Dobuans, South Pacific yam gardeners and fishermen of the Admiralty Islands, have what seems to be an incipient phase of a particularized ancestor religion. When the leader of a Dobuan household died, his children cleaned his skull, hung it from the rafters of their house, and provided it with food and drink. Addressing it as "Sir Ghost," they solicited protection against disease and misfortune, and through oracles, asked him for advice. If Sir Ghost did not cooperate, his heirs threatened to get rid of him. Actually, Sir Ghost could never win. The death of his children finally proved that he was no longer of any use. So when the grandchildren took charge, they threw Sir Ghost into the lagoon, substituting their own father's skull as the symbol of the household's new spiritual patron.

With the development of chiefdoms, ruling elites employed specialists whose job was to memorize the names of the chief's ancestors. To make sure that the remains of these dignitaries did not get thrown away like Sir Ghost's skull, paramount chiefs built elaborate tombs that preserved links between generations in a tangible form. Finally, with the emergence of states and empires, as the rulers' souls rose to take their places in the firmament alongside the high gods, their mummified mortal remains, surrounded by exquisite furniture, rare jewels, gold-encrusted chariots and other preciosities, were interred in gigantic crypts and pyramids that only a true god could have built.

Religious Perspectives in Anthropology

Dorothy Lee

At first glance, the study of the religion of non-Western cultures may appear somewhat esoteric, albeit interesting. In reality, however, religion is very much a part of everyday, practical activities in these cultures, and knowledge of a society's religion is essential for the successful introduction of social changes. In the following article, Dorothy Lee dramatically shows how religion is part and parcel of preliterate people's world view, or Weltanschauung: *the corpus of beliefs about the life and environment in which members of a society find themselves. Among preliterate societies, economic, political, and artistic behavior is permeated by religion. Lee points out that anthropologists make every attempt to understand the insiders' "emic" view of their universe, which they share with other members of their group, and demonstrates that an outsider's "etic" view is too limited a base of cultural knowledge on which to introduce innovations that do not violate the religious tenets of the society and meet with acceptance.*

Reprinted from Lowell D. Holmes, ed., *Readings in General Anthropology* (New York: Ronald Press, 1971), pp. 416–27.

IN PRIMITIVE SOCIETIES, WE DO NOT ALWAYS FIND the worship of God or a god, nor the idea of the supernatural. Yet religion is always present in man's view of his place in the universe, in his relatedness to man and nonhuman nature, to reality and circumstance. His universe may include the divine or may itself be divine. And his patterned behavior often has a religious dimension, so that we find religion permeating daily life—agriculture and hunting, health measures, arts and crafts.

We do find societies where a Supreme Being is recognized; but this Being is frequently so far removed from mundane affairs, that it is not present in the consciousness of the people except on the specific occasions of ceremonial or prayer. But in these same societies, we find communion with the unperceivable and unknowable in nature, with an ultimate reality, whether spirit, or power, or intensified being, or personal worth, which evokes humility, respect, courtesy or sometimes fear, on man's part. This relationship to the ultimate reality is so pervasive, that it may determine, for example, which hand a man will use in adjusting his loin cloth, or how much water he will drink at a time, or which way his head will point when he sleeps, or how he will butcher and utilize the carcass of a caribou. What anthropologists label "material culture," therefore, is never purely material. Often we would be at least as justified to call the operation involved religious.

All economic activities, such as hunting, gathering fuel, cultivating the land, storing food, assume a relatedness to the encompassing universe, and with many cultures, this is a religious relationship. In such cultures, men recognize a certain spiritual worth and dignity in the universe. They do not set out to control, or master, or exploit. Their ceremonials are often periods of intensified communion, even social affairs, in a broad sense, if the term may be extended to include the forces of the universe. They are not placating or bribing or even thanking; they are rather a formal period of concentrated, enjoyable association. In their relationships with nature, the people may see themselves as the offspring of a cherishing mother, or the guests of a generous hostess, or as members of a democratic society which proceeds on the principle of consent. So, when the Baiga in India were urged to change over to the use of an iron plow, they replied with horror that they could not tear the flesh of their mother with knives. And American Indians have hunted many animals with the consent of the generic essence of these—of which the particular animal was the carnal manifestation—only after establishing a relationship or reciprocity; with man furnishing the ceremonial, and Buffalo or Salmon or Caribou making a gift of the countless manifestations of his flesh.

The great care with which so many of the Indian groups utilized every portion of the carcass of a hunted animal, was an expression, not of economic thrift, but of courtesy and respect; in fact, an aspect of the religious relationship to the slain. The Wintu Indians of California, who lived on land so wooded that it was difficult to find clear land for putting up a group of houses, nevertheless used only dead wood for fuel, out of respect for nature. An old Wintu woman, speaking in prophetic vein, expressed this: "The White people never cared for land or deer or bear. When we Indians kill meat, we eat it all up. When we dig roots we make little holes. When we build houses, we make little holes. When we burn grass for grasshoppers, we don't ruin things. We shake down acorns and pinenuts. We don't chop down the trees. We only use dead wood. But the White people plow up the ground, pull up the trees, kill everything. The tree says, 'Don't. I am sore. Don't hurt me.' But they chop it down and cut it up. The spirit of the land hates them. They blast out trees and stir it up to its depths. They saw up the trees. That hurts them. The Indians never hurt anything, but the White people destroy all. They blast rocks and scatter them on the ground. The rock says, 'Don't! You are hurting me.' But the White people pay no attention. When the Indians use rocks, they take little round ones for their cooking. . . . How can the spirit of the earth like the White man? . . . Everywhere the White man has touched it, it is sore.'"

Here we find people who do not so much *seek* communion with environing nature as *find themselves* in communion with it. In many of these societies, not even mysticism is to be found, in our sense

of the word. For us, mysticism presupposes a prior separation of man from nature; and communion is achieved through loss of self and subsequent merging with that which is beyond; but for many cultures, there is no such distinct separation between self and other, which must be overcome. Here, man is *in* nature already, and we cannot speak properly of man *and* nature.

Take the Kaingang, for example, who chops out a wild beehive. He explains his act to the bees, as he would to a person whom he considered his coordinate. "Bee, produce! I chopped you out to make beer of you! Yukui's wife died, and I am making beer of you so that I can cut his hair." Or he may go up to a hive and say simply, "Bee, it is I." And the Arapesh of New Guinea, going to his yam garden, will first introduce to the spirit of the land, the brother-in-law whom he has brought along to help him with the gardening. This is not achieved communication, brought about for definite ends. It implies an already present relatedness with the ultimate reality, with that which is accepted in faith, and which exists irrespective of man's cognition or perception or logic. If we were to abstract, out of this situation, merely the food getting or the operational techniques, we would be misrepresenting the reality.

The same present relatedness is to be found in some societies where the deity is more specifically defined. The Tikopia, in the Solomon Islands Protectorate, sit and eat their meals with their dead under the floor, and hand food and drink to them; the dead are all somewhat divine, progressively so as they come nearer to the original, fully divine ancestor of the clan. Whatever their degree of divinity, the Tikopia is at home with them; he is aware of their vague presence, though he requires the services of a medium whenever he wants to make this presence definite.

Firth describes an occasion when a chief, having instructed a medium to invite his dead nephew to come and chew betel with him, found himself occupied with something else when the dead arrived, and so asked the medium to tell the spirit—a minor deity—to chew betel by himself. At another time, during an important ceremonial, when this chief was receiving on his forehead the vertical stripe which was the symbol that he was now the incarnation of the highest god, he jokingly jerked his head aside, so that the stripe, the insignium of the presence of the god, went crooked. These are the acts of a man who feels accepted by his gods, and is at one with them. And, in fact, the Tikopia appear to live in a continuum which includes nature and the divine without defining bounds; where communion is present, not achieved; where merging is a matter of being, not of becoming.

In these societies, where religion is an everpresent dimension of experience, it is doubtful that religion as such is given a name; Kluckhohn reports that the Navaho have no such word, but most ethnographers never thought to inquire. Many of these cultures, however, recognized and named the spiritual ingredient or attribute, the special quality of the wonderful, the very, the beyondness, in nature. This was sometimes considered personal, sometimes not. We have from the American Indians terms such as *manitou*, or *wakan*, or *yapaitu*, often translated as power; and we have the well-known Melanesian term *mana*. But this is what they reach through faith, the other end of the relationship; the relationship itself is unnamed. Apparently, to behave and think religiously, is to behave and think. To describe a way of life in its totality is to describe a religious way of life.

When we speak of agricultural taboos and rites, therefore, we often introduce an analytical factor which violates the fact. For example, when preparing seed for planting, one of the several things a Navaho traditionally does is to mix ground "mirage stone" with the seed. And in the process of storing corn, a double-eared stalk is laid at the bottom of the storage pit. In actual life, these acts are a continuous part of a total activity.

The distinction between the religious and the secular elements may even separate an act from the manner of performance, a verb from its adverb. The direction in which a man is facing when performing a secular act, or the number of times he shakes his hand when spattering water, often have their religious implications. When the Navaho planted his corn sunwise, his act reflected a total world view, and it would be nonsense for us to separate the planting itself from the direction of the planting.

Those of us who present religion as separate from "everyday" living, reflect moreover the distinctions of a culture which will identify six days with the secular in life and only the seventh with religion. In many primitive societies, religion is rarely absent from the details of everyday living, and the ceremonials represent a formalization and intensification of an everpresent attitude. We have societies such as that of the Hopi of Arizona, where ceremonials, and the preparation for them, cover most of the year. Some years ago, Crowwing, a Hopi, kept a journal for the period of a year, putting down all events of ceremonial import. Day after day, there are entries containing some casual reference to a religious activity, or describing a ritual, or the preparation for a ceremonial. After a few weeks of such entries, we come to a sequence of four days' entries which are devoted to a description of a ball game played by two opposing groups of children and enjoyed by a large number of spectators. But, in the end, this also turns out to have been ceremonial in nature, helping the corn to grow.

Among many groups, agriculture is an expression of man's religious relatedness to the universe. As Robert Redfield and W. Lloyd Warner have written: "The agriculture of the Maya Indians of southeastern Yucatan is not simply a way of securing food. It is also a way of worshipping the gods. Before a man plants, he builds an altar in the field and prays there. He must not speak boisterously in the cornfield; it is a sort of temple. The cornfield is planted as an incident in a perpetual sacred contract between supernatural beings and men. By this agreement, the supernaturals yield part of what is theirs—the riches of the natural environment—to men. In exchange, men are pious and perform the traditional ceremonies in which offerings are made to the supernaturals. . . . The world is seen as inhabited by the supernaturals; each has his appropriate place in the woods, the sky, or the wells from which the water is drawn. The village is seen as a reflection of the quadrilateral pattern of the cosmos; the cornfield too is oriented, laid out east, west, north, and south, with reference to the supernaturals that watch over the cardinal points; and the table altars erected for the ceremonies again remind the individual of this pattern. The stories that are told at the time when men wait to perform the ceremony before the planting of the corn or that children hear as they grow up are largely stories which explain and further sanction the traditional way of life."

Art also is often so permeated with religion that sometimes, as among the Navaho, what we classify as art is actually religion. To understand the rhythm of their chants, the "plot" of their tales, the making of their sand paintings, we have to understand Navaho religion: the concept of harmony between man and the universe as basic to health and well being; the concept of continuity, the religious significance of the groups of four, the door of contact opened through the fifth repetition, the need to have no completely enclosing frame around any of their works so that continuity can be maintained and the evil inside can have an opening through which to leave.

The sand paintings are no more art than they are ritual, myth, medical practice or religious belief. They are created as an integral aspect of a ceremonial which brings into harmony with the universal order one who finds himself in discord with it; or which intensifies and ensures the continuation of a harmony which is already present. Every line and shape and color, every interrelationship of form, is the visible manifestation of myth, ritual and religious belief. The making of the painting is accompanied with a series of sacred songs sung over a sick person, or over someone who, though healed of sickness by emergency measures has yet to be brought back into the universal harmony; or in enhancing and giving emphasis to the present harmony. What we would call purely medical practices may or may not be part of all this. When the ceremonial is over, the painting is over too; it is destroyed; it has fulfilled its function.

This is true also of the art of the neighboring Hopi; where the outstanding form of art is the drama. In this we find wonderfully humorous clowning, involving careful planning and preparation, creation of magnificent masks and costumes, rehearsals, organization. Everyone comes to see and responds with uproarious hilarity. But this is not mere art. It is an important way of helping nature in her work of growing the corn. Even the laughter of the audience helps in this.

More than dramatic rehearsal and creation of costumes has gone into the preparation. The actors have prepared themselves as whole persons. They have refrained from sexual activity, and from anything involving conflict. They have had good thoughts only. They have refrained from anger, worry and grief. Their preparations as well as their performance have had a religious dimension. Their drama is one act in the great process of the cyclical growing of corn, a divinity indispensable to man's well being, and to whose well being man is indispensable. Corn wants to grow, but cannot do so without the cooperation of the rest of nature and of

man's acts and thoughts and will. And, to be happy, corn must be danced by man and participate in his ceremonials. To leave the religious dimension out of all this, and to speak of Hopi drama as merely a form of art, would be to present a fallacious picture. Art and agriculture and religion are part of the same totality for the Hopi.

In our own culture, an activity is considered to be economic when it deals with effective utilization or exploitation of resources. But this definition cannot be used when speaking of Hopi economics. To begin with, it assumes an aggressive attitude toward the environment. It describes the situation of the homesteader in Alaska, for example, who works against tremendous odds clearing land for a dairy farm, against the inexorable pressure of time, against hostile elements. By his sweat, and through ingenuity and know-how and the use of brutally effective tools, he tames nature; he subjugates the land and exploits its resources to the utmost.

The Hopi Talayesua, however, describing his work on the land, does not see himself in opposition to it. He works *with* the elements, not *against* them. He helps the corn to grow; he cooperates with the thunderstorm and the pollen and the sun. He is in harmony with the elements, not in conflict; and he does not set out to conquer an opponent. He depends on the corn, but this is part of a mutual interdependence; it is not exploitation. The corn depends on him too. It cannot grow without his help; it finds life dull and lonely without his company and his ceremonials. So it gives its body for his food gladly, and enjoys living with him in his granary. The Hopi has a personal relationship with it. He treats it with respect, and houses it with the care and courtesy accorded to an honored guest. Is this economics?

In a work on Hopi economics we are given an account of the Hopi Salt Journey, under the heading, "Secondary Economic Activities." This expedition is also described in a Hopi autobiography, and here we discover that only those men who have achieved a certain degree of experience in the Hopi way, can go on this journey, and then, only if their minds are pure and they are in a state of harmony with the universe. There is a period of religious preparation, followed by the long and perilous journey which is attended by a number of rituals along the way. Old men, lowering themselves from the overhanging ledge onto the salt deposits, tremble with fear, knowing that they may be unable to make the ascent. The occasion is solemnly religious. This is no utilization of resources, in the eyes of the Hopi who makes the journey. He goes to help the growing corn; the Salt Journey brings needed rain. Twelve adult men will spend days and court dangers to procure salt which they can buy for two dollars from the itinerant peddler. By our own economic standards, this is not an efficient use of human resources. But Hopi ends transcend our economic categories and our standards of efficiency are irrelevant to them.

In many societies, land tenure, or the transference of land, operations involved in hunting and agriculture, are often a part of a religious way of life. In our own culture, man conceives of his relationship to his physical environment, and even sometimes his human environment, as mechanistic and manipulative; in other cultures, we often find what Ruth Benedict has called the animistic attitude toward nature and man, underlying practices which are often classified miscellaneously together in ethnographics, under the heading of superstitions or taboos. The courteous speech to the bear about to be killed, the offering to the deer world before the hunter sets out, the introduction of the brother-in-law to the garden spirit, or the sacrifice to the rice field about to be sold, the refraining from intercourse, or from the eating of meat or from touching food with the hand, are expressive of such an attitude. They are the practices we find in a democratic society where there is consideration for the rights of everyone as opposed to the brutal efficiency of the dictator who feels free to exploit, considering the rights of none. They reflect the attitude of people who believe in conference and consent, not in coercion; of people who generally find personality or mana in nature and man, sometimes more, sometimes less. In this framework, taboo and superstitious act mean that man acts and refrains from acting in the name of a wider democracy which includes nature and the divine.

With such a conception of man's place in nature, what is for us land tenure, or ownership, or rights of use and disposal, is for other societies an intimate belongingness. So the Arapesh conceive of themselves as belonging to the land, in the way that flora and fauna belong to it. They cultivate the land by the grace of the immanent spirits, but they cannot dispose of it and cannot conceive of doing so.

This feeling of affinity between society and land is widespread and appears in various forms and varying degrees of intensity, and it is not found only among sedentary peoples. We have Australian tribes where the very spirit of the men is believed to reside in the land, where a bush or a rock or a peculiar formation is the present incarnation of myth, and contains security and religious value; where a social class, a structured group of relatives, will contain in addition to human beings, an animal and a feature of the landscape. Here, when a man moves away from the land of his group, he leaves the vital part of himself behind. When a magistrate put people from such societies in jail in a distant city, he had no idea of the terrifying severity of the punishment he was meting; he was cutting the tribesman off from the very source of his life and of his self, from the past, and the future which were incorporated and present in his land.

In the technology of such societies we are again dealing with material where the religious and secular are not distinct from each other. We have, for example, the description which Raymond Firth gives of the replacing of a wornout wash strake on a canoe, among the Tikopia. This operation is expertly and coherently carried out, with secular and religious acts performed without distinction in continuous succession or concurrently. A tree is cut down for the new wash strake, a libation is poured out to the deities of the canoe to announce this new timber, and a kava rite is performed to persuade the deities to step out of the canoe and on to a piece of bark cloth, where they can live undisturbed, while the canoe is being tampered with. Then comes the unlashing of the old wash strake, the expert examination of the body of the canoe in search of lurking defects, the discovery of signs indicating the work of a borer, the cutting of the body of the canoe with a swift stroke to discover whether the borer is there, accompanied by an appeal to the deities of the canoe by the expert, to witness what he is doing, and the necessity for doing it.

Now a kinsman of the original builder of the canoe, now dead and a tutelary deity, spontaneously drops his head on to the side of the canoe and wails over the wounding of the body of the canoe. The borer is discovered, in the meantime, to be still there; but only a specially consecrated adze can deal with him successfully. The adze is sent for, dedicated anew to the deity, invoked, and finally wielded with success by the expert.

All this is performed with remarkable expedition and economy of motion yet the Tikopia workers are not interested in saving time; they are concerned neither with time limits not with speed in itself.

Their concern is with the dispossessed deities whose home must be made ready against their return; and the speed of their work is incidental to this religious concern. The end result is efficiency; but unlike our own efficiency, this is not rooted in the effort to utilize and exploit material and time resources to the utmost; it is rooted in that profound religious feeling which also gives rise to the time-consuming rites and the wailing procedures which, from the purely economic point of view, are wasteful and interfering.

The world view of a particular society includes that society's conception of man's own relation to the universe, human and non-human, organic and inorganic, secular and divine, to use our own dualisms. It expresses man's view of his own role in the maintenance of life, and of the forces of nature. His attitude toward responsibility and initiative is inextricable from his conception of nature as deity-controlled, man-controlled, regulated through a balanced cooperation between god and man, or perhaps maintained through some eternal homeostasis, independent of man and perhaps of any deity. The way a man acts, his feeling of guilt and achievement, and his very personality, are affected by the way he envisions his place within the universe.

For example, there are the Tiv of Southern Nigeria who as described by one of them in the thirties, people the universe with potentially hostile and harmful powers, the *akombo*. Man's function in the maintenance of his own life and the moderate well-being of the land and of his social unit, is to prevent the manifestation of *akombo* evil, through performing rites and observing taboos. So his rites render safe through preventing, through expulsion and purging. His role is negative, defending the normal course against the interference. Vis-à-vis the universe, his acts arise out of negative motives. Thus what corresponds to a gift of first fruits to a deity in other cultures is phrased as a rite for preventing the deities from making a man's food go bad or diminish too quickly; fertility rites for a field are actually rites preventing the evil-intentioned from robbing the fields of their normal fertility.

In the writings of R. F. Barton, who studied the Ifugao of Luzon in the early part of this century, these people also appear to see deities as ready to interfere and bring evil; but their conception of man's role within the structure of the universe is a different one from that of the Tiv. In Barton's descriptive accounts, the Ifugao either accept what comes as deity-given, or act without being themselves the agents;

they believe that no act can come to a conclusive end without the agency of a specific deity. They have a specific deity often for every step within an operation and for every part of the implement to be used. R. F. Barton recorded the names of 1,240 deities and believed that even so he had not exhausted the list.

The Ifugao associate a deity with every structured performance and at least a large number of their deliberate acts. They cannot go hunting, for example, without enlisting the aid of the deity of each step of the chase, to render each effective, or to nullify any lurking dangers. There is a deity for the level spot where "the hunter stands watching and listening to the dogs"; one for when the dogs "are sicced on the game"; one for when "the hunter leans on his spear transfixing the quarry"; twelve are listed as the deities of specific ways of rendering harmless to the hunter's feet the snags and fangs of snakes which he encounters. If he is to be successful in the hunt, a man does not ask the blessing of a deity. He pays all the particular deities of every specific spot and act, getting them to transitivize each act individually.

Even so, in most cases an Ifugao remains non-agentive, since the function of many of the deities is to save man from encounter, rather than to give him success in his dealing with it. For example, in the area of interpersonal relations, we have Tupya who is invoked so that, "the creditor comes for dun for what is owed, but on the way he forgets and goes about other business"; and Dulaiya, who is invoked so that "the enemies just don't think about us, so they don't attack." His tools, also, are ineffective of themselves; so that, when setting a deadfall, he invokes and bribes such deities as that for the Flat Stone of the Deadfall, the Main Posts of the Deadfall, the Fall of the Deadfall, the Trigger of the Deadfall. Most of the Ifugao economy is involved in providing sacrifices to the deities, big or little according to the magnitude of the operation and the importance of the deities. There is no warmth in the sacrifices; no expression of gratitude or appeal or belongingness. As the Ifugaos see it, the sacrifice is a bribe. With such bribes, they buy the miraculous intervention and transitivization which are essential for achievement, health, and good personal relations.

The Ifugao show no humility in the face of this ineffective role in the universe; they merely accept it as the state of things. They accept their own failures, the frequent deaths, the sudden and disastrous flaring up of tempers, as things that are bound to happen irrespective of their own desires and efforts. But they are neither passive nor helpless. They carry on great undertakings, and, even now they go on forbidden head hunts. They know when and how and whom to bribe so as to perfect their defective acts. When however, a deity states a decision, they accept it as immutable. A Catholic priest tells a story about the neighboring Iloko which illustrates this acceptance. A Christian Iloko was on his deathbed, and the priest, trying to persuade him to repent of his sin, painted to him vividly the horrors of hell; but the dying man merely answered, "If God wants me to go to hell, I am perfectly willing."

Among the Wintu Indians of California we find that man sees himself as effective but in a clearly limited way. An examination of the myths of the Wintu shows that the individual was conceived as having a limited agentive role, shaping, using, intervening, actualizing and temporalizing the given, but never creating; that man was viewed as needing skill for his operations, but that specific skill was useless without "luck" which a man received through communion and pleading with some universal power.

It is to this limited role of man, geared to the working of the universe, that I referred when I spoke earlier of Hopi drama and agriculture. Without an understanding of this role, no Hopi activity or attitude or relationship can be understood. The Hopi have developed the idea of man's limited effectiveness in their own fashion, and have elaborated it systematically in what they call the "Hopi Way." Laura Thompson says of the Hopi, "All phenomena relevant to the life of the tribe—including man, the animals, and plants, the earth, sun, moon, clouds, the ancestors, and the spirits—are believed to be interdependent. . . . In this system each individual—human and non-human—is believed to have . . . a definite role in the universal order." Traditionally, fulfillment of the law of nature—the growth of the corn, the movements of the sun—can come only with man's participation, only with man's performance of the established ceremonials. Here man was effective, but only in cooperation with the rest of the phenomena of nature.

The Indians of the Plains, such as the Crow and the Sioux, have given a somewhat different form to this conception of man's circumscribed agency. The aggressive behavior for which they have been known, their great personal autonomy, their self-assurance and assertiveness and in recent years, their great dependence and apathy, have been explained as an expression of this conception. These societies envisioned the universe as pervaded by an undifferentiated religious force on which they were dependent for success in their undertakings and in life generally. The specific formulation differed in the different tribes, but, essentially, in all it was believed that each individual and particularly each man, must tap this universal force if his undertakings were to be successful. Without this "power" a man could not achieve success in any of the valued activities, whether warfare or the hunt; and no leadership was possible without this power. This was a force enhancing and intensifying the being of the man who acted; it was not, as with the Ifugao, an effectiveness applied to specific details of activities. The invididual himself prepared himself in the hardihood, self-control, skills and areas of knowledge necessary. Little boy of five or seven took pride in their ability to withstand pain, physical hardship, and the terrors of running errands alone in the night. The Sioux did not appeal for divine intervention; he did not want the enemy to forget to come. Yet neither was he fearless. He appealed for divine strength to overcome his own fears as well as the external enemy.

The relationship with the divine, in this case, is personal and intense. The Plains Indian Sioux did not, like the Hopi, inherit a specific relatedness when he was born in a specific clan. Each man, each pre-adolescent boy, had to achieve the relationship for himself. He had to go out into the wilderness and spend days and nights without food or drink, in the cold, among wild beasts, afraid and hungry and anxious, humbling himself and supplicating, sometimes inflicting excruciating pain upon himself, until some particular manifestation of the universal force took pity upon him and came to him to become his life-long guardian and power. The appeals to the universal force were made sometimes in a group, through the institution of the Sun Dance. But here also they were individual in nature. The relationship with the divine was an inner experience; and when the Dakota Black Elk recounted his autobiography, he spoke mainly of these intense, personal religious experiences. Within this range of variation in form and concept and world view, we find expressed by all the same immediate relatedness to the divine.

Steel Axes for Stone-Age Australians

Lauriston Sharp

In this article, Lauriston Sharp discusses the introduction of the steel axe into the Yir Yoront culture and the startling impact this seemingly minor innovation had on their religion and social structure. He outlines a classic example of the cultural disruption that can occur when an outside group intervenes in the life of another group without careful consideration of the various consequences that may occur. Sharp's article is a good selection for Chapter 1 because it gives us an excellent account of the anthropological fieldworker's traditional stance of noninvolvement in a group's religious life versus the missionary's tendency to plunge wholeheartedly into the everyday life and decision making of a people.

Reproduced by permission of the Society for Applied Anthropology from *Human Organization*, Vol. 11, no. 2 (1952) pp. 457–64.

LIKE OTHER AUSTRALIAN ABORIGINALS, THE YIR Yoront group, which lives at the mouth of the Coleman River on the west coast of Cape York Peninsula originally had no knowledge of metals. Technologically their culture was of the old stone age or paleolithic type. They supported themselves by hunting and fishing, and obtained vegetables and other materials from the bush using simple gathering techniques. Their only domesticated animal was the dog, and they had no cultivated plants of any kind. Unlike some other aboriginal groups, however, the Yir Yoront did have polished stone axes hafted in short handles, which were most important in their economy.

Towards the end of the nineteenth century, metal tools and other European artifacts began to filter into the Yir Yoront territory. The flow increased with the gradual expansion of the white frontier outward from southern and eastern Queensland. Of all the items of western technology made available by this expansion, the hatchet, or shorthandled steel axe, was the most acceptable to and the most highly valued by all aboriginals.

During the mid 1930s an American anthropologist lived alone in the bush among the Yir Yoront for thirteen months without seeing another white man. The Yir Yoront were thus still relatively isolated and they continued to live an essentially independent economic existence, supporting themselves entirely by means of their old stone age techniques. Even so, their polished stone axes were disappearing quickly and being replaced by steel axes, which came to them in considerable numbers, either directly or indirectly, from various European sources to the south.

What changes in the life of the Yir Yoront still living under aboriginal conditions in the Australian bush could be expected as a result of their increasing possession and use of the steel axe?

Relevant Factors

If we concentrate our attention on Yir Yoront behavior centering about the original stone axe (rather than on the axe—the object—itself) as a cultural trait or item of cultural equipment, we should get some conception of the role this implement played in aboriginal culture. This, in turn, should enable us to foresee with considerable accuracy some of the results stemming from the displacement of the stone axe by the steel axe.

The production of a stone axe required a number of simple technological skills. With the various details of the axe well in mind, adult men could set about producing it (a task not considered appropriate for women or children). First of all a man had to know the location and properties of several natural resources found in his immediate environment: pliable wood for a handle, which could be doubled or bent over the axe head and bound tightly; bark, which could be rolled into cord for the binding; and gum, to fix the stone head in the haft. These materials had to be correctly gathered, stored, prepared, cut to size, and applied or manipulated. They were in plentiful supply, and could be taken from anyone's property without special permission. Postponing consideration of the stone head, the axe could be made by any normal man who had a simple knowledge of nature and of the technological skills involved, together with fire (for heating the gum), and a few simple cutting tools—perhaps the sharp shells of plentiful bivalves.

The use of the stone axe as a piece of capital equipment used in producing other goods indicates its very great importance to the subsistence economy of the aboriginal. Anyone—man, woman, or child—could use the axe; indeed, it was used primarily by women, for theirs was the task of obtaining sufficient wood to keep the family campfire burning all day, for cooking or other purposes, and all night against mosquitoes and cold (for in July, winter temperature might drop below 40 degrees). In a normal lifetime a woman would use the axe to cut or knock down literally tons of firewood. The axe was also used to make other tools or weapons, and a variety of material equipment required by the aboriginal in his daily life. The stone axe was essential in the construction of the wet-season domed huts which keep out some rain and some insects; of platforms which provide dry storage; of shelters which give shade in the dry summer when days are bright and hot. In hunting and fishing and in gathering vegetable or animal food the axe was also a necessary tool, and in this tropical culture, where preservatives or other means of storage are lacking, the natives spend more time obtaining food than in any other occupation—except sleeping. In only two instances was the use of the stone axe strictly limited to adult men: for gathering wild honey, the most prized food known to the Yir Yoront; and for making the secret paraphernalia for ceremonies. From this brief listing of some of the activities involving the use of the axe, it is easy to understand why there was at least one stone axe in every camp, in every hunting or fighting party, and in every group out on a "walk-about" in the bush.

The stone axe was also prominent in interpersonal relations. Yir Yoront men were dependent upon interpersonal relations for their stone axe heads, since the flat, geologically recent, alluvial country over which they range provides no suitable stone for this purpose. The stone they used came from quarries four hundred miles to the south, reaching the Yir Yoront through long lines of male trading partners. Some of these chains terminated with the Yir Yoront men; others extended on farther north to other groups, using Yir Yoront men as links. Almost every older adult man had one or more regular trading partners, some to the north and some to the south. He provided his partner or partners in the south with surplus spears, particularly fighting spears tipped with the barbed spines of sting ray, which snap into vicious fragments when they penetrate human flesh. For a dozen such spears, some of which he may have obtained from a partner to the north, he would receive one stone axe head. Studies have shown that the sting-ray barb spears increased in value as they moved south and farther from the sea. One hundred and fifty miles south of Yir Yoront one such spear may be exchanged for one stone axe head. Although actual investigations could not be made, it was presumed that farther south, nearer the quarries, one sting-ray barb spear would bring several stone axe heads. Apparently people who acted as links in the middle of the chain and who made neither spears nor axe heads would receive a certain number of each as a middle man's profit.

Thus trading relations, which may extend the individual's personal relationships beyond that of his own group, were associated with spears and axes, two of the most important items in a man's equipment. Finally, most of the exchanges took place during the dry season, at the time of the great aboriginal celebrations centering about initiation rites or other totemic ceremonials which attracted hundreds and were the occasion for much exciting activity in addition to trading.

Returning to the Yir Yoront, we find that adult men kept their axes in camp with their other equipment, or carried them when traveling. Thus a woman or child who wanted to use an axe—as might frequently happen during the day—had to get one from a man, use it promptly, and return it in good condition. While a man might speak of "my axe," a woman or child could not.

This necessary and constant borrowing of axes from older men by women and children was in accordance with regular patterns of kinship behavior. A woman would expect to use her husband's axe unless he himself was using it; if unmarried, or if her husband was absent, a woman would go first to her older brother or to her father. Only in extraordinary circumstances would she seek a stone axe from other male kin. A girl, boy, or a young man would look to a father or an older brother to provide an axe for their use. Older men, too, would follow similar rules if they had to borrow an axe.

It will be noted that all of these social relationships in which the stone axe had a place are pair relationships and that the use of the axe helped to define and maintain their character and the roles of the two individual participants. Every active relationship among the Yir Yoront involved a definite and accepted status of superordination or subordination. A person could have no dealings with another on exactly equal terms. The nearest approach to equality was between brothers, although the older was always superordinate to the younger. Since the exchange of goods in a trading relationship involved a mutual reciprocity, trading partners usually stood in a brotherly type of relationship, although one was always classified as older than the other and would have some advantage in case of dispute. It can be seen that repeated and widespread conduct centering around the use of the axe helped to generalize and standardize these sex, age, and kinship roles both in their normal benevolent and exceptional malevolent aspects.

The status of any individual Yir Yoront was determined not only by sex, age, and extended kin relationships, but also by membership in one of two dozen patrilineal totemic clans into which the entire community was divided. Each clan had literally hundreds of totems from one or two of which the clan derived its name, and the clan members their personal names. These totems included natural species or phenomena such as the sun, stars, and daybreak, as well as cultural "species": imagined ghosts, rainbow serpents, heroic ancestors; such eternal cultural verities as fires, spears, huts; and such human activities, conditions, or attributes as eating, vomiting, swimming, fighting, babies and corpses, milk and blood, lips and loins. While individual members of such totemic classes or species might disappear or be destroyed, the class itself was obviously ever-present and indestructible. The totems, therefore, lent permanence and stability to the clans, to the groupings of human individuals who generation after generation were each associated with a set of totems which distinguished one clan from another.

The stone axe was one of the most important of the many totems of the Sunlit Cloud Iguana clan. The names of many members of this clan referred to the axe itself, to activities in which the axe played a vital part, or to the clan's mythical ancestors with whom the axe was prominently associated. When it was necessary to represent the stone axe in totemic ceremonies, only men of this clan exhibited it or pantomimed its use. In secular life, the axe could be made by any man and used by all; but in the sacred realm of the totems it belonged exclusively to the Sunlit Cloud Iguana people.

Supporting those aspects of cultural behavior which we have called technology and conduct is a third area of culture which includes ideas, sentiments, and values. These are most difficult to deal with, for they are latent and covert, and even unconscious, and must be deduced from overt actions and language or other communicating behavior. In this aspect of the culture lies the significance of the stone axe to the Yir Yoront and to their cultural way of life.

The stone axe was an important symbol of masculinity among the Yir Yoront (just as pants or pipes are to us). By a complicated set of ideas the axe was defined as "belonging" to males, and everyone in the society (except untrained infants) accepted these ideas. Similarly spears, spear throwers, and fire-making sticks were owned only by men and were also symbols of masculinity. But the masculine values represented by the stone axe were constantly being impressed on all members of society by the fact that females borrowed axes but not other masculine artifacts. Thus the axe stood for an important theme of Yir Yoront culture: the superiority and rightful dominance of the male, and the greater value of his concerns and of all things associated with him. As the axe also had to be borrowed by the younger people it represented the prestige of age, another important theme running through Yir Yoront behavior.

To understand the Yir Yoront culture it is necessary to be aware of a system of ideas which may be called their totemic ideology. A fundamental belief of the aboriginal divided time into two great epochs: (1) a distant and sacred period at the beginning of the world when the earth was peopled by mildly marvelous ancestral beings or culture heroes who are in a special sense the forebears of the clans; and (2) a period when the old was succeeded by a new order which includes the present. Originally there was no anticipation of another era supplanting the present. The future would simply be an eternal continuation and reproduction of the present which itself had remained unchanged since the epochal revolution of ancestral times.

The important thing to note is that the aboriginal believed that the present world, as a natural and cultural environment, was and should be simply a detailed reproduction of the world of the ancestors. He believed that the entire universe "is now as it was in the beginning" when it was established and left by the ancestors. The ordinary cultural life of the ancestors became the daily life of the Yir Yoront camps, and the extraordinary life of the ancestors remained extant in the recurring symbolic pantomimes and paraphernalia found only in the most sacred atmosphere of the totemic rites.

Such beliefs, accordingly, open the way for ideas of what *should be* (because it supposedly *was*) to influence or help determine what actually *is*. A man called Dog-chases-iguana-up-a-tree-and-barks-at-him-all-night had that and other names because he believed his ancestral alter ego had also had them; he was a member of the Sunlit Cloud Iguana clan because his ancestor was; he was associated with particular countries and totems of this same ancestor; during an initiation he played the role of a dog and symbolically attacked and killed certain members of other clans because his ancestor (conveniently either anthropomorphic or kynomorphic) really did the same to the ancestral alter egos of these men; and he would avoid his mother-in-law, joke with a mother's distant brother, and make spears in a certain way because his and other people's ancestors did these things. His behavior in these specific ways was outlined, and to that extent determined for him, by a set of ideas concerning the past and the relation of the present to the past.

But when we are informed that Dog-chases-etc. had two wives from the Spear Black Duck clan and one from the Native Companion clan, one of them being blind, that he had four children with such and such names, that he had a broken wrist and was left handed, all because his ancestor had exactly these same attributes, then we know (though he apparently didn't) that the present has influenced the past, that the mythical world has been somewhat adjusted to meet the exigencies and accidents of the inescapably real present.

There was thus in Yir Yoront ideology a nice balance in which the mythical was adjusted in part to the real world, the real world in part to the ideal pre-existing mythical world, the adjustments occurring to maintain a fundamental tenet of native faith that the present must be a mirror of the past. Thus the stone axe in all its aspects, uses, and associations was integrated into the context of Yir Yoront technology and conduct because a myth, a set of ideas, had put it there.

The Outcome

The introduction of the steel axe indiscriminately and in large numbers into the Yir Yoront technology occurred simultaneously with many other changes. It is therefore impossible to separate all the results of this single innovation. Nevertheless, a number of specific effects of the change from stone to steel axes may be noted, and the steel axe may be used as an epitome of the increasing quantity of European goods and implements received by the aboriginals and of their general influence on the native culture. The use of the steel axe to illustrate such influences would seem to be justified. It was one of the first European artifacts to be adopted for regular use by the Yir Yoront, and whether made of stone or steel, the axe was clearly one of the most important items of cultural equipment they possessed.

The shift from stone to steel axes provided no major technological difficulties. While the aboriginals themselves could not manufacture steel axe heads, a steady supply from outside continued; broken wooden handles could easily be replaced from bush timbers with aboriginal tools. Among the Yir Yoront the new axe was never used to the extent it was on mission or cattle stations (for carpentry work, pounding tent pegs, as a hammer, and so on); indeed, it had so few more uses than the stone axe that its practical effect on the native standard of living was negligible. It did some jobs better, and could be used longer without breakage. These factors were sufficient to make it of value to the native. The white man believed that a shift from steel to stone axe on his part would be a definite regression. He was convinced that his axe was much more efficient, that its use would save time, and that it therefore represented technical "progress" towards goals which he had set up for the native. But this assumption was hardly born out in aboriginal practice. Any leisure time the Yir Yoront might gain by using steel axes or other western tools was not invested in "improving the conditions of life," nor certainly, in developing aesthetic activities, but in sleep—an art they had mastered thoroughly.

Previously, a man in need of an axe would acquire a stone axe head through regular trading partners from whom he knew what to expect, and was then dependent solely upon a known and adequate natural environment, and his own skills or easily acquired techniques. A man wanting a steel axe, however, was in no such self-reliant position. If he attended a mission festival when steel axes were handed out as gifts, he might receive one either by chance or by happening to impress upon the mission staff that he was one of the "better" bush aboriginals (the missionaries definition of "better" being quite different from that of his bush fellows). Or, again almost by pure chance, he might get some brief job in connection with the mission which would enable him to earn a steel axe. In either case, for older men a preference for the steel axe helped change the situation from one of self-reliance to one of dependence, and a shift in behavior from well-structured or defined situations in technology or conduct to ill-defined situations in conduct alone. Among the men, the older ones whose earlier experience or knowledge of the white man's harshness made them suspicious were particularly careful to avoid having relations with the mission, and thus excluded themselves from acquiring steel axes from that source.

In other aspects of conduct or social relations, the steel axe was even more significantly at the root of psychological stress among the Yir Yoront. This was the result of new factors which the missionary considered beneficial: the simple numerical increase in axes per capita as a result of mission distribution, and distribution directly to younger men, women, and even children. By winning the favor of the mission staff, a woman might be given a steel axe which was clearly intended to be hers, thus creating a situation quite different from the previous custom which necessitated her borrowing an axe from a male relative. As a result a woman would refer to the axe as "mine," a possessive form she was never able to use of the stone axe. In the same fashion, young men or even boys also obtained steel axes directly from the mission, with the result that older men no longer had a complete monopoly of all the axes in the bush community. All this led to a revolutionary confusion of sex, age, and kinship roles, with a major gain in independence and loss of subordination on the part of those who now owned steel axes when they had previously been unable to possess stone axes.

The trading partner relationship was also affected by the new situation. A Yir Yoront might have a trading partner in a tribe to the south whom he defined as a younger brother and over whom he would therefore have some authority. But if the partner were in contact with the mission or had other access to steel axes, his subordination obviously decreased. Among other things, this took some of the excitement away from the dry season fiesta-like tribal gatherings centering around initiations. These had traditionally been the climactic annual occasions for exchanges between trading partners, when a man might seek to acquire a whole year's supply of stone axe heads. Now he might find himself prostituting his wife to almost total strangers in return for steel axes or other white man's goods. With trading partnerships weakened there was less reason to attend the ceremonies, and less fun for those who did.

Not only did an increase in steel axes and their distribution to women change the character of the relations between individuals (the paired relationships that have been noted), but a previously rare type of relationship was created in the Yir Yoront's conduct towards whites. In the aboriginal society there were few occasions outside of the immediate family when an individual would initiate action to several other people at once. In any average group, in accordance with the kinship system, while a person might be superordinate to several people to whom he could suggest or command action, he was also subordinate to several others with whom such behavior would be tabu. There was thus no overall chieftainship or authoritarian leadership of any kind. Such complicated operations as grass-burning animal drives or totemic ceremonies could be carried out smoothly because each person was aware of his role.

On both mission and cattle stations, however, the whites imposed their conception of leadership roles upon the aboriginals, consisting of one person in a controlling relationship with a subordinate group. Aboriginals called together to receive gifts, including axes, at a mission Christmas party found themselves facing one or two whites who sought to control their behavior for the occasion, who disregarded the age, sex, and kinship variables of which the aboriginals were so conscious, and who considered them all at one subordinate level. The white also sought to impose similar patterns on work parties. (However, if he placed an aboriginal in charge of a mixed group of post-hole diggers, for example, half of the group, those subordinate to the "boss," would work while the other half, who were superordinate to him, would sleep.) For the aboriginal, the steel axe and other European goods came to symbolize this new and uncomfortable form of social organization, the leader-group relationship.

The most disturbing effects of the steel axe, operating in conjunction with other elements also being introduced from the white man's several subcultures, developed in the realm of traditional ideas, sentiments, and values. These were undermined at a rapidly mounting rate, with no new conceptions being defined to replace them. The result was the erection of a mental and moral void which foreshadowed the collapse and destruction of all Yir Yoront culture, if not, indeed, the extinction of the biological group itself.

From what has been said it should be clear how changes in overt behavior, in technology and conduct, weakened the values inherent in a reliance on nature, in the prestige of masculinity and of age, and in the various kinship relations. A scene was set in which a wife, or a young son whose initiation may

not yet have been completed, need no longer defer to the husband or father who, in turn, became confused and insecure as he was forced to borrow a steel axe from them. For the woman and boy the steel axe helped establish a new degree of freedom which they accepted readily as an escape from the unconscious stress of the old patterns—but they, too, were left confused and insecure. Ownership became less well defined with the result that stealing and trespassing were introduced into technology and conduct. Some of the excitement surrounding the great ceremonies evaporated and they lost their previous gaiety and interest. Indeed, life itself became less interesting, although this did not lead the Yir Yoront to discover suicide, a concept foreign to them.

The whole process may be most specifically illustrated in terms of totemic system, which also illustrates the significant role played by a system of ideas, in this case a totemic ideology, in the breakdown of a culture.

In the first place, under pre-European aboriginal conditions where the native culture has become adjusted to a relatively stable environment, few, if any, unheard of or catastrophic crises can occur. It is clear, therefore, that the totemic system serves very effectively in inhibiting radical cultural changes. The closed system of totemic ideas, explaining and categorizing a well-known universe as it was fixed at the beginning of time, presents a considerable obstacle to the adoption of new or the dropping of old culture traits. The obstacle is not insurmountable and the system allows for the minor variations which occur in the norms of daily life. But the inception of major changes cannot easily take place.

Among the bush Yir Yoront the only means of water transport is a light wood log to which they cling in their constant swimming of rivers, salt creeks, and tidal inlets. These natives know that tribes forty-five miles further north have a bark canoe. They know these northern tribes can thus fish from midstream or out at sea, instead of clinging to the river banks and beaches, that they can cross coastal waters infested with crocodiles, sharks, sting rays, and Portuguese men-of-war without danger. They know the materials of which the canoe is made exist in their own environment. But they also know, as they say, that they do not have canoes because their own mythical ancestors did not have them. They assume that the canoe was part of the ancestral universe of the northern tribes. For them, then, the adoption of the canoe would not be simply a matter of learning a number of new behavioral skills for its manufacture and use. The adoption would require a much more difficult procedure; the acceptance by the entire society of a myth, either locally developed or borrowed, to explain the presence of the canoe, to associate it with some one or more of the several hundred mythical ancestors (and how decide which?), and thus establish it as an accepted totem of one of the clans ready to be used by the whole community. The Yir Yoront have not made this adjustment, and in this case we can only say that for the time being at least, ideas have won out over very real pressures for technological change. In the elaborateness and explicitness of the totemic ideologies we seem to have one explanation for the notorious stability of Australian cultures under aboriginal conditions, an explanation which gives due weight to the importance of ideas in determining human behavior.

At a later stage of the contact situation, as has been indicated, phenomena unaccounted for by the totemic ideological system begin to appear with regularity and frequency and remain within the range of native experience. Accordingly, they cannot be ignored . . . and there is an attempt to assimilate them and account for them along the lines of principles inherent in the ideology. The bush Yir Yoront of the mid-thirties represent this stage of the acculturation process. Still trying to maintain their aboriginal definition of the situation they accept European artifacts and behavior patterns, but fit them into their totemic system, assigning them to various clans on a par with original totems. There is an attempt to have the myth-making process keep up with these cultural changes so that the idea system can continue to support the rest of the culture. But analysis of overt behavior, of dreams, and of some of the new myths indicates that this arrangement is not entirely satisfactory, that the native clings to his totemic system with intellectual loyalty (lacking any substitute ideology), but that associated sentiments and values are weakened. His attitudes towards his own and towards European culture are found to be highly ambivalent.

All ghosts are totems of the Head-to-the-East Corpse clan, are thought of as white, and are of course closely associated with death. The white man, too, is closely associated with death, and he

and all things pertaining to him are naturally assigned to the Corpse clan as totems. The steel axe, as a totem, was thus associated with the Corpse clan. But as an "axe," clearly linked with the stone axe, it is a totem of the Sunlit Cloud Iguana clan. Moreover, the steel axe, like most European goods, has no distinctive origin myth, nor are mythical ancestors associated with it. Can anyone, sitting in the shade of a *ti* tree one afternoon, create a myth to resolve this confusion? No one has, and the horrid suspicion arises as to the authenticity of the origin myths, which failed to take into account this vast new universe of the white man. The steel axe, shifting hopelessly between one clan and the other, is not only replacing the stone axe physically, but is hacking at the supports of the entire culture system.

The aboriginals to the south of the Yir Yoront have clearly passed beyond this stage. They are engulfed by European culture, either by the mission or cattle station subcultures or, for some natives, by a baffling, paradoxical combination of both incongruent varieties. The totemic ideology can no longer support the inrushing mass of foreign culture traits, and the myth-making process in its native form breaks down completely. Both intellectually and emotionally a saturation point is reached so that the myriad new traits which can neither be ignored nor any longer assimilated simply force the aboriginal to abandon his totemic system. With the collapse of this system of ideas, which is so closely related to so many other aspects of the native culture, there follows an appallingly sudden and complete cultural disintegration, and a demoralization of the individual such as has seldom been recorded elsewhere. Without the support of a system of ideas well devised to provide cultural stability in a stable environment, but admittedly too rigid for the new realities pressing in from outside, native behavior and native sentiments and values are simply dead. Apathy reigns. The aboriginal has passed beyond the realm of any outsider who might wish to do him well or ill.

Returning from the broken natives huddled on cattle stations or on the fringes of frontier towns to the ambivalent but still lively aboriginals settled on the Mitchell River mission, we note one further devious result of the introduction of European artifacts. During a wet season stay at the mission, the anthropologist discovered that his supply of tooth paste was being depleted at an alarming rate. Investigation showed that it was being taken by old men for use in a new tooth paste cult. Old materials of magic having failed, new materials were being tried out in a malevolent magic directed towards the mission staff and some of the younger aboriginal men. Old males, largely ignored by the missionaries, were seeking to regain some of their lost power and prestige. The mild aggression proved hardly effective, but perhaps only because confidence in any kind of magic on the mission was by this time at a low ebb.

For the Yir Yoront still in the bush, a time could be predicted when personal deprivation and frustration in a confused culture would produce an overload of anxiety. The mythical past of the totemic ancestors would disappear as a guarantee of a present of which the future was supposed to be a stable continuation. Without the past, the present could be meaningless and the future unstructured and uncertain. Insecurities would be inevitable. Reaction to this stress might be some form of symbolic aggression, or withdrawal and apathy, or some more realistic approach. In such a situation the missionary with understanding of the processes going on about him would find his opportunity to introduce his forms of religion and to help create a new cultural universe.

2

Myth, Ritual, Symbolism, and Taboo

Tales, legends, proverbs, riddles, adages, and myths make up what anthropologists call *folklore,* an important subject for the study of culture. Because of its sacred nature, myth is especially significant in the analysis of comparative religion. Myth functions in a society as a "charter," as Bronislaw Malinowski puts it—a model for behavior that also explains the origins of the world, life on earth, death, and all other experiences of human existence:

> [Myth] is a statement of primeval reality which lives in the institutions and pursuits of a community. It justifies by precedent the existing order and it supplies a retrospective pattern of moral values, of sociological discriminations and burdens and of magical belief. . . . The function of myth is to strengthen tradition and to endow it with a greater value and prestige by tracing it back to a higher, better, more supernatural, and more effective reality of initial events. (1931: 640–41)

Some anthropologists apply a psychological approach to myth analysis and see myths as symbolic expressions of sibling rivalry, male–female

Indian mask of painted wood, Northwest Coast, North America.

tensions, and other themes. Others—structural anthropologists such as Claude Lévi-Strauss—view myths as cultural means of resolving critical binary oppositions (life–death, matrilineal–patrilineal, nature–culture) that serve as models for members of a society (Hunter and Whitten 1976: 280–81). Whether in Judeo-Christian and Muslim cultures, where myths have been transcribed to form the Torah, Bible, and Koran, or in other, less familiar cultures, these sacred narratives still serve their time-honored function for the bulk of humanity as the basis of religious belief. What is important to remember is that myths in traditional societies are considered to be truthful accounts of the past, just as are the writings of the so-called great religions.

Like myth, ritual and ceremony are of crucial significance to all human societies and are important for the understanding of religion in culture. According to Victor Turner, in a definition widely quoted, "A ritual is a stereotyped sequence of activities involving gestures, words, and objects, performed in a sequestered place and designed to influence preternatural [magical] entities or forces on behalf of the actors' goals and interests." As described by Anthony Wallace, ritual is "the primary phenomenon of religion": "Ritual is religion in action; it is the cutting edge of the tool. Belief, although its recitation may be part of the ritual, or a ritual in its own right, serves to explain, to rationalize, to interpret and direct the energy of the ritual performance. . . . It is ritual which accomplishes what religion sets out to do" (1966: 102). "The prescriptive nature of ritual, that it must be done, is recognized in most anthropological definitions of ritual. . . . Conventional behavior, however, regularly repeated, is not ritual" (La Fontaine 1985: 11).

It is through ritual that religion is able to impress on people a commitment to their system of religious beliefs. Participants in a religious ritual are able to express group solidarity and loyalty. Indeed, Emile Durkheim argued that the true nature of religion was ritual participation. Of course, history abounds with examples of the importance of the individual experience in religion; yet there is no denying the overwhelming effect of group participation. As William Howells has pointed out, ritual helps individuals but does so by treating them as a whole group: "they are like a tangled head of hair, and ritual is the comb" (1962: 243).

Although in this chapter Max Gluckman urges the rejection of any simple explanation of ritual as a response to anxiety, most anthropologists believe, along with Malinowski and other early functionalists, that ritual at least allays anxiety. Through the shared performance of group dances and ceremonies, humans are able to reduce the fears that often come when life's events threaten their security and sense of well-being. Other scholars, such as A. R. Radcliffe-Brown, have taken the opposite tack, claiming that ritual may actually create rather than allay anxiety and fears.

Most introductory textbooks in anthropology divide religious ritual into rites of passage and rites of intensification. Rites of passage mark transition points in the lives of individuals—for example, birth, puberty, marriage, and death. Rites of intensification occur during a crisis for a group and are thus more important in maintaining group equilibrium and solidarity. They are typically associated with natural phenomena, such as seasonal changes or a lack of rain, but other events, such as impending warfare, could also trigger a rite of intensification. Whatever precipitates the crisis, there is need of a ritual to lessen the anxiety that is felt by the group.

Although the division of rituals into this twofold scheme is useful, it does not adequately represent the variety of ritual occurring in the world's cultures. Wallace, for example, has outlined five major categories of ritual (1966: 107–66).

1. *Technological rituals,* designed to control nature for the purpose of human exploitation, comprise three subdivisions:

   a. Divination rites, which help predict the future and gain hidden information.

   b. Rites of intensification, designed to help obtain food and alcohol.

   c. Protective rites, aimed at coping with the uncertainty of nature (for example, stormy seas, floods, crop disease, and bad luck).

2. *Therapy and antitherapy rituals* are designed to control human health. Curative rites exemplify therapy rituals; witchcraft and sorcery, antitherapy.

3. *Ideological rituals,* according to Wallace, are "intended to control, in a conservative way, the behav-

ior, the mood, the sentiments and values of groups for the sake of the community as a whole." They consist of four subcategories:

a. Rites of passage, which deal with role change and geographic movement (for example, marriages).

b. Rites of intensification, to ensure people adhere to values and customs (for example, Sunday church service).

c. Taboos (ritual avoidances), courtesies (positive actions), and other arbitrary ceremonial obligations, which serve to regulate human behavior.

d. Rites of rebellion, which provide a form of "ritualized catharsis" that contributes to order and stability by allowing people to vent their frustrations.

4. *Salvation rituals* aim at repairing damaged self-esteem and other forms of impaired identity. Wallace sees three common subdivisions in this category:

a. Possession, in which an individual's identity is altered by the presence of an alien spirit that occupies the body (exorcism is the usual treatment).

b. Ritual encouragement of an individual to accept an alternate identity, a process similar to the ritual procedure shamans undergo upon assuming a shamanic role.

c. The mystic experience—loss of personal identity by abandoning the old self and achieving salvation by identifying with a sacred being.

5. *Revitalization rituals* are aimed at what can be described as an identity crisis of an entire community. The revitalization movement may be seen as a religious movement (a ritual) that, through the help of a prophet, strives to create a better culture.

Just as myth and ritual are expressions of ideology, the study of symbolism too is vital to the study of religion. In fact, "the human beings who perform the rituals . . . , and those who are ostensibly a ritual's objects, are themselves representations of concepts and ideas, and therefore symbolic" (La Fontaine 1985: 13). Anthropology has been less than clear in its attempt to define the meaning of this important concept. Minimally, a symbol may be thought of as something that represents something else. The development of culture, for example, was dependent on human beings having the ability to assign symbolic meanings of words—to create and use a language. Religion is also a prime example of man's proclivity to attach symbolic meanings to a variety of behavior and objects. "The object of symbolism," according to Alfred North Whitehead, "is the enhancement of the importance of what is symbolized" (1927: 63).

That anthropological interest in the topic of symbolism had its start with the study of religious behavior is not surprising, especially in light of the plethora of symbols present in religious objects and ceremonies. Reflect for a moment on any religious service. Immediately on entering the building, be it a church, synagogue, or mosque, one is overwhelmed by symbolic objects—the Christian cross, the Star of David, paintings, statues, tapestries, and assorted ceremonial paraphernalia—each representing a religious principle. Fittingly, Clifford Geertz has noted that a religious system may be viewed as a "cluster of sacred symbols" (1957: 424). Unlike the well-defined symbols in mathematics and the physical sciences, these religious symbols assume many different forms and meanings: witness Turner's concept of the multivocalic nature of symbols (their capacity to have many meanings).

More than a simple reminder of some remote aspect of a religion's history, religious symbols are often considered to possess a power or force (*mana*) emanating from the spiritual world itself. The symbols provide people with an emotional and intellectual commitment to their particular belief system, telling them what is important to their society, collectively and individually, and helping them conform to the group's value system. Durkheim accounted for the universality of symbols by arguing that a society kept its value system through their use; that is, the symbols stood for the revered values. Without the symbols, the values and, by extension, the society's existence would be threatened.

Whereas symbols, like myths and rituals, prescribe thoughts and behaviors of people, taboos restrict actions. Because the term *taboo* (also known as *tabu* and *kapu*) originated in the Pacific Islands, beginning anthropology students often associate it with images of "savage" Polynesians observing mystical prohibitions. It is true that Pacific Islanders did cautiously regard these restrictions, being careful to avoid the supernatural retribution that was certain to follow violations. Taboos are not limited to the Pacific, however; every society has restrictions that limit behavior in one respect or another, usually in association with sex, food, rites of passage, sacred objects, and sacred people. The incest taboo is unique in that it is found in all societies. Although anthropologists have yet to explain adequately why the incest taboo exists everywhere, they have demonstrated that most taboos are reinforced by the threat of punishments meted out by supernatural forces.

As anthropologists have pointed out, taboos are adaptive human mechanisms: they function to counter dangers of both the phenomenal and ideational world. It is possible to theorize that the existence of fewer real or imagined dangers would result in fewer taboos, but it is equally safe to argue that all societies will continue to establish new taboos as new threats to existence or social stability arise. Certainly taboos function at an ecological level—for example, to preserve plants, animals, and resources of the sea. Taboos also function to distinguish between and control social groups, threatening violators with supernatural punishments as severe as the denial of salvation. Depending on the culture, sacred authority is often as compelling as the civil codes to which people are required to comply. Simply stated, the breaking of a sacred taboo, as opposed to a civil sanction, is a sin. The impersonal power of *mana* made certain objects and people in Pacific cultures taboo. Although the concept of *mana* does not exist in contemporary Western cultures, certain symbols and objects are similarly imbued with such an aura of power or sacredness that they too are considered taboo.

Using both a case study and an encyclopedic approach to myth, ritual, symbolism, and taboo, the seven articles selected for this chapter clearly show the importance of these topics to the study of comparative religion. Leach, Turner, Gordon, Firth, and Douglas bring to the reader the results of their field work in the non-Western world; Dubisch, on the other hand, discusses the religious aspects evidenced in the American health food movement—a phenomenon that displays common elements of all this chapter's major topics. In the final article, Miner examines the body rituals of the Nacirema, a North American group who devote a considerable portion of the day to ritual activity.

References

Geertz, Clifford
1957 "Ethos, World-View and the Analysis of Sacred Symbols," *Antioch Review* 17: 421–37.

Howells, William
1962 *The Heathens.* Garden City, N.Y.: Doubleday.

Hunter, David E., and Phillip Whitten
1976 *Encyclopedia of Anthropology.* New York: Harper and Row.

La Fontaine, Joan S.
1985 *Initiation.* Harmondsworth, England: Penguin Books.

Malinowski, Bronislaw
1931 "Culture." In David L. Sills, ed., *Encyclopedia of the Social Sciences,* Vol. 4, pp. 621–46. New York: Macmillan Free Press.

Wallace, A. F. C.
1966 *Religion: An Anthropological View.* New York: Random House.

Whitehead, Alfred N.
1927 *Symbolism.* New York: G. P. Putnam's Sons.

Genesis as Myth

Edmund R. Leach

Rather than analyze myths that have originated in non-Western societies, the late Edmund Leach here dissects a familiar story: the Old Testament recounting of the beginning of the world. Leach argues that although myths such as the Book of Genesis are repetitive, intricate, and contradictory, their construction is logical. He also shows how modern information theory sheds new light on myths as a form of communication. Leach notes that it is common to all mythological systems that important stories occur in several different versions. Because to the true believer these messages are the work of God, their very redundancy is reassuring. Each version confirms and reinforces the meaning of all the others and thereby reifies people's faith in the unknowable, making it the known. Leach explains the role of opposites as a basic construct of human minds, and he maintains that the structure of binary opposites in myth reflects our natural cognitive map as we separate, for example, God from man. Myth not only creates the oppositions but provides a common mythic element as a means of eliminating these separations through supernatural intermediaries and rituals, which bring the opposites together.

Reprinted from *Discovery* (May 1982), pp. 30–35, by permission of the author.

A DISTINGUISHED GERMAN THEOLOGIAN HAS defined myth as "the expression of unobservable realities in terms of observable phenomena" (Bartsch 1953). All stories which occur in the Bible are myths for the devout Christian, whether they correspond to historical fact or not. All human societies have myths in this sense, and normally the myths to which the greatest importance is attached are those which are the least probable. The non-rationality of myth is its very essence, for religion requires a demonstration of faith by the suspension of critical doubt.

But if myths do not mean what they appear to mean, how do they come to mean anything at all? What is the nature of the esoteric mode of communication by which myth is felt to give "expression" to unobservable realities"?

This is an old problem which has lately taken on a new shape because, if myth be a mode of communication, then a part of the theory which is embodied in digital computer systems ought to be relevant. The merit of this approach is that it draws special attention to precisely those features of myth which have formerly been regarded as accidental defects. It is common to all mythological systems that all important stories recur in several different versions. Man is created in Genesis (chapter I, verse 27) and then he is created all over again (II, 7). And, as if the two first men were not enough, we also have Noah in chapter VIII. Likewise in the New Testament, why must there be four gospels each telling "the same" story yet sometimes flatly contradictory on details of fact? Another noticeable characteristic of mythical stories is their markedly binary aspect; myth is constantly setting up opposing categories: "In the beginning God created the heaven and the earth," "they crucified Him and two others with him, on either side one, and Jesus in the midst," "I am the Alpha and the Omega, the beginning and the end, saith the Lord." So always it is in myth—God against the world and the world itself forever dividing into opposites on either side—male and female, living and dead, good and evil, first and last . . .

Now, in the language of communication engineers, the first of these common characteristics of myth is called *redundancy,* while the second is strongly reminiscent of the unit of information—the *bit.* "Information" in this technical sense is a measure of the freedom of choice in selecting a message. If there are only two messages and it is arbitrary which you choose then "information is unity," that is = 1 bit (*bit* stands for "binary digit") (Shannon and Weaver 1949).

Communication engineers employ these concepts for the analysis of problems which arise when a particular individual (the sender) wishes to transmit a coded message correctly to another individual (the receiver) against a background of interference (noise). "Information" refers on the one hand to the degrees of choice open to the sender in encoding his transmission and on the other to the degrees of choice open to the receiver in interpreting what he receives (which will include noise in addition to the original transmitted signal). In this situation a high level of redundancy makes it easy to correct errors introduced by noise.

Now in the mind of the believer, myth does indeed convey messages which are the Word of God. To such a man the redundancy of myth is a very reassuring fact. Any particular myth in isolation is like a coded message badly snarled up with noisy interference. Even the most confident devotee might feel a little uncertain as to what precisely is being said. But, as a result of redundancy, the believer can feel that, even when the details vary, each alternative version of a myth confirms his understanding and reinforces the essential meaning of all the others.

Binary Structure of Myth

The anthropologist's viewpoint is different. He rejects the idea of a supernatural sender. He observes only a variety of possible receivers. Redundancy increases information—that is the uncertainty of the possible means of decoding the message. This explains what is surely the most striking of all religious phenomena—the passionate adherence to sectarian belief. The whole of Christendom shares a single corpus of mythology so it is surely very remarkable that the members of each particular Christian sect are able to convince themselves that they

alone possess the secret of revealed truth. The abstract propositions of communication theory help us to understand this paradox.

But if the true believer can interpret his own mythology in almost any way he chooses, what principle governs the formation of the original myth? Is it random chance that a myth assumes one pattern rather than another? The binary structure of myth suggests otherwise.

Binary oppositions are intrinsic to the process of human thought. Any description of the world must discriminate categories in the form "*p* is what not-*p* is not." An object is alive or not alive and one could not formulate the concept "alive" except as the converse of its partner "dead." So also human beings are male or not male, and persons of the opposite sex are either available as sexual partners or not available. Universally these are the most fundamentally important oppositions in all human experience.

Religion everywhere is preoccupied with the first, the antinomy of life and death. Religion seeks to deny the binary link between the two words; it does this by creating the mystical idea of "another world," a land of the dead where life is perpetual. The attributes of this other world are necessarily those which are not of this world; imperfection here is balanced by perfection there. But this logical ordering of ideas has a disconcerting consequence— God comes to belong to the other world. The central "problem" of religion is then to reestablish some kind of bridge between Man and God.

This pattern is built into the structure of every mythical system; the myth first discriminates between gods and men and then becomes preoccupied with the relations and intermediaries which link men and gods together. This much is already implicit in our initial definition.

So too with sex relations. Every human society has rules of incest and exogamy. Though the rules vary they always have the implication that for any particular male individual all women are divided by at least one binary distinction, there are women of *our kind* with whom sex relations would be incestuous and there are women of the *other kind* with whom sex relations are allowed. But here again we are immediately led into paradox. How was it in the beginning? If our first parents were persons of two kinds, what was that other kind? But if they were both of our kind, then their relations must have been incestuous and we are all born in sin. The myths of the world offer many different solutions to this childish intellectual puzzle, but the prominence which it receives shows that it entails the most profound moral issues. The crux is as before. If the logic of our thought leads us to distinguish *we* from *they*, how can we bridge the gap and establish social and sexual relations with "the others" without throwing our categories into confusion?

So, despite all variations of theology, this aspect of myth is a constant. In every myth system we will find a persistent sequence of binary discriminations as between human/superhuman, mortal/immortal, male/female, legitimate/illegitimate, good/bad . . . followed by a "mediation" of the paired categories thus distinguished.

"Mediation" (in this sense) is always achieved by introducing a third category which is "abnormal" or "anomalous" in terms of ordinary "rational" categories. Thus myths are full of fabulous monsters, incarnate gods, virgin mothers. This middle ground is abnormal, non-natural, holy. It is typically the focus of all taboo and ritual observance.

This approach to myth analysis derives originally from the techniques of structural linguistics associated with the name of Roman Jakobson (Jakobson and Halle 1956) but is more immediately due to C. Lévi-Strauss, one of whose examples may serve to illustrate the general principle.

Certain Pueblo Indian myths focus on the opposition between life and death. In these myths we find a threefold category distinction: agriculture (means to life), war (means to death), and hunting (a mediating category since it is means to life for men but means to death for animals). Other myths of the same cluster deploy a different triad: grass-eating animals (which live without killing), predators (which live by killing), and carrion-eating creatures (mediators, since they eat meat but do not kill in order to eat). In accumulation this total set of associated symbols serves to imply that life and death are *not* just the back and the front of the same penny, that death is *not* the necessary consequence of life (Lévi-Strauss 1955).

My Figure 1 has been designed to display an analogous structure for the case of the first four chapters of Genesis. The three horizontal bands of the diagram correspond to (i) the story of the seven-day creation, (ii) the story of the Garden of Eden, and (iii) the story of Cain and Abel. The diagram can also be read vertically: column 1 in band (ii) corre-

sponds to column 1 in band (i) and so on. The detailed analysis is as follows:

Upper Band

First Day (I, 1–5; not on diagram). Heaven distinguished from Earth; Light from Darkness; Day from Night; Evening from Morning.

Second Day (I, 6–8; col. 1 of diagram). (Fertile) water (rain) above; (infertile) water (sea) below. Mediated by firmament (sky).

Third Day (I, 9–10; col. 2 and I, 11–12; col. 3). Sea opposed to dry land. Mediated by "grass, herb yielding seed (cereals), fruit trees." These grow on dry land but need water. They are classed as things "whose seed is in itself" and thereby contrasted with bisexual animals, birds, etc.

The creation of the world as a static (that is, dead) entity is now complete and this whole phase of the creation is opposed to the creation of moving (that is, living) things.

Fourth Day (I, 13–18; col. 4). Mobile sun and moon are placed in the fixed firmament of col. 1. Light and darkness become alternations (life and death become alternates).

Fifth Day (I, 20–23; col. 5). Fish and birds are living things corresponding to the sea/land opposition of col. 2 but they also mediate the col. 1 oppositions between sky and earth and between salt water and fresh water.

Sixth Day (I, 24–25; col. 6). Cattle (domestic animals), beasts (wild animals), creeping things. These correspond to the static triad of col. 3. But only the grass is allocated to the animals. Everything else, including the meat of the animals, is for Man's use (I, 29–30). Later at Leviticus XI creatures which do not fit this exact ordering of the world—for instance, water creatures with no fins, animals and birds which eat meat or fish, etc.—are classed as "abominations." Creeping Things are anomalous with respect to the major categories, Fowl, Fish, Cattle, Beast and are thus abominations *ab initio* (Leviticus XI, 41–42). This classification in turn leads to an anomalous contradiction. In order to allow the Israelites to eat locusts the author of Leviticus XI had to introduce a special qualification to the prohibition against eating creeping things: "Yet these ye *may* eat: of every flying creeping thing that goeth on all four which have legs above their feet, to leap withal upon the earth" (v. 21). The procedures of binary discrimination could scarcely be carried further!

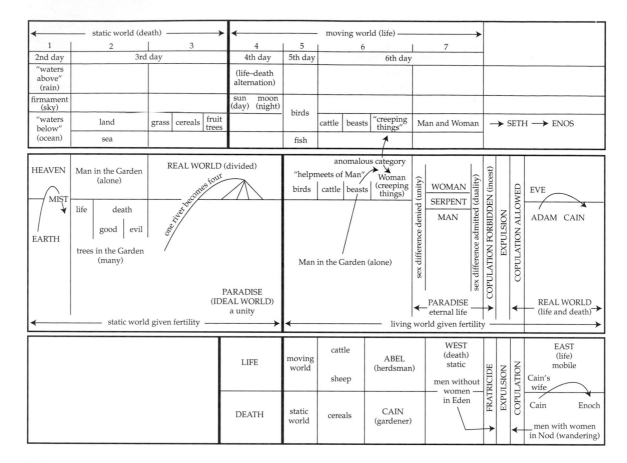

FIGURE 1

The first four chapters of Genesis contain three separate creation stories. Horizontal bands correspond to (a) 7-day creation; (b) Garden of Eden; (c) Cain and Abel. Each story sets up opposition of Death versus Life, God versus Man. World is "made alive" by using categories of "woman" and "creeping things" to mediate this opposition.

(I, 26–27; col. 7), Man and Woman are created simultaneously. The whole system of living creatures is instructed to "be fruitful and multiply" but the problems of Life versus Death, and Incest versus Procreation are not faced at all.

Center Band

The Garden of Eden story which now follows tackles from the start these very problems which have been evaded in the first version. We start again with the opposition Heaven versus Earth, but this is mediated by a fertilizing mist drawn from the dry infertile earth (II, 4–6). This theme, which blurs the distinction life/death, is repeated. Living Adam is formed from the dead dust of the ground (II, 7); so are the animals (II, 19); the garden is fertilised by a river which "went out of Eden" (II, 10); finally fertile Eve is formed from a rib of infertile Adam (II, 22–23).

The opposition Heaven/Earth is followed by further oppositions—Man/Garden (II, 15); Tree of Life/Tree of Death (II, 9, 17); the latter is called the tree of the "knowledge of good and evil" which means the knowledge of sexual difference.

Recurrent also is the theme that unity in the other world (Eden, Paradise) becomes duality in this world. Outside Eden the river splits into four and divides the world into separate lands (II, 10–14). In Eden, Adam can exist by himself, Life can exist by itself; in this world, there are men and women, life and death. This repeats the contrast between monosexual plants and bisexual animals which is stressed in the first story.

The other living creatures are now created specifically because of the loneliness of Man in Eden (II, 18). The categories are Cattle, Birds, Beasts. None of these is adequate as a helpmeet for Man. So finally Eve is drawn from Adam's rib . . . "they are of one flesh" (II, 18–24).

Comparison of Band 1 and Band 2 at this stage shows that Eve in the second story replaces the "Creeping Things" of the first story. Just as Creeping Things were anomalous with respect to Fish, Fowl, Cattle and Beast so Eve is anomalous to the opposition Man versus Animal. And, as a final mediation (chapter III), the Serpent, a creeping thing, is anomalous to the opposition Man versus Woman. Christian artists have always been sensitive to this fact; they manage to give the monster a somewhat hermaphrodite appearance while still indicating some kind of identification between the Serpent and Eve herself.

Hugo Van der Goes puts Eve and the Serpent in the same posture; Michelangelo makes Adam and Eve both gaze with loving adoration on the Serpent, but the Serpent has Eve's face.

Adam and Eve eat the forbidden fruit and become aware of sexual difference, death becomes inevitable (III, 3–8). But now for the first time pregnancy and reproduction become possible. Eve does not become pregnant until after she has been expelled from Paradise (IV, 1).

Lower Band

Cain the Gardener and Abel the Herdsman repeat the antithesis between the first three days of the creation and the last three days in the first story. Abel's living world is more pleasing to God (IV, 4–5). Cain's fratricide compares with Adam's incest and so God's questioning and cursing of Cain (IV, 9–12) has the same form and sequence as God's questioning and cursing of Adam, Eve and the Ser-

pent (III, 9–19). The latter part of III, 16, is later repeated exactly (IV, 7) so Cain's sin was not only fratricide but also incestuous homosexuality. In order that immortal monosexual existence in Paradise may be exchanged for fertile heterosexual existence in reality, Cain, like Adam, must acquire a wife (IV, 17). To this end Adam must eliminate a sister; Cain a brother. The symmetry is complete.

Cross-Cultural Comparison

The issue here is the logical basis of incest categories and closely analogous patterns must occur in all mythologies regardless of their superficial content. Cross-cultural comparison becomes easier if we represent the analysis as a systematic pattern of binary discriminations as in Figure 2.

Adam/Eve and Cain/Abel are then seen to be variants of a theme which can also occur in other forms as in the well-known myth of Oedipus. The actual symbolism in these two cases is nearly identical. Oedipus, like Adam and Cain, is initially earthbound and immobile. The conclusion of the Athenian version of the Oedipus story is that he is an exiled wanderer, protected by the gods. So also is Cain (IV, 14–15). The Bible also includes the converse of this pattern. In Genesis XXVIII Jacob is a lonely exile and wanderer under God's protection but (XXXII, 24–32) he is renamed Israel and thus given the status of a first ancestor with a territorial autochthonous base, and he is lamed by God. Although Jacob dies abroad in Egypt he is buried on his own ancestral soil in Israel (XL, 29–32; L, 5–7).

In the Oedipus story, in place of Eve's Serpent we have Jocasta's Sphinx. Like Jocasta the Sphinx is female, like Jocasta the Sphinx commits suicide, like the Serpent the Sphinx leads men to their doom by verbal cunning, like the Serpent the Sphinx is an anomalous monster. Eve listens to the Serpent's words and betrays Adam into incest; Oedipus solves the Sphinx riddle and is led into incest. Again, Oedipus's patricide replaces Cain's fratricide—Oedipus, incidentally, meets Laius "at a cross roads."

Parallels of this kind seem too close to be accidental but this kind of algebra is unfamiliar and more evidence will be needed to convince the sceptical. Genesis contains several further examples of first ancestors.

Firstly, Noah survived the destruction of the world by flood together with three sons and their

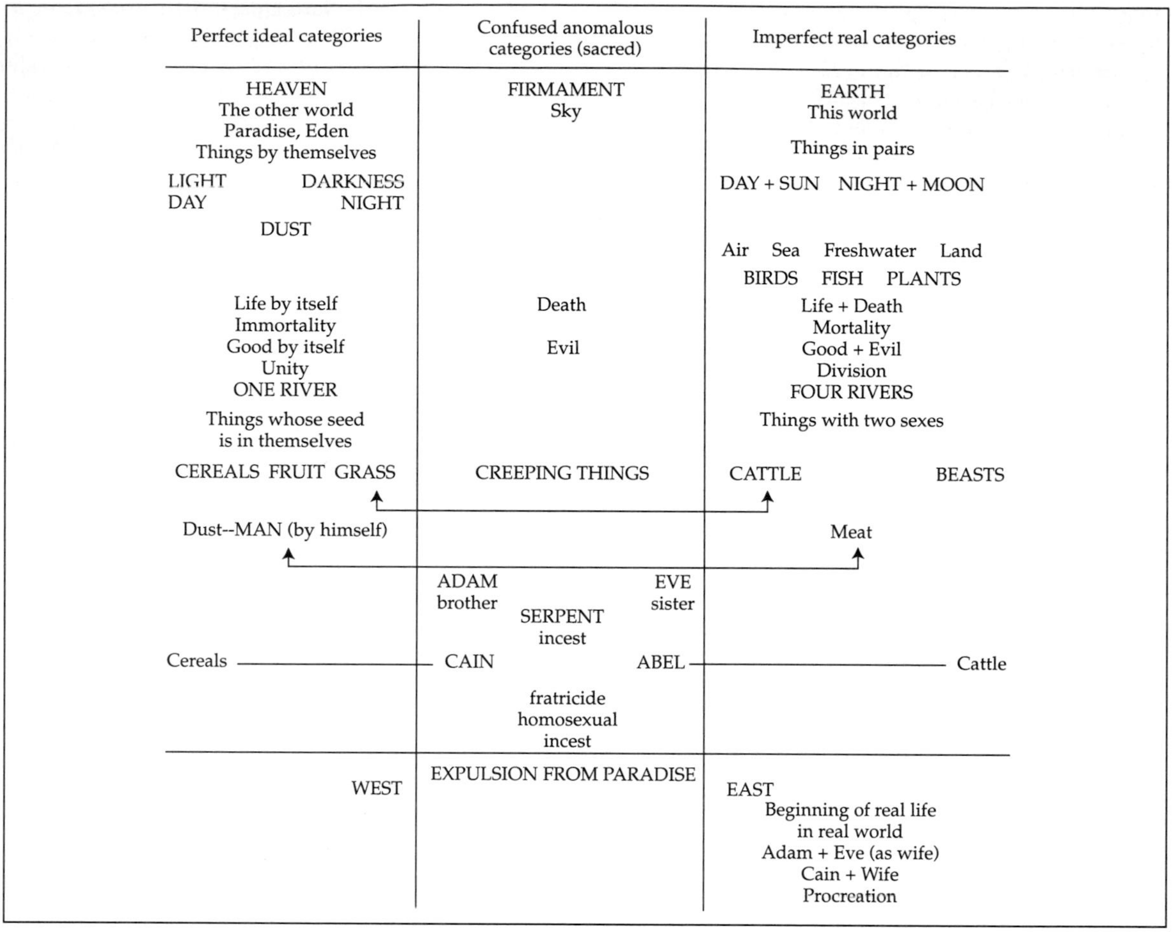

Perfect ideal categories	Confused anomalous categories (sacred)	Imperfect real categories
HEAVEN The other world Paradise, Eden Things by themselves	FIRMAMENT Sky	EARTH This world Things in pairs
LIGHT DARKNESS DAY NIGHT DUST		DAY + SUN NIGHT + MOON
		Air Sea Freshwater Land BIRDS FISH PLANTS
Life by itself Immortality Good by itself Unity ONE RIVER	Death Evil	Life + Death Mortality Good + Evil Division FOUR RIVERS
Things whose seed is in themselves		Things with two sexes
CEREALS FRUIT GRASS	CREEPING THINGS	CATTLE BEASTS
Dust--MAN (by himself)		Meat
	ADAM EVE brother sister SERPENT incest	
Cereals —————— CAIN		ABEL ————————— Cattle
	fratricide homosexual incest	
WEST	EXPULSION FROM PARADISE	EAST Beginning of real life in real world Adam + Eve (as wife) Cain + Wife Procreation

FIGURE 2
Incest categories have a logical basis in all myths. Similarity between myths is seen most clearly if they are analysed in a binary form as shown in this table.

wives. Prior to this the population of the world had included three kinds of being—"sons of God," "daughters of men" and "giants" who were the offspring of the union of the other two (VI, 1–4). Since the forbears of Noah's daughters-in-law have all been destroyed in the Flood, Noah becomes a unique ancestor of all mankind without the implication of incest. Chapter IX, 1–7, addressed to Noah is almost the duplicate of I, 27–30, addressed to Adam.

Though heterosexual incest is evaded, the theme of homosexual incest in the Cain and Abel story recurs in the Noah saga when drunken Noah is seduced by his own son Ham (IX, 21–25). The Canaanites, descendants of Ham, are for this reason accursed. (That a homosexual act is intended is evident from the language "Ham saw the nakedness of his father." Compare Leviticus XVIII, 6–19, where "to uncover the nakedness of" consistently means to have sexual relations with.)

In the second place Lot survives the destruction of the world by fire together with two nubile daughters. Drunken Lot is seduced by his own daughters (XIX, 30–38). The Moabites and the Ammonites, descendants of these daughters, are for this reason accursed. In chapter XIX the men of Sodom endeavour to have homosexual relations with two angels who are visiting Lot. Lot offers his nubile daughters instead but they escape unscathed. The implication is that Lot's incest is less grave than heterosexual relations with a foreigner, and still less grave than homosexual relations.

Thirdly, the affair of the Sodomites and the Angels contains echoes of "the sons of God" and "the daughters of men" but links specifically with chapter XVIII where Abraham receives a visit from God and two Angels who promise that his ageing and barren wife Sarah shall bear a son. Sarah is Abraham's half-sister by the same father (XX, 12) and his relations with her are unambiguously incestuous (Leviticus XVIII, 9). Abraham loans Sarah to Pharaoh saying that she is his sister (XII, 19). He does the same with King Abimelech (XX, 2). Isaac repeats the game with Abimelech (XXVI, 9–11) but with a difference. Isaac's wife Rebekah is his father's brother's son's daughter (second cousin) and the relation is *not* in fact incestuous. The barrenness of Sarah is an aspect of her incest. The supernatural intervention which ultimately ensures that she shall bear a child is evidence that the incest is condoned. Pharaoh and Abimelech both suffer supernatural penalties for the lesser offence of adultery, but Abraham, the incestuous husband, survives unscathed.

There are other stories in the same set. Hagar, Sarah's Egyptian slave, bears a son Ishmael to Abraham, whose descendants are wanderers of low status. Sarah's son Isaac is marked out as of higher status than the sons of Abraham's concubines, who are sent away to "the east country" (c.f. wandering Cain who made his home in Nod "eastward of Eden"). Isaac marries a kinswoman in preference to a Canaanite woman. Esau's marriage to a Hittite woman is marked as a sin. In contrast his younger and favoured twin brother Jacob marries two daughters of his mother's brother, who is in turn Jacob's father's father's brother's son's son.

All in all, this long series of repetitive and inverted tales asserts:

1. the overriding virtue of close kin endogamy;

2. that the sacred hero ancestor Abraham can carry this so far that he marries his paternal half-sister (an incestuous relationship). Abraham is thus likened to Pharaoh, for the Pharaohs of Egypt regularly married their paternal half-sisters; and

3. that a rank order is established which places the tribal neighbours of the Israelites in varying degrees of inferior status depending upon the nature of the defect in their original ancestry as compared with the pure descent of Jacob (Israel).

The myth requires that the Israelites be descended unambiguously from Terah, the father of Abraham. This is achieved only at the cost of a breach of the incest rule; but by reciting a large number of similar stories which entail even greater breaches of sexual morality the relations of Abraham and Sarah finally stand out as uniquely virtuous. Just as Adam and Eve are virtuous as compared to Cain and Abel, so Abraham's incest can pass unnoticed in the context of such outrageous characters as Ham, Lot's daughters, and the men of Sodom.

I have concentrated here upon the issue of sexual rules and transgressions so as to show how a multiplicity of repetitions, inversions, and variations can add up to a consistent "message." I do not wish to imply that this is the only structural pattern which these myths contain.

The novelty of the analysis which I have presented does not lie in the facts but in the procedure. Instead of taking each myth as a thing in itself with a "meaning" peculiar to itself it is assumed, from the start, that every myth is one of a complex and that any pattern which occurs in one myth will recur, in the same or other variations, in other parts of the complex. The structure that is common to all variations becomes apparent when different versions are "superimposed" one upon the other.

Whenever a corpus of mythology is recited in its religious setting such structural patterns are "felt" to be present, and convey meaning much as poetry conveys meaning. Even though the ordinary listener is not fully conscious of what has been communicated, the "message" is there in a quite objective sense. If the labour of programming could be performed the actual analysis could be done by a computer far better than by any human. Furthermore, it seems evident that much the same patterns exist in the most diverse kinds of mythology. This seems to me to be a fact of great psychological, sociological, and scientific significance. Here truly are observable phenomena which are the expression of unobservable realities.

Betwixt and Between: The Liminal Period in *Rites de Passage*

Victor W. Turner

The following selection could not have been written were it not for the seminal writing on ritual by the French anthropologist Arnold van Gennep (1873–1957). Van Gennep is recognized by scholars as the first anthropologist to study the significance of rituals accompanying the transitional stages in a person's life —birth, puberty, marriage, and death. Ever since the publication of Les Rites de Passage *in 1909, the phrase "rites of passage" has become part and parcel of anthropological literature. Van Gennep saw in human rituals three successive but separate stages: separation, margin, and aggregation. In the following selection, Victor Turner singles out the marginal, or liminal, period for examination. The liminal stage in rites of passage is when the initiates are removed and typically secluded from the rest of society—in effect they become invisible, or, as in the title of this article, "betwixt and between." It is Turner's belief that the neophyte at the liminal stage has nothing—no status, property rank, or kinship position. He describes this condition as one of "sacred poverty." Turner concludes his article with an invitation to researchers of ritual to concentrate their efforts on the marginal stage, believing that this is where the basic building blocks of culture are exposed and therefore open for cross-cultural comparison. Victor Turner taught at Cornell and the University of Chicago. His major field research was done in Uganda, Zambia, and Mexico.*

Reprinted from Victor W. Turner, "Betwixt and Between: The Liminal Period in *Rites de Passage*," *The Proceedings of the American Ethnological Society* (1964), Symposium on New Approaches to the Study of Religion, pp. 4–20.

IN THIS PAPER, I WISH TO CONSIDER SOME OF THE sociocultural properties of the "liminal period" in that class of rituals which Arnold van Gennep has definitively characterized as *"rites de passage."* If our basic model of society is that of a "structure of positions," we must regard the period of margin or "liminality" as an interstructural situation. I shall consider, notably in the case of initiation rites, some of the main features of instruction among the simpler societies. I shall also take note of certain symbolic themes that concretely express indigenous concepts about the nature of "interstructural" human beings.

Rites de passage are found in all societies but tend to reach their maximal expression in small-scale, relatively stable and cyclical societies, where change is bound up with biological and meteorological rhythms and recurrences rather than with technological innovations. Such rites indicate and constitute transitions between states. By "state" I mean here "a relatively fixed or stable condition" and would include in its meaning such social constancies as legal status, profession, office or calling, rank or degree. I hold it to designate also the condition of a person as determined by his culturally recognized degree of maturation as when one speaks of "the married or single state" or the "state of infancy." The term "state" may also be applied to ecological conditions, or to the physical, mental or emotional condition in which a person or group may be found at a particular time. A man may thus be in a state of good or bad health; a society in a state of war or peace or a state of famine or of plenty. State, in short, is a more inclusive concept than status or office and refers to any type of stable or recurrent condition that is culturally recognized. One may, I suppose, also talk about "a state of transition," since J. S. Mill has, after all, written of "a state of progressive movement," but I prefer to regard transition as a process, a becoming, and in the case of *rites de passage* even a transformation—here an apt analogy would be water in process of being heated to boiling point, or a pupa changing from grub to moth. In any case, a transition has different cultural properties from those of a state, as I hope to show presently.

Van Gennep himself defined *"rites de passage"* as "rites which accompany every change of place, state, social position and age." To point up the contrast between "state" and "transition," I employ "state" to include all his other terms. Van Gennep has shown that all rites of transition are marked by three phases: separation, margin (or *limen*), and aggregation. The first phase of separation comprises symbolic behavior signifying the detachment of the individual or group either from an earlier fixed point in the social structure or a set of cultural conditions (a "state"); during the intervening liminal period, the state of the ritual subject (the "passenger") is ambiguous; he passes through a realm that has few or none of the attributes of the past or coming state; in the third phase the passage is consummated. The ritual subject, individual or corporate, is in a stable state once more and, by virtue of this, has rights and obligations of a clearly defined and "structural" type, and is expected to behave in accordance with certain customary norms and ethical standards. The most prominent type of *rites de passage* tends to accompany what Lloyd Warner (1959, 303) has called "the movement of a man through his lifetime, from a fixed placental placement within his mother's womb to his death and ultimate fixed point of his tombstone and final containment in his grave as a dead organism—punctuated by a number of critical moments of transition which all societies ritualize and publicly mark with suitable observances to impress the significance of the individual and the group on living members of the community. These are the important times of birth, puberty, marriage, and death." However, as Van Gennep, Henri Junod, and others have shown, *rites de passage* are not confined to culturally defined life-crises but may accompany any change from one state to another, as when a whole tribe goes to war, or when it attests to the passage from scarcity to plenty by performing a first-fruits or a harvest festival. *Rites de passage,* too, are not restricted, sociologically speaking, to movements between ascribed statuses. They also concern entry into a new achieved status, whether this be a political office or membership of an exclusive club or secret society. They may admit persons into membership of a religious group where such a group does not include the whole society, or qualify them for the official duties of the cult, sometimes in a graded series of rites.

Since the main problem of this study is the nature and characteristics of transition in relatively stable societies, I shall focus attention on *rites de passage* that tend to have well-developed liminal periods. On the whole, initiation rites, whether into social maturity or cult membership, best exemplify transition, since they have well-marked and protracted marginal or liminal phases. I shall pay only brief heed here to rites of separation and aggregation, since these are more closely implicated in social structure than rites of liminality. Liminality during initiation is, therefore, the primary datum of this study, though I will draw on other aspects of passage ritual where the argument demands this. I may state here, partly as an aside, that I consider the term "ritual" to be more fittingly applied to forms of religious behavior associated with social transitions, while the term "ceremony" has a closer bearing on religious behavior associated with social states, where politico-legal institutions also have greater importance. Ritual is transformative, ceremony confirmatory.

The subject of passage ritual is, in the liminal period, structurally, if not physically, "invisible." As members of society, most of us see only what we expect to see, and what we expect to see is what we are conditioned to see when we have learned the definitions and classifications of our culture. A society's secular definitions do not allow for the existence of a not-boy-not-man, which is what a novice in a male puberty rite is (if he can be said to be anything). A set of essentially religious definitions co-exist with these which do set out to define the structurally indefinable "transitional-being." The transitional-being or "liminal *persona*" is defined by a name and by a set of symbols. The same name is very frequently employed to designate those who are being initiated into very different states of life. For example, among the Ndembu of Zambia the name *mwadi* may mean various things: it may stand for "a boy novice in circumcision rites," or "a chief-designate undergoing his installation rites," or, yet again, "the first or ritual wife" who has important ritual duties in the domestic family. Our own terms "initiate" and "neophyte" have a similar breadth of reference. It would seem from this that emphasis tends to be laid on the transition itself, rather than on the particular states between which it is taking place.

The symbolism attached to and surrounding the liminal *persona* is complex and bizarre. Much of it is modeled on human biological processes, which are conceived to be what Lévi-Strauss might call "isomorphic" with structural and cultural processes. They give an outward and visible form to an inward and conceptual process. The structural "invisibility" of liminal *personae* has a twofold character. They are at once no longer classified and not yet classified. In so far as they are no longer classified, the symbols that represent them are, in many societies, drawn from the biology of death, decomposition, catabolism, and other physical processes that have a negative tinge, such as menstruation (frequently regarded as the absence or loss of a fetus). Thus, in some boys' initiations, newly circumcised boys are explicitly likened to menstruating women. In so far as a neophyte is structually "dead," he or she may be treated, for a long or short period, as a corpse is customarily treated in his or her society. (See Stobaeus' quotation, probably from a lost work of Plutarch, "initiation and death correspond word for word and thing for thing." The neophyte may be buried, forced to lie motionless in the posture and direction of customary burial, may be stained black, or may be forced to live for a while in the company of masked and monstrous mummers representing, *inter alia,* the dead, or worse still, the un-dead. The metaphor of dissolution is often applied to neophytes; they are allowed to go filthy and identified with the earth, the generalized matter into which every specific individual is rendered down. Particular form here becomes general matter; often their very names are taken from them and each is called solely by the generic term for "neophyte" or "initiand." (This useful neologism is employed by many modern anthropologists.)

The other aspect, that they are not yet classified, is often expressed in symbols modeled on processes of gestation and parturition. The neophytes are likened to or treated as embryos, newborn infants, or sucklings by symbolic means which vary from culture to culture. I shall return to this theme presently.

The essential feature of these symbolizations is that the neophytes are neither living nor dead from one aspect, and both living and dead from another. Their condition is one of ambiguity and paradox, a confusion of all the customary categories. Jakob Boehme, the German mystic whose obscure writings gave Hegel his celebrated dialectical "triad," liked to say that "In Yea and Nay all things consist." Liminality may perhaps be regarded as the Nay to all positive structural assertions, but as in some sense the source of them all, and, more than that, as a realm of pure possibility whence novel configurations of ideas and relations may arise. I will not pursue this point here but, after all, Plato, a speculative philosopher, if there ever was one, did acknowledge his philosophical debt to the teachings of the Eleusinian and Orphic initiations of Attica. We have no way of knowing whether primitive initiations merely conserved lore. Perhaps they also generated new thought and new custom.

Dr. Mary Douglas, of University College, London, has recently advanced (in a magnificent book *Purity and Danger* [1966]) the very interesting and illuminating view that the concept of pollution "is a reaction to protect cherished principles and categories from contradiction." She holds that, in effect, what is unclear and contradictory (from the perspective of social definition) tends to be regarded as (ritually) unclean. The unclear is the unclean: e.g., she examines the prohibitions on eating certain animals and crustaceans in Leviticus in the light of this hypothesis (these being creatures that cannot be unambiguously classified in terms of traditional criteria). From this standpoint, one would expect to find that transitional beings are particularly polluting, since they are neither one thing nor another; or may be both; or neither here nor there; or may even be nowhere (in terms of any recognized cultural topography), and are at the very least "betwixt and between" all the recognized fixed points in space-time of structural classification. In fact, in confirmation of Dr. Douglas's hypothesis, liminal *personae* nearly always and everywhere are regarded as polluting to those who have never been, so to speak, "inoculated" against them, through having been themselves initiated into the same state. I think that we may perhaps usefully discriminate here between the statics and dynamics of pollution situations. In other words, we may have to distinguish between pollution notions which concern states that have been ambiguously or contradictorily defined, and those which derive from ritualized transitions between states. In the first case, we are dealing with what has been defectively defined or ordered, in the second with what cannot be defined in static terms. We are not dealing with structural contradictions when we discuss liminality, but with the essentially unstructured (which is at once destructured and prestructured) and often the people themselves see this in terms of bringing neophytes into close connection with deity or with superhuman power, with what is, in fact, often regarded as the unbounded, the infinite, the limitless. Since neophytes are not only structurally "invisible" (though physically visible) and ritually polluting, they are very commonly secluded, partially or completely, from the realm of culturally defined and ordered states and statuses. Often the indigenous term for the liminal period is, as among Ndembu, the locative form of a noun meaning "seclusion site" (*kunkunka, kung'ula*). The neophytes are sometimes said to "be in another place." They have physical but not social "reality," hence they have to be hidden, since it is a paradox, a scandal, to see what ought not to be there! Where they are not removed to a sacred place of concealment they are often disguised, in masks or grotesque costumes or striped with white, red, or black clay, and the like.

In societies dominantly structured by kinship institutions, sex distinctions have great structural importance. Patrilineal and matrilineal moieties and clans, rules of exogamy, and the like, rest and are built up on these distinctions. It is consistent with this to find that in liminal situations (in kinship-dominated societies) neophytes are sometimes treated or symbolically represented as being neither male nor female. Alternatively, they may be symbolically assigned characteristics of both sexes, irrespective of their biological sex. (Bruno Bettelheim [1954] has collected much illustrative material on this point from initiation rites.) They are symbolically either sexless or bisexual and may be regarded as a kind of human *prima materia*—as undifferentiated raw material. It was perhaps from the rites of the Hellenic mystery religions that Plato derived his notion expressed in his *Symposium* that the first humans were androgynes. If the liminal period is seen as an interstructural phase in social dynamics, the symbolism both of androgyny and sexlessness immediately becomes intelligible in sociological terms without the need to import psychological (and especially depth-psychological) explanations. Since sex distinctions are important components of structural status, in a structureless realm they do not apply.

A further structurally negative characteristic of transitional beings is that they *have* nothing. They have no status, property, insignia, secular clothing, rank, kinship position, nothing to demarcate them structurally from their fellows. Their condition is indeed the very prototype of sacred poverty. Rights over property, goods, and services inhere in positions in the politico-jural structure. Since they do not occupy such positions, neophytes exercise no such rights. In the words of King Lear they represent "naked unaccommodated man."

I have no time to analyze other symbolic themes that express these attributes of "structural invisibility," ambiguity and neutrality. I want now to draw attention to certain positive aspects of liminality. Already we have noted how certain liminal processes are regarded as analogous to those of gestation, parturition, and suckling. Undoing, dissolution, decomposition are accompanied by processes of growth, transformation, and the reformulation of old elements in new patterns. It is interesting to note how, by the principle of the economy (or parsimony) of symbolic reference, logically antithetical processes of death and growth may be represented by the same tokens, for example, by huts and tunnels that are at once tombs and wombs, by lunar symbolism (for the same moon waxes and wanes), by snake symbolism (for the snake appears to die, but only to shed its old skin and appear in a new one), by bear symbolism (for the bear "dies" in autumn and is "reborn" in spring), by nakedness (which is at once the mark of a newborn infant and a corpse prepared for burial), and by innumerable other symbolic formations and actions. This coincidence of opposite processes and notions in a single representation characterizes the peculiar unity of the liminal: that which is neither this nor that, and yet is both.

I have spoken of the interstructural character of the liminal. However, between neophytes and their instructors (where these exist), and in connecting neophytes with one another, there exists a set of relations that compose a "social structure" of highly specific type. It is a structure of a very simple kind: between instructors and neophytes there is often complete authority and complete submission; among neophytes there is often complete equality. Between incumbents of positions in secular politico-jural systems there exist intricate and situationally shifting networks of rights and duties proportioned to their rank, status, and corporate affiliation. There are many different kinds of privileges and obligations, many degrees of superordination and subordination. In the liminal period such distinctions and gradations tend to be eliminated. Nevertheless, it must be understood that the authority of the elders over the neophytes is not based on legal sanctions; it is in a sense the personification of the self-evident authority of tradition. The authority of the elders is absolute, because it represents the absolute, the axiomatic values of society in which are expressed the "common good" and the common interest. The essence of the complete obedience of the neophytes is to submit to the elders but only in so far as they are in charge, so to speak, of the common good and represent in their persons the total community. That the authority in question is really quintessential tradition emerges clearly in societies where initiations are not collective but individual and where there are no instructors or *gurus.* For example, Omaha boys, like other North American Indians, go alone into the wilderness to fast and pray (Hocart, 1952, 160). This solitude is liminal between boyhood and manhood. If they dream that they receive a woman's burden-strap, they feel compelled to dress and live henceforth in every way as women. Such men are known as *mixuga.* The authority of such a dream in such a situation is absolute. Alice Cummingham Fletcher tells of one Omaha who had been forced in this way to live as a woman, but whose natural inclinations led him to rear a family and to go on the warpath. Here the *mixuga* was not an invert but a man bound by the authority of tribal beliefs and values. Among many Plains Indians, boys on their lonely Vision Quest inflicted ordeals and tests on themselves that amounted to tortures. These again were not basically self-tortures inflicted by a masochistic temperament but due to obedience to the authority of tradition in the liminal situation—a type of situation in which there is no room for secular compromise, evasion, manipulation, casuistry, and maneuver in the field of custom, rule, and norm. Here again a cultural explanation seems preferable to a psychological one. A normal man acts abnormally because he is obedient to tribal tradition, not out of disobedience to it. He does not evade but fulfills his duties as a citizen.

If complete obedience characterizes the relationship of neophyte to elder, complete equality usually characterizes the relationship of neophyte to neophyte, where the rites are collective. This comradeship must be distinguished from brotherhood or sibling relationship, since in the latter there is always the inequality of older and younger, which often achieves linguistic representation and may be maintained by legal sanctions. The liminal group is a community or comity of comrades and not a structure of hierarchically arrayed positions. This comradeship transcends distinctions of rank, age, kinship position, and, in some kinds of cultic group, even of sex. Much of the behavior recorded by ethnographers in seclusion situations falls under the principle: "Each for all, and all for each." Among the Ndembu of Zambia, for example, all food brought for novices in circumcision seclusion by their mothers is shared out equally among them. No special favors are bestowed on the sons of chiefs or headmen. Any food acquired by novices in the bush is taken by the elders and apportioned among the group. Deep friendships between novices are encouraged, and they sleep around lodge fires in clusters of four or five particular comrades. However, all are supposed to be linked by special ties which persist after the rites are over, even into old age. This friendship, known as *wubwambu* (from a term meaning "breast") or *wulunda,* enables a man to claim privileges of hospitality of a far-reaching kind. I have no need here to dwell on the lifelong ties that are held to bind in close friendship those initiated into the same age-set in East African Nilo-Hamitic and Bantu societies, into the same fraternity or sorority on an American campus, or into the same class in a Naval or Military Academy in Western Europe.

This comradeship, with its familiarity, ease and, I would add, mutual outspokenness, is once more the product of interstructural liminality, with its scarcity of jurally sanctioned relationships and its emphasis on axiomatic values expressive of the common weal. People can "be themselves," it is frequently said, when they are not acting institutionalized roles. Roles, too, carry responsibilities and in the liminal situation the main burden of responsibility is borne by the elders, leaving the neophytes free to develop interpersonal relationships as they will. They confront one another, as it were, integrally and not in compartmentalized fashion as actors of roles.

The passivity of neophytes to their instructors, their malleability, which is increased by submission to ordeal, their reduction to a uniform condition, are signs of the process whereby they are ground down to be fashioned anew and endowed with additional powers to cope with their new station in life. Dr. Richards, in her superb study of Bemba girls' puberty rites, *Chisungu,* has told us that Bemba speak of "growing a girl" when they mean initiating her (1956, 121). This term "to grow" well expresses how many peoples think of transition rites. We are inclined, as sociologists, to reify our abstractions (it is indeed a device which helps us to understand many kinds of social interconnection) and to talk about persons "moving through structural positions in a hierarchical frame" and the like. Not so the Bemba and the Shilluk of the Sudan who see the status or condition embodied or incarnate, if you like, *in the* person. To "grow" a girl into a woman is to effect an ontological transformation; it is not merely to convey an unchanging substance from one position to another by a quasi-mechanical force. Howitt saw Kuringals in Australia and I have seen Ndembu in Africa drive away grown-up men before a circumcision ceremony because they had not been initiated. Among Ndembu, men were also chased off because they had only been circumcised at the Mission Hospital and had not undergone the full bush seclusion according to the orthodox Ndembu rite. These biologically mature men had not been "made men" by the proper ritual procedures. It is the ritual and the esoteric teaching which grows girls and makes men. It is the ritual, too, which among Shilluk makes a prince into a king, or, among Luvale, a cultivator into a hunter. The arcane knowledge or *"gnosis"* obtained in the liminal period is felt to change the inmost nature of the neophyte, impressing him, as a seal impresses wax, with the characteristics of his new state. It is not a mere acquisition of knowledge, but a change in being. His apparent passivity is revealed as an absorption of powers which will become active after his social status has been redefined in the aggregation rites.

The structural simplicity of the liminal situation in many initiations is offset by its cultural complexity. I can touch on only one aspect of this vast subject matter here and raise three problems in connection with it. This aspect is the vital one of the communication of the *sacra,* the heart of the liminal matter.

Jane Harrison has shown that in the Greek Eleusinian and Orphic mysteries this communication of the *sacra* has three main components (1903, 144–160). By and large, this threefold classification holds good for initiation rites all over the world. *Sacra* may be communicated as: (1) exhibitions, "what is shown"; (2) actions, "what is done"; and (3) instructions, "what is said."

"Exhibitions" would include evocatory instruments or sacred articles, such as relics of deities, heroes or ancestors, aboriginal *churingas,* sacred drums or other musical instruments, the contents of Amerindian medicine bundles, and the fan, cist and tympanum of Greek and Near Eastern mystery cults. In the Lesser Eleusinian Mysteries of Athens, *sacra* consisted of a bone, top, ball, tambourine, apples, mirror, fan, and woolly fleece. Other *sacra* include masks, images, figurines, and effigies; the pottery emblem *(mbusa)* of the Bemba would belong to this class. In some kinds of initiation, as for example the initiation into the shaman-diviner's profession among the Saora of Middle India, described by Verrier Elwin (1955), pictures and icons representing the journeys of the dead or the adventures of supernatural beings may be shown to the initiands. A striking feature of such sacred articles is often their formal simplicity. It is their interpretation which is complex, not their outward form.

Among the "instructions" received by neophytes may be reckoned such matters as the revelation of the real, but secularly secret, names of the deities or spirits believed to preside over the rites—a very frequent procedure in African cultic or secret associations (Turner, 1962, 36). They are also taught the main outlines of the theogony, cosmogony, and mythical history of their societies or cult, usually with reference to the *sacra* exhibited. Great importance is attached to keeping secret the nature of the *sacra,* the formulas chanted and instructions given about them. These constitute the crux of liminality, for while instruction is also given in ethical and social obligations, in law and in kinship rules, and in technology to fit neophytes for the duties of future office, no interdiction is placed on knowledge thus imparted since it tends to be current among uninitiated persons also.

I want to take up three problems in considering the communication of *sacra.* The first concerns their frequent disproportion, the second their monstrousness, and the third their mystery.

When one examines the masks, costumes, figurines, and such displayed in initiation situations, one is often struck, as I have been when observing

Ndembu masks in circumcision and funerary rites, by the way in which certain natural and cultural features are represented as disproportionately large or small. A head, nose, or phallus, a hoe, bow, or meal mortar are represented as huge or tiny by comparison with other features of their context which retain their normal size. (For a good example of this, see "The Man Without Arms" in *Chisungu* [Richards, 1956, 211], a figurine of a lazy man with an enormous penis but no arms.) Sometimes things retain their customary shapes but are portrayed in unusual colors. What is the point of this exaggeration amounting sometimes to caricature? It seems to me that to enlarge or diminish or discolor in this way is a primordial mode of abstraction. The outstandingly exaggerated feature is made into an object of reflection. Usually it is not a univocal symbol that is thus represented but a multivocal one, a semantic molecule with many components. One example is the Bemba pottery emblem *Coshi wa ng'oma,* "The Nursing Mother," described by Audrey Richards in *Chisungu*. This is a clay figurine, nine inches high, of an exaggeratedly pregnant mother shown carrying four babies at the same time, one at her breast and three at her back. To this figurine is attached a riddling song:

> My mother deceived me!
> Coshi wa ng'oma!
> So you have deceived me;
> I have become pregnant again.

Bemba women interpreted this to Richards as follows:

> *Coshi wa ng'oma* was a midwife of legendary fame and is merely addressed in this song. The girl complains because her mother told her to wean her first child too soon so that it died; or alternatively, told her that she would take the first child if her daughter had a second one. But she was tricking her and now the girl has two babies to look after. The moral stressed is the duty of refusing intercourse with the husband before the baby is weaned, i.e., at the second or third year. This is a common Bemba practice.

In the figurine the exaggerated features are the number of children carried at once by the woman and her enormously distended belly. Coupled with the song, it encourages the novice to ponder upon two relationships vital to her, those with her mother and her husband. Unless the novice observes the Bemba weaning custom, her mother's desire for

grandchildren to increase her matrilineage and her husband's desire for renewed sexual intercourse will between them actually destroy and not increase her offspring. Underlying this is the deeper moral that to abide by tribal custom and not to sin against it either by excess or defect is to live satisfactorily. Even to please those one loves may be to invite calamity, if such compliance defies the immemorial wisdom of the elders embodied in the *mbusa*. This wisdom is vouched for by the mythical and archetypal midwife *Coshi wa ng'oma*.

If the exaggeration of single features is not irrational but thought-provoking, the same may also be said about the representation of monsters. Earlier writers—such as J. A. McCulloch (1913) in his article on "Monsters" in *Hastings Encyclopaedia of Religion and Ethics*—are inclined to regard bizarre and monstrous masks and figures, such as frequently appear in the liminal period of initiations, as the product of "hallucinations, night-terrors and dreams." McCulloch goes on to argue that "as man drew little distinction (in primitive society) between himself and animals, as he thought that transformation from one to the other was possible, so he easily ran human and animal together. This in part accounts for animal-headed gods or animal-gods with human heads." My own view is the opposite one: that monsters are manufactured precisely to teach neophytes to distinguish clearly between the different factors of reality, as it is conceived in their culture. Here, I think, William James's so-called "law of dissociation" may help us to clarify the problem of monsters. It may be stated as follows: when *a* and *b* occurred together as parts of the same total object, without being discriminated, the occurrence of one of these, *a,* in a new combination *ax,* favors the discrimination of *a, b,* and *x* from one another. As James himself put it, "What is associated now with one thing and now with another, tends to become dissociated from either, and to grow into an object of abstract contemplation by the mind. One might call this the law of dissociation by varying concomitants." (1918, 506).

From this standpoint, much of the grotesqueness and monstrosity of liminal *sacra* may be seen to be aimed not so much at terrorizing or bemusing neophytes into submission or out of their wits as at making them vividly and rapidly aware of what may be called the "factors" of their culture. I have myself seen Ndembu and Luvale masks that combine features of both sexes, have both animal and human attributes, and unite in a single representation human characteristics with those of the natural landscape. One *ikishi* mask is partly human and partly represents a grassy plain. Elements are withdrawn from their usual settings and combined with one another in a totally unique configuration, the monster or dragon. Monsters startle neophytes into thinking about objects, persons, relationships, and features of their environment they have hitherto taken for granted.

In discussing the structural aspect of liminality, I mentioned how neophytes are withdrawn from their structural positions and consequently from the values, norms, sentiments, and techniques associated with those positions. They are also divested of their previous habits of thought, feeling, and action. During the liminal period, neophytes are alternately forced and encouraged to think about their society, their cosmos, and the powers that generate and sustain them. Liminality may be partly described as a stage of reflection. In it those ideas, sentiments, and facts that had been hitherto for the neophytes bound up in configurations and accepted unthinkingly are, as it were, resolved into their constituents. These constituents are isolated and made into objects of reflection for the neophytes by such processes as componental exaggeration and dissociation by varying concomitants. The communication of *sacra* and other forms of esoteric instruction really involves three processes, though these should not be regarded as in series but as in parallel. The first is the reduction of culture into recognized components or factors; the second is their recombination in fantastic or monstrous patterns and shapes; and the third is their recombination in ways that make sense with regard to the new state and status that the neophytes will enter.

The second process, monster- or fantasy-making, focuses attention on the components of the masks and effigies, which are so radically ill-assorted that they stand out and can be thought about. The monstrosity of the configuration throws its elements into relief. Put a man's head on a lion's body and you think about the human head in the abstract. Perhaps it becomes for you, as a member of a given culture and with the appropriate guidance, an emblem of chieftainship; or it may be explained as representing the soul as against the body; or intellect as contrasted with brute force, or innumerable other things. There could be less encouragement to reflect on heads and

headship if that same head were firmly ensconced on its familiar, its all too familiar, human body. The man-lion monster also encourages the observer to think about lions, their habits, qualities, metaphorical properties, religious significance, and so on. More important than these, the relation between man and lion, empirical and metaphorical, may be speculated upon, and new ideas developed on this topic. Liminality here breaks, as it were, the cake of custom and enfranchises speculation. That is why I earlier mentioned Plato's self-confessed debt to the Greek mysteries. Liminality is the realm of primitive hypothesis, where there is a certain freedom to juggle with the factors of existence. As in the works of Rabelais, there is a promiscuous intermingling and juxtaposing of the categories of event, experience, and knowledge, with a pedagogic intention.

But this liberty has fairly narrow limits. The neophytes return to secular society with more alert faculties perhaps and enhanced knowledge of how things work, but they have to become once more subject to custom and law. Like the Bemba girl I mentioned earlier, they are shown that ways of acting and thinking alternative to those laid down by the deities or ancestors are ultimately unworkable and may have disastrous consequences.

Moreover, in initiation, there are usually held to be certain axiomatic principles of construction, and certain basic building blocks that make up the cosmos and into whose nature no neophyte may inquire. Certain *sacra*, usually exhibited in the most arcane episodes of the liminal period, represent or may be interpreted in terms of these axiomatic principles and primordial constituents. Perhaps we may call these *sacerrima*, "most sacred things." Sometimes they are interpreted by a myth about the world-making activities of supernatural beings "at the beginning of things." Myths may be completely absent, however, as in the case of the Ndembu "mystery of the three rivers".... This mystery (*mpang'u*) is exhibited at circumcision and funerary cult association rites. Three trenches are dug in a consecrated site and filled respectively with white, red, and black water. These "rivers" are said to "flow from Nzambi," the High God. The instructors tell the neophytes, partly in riddling songs and partly in direct terms, what each river signifies. Each "river" is a multivocal symbol with a fan of referents ranging from life values, ethical ideas, and social norms, to grossly physiological processes and phenomena.

They seem to be regarded as powers which, in varying combination, underlie or even constitute what Ndembu conceive to be reality. In no other context is the interpretation of whiteness, redness, and blackness so full; and nowhere else is such a close analogy drawn, even identity made, between these rivers and bodily fluids and emissions: whiteness = semen, milk; redness = menstrual blood, the blood of birth, blood shed by a weapon, etc.; blackness = feces, certain products of bodily decay, etc. This use of an aspect of human physiology as a model for social, cosmic, and religious ideas and processes is a variant of a widely distributed initiation theme: that the human body is a microcosm of the universe. The body may be pictured as androgynous, as male or female, or in terms of one or other of its developmental stages, as child, mature adult, and elder. On the other hand, as in the Ndembu case, certain of its properties may be abstracted. Whatever the mode of representation, the body is regarded as a sort of symbolic template for the communication of *gnosis,* mystical knowledge about the nature of things and how they came to be what they are. The cosmos may in some cases be regarded as a vast human body; in other belief systems, visible parts of the body may be taken to portray invisible faculties such as reason, passion, wisdom and so on; in others again, the different parts of the social order are arrayed in terms of a human anatomical paradigm.

Whatever the precise mode of explaining reality by the body's attributes, *sacra* which illustrates this are always regarded as absolutely sacrosanct, as ultimate mysteries. We are here in the realm of what Warner (1959, 3–4) would call "nonrational or nonlogical symbols" which

> arise out of the basic individual and cultural assumptions, more often unconscious than not, from which most social action springs. They supply the solid core of mental and emotional life of each individual and group. This does not mean that they are irrational or maladaptive, or that man cannot often think in a reasonable way about them, but rather that they do not have their source in his rational processes. When they come into play, such factors as data, evidence, proof, and the facts and procedures of rational thought in action are apt to be secondary or unimportant.

The central cluster of nonlogical *sacra* is then the symbolic template of the whole system of beliefs and values in a given culture, its archetypal paradigm and ultimate measure. Neophytes shown these are often told that they are in the presence of forms established from the beginning of things. . . . I have used the metaphor of a seal or stamp in connection with the ontological character ascribed in many initiations to arcane knowledge. The term "archetype" denotes in Greek a master stamp or impress, and these *sacra,* presented with a numinous simplicity, stamp into the neophytes the basic assumptions of their culture. The neophytes are told also that they are being filled with mystical power by what they see and what they are told about it. According to the purpose of the initiation, this power confers on them capacities to undertake successfully the tasks of their new office, in this world or the next.

Thus, the communication of *sacra* both teaches the neophytes how to think with some degree of abstraction about their cultural milieu and gives them ultimate standards of reference. At the same time, it is believed to change their nature, transform them from one kind of human being into another. It intimately unites man and office. But for a variable while, there was an uncommitted man, an individual rather than a social *persona,* in a sacred community of individuals.

It is not only in the liminal period of initiations that the nakedness and vulnerability of the ritual subject receive symbolic stress. Let me quote from Hilda Kuper's description of the seclusion of the Swazi chief during the great *Incwala* ceremony. The *Incwala* is a national First-Fruits ritual, performed in the height of summer when the early crops ripen. The regiments of the Swazi nation assemble at the capital to celebrate its rites, "whereby the nation receives strength for the new year." The *Incwala* is at the same time "a play of kingship." The king's well-being is identified with that of the nation. Both require periodic ritual strengthening. Lunar symbolism is prominent in the rites, as we shall see, and the king, personifying the nation, during his seclusion represents the moon in transition between phases, neither waning nor waxing. Dr. Kuper, Professor Gluckman, and Professor Wilson have discussed the structural aspects of the *Incwala* which are clearly present in its rites of separation and aggregation. What we are about to examine are the interstructural aspects.

During his night and day of seclusion, the king, painted black, remains, says Dr. Kuper, "painted in blackness" and "in darkness"; he is unapproachable, dangerous to himself and others. He must cohabit that night with his first ritual wife (in a kind of "mystical marriage"—this ritual wife is, as it were, consecrated for such liminal situations).

> The entire population is also temporarily in a state of taboo and seclusion. Ordinary activities and behavior are suspended; sexual intercourse is prohibited, no one may sleep late the following morning, and when they get up they are not allowed to touch each other, to wash the body, to sit on mats, to poke anything into the ground, or even to scratch their hair. The children are scolded if they play and make merry. The sound of songs that has stirred the capital for nearly a month is abruptly stilled; it is the day of *bacisa* (cause to *hide*). The king remains secluded; . . . all day he sits naked on a lion skin in the ritual hut of the harem or in the sacred enclosure in the royal cattle byre. Men of his inner circle see that he breaks none of the taboos . . . on this day the identification of the people with the king is very marked. The spies (who see to it that the people respect the taboos) do not say, "You are sleeping late" or "You are scratching," but "You cause the king to sleep," "You scratch him (the king)"; etc. (Kuper, 1947, 219–220).

Other symbolic acts are performed which exemplify the "darkness" and "waxing and waning moon" themes, for example, the slaughtering of a black ox, the painting of the queen mother with a black mixture—she is compared again to a half-moon, while the king is a full moon, and both are in eclipse until the paint is washed off finally with doctored water, and the ritual subject "comes once again into lightness and normality."

In this short passage we have an embarrassment of symbolic riches. I will mention only a few themes that bear on the argument of this paper. Let us look at the king's position first. He is symbolically invisi-

ble, "black," a moon between phases. He is also under obedience to traditional rules, and "men of his inner circle" see that he keeps them. He is also "naked," divested of the trappings of his office. He remains apart from the scenes of his political action in a sanctuary or ritual hut. He is also, it would seem, identified with the earth which the people are forbidden to stab, lest the king be affected. He is "hidden." The king, in short, has been divested of all the outward attributes, the "accidents," of his kingship and is reduced to its substance, the "earth" and "darkness" from which the normal, structured order of the Swazi kingdom will be regenerated "in lightness."

In this betwixt-and-between period, in this fruitful darkness, king and people are closely identified. There is a mystical solidarity between them, which contrasts sharply with the hierarchical rank-dominated structure of ordinary Swazi life. It is only in darkness, silence, celibacy, in the absence of merriment and movement that the king and people can thus be one. For every normal action is involved in the rights and obligations of a structure that defines status and establishes social distance between men. Only in their Trappist sabbath of transition may the Swazi regenerate the social tissues torn by conflicts arising from distinctions of status and discrepant structural norms.

I end this study with an invitation to investigators of ritual to focus their attention on the phenomena and processes of mid-transition. It is these, I hold, that paradoxically expose the basic building blocks of culture just when we pass out of and before we re-enter the structural realm. In *sacerrima* and their interpretations we have categories of data that may usefully be handled by the new sophisticated techniques of cross-cultural comparison.

Female Circumcision in Egypt and Sudan: A Controversial Rite of Passage

Daniel Gordon

Anthropologists have known and written about female genital operations for many years, but the subject has only recently been brought to the attention of a startled Western public. The practice, taboo to the non-Western media prior to the airing of CNN International's video of an actual operation in 1994 (and subsequent report on the film in Time*), is now a hot issue in Egypt where human rights advocates, including women's groups and many physicians, are pitted against its proponents. Also termed* female genital mutilation *and (erroneously)* female circumcision, *this operation is widespread in Africa south of the Sahara, but although practiced in several Islamic countries of North Africa, it is not present in 80 percent of the Muslim world.*

Blending physiological and cultural data, Daniel Gordon's research focuses on the types of genital surgery common in Egypt and Sudan and the rationales employed by members of these societies to defend the practice. Although not a ritual marking the physiological change from adolescence to adulthood, as is the case in Black Africa, female genital surgery in Egypt and Sudan is a rite of passage that moves immature females into what Gordon calls "social puberty," giving a child the status of a woman after the operation.

Gordon's work challenges the validity of cultural relativism and accuses anthropologists of advocating female genital surgery because of their nonjudgmental position. Yet he makes plain that although these operations are deeply imbedded in the male-dominated cultures of Egypt and Sudan, which stress female constraint and the separation of male and female worlds, women themselves are the strongest proponents of genital surgery for their daughters and granddaughters. This fact demands explanation that can be found only in the intricate weave of the fabric of Egyptian and Sudanic cultures.

Reproduced by permission of the American Anthropological Association from *Medical Anthropology Quarterly* 5:1, March 1991. Not for further reproduction.

DESPITE ITS LONG HISTORY, ITS ENDURING PREVALENCE, and the capacity of its practice to arouse emotional response, the literature on female circumcision in the Arab world is surprisingly scant. . . . In the last decade, finally, with the development of feminist consciousness and the advent of an international women's health movement, there has been a growing perception that the largely descriptive approach taken in much of the existing literature is inappropriately passive in its response to the international health issue of "female genital mutilation" (Hosken 1982).

In beginning, I must make it clear that the term "female circumcision," although common throughout much of the literature, is an incorrect, euphemistic description for what is really a variety of operations which can be categorized into three main types. Literal circumcision is the least mutilating of the three procedures and is referred to as *sunna* ("duty") in Arabic, since it is thought to be commanded or at least recommended by Islam. It corresponds most closely to the operation in males, involving removal of the clitoral prepuce (foreskin) by razor, knife, or smoldering stone, depending on where and by whom it is practiced. The second form, excision or clitoridectomy, involves the cutting out of the whole clitoris as well as parts or all of the labia minora. In its varying degrees it is the most common form practiced in Egypt. In the Sudan excision is not performed, but a similar operation, referred to as "intermediate circumcision" (El Dareer 1982: 4), involves removal of the clitoris, the anterior or all of the labia minora, and slices of the labia majora. El Dareer suggests that this procedure was invented as a compromise by Sudanese midwives when British legislation forbade the most extreme operations in 1946.

Pharaonic circumcision, or *tahara farowniyya* in Arabic, is the oldest of the three operations, attributed in folk legend to the time of the ancient Pharaohs (hence the name). It is most prevalent in the Sudan and Nubian Egypt. The most radical of the operations, it is often referred to as infibulation, because of its association with the ancient Roman practice of fastening a clasp, or fibula, through the labia majora of a woman to ensure her chastity. Pharaonic circumcision involves complete removal of the clitoris, labia minora and majora, with the two sides of the wound then stitched together, leaving a small pinhole opening for the drop by drop passage of urine and menstrual blood. The operation is done in a variety of ways, depending on where it is practiced. In rural settings, a small stick is often inserted to maintain the opening, and the two sides stitched together with thorns. Adhesives such as egg, oil, or wet cigarette paper are placed over the wound to promote healing. The girl's legs are often bound together for as long as 40 days to ensure the desired tightly scarred aperture (El Dareer 1982: 1–20). In urban settings, stitching is likely to be done with catgut or silk sutures, and anesthesia and antibiotics are likely to be used.

The most extensive statistical survey of female genital operations done to date was carried out in the Sudan between 1977 and 1981 by the Faculty of Medicine at the University of Khartoum, with Dr. Asma El Dareer as chief investigator (El Dareer 1982). El Dareer's team interviewed 3,210 women and 1,545 men, representing a random sampling of households throughout Northern Sudan. In addition to El Dareer, interviewers were Sudanese social workers and medical and college students, who all received a standardized training in administration of the questionnaire. The questionnaire included demographic information on age, religion, education, occupation, income, marital status, and circumcision history (method, type, operator, healing, complications, need for treatment). Cooperative respondents were followed further with open-ended questions on their recollections of the procedure, their support or opposition, and plans for their daughters. When permitted, a physical exam was performed to corroborate type of circumcision and evidence of complications. Ninety-five percent of the sample population responded to the questionnaire, and 95% of this group proceeded to the open-ended questions. Only 12 women were willing to undergo examination, meaning that nearly all information on operation type and on sequelae was reported and could not be corroborated.

What the survey showed was that a genital operation of some sort is nearly universal. Over 98% of the women questioned were circumcised—3% with the *sunna* procedure; 12% "intermediate"; and 83%, pharaonic (El Dareer 1982: 1). The strongest predictor of operation type was level of education. Seventy-five percent of pharaonically circumcised girls were from illiterate families, while educated parents were more likely to opt for the milder forms (El Dareer 1982: 22). Over 90% of the operations in the Sudan were performed by *dayas,* or midwives, the rest by doctors, nurses, or old men and women who inherited the role (El Dareer 1982: 17).

Survey information for Egypt is not nearly so extensive, but the incidence of female genital operations is certainly much lower. Estimates range from one-third (Hosken 1978: 152) to one-half (Rugh 1984: 160) of all Egyptian women. In addition, the variety of procedures is more moderate. Except for the Nubian south, virtually no pharaonic operations are performed. A 1965 study of 651 circumcised women by two male Egyptian gynecologists reported that all circumcisions were variations of *sunna* and excision (Hansen 1972/73: 15).

That both the Egyptian and Sudanese governments recognize female genital operations as a health concern is evidenced by statutes in both countries which ban all but the most moderate forms. Sudan seems to have inherited a tradition of concern from the British Health Service, dating from the 1920s and 1930s, and now sponsors conferences and epidemiological research, such as El Dareer's, which use the language of medicine and epidemiology to oppose the practices. El Dareer, for example, is active in programs that educate rural Sudanese about the health hazards of female genital operations. In introducing the data from her survey, she explicitly states that her goal in carrying out such work is to reveal how the genital operations can best be eradicated.

Despite efforts to curb these practices, however, inadequate reporting renders the precise nature and extent of the health problem very difficult to assess. Perhaps most misleading is that few women relate the complications of circumcision to the operation, since it is generally believed to be harmless (El Dareer 1982: 28). Infections, for example, which are among the most common complications, are more likely to be attributed to the evil eye and treated by amulets, incantations, or a dip in the Nile (El Dareer 1982: 33). In addition, many women are reluctant to seek help from male physicians because of the area of the body they would have to expose on examination, and they therefore accept the painful consequences (El Dareer 1982: 28). Sufferers from the complications of the pharaonic procedure will often remain quiet because of the known illegality of the operation and the shame attached to endangering one's *daya* (El Dareer 1982: 28). El Dareer noted that of the 790 immediate complications reported to her, only 10% had been shown to medical personnel, and 85% of cases that in her opinion had later required serious medical attention went unreported (El Dareer 1982: 28). Mortality records are particularly incomplete. Primary fatalities (e.g., from hemorrhagic shock) are concealed for fear of legal repercussions, while secondary fatalities, such as death in childbirth, are not reported in a way that they can be related to the operations (Hosken 1982: 4).

Although the incidence of mortality is not known and the extent of morbidity is sketchy at best, the complications of female genital operations have been described, if not quantified, with some consistency (e.g., Dewhurst and Michelson 1964; El Dareer 1982; El Saadawi 1980; Hathout 1963; Huddleston 1944; Koso-Thomas 1987; Mustafa 1966; Worsley 1938). The most immediate of these complications include pain from lack of anesthesia, hemorrhage of major blood vessels, and fatal shock from loss of blood. Pain and the fear associated with it can lead to acute urinary retention, as can trauma to the urethra. The nearly complete sealing off of the vagina in infibulation makes chronic urinary retention a standard complaint after this operation. Inability to void urine can lead to the formation of painful stones and, particularly when preceded by the use of unsterilized equipment and dressings, makes urinary tract infections a virtual certainty. Untreated lower urinary tract infections can ascend to the bladder and kidneys (pyelonephritis) with devastating consequences, including renal failure, septicemia, and death. Pelvic inflammatory disease (infection of the uterus and fallopian tubes) is also common, excruciatingly painful, and can render a woman infertile. Local infection, often accompanied by anemia from blood loss, causes slow and incomplete healing, a condition which favors formation of excessive scar tissue, or keloid. Keloid is a particular problem in Nubian Egypt and the Sudan, as its formation is most characteristic of the healing process of blacks. By one estimation, keloids occur in about half of infibulated women in the Sudan (Worsley 1938: 687). Keloids can cause vaginal obstruction, predisposing women to urinary and menstrual blockage even in the noninfibulated. At the extreme, complete obstruction of the vagina (whether secondary to infibulation or keloids) can lead to hematocolpos, the accumulation of menstrual blood in the vagina. This condition can persist for months or even years. There are, in fact, documented cases of young women who have been put to death by their families when an abnormal swelling caused by accumulated blood was incorrectly interpreted as pregnancy out of wedlock (El Saadawi 1980: 26). Vulvar abscesses and cysts, finally, are common in operations that involve stitching (pharaonic and intermediate) and are caused by inclusion of skin into the stitched wound. These can swell to an enormous size and persist for years.

Medical sequelae, particularly of the pharaonic operations, also have a profound effect on childbirth. Accumulated scarring favors a prolonged and painful labor, as fibrous vulvar tissue fails to dilate during contractions. Hemorrhage often results from tearing through scar tissue or through the cervix or perineum. Rupture of the vagina leads to formation of fistulae with rectum or bladder, causing lifelong incontinence, discomfort, and odor. Furthermore, in all cases of pharaonic circumcision, the woman must be disinfibulated, or cut open along the original scar, to permit passage of the baby. For its part, the child can be stillborn, brain damaged, or suffer malformations from the obstructed labor, lack of oxygen during the excessive time spent in the vaginal canal, or errant episiotomy cuts dealt by the *daya*.

While recognizing the difficulty of achieving an accurate quantification of these complications, a 1979 conference of the World Health Organization in Khartoum reported extensive experience of unanesthetized pain, hemorrhage, urinary retention, and infection in all forms of genital operation, but particularly in the pharaonic (Hosken 1982: 45). In El Dareer's survey, one-quarter of respondents reported immediate complications, with dysuria and hemorrhage the most common (each about 20% of all reported complications) (El Dareer 1982: 37).

When women in the sample were asked if they suffered from any of a list of known sequelae, 30% reported long-term consequences. Chronic urinary tract and pelvic infections were most commonly cited at about 25% each of all reported sequelae (El Dareer 1982: 28). In addition, the highest mortality rates in childbirth are reported from areas practicing circumcision (Hosken 1982: 110), although a cause and effect relationship cannot necessarily be inferred from this fact, since areas where the more radical procedures are done are also those regions with the lowest standard of living and the least adequate health care.

Evaluation of the immediate and long-term psychological impact of the operations has not been addressed, but the effects on sexual response seem fairly clear, despite the reluctance of women to discuss this topic (Rugh 1984: 110). Seventy-five percent of women in El Dareer's survey report either never experiencing sexual pleasure, or being totally indifferent to the notion (El Dareer 1982: 48). Scar tissue often makes sex painful, and with the substantial narrowing of the vaginal orifice in pharaonic circumcision, tearing and bleeding are greatly increased, making first-time sex particularly feared (El Dareer 1982: 41). What is more, an infibulated woman usually needs to be cut open to allow intercourse. If not, full penetration can be a long and painful process taking many months (Boddy 1982: 686).

Although circumcised women do not consider many of the subsequent pains and complications they endure to be connected with their operations, one has to wonder why these operations are done in view of the immediate suffering alone. This question is intensified by the fact that on the books, at least, pharaonic circumcision in the Sudan and total clitoral excision in Egypt are forbidden, yet they continue to be practiced. Indeed, leniency of enforcement has been attributed to local riots and protests which accompanied the initial attempts to apply these laws (Hosken 1982: 105).

Several authors suggest that associations with and overtones of religious tradition make these practices more persistent than parallel customs in other cultures, such as foot binding in China, which simply disappeared when outlawed (Beck and Keddie 1980: 24). Indeed, El Dareer points out that religion and tradition are the most common reasons given by both women and men for the practice of these operations (El Dareer 1982: 67). The name *sunna,* or religious duty, which has become associated with one type of operation, implies unquestionable adherence for Muslims. When asked about these practices, people commonly respond, "We are following our religious teachings" (El Dareer 1982: 71), yet, interestingly, this same response is given even when non-*sunna* operations are being described (El Dareer 1982: 70). Thus, even to its religious defenders, the precise relationship of female genital operations to Islamic tradition, though apparently closely associated, is not so clear.

There is good evidence, in fact, that the custom is not even originally Islamic. Clitoridectomy and excision are practiced in West Africa from Mauritania to Cameroon, across central Africa to Chad, and in the East from Tanzania to Ethiopia; infibulation is customary in Mali, Somalia, Ethiopia, and Nigeria. This wide distribution of these practices in non-Islamic parts of Africa suggests that these operations are originally an African institution, adopted by Islam in its conquest of Egypt (Hansen 1972/73: 18). It should be noted in this regard that while female genital operations are practiced in several Islamic countries, they are unknown in 80% of the Islamic world, most notably Saudi Arabia, Jordan, Iran, and Iraq. Searching for precedent in Islamic texts, one finds that the operations are not mentioned anywhere in the Qur'an, although several statements from the companion *hadith,* the sayings of the Prophet, have a tradition of being interpreted as referring to female circumcision (Al Hibri 1982: 204). Even so, the traditions of *hadith* interpretation support only the most moderate of the operations. Egypt's 1959 statute banning all but partial clitoridectomy was based on a summary of religious opinion by the Ministry of Public Health. According to this source, it is unclear whether the *hadith* consider *khafd* (literally, reduction; in this context, the *sunna* operation) to be *sunna* (duty) or merely *makrama* (embellishment), but all interpretations agree that total excision is forbidden (Hosken 1982: 133).

In short, the commonly held conception among those who practice these operations, that they are dictated by religious tenets, has not been validated. Perhaps the interplay that arises between doctrine and a culturally embedded sense of what is right is more vague in Islam than some other religions, because there is no central religious authority to interpret and disseminate dogma to a largely illiterate populace. Religion and "tradition" are offered almost reflexively as an explanation for behavior patterns that are woven into the texture of society. This can be seen by the fact that many interviewees who supported the practice of female genital operations admitted to no clear or conscious rationale for doing so, or perhaps they were responding out of a deep fear of social criticism (El Dareer 1982: 78). Furthermore, many who opposed the operations still intended to subject their own daughters to them (El Dareer 1982: 82).

A window into understanding the belief patterns which undergird this sense of what is proper is offered by another popular explanation given by interviewees: cleanliness (El Dareer 1982: 73). The important role of this quality can be seen in the folk name for all the female genital operations: *tahara,* or purity. There is an extensive body of anecdotal material linking the operations to improved health, including prevention of stillbirth (Koso-Thomas 1987: 5) and relief from the generalized affliction of *el duda,* the "worm," which *dayas* sometimes claim to see jumping out when a girl is circumcised (El Dareer 1982: 13). As the name and the healing associated with it imply, *tahara* refers to cleanliness rooted in deeper concerns.

What these concerns might be brings us to the most venerated anthropological explanation for mutilation operations—the rite of passage. In this construction, the operation serves as a marker of the movement from child to adult, in which the similarity between male and female is removed, permitting a ritual differentiation of the sexes (van Gennep 1960[1908]: 72). There is certainly support for this argument among many African tribes, where the operation takes place at puberty and is accompanied by a naming ceremony. In the Sudan and Egypt, however, female genital surgery is performed well before puberty, usually between the ages of about five to nine, and does not, therefore, correspond to actual physiological change.

The key to understanding these operations is to recognize that they serve as something of a "social puberty," powerfully signifying the young girl's future passage into sexuality. In some areas of the Sudan and Nubian Egypt, this passage is ritualized by investing the operations with the form and symbolism of a wedding. The girl is adorned with gold and henna in the style of a bride, while Qur'anic verses are chanted and a groom is exhorted to come forward (Kennedy 1970: 179). In this way, the operation becomes part of the same ceremonial complex as marriage and childbirth. The involvement with blood and genitalia foreshadows the young girl's future role as wife and mother (Kennedy 1970: 179).

Although a circumcised girl may still be a child biologically, her status becomes that of a woman after her operation. She is no longer permitted to play outside or to socialize with boys her age; in some areas even school is forbidden, as she begins the task of waiting for a husband (El Dareer 1982: 71). As a woman, she is now subject to a strict code of modesty, one of the most fundamental patterns of belief and behavior in the Arab world as a whole, involving appropriate bodily covering, character traits such as bashfulness and naiveté, and associated customs and belief relating to chastity, fidelity, separation, and seclusion (Antoun 1968: 672).

The traditional pattern of female constraint involves a separation of male and female worlds, with propriety and honor accorded women at home and men in public. If they must go out, women should be accompanied by symbols of virtuous intent: modest clothes, clear evidence of destination, the company of a child or adult relative (Rugh 1984: 186). There are separate male and female lines in stores and at bus depots, underscoring the forbidden nature of even the most superficial contact between unmarried men and women.

The reward for adherence to this code of modesty and separation is honor to the family and improved marriage prospects for the girl and her sisters. The punishment for its violation is shame (Rugh 1984: 160). An unmarried pregnant woman, for example, is considered bereft of honor and utterly alone. In certain areas it would not be unusual for her to commit suicide, or even to be murdered by her own family (El Saadawi 1980: 23).

Understanding the broader Arabic code of modesty and conceptions of female sexuality offers a clearer insight into the role of female genital operations. That the separation and seclusion of women is deeply connected to a particular orientation toward sexuality is not only intuitively plausible, but it is borne out by how early (prepubertally) these constraints are imposed and by their removal in old age. When a woman is no longer considered sexual, she is permitted to mix freely with men, often in a position of veneration and status (Antoun 1968: 677).

At the heart of the code of modesty is an ideology of female appetite, unpredictability, and lack of self-control (Antoun 1968: 678). The education of a young girl is a litany of what she is by nature likely to do but must avoid, because it is harmful, shameful, or religiously outlawed (El Saadawi 1980: 13). The ideal form of the code dictates the complete separation of the female threat to the public sphere. Absolute seclusion, however, is rarely an economically feasible option. Most Egyptians and Sudanese do not have the resources to maintain the required accoutrements of harems: extra servants, large gardens, high walls (Rugh 1984: 156). These features are more characteristic of countries, such as Saudi Arabia and Kuwait, where genital operations are not practiced. That these operations have, however, been reported as universal among nomadic Bedouin (Hosken 1982: 110) supports the contention that the genital operations, with the physical and symbolic barriers that they present, serve as a substitute for a more complete seclusion of women.

A man from the poor Bulaq community of Cairo is quoted by Rugh as saying,

> In the cold countries of the north where the blood runs slowly, you do not have the need for the operation. But here in the warm countries we are more emotional and less restricted. Without this operation there is no telling what our women might do. For sure, one man would not be enough to satisfy them. (1984: 160)

It has been argued that this fear of female sexuality is a product of Arab concern with patrilineal purity (Beck and Keddie 1980: 8). Family and lineage are certainly of great importance in the Arab world, as evidenced by the slant of Islamic law and practice which, for example, do not recognize adoption (Antoun 1968: 689). Thus the genital operations can serve as a means for protecting lineage purity and, by extension, the honor of the woman's agnatic group (Beck and Keddie 1980). With extramarital sexuality at least symbolically prevented, there is a reduction of the destabilizing possibility that a given child may actually belong to another lineage. The genital scar—proudly called *nafsi*, "my own self," by

the bearer (Worsley 1938: 687)—attests to the value of definite possessions for the families involved: honor for the women's family of birth and purity of patrilineage for the family of her husband (Oldfield Hayes 1975: 623). A particularly tight infibulation, in fact, is often rewarded by an increased brideprice and by gifts from the groom to the bride's family (El Dareer 1982: 41). Likewise, to call a man the son of an uncircumcised mother is one of the severest insults in the Arab world (Hansen 1972/73: 19).

A fascinating proof for the undergirding of infibulation by the issue of patrilineage is provided by Kennedy's fieldwork among the Nubians, who inhabit the Nile between Aswan, Egypt, and Dongola, Sudan. When much of their agricultural land was inundated after construction of the Aswan High Dam, their forced dependence on urban wage labor began to shift emphasis to the nuclear family, eroding the centrality of land inheritance and lineage continuity. The result has been that Nubian girls are being subjected increasingly to the milder excision operation instead of full-scale infibulation (Kennedy 1970: 186).

Despite the emphasis or the preceding arguments on a male conception of sexuality, one cannot ignore the fact that women are the strongest proponents of the operations (Oldfield Hayes 1975: 624). It is the grandmothers who make all arrangements and preparations, often without the father's consent (Oldfield Hayes 1975: 619). An argument can be made for there being significant economic impetus to perpetuate the respected role of the *daya*, the only achieved position of prestige that is available to women. The *daya*'s work provides a substantial contribution to the village economy, particularly in areas where pharaonic circumcision is the norm (Oldfield Hayes 1975: 627). In addition to the initial infibulation, a woman often needs to be deinfibulated on her wedding night, usually at a substantial fee, since the *daya* is brought in secretly to protect the husband from the public shame of having been unable to achieve penetration (Oldfield Hayes 1975: 627). Deinfibulation and subsequent reinfibulation are done also for infections, infertility, urinary and menstrual retention, and childbirth (El Dareer 1982: 51). There is also the additional phenomenon of widows, divorcees, and married women reinfibulating to appear virginal, some of them actually going through the procedure at regular intervals (El Dareer 1982: 51).

Another argument suggests that while men view these practices in terms of chastity and honor, women understand genital operations by focusing on fertility and deemphasizing sexuality (Boddy 1982). Based on her fieldwork in the Sudan, Boddy developed a linguistic and cultural exegesis which links fertility with enclosedness—a characteristic of infibulated genitalia. The idiom of enclosure is echoed in Sudanese folk medicine, where an accumulation of demons (*djinn*) is feared at all orifices, and many remedies are based on the assumption that illness is caused by things opening or coming apart. The enclosed womb protects a woman's truest possession, her fertility, as well as the future lineage of her husband. In this way, Boddy argues, infibulation is an assertive and symbolic act, controlled by women, in which the womb becomes a social space —enclosed, guarded, and impervious.

Analyses such as this present a stumbling block to Western political agitation against female genital operations. While it may be true, as Hosken asserts, that without "the [male] preference for women who have undergone the operations, the practice would die out" (Hosken 1982: 11), hopeful assertions such as this miss the cultural point. Preferences for ritual are not so much matters of personal predilection as they are deeply embedded solutions to group concerns—in this case to issues such as sexuality, fertility, and patrilineage.

From the perspective of those who would like to see these practices completely eradicated, one of the most frustrating aspects of the current practice of female genital operations has been its peripheral incorporation into the biomedical health care system. Thus, while the World Health Organization and other medical groups assume a "passive stance" (Hosken 1982: 272) with regard to these procedures, trained medical personnel, drugs, and equipment are being disseminated and used to perform genital operations (Hosken 1982: 287). In urban Sudan there has been an official policy of using the health care system for the operations in order to reduce complications through improved surgical conditions (Hosken 1982: 47). Physicians do about 2% of the urban operations, while *dayas* with government sponsored midwifery training (a legacy of the British) do about 35% (El Dareer 1982: 15).

From a medical perspective, this development has to be seen as encouraging. Sanitation is greatly improved, and antibiotics, anesthetics, and better aseptic techniques are all more likely to be used when trained operators perform the surgery (El Dareer 1982: 16). Perhaps even more important, particularly for the future, is what seems to be a slow turning away from the more extreme operations. The most sensitive barometer of potential change is probably the opinions of those who have been subjected to operations and are now themselves the parents of young girls. The interviews conducted by El Dareer throughout the Sudan show a striking discordance between the type of operation previously performed and that currently favored. While over 80% were infibulated, only 23% of women and 16% of men actually preferred this procedure, with the majority of men opting for *sunna* instead, most women favoring intermediate, and approximately 15% of respondents preferring no operation at all (El Dareer 1982: 69). While El Dareer's survey is not exhaustive, it represents the best statistical information available, at least for the Sudan, and could well be predictive of substantial moderation of future practice.

The most significant change in these practices is likely to be rooted in the inexorable Western influences of industrialization and urbanization. Kennedy has shown how Nubian custom changed as the importance of tribal descent was replaced by the urban focus on paid labor and the nuclear family. A similar case can be made for the major urban centers of the Sudan, where the incidence of pharaonic operations is dropping in favor of the intermediate form (El Dareer 1982: 22). In Egypt, the process of urbanization is farther along, and a majority of the middle class now abstains from genital operations altogether (Hosken 1978: 152).

These small seeds of change leave us, still, with a dilemma of cross-cultural ethics. Konner's admonition that "female circumcision is one place where we ought to draw the line" argues for the increasingly popular Western movement of opposition to an alien practice that is painful, physically disfiguring, medically treacherous, and oppressive to women. There is considerable moral force to this stance, yet it is diluted in the end by a failure to place the female genital operations within the context of anthropological thought. Hosken even asserts that the practice, in its violence and subjugation, has "nothing to do with culture" (Hosken 1982: 1). This skirts not only the issue of culturally embedded meaning for those who practice and experience female genital operations but also our own cultural assumptions.

Cultural relativism, although it is not generally considered to be so, is also a position of advocacy. The anthropological enterprise of exploring what it means to be human through consideration of alien behavior has shown how customs and rituals are not isolated practices to be chosen or discarded at will, but they form a framework of interrelated idioms, a logic of daily life through which reality is ordered and experience mediated. Numerous studies have demonstrated how an entire culture is stressed when its customs are devalued, "modernized," or eliminated by the processes of urbanization and acculturation. Hypertension, loss of respect for the elders, fragmentation of families, increased prevalence of depression and suicide have been documented among both urbanized Zulu (Scotch 1963) and Ethiopian immigrants to Israel (Weingrod 1987), to cite two examples.

The failings of anthropology in its study of female genital operations in Egypt and the Sudan have been its inability to integrate a consideration of the medical complications of the practice into its description and a denial of its own position of moral advocacy. Because of this, the international women's rights movement has not been far off base in considering anthropologists as perpetuating a cover-up. Although this has doubtless taken place outside of conscious awareness for the most part, with no intention to mislead, a decision to describe without judging does require certain blindspots.

With a capacity perhaps unique among non-Western practices in its ability to generate emotional debate and misunderstanding, the phenomenon of female genital operations can be seen as a compelling test-case in cross-cultural ethics for medical anthropology. The challenge is to develop an explanatory model that can integrate anthropological description, public health concerns, and our own cultural sensitivities. This last point is the most likely to be ignored because of its perceived antagonism to anthropology's nonjudgmental relativism. At the limits of our ability to understand another culture's practices, however, an articulated self-awareness helps to remind us that we are ourselves looking at the world through culturally trained eyes. While relativism is a powerful descriptive tool for getting inside another culture, both the describer and his audience have cultural agendas that must be considered as well.

An Anthropologist's Reflections on Symbolic Usage

Raymond Firth

*In the following selection, Raymond Firth discusses
the power of symbolism and the contribution of
anthropology to its understanding. Firth argues that
because anthropologists have traditionally explored the
meaning and importance of symbols used by the
world's cultures, they are especially prepared to help
others understand the impact of symbols on behavior.
Firth contends that the anthropological approach to
symbolism can help us understand the problem of
disjunction, a term that he uses to describe the
difference between an overt action and its real or
underlying meaning. Referring to his own fieldwork
in the Pacific, Firth compares disjunctions among
various Tikopian religious ceremonies with
disjunctions easily observable in certain Christian
rituals. Firth also observes that anthropologists use
their knowledge of Western religious symbolism to aid
them in understanding symbolism in preliterate
cultures.*

*It is important to note that although the article
focuses on the relevance of anthropology to symbolism
and religious symbols in particular, the material has
been excerpted from a larger general work by Firth on
public and private symbols, one in which he explores
the power of symbolism in art, literature, philosophy,
and everyday life.*

*Professor Raymond Firth is a scholar of
international fame and is especially known for his
pioneering studies in the Solomon Islands and
Malaysia. His book,* Rank and Religion in Tikopia,
*is regarded as one of the outstanding works in the
anthropology of comparative religion.*

Reprinted from *Symbols: Public and Private* (Ithaca, New
York: Cornell University Press, 1973). © 1973 George
Allen and Unwin Ltd.

SYMBOLIZATION IS A UNIVERSAL HUMAN PRO-
cess. But we still need to understand much more
about it, especially in its comparative aspects, in
different societies, different classes, different religions. Pervasive in communication, grounded in
the very use of language, symbolization is part of
the living stuff of societal relationships. Western
literature is shot through with references which
recall to us questions of existence and identity in
symbol terms. In an essay on The Poet, Emerson
wrote of the universality of the symbolic language: 'things admit of being used as symbols because nature is a symbol' (but so is culture)—'we
are symbols and inhabit symbols'. In *Sartor Resar-
tus* Carlyle held that in a symbol there is both concealment and revelation. Oriental writings show
analogous views. What is it in such statements
that some of us find so attractive? Is it truth or illusion about human personality? And if these are
not questions for anthropologists to answer, can
we at least comment meaningfully upon the
forms of such statements, the conditions of their
utterance, and their social effects?

In intellectual circles, symbolism in literature,
art and religion has long been a subject of study;
philosophers and linguists have scrutinized the
concept of symbol in its more abstract significance. I show later why I think such treatment is
of interest to anthropologists. But anthropologists
are also concerned with the ways in which ordinary people think about symbols, behave symbolically in their daily life as members of a society,
and consciously interpret what they do as having
symbolic meaning.

The essence of symbolism lies in the recognition of one thing as standing for (re-presenting)
another, the relation between them normally
being that of concrete to abstract, particular to
general. The relation is such that the symbol by itself appears capable of generating and receiving

effects otherwise reserved for the object to which it refers—and such effects are often of high emotional charge.

An Anthropological Approach

I have shown the existence of a very wide range of symbolic material—things called symbols and ideas about symbols—in the current social milieu in which we all move. I have suggested too that such material can be relevant to any general anthropological study of symbols because of the problems of definition and image it raises.

But what can be a specifically anthropological contribution to the understanding of symbolism? What can an anthropologist do that has not been done already by logicians, metaphysicians, linguists, psychologists, theologians, art historians and the rest? Essentially as I see it, the anthropological approach is comparative, observationalist, functionalist, relatively neutralist. It links the occurrence and interpretations of symbolism to social structures and social events in specific conditions. Over a wide range of instances, anthropologists have observed what symbols people actually use, what they have said about these things, the situations in which the symbols emerge, and the reactions to them. Consequently, anthropologists are equipped to explain the meanings of symbols in the cultures they have studied, and to use such explanations as a means of furthering understanding of the processes of social life. Victor Turner has said of one of his studies—which have played a great part in modern developments—that it is a demonstration of the use of rite and symbol as a key to the understanding of social structure and social process. Others have explicitly examined symbolic actions in their social contexts to clarify the understanding of phenomena of political or religious change. But I think that for many of us the prime relevance of an anthropological approach to the study of symbolism is its attempt to grapple as empirically as possible with the basic human problem of what I would call disjunction—a gap between the overt superficial statement of action and its underlying meaning. On the surface, a person is saying or doing something which our observations or inferences tell us should not be simply taken at face value—it stands for something else, of greater significance to him.

I take an illustration from my own experience in the Pacific, years ago. I remember seeing a Tikopia chief in pagan times stand up in his temple and rub the great centre post of the building with aromatic leaves drenched in coconut oil. Now you can oil wood to preserve it or give it a polish, as decoration. And in the Pacific you can oil your body and scent it with leaves, when you decorate yourself, as for a dance. But as the chief did this rubbing he murmured: 'May your body be washed with power.' Now scrubbing a baulk of timber with a hunk of oily leaves is not a very elevated intellectual act. But think of the timber as a *body* and of the fragrant oil as a decorative medium. Think too not of a material body, but of an invisible body—not necessarily with the shape of a post, but in another context, an anthropomorphic body, of a spiritual being, believed to control crops and fish and the health of men. Think too of washing as cleansing, and cleansing as a preface to adornment, and adornment as pleasing to oneself as well as to others. So you can see this act as symbolizing the anointing of the body of a god with fragrant scents to express the status relations and emotions of worship—and to render the god more amenable to the requests of his worshippers. This may seem a very faraway symbolism. Yet think further of Christ's washing of the feet of his disciples; the anointing of Christ by Mary of Bethany; the symbolic value to Christians of the Cross, with its synonyms of the Wood, the Tree; and think also of conceptions of the Eucharist, of the Mystical Body of Christ, of the Glorified Body of the Virgin. It is not difficult to see that what we are dealing with in the Tikopia case is a set of symbolic counters which though superficially very dissimilar to the Christian ones, share some of the basic modes of symbolic conceptualization and patterning. But the symbolic arrangement is set in a social matrix of clans, chieftainship, modes of bodily decoration, even of architectural design which need intensive study for the symbolism to become fully intelligible.

The anthropological approach, fully applied, has as its objective to provide a systematic description and analysis of such a symbolic act in its verbal and non-verbal aspects; to distinguish those parts of the action held to be significant from those which are incidental; to mark the routine or standard elements as against those which are personal and idiosyncratic; to get elucidation from actor, participants and non-participants of the meanings they attach to the act;

and to set all this in its general conceptual and institutional framework, and in the more specific framework of the statuses and group relationships of the people concerned. This is a demanding task. But it has been admirably done by many anthropologists —to mention here only Audrey Richards, Monica Wilson and Victor Turner. . . . Some anthropologists have also studied change in symbolic idiom—as I myself have done in the field of Tikopia religion.

The study of symbolism, especially religious symbolism, is fashionable now in social anthropology. There is a tendency to look on this study as a totally new development, but in fact, anthropological interest in symbols goes back at least 100 years, before the days of McLennan and Tylor. It is true that until recently this interest was rarely intense, systematic or sustained, and the modern interest is much more sophisticated, analytical and highly focused. I think there are several reasons for this delayed development. Firstly, as a purely professional sequence of operations, systematic studies of symbolism have had to wait until a substantial measure of progress had been made in the more formal fields of social structure, such as kinship and politics. Now that so much groundwork has been laid we can build loftier constructions of interpretation. Secondly, developments in the theory of communication and of semantics, of signs and their meanings, have focused attention on the interpretation of those elements of behaviour where the meaning of the sign has often seemed most complex and obscure. Thirdly, the growing interest in culturally-defined systems of thought, and in concepts and thought-processes more generally, has stimulated inquiry in fields such as symbolism, where the relationships between elements seem above all to be of a conceptual kind. All this is part of the relatively straightforward operations of scholarship.

But I think two other reasons may be significant also. It is in keeping with the general temper of our time to be attracted to studies which concern themselves with the less rational aspects of human behaviour, which tend to reject or criticize a positivist approach, which make play with ideas of ambiguity, uncertainty, mystery. This is probably in part a counter to or a relief from the demands for rationality and precision of our industrial, machine-governed society. The other reason is more personal. Some anthropologists (and I think I should probably have to include myself here) find in working out

their position on symbolism a means of examining and stating, perhaps resolving, some of their individual views about the nature and determinants of human social relationships and activity. Here I should say that while I am much impressed by a great deal of the modern anthropological work on symbolism, I do not share all the perspective of some of its most distinguished exponents.

It seems to me to make sense, and to be relevant in the world today, that anthropologists should try to interpret symbolical language and symbolical behaviour and relate them to the range of social forms and social values. In such study political symbols are important. But I do not think that only those issues are relevant which refer to political affairs—unless one conceives of the political, as some of my colleagues do, as involving any kind of relations between persons where power is concerned, irrespective of scale. Religious symbols are important too, but I look upon them as referring to the same order of reality as the rest, categorized by the quality of attention given to them, not by the uniqueness of the objects to which they refer. So while I include both political and religious symbols in my examination, I deliberately take in material from ordinary daily life —such as the symbolism of ways of wearing the hair, of greeting and parting, of making and of accepting gifts, of showing flags. I deliberately also try to consider private as well as public aspects of symbolic behaviour and concepts, because I think that the inter-relationship between them has often been neglected, by anthropologists as well as by other students of symbolism. I think this relation between public and private, social and personal symbols is important to consider because certainly nowadays it seems that there are strong trends within society for the rejection of traditional symbols and for the discovery, even the invention, of new symbols—trends in which individual interests and decisions are brought to bear upon the recognition of communal symbolic forms.

Popular, unanalysed expressions of symbolism are of interest to anthropologists because they are part of the raw material for comparative study of processes of human thought and action. They reveal the direction and extent of peoples' involvement in social processes of various kinds, and the quality of abstraction applied to these processes. But at a more analytical level, specialized treatments of symbolism also have their anthropological importance. Much that philosophers, artists, art historians, literary critics, theologians, have written about symbolism is not immediately germane to anthropological studies. But I think it has distinct value for anthropological purposes. Firstly, I find it a very proper satisfaction of an intellectual curiosity to know at least the outline of the arguments put forward about symbolism by specialists in other disciplines, and the range of material they cover. Secondly, some of the illustrations they give recall obliquely some of the data anthropologists deal with, and suggest possible alternative lines of treatment. Finally, some of the hypotheses they put forward about criteria for identification of symbols, the relation between public and private symbols, the relation of symbolization to expression and communication provide parallel or challenge to anthropological views. Yet they often seem to lack that social dimension which is vital to an anthropologist, and to make assertions which seem to an anthropologist to be culture-bound, or 'ethnocentric'. So I think that no systematic theoretical exploration of symbolism by anthropologists should ignore the existence of such an interest by these other disciplines.

Taboo

Mary Douglas

One of the most difficult tasks anthropologists face in their study of non-Western cultures is isolating the bases for rules of right conduct. In the following article, Mary Douglas succinctly demonstrates that unlike modern industrialized nations, which have shared common experiences for centuries, primitive cultures have remained separated by distance and language and have developed unique worldviews. Pointing out, for example, that Westerners' separation of the natural and the supernatural is peculiar to us, Douglas explains how our reality and, therefore, our taboos are so different from those of the non-Western world.

Douglas's functional analysis of taboos shows that they underpin social structure everywhere. Anthropologists, studying taboos over extensive periods of time, have learned that taboo systems are not static and forever inviolate; on the contrary, they are dynamic elements of learned behavior that each generation absorbs. Taboos, as rules of behavior, are always part of a whole system and cannot be understood outside their social context. Douglas's explanation of taboos holds as much meaning for us in the understanding of ourselves as it does for our understanding of rules of conduct in the non-Western world. Whether considering the taboos surrounding a Polynesian chief's mana *or the changing sexual taboos in the Western world, it is apparent that taboo systems function to maintain cultural systems.*

Reprinted from Richard Cavendish, ed., *Man, Myth, and Magic* (London, 1979), Vol. 20, pp. 2767–71, by permission of the author and BPCC/Phoebus Publishing.

A TABOO (SOMETIMES SPELLED TABU) IS A BAN OR prohibition; the word comes from the Polynesian languages where it means a religious restriction, to break which would entail some automatic punishment. As it is used in English, taboo has little to do with religion. In essence it generally implies a rule which has no meaning, or one which cannot be explained. Captain Cook noted in his log-book that in Tahiti the women were never allowed to eat with the men, and as the men nevertheless enjoyed female company he asked the reason for this taboo. They always replied that they observed it because it was right. To the outsider the taboo is irrational, to the believer its rightness needs no explaining. Though supernatural punishments may not be expected to follow, the rules of any religion rate as taboos to outsiders. For example, the strict Jewish observance forbids the faithful to make and refuel the fire, or light lamps or put them out during the Sabbath, and it also forbids them to ask a Gentile to perform any of these acts. In his book *A Soho Address*, Chaim Lewis, the son of poor Russian Jewish immigrants in London's Soho at the beginning of this century, describes his father's quandary every winter Sabbath: he did not want to let the fire go out and he could not ask any favor outright. Somehow he had to call in a passerby and drop oblique hints until the stranger understood what service was required. Taboos always tend to land their observers in just such a ridiculous situation, whether it is a Catholic peasant of the Landes who abstains from meat on Friday, but eats teal (a bird whose fishy diet entitles it in their custom to be counted as fish), or a Maori hairdresser who after he had cut the chief's hair was not allowed to use his own hands even for feeding himself and had to be fed for a time like a baby.

In the last century, when the word gained currency in European languages, taboo was understood to arise from an inferior mentality. It was argued that primitive tribes observed countless taboos as part of their general ignorance about the physical world. These rules, which seemed so peculiar to Europeans, were the result of false science, leading to mistaken hygiene, and faulty medicine. Essentially the taboo is a ban on touching or eating or speaking or seeing. Its breach will unleash dangers, while keeping the rules would amount to avoiding dangers and sickness. Since the native theory of taboo was concerned to keep certain classes of people and things apart lest misfortune befall, it was a theory about contagion. Our scholars of the last century contrasted this false, primitive fear of contagion with our modern knowledge of disease. Our hygiene protects from a real danger of contagion, their taboos from imaginary danger. This was a comfortably complacent distinction to draw, but hygiene does not correspond to all the rules which are called taboo. Some are as obviously part of primitive religion in the same sense as Friday abstinence and Sabbath rest. European scholars therefore took care to distinguish on the one hand between primitive taboo with a mainly secular reference, and on the other hand rules of magic which infused the practice of primitive religion. They made it even more difficult to understand the meaning of foreign taboos by importing a classification between true religion and primitive magic, and modern medicine and primitive hygiene; and a very complicated web of definitions was based on this misconception.

In the Eye of the Beholder

The difficulty in understanding primitive taboo arose from the difficulty of understanding our own taboos of hygiene and religion. The first mistake was to suppose that our idea of dirt connotes an objectively real class from which real dangers to health may issue, and whose control depends on valid rules of hygiene. It is better to start by realizing that dirt, like beauty, resides in the eye of the beholder. We must be prepared to put our own behavior under the same microscope we apply to primitive tribes. If we find that they are busy hedging off this area from that, stopping X from touching Y, preventing women from eating with men, and creating elaborate scales of edibility and inedibility among the vegetable and animal worlds, we should realize that we too are given to this ordering and classifying activity. No taboo can ever make sense by itself. A taboo is always part of a whole system of rules. It makes sense as part of a classification whose meaning is so basic to those who live by it that no piecemeal explanation can be given. A native cannot explain the meaning of a taboo because it forms part of his own machinery of learning. The separate compartments which a taboo system constructs are the framework or instrument of understanding. To turn round and inspect that instrument may seem to be an advanced philosophic exercise, but it is necessary if we are to understand the subject.

The nineteenth-century scholars could not understand taboo because they worked within the separate compartments of their own taboo system. For them religion, magic, hygiene, and medicine were as distinct as civilized and primitive; the problem of taboo for them was only a problem about native thought. But put in that form it was insoluble. We approach it nowadays as a problem in human learning.

First, discard the idea that we have anything like a true, complete view of the world. Between what the scientists know and what we make of their knowledge there is a synthesis which is our own rough-and-ready approximation of rules about how we need to behave in the physical world. Second, discard the idea that there can ever be a final and correct world view. A gain in knowledge in one direction does not guarantee there will be no loss or distortion in another; the fullness of reality will always evade our comprehension. The reasons for this will become clear. Learning is a filtering and organizing process. Faced with the same events, two people will not necessarily register two identical patterns, and faced with a similar environment, two cultures will construe two different sets of natural constraints and regular sequences. Understanding is largely a classifying job in which the classifying human mind is much freer than it supposes itself to be. The events to be understood are unconsciously trimmed and filtered to fit the classification being used. In this sense every culture constructs its own universe. It attributes to its own world a set of powers to be harnessed and dangers to be avoided. Each primitive culture, because of its isolation, has a unique world view. Modern industrial nations, because and insofar as they share a common experience, share the same rules about the powers and dangers aroused. This is a valid difference between "Us" and "Them," their primitive taboos and ours.

For all humans, primitive or not, the universe is a system of imputed rules. Using our own distinctions, we can distinguish firstly, physical Nature, inorganic (including rocks, stars, rivers) and organic (vegetable and animal bodies, with rules governing their growth, lifespan and death); secondly, human behavior; thirdly, the interaction between these two groups; fourthly, other intelligent beings whether incorporeal like gods, devils and ghosts or mixtures of human and divine or human and animal; and lastly, the interaction between this fourth group and the rest.

The use of the word supernatural has been avoided. Even a small amount of reading in anthropology shows how very local and peculiar to our own civilization is the distinction between natural and supernatural. The same applies even to such a classification as the one just given. The fact that it is our own local classification is not important for this argument as the present object is to make clear how taboos should be understood. Taboos are rules about our behavior which restrict the human uses of things and people. Some of the taboos are said to avoid punishment or vengeance from gods, ghosts and other spirits. Some of them are supposed to produce automatically their dreaded effects. Crop failures, sickness, hunting accidents, famine, drought, epidemic (events in the physical realm), they may all result from breach of taboos.

The Seat of Mana

Taboos can have the effect of expressing political ideas. For example, the idea of the state as a hierarchy of which the chief is the undisputed head and his officials higher than the ordinary populace easily lends itself to taboo behavior. Gradings of power in the political body tend to be expressed as gradings of freedom to approach the physical body of the person at the top of the system. As Franz Steiner says, in *Taboo* (1956):

> In Polynesian belief the parts of the body formed a fixed hierarchy which had some analogy with the rank system of society. . . . Now the backbone was the most important part of the body, and the limbs that could be regarded as continuations of the backbone derived importance from it. Above the body was, of course, the head, and it was the seat of mana. When we say this, we must realize that by "mana" are meant both the soul aspect, the life force, and a man's ritual status. This grading of the limbs concerned people of all ranks and both sexes.

It could, for example, be so important to avoid stepping over people's heads that the very architecture was involved: the arrangements of the sleeping rooms show such an adaptation in the Marquesas. The commoner's back or head is thus not without its importance in certain contexts. But the real significance of this grading seems to have been in the possibilities it provided for cumulative effects in association with the rank system. The head of a chief was the most concentrated mana object of Polynesian society, and was hedged around with the most terrifying taboos which operated when things were to enter the head or when the head was being diminished; in other words when the chief ate or had his hair cut. . . . The hands of some great chiefs were so dangerous that they could not be put close to the head.

Since the Polynesian political systems was very competitive and chiefs had their ups and downs, great triumphs or total failures, the system of taboo was a kind of public vote of confidence and register of current distributions of power. This is important to correct our tendency to think of taboo as a rigidly fixed system of respect.

We will never understand a taboo system unless we understand the kind of interaction between the different spheres of existence which is assumed in it. Any child growing up learns the different spheres and interactions between them simultaneously. When the anthropologist arrives on the scene, he finds the system of knowledge a going concern. It is difficult for him to observe the changes being made, so he gets the wrong impression that a given set of taboos is something hard-and-fast handed down the generations.

In fact, the classifying process is always active and changing. New classifications are being pushed by some and rejected by others. No political innovation takes place without some basic reclassification. To take a currently live issue, in a stratified society, if it is taboo for lower classes or Negroes to sit down at table or to join sporting events with upper classes or whites, those who assert the rule can make it stronger if they find a basis in Nature to support the behavior they regard as right. If women in Tahiti are forbidden to eat with men, or in Europe to enter certain male occupations, some ultimate justification for the rule needs to be found. Usually it is traced back to their physical nature. Women are said to be constitutionally feeble, nervous or flighty; Negroes to smell; lower classes to be hereditarily less intelligent.

Rules of the Game

Perhaps the easiest approach is to try to imagine what social life would be like without any classification. It would be like playing a game without any rules; no one would know which way to run, who is on his side or against him. There would be no game. It is no exaggeration to describe social life as the process of building classification systems. Everyone is trying to make sense of what is happening. He is trying to make sense of his own behavior, past and present, so as to capture and hold some sense of identity. He is trying to hold other people to their promises and ensure some kind of regular future. He is explaining continually, to himself and to everyone else. In the process of explaining, classifications are developed and more and more meanings successfully added to them, as other people are persuaded to interpret events in the same way. Gradually even the points of the compass get loaded with social meanings. For example, the west room in an Irish farmer's house used to be the room where the old couple retired to, when the eldest son married and brought his wife to the farm. West meant retirement as well as sundown. In the Buddhist religion, east is the high status point; Buddha's statue is on a shelf on the east wall of the east room; the husband always sleeps to the east of his wife. So east means male and social superior. Up and down, right and left, sun and moon, hot and cold, all the physical antitheses are able to carry meanings from social life, and in a rich and steady culture there is a steady core of such agreed classifications. Anyone who is prepared to support the social system finds himself impelled to uphold the classification system which gets meaning from it. Anyone who wants to challenge the social system finds himself up against a set of manifold classifications which will have to be rethought. This is why breach of taboo arouses such strong feeling. It is not because the minor classification is threatened, but because the whole social system (in which a great investment has been made) looks like tottering, if someone can get away with challenging a taboo.

Classification involves definition; definition involves reducing ambiguity; ambiguity arises in several ways and it is wrong to think it can ever be excluded. To take the classification of animal species, they can be classified according to their obvious features, and according to the habitat they live in, and according to how they behave. This gives three ways of classifying animals which could each place the same beasts in different classes. Classed by behavior, using walking, swimming or flying as basic types, penguins would be nearer to fish; classed by bone structure and egg laying, penguins would count more clearly as birds than would flying fish, which would be birds in the other classification. Animal life is much more untidy and difficult to fit into a regular system of classification than at first appears. Human social life is even more untidy. Girls behave like boys, there are adults who refuse to grow up, every year a few are born whose physical make-up is not clearly male or female. The rules of marriage and inheritance require clear-cut categories but always there will be some cases which do not fit the regularities of the system. For human classifications are always too crude for reality. A system of taboos covers up this weakness of the classification system. It points in advance to defects and insists that no one shall give recognition to the inconvenient facts or behave in such a way as to undermine the acceptability and clarity of the system as a whole. It stops awkward questions and prevents awkward developments.

Sometimes the taboo ban appears in ways that seem a long way from their point of origin. For example, among the Lele tribe, in the Kasai district of the Congo, it was taboo to bring fishing equipment direct into the village from the streams or lakes where it had been in use. All round the village fishing traps and baskets would be hung in trees overnight. Ask the Lele why they did this and they replied that coughs and disease would enter the village if the fishing things were not left out one night. No other answer could be got from them except elaboration of the danger and how sorcerers could enter the village if this barrier were not kept up. But another kind of answer lay in the mass of other rules and regulations which separated the village and its human social life from the forest and streams and animal life. This was the basic classification at stake; one which never needed to be explained because it was too fundamental to mention.

Injecting Order into Life

The novelist William Burroughs describes the final experiences of disgust and depression of some forms of drug addiction. What he calls the "Naked Lunch" is the point where all illusions are stripped away and every thing is seen as it really is. When everyone can see what is on everyone's fork, nothing is classed as edible. Meat can be animal or human flesh, caterpillars, worms, or bugs; soup is equally urine, lentils, scotch broth, or excreta; other people are neither friends nor enemies, nor is oneself different from other people since neither has any very clear definition. Identities and classifications are merged into a seething, shapeless experience. This is the potential disorder of the mind which taboo breaks up into classes and rules and so judges some activities as right and proper and others as horrifying.

This kind of rationality is the justification for the taboos which we ourselves observe when we separate the lavatory from the living room and the bed from the kitchen, injecting order into the house. But the order is not arbitrary; it derives from social categories. When a set of social distinctions weakens, the taboos that expressed it weaken too. For this reason sex taboos used to be sacred in England but are no longer so strong. It seems ridiculous that women should not be allowed in some clubs or professions, whereas not so long ago it seemed obviously right. The same for the sense of privacy, the same for hierarchy. The less we ourselves are forced to adopt unthinking taboo attitudes to breaches of these boundaries, the easier it becomes to look dispassionately at the taboos of other societies and find plenty of meaning in them.

In some tribal societies it is thought that the shedding of blood will cause droughts and other environmental disasters. Elsewhere any contact with death is dangerously polluting, and burials are followed by elaborate washing and fumigation. In other places they fear neither homicide nor death pollution but menstrual blood is thought to be very dangerous to touch. And in other places again, adultery is liable to cause illness. Some people are thickly beset with taboos so that everything they do is charged with social symbolism. Others observe only one or two rules. Those who are most taboo-minded have the most complex set of social boundaries to preserve. Hence their investment of so much energy into the control of behavior.

A taboo system upholds a cultural system and a culture is a pattern of values and norms; social life is impossible without such a pattern. This is the dilemma of individual freedom. Ideally we would like to feel free to make every choice from scratch and judge each case on its merits. Such a freedom would slow us down, for every choice would have to be consciously deliberated. On the one hand, education tries to equip a person with means for exercising private judgment, and on the other hand, the techniques of education provide a kind of mechanical decision-making, along well-oiled grooves. They teach strong reactions of anxiety about anything which threatens to go off the track. As education transmits culture, taboos and all, it is a kind of brainwashing. It only allows a certain way of seeing reality and so limits the scope for private judgment. Without the taboos, which turn basic classifications into automatic psychological reflexes, no thinking could be effective, because if every system of classification was up for revision at every moment, there would be no stability of thought. Hence there would be no scope for experience to accumulate into knowledge. Taboos bar the way for the mind to visualize reality differently. But the barriers they set up are not arbitrary, for taboos flow from social boundaries and support the social structure. This accounts for their seeming irrational to the outsider and beyond challenge to the person living in the society.

You Are What You Eat: Religious Aspects of the Health Food Movement

Jill Dubisch

In this article Jill Dubisch shows that the health food movement in this country may be seen as more than a way of eating and more than an alternative healing system. Using Clifford Geertz's definition of religion as a "system of symbols," Dubisch maintains that the health food movement has many of the characteristics of a religion. For example, the anthropological concepts of mana *and* taboo *are used in a discussion of the merits of "health foods" (mana) versus the detrimental nature of "junk foods" (taboo). The health food movement, like religion, offers its adherents salvation of the body, psyche, and even society itself. Followers strive to gain new values and a new worldview. Comparing health food devotees to people undergoing a religious revitalization, Dubisch describes how converts learn to criticize prevailing social values and institutions. She notes the process of conversion that individuals entering the movement undergo, their concern for the maintenance of purity, the "temples" (health food stores), the "rabbis" (health food experts), and the sacred writing that establish the movement's principles. Provocative and entertaining, Dubisch's analysis of the religious aspects of the health food movement is sound anthropology and is certain to remind each of us of our own, or an acquaintance's, "religious" involvement with health food.*

Reprinted from Susan P. Montague and W. Arens, eds., *The American Dimension: Culture Myths and Social Realities,* 2nd ed. (Palo Alto, Calif., 1981), pp. 115–27, by permission of the author.

Dr. Robbins was thinking how it might be interesting to make a film from Adelle Davis' perennial best seller, *Let's Eat Right to Keep Fit.* Representing a classic confrontation between good and evil—in this case nutrition versus unhealthy diet—the story had definite box office appeal. The role of the hero, Protein, probably should be filled by Jim Brown, although Burt Reynolds undoubtedly would pull strings to get the part. Sunny Doris Day would be a clear choice to play the heroine, Vitamin C, and Orson Welles, oozing saturated fatty acids from the pits of his flesh, could win an Oscar for his interpretation of the villainous Cholesterol. The film might begin on a stormy night in the central nervous system. . . .

—Tom Robbins, *Even Cowgirls Get the Blues*

I INTEND TO EXAMINE A CERTAIN WAY OF EATING, that which is characteristic of the health food movement, and try to determine what people are communicating when they choose to eat in ways which run counter to the dominant patterns of food consumption in our society. This requires looking at health foods as a system of symbols and the adherence to a health food way of life as being, in part, the expression of belief in a particular world view. Analysis of these symbols and the underlying world view reveals that, as a system of beliefs and practices, the health food movement has some of the characteristics of a religion.

Such an interpretation might at first seem strange since we usually think of religion in terms of a belief in a deity or other supernatural beings. These notations, for the most part, are lacking in the health food movement. However, anthropologists do not always consider such beliefs to be a necessary part of a religion. Clifford Geertz, for example, suggests the following broad definition:

> A *religion* is (1) a system of symbols which acts to (2) establish powerful, pervasive, and long-lasting moods and motivations in men by (3) formulating conceptions of a general-order of existence and (4) clothing these conceptions with such an aura of factuality that (5) the moods and motivations seem uniquely realistic (Geertz 1965: 4).

Let us examine the health food movement in the light of Geertz's definition.

History of the Health Food Movement

The concept of "health foods" can be traced back to the 1830s and the Popular Health movement, which combined a reaction against professional medicine and an emphasis on lay knowledge and health care with broader social concerns such as feminism and the class struggle (see Ehrenreich and English 1979). The Popular Health movement emphasized self-healing and the dissemination of knowledge about the body and health to laymen. One of the early founders of the movement, Sylvester Graham (who gave us the graham cracker), preached that good health was to be found in temperate living. This included abstinence from alcohol, a vegetarian diet, consumption of whole wheat products, and regular exercise. The writings and preachings of these early "hygienists" (as they called themselves) often had moral overtones, depicting physiological and spiritual reform as going hand in hand (Shryock 1966).

The idea that proper diet can contribute to good health had continued into the twentieth century. The discovery of vitamins provided for many health food people a further "natural" means of healing which could be utilized instead of drugs. Vitamins were promoted as health-giving substances by various writers, including nutritionist Adelle Davis, who has been perhaps the most important "guru" of health foods in this century. Davis preached good diet as well as the use of vitamins to restore and maintain health, and her books have become the best sellers of the movement. (The titles of her books, *Let's Cook It Right, Let's Get Well, Let's Have Healthy Children,* give some sense of her approach.) The health food movement took on its present form,

however, during the late 1960s, when it became part of the "counterculture."

Health foods were "in," and their consumption became part of the general protest against the "establishment" and the "straight" life-style. They were associated with other movements centering around social concerns, such as ecology and consumerism (Kandel and Pelto 1980: 328). In contrast to the Popular Health movement, health food advocates of the sixties saw the establishment as not only the medical profession but also the food industry and the society it represented. Food had become highly processed and laden with colorings, preservatives, and other additives so that purity of food became a new issue. Chemicals had also become part of the food-growing process, and in reaction terms such as "organic" and "natural" became watchwords of the movement. Health food consumption received a further impetus from revelations about the high sugar content of many popular breakfast cereals which Americans had been taught since childhood to think of as a nutritious way to start the day. (Kellogg, an early advocate of the Popular Health movement, would have been mortified, since his cereals were originally designed to be part of a hygienic regimen.)

Although some health food users are members of formal groups (such as the Natural Hygiene Society, which claims direct descent from Sylvester Graham), the movement exists primarily as a set of principles and practices rather than as an organization. For those not part of organized groups, these principles and practices are disseminated, and contact is made with other members of the movement, through several means. The most important of these are health food stores, restaurants, and publications. The two most prominent journals in the movement are *Prevention* and *Let's Live,* begun in 1920 and 1932 respectively (Hongladarom 1976).

These journals tell people what foods to eat and how to prepare them. They offer advice about the use of vitamins, the importance of exercise, and the danger of pollutants. They also present testimonials from faithful practitioners. Such testimonials take the form of articles that recount how the author overcame a physical problem through a health food approach, or letters from readers who tell how they have cured their ailments by following methods advocated by the journal or suggested by friends in the movement. In this manner, such magazines not only educate, they also articulate a world view and provide evidence and support for it. They have become the "sacred writings" of the movement. They are a way of "reciting the code"—the cosmology and moral injunctions—which anthropologist Anthony F. C. Wallace describes as one of the important categories of religious behavior (1966: 57).

Ideological Content of the Health Food Movement

What exactly is the health food system? First, and most obviously, it centers around certain beliefs regarding the relationship of diet to health. Health foods are seen as an "alternative" healing system, one which people turn to out of their dissatisfaction with conventional medicine (see, for example, Hongladarom 1976). The emphasis is on "wellness" and prevention rather than on illness and curing. Judging from letters and articles found in health food publications, many individuals' initial adherence to the movement is a type of conversion. A specific medical problem, or a general dissatisfaction with the state of their health, leads these converts to an eventual realization of the "truth" as represented by the health food approach, and to a subsequent change in life-style to reflect the principles of that approach. "Why This Psychiatrist 'Switched'," published in *Prevention* (September 1976), carries the following heading: "Dr. H. L. Newbold is a great advocate of better nutrition and a livelier life style. But it took a personal illness to make him see the light." For those who have experienced such conversion, and for others who become convinced by reading about such experiences, health food publications serve an important function by reinforcing the conversion and encouraging a change of life-style. For example, an article entitled "How to Convert Your Kitchen for the New Age of Nutrition" (*Prevention*, February 1975) tells the housewife how to make her kitchen a source of health for her family. The article suggests ways of reorganizing kitchen supplies and reforming cooking by substituting health foods for substances detrimental to health, and also offers ideas on the preparation of nutritious and delicious meals which will convert the family to this new way of eating without "alienating" them. The pamphlet *The Junk Food Withdrawal Manual* (Kline 1978), details how an individual can, step by step, quit eating junk foods and adopt more healthful eating habits. Publi-

cations also urge the readers to convert others by letting them know how much better health foods are than junk foods. Proselytizing may take the form of giving a "natural" birthday party for one's children and their friends, encouraging schools to substitute fruit and nuts for junk food snacks, and even selling one's own baking.

Undergoing the conversion process means learning and accepting the general features of the health food world view. To begin with, there is great concern, as there is in many religions, with purity, in this case, the purity of food, of water, of air. In fact, there are some striking similarities between keeping a "health food kitchen" and the Jewish practice of keeping kosher. Both make distinctions between proper and improper foods, and both involve excluding certain impure foods (whether unhealthful or non-kosher) from the kitchen and table. In addition, a person concerned with maintaining a high degree of purity in food may engage in similar behavior in either case—reading labels carefully to check for impermissible ingredients and even purchasing food from special establishments to guarantee ritual purity.

In the health food movement, the basis of purity is healthfulness and "naturalness." Some foods are considered to be natural and therefore healthier; this concept applies not only to foods but to other aspects of life as well. It is part of the large idea that people should work in harmony with nature and not against it. In this respect, the health food cosmology sets up an opposition of nature (beneficial) versus culture (destructive), or, in particular, the health food movement against our highly technological society. As products of our industrialized way of life, certain foods are unnatural; they produce illness by working against the body. Consistent with this view is the idea that healing, like eating, should proceed in harmony with nature. The assumption is that the body, if allowed to function naturally, will tend to heal itself. Orthodox medicine, on the other hand, with its drugs and surgery and its non-holistic approach to health, works against the body. Physicians are frequently criticized in the literature of the movement for their narrow approach to medical problems, reliance on drugs and surgery, lack of knowledge of nutrition, and unwillingness to accept the validity of the patient's own experience in healing himself. It is believed that doctors may actually cause further health problems rather than effecting a cure. A short item in *Prevention*, "The Delivery Is Normal—But the Baby Isn't," recounts an incident in which drug-induced labor in childbirth resulted in a mentally retarded baby. The conclusion is "nature does a good job—and we should not, without compelling reasons, try to take over" (*Prevention*, May 1979: 38).

The healing process is hastened by natural substances, such as healthful food, and by other "natural" therapeutic measures such as exercise. Vitamins are also very important to many health food people, both for maintaining health and for healing. They are seen as components of food which work with the body and are believed to offer a more natural mode of healing than drugs. Vitamins, often one of the most prominent products offered in many health food stores, provide the greatest source of profit (Hongladarom 1976).

A basic assumption of the movement is that certain foods are good for you while others are not. The practitioner of a health food way of life must learn to distinguish between two kinds of food: those which promote well-being ("health foods") and those which are believed to be detrimental to health ("junk foods"). The former are the only kind of food a person should consume, while the latter are the antithesis of all that food should be and must be avoided. The qualities of these foods may be described by two anthropological concepts, *mana* and *taboo*. Mana is a type of beneficial or valuable power which can pass to individuals from sacred objects through touch (or, in the case of health foods, by ingestion). Taboo, on the other hand, refers to power that is dangerous; objects which are taboo can injure those who touch them (Wallace 1966: 60–61). Not all foods fall clearly into one category or the other. However, those foods which are seen as having health-giving qualities, which contain *mana*, symbolize life, while *taboo* foods symbolize death. ("Junk food is . . . dead . . . Dead food produces death," proclaims one health food manual [Kline 1978: 2–4].) Much of the space in health food publications is devoted to telling the reader why to consume certain foods and avoid others ("Frozen, Creamed Spinach: Nutritional Disaster," *Prevention*, May 1979; "Let's Sprout Some Seeds," *Better Nutrition*, September 1979).

Those foods in the health food category which are deemed to possess an especially high level of *mana* have come to symbolize the movement as a whole. Foods such as honey, wheat germ, yogurt,

and sprouts are seen as representative of the general way of life which health food adherents advocate, and Kandel and Pelto found that certain health food followers attribute mystical powers to the foods they consume. Raw food eaters speak of the "life energy" in uncooked foods. Sprout eaters speak of their food's "growth force" (1980: 336).

Qualities such as color and texture are also important in determining health foods and may acquire symbolic value. "Wholeness" and "whole grain" have come to stand for healthfulness and have entered the jargon of the advertising industry. Raw, coarse, dark, crunchy, and cloudy foods are preferred over those which are cooked, refined, white, soft, and clear. (See chart.)

Thus dark bread is preferred over white, raw milk over pasteurized, brown rice over white. The convert must learn to eat foods which at first seem strange and even exotic and to reject many foods which are components of the Standard American diet. A McDonald's hamburger, for example, which is an important symbol of America itself (Kottak 1978), falls into the category of "junk food" and must be rejected.

Just as the magazines and books which articulate the principles of the health food movement and serve as a guide to the convert can be said to comprise the sacred writings of the movement, so the health food store or health food restaurant is the temple where the purity of the movement is guarded and maintained. There individuals find for sale the types of food and other substances advocated by the movement. One does not expect to find items of questionable purity, that is, substances which are not natural or which may be detrimental to health. Within the precincts of the temple adherents can feel safe from the contaminating forces of the larger society, can meet fellow devotees, and can be instructed by the guardians of the sacred area (see, for example, Hongladarom 1976). Health food stores may vary in their degree of purity. Some sell items such as coffee, raw sugar, or "natural" ice cream which are considered questionable by others of the faith. (One health food store I visited had a sign explaining that it did not sell vitamin supplements, which it considered to be "unnatural," i.e., impure.)

People in other places are often viewed as living more "naturally" and healthfully than contemporary Americans. Observation of such peoples may be

HEALTH FOOD WORLD VIEW

	Health Foods	Junk Foods	
cosmic oppositions	LIFE NATURE	DEATH CULTURE	
	holistic, organic	fragmented, mechanistic	
basic	harmony with body	working against body	undesirable
values	and nature	and nature	attributes
and	natural and real	manufactured and	
desirable	harmony, self-	artificial disharmony,	
attributes	sufficiency, independence	dependence	
	homemade, small scale	mass-produced	
	layman competence	professional esoteric	
	and understanding	knowledge and jargon	
beneficial qualities of food	whole coarse dark crunchy raw cloudy	processed refined white soft cooked clear	harmful qualities
specific foods with mana	yogurt* honey* carob soybeans* sprouts* fruit juices herb teas foods from other cultures: humus, falafel, kefir, tofu, stir-fried vegetables, pita bread	ice cream, candy sugar* chocolate beef overcooked vegetables soft drinks* coffee,* tea "all-American" foods: hot dogs, McDonald's hamburgers,* potato chips, Coke	specific taboo foods
	return to early American values, "real" American way of life	corruption of this original and better way of life and values	

*Denotes foods with especially potent mana or taboo.

used to confirm practices of the movement and to acquire ideas about food. Healthy and long-lived people like the Hunza of the Himalayas are studied to determine the secrets of their strength and longevity. Cultures as yet untainted by the food systems of industrialized nations are seen as examples of what better diet can do. In addition, certain foods from other cultures—foods such as humus, falafel, and tofu—have been adopted into the health food repertoire because of their presumed healthful qualities.

People of other times can also serve as models for a more healthful way of life. There is in the health food movement a concept of a "golden age," a past which provides an authority for a better way of living. This past may be scrutinized for clues about how to improve contemporary American society. An archaeologist, writing for *Prevention* magazine, recounts how "I Put Myself on a Caveman Diet—Permanently" (*Prevention*, September 1979). His article explains how he improved his health by utilizing the regular exercise and simpler foods which he had concluded from his research were probably characteristic of our prehistoric ancestors. A general nostalgia about the past seems to exist in the health food movement, along with the feeling that we have departed from a more natural pattern of eating practiced by earlier generations of Americans (see, for example, Hongladarom 1976). (Sylvester Graham, however, presumably did not find the eating habits of his contemporaries to be very admirable.)

The health food movement is concerned with more than the achievement of bodily health. Nutritional problems are often seen as being at the root of emotional, spiritual, and even social problems. An article entitled "Sugar Neurosis" states "Hypoglycemia (low blood sugar) is a medical reality that can trigger wife-beating, divorce even suicide" (*Prevention,* April 1979: 110). Articles and books claim to show the reader how to overcome depression through vitamins and nutrition and the movement promises happiness and psychological well-being as well as physical health. Social problems, too, may respond to the health food approach. For example, a probation officer recounts how she tried changing offenders' diets in order to change their behavior. Testimonials from two of the individuals helped tell "what it was like to find that good nutrition was their bridge from the wrong side of the law and a frustrated, unhappy life to a vibrant and useful one" (*Prevention,* May 1978: 56). Thus, through more healthful eating and a more natural life-style, the health food movement offers its followers what many religions offer: salvation—in this case salvation for the body, for the psyche, and for society.

Individual effort is the keystone of the health food movement. An individual can take responsibility for his or her own health and does not need to rely on professional medical practitioners. The corollary of this is that it is a person's own behavior which may be the cause of ill health. By sinning, by not listening to our bodies, and by not following a natural way of life, we bring our ailments upon ourselves.

The health food movement also affirms the validity of each individual's experience. No two individuals are alike: needs for different vitamins vary widely; some people are more sensitive to food additives than others; each person has his or her best method of achieving happiness. Therefore, the generalized expertise of professionals and the scientifi-

cally verifiable findings of the experts may not be adequate guides for you, the individual, in the search of health. Each person's experience has meaning; if something works for you, then it works. If it works for others also, so much the better, but if it does not, that does not invalidate your own experience. While the movement does not by any means disdain all scientific findings (and indeed they are used extensively when they bolster health food positions), such findings are not seen as the only source of confirmation for the way of life which the health food movement advocates, and the scientific establishment itself tends to be suspect.

In line with its emphasis on individual responsibility for health, the movement seeks to deprofessionalize knowledge and place in every individual's hands the information and means to heal. Drugs used by doctors are usually available only through prescription, but foods and vitamins can be obtained by anyone. Books, magazines, and health food store personnel seek to educate their clientele in ways of healing themselves and maintaining their own health. Articles explain bodily processes, the effects of various substances on health, and the properties of foods and vitamins.

The focus on individual responsibility is frequently tied to a wider concern for self-sufficiency and self-reliance. Growing your own organic garden, grinding your own flour, or even, as one pamphlet suggests, raising your own cow are not simply ways that one can be assured of obtaining healthful food; they are also expressions of independence and self-reliance. Furthermore, such practices are seen as characteristic of an earlier "golden age" when people lived naturally lives. For example, an advertisement for vitamins appearing in a digest distributed in health food stores shows a mother and daughter kneading bread together. The heading reads "America's discovering basics." The copy goes on, "Baking bread at home has been a basic family practice throughout history. The past several decades, however, have seen a shift in the American diet to factory-produced breads. . . . Fortunately, today there are signs that more and more Americans are discovering the advantage of baking bread themselves." Homemade bread, home-canned produce, sprouts growing on the window sill symbolize what are felt to be basic American values, values supposedly predominant in earlier times when people not only lived on self-sufficient farms and produced their own fresh and more natural food, but also stood firmly on their own two feet and took charge of their own lives. A reader writing to *Prevention* praises an article about a man who found "new life at ninety without lawyers or doctors," saying "If that isn't the optimum in the American way of living, I can't imagine what is!" (*Prevention,* May 1978: 16). Thus although it criticizes the contemporary American way of life (and although some vegetarians turn to Eastern religions for guidance—see Kandel and Pelto 1980), the health food movement in general claims to be the true faith, the proponent of basic Americanness, a faith from which the society as a whole has strayed.

Social Significance of the Health Food Movement for American Actors

Being a "health food person" involves more than simply changing one's diet or utilizing an alternative medical system. Kandel and Pelto suggest that the health food movement derives much of its popularity from the fact that "food may be used simultaneously to cure or prevent illness, as a religious symbol and to forge social bonds. Frequently health food users are trying to improve their health, their lives, and sometimes the world as well" (1980: 332). Use of health foods becomes an affirmation of certain values and a commitment to a certain world view. A person who becomes involved in the health food movement might be said to experience what anthropologist Anthony F. C. Wallace has called "mazeway resynthesis." The "mazeway" is the mental "map" or image of the world which each individual holds. It includes values, the environment and the objects in it, the image of the self and of others, the techniques one uses to manipulate the environment to achieve desired end states (Wallace 1966: 237). Resynthesis of this mazeway—that is, the creation of new "maps," values, and techniques—commonly occurs in times of religious revitalization, when new religious movements are begun and converts to them are made. As individuals, these converts learn to view the world in a new manner and to act accordingly. In the case of the health food movement, those involved learn to see their health problems and other dissatisfactions with their lives as stemming from improper diet and living in disharmony with nature. They are provided with new values, new ways of viewing their environ-

ment, and new techniques for achieving their goals. For such individuals, health food use can come to imply "a major redefinition of self-image, role, and one's relationship to others" (Kandel and Pelto 1980: 359). The world comes to "make sense" in the light of this new world view. Achievement of the desired end states of better health and an improved outlook on life through following the precepts of the movement gives further validation.

It is this process which gives the health food movement some of the overtones of a religion. As does any new faith, the movement criticizes the prevailing social values and institutions, in this case the health-threatening features of modern industrial society. While an individual's initial dissatisfaction with prevailing beliefs and practices may stem from experiences with the conventional medical system (for example, failure to find a solution to a health problem through visits to physician), this dissatisfaction often comes to encompass other facets of the American way of life. This further differentiates the "health food person" from mainstream American society (even when the difference is justified as a return to "real" American values).

In everyday life the consumption of such substances as honey, yogurt, and wheat germ, which have come to symbolize the health food movement, does more than contribute to health. It also serves to represent commitment to the health food world view. Likewise, avoiding those substances, such as sugar and white bread, which are considered "evil" is also a mark of a health food person. Ridding the kitchen of such items—a move often advocated by articles advising readers on how to "convert" successfully to health foods—is an act of ritual as well as practical significance. The symbolic nature of such foods is confirmed by the reactions of outsiders to those who are perceived as being inside the movement. An individual who is perceived as being a health food person is often automatically assumed to use honey instead of sugar, for example. Conversely, if one is noticed using or not using certain foods (e.g., adding wheat germ to food, not eating white sugar), this can lead to questions from the observer as to whether or not that individual is a health food person (or a health food "nut," depending upon the questioner's own orientation).

The symbolic nature of such foods is especially important for the health food neophyte. The adoption of a certain way of eating and the renunciation of mainstream cultural food habits can constitute "bridge-burning acts of commitment" (Kandel and Pelto 1980: 395), which function to cut the individual off from previous patterns of behavior. However, the symbolic activity which indicates this cutting off need not be as radical as a total change of eating habits. In an interview in *Prevention,* a man who runs a health-oriented television program recounted an incident in which a viewer called up after a show and announced excitedly that he had changed his whole life-style—he had started using honey in his coffee! (*Prevention,* February 1979: 89). While recognizing the absurdity of the action on a practical level, the program's host acknowledged the symbolic importance of this action to the person involved. He also saw it as a step in the right direction since one change can lead to another. Those who sprinkle wheat germ on cereal, toss alfalfa sprouts with a salad, or pass up an ice cream cone for yogurt are not only demonstrating a concern for health but also affirming their commitment to a particular life-style and symbolizing adherence to a set of values and a world view.

Conclusion

As this analysis has shown, health foods are more than simply a way of eating and more than an alternative healing system. If we return to Clifford Geertz's definition of religion as a "system of symbols" which produces "powerful, pervasive, and long-lasting moods and motivations" by "formulating conceptions of a general order of existence" and making them appear "uniquely realistic," we see that the health food movement definitely has a religious dimension. There is, first, a system of symbols, in this case based on certain kinds and qualities of food. While the foods are believed to have health-giving properties in themselves, they also symbolize a world view which is concerned with the right way to live one's life and the right way to construct a society. This "right way" is based on an approach to life which stresses harmony with nature and the holistic nature of the body. Consumption of those substances designated as "health foods," as well as participation in other activities associated with the movement which also symbolize its world view (such as exercising or growing an organic garden) can serve to establish the "moods and motivations"

of which Geertz speaks. The committed health food follower may come to experience a sense of spiritual as well as physical well-being when he or she adheres to the health food way of life. Followers are thus motivated to persist in this way of life, and they come to see the world view of this movement as correct and "realistic."

In addition to its possession of sacred symbols and its "convincing" world view, the health food movement also has other elements which we usually associate with a religion. Concepts of mana and taboo guide the choice of foods. There is a distinction between the pure and impure and a concern for the maintenance of purity. There are "temples" (health food stores and other such establishments) which are expected to maintain purity within their confines. There are "rabbis," or experts in the "theology" of the movement and its application to everyday life. There are sacred and instructional writings which set out the principles of the movement and teach followers how to utilize them. In addition, like many religious movements, the health food movement harkens back to a "golden age" which it seeks to recreate and assumes that many of the ills of the contemporary world are caused by society's departure from this ideal state.

Individuals entering the movement, like individuals entering any religious movement, may undergo a process of conversion. This can be dramatic, resulting from the cure of an illness or the reversal of a previous state of poor health, or it can be gradual, a step-by-step changing of eating and other habits through exposure to health food doctrine. Individuals who have undergone conversion and mazeway resynthesis, as well as those who have tested and confirmed various aspects of the movement's prescriptions for better health and a better life, may give testimonials to the faith. For those who have adopted, in full or in part, the health food world view, it provides, as do all religions, explanations for existing conditions, answers to specific problems, and a means of gaining control over one's existence. Followers of the movement are also promised "salvation," not in the form of afterlife, but in terms of enhanced physical well-being, greater energy, longer life-span, freedom from illness, and increased peace of mind. However, although the focus is this-worldly, there is a spiritual dimension to the health food movement. And although it does not center its world view around belief in supernatural beings, it does posit a higher authority—the wisdom of nature —as the source of ultimate legitimacy for its views.

Health food people are often dismissed as "nuts" or "food faddists" by those outside the movement. Such a designation fails to recognize the systematic nature of the health food world view, the symbolic significance of health foods, and the important functions which the movement performs for its followers. Health foods offer an alternative or supplement to conventional medical treatment, and a meaningful and effective way for individuals to bring about changes in lives which are perceived as unsatisfactory because of poor physical and emotional health.

It can also provide for its followers a framework of meaning which transcends individual problems. In opposing itself to the predominant American lifestyle, the health food movement sets up a symbolic system which opposes harmony to disharmony, purity to pollution, nature to culture, and ultimately, as in many religions, life to death. Thus while foods are the beginning point and the most important symbols of the health food movement, food is not the ultimate focus but rather a means to an end: the organization of a meaningful world view and the construction of a satisfying life.

Body Ritual among the Nacirema

Horace Miner

This article is a classic of anthropological literature. In it Horace Miner gives readers a thorough and exciting ethnographic account of the myriad of taboos and ceremonial behaviors that permeate the everyday activities of the members of a magic-ridden society. Focusing on secret rituals that are believed to prevent disease while simultaneously beautifying the body, Miner demonstrates the importance of ceremonial specialists such as the "holy-mouth-men" and the "listeners" in directing even the most routine aspects of daily life among the Nacirema. Miner finds it difficult to understand how the Nacirema have managed to exist so long under the burdens that they have imposed on themselves.

Reprinted by permission of the American Anthropological Association from *American Anthropologist*, Vol. 58 (1956), pp. 503–507. Not for further reproduction.

THE ANTHROPOLOGIST HAS BECOME SO FAMILIAR with the diversity of ways in which different peoples behave in similar situations that he is not apt to be surprised by even the most exotic customs. In fact, if all of the logically possible combinations of behavior have not been found somewhere in the world, he is apt to suspect that they must be present in some yet undescribed tribe. This point has, in fact, been expressed with respect to clan organization by Murdock (1949: 71). In this light, the magical beliefs and practices of the Nacirema present such unusual aspects that it seems desirable to describe them as an example of the extremes to which human behavior can go.

Professor Linton first brought the ritual of the Nacirema to the attention of anthropologists twenty years ago (1936: 326), but the culture of this people is still very poorly understood. They are a North American group living in the territory between the Canadian Cree, the Yaqui and Tarahumare of Mexico, and the Carib and Arawak of the Antilles. Little is known of their origin, though tradition states that they came from the east. According to Nacirema mythology, their nation was originated by a culture hero, Notgnishaw, who is otherwise known for two great feasts of strength—the throwing of a piece of wampum across the river Pa-To-Mac and the chopping down of the cherry tree in which the Spirit of Truth resided.

Nacirema culture is characterized by a highly developed market economy which has evolved in a rich natural habitat. While much of the people's time is devoted to economic pursuits, a large part of the fruits of these labors and a considerable portion of the day are spent in ritual activity. The focus of this activity is the human body, the appearance and health of which loom as a dominant concern in the ethos of the people. While such a concern is certainly not unusual, its ceremonial aspects and associated philosophy are unique.

The fundamental belief underlying the whole system appears to be that the human body is ugly and that its natural tendency is to debility and disease. Incarcerated in such a body, man's only hope is to avert these characteristics through the use of the powerful influences of ritual and ceremony. Every household has one or more shrines devoted to this purpose. The more powerful individuals in the society have several shrines in their houses and, in fact, the opulence of a house is often referred to in terms of the number of such ritual centers it possesses. Most houses are of wattle and daub construction, but the shrine rooms of the more wealthy are walled with stone. Poorer families imitate the rich by applying pottery plaques to their shrine walls.

While each family has at least one such shrine, the rituals associated with it are not family ceremonies but are private and secret. The rites are normally only discussed with children, and then only during the period when they are being initiated into these mysteries. I was able, however, to establish sufficient rapport with the natives to examine these shrines and to have the rituals described to me.

The focal point of the shrine is a box or chest which is built into the wall. In this chest are kept the many charms and magical potions without which no native believes he could live. These preparations are secured from a variety of specialized practitioners. The most powerful of these are the medicine men, whose assistance must be rewarded with substantial gifts. However, the medicine men do not provide the curative potions for their clients, but decide what the ingredients should be and then write them down in an ancient and secret language. This writing is understood only by the medicine men and by the herbalists who, for another gift, provide the required charm.

The charm is not disposed of after it has served its purpose, but is placed in the charm-box of the household shrine. As these magical materials are specific for certain ills, and the real or imagined maladies of the people are many, the charm-box is usually full to overflowing. The magical packets are so numerous that people forget what their purposes were and fear to use them again. While the natives are very vague on this point, we can only assume that the idea in retaining all the old magical materials is that their presence in the charm-box, before which the body rituals are conducted, will in some way protect the worshipper.

Beneath the charm-box is a small font. Each day every member of the family, in succession, enters the shrine room, bows his head before the charm-box, mingles different sorts of holy water in the font, and proceeds with a brief rite of ablution. The holy waters are secured from the Water Temple of the community, where the priests conduct elaborate ceremonies to make the liquid ritually pure.

In the hierarchy of magical practitioners, and below the medicine men in prestige, are specialists whose designation is best translated "holy-mouth-men." The Nacirema have an almost pathological horror and fascination with the mouth, the condition of which is believed to have supernatural influence on all social relationships. Were it not for the rituals of the mouth, they believe that their teeth would fall out, their gums bleed, their jaws shrink, their friends desert them, and their lovers reject them. (They also believe that a strong relationship exists between oral and moral characteristics. For example, there is a ritual ablution of the mouth for children which is supposed to improve their moral fiber.)

The daily body ritual performed by everyone includes a mouth-rite. Despite the fact that these people are so punctilious about care of the mouth, this rite involves a practice which strikes the uninitiated stranger as revolting. It was reported to me that the ritual consists of inserting a small bundle of hog hairs into the mouth, along with certain magical powders, and then moving the bundle in a highly formalized series of gestures.

In addition to the private mouth-rite, the people seek out a holy-mouth-man once or twice a year. These practitioners have an impressive set of paraphernalia, consisting of a variety of augers, awls, probes, and prods. The use of these objects in the exorcism of the evils of the mouth involves almost unbelievable ritual torture of the client. The holy-mouth-man opens the client's mouth and, using the above-mentioned tools, enlarges any holes which decay may have created in the teeth. Magical materials are put into these holes. If there are no naturally occurring holes in the teeth, large sections of one or more teeth are gouged out so that the supernatural substance can be applied. In the client's view, the purpose of these ministrations is to arrest decay and to draw friends. The extremely sacred and traditional character of the rite is evident in the fact that the natives return to the holy-mouth-men year after year, despite the fact that their teeth continue to decay.

It is to be hoped that, when a thorough study of the Nacirema is made, there will be a careful inquiry into the personality structure of these people. One has but to watch the gleam in the eye of a holy-mouth-man, as he jabs an awl into an exposed nerve, to suspect that a certain amount of sadism is involved. If this can be established, a very interesting pattern emerges, for most of the population shows definite masochistic tendencies. It was to these that Professor Linton referred in discussing a distinctive part of the daily body ritual which is performed only by men. This part of the rite involves scraping and lacerating the surface of the face with a sharp instrument. Special women's rites are performed only four times during each lunar month, but what they lack in frequency is made up in barbarity. As part of this ceremony, women bake their heads in small ovens for about an hour. The theoretically interesting point is that what seems to be a preponderantly masochistic people have developed sadistic specialists.

The medicine men have an imposing temple, or *latipso,* in every community of any size. The more elaborate ceremonies required to treat very sick patients can only be performed at this temple. These ceremonies involve not only the thaumaturge but a permanent group of vestal maidens who move sedately about the temple chambers in distinctive costume and headdress.

The *latipso* ceremonies are so harsh that it is phenomenal that a fair proportion of the really sick natives who enter the temple ever recover. Small children whose indoctrination is still incomplete have been known to resist attempts to take them to the temple because "that is where you go to die." Despite this fact, sick adults are not only willing but eager to undergo the protracted ritual purification, if they can afford to do so. No matter how ill the supplicant or how grave the emergency, the guardians of many temples will not admit a client if he cannot give a rich gift to the custodian. Even after one has gained admission and survived the ceremonies, the guardians will not permit the neophyte to leave until he makes still another gift.

The supplicant entering the temple is first stripped of all his or her clothes. In every-day life the Nacirema avoids exposure of his body and its natural functions. Bathing and excretory acts are performed only in the secrecy of the household shrine, where they are ritualized as part of the body-rites. Psychological shock results from the fact that body secrecy is suddenly lost upon entry into the *latipso.* A man, whose own wife has never seen him in an excretory act, suddenly finds himself naked and assisted by a vestal maiden while he performs his natural functions into a sacred vessel. This sort of ceremonial treatment is necessitated by the fact that the excreta are used by a diviner to ascertain the course and nature of the client's sickness. Female clients, on the other hand, find their naked bodies are subjected to the scrutiny, manipulation, and prodding of the medicine men.

Few supplicants in the temples are well enough to do anything but lie on their hard beds. The daily ceremonies, like the rites of the holy-mouth-men, involve discomfort and torture. With ritual precision, the vestals awaken their miserable charges each dawn and roll them about on their beds of pain while performing ablutions, in the formal movements of which the maidens are highly trained. At other times they insert magic wands in the supplicant's mouth or force him to eat substances which are supposed to be healing. From time to time the medicine men come to their clients and jab magically treated needles into their flesh. The fact that these temple ceremonies may not cure, and may even kill the neophyte, in no way decreases the people's faith in the medicine men.

There remains one other kind of practitioner, known as a "listener." This witch-doctor has the power to exorcise the devils that lodge in the heads of people who have been bewitched. The Nacirema believe that parents bewitch their own children. Mothers are particularly suspected of putting a curse on children while teaching them the secret body rituals. The counter-magic of the witch-doctor is unusual in its lack of ritual. The patient simply tells the "listener" all his troubles and fears, beginning with the earliest difficulties he can remember. The memory displayed by the Nacirema in these exorcism sessions is truly remarkable. It is not uncommon for the patient to bemoan the rejection he felt upon being weaned as a babe, and a few individuals even see their troubles going back to the traumatic effects of their own birth.

In conclusion, mention must be made of certain practices which have their base in native esthetics but which depend upon the pervasive aversion to the natural body and its functions. There are ritual fasts to make fat people thin and ceremonial feasts to make thin people fat. Still other rites are used to make women's breasts large if they are small, and smaller if they are large. General dissatisfaction with breast shape is symbolized in the fact that the ideal form is virtually outside the range of human variation. A few women afflicted with almost inhuman hyper-mammary development are so idolized that they make a handsome living by simply going from village to village and permitting the natives to stare at them for a fee.

Reference has already been made to the fact that excretory functions are ritualized, routinized, and relegated to secrecy. Natural reproductive functions are similarly distorted. Intercourse is taboo as a topic and scheduled as an act. Efforts are made to avoid pregnancy by the use of magical materials or by limiting intercourse to certain phases of the moon. Conception is actually very infrequent. When pregnant, women dress so as to hide their condition. Parturition takes place in secret, without friends or relatives to assist, and the majority of women do not nurse their infants.

Our review of the ritual life of the Nacirema has certainly shown them to be a magic-ridden people. It is hard to understand how they have managed to exist so long under the burdens which they have imposed upon themselves. But even such exotic customs as these take on real meaning when they are viewed with the insight provided by Malinowski when he wrote (1948: 70):

> Looking from far and above, from our high places of safety in the developed civilization, it is easy to see all the crudity and irrelevance of magic. But without its power and guidance early man could not have mastered his practical difficulties as he has done, nor could man have advanced to the higher stages of civilization.

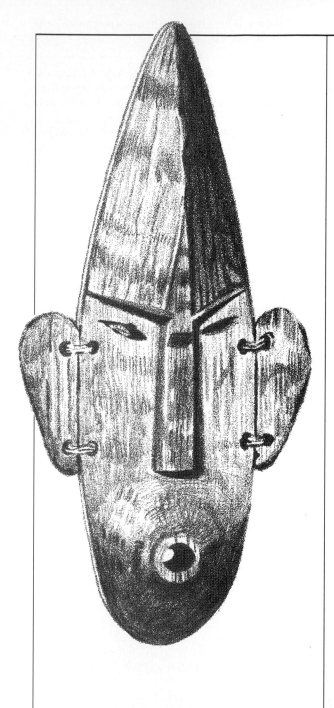

3
Shamans, Priests, and Prophets

In Chapters 1 and 2 the reader was introduced to the anthropological approach to the study of religion and to the complex variety of symbols, rites, ceremonies, and belief structures that constitute the heart of supernatural belief systems everywhere. We now turn to the role and place of the supernatural leader. Where and how do religious leaders get their power? What is the distinction between a shaman and a priest, or a prophet and a priest? How do sorcerers, diviners, and magicians differ? In short, this chapter introduces the topic of religious specialists.

Any member of society may approach the supernatural on an individual basis; for example, a person may kneel to the ground, all alone, and recite a prayer for help from the spiritual world. But the religions of the world, whether small animistic cults or the "great faiths," also have intermediaries: religious people who, acting as part-time or full-time specialists, intervene on behalf of an individual client or an entire community. Paul Radin (1937: 107) argued that the development of religion can be traced to the social roles undertaken by each of these "priest-thinkers"—at once, a philosopher of religion, a theologian of beliefs, a person who is the recognized master of worship.

Eskimo mask, Ingalik, Alaska.

If all religions appear to have specialists, anthropologists have also found that some societies place more emphasis on these religious experts than others do. Robert Textor has noted, for example, that the societies that are more likely to have religious specialists tend to produce food rather than collect it, use money as a medium of exchange, and display different social classes and a complex political system (1967). In other words, the more complex the society, the greater is the likelihood of having religious intermediaries.

Early anthropologists were drawn to the view of unilineal evolution: how institutions progressed from savagery to barbarism, finally achieving a civilized state. As societies advance, all institutions become more complex and specialized. In this classic work *Primitive Culture* (1871), E. B. Tylor posited an early definition of religion that prompted his colleagues to concern themselves with religious specialization. Describing religion as the belief in spiritual beings, what he called "animism," Tylor implied that a society's degree of religious specialization was directly related to its position on the evolutionary scale. Unilineal evolutionary theory was pockmarked with faulty premises, of course: Although cultures do evolve, they do not necessarily follow a prescribed series of stages. What is important to note here, however, is that Tylor and his contemporaries began to look carefully at religious specialization and categories of religious phenomena. J. G. Frazer, in the *Golden Bough* (1890), distinguished between magic and religion and described the role of specialists. And Herbert Spencer's approach, in the *Principles of Sociology* (1896), that religious stages could be comprehended only if the functions of religion and the interrelationships of religion with other institutions were known, demanded that religious specialization be studied in terms of its functions in society—an approach that anthropologists still adhere to today. Anthropological data have shown the importance of shamans, priests, prophets, and other specialists to the maintenance of economic, political, social, and educational institutions of their societies.

The anthropological literature devoted to religious specialists is extensive; much work remains, however, to define and distinguish adequately between the actual functions they perform for members of their societies. It is important to note here that because of limitations on the application of biomedical (Western) therapy in the Third World, traditional doctors play a crucial role in healing (Hepburn 1988: 68). Shamans, for example, have duties and religious obligations that differ from society to society, although their basic duty of curing through the use of the supernatural is accepted by anthropologists. J. M. Atkinson's review article, "Shamanisms Today" (1992), demonstrates the continuing importance of shamanic practices in the contemporary non-Western world. The same kinds of differences exist in the tasks performed by prophets, priests, sorcerers, and others designated as "intermediaries" with the supernatural. Without a clear understanding of these distinctions, systematic cross-cultural comparisons would be impossible. Differentiation of specialists through an analysis of their functions tells anthropologists a great deal about the structure of society.

In addition to the definitional problem associated with specialists, anthropologists must also determine whether to place the tasks performed by these experts under the rubric of "the religious" or to create other categories for such activities. Is the performance of magic, witchcraft, and sorcery "religious" behavior, or are these examples of nonreligious, indeed antireligious acts? If those who practice these acts are outside the religious realm, then what, if any, connection do they have with the sacred? The real question becomes, What is religion? In Western culture, witchcraft, magic, and sorcery are assigned to the occult and are considered outside of and, ordinarily, counter to religion. In the non-Western world, however, specialists who take part in these kinds of activities are often considered to be important parts of the total religious belief system. It is a common view in Africa south of the Sahara that people are often designated witches by God, and that sorcerers and magicians receive their power from the spirit world, that is, from supernatural agencies controlled by God. In these terms, is drawing upon supernatural aid from shamans, priests, or prophets more "religious" than turning to magicians, sorcerers, and other specialists who also call upon supernatural agents but for different ends? In light of these questions, anthropologists have found it necessary to consider all specialists whose power emanates from supernatural agents to be in the realm of the religious, although some specialists serve whereas others harm society through their actions.

Because not all societies contain identical religious specialists, determining why certain specialists exist and others do not is important to our understanding both of the structure of a society and its supernatural world, and of the causal forces behind good and bad fortune. In societies where witches do not exist, for example, it is frequently malicious ghosts or ancestors who are believed to bring misfortune and illness. In such cases, elders may play an important role as diviners, in contrast to the diviner specialists that exist in other groups. Such data not only aid our understanding of supernatural causation and specialization but also demonstrate the connection between the social structure of the living—the position of the elder in society—and that of the ancestor or ghost in the afterworld. The example of the elder as religious specialist is problematic in some societies. Eugene Mendonsa, in speaking of the Sisala of Ghana, for example, makes clear that not all elders have the ability to divine, and those who can are only specialists in a part-time sense (1976).

The difficulty inherent in making distinctions among non-Western specialists may be further realized by considering the position of the religious layperson in this country. Although not a specialist in the traditional sense, this individual is nevertheless more involved and usually more knowledgeable than the typical church member. Is the layperson significantly different from one of the more traditional part-time specialists? Immediately, the problem of the degree of participation comes to mind—part-time versus full-time—accompanied by the complicating factor of training—formal versus on-the-job learning. Making distinctions such as these is an important part of analytic accounts of religious functionaries.

The five excellent articles that follow tell us much about the religious specialist. Victor Turner's lead-off essay provides a broad-spectrum account of the various specialists who appear in ethnographic descriptions of religions around the world. Next, C. Von Furer-Haimendorf delineates the role of priests, and William Howells discusses the positive functions offered by Siberian shamans to the societies they serve. Shamanistic leadership, the result of psychological and physiological aid given their followers, is also based on their control of malevolent powers that can be dangerous to the people. But these powers, for good or evil, contribute to the awe in which the shaman is held. How does trickery assist the shaman? Do shamans really believe they have the power to cure? Or is shamanism a charlatan's game? Michael Fobes Brown clearly demonstrates that shamans do have a dark, dangerous side, and Michael Barkun concludes the chapter with an in-depth look into the minds of the Branch Davidians and their prophetic leader, David Koresh, as well as the FBI and ATF authorities and the tragic clash at Waco.

References

Atkinson, J. M.
  1992 "Shamanisms Today." *Annual Reviews in Anthropology* 21: 307–30.

Frazer, J. G.
  1890 *The Golden Bough.* London: MacMillan.

Hepburn, Sharon J.
  1988 "Western Minds, Foreign Bodies." *Medical Anthropology Quarterly* 2 (New Series): 59–74.

Mendonsa, Eugene L.
  1976 "Characteristics of Sisala Diviners." In *The Realm of the Extra-Human: Agents and Audiences*, pp. 179–95. World Anthropology Series, ed. Agehanarda Bharati. The Hague: Mouton Publishers.

Radin, Paul
  1937 *Primitive Religion: Its Nature and Origin.* New York: Dover Publications.

Spencer, H.
  1896 *Principles of Sociology.* New York: D. Appleton.

Textor, Robert
  1967 *A Cross-Cultural Summary.* New Haven, Conn.: HRAF Press.

Tylor, E. B.
  1871 *Primitive Culture: Researches into the Development of Mythology, Philosophy, Religion, Language, Art and Custom.* London: J. Murray.

Religious Specialists

Victor W. Turner

*Noted for his concentration in the study of symbolism
and symbolic behavior, Victor Turner here presents an
outstanding general discussion of religious specialists
and lays the groundwork for the more specialized
articles to follow, which deal specifically with
shamans, priests, and prophets. Turner not only
deals with these avocations but includes other, less
prominent but often equally important religious
specialists—diviners, seers, mediums, witches,
sorcerers, and magicians. Unlike many theorists of the
past, Turner stresses that all should be included under
the umbrella of the term* religion, *for all, in special
ways, manipulate the supernatural to their own or
society's ends.*

*Turner's is no small theoretical accomplishment,
for controversy over the definition of the term* religion
*has long occupied anthropologists. His discussion
illuminates the subtle but important differences
among specialists, without which religions of the
non-Western world would remain unintelligible.*

Reprinted by permission of the publisher from the
International Encyclopedia of the Social Sciences, David L.
Sills, Editor. Vol. 13, pp. 437–44. Copyright © 1972 by
Crowell Collier and Macmillan.

A RELIGIOUS SPECIALIST IS ONE WHO DEVOTES
himself to a particular branch of religion or,
viewed organizationally, of a religious system.
"Religion" is a multivocal term whose range of
meanings varies in different social and historical
contexts. Nevertheless, most definitions of religion refer to the recognition of a transhuman controlling power that may be either personal or
impersonal. A religious specialist has a culturally
defined status relevant to this recognition. In societies or contexts where such power is regarded as
impersonal, anthropologists customarily describe
it as *magic*, and those who manipulate the power
are magicians. Wherever power is personalized, as deity, gods, spirits, daemons, genii, ancestral shades, ghosts, or the like, anthropologists
speak of *religion*. In reality, religious systems
contain both magical and religious beliefs and
procedures: in many of them the impersonal
transhuman (or mystical, or non-empirical, or
supernatural) power is considered to be a devolu-
tion of personal power, as in the case of the mystical efficacy of rites established *in illo tempore* by a
deity or divinized ancestor.

Priest and Prophet

Scholars have tended to distinguish between two
polarities of religious specialization. Max Weber,
for example, although well aware of numerous
historical instances of their overlap and interpen-
etration, contrasts the roles of priest and prophet.
He begins by making a preliminary distinction
between priest and magician. A priest, he writes,
is always associated with "the functioning of a
regularly organized and permanent enterprise
concerned with influencing the gods—in contrast
with the individual and occasional efforts of magicians." Accordingly, the crucial feature of priesthood is that it represents the "specialization of a
particular group of persons in the continuous operation of a cultic enterprise, permanently associated with particular norms, places and times, and

related to specific social groups." In Weber's view, the prophet is distinguished from the priest by "personal call." The priest's claim to religious authority derives from his service in a sacred tradition; the authority of the prophet is founded on revelation and personal "charisma." This latter term has been variously defined by Weber (in some contexts it seems almost to represent the *Führerprinzip*), but it may broadly be held to designate extraordinary powers. These include, according to Weber, "the capacity to achieve the ecstatic states which are viewed, in accordance with primitive experience, as the preconditions for producing certain effects in meteorology, healing, divination and telepathy." But charisma may be either ascribed or achieved. It may be an inherent faculty ("primary charisma") or it may be "produced artificially in an object or person through some extraordinary means." Charisma may thus be "merited" by fastings, austerities, or other ordeals. Even in such cases, Weber asserts, there must be some dormant capacity in the persons or objects, some "germ" of extraordinary power, already vested in them. The prophet, then, is a "purely individual bearer of charisma," rather than the representative of a sacred tradition. He produces discontinuity in that cultic enterprise which it is the priest's major role to keep "in continuous operation." Weber's prophet feels that he has a "mission" by virtue of which he "proclaims religious doctrine or divine commandment." Weber refuses to distinguish sharply between a "renewer of religion" who preaches "an older revelation, actual or suppositious" and a "founder of religion" who claims to bring completely new "deliverances," for, he says, "the two types merge into one another." In Weber's view, the charisma of a prophet appears to contain, in addition to ecstatic and visionary components, a rational component, for he proclaims "a systematic and distinctively religious ethic based upon a consistent and stable doctrine which purports to be a revelation" [(1922)].

Weber's distinction between priest and prophet has its main relevance in an analytical frame of reference constructed to consider the relationship between religion as "a force for dynamic social change" and religion as "a reinforcement of the stability of societies" (Parsons 1963). It has been found effective by such anthropologists as Evans-Pritchard ([1956] 1962) and Worsley (1957a; 1957b) who are dealing directly with social transitions and "the

prophetic break," or what Parsons calls "the primary decision point [between] a direction which makes for a source of evolutionary change in the . . . established or traditional order, and a direction which tends either to reinforce the established order or at least not to change it drastically" (1963; p. xxix in 1964 edition).

Priest and Shaman

Anthropologists who are less concerned than Weber with the genesis of religions and with internal developments in complex societies or their impact on the "primitive" world are inclined to contrast priest not with prophet but with shaman or spirit medium and to examine the relationship between these statuses as part of the normal working of the religious system in the simpler societies. In their excellently representative *Reader in Comparative Religion* (1958), the editors W. A. Lessa and E. Z. Vogt devote a whole section to this distinction.

Often, where there is a priest the shaman is absent, and vice versa, although both these roles may be found in the same religion, as among the Plains Indians. According to Lowie (1954), a Plains Indian shaman is a ritual practitioner whose status is acquired through a personal communication from a supernatural being, whereas a priest does not necessarily have a face-to-face relationship with the spirit world but must have competence in conducting ritual. Lessa and Vogt ([1958] 1965, p. 410) expand these differences: a shaman's powers come by "divine stroke," a priest's power is inherited or is derived from the body of codified and standardized ritual knowledge that he learns from older priests and later transmits to successors. They find that shamanism tends to predominate in food-gathering cultures, where the shaman most frequently performs a curing rite for the benefit of one or more patients and within the context of an extended family group. Shamanistic rites are "non-calendrical," or contingent upon occasions of mishap and illness. The priest and priestly cult organization are characteristically found in the more structurally elaborated food-producing—usually agricultural—societies, where the more common ceremonial is a public rite performed for the benefit of a whole village or community. Such rites are often calendrical, or performed at critical points in the ecological cycle.

Shaman and Medium

Raymond Firth (1964a, p. 638) regards shamanism as itself "that particular form of spirit mediumship in which a specialist (the *shaman*) normally himself a medium, is deemed to exercise developed techniques of control over spirits, sometimes including mastery of spirits believed to be possessing another medium." This definition, like that of Howells (1948), stresses the *control* exercised over spirits. Howells describes the shaman as "bullyragging" gods or spirits and emphasizes his intellectual qualities as a leader. This element of mastery makes the shaman a distinctive type of spirit medium, one who is believed to be "possessed by a spirit (or closely controlled by a spirit) [and who] can serve as a means of communication between other human beings and the spirit world" (Firth 1964b, p. 689). The spirit medium per se need not exert mastery; he is rather the vessel or vehicle of the transhuman entity.

Thus, although we sometimes find the two functions of priest and shaman combined in the same individual (Piddington 1950), mediums, shamans, and prophets clearly constitute subtypes of a single type of religious functionary. The priest communicates with transhuman entities through ritual that involves cultural objects and activities. The medium, shaman, and prophet communicate in a person-to-person manner: they are in what Buber (1936) would describe as an I-thou relationship with the deities or spirits. The priest, on the other hand, is in what may be called an I-it relationship with the transhuman. Between the priest and the deity intervenes the institution. Priests may therefore be classified as institutional functionaries in the religious domain, while medium, shaman, and prophet may be regarded as subtypes of inspirational functionaries. This distinction is reflected in characteristically different modes of operation. The priest presides over a rite; the shaman or medium conducts a seance. Symbolic forms associated with these occasions differ correlatively: the symbols of a rite are sensorily perceptible to a congregation and have permanence in that they are culturally transmissible, while those of a seance are mostly in the mind of the entranced functionary as elements of his visions or fantasies and are often generated by and limited to the unique occasion. The inspirational functionary may describe what he has clairvoyantly perceived (or "been shown" as he might put it), but the institutional functionary manipulates symbolic objects with prescribed gestures in full view of this congregation.

Sociocultural Correlates

Since the priest is an actor in a culturally "scripted" drama, it is but rarely that priests become innovators, or "dramatists." If they do assume this role it is mainly as legislative reformers—by altering the details of liturgical procedure—that they do so. If a priest becomes a radical innovator in religion, he is likely to become a prophet to his followers and a heretic to his former superiors. From the priestly viewpoint it is the office, role, and script that are sacred and "charismatic" and not the incumbent of priestly office. The priest is concerned with the conservation and maintenance of a deposit of beliefs and practices handed down as a sacred trust from the founders of the social or religious system. Since its symbols at the semantic level tend to condense the critical values, norms, and principles of the total cultural system into a few sensorily perceptible representations, the sanctification of these symbols is tantamount to a preservative of the entire culture. What the priest is and does keeps cultural change and individual deviation within narrow limits. But the energy and time of the inspirational functionary is less bound up with the maintenance of the total cultural system. His practice has more of an ad hoc flavor; he is more sensitive and responsive than the priest to the private and personal, to the mutable and idiosyncratic. This type of functionary thrives in loosely structured food-gathering cultures, where he deals individually with specific occasions of trouble, or during periods of social turbulence and change, when societal consensus about values is sharply declining and numerically significant classes of persons and social groups are becoming alienated from the orthodox social order. The shaman subtype is completely a part of the cultural system of the food-gatherers; the prophet may well stand outside the cultural system during such a period of decomposition and propose new doctrines, ethics, and even economic values.

The shaman is not a radical or a reformer, since the society he services is traditionally flexible and mobile; the prophet is an innovator and reformer, for he confronts a tightly structured order that is moribund and points the way to religious forms that will either provide an intensified cognitive dynamic for sociocultural change or codify the new moral, ideational, and social structures that have been inarticulately developing.

There are of course significant differences in the scale of the societies in which shaman and prophet operate. The shaman enacts his roles in small-scale, multifunctional communities whose religious life incorporates beliefs in a multitude of deities, daemons, nature spirits, or ancestral shades—societies that Durkheim might have described as possessing mechanical solidarity, low moral density, and segmental organization. The prophet tends to come into his own when the division of labor is critically replacing "mechanical" by "organic" solidarity, when class antagonisms are sharpened, or when small-scale societies are decisively invaded by the powerful personnel, ideas, techniques, and cultural apparatus (including military skills and armaments) of large-scale societies. The shaman deals in a personal and specific way with spirits and lesser deities; the prophet enters into dialogue, on behalf of his whole community, with the Supreme Being or with the major deities of a traditional pantheon, whose tutelary scope embraces large numbers of persons and groups, transcending and transecting their traditional divisions and animosities. Alternatively he communicates with the generalized ancestors or *genii loci,* conceived to be a single anonymous and homogeneous collectivity rather than a structure of known and named shades, each representing a specific segment of society. Whereas the shaman's function is associated with looseness of structure in small-scale societies, the prophet's is linked with loosening of structure in large-scale societies or with incompatibilities of scale in culture-contact situations.

Divination and Religious Specialists

In its strict etymological sense the term "divination" denotes inquiry about future events or matters, hidden or obscure, directed to a deity who, it is believed, will reply through significant tokens. It usually refers to the process of obtaining knowledge of secret or future things by mechanical means or manipulative techniques—a process which may or may not include invoking the aid of non-empirical (transhuman) persons or powers but does not include the empirical methods of science.

In the analysis of preliterate societies divination often is concerned with the immediate problems and interests of individuals and subgroups and but seldom with the destinies of tribes and nations. It is this specificity and narrowness of reference that primarily distinguishes divination from prophecy. Nadel (1954, p. 64) has called the kind of guidance it offers "mechanical and of a case-to-case kind." The diviner "can discover and disentangle some of the hidden influences which are at work always and everywhere. . . . He cannot uncover any more embracing design. . . . Yet within the limits set to it divination has a part to play, providing some of the certainty and guidance required for provident action." Thus, although its range and scope are more circumscribed than those of prophecy, divination is believed to reveal what is hidden and in many cases to forecast events, auspicious and inauspicious.

Divination further refers to the analysis of past events, especially untoward events; this analysis often includes the detection and ascription of guilt with regard to their perpetrators, real or alleged. Where such untoward events are attributed to sorcerers and witches the diviner has great freedom of judgment in detecting and determining guilt. Diviners are frequently consulted by victims' relatives and show intuitive and deductive virtuosity in discovering quarrels and grudges in their clients' kin groups and local communities. Social anthropologists find important clues to areas and sources of social strain and to the character and strength of supportive social norms and values in the diviners' diagnoses.

There is evidence that mediums, shamans, and priests in various cultures have practiced divination. The medium and shaman often divine without mechanical means but with the assistance of a tutelary spirit. In the work of Lessa and Vogt there is a translation of a vivid first-person account by a Zulu informant of a diviner's seance. This mediumistic female diviner

> dramatically utilizes some standard procedures of her art—ventriloquism, prior knowledge of the clients, the overhearing of the client's unguarded conversation, and shrewd common sense—to enable her spirits to provide the clients with advice. In this example, . . . a boy is suffering from a convulsive ailment. The spirits discover that an ancestral spirit is spitefully causing the boy's illness: the spirits decree that the location of the family's village must be moved; a goat must be sacrificed to the an-

cestor and the goat's bile poured over the boy; the boy must drink *Itongo* medicine. The treatment thus ranges from physical to social actions—from propitiation of wrathful ancestors to prescription of a medicinal potion (Lessa & Vogt [1958] 1965, p. 340).

Similar accounts of shamanistic divinatory seances have been recorded by anthropologists working among North and South American Indians, Eskimos, and Siberian tribes, in many parts of Africa, and among Afro-Americans.

Divination was a function of members of the priesthood in many of the complex religious systems of Polynesia, west Africa, and ancient Mexico; in the religions of Israel, Greece, Etruria, and Rome; in Babylonia, India, China, Japan, and among the Celts. According to Wach,

> The Etruscans made these practices so much a part of their culture that the discipline has been named after them (*disciplina Etrusca* or *auguralis*). Different phenomena and objects were used as media to ascertain the desires of the gods (regular and irregular celestial events, lightning, fire, and earthquakes, the shape or utterances of animals, flights of birds, movements of serpents, barking of dogs, forms of liver or entrails). Both in Etruria and Rome a numerous and well-organized hierarchy of functionaries existed for practice of the sacred arts (1958, p. 111 in 1961 edition).

Indeed, diffused through the Roman world, many of these techniques passed into medieval and modern culture.

Diviner and Doctor

Callaway's account (1868–1870) of the combined divinatory and curative seance in Zululand emphasizes the close relationship believed to hold in many preliterate societies between the functions of divination and therapy. Sometimes, as in the case cited, the diviner and "doctor" are the same person, but more often the roles are specialized and performed by different individuals. Modern therapy is taking increasingly into account the psychosomatic character of many maladies and the importance of sociological factors in their etiology. In most preliterate societies bodily symptoms are regarded as signs that the soul or life principle of the patient is under attack or has been abstracted by spiritual forces or beings. Furthermore, it is widely held that these attacks are motivated by animosities provoked by breaches of cultural, mainly religious, prescriptions and/or breaches of social norms regarded as binding on members of kin groups or local communities. Thus, to acquire a comprehensive understanding of why and how a patient was afflicted with certain symptoms by a spirit or witch, primitives seek out a diviner who will disclose the secret antagonisms in social relations or the perhaps unconscious neglect of ritual rules (always a threat to the cultural order) that incited mystical retribution or malice. The diviner is a "diagnostician" who refers his clients to his colleague, the doctor or "therapist." The doctor in question has both shamanistic and priestly attributes. The division of labor which in more complex societies segregates and institutionalizes the functions of priest and medical man has hardly begun to make its influence felt. The diviner-doctor dichotomy does not depend, as does the priest-shaman dichotomy, upon contrasting roles in regard to the transhuman realm but upon different phases in a social process which involves *total* human phenomena —integral personalities, many psychosomatic complexes, multiple social relationships, and multiform communities.

Modes of Religious Specialization

As the scale and complexity of society increase and the division of labor develops, so too does the degree of religious specialization. This process accompanies a contraction in the domain of religion in social life. As Durkheim stated with typical creative exaggeration in his *Division of Labor in Society* ([1893] 1960, p. 169): "Originally [religion] pervades everything; everything social is religious; the two words are synonymous. Then, little by little, political, economic, scientific functions free themselves from the religious function, constitute themselves a part and take on a more and more acknowledged temporal character."

Simple Societies

In the simplest societies every adult has some religious functions and the elders have most; as their capacity to hunt or garden wanes, their priestlike role comes into ever greater prominence. Women tend to receive more recognition and scope as religious functionaries than in more developed societies. There is some tendency toward religious specialization in such societies, based on a variety of attributes, such as knowledge of herbalistic lore, skill in leechcraft, the capacity to enter a state of trance or dissociation, and sometimes physical handicap that compels a man or woman to find an alternative means of support to subsistence activities. (I have met several diviners in central Africa with maimed hands or amputated limbs.) But such specialization can hardly be defined, in the majority of cases, as more than part-time or even spare-time specialization. Michael Gelfand's description of the Shona *nganga*, variously translated in the ethnographic literature as "medicine man," "doctor," or "witch doctor," exemplifies the sociocultural situation of similar practitioners in very many preliterate societies (1964). The Shona *nganga* is at once a herbalist, a medium, and also a diviner who, possessed by a spirit of a dead relative, diagnoses both the cause of illness and of death. Yet, reports Gelfand,

> when he is not engaged in his medical practice he leads exactly the same life as the other men of his village. He cultivates his land, looks after his cattle, repairs his huts, makes blankets or other equipment needed by his family. And the same applies to a woman *nganga*, who busies herself with the tasks expected of every Shona woman. . . . The amount the *nganga* does in his village depends, of course, on the demands of his patients, but on the average he has a fair amount of spare time. . . . A fair guess would be [that there is a *nganga*] to every 800 to 1,000 persons. . . . The *nganga* is given no special status in his village, his chances of being appointed headman are the same as anyone else's (1964, pp. 22–23).

Complex Societies

To bring out best the effects of increase in scale and the division of labor it is necessary to examine religious systems at the opposite end of the gradient of complexity. Religion no longer pervades all social domains; it is limited to its own domain. Furthermore, it has acquired a contractual and associational character; people may choose both the form and extent of their religious participation or may opt out of any affiliation. On the other hand, within each religious group a considerable amount of specialization has taken place. Much of this has been on the organizational level. Processes of bureaucratization, involving rationality in decision making, relative

impersonality in social relations, routinization of tasks, and a hierarchy of authority and function, have produced a large number of types, grades, and ranks of religious specialists in all the major religious systems.

For example, the Catholic clerical hierarchy may be considered as (1) the hierarchy of order, whose powers are exercised in worship and in the administration of the sacraments, and (2) as the hierarchy of jurisdiction, whose power is over the members of the church. Within the hierarchy of jurisdiction alone we find such manifold statuses as pope and bishop (which are held to be of divine institution); cardinal, patriarch, exarch, and primate (whose powers are derived by delegation expressed or implied from the holy see); metropolitan and archbishop (who derive their powers from their patriarch, exarch, or primate); archdeacon, vicar general, vicar forane, rural dean, pastor, and rector (who derive their powers from their diocesan bishop).

In addition to the clerical hierarchy there are in the Catholic church numerous institutes of the religious, that is, societies of men and women approved by ecclesiastical superiors, in which the members in conformity with the special laws of their association take vows, perpetual or temporary, and by this means aspire to religious perfection. This is defined as "the heroic exercise of the virtue of supernatural charity" and is pursued by voluntary maintenance of the vows of poverty, chastity, and obedience, by ascetical practices, through charitable works, such as care of the poor, sick, aged, and mentally handicapped, and by contemplative techniques, such as prayer. Within each religious institution or congregation there is a marked division of function and gradation of office.

Thus there are many differences of religious status, rank, and function in a developed religious system such as the Catholic church. Differences in charismata are also recognized in such terms as "contemplative," "ascetic," "mystic," "preacher," "teacher," "administrator." These gifts may appear in any of the major divisions of the church: among clergy or laity, among hermits, monks, or friars, among female as well as male religious. Certain of these charismata are institutionalized and constitute the devotional pattern particular to certain religious institutions: thus there are "contemplative orders," "friars preachers," and the like.

Medium-Scale Societies

Other developed religions, churches, sects, cults, and religious movements exhibit degrees of bureaucratic organization and specialization of role and function. Between the situational specialization of religious activities found in small-scale societies and the full-time and manifold specialization in large-scale societies falls a wide variety of intermediate types. A characteristic religious dichotomy is found in many of the larger, politically centralized societies of west and east Africa, Asia, Polynesia, and pre-Columbian Central and South America. National and tribal gods are worshiped in the larger towns, and minor deities, daemons, and ancestral shades are venerated in the villages. At the village level we find once more the multifunctional religious practitioner. But where there are national gods there are usually national priests, their official servants, and worship tends to take place in temples or at fixed and elaborate shrines. Parrinder writes:

> In the cults of the West African gods [for example, in Dahomey, Yoruba, and Ashanti] there are priests who are highly trained to do their work. These priests are often set aside from birth, or they may be called to the service of the god by being possessed by his spirit. They will then retire from their families and public life, and submit to the training of an older priest. The training normally lasts several years, during which time the novice has to apply himself to learn all the secrets of consulting and serving the god. The training of a priest is an arduous matter. . . . [He] has to observe chastity and strict taboos of food and actions. He frequently has to sleep on a hard floor, have insufficient food, and learn to bear hardship. He is regarded as married to the god, though later he may take a wife. Like an Indian devotee, he seeks by self-discipline to train himself to hear the voice of his god. He learns the ritual and dances appropriate to the cult, receives instruction in the laws and taboos of the god, and gains some knowledge of magical medicines (1954, pp. 100–101).

In these west African cults of deities there is a formal division of function between priests and mediums. In general, priests control mediums and carefully regulate their experience of possession. This situation is one solution to the perennial problem posed for priesthoods by what Ronald Knox (1950) has termed "enthusiasm," that is, the notion that one can become possessed by or identified with a god or God and that one's consequent acts and words are divinely inspired, even if they transgress religious or secular laws. In Dahomey, for example (Herskovits 1938), there are communal training centers, called cult houses or "convents," for mediums and assistants to priests. Here the novices are secluded for considerable periods of time. Part of their training involves the attempt to induce the return of the initial spirit possession that marked their calling. They learn later to produce coherent messages in a state of trance. During this period they are under the surveillance of priests. The Catholic church has similarly brought under its control as members of contemplative orders mystics and visionaries who claim "experimental knowledge of God's presence."

Religious and Political Specialization

In many primitive societies an intimate connection exists between religion and politics. If by politics we denote those behavioral processes of resolution of conflict between the common good and the interests of groups by the use of or struggle for power, then religion in such societies is pragmatically connected with the maintenance of those values and norms expressing the common good and preventing the undue exercise of power. In centralized political systems that have kings and chiefs, these dignitaries themselves have priestly functions; in many parts of Africa, for example, they take charge of observances which safeguard many of the basic needs of existence, such as rainmaking, sowing, and harvest rites, rituals to promote the fertility of men, domestic and wild animals, and so on. On the other hand, even where this is the case, there are frequently other specialized religious functionaries whose duties are bound up with the office of kingship. An illustration of this occurs among the Bemba of Zambia, where the *Bakabilo*

> are in charge of ceremonies at the sacred relic shrines and take possession of the *babenye* when the chief dies. They alone can purify the chief from the defilement of sex intercourse so that he is able to enter his relic shrine and perform the necessary rites there. They are in complete charge of the accession ceremonies of the paramount and the bigger territorial chiefs, and some of their number are described as *bafingo*, or hereditary buriers of the chief.

Besides this, each individual *mukabilo* has his own small ritual duty or privilege, such as lighting the sacred fire, or forging the blade of the hoe that is to dig the foundations of the new capital (Richards 1940, p. 109 in 1955 edition).

The *Bakabilo* constitute a council that exerts a check on the paramount's power, since the members are hereditary officials and cannot be removed at will. They are immune to the paramount's anger and can block the implementation of decisions that they consider to be detrimental to the interests of the Bemba people by refusing to perform the ritual functions that are necessary to the exercise of his office. A priesthood of this type thus forms a constituent part of the interior structure of the government of a primitive state.

In stateless societies in Africa and elsewhere, incumbents of certain ritual positions have similar functions in the maintenance of order and the resolution of conflict. The "leopard-skin chief" or "priest of the earth" (as this specialist has been variously called) among the Nuer of the Nilotic Sudan is a person whose ritual relationship with the earth gives him power to bless or curse, to cleanse a killer from the pollution of bloodshed, and, most important, to perform the rites of reconciliation between persons who are ready to terminate a blood feud. A similar role is performed by the "masters of the fishing spear" among the Dinka and the *tendaanas,* or earth priests, among the Tallensi and their congeners in the northern territories of Ghana. Similar religious functionaries are found in many other regions of Africa. They serve to reduce, if not to resolve, conflict within the society. As against sectional and factional interests they posit the commonweal. In these contexts, moreover, the commonweal is regarded as part of the cosmic order; breach, therefore, is mystically punished. The religious specialists are accorded the function of restoring the right relation that should obtain between society, the cosmos, and the deities or ancestral shades.

Priests

C. Von Furer-Haimendorf

In the following article Von Furer-Haimendorf, a specialist in the ethnology of Asian societies, calls on his own field data to demonstrate the important roles of priests in society. Utilizing case studies of the aboriginal Hill Reddis and the Saora tribe of India, the Ifugao of the Philippines, and West African societies, he focuses on the functions of priests as experts on ritual, preservers of myths and religious belief systems, and conduits for communication with the supernatural.

Distinguishing among priests, shamans, magicians, and prophets, Professor Von Furer-Haimendorf also demonstrates that the functions of these religious specialists often overlap. Unlike other specialists, the position of priest is more precarious and constantly threatened with loss of power from a variety of sources, both human and superhuman. As a result, taboos evolved into important protective mechanisms for priests, functioning to guard them against innumerable forms of pollution that could drain away the priestly powers necessary to properly serve society. The respect given priests and the awe surrounding their station can be, in part, correlated with their quality of charisma.

Reprinted from Richard Cavendish, ed., *Man, Myth, and Magic* (London, 1970), vol. 16, pp. 2248–55, by permission of the author and BPCC/Phoebus Publishing.

The priests, medicine men, or shamans of primitive societies are "specialists in the supernatural" who provide a channel of communication between human beings and the divine: more sophisticated societies also have specialist priesthoods.

AT MOST LEVELS OF CIVILIZATION PRIESTS ACT AS the socially recognized mediators between men and supernatural beings. They are the experts in the performances of rituals, and in preliterate societies it is they who preserve, by oral tradition, the myths and the body of religious concepts and ideas which constitute a people's intellectual heritage. The functions, selection, training, and social position of priests differ widely even within simpler societies, and the designation "priest" has been applied to a large variety of religious practitioners, who may have little in common except for their alleged ability to establish contact with gods and spirits, or to manipulate supernatural forces.

In some societies there is a distinction between priests, who are the official religious leaders and representatives of the community, and magicians, shamans, and prophets, whose power derives from individual supernatural experiences or what is presumed to be direct inspiration by deities or spirits. In practice, the functions of these two types of religious practitioners often overlap, and the distinction is not universal.

At the lowest level of economic development, there is little scope for the emergence of ritual experts or any other form of occupational specialization. Most societies of nomadic food gatherers and hunters lack religious specialists comparable to the priests of more advanced peoples. All adults are considered capable of invoking gods or spirits and of soliciting their favor by way of prayers and offerings. Cult acts involving all the members of a group may be conducted by old men experienced in the performance of ritual, but no training or hereditary qualification is required for such activity, nor do those engaging in the organization of religious rites enjoy any special privileges.

Priest and Magician

Where larger and more stable social groups have developed, increased economic efficiency enables man to divert some energies to the elaboration of religious practices. In most societies of some complexity the task of establishing contact with transcendental powers tends to be vested in individuals who act as the representatives of their clan or village. Such individuals need not possess outstanding intellectual gifts, but the ability and the right to perform priestly functions may be hereditary in certain families, lineages or clans. Another claim to priesthood is derived from psychological states interpreted as possession or selection by a divinity or spirit, who is supposed to invest the priest with powers and knowledge not accessible to other men. Priests who base their position on hereditary rights and priests called to their vocation by the gods may coexist in the same society.

The Hill Reddis, an aboriginal tribe of southern India, for instance, depend on two classes of intermediaries in their relations with the supernatural world: the hereditary priest of the local group or village and the magician who derives his powers from an intimate connection with a specific god or spirit. The hereditary priest is normally a descendant of the village-founder, and membership of the lineage of the man who first settled in the locality is sufficient qualification for this office. He is regarded as the head of the village, and as the appropriate mediator between man and the deities and spirits who dwell in the area.

As representative of the village he performs those rites and ceremonies that are believed to secure the prosperity of the community as a whole. And since this prosperity is intimately linked with the thriving of the crops, it is above all the agricultural rites that call for the intercession of the priest. He must inaugurate the sowing of the grain, propitiate the earth deity with sacrifices, and perform the rites at the great seasonal feasts. No special intuition or skill is required for these tasks.

Less simple are those that fall to the magician. While the hereditary spiritual head of the community follows the broad and well-trodden path of long-established ritual, the magician must battle through the wilderness of the supernatural world to discover the cause of disease and threatening disaster, and must devise the means of placating the wrath of malignant spirits. The priest acts, so to speak, while all is well; his offerings are tendered to gods while their mood is benevolent, and his prayers are designed to solicit their favor for the welfare of the community, and their protection against dangers not yet arisen. It is only when misfortune is rife that the magician is called in to restore the disturbed relations with supernatural powers, to draw the sick from the jaws of death or to counteract the black magic of an enemy. This power, which he could not wield unless he himself possessed a thorough knowledge of magical practices, justifies his being called a "magician."

Every Reddi village must have a priest, but there may or may not be a magician in the community. Being a magician is an art, acquired by learning or bestowed by supernatural beings on an eager apprentice. It is an art and a power within reach only of those men and women who are predisposed towards it by particular mental qualities. Naturally these may occur in a priest as well as in any other man, and his frequent performance of ritual acts is bound to favor their development. Nothing debars a priest from learning the practices of a magician, and the combination of both functions is fairly common.

No Reddi is born a magician and aptitude for the work does not manifest itself in childhood. A magician frequently owes his knowledge to the instruction of his father or an older kinsman, but not every son of a famous magician has the talent or the desire to assimilate his parent's teaching. The cooperation of a deity is indispensable to the process of becoming a magician, and it is not only men who seek the gods; on occasion the gods themselves take the initiative. Reddi magicians agree that they receive their inspiration and knowledge from the gods, either while in a state of trance or through the medium of dreams. When a magician is called on to treat a sick person, it is usually his guardian deity who tells him what medicines to apply and what animals to sacrifice.

Married to a Spirit

While the roles of priest and magician are clearly distinguished in some of the simpler societies, they overlap in others and a distinction between the functions of priests and magicians is hardly perceptible. Both deal with the control of supernatural forces and priests are generally expected to influence the gods through prayer and ritual performances, while magicians exert their power through spells and the manipulation of certain material objects possessed of mysterious efficacy. But as the principal duty of priests is to mediate between mankind and the higher powers, the faculty of communicating with gods and spirits is a primary qualification for the priesthood in many societies. This ability may be proved in different ways. When a person falls into a state of trance or ecstasy, people think that he or she is under the influence of a supernatural power, and therefore suitable for the role of mediator between men and gods. Or the supposed connection between priests and the spirit world may be that they have one or more tutelary deities of their own who assist them when required.

A striking example of this type of link between priests and supernatural beings occurs among the Saora tribe of Orissa in India. Among these primitive hill farmers, placating the vast otherworld of invisible and often hostile beings occupies the energy of a small band of dedicated men and women. Armed with a few fragile implements, and devoting themselves to supplication of spirits and the sacrifice of animals, these people strive bravely to protect mankind.

There are two types of religious practitioner among the Saoras, the village priest and the shaman or magician. The priest's special function is to maintain the cult of the local shrines and to guard the village lands from the interference of hostile spirits and sorcerers. When a new priest is to be appointed a shaman is called and, falling into a trance, he asks the gods and ancestors whether the proposed candidate is acceptable to them. If they agree that he is, the shaman summons the ghost of the last priest to hold office in the village. If he too approves, the shaman—possessed by, and representing, the dead man—puts his hands on the head of the new priest and tells him to do his work well. This selection and installation of a Saora village priest demonstrates the coexistence and friendly cooperation of two quite different types of ritual expert.

For practical purposes, however, the shaman, who may be male or female, is the most important religious figure in a Saora village. He has the power not only to diagnose the source of trouble or disease, but to cure it. He is doctor as well as priest, psychol-ogist as well as magician, the repository of tradition, the source of sacred knowledge. His primary duty is that of divination; in case of sickness he seeks the cause in trance or dream. Every male shaman has a spirit-wife in the underworld and every female shaman has a spirit-husband, whom she visits in her dreams. These tutelary spouses are the strength and inspiration of Saora shamans. The marriages are absolutely real in their own minds, and they believe themselves to be chosen by the direct intervention of the guardian spirit, through whom they subsequently have immediate access to the world of spirits and deities. A female shaman may have to be wooed by a spirit for a long time before she consents to accept him as husband. Usually such calls from the spirit world come as hallucinations or dream experiences, and a girl may appear to be deranged and ill until the "marriage" to her suitor from the underworld has been performed.

After the marriage, the shaman's spirit-husband visits her regularly and lies with her till dawn. He may even take her away into the jungle for days at a time. In due course a spirit-child is born, and the ghostly father brings it every night to be nursed by the human wife. This imaginary marriage is no bar to marrying a human husband, but the dream-spouse seems as real to a Saora shaman as her husband of flesh and blood, and it is believed that she will become a spirit herself after death.

The Master of Ecstasy

The term "shaman," now widely current in anthropological literature, was first applied to the religious practitioners of central and northern Asia, where the magico-religious life of most of the indigenous population traditionally centers on the shaman. He is the dominating figure, though in many tribes there are also priests concerned with the performance of animal sacrifices, and every head of a family is also the head of the domestic cult. The ecstatic state is considered to be the supreme religious experience, and the shaman is the great master of ecstasy. Unlike persons possessed by spirits and temporarily in their power, the shaman controls spirits. He is able to communicate with the dead, or with demons and Nature spirits, without becoming their instrument.

Shamans are separated from the rest of society by the intensity of their religious experience, and in this sense they resemble the mystics of historic religions. The mental disposition which qualifies a person for the functions of a shaman points to an important feature of early priesthood. Among many peoples, priests must display a certain excitability of temperament, which in modern Western society might be considered as bordering on a psychopathic condition. The ability to fall into trance may be an essential prerequisite for the performance of certain rites, in which case only those capable of such psychological states are suitable as priests.

The importance attached to ecstasy as a visible means of divine inspiration is shown in the numerous instances of priests obtaining their initiation by inducing a state of delirium or trance through the use of narcotics or fasting. The convulsive movements and seemingly irrational utterances of the inspired person suggest that his own controlling will is in abeyance, and that an external force or being has taken possession of his body. In many cases a god or spirit is supposed to speak through his mouth and determine his actions.

Not all priests need to undergo a formal course of training, or be initiated into the mystery of relations with supernatural powers by a specific ritual. Those who succeed to the priesthood through inheritance, for example, are usually believed to have powers acquired by birth into a family or clan. On the other hand, there are many preliterate societies which require potential religious practitioners to be subjected to a rigorous training in self-control and in the sacred lore of the tribe. Among the Eskimo, for instance, the priests are trained in their profession from childhood.

Where priests receive formal instruction, their education often consists of two different phases. During the first period the novice is under the care of an experienced practitioner, who initiates him into the body of religious beliefs and teaches him how to perform various rites. A later phase is devoted mainly to self-training, in the course of which the novice seeks mystic experiences, and through them a direct relationship with supernatural powers. During this preparation for the priesthood he may have to live in seclusion or submit himself to austerities such as prolonged fasting or exposure to the elements.

In some primitive societies the period of instruction and training culminates in an elaborate initiation ceremony which confirms upon the candidate the full status of an ordained priest.

In many societies, however, priests are trained in a much more casual way. Among the Ifugao tribe of the Philippines, for instance, there is no institutionalized method of initiating priests into the labyrinth of an immensely rich and complicated mythology. There is no organized priesthood recruited from a special social class. Any Ifugao possessing intellectual ability and a good memory may attach himself to an experienced priest of his kingroup or locality as an apprentice; but in many cases sons follow in the footsteps of fathers enjoying a reputation as knowledgeable and successful priests. Ifugao priests also act as chroniclers and genealogists, for the frequently repeated incantations of ancestors give them an unrivalled knowledge of genealogies. The ministrations of priests form an essential part of all the innumerable rituals by which Ifugaos mark social as well as religious occasions.

Some of these rituals may extend over a whole day or even over several days, and the demands they make on the memory can be prodigious. The priests are of supreme importance to the Ifugao, for only they are thought to be capable of manipulating the gods and coaxing them to aid human endeavor. The relation between man and deities is looked upon as one of bargaining and of give and take, and the priests must exert all their skill to get favorable terms for their clients. Ifugao gods are regarded as morally neutral and unconcerned with the ethical conduct of men, and the priests do not take any stand on moral questions. They do not feel any need to behave in an exemplary way in their private lives, nor do they attempt to influence the moral conduct of their clients and fellow villagers.

Unlike Christian priests or other holy men who regard themselves as representatives of a moral order that derives its sanction from a supreme deity, most priests in primitive societies act simply as the agents of their fellow men, and are intent only on obtaining material benefits for them. They have no interest in giving them any guidance in moral matters. Priests of this kind do not preach to men, but address themselves solely to the deities they seek to influence.

In addition, whatever the circumstances in which a priest acts as an intermediary between men and gods, the quality which makes his mediation effective often resides in his office rather than in himself as an individual. Consequently it may not greatly matter what sort of person he is, socially, psychologically, or morally.

A Sense of Awe

Because of his usefulness and power a priest may enjoy considerable prestige and authority, but his position is so precarious and easily damaged that he tends to be surrounded with taboos to protect him against harmful contacts with forces that might render him ineffective. The social position of priests varies greatly from one society to another. The ability to experience states of trance and spirit-possession is usually not combined with great economic efficiency or political acumen, and priests who on ritual occasions will act as the mouthpiece of gods may be withdrawn and comparatively ineffective personalities in ordinary life. On the other hand, someone who holds the position of clan priest by hereditary right, and functions as the sole mediator between a powerful clan and its protective deities, may derive considerable prestige and material advantages from his office.

In some societies, as among certain West African tribes for instance, priests tend to increase the respect in which they are held by enveloping their proceedings in mystery. They often create a sense of awe and fear among the laity, in order to enhance their power. The special and sometimes fantastic attire donned by some priests is intended partly to distinguish them from the rest of the population, and partly to impress deities and spirits or avert malignant forces. Masks worn by priests have similar purposes, and occasionally signify a mystical connection between the priest and an ancestor spirit or deity whom he embodies.

In primitive societies priesthood is not exclusively a male occupation, and there are many instances of women functioning as priestesses and magicians. It is rare for them to be debarred from marriage, just as male priests are usually expected to marry and lead a life not basically different from that of other members of their society. Though their priestly status may provide them with certain privileges and material benefits, occupational specialization among primitive populations normally does not go far enough to free religious practitioners from the need to till the soil or herd cattle. At that level of material development priesthood is seldom an exclusive profession, and a priest does not diminish his spiritual status or prestige by engaging in normal secular occupations.

Restrictions on the sexual life of priests and priestesses are usually found in the more advanced civilizations. Primitive peoples rarely place any value on celibacy and chastity, and priests are expected to have normal family lives. They may be obliged to abstain from sexual activities during periods of training or at the time of major rituals, in the same way as fasting is regarded as a preparation for spiritual experiences; but in general primitive priests are not expected to lead a life basically different from that of laymen.

The Shaman: A Siberian Spiritualist

William Howells

In this classic work, William Howells demonstrates the many positive functions of Siberian and Eskimo shamans in their roles as mediums and diviners, clearly differentiating their character from the evil nature of witches. Like witches, however, shamans have "familiars"—animal souls that give them their powers. Through their familiars, for example, shamans might travel into all three realms of nature (upper, middle, and lower) to recapture the lost souls of villagers enticed into the lower realm of darkness and evil by a demon. At the same time, the power of animal souls allows the shamans to do witchlike harm, and this, along with their ability to cure and keep the balance between the spirits of the upper and lower realms of nature, inspires awe in the villagers' minds. The shamans foster this awe through their artful use of prestidigitation and ventriloquism, justifying their trickery because it enables them to help their followers in the cause of good and to perpetuate their religion.

Although shamanism is both dangerous and burdensome, in Siberia as many women as men become shamans, and each sex often takes on the behavior of its opposite. Members of society may disapprove of this behavior but don't voice their disapproval due to fear of shamanic retribution. It is the shaman's power, expressed in dramatic performance, that provides the psychological benefits for the society by reducing tensions in both individuals and groups and thereby returning emotional balance.

Howells's view of the functions of shamanism anticipated the current view of medical anthropologists who have positively reappraised the role of the traditional healer.

WITCHES ARE ALL EVIL, AND HIDE THEMSELVES from common men; they are "secret, black and midnight hags"; fell creatures, they hypocritically put on the mien of ordinary folk, the better to stalk and strike their prey unknown. But there are other men and women with extraordinary powers of their own, who have no need to skulk, because their purposes are good, and who are given public recognition and respect. The type specimen of such people is known under the Tungus word *shaman,* and the shaman is a figure of importance among the aboriginal people of Siberia and the Eskimos, among most of the American Indians, and to a lesser extent among various other primitive tribes elsewhere in the world. He has been sometimes called a witch doctor, especially with reference to Africa.

A shaman is a medium and a diviner, but his powers do not stop there. He differs from men in general, and resembles a witch, because he can shift gears and move in the plane of the supernatural. He can go at will to the other world, and he can see and treat with souls or spirits, meeting them on their own ground. And that is his business. He differs from a witch, who exists solely in the heads of the victimized, in that he is an actual person, who not only conducts his profession publicly, making the people think that he goes on brave errands among ghosts and goblins, but in many if not most cases really believes he has the powers he claims. This, of course, would be something difficult to get the truth of. Nonetheless he acts as though he can and does do the things which are traditionally his to do, and the public believes and acclaims him. That is the important thing.

His duties are to ride herd on the souls of the departed and to discover the general disposition of other important spirits, according as it is swayed by the behavior of human beings. He may do only a little of this; among some people there is a shaman in every family, who simply makes contact with the spirits from time to time to flatter them and assure himself of their serene humor, as we look at a barometer. Elsewhere he may do it as his trade: general divining, diagnosis of sickness, and ghost chasing. And he may be the most important person of the village, as well as the center of religion; this position he has in easternmost Siberia and among the Eskimos. With such people communities are small and religion is otherwise crude, and the people look to the shaman to take care of their relations with the supernatural both public and private. While he thus acts for them much as does a medicine man or a diviner, he is no magician. He does not endeavor to find the formula to the supernatural, working it as though it were made up of wires and joints, while remaining on the outside; instead, he boldly enters it himself and meets its inhabitants man to man. Nor is he a priest, who leads the people in supplication and represents them before their gods. He may work in their behalf, but he does not represent them; he is acting on his own hook, and through skill and power, not through supplication.

The stronghold of the shaman is among the reindeer herders and fishers of northeast Asia: the Yakuts and the Tungus, two widespread groups of tribes, and others living around the western shore of the Bering Sea: the Chuckchis, the Koryaks, the Gilyaks, and the Kamchadals of Kamchatka. Some of these live nomadically in felt tents and others in wooden villages, and in the long arctic nights of their bleak environment the comfort and entertainment that the shaman gives them is very well received. Typically it is believed that there are three realms of nature: an upper one, of light and of good spirits; a middle one, which is the world of men and of the spirits of the earth; and a lower one, for darkness and evil spirits. Men of the usual sort can move about the middle realm, and have some dealings with its spirits, but only a shaman can go above or below. A shaman also has the power of summoning spirits to come to him. Thus he can speak directly to spirits and ask what they want, which is his form of divining. Not only this, but a shaman deals with sickness in various ways through these same powers. If you have a disease spirit inside you, he can detect it and he knows how to send it off, perhaps by having a personal contest with it. Or you may have lost your soul—this explanation of illness turns up almost everywhere in the world—and the shaman

gets it back. It has probably been enticed against its will by a stronger demon, and taken to the lower regions, and only the shaman can go after it, see it, identify it, and return it.

Both in Asia and America shamans, like witches, are generally believed to have familiar spirits, or animal souls, which are the things that give them their peculiar qualities and powers. A Yakut shaman has two or three (Casanowicz 1924; Czaplicka 1914). One, called *emekhet,* is the shaman's own guardian angel, which is not only a sort of impersonal power like mana but also a definite spirit, usually that of a shaman already dead. This spirit hovers around its protégé, guiding and protecting him all the time, and comes at once when he calls for it, and gives him the advice he needs. Another spirit, the *yekyua,* has more character but is less accommodating. This one is an external soul, which belongs both to the shaman and to a living wild animal, which may be a stallion, a wolf, a dog, an eagle, a hairy bull, or some mythical creature, like a dragon. The yekyua is unruly and malevolent; it is dangerous and enables the shaman to do harm, rather like a witch, so that the people are in awe of him, but at the same time it has no consideration for the shaman himself and gives him continual trouble and anxiety, because his own fortunes are bound up with it. It is independent and lives far away, rather than upon the immediate tribal scene, and only another shaman can see it anyway.

"Once a year, when the snow melts and the earth is black, the yekyua arise from their hiding places and begin to wander" (Czaplicka 1914). When two of them meet, and fight, the human shamans to whom they are linked undergo the evil effects and feel badly. If such an animal dies or is killed, its shaman dies as well, so that a shaman whose yekyua is a bear or a bull can congratulate himself that his life expectancy is good. Of this phantasmal zoo the least desirable soul partners to have are carnivorous animals, especially dogs, because the shaman must keep them appeased, and if they go hungry they are not above taking advantage of their connection with the poor shaman to gnaw at his vitals to stay their appetites. When a person takes to shamanizing, the other shamans round about can tell whether a new yekyua has made its appearance far away, which will cause them to recognize the new shaman and accept him into the profession.

Siberian shamans all dress the part, as do so many shamans and medicine men of North America. The north-eastern Asiatics wear clothing which is made of skin and tailored. A shaman has a cap and a mask, but it is his coat which distinguishes him like a collar turned around. It is a tunic made of hide—goat, elk, etc.—and usually comes down to his knees in front and to the ground behind, and is decorated to the point of being a textbook of shamanistic lore. On the front may be sewed metal plates which protect him from the blows of hostile spirits which he is always encountering. One of these plates represents his emekhet, and usually two others suggest a feminine appearance, since shamans have a hermaphroditic character, as we shall see. All over the tunic are embroidered or appliquéd the figures of real and mythical animals, to represent those he must face on his travels in spirit realms, and from the back there hang numerous strips of skin falling clear to the ground, with small stuffed animals attached to some of them, all this alleged to be for attracting to the shaman any spiritual waifs of the vicinity, who might like to join his retinue. The whole getup would remind you of the unusual headdresses and paraphernalia in which medicine men are turned out among Indians of the Plains and Canada.

Siberian shamans have a tambourine drum whenever they are working, and this is true of Eskimo shamans as well. It is a round or oval drum, covered like a tambourine on one side only, and decorated with the same kind of symbolism as the coat. It is held by a crosspiece or strips of hide in the frame, and is beaten to accompany all the invocations of spirits.

When a shaman goes into action the result is not a rite but a séance, which is full of drama and which the people enjoy immensely. A typical performance is a summoning of spirits, and is carried out in the dark (for the same reasons as among ourselves—i.e., to hide the shenanigans), in a house, a tent, or an Eskimo igloo. The people all gather, and the shaman says what he is going to do, after which he puts out the lamps and the fire, being sure that there is little or no light. Then he begins to sing. There may be a wait, and he beats his tambourine drum first of all, an immediate dramatic effect. The song starts softly. The sense of the song is of no consequence as far as

the listeners are concerned; it is often incomprehensible, and may have no words at all. Jochelson knew a Tungus shaman who sang his songs in Koryak (1908). He explained that his spirits were Koryak and said that he could not understand Koryak himself. Jochelson found this last suspicious statement to be quite true; the shaman had memorized the songs subconsciously when he had first heard them.

As the singing goes on, other sounds begin to make themselves heard, supposedly made by animal spirits and said to be remarkably good imitations. The shaman may announce to the audience that the spirits are approaching, but he is apt to be too absorbed or entranced himself to bother. Soon voices of all kinds are heard in the house, in the corners and up near the roof. The house now seems to have a number of independent spirits in it, all moving around, speaking in different voices, and all the time the drum is sounding, changing its tempo and its volume; the people are excited, and some of them who are old hands help the shaman out by making responses and shouting encouragement, and the shaman himself is usually possessed by a spirit or spirits, who are singing and beating the drum for him. The confusion of noises goes on increasing in intensity, with animal sounds and foreign tongues as well as understandable communications (among the Chuckchis, the wolf, the fox, and the raven can speak human language), until it finally dies down; the spirits give some message of farewell, the drumming ceases, and the lights are lit. Often the shaman will be seen lying exhausted or in a faint, and on coming to he will assert that he cannot say what has been happening.

This is all a combination of expert showmanship and management and of autohypnosis, so that while the shaman knows perfectly well he is faking much of the performance he may at the same time work himself into a trance in which he does things he believes are beyond his merely human powers. He warns his audience strictly to keep their places and not try to touch the spirits, who would be angered and assault the offender, and perhaps even kill the shaman. When the show starts, the shaman produces his voices by moving around in the dark and by expert ventriloquism, getting the audience on his side and rapidly changing the nature and the force of the spirit sounds he is making. He may allow the impression that some of the visiting spirits are possessing him and speaking through his mouth and beating on his drum, but he may hide the fact that he is using his own mouth at all.

A shaman does not perform only in the dark. He carries out some of his business in full view, especially when it is a matter of his going to the spirit world himself, rather than summoning the spirits to this world. The idea seems to be that he is in two places at once; i.e., his soul is traveling in spiritdom while he himself is going through the same actions before his watchers. He does a furious dramatic dance, rushing about, advancing and retreating, approaching the spirits, fighting them or wheedling them, all in a seeming trance. He may foam at the mouth and be so wild that he must be held for safety in leather thongs by some of the onlookers. After vivid adventures in the other realms, portrayed in his dance, he will accomplish his purpose, which may be to capture a wandering soul or to get some needed information from his spectral hosts. Then he becomes his normal self again and gives an account of what he has done.

After a death it is a regular thing for a Mongolian shaman to be called in to "purify" the *yurt* (felt hut) of the deceased's family, by getting rid of the soul of the dead, which of course cannot be allowed to hang around indefinitely. The mourners assemble late in the day, and at dusk the shaman himself comes, already drumming in the distance. He enters the yurt, still drumming, lowering the sound until it is only a murmur. Then he begins to converse with the soul of the newly departed, which pitifully implores to be allowed to stay in the yurt, because it cannot bear to leave the children or the scenes of its mortal days. The shaman, faithful to his trust, steels himself and pays no attention to this heartrending appeal. He goes for the soul and corners it by means of the power in his drum, until he can catch it between the drum itself and the drum stick. Then he starts off with it to the underworld, all in play acting. Here at the entrance he meets the souls of other dead members of the same family, to whom he announces the arrival of the new soul. They answer that they do not want it and refuse it admission. To multiply the difficulties, the homesick soul, which is slippery, generally makes its escape from the shaman as the two of them are on the way down, and comes rushing back to the yurt, with the shaman after it; he catches it all over again. It is lucky the people have a shaman! Back at the gate of the lower world he makes himself affable to the older souls and gives

them vodka to drink, and in one way or another he manages to smuggle the new one in.

Europeans who have seen Siberian shamans perform say that it is tremendous and exciting melodrama for them, and it must therefore have still more of an impact on the natives, whose belief and interest are greater. Aside from ventriloquism and histrionics, shamans use other tricks to heighten their effects, and even give small magic shows to maintain the awe of the populace. They are masters of prestidigitation, especially considering that they must work with little apparatus—no trap doors or piano wire. In their séances they can make it appear that there are spirits in several parts of the yurt at once, mischievously throwing things around. Many stick knives into themselves and draw them out again, making the wound heal immediately (all faked, of course). Or they will have themselves trussed up, like Houdini, and call on their spirits, who will set them free. Bogoras saw a Chuckchi woman shaman take a rock between her hands and, without changing it in any way, produce a pile of smaller stones from it, and to defy the skeptics she wore nothing above her waist (Bogoras 1904–09). She repeated the trick at Bogoras's request, but he could not find out what she did.

The shamans know, of course, that their tricks are impositions, but at the same time everyone who has studied them agrees that they really believe in their power to deal with spirits. Here is a point, about the end justifying the means, which is germane to this and to all conscious augmenting of religious illusion.* The shaman's main purpose is an honest one

---

* Shaw has the following to say about it, through two characters in *Saint Joan:*

THE ARCHBISHOP: A miracle, my friend, is an event which creates faith. That is the purpose and nature of miracles. They may seem very wonderful to the people who witness them, and very simple to those who perform them. That does not matter; if they confirm or create faith they are true miracles.

LA TRÉMOUILLE: Even when they are frauds, do you mean?

THE ARCHBISHOP: Frauds deceive. An event which creates faith does not deceive; therefore it is not a fraud, but a miracle.

Elsewhere the archbishop says: "Miracles are not frauds

and he believes in it, and does not consider it incongruous if his powers give him the right to hoodwink his followers in minor technical matters. If shamanism were a conspiracy or a purposeful fraud, it would attract only the clever and the unscrupulous, interested in their own aggrandizement, and the public would shortly see the snare, being no bigger fools than we are. But shamanism is an institution, and the things that keep the public from rejecting it are religious characteristics: shamanism does something to help them, and the shamans themselves are inside the system and believe in it too. A sick shaman will call in a superior shaman to cure him. Actually, shamans are among the most intelligent and earnest people of the community, and their position is one of leadership.

Evans-Pritchard has the same thing to say about Zande witch doctors, who do shamanizing of a less distinct type. They divine for the people, usually dancing in a group. A question will be asked one of them, and he will "dance" to it, very vigorously, working himself into a transport or half frenzy, throwing himself on the ground and perhaps gashing himself. In this state he begins to make an answer to the question, at first tentatively and in a faraway voice, but then more certainly and finally in loud and arrogant tones, although the terms of the answer remain a little obscure, with no names mentioned, and probably phrased in such a way that only the questioner can gather up the meaning. They do not claim to be guided by spirits, and they could be accused of making any answer they chose. It is unlikely, however, that they do such a thing consciously; actually they possess a knowledge of the village and its people, and of the background of any question asked them, so that they have a good basis

for judgment, and they juggle all these elements loosely in their heads until, under the stimulation of their abandoned physical activity, they feel struck by an inspiration, an effect which they would not experience without the dancing. These witch doctors also cure by sucking intrusive magical objects out of their patients, if that is the cause of illness, and at their shindigs the doctors who are not busy dancing to a question will stage contests of shooting the same kind of thing—bones or beetles—into one another, or into the spectators, if they are unruly, and then removing them again. This is generally known by the Azande to be nothing but sleight of hand, good as it is, and the doctors will admit it, saying that their success is really due to their medicines; the people are also often skeptical of them to the point of laughing outright at them, because a doctor may fail completely when tested by so simple a question as what is hidden in a pot. Nonetheless Evans-Pritchard feels that these doctors, who do not occupy as responsible a position as the Asiatic shamans, are basically honest; and also that they are usually above the average mentally. In spite of their higher intelligence, and their awareness of their own trickery, they believe in their magic and their powers as much as anyone else, and the people, laugh as they may, always go to them when taken sick.

In Asia and North America some tribes think that shaman spirits run in the family, and that a boy or young man will sooner or later be seized by such a legacy. This is the usual thing on the Northwest Coast of America, so that normally only the descendants of shamans became shamans. However, a man with none of them in the family tree may nevertheless become one by going to the bier of a newly dead shaman, which in the northern region was set out in a hut on a point of land, and there he will sit and bite the dead man's little finger all night long. This will offend the departed soul, who will react by sending a small spirit to torment the offender, and the latter, if he is courageous and has his wits about him, may capture the spirit for his own ends, and so become a shaman.

The most general belief as to recruitment is simply that a spirit appears, to anyone at all, and insists on the person's becoming a shaman, which is tantamount to accepting the spirit as an internal boarder, whether it is wanted or not. Being a shaman is considered dangerous and burdensome, because you

---

because they are often—I do not say always—very simple and innocent contrivances by which the priest fortifies the faith of his flock. When this girl picks out the Dauphin from among his courtiers, it will not be a miracle for me, because I shall know how it has been done, and my faith will not be increased. But as for the others, if they feel the thrill of the supernatural, and forget their sinful clay in a sudden sense of the glory of God, it will be a miracle and a blessed one. And you will find that the girl herself will be more affected than anyone else. She will forget how she really picked him out. . . ."

are committed to it and have to observe certain tabus, and so people generally try to avoid it. If you play on a drum, or show yourself in any way receptive, you are laying yourself open, and anyone not wishing to become a shaman will be careful to do no such thing. Usually the spirits pick out young men. In Siberia there are as many women shamans as men, and they are by no means subservient to their male colleagues. In this area also, there is something of an assimilation of male and female shamans; the former, as I said, wear some marks suggestive of femininity, and may braid their hair, and vice versa, female shamans acting somewhat like men. They may go so far as to marry someone of their own sex, a woman getting a wife to keep house for her. This is considered strange, as you might think, and it is not approved of by right-thinking people, but right-thinking people do not like to antagonize shamans and so they keep their mouths shut. Actually, shamans are not thought of as bisexual so much as sexless.

This is one significant thing about the temperamental nature of individuals who become shamans. Another is the reason often given as to why they do so deliberately. A Siberian will say that he became ill, and that in desperation over being melancholy, or on the verge of dying, he began to solicit a spirit and prepare for a shaman's career, whereupon he got well; he now has a bull by the tail, however, and must continue to shamanize or fall ill again. He has to undergo a long training, under the tutelage of an older shaman, and during this period he is subject to mental suffering and sickness; but once he is a practicing shaman he regains his balance, and no shamans suffer from insanity. Europeans report that they can distinguish a shaman by his expression, which is nervous and bright compared to that of ordinary people. Furthermore, the Buriats allege that a future shaman can be told while he is still a child, by certain signs: he is meditative and likes to be alone, and he has mysterious dreams, and sometimes fits, in which he faints.

It is clear from these clues that shamanism is a calling for a certain psychological type: those who are less stable and more excitable than the average, but who have at the same time intelligence, ability, and what is vulgarly called "drive." They are famil-

iar to us, perhaps most so in what we think of as the artistic temperament; they fail of the balance and solidity and self-confidence, not to say aggressiveness, that are necessary in a business executive, or a politician, but their mental powers and their quickness demand expression, goaded by their dissatisfaction at being somewhat maladjusted socially. We are given to calling them introverted, and think them somewhat difficult. They find the expression they need mainly in the arts. Now of course I do not mean that every artist must have bats in his belfry, but only that there is some relation between one variety of human temperament and the insistence of artistic expression. There are plenty of placid and well-adjusted artists; nevertheless, we often say that artists are temperamental people, actually meaning that it is temperamental people who become artists. So it is with shamans, who have in their profession a socially useful exhibitionist release, and a device by which they can discipline their own nervous tendencies by orienting them according to a defined pattern. We have a somewhat stereotyped parallel in people who soothe their nerves by playing the piano; and Conan Doyle made Sherlock Holmes (who was such a bad case that he was addicted to the needle) play the violin.

Some of the native diviners of South Africa, of either sex, are much the same as shamans, being recognized as people of a special type (Hoernle 1937). They enter into this life because of an illness, or hallucinations, or spirit possession; and since the novidiate involves months of solitude, training, and medical treatment by an older diviner, few go into it voluntarily, and most will try to resist it as long as possible. When they come out of this phase they are believed to have second sight and spirit connections, and have developed a peculiar faraway look. As elsewhere, the profession automatically picks out people of a high-strung temperament and appears to give them social satisfaction and psychiatric help.

Shamanism is the more adapted to Siberian and North American native cultures because hysterical tendencies seem to be common among the peoples of the Arctic, giving rise to the term "Arctic hysteria" (Czaplicka 1914; Jochelson 1926). Hysterical seizures, cramps, and trances are the simpler expressions of it. Eskimos will suddenly run wild, tearing off their clothes and rushing out, plunging into a snowbank and sometimes freezing before they can be caught. In Siberia, victims fall into a state, generally on being startled, in which they lose command of themselves and cannot help repeating the words and actions of others. Jokers used to tease known sufferers by tricking them in this way into throwing their belongings into the water, and a Russian colonel was once faced with a troop of natives who had gone hysterical in a body, and were helplessly roaring his orders back at him, and his curses too. A native boy, who knew two older men were both subject to this failing, managed to get them each repeating the other, which they kept up until they both collapsed. I do not know what the basis for this is— i.e., whether it is culturally suggested, like running amok among the Malays—but it is not as merry for the people concerned as it sounds, and is a disturber of the normal social welfare of a group. The contribution of shamanism is not only that it exhausts the special tensions of the shaman himself, and makes him a figure of consequence rather than a slightly psychopathic social liability, but also that it drains off the potential hysteria of the whole community, through the excitement and the drama of the shaman's performances.

Shamans seem to flourish, as might be expected, mainly among people whose religion is not highly organized and whose social structure is also simple and loosely knit. Something that can be called shamanizing often exists in other cultures and cults, but when it does, it is apt to be subservient to some higher political or religious authority. A true shaman is a lone wolf, following his own dictates, and so a well-developed cult, with important gods in it, cannot tolerate any such freebooting approach to the supernatural, and is bound to restrict this kind of activity, and to deprecate the importance to shamans, mediums, and their like. Two generally similar examples will show this. I have already described the *kaula* of the Polynesians, the prophet who was temporarily occupied by a god, and who then spoke with the voice of the god, often going into violent frenzies while possessed. These prophets also held séances of an entirely shamanistic kind, conducted in a dark house, with ventriloquism, sleight of hand, and all the other appurtenances of shamans as I have described them. Handy (1927) refers to a well-known story about a Maori priest whom a missionary was assiduously trying to convert: he stopped the missionary in his tracks by holding up a sprig of dry brown leaves and causing it to turn green before the good man's eyes. The report does not say whether the missionary saw the light and became a Maori. At any rate, the public business of the Polynesian prophets was limited to divining—the primary overt, if not actual, office of all shamans—and in their public appearances at Tahitian feasts they were kept under the thumb of the priests proper, who received the word of the gods in the indistinct mutterings and shouts of the kaula, and then interpreted it themselves and divulged it to the people.

A good parallel to this exists in female functionaries, called *woyei* (singular *woyo*) by the Gã of West Africa, and common to many tribes of the same region (Field 1937). It is an area of polytheistic cults, in which worshipers are free to choose their favorite god, with each god having his own temple, manned by a priest. Such a god enters and possesses certain women, who will therefore be officially appointed to his temple; and their duty is to dance and become possessed at any ceremony, and while possessed to speak for the god. They show various typical signs of possession, and dance in a semi-abandoned manner. If a practicing woyo becomes possessed while no ceremony is going on, a dance is organized at once in order to maintain the possession and get the message which the god is transmitting. Such a woman generally has her first seizure at a dance, having an apparently genuine fit, and acting bewildered and abstracted, talking incoherently. This is a sign that the god has chosen her, and she must leave home and go into training. Eventually she becomes able to deliver the words of her god with more coherence. Sometimes one has been found to talk in languages of other tribes, which she once knew but can no longer speak in her ordinary conscious state. On completing her training she resumes her normal life, and may be appointed to a temple, serving under the priest at ceremonies, and becoming possessed; or else she may practice free lance, as she sees fit.

I have not seen any comments of the same sort on Polynesian kaulas, but Miss Field states that Gã women who become woyei are, like shamans, individuals of a more nervous and less stable temperament than the average, and that the satisfactions of office, together with the license to throw a periodic fit of prophylactic hysterics, actually result in their living more serene, well-balanced, and happier everyday lives than perfectly "normal" women.

If you follow native philosophy, shamanism can be made to look something like witchcraft, as I said earlier. And it also resembles witchcraft, as we have seen, in the psychological benefits it bestows. Both of them relieve certain kinds of tensions in individuals, such as can be harmful to the social climate, and both of them do it dramatically, which means artisti-cally, which in turn means in a manner calculated to give emotional satisfaction. Shamanism should be the more successful, because witchcraft is more of a fantasy and brings its own difficulties, while shamanism is a real emotional exercise, with practically no drawbacks. It allows some of the people to let off steam by indulging in uninhibited antics, while it allows the others to enjoy these antics and at the same time to make use of some of the shaman's real gifts.

Dark Side of the Shaman

Michael Fobes Brown

In this brief but vital treatise, Michael Fobes Brown gives evidence of what every field ethnographer who has observed traditional curing firsthand has always known: that despite the romanticism with which the shaman is held by the West, a careful analysis of the shaman's role in the Third World discloses a dark side. Brown's work among the Aguaruna Indians of the tropical forest of northeastern Peru illustrates that life-threatening illness is attributed to sorcerers who attack their victims with deadly spirit darts. In itself, the presence of sorcery at such a level is ordinarily considered by anthropologists as an index of social tension and strain between members of a society. Here sorcerers are ordinary people whose envy and spite lead them to attack their neighbors with magical darts. Aguaruna shaman (iwishín), whose job is to remove the darts from the victim, also have been given spirit darts from an instructor who, as is the case with sorcerers, trained each in their use of these special powers to cure or kill. Ironically, the shamans' darts also have the power to kill and bewitch, causing them to come under suspicion of sorcery themselves while simultaneously heightening the ordinary fears of patients and their families, who dread an attack during treatment. Anthropologists look for the functions of culture traits and institutions in societies. The fact that only shamans can identify sorcerers and effect cures for their attacks perpetuates the belief in sorcery and sustains a high level of anxiety in Aguaruna society. On the other hand, sorcery beliefs function positively to provide the Aguaruna with rules for proper behavior and explanations for misfortune where no others exist. In our culture, however, Brown argues that New Agers' substitution of shamanism for Western biomedicine ignores the cultural context of traditional curing, and, in fact, they "brush aside its stark truths" of violence and death.

Reprinted with permission from *Natural History*, November 1989, pp. 8–10. Copyright © 1989 the American Museum of Natural History.

SANTA FE, NEW MEXICO, IS A STRONGHOLD OF that eclectic mix of mysticism and folk medicine called "New Age" thought. The community bulletin board of the public library, just around the corner from the plaza and the venerable Palace of the Governors, serves as a central bazaar for spiritual guides advertising instruction in alternative healing methods. Many of these workshops—for example, classes in holistic massage and rebirthing—have their philosophical roots in the experiments of the 1960s. Others resist easy classification: What, I've wondered, is Etheric Body Healing and Light Body Work, designed to "resonate the light forces within our being"? For thirty-five dollars an hour, another expert offers consultations in "defense and removal of psychic attack." Most of the classes, however, teach the healing arts of non-Western or tribal peoples. Of particular interest to the New Agers of Santa Fe is the tradition known as shamanism.

Shamans, who are found in societies all over the world, are believed to communicate directly with spirits to heal people struck down by illness. Anthropologists are fond of reminding their students that shamanism, not prostitution, is the world's oldest profession. When, in my role as curious ethnographer, I've asked Santa Feans about their interest in this exotic form of healing, they have expressed their admiration for the beauty of the shamanistic tradition, the ability of shamans to "get in touch with their inner healing powers," and the superiority of spiritual treatments over the impersonal medical practice of our own society. Fifteen years ago, I would have sympathized with these romantic ideas. Two years of fieldwork in an Amazonian society, however, taught me that there is peril in the shaman's craft.

A man I shall call Yankush is a prominent shaman among the Aguaruna, a native people who make their home in the tropical forest of northeastern Peru. Once feared headhunters, the Aguaruna now direct their considerable energies to cultivating cash crops and protecting their lands from encroachment by settlers fleeing the poverty of Peru's highland and coastal regions.

Yankush is a vigorous, middle-aged man known for his nimble wit and ready laugh. Like every other able-bodied man in his village, Yankush works hard to feed his family by hunting, fishing, and helping his wife cultivate their fields. But when his kinfolk or friends fall ill, he takes on the role of *iwishín*—shaman—diagnosing the cause of the affliction and then, if possible, removing the source of the ailment from the patient's body.

In common with most peoples who preserve a lively shamanistic heritage, the Aguaruna believe that life-threatening illness is caused by sorcerers. Sorcerers are ordinary people who, driven by spite or envy, secretly introduce spirit darts into the bodies of their victims. If the dart isn't soon removed by a shaman, the victim dies. Often the shaman describes the dart as a piece of bone, a tiny thorn, a spider, or a blade of grass.

The Aguaruna do not regard sorcery as a quaint and colorful bit of traditional lore. It is attempted homicide, plain and simple. That the evidence of sorcery can only be seen by a shaman does not diminish the ordinary person's belief in the reality of the sorcerer's work, any more than our inability to see viruses with the naked eye leads us to question their existence. The Aguaruna insist that sorcerers, when discovered, must be executed for the good of society.

Shaman and sorcerer might seem locked in a simple struggle of good against evil, order against chaos, but things are not so straightforward. Shamans and sorcerers gain their power from the same source, both receiving spirit darts from a trusted instructor. Because the darts attempt to return to their original owner, apprentice shamans and sorcerers must induce them to remain in their bodies by purifying themselves. They spend months in jungle isolation, fasting and practicing sexual abstinence. By wrestling with the terrifying apparitions that come to plague their dreams, they steel themselves for a life of spiritual struggle.

There the paths of sorcerer and shaman divide. The sorcerer works in secret, using spirit darts to inflict suffering on his enemies. The shaman operates in the public eye and uses his own spirit darts to thwart the sorcerer's schemes of pain and untimely death. (I say "he" because to my knowledge all Aguaruna shamans are men. Occasionally, however, a woman is accused of sorcery.) Yet because shamans possess spirit darts, and with them the power to kill, the boundary between sorcerer and shaman is sometimes indistinct.

The ambiguities of the shaman's role were brought home to me during a healing session I attended in Yankush's house. The patients were two women: Yamanuanch, who complained of pains in her stomach and throat, and Chapaik, who suffered discomfort in her back and lower abdomen. Their illnesses did not seem life threatening, but they were persistent enough to raise fears that sorcery was at the root of the women's misery.

As darkness fell upon us, the patients and their kin waited for Yankush to enter into a trance induced by a bitter, hallucinogenic concoction he had taken just before sunset (it is made from a vine known as *ayahuasca*). While the visitors exchanged gossip and small talk, Yankush sat facing the wall of his house, whistling healing songs and waving a bundle of leaves that served as a fan and soft rattle. Abruptly, he told the two women to lie on banana leaves that had been spread on the floor, so that he could use his visionary powers to search their bodies for tiny points of light, the telltale signature of the sorcerer's darts. As Yankush's intoxication increased, his meditative singing gave way to violent retching. Gaining control of himself, he sucked noisily on the patients' bodies in an effort to remove the darts.

Family members of the patients shouted words of concern and support. "Others know you are curing. They can hurt you, be careful!" one of the spectators warned, referring to the sorcerers whose work the shaman hoped to undo. Torn by anxiety, Chapaik's husband addressed those present: "Who has done this bewitching? If my wife dies, I could kill any man out of anger!" In their cries of encouragement to Yankush, the participants expressed their high regard for the difficult work of the shaman, who at this point in the proceedings was frequently doubled over with nausea caused by the drug he had taken.

Suddenly there was a marked change of atmosphere. A woman named Chimi called out excitedly, "If there are any darts there when she gets back home, they may say that Yankush put them there. So take them all out!" Chimi's statement was an unusually blunt rendering of an ambivalence implicit in all relations between Aguaruna shamans and their clients. Because shamans control spirit darts, people fear that a shaman may be tempted to use the cover of healing as an opportunity to bewitch his own clients for personal reasons. The clients therefore remind the shaman that they expect results—and if such results are not forthcoming, the shaman himself may be suspected of, and punished for, sorcery.

Yankush is such a skilled healer that this threat scarcely caused him to miss a step. He sucked noisily on Yamanuanch's neck to cure her sore throat and, after singing about the sorcery darts lodged in her body, announced she would recover. For good measure, he recommended injections of a commercial antibiotic. Yankush also took pains to emphasize the intensity of his intoxication. Willingness to endure the rigors of a large dose of *ayhausca* is a sign of his good faith as a healer. "Don't say I wasn't intoxicated enough," he reminded the participants.

As Yankush intensified his singing and rhythmic fanning of the leaf-bundle, he began to have visions of events taking place in distant villages. Suddenly he cried out, "In Achu they killed a person. A sorcerer was killed." "Who could it be?" the other participants asked one another, but before they could reflect on this too long, Yankush had moved on to other matters. "I'm concentrating to throw out sickness, like a tireless jaguar," he sang, referring to Chapaik, who complained of abdominal pains. "With my help she will become like the tapir, which doesn't know how to refuse any kind of food."

After two hours of arduous work, Yankush steered the healing session to its conclusion by reassuring the patients that they were well on their way to recovery. "In her body the sickness will end," he sang. "It's all right. She won't die. It's nothing," he added, returning to a normal speaking voice. Before departing, the patients and their kin discussed the particulars of Yankush's dietary recommendations and made plans for a final healing session to take place at a later date. As the sleepy participants left Yankush's house for their beds in other parts of the village, they expressed their contentment with the results of his efforts.

During the year I lived near Yankush, he conducted healing sessions like this one about twice a month. Eventually, I realized that his active practice was only partly a matter of choice. To allay suspicions and demonstrate his good faith as a healer, he felt compelled to take some cases he might otherwise have declined. Even so, when I traveled to other villages, people sometimes asked me how I could live in a community where a "sorcerer" practiced on a regular basis.

When a respected elder died suddenly of unknown causes in 1976, Yankush came under extraordinary pressure to identify the sorcerer responsible. From the images of his *ayahuasca* vision he drew the name of a young man from a distant region who happened to be visiting a nearby village. The man was put to death in a matter of days. Because Yankush was widely known to have fingered the sorcerer, he became the likely victim of a reprisal raid by members of the murdered man's family. Yankush's willingness to accept this risk in order to protect his community from future acts of sorcery was a source of his social prestige, but it was also a burden. I rarely saw him leave his house without a loaded shotgun.

In calling attention to the violent undercurrents of shamanism, my intention is not to disparage the healing traditions of the Aguaruna or of any other tribal people. I have no doubt that the cathartic drama I witnessed in Yankush's house made the two patients feel better. Medical anthropologists agree that rituals calling forth expressions of community support and concern for sick people often lead to a marked improvement in their sense of well-being. Shamans also serve their communities by administering herbal medications and other remedies and even, as in Yankush's case, helping to integrate traditional healing arts with the use of modern pharmaceuticals. At the same time, however, they help sustain a belief in sorcery that exacts a high price in anxiety and, from time to time, in human life.

In their attempts to understand this negative current, anthropologists have studied how shamanism and accusations of sorcery define local patterns of power and control. Belief in sorcery, for example, may provide a system of rules and punishments in societies that lack a police force, written laws, and a formal judicial system. It helps people assign a cause to their misfortunes. And it sustains religions that link human beings with the spirit world and with the tropical forest itself.

What I find unsettling, rather, is that New Age America seeks to embrace shamanism without any appreciation of its context. For my Santa Fe acquaintances, tribal lore is a supermarket from which they choose some tidbits while spurning others. They program computers or pursue other careers by day so that by night they can wrestle with spirit-jaguars and search for their power spots. Yankush's lifetime of discipline is reduced to a set of techniques for personal development, stripped of links to a specific landscape and cultural tradition.

New Age enthusiasts are right to admire the shamanistic tradition, but while advancing it as an alternative to our own healing practices, they brush aside its stark truths. For throughout the world, shamans see themselves as warriors in a struggle against the shadows of the human heart. Shamanism affirms life but also spawns violence and death. The beauty of shamanism is matched by its power—and like all forms of power found in society, it inspires its share of discontent.

Reflections after Waco: Millennialists and the State

Michael Barkun

No question existed in the minds of the Branch Davidians that the predictions of their charismatic prophet, David Koresh, were correct; the apocalypse engineered by God and the millennia it promised were at hand. Their conscious attempt to change their culture under the direction of their messiahlike leader fit well the model of revitalization movements set out by Wallace (see Chapter 9). As Michael Barkun makes clear, parties in the Waco tragedy accurately fulfilled the millennialists' prophecy of the battle between good and evil.

More than simply recounting the events at Waco, Barkun analyzes the characteristics of millenarianism and charismatic leadership and demonstrates that neither the Bureau of Alcohol, Tobacco, and Firearms (ATF) nor the Federal Bureau of Investigation (FBI) understood or took seriously the millenarian beliefs of the Branch Davidians. Falling victim to the "cult concept," the ATF and FBI perceived the activity of Koresh and his followers, not as the manifestation of a religion, but as that of a psychopathology to be dealt with as they would deal with hijackers or hostage takers. The direct assaults on the compound at Waco were, as Barkun points out, fulfillment of the millenarianists' prophecy. It is important to recall the Reverend Jim Jones and the tragedy at Jonestown, Guyana, in November 1978 to put in proper perspective the reaction of the Branch Davidians to federal authority. But it appears that these types of movements may not be exclusively American. The reader is reminded of the mass immolations of fifty-two members of the Order of the Solar Temple in Quebec and Switzerland in 1994 and the murder-suicide ritual that took the lives of sixteen more members of the group in a woods near Grenoble, France, the day before Christmas, 1995, in what appears at this point to be a ritual timed for the winter solstice. At this writing, little is known of the Order of the Solar Temple or its deceased leader, Luc Jouret.

Barkun ends his article with two questions. First, will federal authorities come to understand the worldview of millennialists, particularly those who follow the "post-tribulationists" approaches of some survivalists, and change their agencies' strategies of force? Second, and more important in the long run, will the First Amendment's guarantee of the free exercise of religion be shared equally by all groups in the future?

NOT SINCE JONESTOWN HAS THE PUBLIC BEEN gripped by the conjunction of religion, violence and communal living as they have by the events at the Branch Davidians' compound. All that actually took place near Waco remains unknown or contested. Nonetheless, the information is sufficient to allow at least a preliminary examination of three questions: Why did it happen? Why didn't it happen earlier? Will it happen again?

As a *New York Times* editorialist put it, "The Koresh affair has been mishandled from beginning to end." The government's lapses, errors and misjudgments can be grouped into two main categories: issues of law-enforcement procedure and technique, with which I do not propose to deal; and larger issues of strategy and approach, which I will address.

The single most damaging mistake on the part of federal officials was their failure to take the

Branch Davidians' religious beliefs seriously. Instead, David Koresh and his followers were viewed as being in the grip of delusions that prevented them from grasping reality. As bizarre and misguided as their beliefs might have seemed, it was necessary to grasp the role these beliefs played in their lives; these beliefs were the basis of *their* reality. The Branch Davidians clearly possessed an encompassing worldview to which they attached ultimate significance. That they did so carried three implications. First, they could entertain no other set of beliefs. Indeed, all other views of the world, including those held by government negotiators, could only be regarded as erroneous. The lengthy and fruitless conversations between the two sides were, in effect, an interchange between different cultures—they talked past one another.

Second, since these beliefs were the basis of the Branch Davidians' sense of personal identity and meaning, they were nonnegotiable. The conventional conception of negotiation as agreement about some exchange or compromise between the parties was meaningless in this context. How could anything of ultimate significance be surrendered to an adversary steeped in evil and error? Finally, such a belief system implies a link between ideas and actions. It requires that we take seriously—as apparently the authorities did not—the fact that actions might be based on something other than obvious self-interest.

Conventional negotiation assumes that the parties think in terms of costs and benefits and will calculate an outcome that minimizes the former and maximizes the latter. In Waco, however, the government faced a group seemingly impervious to appeals based upon interests, even where the interests involved were their own life and liberty. Instead, they showed a willingness to take ideas to their logical end-points, with whatever sacrifice that might entail.

The Branch Davidians did indeed operate with a structure of beliefs whose authoritative interpreter was David Koresh. However absurd the system might seem to us, it does no good to dismiss it. Ideas that may appear absurd, erroneous or morally repugnant in the eyes of outsiders continue to drive believers' actions. Indeed, outsiders' rejection may lead some believers to hold their views all the more tenaciously as the group defines itself as an island of enlightenment in a sea of error. Rejection validates

their sense of mission and their belief that they alone have access to true knowledge of God's will.

These dynamics assumed particular force in the case of the Branch Davidians because their belief system was so clearly millenarian. They anticipated, as historian Norman Cohn would put it, total, immediate, collective, imminent, terrestrial salvation. Such commitments are even less subject than others to compromise, since the logic of the system insists that transcendent forces are moving inexorably toward the fulfillment of history.

Federal authorities were clearly unfamiliar and uncomfortable with religion's ability to drive human behavior to the point of sacrificing all other loyalties. Consequently, officials reacted by trying to assimilate the Waco situation to more familiar and less threatening stereotypes, treating the Branch Davidians as they would hijackers and hostage-takers. This tactic accorded with the very human inclination to screen out disturbing events by pretending they are simply variations of what we already know. Further, to pretend that the novel is really familiar is itself reassuring, especially when the familiar has already provided opportunities for law-enforcement officials to demonstrate their control and mastery. The FBI has an admirable record of dealing effectively with hijackers and hostage-takers; therefore, acting as if Waco were such a case encouraged the belief that here too traditional techniques would work.

The perpetuation of such stereotypes at Waco, as well is the failure to fully approach the religious dimension of the situation, resulted in large measure from the "cult" concept. Both the authorities and the media referred endlessly to the Branch Davidians as a "cult" and Koresh as a "cult leader." The term "cult" is virtually meaningless. It tells us far more about those who use it than about those to whom it is applied. It has become little more than a label slapped on religious groups regarded as too exotic, marginal or dangerous.

As soon as a group achieves respectability by numbers or longevity, the label drops away. Thus books on "cults" published in the 1940s routinely applied the term to Christian Scientists, Jehovah's Witnesses, Mormons and Seventh-Day Adventists, none of whom are referred to in comparable terms today. "Cult" has become so clearly pejorative that to dub a group a "cult" is to associate it with irrationality and authoritarianism. Its leaders practice "mind control," its members have been "brain-washed" and its beliefs are "delusions." To be called a "cult" is to be linked not to religion but to psychopathology.

In the Waco case, the "cult" concept had two dangerous effects. First, because the word supplies a label, not an explanation, it hindered efforts to understand the movement from the participants' perspectives. The very act of classification itself seems to make further investigation unnecessary. To compound the problem, in this instance the classification imposed upon the group resulted from a negative evaluation by what appear to have been basically hostile observers. Second, since the proliferation of new religious groups in the 1960s, a network of so-called "cult experts" has arisen, drawn from the ranks of the academy, apostates from such religious groups, and members' relatives who have become estranged from their kin because of the "cult" affiliations. Like many other law-enforcement agencies, the FBI has relied heavily on this questionable and highly partisan expertise—with tragic consequences. It was tempting to do so since the hostility of those in the "anti-cult" movement mirrored the authorities' own anger and frustration.

These cascading misunderstandings resulted in violence because they produced erroneous views of the role force plays in dealing with armed millenarians. In such confrontations, dramatic demonstrations of force by the authorities provoke instead of intimidate. It is important to understand that millenarians possess a "script"—a conception of the sequence of events that must play out at the end of history. The vast majority of contemporary millenarians are satisfied to leave the details of this script in God's hands. Confrontation can occur, however, because groups often conceive of the script in terms of a climactic struggle between forces of good and evil.

How religious prophecy is interpreted is inseparable from how a person or a group connects events with the millenarian narrative. Because these believers' script emphasizes battle and resistance, it requires two players: the millenarians as God's instruments or representatives, and a failed but still resisting temporal order. By using massive force the Bureau of Alcohol, Tobacco, and Firearms on February 28, and the FBI on April 19, unwittingly conformed to Koresh's millenarian script. He wanted

and needed their opposition, which they obligingly provided in the form of the initial assault, the nationally publicized siege, and the final tank and gas attack. When viewed from a millenarian perspective, these actions, intended as pressure, were the fulfillment of prophecy.

The government's actions almost certainly increased the resolve of those in the compound, subdued the doubters and raised Koresh's stature by in effect validating his predictions. Attempts after the February 28 assault to "increase the pressure" through such tactics as floodlights and sound bombardment now seem as pathetic as they were counterproductive. They reflect the flawed premise that the Branch Davidians were more interested in calculating costs and benefits than in taking deeply held beliefs to their logical conclusions. Since the government's own actions seemed to support Koresh's teachings, followers had little incentive to question them.

The final conflagration is even now the subject of dispute between the FBI, which insists that the blazes were set, and survivors who maintain that a tank overturned a lantern. In any case, even if the FBI's account proves correct, "suicide" seems an inadequate label for the group's fiery demise. Unlike Jonestown, where community members took their own lives in an isolated setting, the Waco deaths occurred in the midst of a violent confrontation. If the fires were indeed set, they may have been seen as a further working through of the script's implications. It would not have been the first time that vastly outnumbered millenarians engaged in self-destructive behavior in the conviction that God's will required it. In 1525, during the German Peasants' Revolt, Thomas Münzer led his forces into a battle so hopeless that five thousand of his troops perished, compared to six fatalities among their opponents.

Just as the authorities in Waco failed to understand the connections between religion and violence, so they failed to grasp the nature of charismatic leadership. Charisma, in its classic sociological sense, transcends law and custom. When a Dallas reporter asked Koresh whether he thought he was above the law, he responded: "I *am* the law." Given such self-perception, charismatic figures can be maddeningly erratic; they feel no obligation to remain consistent with pre-existing rules. Koresh's swings of mood and attitude seemed to have been a major factor in the FBI's growing frustration, yet they were wholly consistent with a charismatic style.

Nevertheless, charismatic leaders do confront limits. One is the body of doctrine to which he or she is committed. This limit is often overcome by the charismatic interpreter's ingenuity combined with the texts' ambiguity (Koresh, like so many millennialists, was drawn to the vivid yet famously obscure language of the Book of Revelation).

The other and more significant limit is imposed by the charismatic leader's need to validate his claim to leadership by his performance. Charismatic leadership is less a matter of inherent talents than it is a complex relational and situational matter between leader and followers. Since much depends on followers' granting that a leader possesses extraordinary gifts, the leader's claim is usually subject to repeated testing. A leader acknowledged at one time may be rejected at another. Here too the Waco incident provided an opportunity for the authorities inadvertently to meet millennialist needs. The protracted discussions with Koresh and his ability to tie down government resources gave the impression of a single individual toying with a powerful state. While to the outer world Koresh may have seemed besieged, to those in the community he may well have provided ample evidence of his power by immobilizing a veritable army of law-enforcement personnel and dominating the media.

Given the government's flawed approach, what ought to have been done? Clearly, we will never know what might have resulted from another strategy. Nonetheless, taking note of two principles might have led to a very different and less violent outcome. First, the government benefited more than Koresh from the passage of time. However ample the Branch Davidians' material stockpiles, these supplies were finite and diminishing. While their resolve was extraordinary, we do not know how it might have been tested by privation, boredom and the eventual movement of public and official attention to other matters. Further, the longer the time that elapsed, the greater the possibility that Koresh in his doctrinal maneuvering might have constructed a theological rationalization that would have permitted surrender. Messianic figures, even those cut from seemingly fanatic cloth, have occa-

sionally exhibited unpredictable moments of prudential calculation and submission (one thinks, for example, of the sudden conversion to Islam of the seventeenth century Jewish false messiah Sabbatai Zevi). Time was a commodity the government could afford, more so than Koresh, particularly since a significant proportion of the community's members were almost certainly innocent of directly violating the law.

As important as patience, however, would have been the government's willingness to use restraint in both the application and the appearance of force. The ATF raid, with its miscalculations and loss of life, immediately converted a difficult situation into one fraught with danger. Yet further bloodshed might have been averted had authorities been willing both to wait and to avoid a dramatic show of force. Federal forces should have been rapidly drawn down to the lowest level necessary to prevent individuals from leaving the compound undetected. Those forces that remained should have been as inconspicuous as possible. The combination of a barely visible federal presence, together with a willingness to wait, would have accomplished two things: it would have avoided government actions that confirmed apocalyptic prophecies, and it would have deprived Koresh of his opportunity to validate his charismatic authority through the marathon negotiations that played as well-rehearsed millenarian theater. While there is no guarantee that these measures would have succeeded (events within the compound might still have forced the issue), they held a far better chance of succeeding than the confrontational tactics that were employed.

The events in Waco were not the first time in recent years that a confrontation between a communal group and government forces has ended in violence. Several years ago the Philadelphia police accidentally burned down an entire city block in their attempt to evict the MOVE sect from an urban commune. In 1985 surrender narrowly averted a bloody confrontation at Zarephath-Horeb, the heavily armed Christian Identity community in Missouri organized by the Covenant, Sword and Arm of the Lord. In August 1992 a federal raid on the Idaho mountaintop cabin of a Christian Identity family resulted in an eleven-day armed standoff and the deaths of a U.S. marshal and two family members.

In this case, too, the aim was the arrest of an alleged violator of firearms law, Randy Weaver, whose eventual trial, ironically, took place even as the FBI prepared its final assault on the Branch Davidians. In retrospect, the Weaver affair was Waco in microcosm —one from which, apparently, the ATF learned little.

These cases, which should have been seen to signal new forms of religion-state conflict, were untypical of the relationships with government enjoyed by earlier communal societies. While a few such groups, notably the Mormons, were objects of intense violence, most were able to arrive at some way of living with the established order. Many, like the Shakers, were pacifists who had a principled opposition to violence. Some, like the German pietist sects, were primarily interested in preserving their cultural and religious distinctiveness; they only wanted to be left alone. Still others, such as the Oneida perfectionists, saw themselves as models of an ideal social order—exemplars who might tempt the larger society to reform. In all cases, an implied social contract operated in which toleration was granted in exchange for the community's restraint in testing the limits of societal acceptance. When external pressure mounted (as it did in response to the Oneida Community's practice of "complex marriage"), communitarians almost always backed down. They did so not because they lacked religious commitment, but because these communities placed such a high value on maintaining their separate identities and on convincing fellow citizens that their novel social arrangements had merit.

The Branch Davidians clearly were not similarly motivated, and it is no defense of the government's policy to acknowledge that Koresh and his followers would have sorely tested the patience of any state. Now that the events of Waco are over, can we say that the problem itself has disappeared? Are armed millenarians in America likely to be again drawn or provoked into violent conflict with the established order? The answer, unfortunately, is probably yes. For this reason Waco's lessons are more than merely historically interesting.

The universe of American communal groups is densely populated—they certainly number in the thousands—and it includes an enormous variety of ideological and religious persuasions. Some religious communities are millenarian, and of these some grow out of a "posttribulationist" theology.

They believe, that is, that Armageddon and the Second Coming will be preceded by seven years of turmoil (the Tribulation), but they part company with the dominant strain of contemporary Protestant millennialism in the position they assign to the saved. The dominant millenarian current (dispensational premillennialism) assumes that a Rapture will lift the saved off the earth to join Christ before the tribulation begins, a position widely promulgated by such televangelists as Jerry Falwell. Posttribulationists, on the other hand, do not foresee such as rescue and insist that Christians must endure the tribulation's rigors, which include the reign of the Antichrist. Their emphasis upon chaos and persecution sometimes leads them toward a "survivalist" lifestyle—retreat into defendable, self-sufficient rural settlements where they can, they believe, wait out the coming upheavals.

Of all the posttributionists, those most likely to ignite future Wacos are affiliated with the Christian Identity movement. These groups, on the outermost fringes of American religion, believe that white "Aryans" are the direct descendants of the tribes of Israel, while Jews are children of Satan. Not surprisingly, Identity has become highly influential in the white supremacist right. While its numbers are small (probably between 20,000 and 50,000), its penchant for survivalism and its hostility toward Jews and nonwhites renders the Christian Identity movement a likely candidate for future violent conflict with the state.

When millenarians retreat into communal settlements they create a complex tension between withdrawal and engagement. Many communal societies in the nineteenth century saw themselves as showcases for social experimentation—what historian Arthur Bestor has called "patent office models of society." But posttribulationist, survivalist groups are defensive communities designed to keep at bay a world they despise and fear. They often deny the legitimacy of government and other institutions. For some, the reign of Antichrist has already begun. To white supremacists, the state is ZOG—The Zionist Occupation Government. For them, no social contract can exist between themselves and the enemy— the state. Their sense of besiegement and their links to paramilitary subcultures virtually guarantee that, no matter how committed they may be to lives of isolation, they will inevitably run afoul of the law.

The flash-point could involve firearms regulations, the tax system, or the treatment of children.

These and similar groups will receive a subtle but powerful cultural boost as we move toward the year 2000. Even secularists seem drawn, however irrationally, toward the symbolism of the millennial number. The decimal system invests such dates with a presumptive importance. We unthinkingly assume they are watersheds in time, points that divide historical epochs. If even irreligious persons pause in expectation before such a date, is it surprising that millennialists do so? As we move closer to the year 2000, therefore, millenarian date-setting and expectations of transformation will increase.

If this prognosis is valid, what should government policy be toward millennial groups? As I have suggested, government must take religious beliefs seriously. It must seek to understand the groups that hold these beliefs, rather than lumping the more marginal among them in a residual category of "cults." As Waco has shown, violence is a product of interaction and therefore may be partially controlled by the state. The state may not be able to change a group's doctrinal propensities, but it can control its own reactions, and in doing so may exert significant leverage over the outcome. The overt behavior of some millenarian groups will undoubtedly force state action, but the potential for violence can be mitigated if law-enforcement personnel avoid dramatic presentations of force. If, on the other hand, they naively become co-participants in millenarians' end-time scripts, future Wacos will be not merely proba-ble; they will be inevitable. The government's inability to learn from episodes such as the Weaver affair in Idaho provides little cause for short-term optimism. The lesson the ATF apparently took from that event was that if substantial force produced loss of life, then in the next case even more force must be used. Waco was the result.

Admittedly, to ask the government to be more sensitive to religious beliefs in such cases is to raise problems as well as to solve them. It raises the possibility of significant new constitutional questions connected with the First Amendment's guarantee of the free exercise of religion. If the state is not to consign all new and unusual religious groups to the realm of outcast "cults," how is it to differentiate among them? Should the state monitor doctrine to distinguish those religious organizations that require particularly close observation? News reports suggest that Islamic groups may already be the subjects of such surveillance—a chilling and disturbing prospect. Who decides that a group is dangerous? By what criteria? If beliefs can lead to actions, if those actions violate the law, how should order and security be balanced against religious freedom? Can belief be taken into account without fatally compromising free exercise?

These are difficult questions for which American political practice and constitutional adjudication provide little guidance. They need to be addressed, and soon. In an era of religious ferment and millennial excitation, the problems posed by the Branch Davidians can only multiply.

4

The Religious Use of Drugs

Because the people of the world have such a myriad of uses for and attitudes toward what we call "drugs," it is impossible to define the term to the satisfaction of all. In the West, for example, chemical substances are prescribed to alleviate disease, but they are also used, often illegally, to provide "kicks" for the user; in many non-Western societies religious specialists utilize these materials as a vehicle for entry into the realm of the supernatural. Perhaps Marston Bates has most correctly defined the term, as "almost all materials taken for other than nutritional reasons" (1971: 113). Using this definition, one can count an extraordinary number of substances as falling into the category of drugs.

Every culture, whatever the level of technological accomplishment, has an inventory of drugs and a medical system. The use of drugs is so ancient that Weston La Barre has posited the theory that shamanism itself developed from the use of hallucinogens (1972). The aim of this chapter is to describe the religious functions of drugs. This purpose almost totally eliminates the role of drugs in the West, where they are either medicinal or recreational. At varying periods in Western history, most recently in the social ferment of the 1960s, drug usage was proclaimed by some people to have religious overtones, but few fool

Zapotec mask representing life and death, from Oaxaca, Mexico.

themselves today by believing that drugs provide the taker with a religious experience. Hedonism and escapism leading to addiction are the most prominent characteristics of Western drug use and pose immense problems for governments that recognize the changing values that have encouraged the availability of illicit drugs. Certainly anthropologists have found the pleasure and escape motivation for drug use in non-Western societies as well, but the interrelationship of drugs and religion is dominant in traditional societies, where specialists such as shamans utilize plant and animal substances to contact the spirit world.

In an attempt to better understand the role of drugs in shamanic healing, some anthropologists have ingested hallucinogens themselves. In his book *The Way of the Shaman* (1980), Michael Harner, for example, recounts his use of *ayahuasca* while among the Conibo Indians of Peru, and in *Yanomamo: The Fierce People* (1977), Napoleon Chagnon described his use of *ebene* snuff while carrying out fieldwork in Venezuela.

Cross-cultural comparison demonstrates not only that drugs are perceived differently but also that they may actually have different effects on the users from one society to the next (despite having identical chemical makeup). Indeed, physiological and psychological reactions to drugs vary among individuals in the same society, a phenomenon that is often explained in terms of supernatural intervention.

Because most of us know little of the scientific properties of drugs, it is worthwhile to categorize them as to their effects on users. Lewis Lewin, the famous German toxicologist, whose drug classification is still basically sound and continues to be used by pharmacologists, offered the following categories (after Lewin as quoted by Bates 1971: 115–16):

I. *Euphoria:* sedatives which reduce mental activity and induce mental and physical comfort, such as morphine, cocaine and the like.

II. *Phantastica:* hallucinogens, bringing on visions and illusions which vary greatly in chemical composition, but may be followed by unconsciousness or other symptoms of altered brain states. This group includes: mescal buttons, hashish and its source, marijuana.

III. *Inebriantia:* drugs which produce an initial phase of cerebral excitation followed by a state of depression which sometimes leads to unconsciousness. Chloroform, alcohol, ether, and others are members of this group.

IV. *Hypnotica:* sedatives or sleep producers such as chloral, sulphonol and some recent synthetic barbiturates.

V. *Excitania:* mental stimulants today referred to as analeptics. Coffee, tea, betel, and tobacco; that is, all plants containing caffeine, nicotine and the like.

Today we would add a sixth category to the above —the tranquilizers, sometimes termed *ataraxics*. In reality none are new drugs; rather, they are relatively newly discovered.

Interestingly, none of the first five categories, indeed, even the sixth (ataraxics), was unknown to so-called primitive people. Although the history of the use of these drugs is so ancient as to make attempts at tracing their origins academic exercises, not until the development of synthetics, prompted by the shortages of natural products during World War II, did we learn that hunting and gathering societies knew of and used the same basic chemical substances of medicines as modern technological cultures. For their knowledge of the chemical properties of the plants and animals in their environments, modern man's debt to "primitive man" is great.

The focus of drug use in traditionally based non-Western cultures is on the religious specialist, particularly the shaman, whose duty it is to control the spirit world for the benefit of the members of his society. Of all the categories of drugs, it is the hallucinogens, Lewin's "phantastica," that command our attention, for it is these psychotropic plant and animal substances that provide the shamans with their visions of the supernatural realm. Importantly, what one society considers to be real or unreal is not always shared by another society. Michael Harner's article in this chapter demonstrates, for example, that the Jívaro of the Ecuadorian Amazon consider reality to be what is found in the hallucinogenic state that results from drinking a tea made from the Banisteriopsis vine; the nonhallucinogenic, ordinary state is considered to be an illusion. Indeed, some drugs not considered hallucinogens in Western pharmacology do cause a visionary state; such is the case of the Warao shamans' use of tobacco (Wilbert 1972). The point is that whether we agree or not with the folk categories of drugs in other societies, the mainspring of shamanistic power is centered on drugs that produce visual hallucinations as well as hallucinations of the other senses.

The shamanistic use of a variety of hallucinogenic drugs for trance inducement has not in itself guaranteed that a shaman's patient would recover, or that an enemy would suffer. To this end many other, nonhallucinogenic drugs and practices have also been used, some of which involved effective chemical properties or constituted successful non-drug techniques, such as the sucking-out of evil forces. Even substances having only inert chemicals were often effective in the hands of the shaman. Surely, other reasons must be offered for those successes. The illnesses of non-Western traditional societies have sometimes been described as being due to imbalances or disruptions of the patients' social environment. Physical and mental illnesses are difficult to separate, particularly in groups where belief systems are shared by a high percentage of the population. The treatment offered by shamans is relatively standard and almost always considered correct by patients, as well as by their families and friends, who are often present for the curing process and ceremony. The anxiety of the patient, on the one hand, and the confidence of the shaman, on the other, work to develop a level of suggestibility that literally sets the stage for effective treatment. Shamans, with their secret formulas, chants, and personal contact and control over spirit helpers—knowledge and power the patient does not possess—appear omnipotent and inordinately powerful. The encouragement and support of family and friends in a familiar environment all contribute to the eventual cure. Westerners have learned much from shamanistic treatment, for it treats the physical and the psychological, both of which are irrevocably intertwined with the supernatural causes of illness.

The first four articles in this chapter were chosen because each one focuses on a different aspect of drug use in traditional societies. Francis Huxley takes a broad approach to the subject, discussing the general use of drugs in primitive societies. J. S. Slotkin discusses peyote use among members of the Native American Church. Furst and Coe's work on "Ritual Enemas" is an ethnohistorical reconstruction of Maya drug usage through an analysis of their pottery. In "The Sound of Rushing Water," Michael Harner offers an insight to Jívaro reality, a state that can be achieved only through consumption of the hallucinogenic tea, natema. Finally, in the fifth article, Robert S. de Ropp discusses the dynamic and disruptive history of psychedelic cults of the Flower Children movement of the '60s in the United States.

References

Bates, Marston
1971 *Gluttons and Libertines: Human Problems of Being Natural*. New York: Vintage Books.

Chagnon, Napoleon
1977 *Yanomamo: The Fierce People*, 2nd ed. New York: Holt, Rinehart and Winston.

Harner, Michael
1980 *The Way of the Shaman*. New York: Harper and Row.

La Barre, Weston
1972 "Hallucinogens and the Shamanistic Origins of Religion." In Peter T. Furst, ed., *Flesh of the Gods: The Ritual Use of Hallucinogens*, pp. 261–78. New York: Praeger.

Wilbert, Johannes
1972 "Tobacco and Shamanistic Ecstasy Among the Warao Indians of Venezuela." In Peter T. Furst, ed., *Flesh of the Gods: The Ritual Use of Hallucinogens*, pp. 55–83. New York: Praeger.

Drugs

Francis Huxley

Fieldworkers' interest in religious specialists inevitably drew anthropologists' attention to the religious use of drugs. The important role of drugs in human life, particularly in aboriginal South America where they are used in the most traditional manner, has prompted Marston Bates to refer to us as Homo medicans, *man the drug taker. His definition of drugs as almost all materials taken for other than nutritional reasons may be vague, but it does demonstrate the extraordinary variety of substances that are eaten, drunk, smoked, chewed, or rubbed on the skin but lack food value as their primary function (1971: 112–13). Francis Huxley's article discusses uses of drugs the world over but focuses on such religious purposes as curing illnesses of the soul and body, divining, gaining supernatural knowledge, and contacting spirits. Huxley argues that drugs used in many religious rites tend to be hallucinogenic rather than those that suppress mental and physical activity. Unlike users of hallucinogens in contemporary society, however, primitive groups have long recognized the need for a ritual setting to channel the dangerous forces contained in drugs.*

Reprinted from Richard Cavendish, ed., *Man, Myth, and Magic* (London, 1970), vol. 5, pp. 711–16, by permission of the author and BPCC/Phoebus Publishing.

THE POET BAUDELAIRE DESCRIBED DRUGS WHICH affect the mind as "artificial paradises." The phrase is apt and Lewis Lewin, the German biochemist, repeated it in his pioneering study of these drugs (*Phantastica*, 1924), where he divided paradise into categories: five of them in all, the paradises of narcosis, stimulation, euphoria, intoxication and hallucination. More simply we might say: of dreaming sleep, energetic wakefulness, well-being, drunkenness and the inspired imagination.

In palmistry, a certain small line near the bottom edge of the palm is called the paradise line. Some people, however, refer to this line as the poison line, because it indicates a person's capacity to enjoy a private and rarefied pleasure which in large doses cuts one off from reality and infects one with an unattainable hope. A substance known as a drug in the pejorative sense of that word also has the characteristic of being at once paradisiacal and poisonous, as though it were one product of the serpent coiled about the Tree of Life.

One cannot read widely about drugs these days without coming across persistent references to the "drug problem." Drugs are indeed a problem in that they are addictive and encourage strange forms of narcissism which, though they may end fatally, are still attempts to regain paradise. The desire to regain paradise is one of the fundamental ambitions of human nature which nearly every religion encourages, and this illuminates the drug problem from another aspect. If drugs can be used to enter paradise, what are the uses of paradise itself?

Drugs are used the world over, sometimes for entertainment, often for therapy or as a religious observation. Thus the soma plant celebrated in the early Vedic hymns of the East gave such bliss to those who took its juices that it was regarded as a divinity, and the visionary worlds of splendor praised by its devotees are certainly descriptions of the images which it induced. Opinions are divided as to what plant soma was originally; at one time it was thought to be a species of either *Asclepias* or of *Sarcostemma,* though it has recently been identified as *Amanita muscaria,* the fly agaric.

The use of this toadstool and of other hallucinogenic (hallucination-producing) mushrooms may have been much more widespread in the past than we realize, and its effects quite possibly helped to give form to a number of traditional descriptions of heaven. Indeed, the most famous mysteries of antiquity, those of Eleusis, may have used the fly agaric in order to initiate the worshippers into a realization of the divine, which could well account for the veneration in which the mysteries were held. In Mexico before and after the Spanish Conquest several plants were held sacred because of their illuminating properties, ranging from the peyote cactus from which mescalin is derived to a species of *ipomea* containing a relative of lysergic acid (LSD); the *psilocybe* mushroom which was called *teonanactl* or "god's flesh," whose active principle is psilocybine, and *Datura stramonium* or thornapple with its scopolamine and atropine.

Such plants were used to cure illnesses of the soul and of the body, to divine the future and to gain a sense of supernatural knowledge. In South America other plants are used for similar purposes: one Brazilian curer has tracked down some 80 such plants in his own country, including a hallucinatory tree-toadstool. These plants include lianas like *Banisteria caapi,* peppers like *Piptadenia,* cocaine in the Andes, and at least one hallucinogenic animal, a caterpillar found inside bamboo stems.

In Africa, Asia, Siberia and Australia the list of plants which produce psychotropic (mind-changing) effects is long, and where no such plant is available alcohol may be used instead. Modern pharmacology has added to the number of psychotropic substances with highly potent and dangerous derivatives of opium, with anaesthetics, synthetic narcotics, tranquillizers—the original one being a synthetic based on the active principle of *Rauwolfia,* a plant used for centuries in India to calm the mind—pep pills, hallucinogens, and others. However, no modern doctor considers such substances to be sacred, as they would be amongst traditional cultures and as they are, up to a point, among those who use these products for their own enjoyment. This fact in itself has much to do with the existence of a drug problem.

The Religious Use of Drugs

The widespread use of drugs around the world, and especially in our society, makes it plain that man is a discontented animal beset by psychological and physical troubles, by boredom and spiritual ambitions. He uses drugs to relieve pain and illness, and also to change his entire way of looking at things. In religious language, human nature is always wishing to transcend its usual limitations. For waking consciousness is by no means the only kind which it is possible or desirable to experience, and other states can be reached by the use of psychophysical techniques and also by drugs.

Because they change the degree of alertness of the mind in one way or another, it seems probable that drugs interfere with the sleep cycle, either by allowing one to dream while still awake or by using the force of dreams to power action. It seems hardly credible, however, that maté tea, made from the leaf of a South American shrub and containing caffeine, could ever be used to induce trance. Tea, which contains tannin as well as caffeine in quite large quantities, certainly does not have this effect normally, and it was originally celebrated in India and China for its refreshing qualities that allowed the mind to stay awake during meditation. By itself maté could not bring about an oracular state of trance—as it does amongst Indians still living in the Mato Grosso—unless its actions reinforce a process already set in motion by the seer and, by this working together of a psychological technique with a physiological agent, bring about a state of dissociation in which the mind finds a new faculty of expression.

The religious use of drugs, in fact, usually accompanies the practice of shamanism, though shamanism often does without drugs. Shamanism is a technique by which a man, and sometimes a woman, prepares himself by singing, dancing, training and long periods of seclusion during which he meditates, for an influx of untoward inspiration that can carry him into the world of spirits where events on earth are ordained and carried out. It is often a hereditary calling, but may equally well be embraced by those who have either a surplus of mental energy or who have suffered from what we would call a nervous complaint of some severity. Such unsatisfied or unbalanced states of mind are continually looking for a resolution of their frustrations and ambitions, and they do so by using traditional methods which articulate their powers coherently.

Drugs can help to do this because their effects are so similar to those produced by other methods of shamanistic training. An instructive case concerns tobacco, which like maté was used for getting into trance. Throughout the Americas this plant was used much as we use it today, for pleasure and to aid concentration, though it was sometimes accounted a fault in an ordinary man if he smoked it in private. But its most significant use was by shamans who smoked large amounts at one sitting to achieve their ecstatic experiences. The combination of tobacco smoke and overbreathing (causing oxygen intoxication) produces that kind of giddiness and nausea which most people experience with their first cigarette. Giddiness is one of the universal symptoms of ecstasy—the word giddy comes from the Old English *gidig,* meaning possessed by a god—and it is by entering into this giddiness and following down the physiological pathways which it opens up that a shaman is able to dissociate himself from his normal waking self and arrive at a place in his mind where all is certain and a quite different conscious process begins.

What such people have done is to use the forces within the paradisiacal experience for definite ends. The lack of such ends in modern society, as has already been implied, is one reason why we have a drug problem: without a ritual support the mind is often not strong enough to resist the effects of a drug, and so loses its sense of direction. When we consider the power of some drugs, this is not surprising. The incredibly small quantity of 100 microgrammes of lysergic acid is enough to bring about a psychedelic experience in which the mind is profoundly altered in its normal functioning and of which it previously had but the barest suspicion. Indeed many investigators have been so taken aback by these changes that they prefer to call the drug a psychosomimetic, one which produces a condition resembling madness.

The purpose of a ritual setting for the taking of a drug is to prevent madness, by directing the energies which the drug releases into a number of specific channels, and to put paradise into relation with objects in the outside world by establishing a dogmatic plan within the imagination, through which social events can be seen as psychological ones, psychological as physical ones, and physical ones as spiritual.

By such a method even opium, the grandmother of all narcotics, has occasionally been used not merely to enjoy its sumptuous and pearly visions but to carry out a conscious intention. Such is the habit of shamans in parts of Southeast Asia, who take opium to increase the ecstatic effects of dancing and through them to send their spirits upon a supernatural adventure for the curing of illness or the foretelling of the future. The soporific effect of opium is such, however, that its devotees are much more liable to become physically passive, which must be why it is so seldom used in an active and practical manner. It is true that opium is used in the East for conviviality, but its solitary use is difficult to control. Coleridge, who first took laudanum, a derivative of opium, to dull a particularly ferocious toothache and eventually became addicted to it, did manage to write at least one great poem under its influence: or perhaps we should say that *Kubla Khan* composed itself when his mind, still active in its poetic function, directed the opium into a creative activity. But such feats are rare, for the mind's ability to hold its own against the sweetly insidious effects of opium in large quantities is limited, and the drug soon brings about that passive state in which, as Henri Michaux, the modern French poet, has said, "One no longer dreams, one is dreamed."

"O just, subtle and all-conquering opium!" cried de Quincey, author of *Confessions of an English Opium Eater* (1822), who took laudanum as an elixir for his neurasthenia and declared it to be the center of the true religion of which he was the high priest. But religions have hells as well as heavens, and the last stages of his addiction were marked, as they always are, by psychic and physical horrors from which he at last managed to free himself. What is this paradise, as Baudelaire said of hashish, which one buys at the price of one's eternal damnation? But this progression from paradise to the inferno allows one to draw a most interesting parallel between the possessive effects of a drug and those of a spirit, as in Voodoo.

In Voodoo ceremonies we might say that a pact has been entered into with any one of the many gods or spirits of the Haitian pantheon, which are called *loa*. The worshipper is possessed by the loa in such a way that he no longer has conscious control of his actions, and has no memory of what passed when he was possessed. The loa who rides him, as the phrase goes, always has a definite way of behaving—a stereotype, we might say, or schema—and this ability to act out the character of a loa is only achieved after training and initiation. Those who feel the influx of divine energy before they are initiated into Voodoo suffer not only from unfortunate accidents but often from manic outbursts ending in madness. It is the business of Voodoo to avoid this outcome and to see that its initiates can become possessed by this energy and still remain sane.

A Pact with the Devil

We might thus call an addict one who has been possessed by a drug after a private initiation which has no aim other than the desire continually to be possessed, unlike a Voodoo ceremony with its definite beginning and end. The addict cannot but wish his experience will continue forever, even if he realizes that his body will disintegrate under the impact of the drug and that he then can no longer call his soul his own. The narcotic drugs, which slow down physical activity, and the excitants like amphetamine which speed it up, are particularly apt to bring about this state of living on borrowed time; this is presumably not only because they bring out long-term metabolic changes but also because the will cannot detach itself from the pleasures it seeks.

The question of whether it is ethical to take drugs is a difficult one to answer. They have been and still are being used as an aid to meditation, but the masters of this art are unanimous in condemning them, since they tend to inflame the imagination and give it a wrong idea of its powers. From his own experience, Jean Cocteau has said that no one becomes an opium addict unless he has made a pact with it: a pact in which he dedicates his will to the power of the drug. There is no doubt that the mythology surrounding drug-taking reflects certain basic notions about black magic for this reason. Black magic is rightly regarded as a dangerous pastime because it provides immediate gains without immediate pay-

ment: it is a pact with the Devil, who comes later when it suits him and presents a bill on which are written the ominous words, One Soul.

What does it mean, to enter into a pact with the Devil? Freud was much interested in the subject and wrote a study of it at the time when he was still taking cocaine, which he did for ten years. The traditional reasons for such a pact include the obtaining of wealth, of power over men and Nature, and over the hearts of women. But Freud concluded from the case he studied that the central reason was to overcome depression and to find a father-substitute. About cocaine he wrote: "One senses an increase of self-control and feels more vigorous and more capable of work," and he suggested that its effects were due, not to direct stimulation but to the removal of anxiety symptoms, which produced a return to a state of normal euphoria. Anxiety has to do with the superego in his system, and we can enlarge this description by remarking that by removing the "censor" cocaine also removes anxiety. Because of this cocaine may have been an indispensable tool for Freud during his self-analysis: it allowed him to follow the lines of his reasoning into the subconscious without his mental censor putting up a resistance. That Freud escaped from addiction while one of his friends, to whom he had recommended it, died from its effects, suggests that he only did so because he had found a method by which the effects of the drug became subservient to the force of his intellectual drive. He had created a special form of ritual.

Separating Mind from Body

Without this drive cocaine is undoubtedly a danger, as we may see from the religious taking of coca amongst the Kogi of Colombia. This tribe uses it ceremonially to learn the lengthy genealogies and liturgies of their worship, and to fill their minds with the proper religious awe and sense of significance. Coca however has the unfortunate effect of making its takers impotent after a while, and the Kogi are suspicious of their womenfolk (who are not allowed to chew it) and so inefficient as farmers that their children are undernourished. Ironically, the atheists of the tribe who have dropped out of the religion altogether are much healthier and happier, though their neighbors scorn them for losing their chance of immortality. The petrifying effect of coca, even with a religious system to direct it, is certainly partly caused by the fact that the Kogi way of life is beset on all sides by the creole population and has withdrawn into a state of apathy.

Coca is used elsewhere in the Andes to ward off hunger and fatigue, and it does so by numbing these sensations and dissociating the mind from anxieties arising in the body. But anxiety may persist even if its symptoms disappear with the use of a drug. These symptoms emerge again after a long time in an even more disagreeable form, as the nightmare effects of addiction show. When at such a time the use of the drug is stopped, this anxiety must be at least one of the constituents of the most unpleasant withdrawal symptoms.

Attacking the Self

The drugs used in other religious rites tend to be hallucinogenic rather than narcotic or stupefying, and these have a quite different effect upon anxiety. Common to plants with such different active principles as *Banisteria, Amanita* and *Datura* is the production of a sudden and violent surge of energy with visions in which terror and splendor may be equally present. The Viking berserkers seem to have used *Amanita* to endow themselves with a blind and warlike frenzy no opponent could withstand, a frenzy that might last more than a day and after which they sank into a long torpor of exhaustion.

In South America the Indians who take *Banisteria* and other plants fall victim to a similar frenzy (though they do not use it when on war parties), and European travellers who have tried the drug in their company report experiencing the traditional visions, amongst which are those of beasts of prey about to tear them into pieces. Such drugs seem to work by putting psychological anxieties into touch with the musculature, and what is dissociated is the ego from the imagination rather than, as in narcotics, the imagination from anxiety. There may be a connection between the fact that hallucinogens are not physically addictive and that they do not inhibit anxiety.

All these drugs, however, can be used for delicate purposes as well as frenzied ones. One must remember that all shamanistic traditions speak of an initiatory experience in which the body is felt to be torn apart, after which a crystalline body is given by the spirits. Both the dismemberment and the illumination of the body are commonly felt under hallucinogens, even if in a mild fashion, and one can understand dismemberment as the outcome of a drug-induced dissociation in which the normal persona or expression of the personality, is forced to give up its defensive reactions. What is known as a "bad trip" is caused by the anxiety which the approach of such a psychological dismemberment evokes, and which generates an increasing feeling of loss and horror when it cannot be properly discharged. From all accounts a really bad trip has certain similarities to a schizophrenic attack, and hospitals report many instances of bad trips which last for days or even months. The taking of tranquillizers is certainly one way of bringing such an episode to an end, but the traditional method is to accept the attack which the drug makes on the self without fear, an acceptance which transforms anxiety into knowledge and makes it give up its energy to a higher faculty.

But no two drugs attack the self in quite the same way, and they activate different parts of the same underlying process and give rise to different types of anxiety. The drug found in *Amanita* seems to be particularly effective in putting the motor system into spasm, and the shamans who use it must go through a long education in this experience and have grappled with the startling visions it produces before they can master its immediate effects and use them according to their will. *Datura* also activates a sense of physical power together with a psychic ambition that may lead a man so far out of his normal range that a spasm of timidity at the wrong moment may leave him stranded upon an ungovernable activity. Different is the effect of the *psilocybe* mushroom which clinically is said to be that of depersonalization. But there are two sides of every coin, and what is depersonalization to one man may be dematerialization to another: tribal practitioners in fact call upon this effect when they wish to penetrate material obstacles, to free consciousness from its bodily entanglements and allow it to inhabit bodies other than its own.

Drug of the Aztecs

Peyote traditionally used has yet other consequences. It was one of the first hallucinogens to be experimented with in Europe, and is famous for its visions of fantastic and grotesque architecture, of prodigious landscapes and giant figures striding about or petrified into ancient statuary, and of jewels shining with abundant color. All these visions occur without apparent reason, and the Indians phrase this by saying that peyote is a power in itself that works from the outside, a teacher who can show a man the right way to live and answer his questions by giving him an experience to live through.

This quality of the peyote experience allows one to qualify the remark of Michaux that under such drugs one does not dream, one is dreamed. If used correctly peyote has the power of personifying a dream in such a way that it allows the dreamer to keep some part of his self-awareness intact and still questioning. The consequence of searching for a meaning within the visions which inhabit one is that they become increasingly full of meaning themselves.

Peyote is of particular interest because it is the sacrament of the Native American Church, a religion based upon Indian practices and having Christianity for its justification. In was used by the Aztecs for divinatory purposes, and by the Tarahumara and Huichol of northern Mexico as the body of divinity on which all their beliefs centered. This religion was picked up by the Plains Indians at the time of their defeat by the whites and used to rally the wisdom of the Indian past to cope with the degrading changes that overcame them. It was in fact a type of cult such as we often find springing into existence when old ways of life are being destroyed by a powerful and technically more advanced culture, and it is also the only surviving one of several such cults which arose in the Plains.

The Search for Power

The drug problem in the West should probably be seen in the same light: the popularity of drugs is at least partly due to the very rapid changes now occurring in our society. Drugs have always been used to search for power, a power which can be used to enlarge the capacity of the imagination and to bring about change in society. When society itself changes, drugs give a certain kind of life to the imagination which is being stripped of its ancient forms, and a confidence in its ability to live in a strange world. Cannabis has certainly been used in this way from time to time: in Jamaica, for instance, the Rastafari smoke it both for religious and political reasons in the hope that they may soon return to their promised land—Abyssinia, where the Lion of Judah still reigns. Half a century ago or more, cannabis was also the motive cause for a new religion being set up by the Baluba of the Congo: they destroyed their fetish houses, and proclaimed the drug to be a power under which they could live in perpetual friendship and protected from calamity. The drinking of alcohol was forbidden, and those who had committed misdeeds were condemned to smoke a number of pipes of cannabis in order to reform their misconceptions.

Wherever a drug is used by a religion to gain a view and foretaste of divinity, it is treated as though it were a god itself. "We have drunk Soma, we have become immortals, we have arrived at the light, we have reached the gods: what power has malevolence over us now, what can the perfidy of mortals do to us, O Immortal?" So runs one of the hymns of the *Rig Veda,* one of the sacred texts of the East. Opium has been called the hand of God and anchor of salvation, though Cocteau has remarked that it resembles religion as an illusionist resembles Jesus. Tobacco has been called the blessed plant, honor of the earth and gift from Olympus, and both wine and beer have been similarly praised down the centuries. "Our glass was the full moon, the wine is the sun. If the grave is moistened with such a wine, the dead man will rediscover his soul and the corpse will revive," said Ibn al Farid, the medieval Arabian poet. But the wine he talks of here is that of the Spirit, which also descended upon the Apostles at Pentecost so that they spoke with tongues and were accused of being drunk.

A drug is nothing unless it kindles the spirit in a man, though this spirit may be thought of as divine or demoniacal according to predilection. Whichever it may be, the spirit is not man's possession but a gift made to him, and as a gift it has a nature and a morality of its own which must be both wrestled with and obeyed if it is not to bring harm to its host. Every religion has its own way of experiencing and ordering this power, and their often stringent ritual requirements are the product of a long experience in bringing the spirit in touch with the world of men. The religious taking of drugs is one particular example of this: it says plainly enough that amateurism in these matters does little but create a problem, and that if the mind is to reach beyond itself by the use of a drug it must be placed in the service of an idea and a method that makes for wisdom and communion rather than folly and isolation.

The Peyote Way

J. S. Slotkin

In this selection, James Sydney Slotkin provides the reader with an insightful description of the Peyote religion, or "Peyote Way," as it is known by its members. Peyote (the name derived from the Aztec word peyotl*) was used by Indians in central and northern Mexico in pre-Columbian years, its use spreading north to the Indians in the United States and Canada around 1890. Since 1918, Peyotists have been organized as the Native American Church, and, despite recurring legal issues (peyote contains the hallucinogenic agent mescaline and thus is classified as a controlled substance), it has become an important religious movement among North American Indians. Slotkin observes that Peyotists believe their religion is an Indian version of Christianity. Just as there are differences among Christians and their beliefs toward Christianity, so too are there tribal and community differences in the ceremonies and beliefs of Native American Church members. Yet, the practice of Peyotism remains decidedly similar. Slotkin describes the basic structure of a Peyote meeting and the ritual behavior followed by the participants. As an anthropologist and as an officer of the Native American Church, Slotkin himself ingested peyote and here discusses the positive effects it had in curing the various illnesses he incurred while conducting his field research.*

Reprinted from *Tomorrow*, IV, No. 3 (1955–1956), pp. 64–70.

PEYOTE (*LOPHOPHORA WILLIAMSI*) IS A SPINELESS cactus which grows in the northern half of Mexico and for a short distance north of the Texas border. It has attracted attention because it is used as a sacrament in religious rites conducted by Indians in the United States and Canada belonging to the Native American Church. The Peyote Religion or Peyote Way, as it is called by members, is the most widespread contemporary religion among the Indians, and is continually spreading to additional tribes.

From the viewpoint of almost all Peyotists, the religion is an Indian version of Christianity. White Christian theology, ethics, and eschatology have been adopted with modifications which make them more compatible with traditional Indian culture. The religion probably originated among the Kiowa and Comanche in Oklahoma about 1885.

The Peyote rite is an all-night ceremony, lasting approximately from sunset to sunrise, characteristically held in a Plains type tipi. Essentially the rite has four major elements: prayer, singing, eating the sacramental Peyote, and contemplation. The ritual is well defined, being divided into four periods: from sunset to midnight, from midnight to three o'clock, from three o'clock to dawn, and from dawn to morning. Four fixed songs sung by the rite leader, analogous to the fixed songs in the Catholic Mass, mark most of these divisions.

The rite within the tipi begins with the Starting Song; the midnight period is marked by the Midnight Water Song; there is no special song at three o'clock; at dawn there is the Morning Water Song, and the rite ends with the Quitting Song. At midnight sacred water is drunk again and a communion meal eaten.

Usually five people officiate at the rite. Four are men: the leader, often referred to as the Roadman because he leads the group along the Peyote Road (that is, the Peyotist way of life) to salvation; the drum chief who accompanies the leader when he sings; the cedar chief who is in charge of the cedar incense; and the fire chief who maintains a ritual fire and acts as sergeant-at-arms. A close female relative of the leader, usually his wife, brings in, and prays over, the morning water.

In clockwise rotation, starting with the leader, each male participant sings a set of four solo songs; he is accompanied on a water drum by the man to his right. The singing continues from the time of the Starting Song to that of the Morning Water Song; the number of rounds of singing therefore depends upon the number of men present. On most occasions there are four rounds, so that each man sings a total of sixteen songs.

During the rite Peyote is taken in one of the following forms: the fresh whole plant except for roots (green Peyote), the dried top of the plant (Peyote button), or an infusion of the Peyote button in water (Peyote tea). Some people have no difficulty taking Peyote. But many find it bitter, inducing indigestion or nausea. A common complaint is, "It's hard to take Peyote."

The amount taken depends upon the individual, and the solemnity of the ritual occasion. There is great tribal variability in amount used, and accurate figures are virtually impossible to obtain. But in general one might say that under ordinary circumstances the bulk of the people take less than a dozen Peyotes. On the most serious occasions, such as rites held for someone mortally sick, those present take as much Peyote as they can; the capacity of most people seems to range from about four to forty Peyote buttons.

Peyotists have been organized into the Native American Church since 1918. These church groups run the gamut of comprehensiveness from the single local group on the one extreme, to the intertribal and international federation known as the Native American Church of North America, on the other extreme.

In a series of other publications I have discussed the early history of Peyotism ("Peyotism, 1521–1891," *American Anthropologist*, LVII [1955], pp. 202–30), presented an historical and generalized account of the religion (in a book to be published in 1956), and given a detailed description of the Peyote Religion in a single tribe ("Menomini Peyotism," *Transactions of the American Philosophical Society*, XLII [1952], Part 4)—all from the viewpoint of a relatively detached anthropologist. The present essay is different. Here I concentrate on the contemporary uses of, and attitudes toward, sacramental Peyote, and write

as a member and officer of the Native American Church of North America. Of course the presentation is mine, but I think substantially it represents the consensus of our membership.

Long ago God took pity on the Indian. (Opinions vary as to when this happened: when plants were created at the origin of the world, when Jesus lived, or after the white man had successfully invaded this continent.) So God created Peyote and put some of his power into it for the use of Indians. Therefore the Peyotist takes the sacramental Peyote to absorb God's power contained in it, in the same way that the white Christian takes the sacramental bread and wine.

Power is the English term used by Indians for the supernatural force called *mana* by anthropologists; it is equivalent to the New Testament *pneuma*, translated as Holy Spirit or Holy Ghost. Power is needed to live. As a Crow Indian once remarked to me as we were strolling near a highway, man is like an auto; if the car loses its power it cannot go. Physically, power makes a person healthy, and safe when confronted by danger. Spiritually, power gives a person knowledge of how to behave successfully in everyday life, and what to make of one's life as a whole. The Peyotist obtains power from the sacramental Peyote.

Physically, Peyote is used as a divine healer and amulet.

For sick people Peyote is used in various ways. In a mild illness Peyote is taken as a home remedy. Thus when a man has a cold, he drinks hot Peyote tea and goes to bed. In more serious illnesses Peyote is taken during the Peyote rite. Such an illness is due not only to lack of sufficient power, but also to a foreign object within the body. Therefore a seriously sick person who takes Peyote usually vomits, thus expelling the foreign object which is the precipitating cause of the illness; then more Peyote is taken in order to obtain the amount of power needed for health.

In cases of severe illness, the rite itself is held for the purpose of healing the patient; it is often referred to as a doctoring meeting. In addition to having the sick person take Peyote, as in less desperate cases, everyone else present prays to God to give the patient extra power so he or she will recover.

Members may keep a Peyote button at home, or on their person, to protect them from danger. The latter is particularly true of men in the armed forces.

The power within the Peyote wards off harm from anything in the area of its influence. In cases of great danger, as when a young man is about to leave for military service, a prayer meeting is held at which everyone present beseeches God to give the man extra power to avoid harm.

Spiritually, Peyote is used to obtain knowledge. This is known as learning from Peyote. Used properly, Peyote is an inexhaustible teacher. A stock statement is, "You can use Peyote all your life, but you'll never get to the end of what there is to be known from Peyote. Peyote is always teaching you something new." Many Peyotists say that the educated white man obtains his knowledge from books —particularly the Bible; while the uneducated Indian has to obtain his knowledge from Peyote. But the Indian's means of achieving knowledge is superior to that of the white man. The latter learns from books merely what other people have to say; the former learns from Peyote by direct experience.

A Comanche once said, "The white man talks *about* Jesus; we talk *to* Jesus." Thus the individual has a vividly direct experience of what he learns, qualitatively different from inference or hearsay. Therefore the Peyotist, epistemologically speaking, is an individualist and empiricist; he believes only what he himself has experienced.

A Peyotist maxim is, "The only way to find out about Peyote is to take it and learn from Peyote yourself." It may be interesting to know what others have to say; but all that really matters is what one has directly experienced—what he has learned himself from Peyote. This conception of salvation by knowledge, to be achieved by revelation (in this case, through Peyote) rather than through verbal or written learning, is a doctrine similar to that of early Middle Eastern Gnosticism.

The mere act of eating Peyote does not itself bring knowledge. The proper ritual behavior has to be observed before one is granted knowledge through Peyote. Physically, one must be clean, having bathed and put on clean clothes. Spiritually, one must put away all evil thought. Psychologically, one must be conscious of his personal inadequacy, humble, sincere in wanting to obtain the benefits of Peyote, and concentrate on it.

Peyote teaches in a variety of ways.

One common way in which Peyote teaches is by heightening the sensibility of the Peyotist, either in reference to himself or to others.

Heightened sensibility to oneself manifests itself as increased powers of introspection. One aspect of introspection is very important in Peyotism. During the rite a good deal of time is spent in self-evaluation. Finally the individual engages in silent or vocal prayer to God, confessing his sins, repenting, and promising to follow the Peyote Road (that is, the Peyotist ethic) more carefully in the future. If he has spiritual evil within him, Peyote makes him vomit, thus purging him of sin.

Heightened sensibility to others manifests itself as what might be called mental telepathy. One either feels that he knows what others are thinking, or feels that he either influences, or is influenced by, the thoughts of others. In this connection a frequent phenomenon is speaking in tongues, which results from the fact that people from different tribes participate in a rite together, each using his own language; Peyote teaches one the meaning of otherwise unknown languages.

For example, during the rite each male participant in succession sings solo four songs at a time. Recently a Winnebago sitting next to me sang a song with what I heard as a Fox text (Fox is an Algonquian language closely related to Menomini, the language I use in the rite), sung so clearly and distinctly I understood every word.

When he was through, I leaned over and asked, "How come you sang that song in Fox rather than Winnebago (a Siouan language unintelligible to me)?"

"I did sing it in Winnebago," he replied. The afternoon following the rite he sat down next to me and asked me to listen while he repeated the song; this time it was completely unintelligible to me because the effects of Peyote had worn off.

A second common way in which Peyote teaches is by means of revelation, called a vision. The vision is obtained because one has eaten enough Peyote under the proper ritual conditions to obtain the power needed to commune with the spirit world. The vision provides a direct experience (visual, auditory, or a combination of both) of God or some intermediary spirit, such as Jesus, Peyote Spirit (the personification of Peyote), or Waterbird.

The nature of the vision depends upon the personality and problems of the individual. The following are typical: He may be comforted by seeing or hearing some previously unexperienced item of Peyotist belief, or departed loved ones now in a happy existence. He may be guided on the one hand by being shown the way to solve some problem in daily life; on the other hand, he may be reproved for evil thoughts or deeds, and warned to repent.

A third way in which Peyote teaches is by means of mystical experience. This is relatively uncommon. It is limited to Peyotists of a certain personality type among the more knowledgeable members of the church; roughly speaking, they have what white people would call a mystical temperament. These Peyotists, in turn, rarely have visions, and tend to look upon them as distractions. The mystical experience may be said to consist in the harmony of all immediate experience with whatever the individual conceives to be the highest good.

Peyote has the remarkable property of helping one to have a mystical experience for an indefinite period of time, as opposed to most forms of mystical discipline under which the mystical experience commonly lasts for a matter of minutes. Actually I have no idea of how long I could maintain such an experience with Peyote for after about an hour or so it is invariably interrupted by some ritual detail I am required to perform.

What happens to the Peyotist phenomenologically that makes possible the extraordinary results I have described? It seems to depend on both the physiological and psychological effects of Peyote.

Physiologically, Peyote seems to have curative properties. Many times, after a variety of illnesses brought about by fieldwork conditions, I have left a Peyote meeting permanently well again.

Another physiological effect of Peyote is that it reduces the fatigue to an astonishing extent. For instance, I am not robust, but after taking Peyote I can participate in the rite with virtually no fatigue—a rite which requires me to sit on the ground, cross-legged, with no back rest, and without moving, for 10 to 14 hours at a stretch; all this in the absence of food and water.

Psychologically, Peyote increases one's sensitivity to relevant stimuli. This applies to both external and internal stimuli. Externally, for example, the ritual fire has more intense colors when I am under the influence of Peyote. Internally, I find it easier to introspect upon otherwise vague immediate experiences.

At the same time, Peyote decreases one's sensitivity to irrelevant external and internal stimuli. Very little concentration is needed for me to ignore distracting noises inside or outside the tipi. Similarly, extraneous internal sensations or ideas are easily ignored.

Thus, on one occasion I wrote in my field diary, "I could notice no internal sensations. If I paid very close attention, I could observe a vague and faint feeling that suggested that without Peyote my back would be sore from sitting up in one position all night; the same was true of my crossed legs. Also, my mouth might be dry, but I couldn't be sure."

The combination of such effects as absence of fatigue, heightened sensitivity to relevant stimuli, and lowered sensitivity to irrelevant stimuli, should make it easier to understand how the individual is disposed to learn from Peyote under especially created ritual conditions.

To any reader who becomes intrigued by Peyote, two warnings should be given. First, I have discussed the effects of Peyote on those who used it as a sacrament under ritual conditions. The described responses of white people to Peyote under experimental conditions are quite different; in fact, they tend to be psychologically traumatic. Second, Peyote is a sacrament in the Native American Church, which refuses to permit the presence of curiosity seekers at its rites, and vigorously opposes the sale or use of Peyote for nonsacramental purposes.

Ritual Enemas

Peter T. Furst
Michael D. Coe

As we have seen in earlier articles, many of the world's cultures contain religious specialists and laypeople who routinely undergo, for ritual purposes, an altering of their normal state of consciousness. Although this state can be obtained by non-drug related methods, it is not uncommon to find ethnographic accounts of drugs being used to enhance and quicken an altered state of consciousness. This article is about the religious use of various psychoactive substances among the Mayan Indians of Central Mexico. The authors note that although hallucinogenic mushrooms, morning glories, and other psychedelic plants were known and used by the Maya, yet another substance seems to have been employed— intoxicating enemas. This phenomenon quite clearly appears in Maya art as early as the first millennium A.D.; it is curious that it has not been described in the literature over the years. Ritual enemas were well known in South America, where rubber-tree sap was used for bulbed syringes. Furst and Coe reason that a rectal infusion of intoxicants could result in a more quickly and more radically changed state of consciousness, with fewer negative side effects.

Reprinted with permission from *Natural History,* vol. 86, no. 3 (1977), pp. 88–91. Copyright © 1977 the American Museum of Natural History.

WHEN THE SPANIARDS CONQUERED MEXICO IN the sixteenth century, they were at once fascinated and repelled by the Indians' widespread use not only of alcoholic beverages but also of numerous hallucinogenic plants.

From the Spaniards' point of view, however, both served the same purpose—to conjure up visions of demons and devils and to take imbibers from their daily life to supernatural realms.

Distillation was unknown in the New World before the conquest, but Mesoamerican Indians were making, as they still do, a variety of intoxicating ritual drinks, principally by fermenting cactus fruit; agave, or century plant, sap; or maize kernels. Among the Maya, the ritual beverage was balche, made from fermented honey mixed with a bark extract from the balche tree, *Lonchocarpus longistylus*. These concoctions were all taken orally.

But according to a Spanish writer known only as the Anonymous Conqueror, the Huastec people of northern Veracruz and southern Tamaulipas had pulque (fermented agave sap) "squirted into their breech," meaning that they used intoxicating enemas. There are indications that the Aztecs, as well as several other Mesoamerican groups, also followed this practice.

Mesoamerican Indians generally used liquor only on sacred occasions, when, according to such sixteenth-century observers as Bishop Diego de Landa of Yucatán, the Indians often drank themselves into states approaching oblivion. Similarly, the use of many botanical hallucinogens, first described by Fray Bernardino de Sahagún and his contemporaries, was strictly limited to occasions when direct communication with the otherworld was required. Today, the best known of these is peyote, *Lophophora williamsii*, a small, spineless cactus native to the north-central desert of Mexico and southern Texas. The plant now serves as sacrament for 225,000 adherents of the Native American Church and also plays an important role in the religious life of the Huichol Indians of western Mexico. Before the conquest, peyote was widely traded throughout Mexico, where the Aztec priests numbered it among their important magical and medicinal plants.

At the time of the conquest the seeds of the white-flowered morning glory *Turbina corymbosa* were a widely used hallucinogen. In 1960, Albert Hofmann, the Swiss discoverer of LSD (a synthetic hallucinogenic drug), isolated the active alkaloids in this morning glory species and a related species, the purple- or blue-flowered *Ipomoea violacea,* and found them to be lysergic acid derivatives closely resembling LSD-25. The latter species is often referred to as "heavenly blue" in the United States.

Mushrooms also played an important role in pre-conquest Mesoamerican Indian life. Certain species, most of them now known to belong to the genus *Psilocybe,* were perhaps the most extraordinary natural hallucinogens in use in Mexico. The Aztecs called them *teonanácatl,* or "God's flesh." Psychedelic fungi were widely employed in Mexico when the Spaniards came, and their use in divination and supernatural curing survives to this day in central Mexico, as well as in the state of Oaxaca (*see* "Drugs, Chants, and Magic Mushrooms," *Natural History,* December 1975). The Indians even used tobacco to induce ecstatic trance states, which the Spanish only saw as diabolic communication.

While Spanish writers of the sixteenth and seventeenth centuries left us relatively detailed accounts of the use of hallucinogens in central Mexico, there is little mention of this intriguing aspect of native religion among the Maya, who lived farther to the south. The silence is the more puzzling because we have circumstantial evidence of a very early cult of sacred mushrooms in the Maya highlands of Guatemala and the adjacent lowlands, in the form of more than 250 mushroom effigies made of carved stone, many dating to the first millennium B.C.

The Maya were an integral part of Mesoamerican civilization and shared many of its basic assumptions about the nature of the universe and the relationship of humans to the natural and supernatural environment. Like the central Mexicans, they divided the cosmos into upperworlds and underworlds with their respective gods, believed in the cyclical destruction and regeneration of the earth and its inhabitants, and followed the 260-day ritual calendar.

In view of these many similarities, as the Maya scholar J. Eric Thompson has written, it was hard to believe that the Maya did not use intoxicating plants. Thompson searched the pages of sacred traditional books of the Yucatec Maya, set down in the European alphabet in the colonial period, for hints of ecstatic visionary trances through which the priests made their prophecies. In the *Books of Chilam Balam* (jaguar-priest) of Tizimín and Maní, he found mention of trancelike states but no hint whatever of any hallucinogenic plants. He also discovered scattered scenes in Maya relief sculpture that suggested visionary experiences characteristic of hallucinogenic ritual.

This is slim evidence, however, compared with the data from central Mexico, and some Maya scholars are not convinced that the Maya practiced the kinds of ecstatic shamanistic rituals or vision quests with botanical hallucinogens that played so pervasive a role in central Mexico, or among the Zapotecs, Mixtecs, Mazatecs, and other peoples of Oaxaca.

The silence of Spanish colonial writers on the subject of hallucinogenic plants or rituals among the Maya accords well with the view, once widely held among scholars, that the Maya were quite unlike their Mexican contemporaries in temperament, being less preoccupied with warfare and the Dionysian excesses than with the contemplative interpretation of the heavens and the passage of time. But the discovery at Bonampak, Chiapas, of mural paintings that depict, among other events, a fierce battle among Maya warriors, indicate that this traditional view is very wide of the mark.

As specialists have more closely examined Maya art and iconography in recent years, they have accumulated increasing evidence that among the classic Maya, ecstatic ritual was important. One suggestion for this is that some of the major Mexican hallucinogens—among them the morning glories and the hallucinogenic mushroom *Stropharia cubensis*—occur in the Maya country. These and other psychedelic plants were undoubtedly known to the Maya.

Had Maya specialists looked more closely at the earliest dictionaries of the Quiché and Cakchiquel languages, compiled in the first centuries after the conquest of highland Guatemala, they would have discovered mention of several varieties of mushrooms with hallucinogenic properties. One is called *xibalbaj okox (xibalba* means "underworld," or "land of the dead," and *okox,* "mushroom"), said by the sixteenth-century compiler to give those who eat it visions of hell. If the association of this species with the Maya underworld left any doubt of its psychedelic nature, it is dispelled by a later reference to the same species in Fray Tomas Coto's dictionary of the Cakchiquel language. According to him, *xibalbaj okox* was also called *k'aizalah okox,* which translates as the "mushroom that makes one lose one's judgment." Still another fungus, *k'ekc'un,* had inebriating characteristics, and another, *muxan okox,* apparently brought on insanity or caused one to "fall into a swoon."

We have recently come across a wholly unexpected use of psychoactive substances among the Maya—the ritual use of intoxicating enemas, unmistakably depicted in classic Maya art of the first millennium A.D., but not mentioned either in the colonial or the modern literature. This practice is well documented among the inhabitants of South American tropical forests as well as among the Inca and their contemporaries in the Andes, where archeologists have discovered enema syringes.

Sixteenth-century sources describe the Incas as regularly intoxicating themselves with infusions of *willka,* now known to be the potent hallucinogenic seeds of the acacialike *Anadenanthera colubrina* tree. Lowland Indians also used tobacco enemas.

South American Indians were the first people known to use native rubber tree sap for bulbed enema syringes. While medical enemas had a long history in the Old World, having been used by ancient Sumerians and Egyptians, as well as by Hindus, Arabs, Chinese, Greeks, and Romans, the rubber bulb syringe was unknown in Europe until two centuries after the discovery of the New World.

The native Amerindian enema was distinguished from its Old-World counterpart in that its primary purpose was to introduce medicines and intoxicants into the body, while the Old World enema was employed principally to clear the bowels. During the seventeenth and eighteenth centuries, the enema as a relief for constipation, real or imagined, became a craze in Europe—so much so, that Louis XIV had more than 2,000 enemas administered to him during his reign, sometimes even receiving court functionaries and foreign dignitaries during the procedure.

The wide dissemination of the intoxicating enema in South America suggests the discovery by Indians that the rectal administration of intoxicants could radically alter one's state of consciousness more rapidly, and with fewer undesirable side effects, such as nausea, than oral administration. The physiological reason is simple: Substances injected into the rectum enter the colon, the last segment of the large intestine; the principal function of the large intestine is the reabsorption of liquids into the system and the storage of wastes until they can be evacuated. The absorbed liquid immediately enters the bloodstream, which carries it to the brain. An intoxicant or hallucinogen injected rectally closely resembles an intravenous injection in the rapidity of its effects.

The first evidence that not only the Huastecs, whose language is related to the Maya languages, but also the classic Maya knew of and employed the intoxicating enema came to light this past year through the examination of a painted vase in a private collection in New York. This polychrome jar, with a high, vertical neck and flaring rim, was probably painted in the heavily forested Petén district of northern Guatemala during the classic Maya phase, which dated from the third century A.D. to the first decades of the seventh century. Seven male-female pairs, the women easily distinguished by their robes and long hair, are depicted in two horizontal rows. That one woman is fondling a child suggests a familial setting. The activity being portrayed would have brought blushes to the cheeks of the traditional Maya specialist, for while one man is inserting a syringe into his rectum, this delicate task is being carried out for another male by his consort. One male also has a bulbed enema syringe tucked into his belt.

Nine vases, identical in shape to the actual vessel, are painted between the couples, and painted dots at the mouth of each represents a foaming, fermented liquid that is probably balche, the common alcoholic drink among the Maya at the time of the conquest. We must conclude that the people on the vase are taking intoxicating enemas, a practice previously unrecorded for this culture.

An understanding of the scenes depicted on the Maya vase was only the first link in a chain of iconographic discovery of the Mesoamerican enema phenomenon. Suddenly, several previously enigmatic scenes and objects in classic Maya art had new meaning. A small clay figurine from a burial excavated in 1964 by Mexican archeologists on the island of Jaina, in the Gulf of Campeche, depicts a male in squatting position, his hand reaching back to his rectum. For a long time Maya experts were puzzled because the figure's position seemed to represent defecation. But would the Maya have interred such a scene as an offering to their dead?

A small hole in the anus suggested that a piece was missing—that some small object previously inserted there had either become lost during excavation or had been made of some perishable material, long since decayed. The discovery of the enema vase from the Petén district seems to have solved the riddle. The little Maya was probably not defecating but was in the act of giving himself an enema.

The gods themselves were also depicted as indulging in the enema ritual. One Maya vase has the figures of thirty-one underworld deities painted on it. A naturalistically designed enema syringe dangles from the paw of one of the principal figures. Maya experts did not recognize the significance of the object until they had examined the enema vase in New York. As another example, a polychrome bowl from Yucatán, now in the National Museum of Anthropology in Mexico City, shows a naked being with a pointed head injecting himself with liquid.

The ritual importance of the intoxicating enema is highlighted by the involvement in the rite of one of the greatest underworld deities, an old lord associated with earth, water, and agricultural fertility. The Maya may have believed that this god—now identified by Mayanists only by the letter N, but very likely the same deity as the ancient Yucatecan god Pauhatun—consisted of four parts, each part living in the underworld and supporting the four corners of the earth.

The quadripartite god is depicted on a fine vase in a private collection in Chicago. Each of the four parts has a characteristically chapfallen face. Four young and fetching consorts are apparently preparing each of the god's representations for the enema rite. Enema pots with syringes on top are in front of two of the consorts. The female consorts may well represent the important Mother Goddess of the Maya, known as Ixchel, as several figurine examples of the god N embracing this goddess have been found.

The same association of the god N, females and enemas is depicted on another pottery vase, with a consort shown standing behind each god representation and untying his loincloth. Again, the same enema pots are in front of the consorts. So often are the pottery forms and syringes encountered together that we must conclude that they were commonly used in the enema rite.

The explicit depiction of enema rituals on Maya vases has led us to take a new look at a hitherto puzzling type of clay figurine from central Veracruz, which also dates from the classic Maya period. Some archeologists have interpreted these curious sculptures as representing human sacrifice. They are usually of males whose facial expressions suggest pleasure or ecstatic trance, not death. Their legs are raised, either draped over a high pillow or some other type of support of else slightly spread, with the feet up in the air. The posture—and the enraptured look—suggest the intoxicating enema. The reclining position also conforms to the Anonymous Conqueror's description of the method of enema intoxication among the Huastecs.

The hallucinogenic, or intoxicating enema has apparently not disappeared altogether from Middle America. While conducting linguistic research in the Sierra Madre Occidental in western Mexico some years ago, ethnographer Tim Knab was shown a peyote apparatus reportedly used by an elderly woman curer. The bulb was made from a deer's bladder and the tube from the hollow femur of a small deer. The curer prepared peyote by grinding it to a fine pulp and diluting it with water. Instead of taking the peyote by mouth, as for example, the Huichols normally do, either whole or ground (*see* "An Indian Journey to Life's Source," *Natural History*, April 1973), she injected it rectally, experiencing its effects almost at once while avoiding its bitter and acrid taste and the nausea that even some experienced Indian *peyoteros* continue to feel as they chew the sacred plant.

We do not know what materials the ancient Maya used for their syringes. The deer was sacred to the Maya, as it still is to Indians in western Mexico. Still, to make the transition from contemporary western Mexico to the Maya requires an enormous jump in time and space. Fish bladders and the bones of birds, which are prominent in Maya art, might have served for the syringe, as might rubber from the latex tree, which is native to the Maya region. More important than the precise technology, however, is the discovery that, no less than the simpler folk of the South American tropical rain forests, the creators of the most flamboyant and intellectually advanced native civilization in the New World hit upon the enema as a technique of intoxication or ecstasy—a practical means of ritually altering or transforming the ordinary state of consciousness.

The Sound of Rushing Water

Michael Harner

Amazonian Indians, as in the case of forest dwellers everywhere, have a tremendous depth of understanding of the chemical properties of plants indigenous to their habitats. Extracts of plants are prepared as medicines that are used both in the Western pharmacological sense and in the supernatural sense. Preparations take a variety of forms and range from ebene, *the snuff used by the Yanomamo of Brazil and Venezuela, to the tealike drink* natema, *used by the Jívaro of Ecuador. Both contain hallucinogenic properties, provide the taker entry into the spirit world, and offer powers otherwise unattainable without ingestion of potent alkaloid compounds. Yet, elsewhere, as among the Warao of South America, nonhallucinogenic drugs such as tobacco are consumed by shamans to achieve a similar ecstatic state, which, as in the case of* ebene *and* natema, *provides visions of spirit helpers and other agents of the supernatural world (Wilbert 1972). Comparisons such as these give anthropologists insight into the importance of shared belief systems and suggestibility. Describing the use of the Banisteriopsis vine by Jívaro shamans, Michael Harner draws on his field data to illustrate the use of the hallucinogenic drink* natema. *Called by a variety of names in other Amazonian societies, this drug gives extraordinary powers to cure or bewitch, and shamans specialize in either one or the other.*

HE HAD DRUNK, AND NOW HE SOFTLY SANG. Gradually, faint lines and forms began to appear in the darkness, and the shrill music of the *tsentsak,* the spirit helpers, arose around him. The power of the drink fed them. He called, and they came. First, *pangi,* the anaconda, coiled about his head, transmuted into a crown of gold. Then *wampang,* the giant butterfly, hovered above his shoulder and sang to him with its wings. Snakes, spiders, birds, and bats danced in the air above him. On his arms appeared a thousand eyes as his demon helpers emerged to search the night for enemies.

The sound of rushing water filled his ears, and listening to its roar, he knew he possessed the power of *tsungi,* the first shaman. Now he could see. Now he could find the truth. He stared at the stomach of the sick man. Slowly, it became transparent like a shallow mountain stream, and he saw within it, coiling and uncoiling, *makanchi,* the poisonous serpent, who had been sent by the enemy shaman. The real cause of the illness had been found.

The Jívaro Indians of the Ecuadorian Amazon believe that witchcraft is the cause of the vast majority of illnesses and non-violent deaths. The normal waking life, for the Jívaro, is simply "a lie," or illusion, while the true forces that determine daily events are supernatural and can only be seen and manipulated with the aid of hallucinogenic drugs. A reality view of this kind creates a particularly strong demand for specialists who can cross over into the supernatural world at will to deal with the forces that influence and even determine the events of the waking life.

These specialists, called "shamans" by anthropologists, are recognized by the Jívaro as being of two types: bewitching shamans or curing shamans. Both kinds take a hallucinogenic drink, whose Jívaro name is *natema,* in order to enter the supernatural world. This brew, commonly called *yagé,* or *yajé,* in Colombia, *ayahuasca* (Inca "vine of the dead") in Ecuador and Peru, and *caapi* in Brazil, is prepared from segments of a species of the vine *Banisteriopsis,* a genus belonging to the Malpighiaceae. The Jívaro boil it with the leaves of a similar vine, which probably is also a species of *Banisteriopsis,* to produce a tea that contains the powerful hallucinogenic alkaloids harmaline, harmine, d-tetrahydroharmine, and quite possibly dimethyltryptamine (DMT). These compounds have chemical structures and effects similar, but not identical, to LSD, mescaline of the peyote cactus, and psilocybin of the psychotropic Mexican mushroom.

When I first undertook research among the Jívaro in 1956–57, I did not fully appreciate the psychological impact of the *Banisteriopsis* drink upon the native view of reality, but in 1961 I had occasion to drink the hallucinogen in the course of field work with another Upper Amazon Basin tribe. For several hours after drinking the brew, I found myself, although awake, in a world literally beyond my wildest dreams. I met bird-headed people, as well as dragon-like creatures who explained that they were the true gods of this world. I enlisted the services of other spirit helpers in attempting to fly through the far reaches of the Galaxy. Transported into a trance where the supernatural seemed natural, I realized that anthropologists, including myself, had profoundly underestimated the importance of the drug in affecting native ideology. Therefore, in 1964 I returned to the Jívaro to give particular attention to the drug's use by the Jívaro shaman.

The use of the hallucinogenic *natema* drink among the Jívaro makes it possible for almost anyone to achieve the trance state essential for the practice of shamanism. Given the presence of the drug and the felt need to contact the "real," or supernatural, world, it is not surprising that approximately one out of every four Jívaro men is a shaman. Any adult, male or female, who desires to become such a practitioner, simply presents a gift to an already practicing shaman, who administers the *Banisteriopsis* drink and gives some of his own supernatural power—in the form of spirit helpers, or *tsentsak*—to the apprentice. These spirit helpers, or "darts," are the main supernatural forces believed to cause illness and death in daily life. To the non-shaman they are normally invisible, and even shamans can perceive them only under the influence of *natema.*

Shamans send these spirit helpers into the victims' bodies to make them ill or to kill them. At other times, they may suck spirits sent by enemy shamans from the bodies of tribesmen suffering from witchcraft-induced illness. The spirit helpers also form shields that protect their shaman masters from attacks. The following account presents the ideology of Jívaro witchcraft from the point of view of the Indians themselves.

To give the novice some *tsentsak,* the practicing shaman regurgitates what appears to be—to those who have taken *natema*—a brilliant substance in which the spirit helpers are contained. He cuts part of it off with a machete and gives it to the novice to swallow. The recipient experiences pain upon taking it into his stomach and stays on his bed for ten days, repeatedly drinking *natema.* The Jívaro believe they can keep magical darts in their stomachs indefinitely and regurgitate them at will. The shaman donating the *tsentsak* periodically blows and rubs all over the body of the novice, apparently to increase the power of the transfer.

The novice must remain inactive and not engage in sexual intercourse for at least three months. If he fails in self-discipline, as some do, he will not become a successful shaman. At the end of the first month, a *tsentsak* emerges from his mouth. With this magical dart at his disposal, the new shaman experiences a tremendous desire to bewitch. If he casts his *tsentsak* to fulfill this desire, he will become a bewitching shaman. If, on the other hand, the novice can control his impulse and reswallow the first *tsentsak,* he will become a curing shaman.

If the shaman who gave the *tsentsak* to the new man was primarily a bewitcher, rather than a curer, the novice likewise will tend to become a bewitcher. This is because a bewitcher's magical darts have such a desire to kill that their new owner will be strongly inclined to adopt their attitude. One informant said that the urge to kill felt by bewitching shamans came to them with a strength and frequency similar to that of hunger.

Only if the novice shaman is able to abstain from sexual intercourse for five months, will he have the power to kill a man (if he is a bewitcher) or cure a victim (if he is a curer). A full year's abstinence is considered necessary to become a really effective bewitcher or curer.

During the period of sexual abstinence, the new shaman collects all kinds of insects, plants, and other objects, which he now has the power to convert into *tsentsak.* Almost any object, including living insects and worms, can become a *tsentsak* if it is small enough to be swallowed by a shaman. Different types of *tsentsak* are used to cause different kinds and degrees of illness. The greater the variety of these objects that a shaman has in his body, the greater is his ability.

According to Jívaro concepts, each *tsentsak* has a natural and supernatural aspect. The magical dart's natural aspect is that of an ordinary material object as seen without drinking the drug *natema*. But the supernatural and "true" aspect of the *tsentsak* is revealed to the shaman by taking *natema*. When he does this, the magical darts appear in new forms as demons and with new names. In their supernatural aspects, the *tsentsak* are not simply objects but spirit helpers in various forms, such as giant butterflies, jaguars, or monkeys, who actively assist the shaman in his tasks.

Bewitching is carried out against a specific, known individual and thus is almost always done to neighbors or, at the most, fellow tribesmen. Normally, as is the case with intratribal assassination, bewitching is done to avenge a particular offense committed against one's family or friends. Both bewitching and individual assassination contrast with the large-scale headhunting raids for which the Jívaro have become famous, and which were conducted against entire neighborhoods of enemy tribes.

To bewitch, the shaman takes *natema* and secretly approaches the house of his victim. Just out of sight in the forest, he drinks green tobacco juice, enabling him to regurgitate a *tsentsak*, which he throws at his victim as he comes out of his house. If the *tsentsak* is strong enough and is thrown with sufficient force, it will pass all the way through the victim's body causing death within a period of a few days to several weeks. More often, however, the magical dart simply lodges in the victim's body. If the shaman, in his hiding place, fails to see the intended victim, he may instead bewitch any member of the intended victim's family who appears, usually a wife or child. When the shaman's mission is accomplished, he returns secretly to his own home.

One of the distinguishing characteristics of the bewitching process among the Jívaro is that, as far as I could learn, the victim is given no specific indication that someone is bewitching him. The bewitcher does not want his victim to be aware that he is being supernaturally attacked, lest he take protective measures by immediately procuring the services of a curing shaman. Nonetheless, shamans and laymen alike with whom I talked noted that illness invariably follows the bewitchment although the degree of the illness can vary considerably.

A special kind of spirit helper, called a *pasuk*, can aid the bewitching shaman by remaining near the victim in the guise of an insect or animal of the forest after the bewitcher has left. This spirit helper has his own objects to shoot into the victim should a curing shaman succeed in sucking out the *tsentsak* sent earlier by the bewitcher who is the owner of the *pasuk*.

In addition, the bewitcher can enlist the aid of a *wakani* ("soul," or "spirit") bird. Shamans have the power to call these birds and use them as spirit helpers in bewitching victims. The shaman blows on the *wakani* birds and then sends them to the house of the victim to fly around and around the man, frightening him. This is believed to cause fever and insanity, with death resulting shortly thereafter.

After he returns home from bewitching, the shaman may send a *wakani* bird to perch near the house of the victim. Then if a curing shaman sucks out the intruding object, the bewitching shaman sends the *wakani* bird more *tsentsak* to throw from its beak into the victim. By continually resupplying the *wakani* bird with new *tsentsak*, the sorcerer makes it impossible for the curer to rid his patient permanently of the magical darts.

While the *wakani* birds are supernatural servants available to anyone who wishes to use them, the *pasuk*, chief among the spirit helpers, serves only a single shaman. Likewise a shaman possesses only one *pasuk*. The *pasuk*, being specialized for the service of bewitching, has a protective shield to guard it from counterattack by the curing shaman. The curing shaman, under the influence of *natema*, sees the *pasuk* of the bewitcher in human form and size, but "covered with iron except for its eyes." The curing shaman can kill this *pasuk* only by shooting a *tsentsak* into its eyes, the sole vulnerable area in the *pasuk*'s armor. To the person who has not taken the hallucinogenic drink, the *pasuk* usually appears to be simply a tarantula.

Shamans also may kill or injure a person by using magical darts, *anamuk*, to create supernatural animals that attack a victim. If a shaman has a small, pointed armadillo bone *tsentsak*, he can shoot this into a river while the victim is crossing it on a balsa raft or in a canoe. Under the water, this bone manifests itself in its supernatural aspect as an anaconda, which rises up and overturns the craft, causing the victim to drown. The shaman can similarly use a tooth from a killed snake as a *tsentsak*, creating a poisonous serpent to bite his victim. In more or less the same manner, shamans can create jaguars and pumas to kill their victims.

About five years after receiving his *tsentsak*, a bewitching shaman undergoes a test to see if he still retains enough *tsentsak* power to continue to kill successfully. This test involves bewitching a tree. The shaman, under the influence of *natema*, attempts to throw a *tsentsak* through the tree at the point where its two main branches join. If his strength and aim are adequate, the tree appears to split the moment the tsentsak is sent into it. The splitting, however, is invisible to an observer who is not under the influence of the hallucinogen. If the shaman fails, he knows that he is incapable of killing a human victim. This means that, as soon as possible, he must go to a strong shaman and purchase a new supply of *tsentsak*. Until he has the goods with which to pay for this new supply, he is in constant danger, in his proved weakened condition, of being seriously bewitched by other shamans. Therefore, each day, he drinks large quantities of *natema*, tobacco juice, and the extract of yet another drug, *pirípirí*. He also rests on his bed at home to conserve his strength, but tries to conceal his weakened condition from his enemies. When he purchases a new supply of *tsentsak*, he can safely cut down on his consumption of these other substances.

The degree of illness produced in a witchcraft victim is a function of both the force with which the *tsentsak* is shot into the body, and also of the character of the magical dart itself. If a *tsentsak* is shot all the way through the body of a victim, then "there is nothing for a curing shaman to suck out," and the patient dies. If the magical dart lodges within the body, however, it is theoretically possible to cure the victim by sucking. But in actual practice, the sucking is not always considered successful.

The work of the curing shaman is complementary to that of a bewitcher. When a curing shaman is called in to treat a patient, his first task is to see if the illness is due to witchcraft. The usual diagnosis and treatment begin with the curing shaman drinking

natema, tobacco juice, and pirípirí in the late afternoon and early evening. These drugs permit him to see into the body of the patient as though it were glass. If the illness is due to sorcery, the curing shaman will see the intruding object within the patient's body clearly enough to determine whether or not he can cure the sickness.

A shaman sucks magical darts from a patient's body only at night, and in a dark area of the house, for it is only in the dark that he can perceive the drug-induced visions that are the supernatural reality. With the setting of the sun, he alerts his *tsentsak* by whistling the tune of the curing song; after about a quarter of an hour, he starts singing. When he is ready to suck, the shaman regurgitates two *tsentsak* into the sides of his throat and mouth. These must be identical to the one he has seen in the patient's body. He holds one of these in the front of the mouth and the other in the rear. They are expected to catch the supernatural aspect of the magical dart that the shaman sucks out of the patient's body. The *tsentsak* nearest the shaman's lips is supposed to incorporate the sucked-out *tsentsak* essence within itself. If, however, this supernatural essence should get past it, the second magical dart in the mouth blocks the throat so that the intruder cannot enter the interior of the shaman's body. If the curer's two *tsentsak* were to fail to catch the supernatural essence of the *tsentsak*, it would pass down into the shaman's stomach and kill him. Trapped thus within the mouth, this essence is shortly caught by, and incorporated into, the material substance of one of the curing shaman's *tsentsak*. He then "vomits" out this object and displays it to the patient and his family saying, "Now I have sucked it out. Here it is."

The non-shamans think that the material object itself is what has been sucked out, and the shaman does not disillusion them. At the same time, he is not lying, because he knows that the only important thing about a *tsentsak* is its supernatural aspect, or essence, which he sincerely believes he has removed from the patient's body. To explain to the layman that he already had these objects in his mouth would serve no fruitful purpose and would prevent him from displaying such an object as proof that he had effected the cure. Without incontrovertible evidence, he would not be able to convince the patient and his family that he had effected the cure and must be paid.

The ability of the shaman to suck depends largely upon the quantity and strength of his own *tsentsak,* of which he may have hundreds. His magical darts assume their supernatural aspect of spirit helpers when he is under the influence of *natema,* and he sees them as a variety of zoomorphic forms hovering over him, perching on his shoulders, and sticking out of his skin. He sees them helping to suck the patient's body. He must drink tobacco juice every few hours to "keep them fed" so that they will not leave him.

The curing shaman must also deal with any *pasuk* that may be in the patient's vicinity for the purpose of casting more darts. He drinks additional amounts of *natema* in order to see them and engages in *tsentsak* duels with them if they are present. While the *pasuk* is enclosed in iron armor, the shaman himself has his own armor composed of his many *tsentsak.* As long as he is under the influence of *netema,* these magical darts cover his body as a protective shield, and are on the lookout for any enemy *tsentsak* headed toward their master. When these *tsentsak* see such a missile coming, they immediately close up together at the point where the enemy dart is attempting to penetrate, and thereby repel it.

If the curer finds *tsentsak* entering the body of his patient after he has killed *pasuk,* he suspects the presence of a *wakani* bird. The shaman drinks *maikua* (*Datura*), an hallucinogen even more powerful than *natema,* as well as tobacco juice, and silently sneaks into the forest to hunt and kill the bird with *tsentsak.* When he succeeds, the curer returns to the patient's home, blows all over the house to get rid of the "atmosphere" created by the numerous *tsentsak* sent by the bird, and completes his sucking of the patient. Even after all the *tsentsak* are extracted, the shaman may remain another night at the house to suck out any "dirtiness" (*pahuri*) still inside. In the cures which I have witnessed, this sucking is a most noisy process, accompanied by deep, but dry, vomiting.

After sucking out a *tsentsak,* the shaman puts it into a little container. He does not swallow it because it is not his own magical dart and would therefore kill him. Later, he throws the *tsentsak* into the air, and it flies back to the shaman who sent it originally into the patient. *Tsentsak* also fly back to a shaman at the death of a former apprentice who had originally received them from him. Besides receiving

"old" magical darts unexpectedly in this manner, the shaman may have *tsentsak* thrown at him by a bewitcher. Accordingly, shamans constantly drink tobacco juice at all hours of the day and night. Although the tobacco juice is not truly hallucinogenic, it produces a narcotized state, which is believed necessary to keep one's *tsentsak* ready to repel any other magical darts. A shaman does not even dare go for a walk without taking along the green tobacco leaves with which he prepares the juice that keeps his spirit helpers alert. Less frequently, but regularly, he must drink *natema* for the same purpose and to keep in touch with the supernatural reality.

While curing under the influence of *natema,* the curing shaman "sees" the shaman who bewitched his patient. Generally, he can recognize the person, unless it is a shaman who lives far away or in another tribe. The patient's family knows this, and demands to be told the identity of the bewitcher, particularly if the sick person dies. At one curing session I attended, the shaman could not identify the person he had seen in his vision. The brother of the dead man then accused the shaman himself of being responsible. Under such pressure, there is a strong tendency for the curing shaman to attribute each case to a particular bewitcher.

Shamans gradually become weak and must purchase *tsentsak* again and again. Curers tend to become weak in power, especially after curing a patient bewitched by a shaman who has recently received a new supply of magical darts. Thus, the most powerful shamans are those who can repeatedly purchase new supplies of *tsentsak* from other shamans.

Shamans can take back *tsentsak* from others to whom they have previously given them. To accomplish this, the shaman drinks *natema,* and, using his *tsentsak,* creates a "bridge" in the form of a rainbow between himself and the other shaman. Then he shoots a *tsentsak* along this rainbow. This strikes the ground beside the other shaman with an explosion and flash likened to a lightning bolt. The purpose of this is to surprise the other shaman so that he temporarily forgets to maintain his guard over his magical darts, thus permitting the other shaman to suck them back along the rainbow. A shaman who has had his *tsentsak* taken away in this manner will discover that "nothing happens" when he drinks *natema.* The sudden loss of his *tsentsak* will tend to make him ill, but ordinarily the illness is not fatal unless a bewitcher shoots a magical dart into him while he is in this weakened condition. If he has not become disillusioned by his experience, he can again purchase *tsentsak* from some other shaman and resume his calling. Fortunately for anthropology some of these men have chosen to give up shamanism and therefore can be persuaded to reveal their knowledge, no longer having a vested interest in the profession. This divulgence, however, does not serve as a significant threat to practitioners, for words alone can never adequately convey the realities of shamanism. These can only be approached with the aid of *natema,* the chemical door to the invisible world of the Jívaro shaman.

Psychedelic Drugs and Religious Experience

Robert S. de Ropp

To members of the older generation, the mere mention of psychedelic drugs immediately brings to mind the Flower Children movement of the 1960s, Timothy Leary's famous line, "turn on, tune in, drop out," and the Vietnam War. Here, Robert S. de Ropp blends a crystal-clear picture of the dynamic and disruptive history of psychedelic cults of the period with both the theo-philosophical dissection of the cause and nature of religious experience and the socio-legal ramifications of drug use in the West. Going far beyond Leary's so-called seven basic spiritual questions, which were actually scientific questions concerned with knowing rather than with being, de Ropp calls up the views of the apostle Paul, William James, Aldous Huxley, and others in order to differentiate religious experience from the varieties of psychedelic experience. To de Ropp all evidence, with minor exception, shatters the theory that psychedelics allow the drug taker to attain a permanent higher level of being. In fact, the effects achieved through the use of psychedelic drugs to gain religious experience may be acquired in a number of less destructive ways such as meditation, hypnosis, or yoga postures.

In the United States today, as in other countries, drug usage is considered a major social problem—the severity of which is so great that we have declared a war on drugs. After a shift in drug use after the 1960s, it is clear that the use of psychedelics is again on the rise. It is also clear that the questions fielded by de Ropp are as pertinent to this generation as they were to the Flower Children.

THE CULT THAT DEVELOPED IN THE UNITED States among the "Flower Children" of the 1960s had some features that distinguished it from the older cults of peyote and *teo-nanacatyl*. First, the drugs used were mainly synthetic; second, the founders of the cult were white Americans—physicians and psychologists—whose interests in the phenomena observed were scientific as well as religious.

The spiritual forefather of the movement was William James, whose studies of the effects of anesthetics on consciousness are described in *The Varieties of Religious Experience* (1902). It was James who declared that both nitrous oxide and ether, when sufficiently diluted with air, "stimulate the mystical consciousness in an extraordinary degree." It was James who made the statement, so often quoted by the high priests of the psychedelic cult, that "our normal waking consciousness, rational consciousness as we call it, is but one special type of consciousness, whilst all about it, parted from it by the filmiest of screens, there lie potential forms of consciousness entirely different."

James concluded that no account of the universe in its totality could be final if it disregarded those other forms of consciousness. He thought that drugs could open a region but that they failed to provide a map of it. Anesthetics, including alcohol, could lead the explorer into that region, but the insights they offered might not be trustworthy. Nitrous oxide, for instance, might seem to reveal "depth after depth of truth to the inhaler," but the truth tended to fade at the moment of awakening. Alcohol, lifeblood of the cult of Dionysus, was the great exciter of the "yes function" in man and brought its votaries "from the chill periphery of things to the radiant core." James found it part of the mystery and tragedy of life that "whiffs and gleams of something we recognize as excellent should be vouchsafed only in the opening phases of what in its totality, is so degrading a poisoning."

The spiritual descendants of William James did not have much faith in either nitrous oxide or alcohol. For the most part they worked with synthetic psychedelics such as psilocybin, mescaline, and LSD. Their approaches ranged from manic enthusiasm (coupled with the feverish urge to proselytize) to cool scientific detachment. The did not limit themselves to investigating responses that could be defined as religious. The drugs were supposed to exert therapeutic effects quite apart from the religious emotions they aroused, and in various experiments psychedelics were given to prison inmates, neurotics, psychotics, and alcoholics, as well as to those who were dying of cancer. Indeed, it seemed for a while that the psychedelics might be a modern version of the universal panacea.

Timothy Leary was the leader of the more aggressive segment of the psychedelic cult. Witty, charming, and erudite, he possessed an extraordinary capacity to inflame the paranoid tendencies of those solid citizens who collectively constituted "the establishment." His own conversion to the psychedelic religion, a result of his having eaten seven sacred mushrooms, left him with an irresistible urge to proselytize. His new religion, summarized in the three commandments "turn on, tune in, drop out," was firmly linked to the use of psychedelics.

Psychedelics and Religious Experience

There was no doubt in Leary's mind that the effects the psychedelics produced were true religious experiences. To support his opinion he quoted the results obtained by Walter Pahnke, in an experiment described in the press as "the miracle of Marsh Chapel." This experiment involved twenty theology students who had never taken psychedelic drugs and ten guides with considerable psychedelic experience. The students were divided into five groups of four, with two guides assigned to each group. After attending the Good Friday service in the chapel two students in each group and one of the guides received thirty milligrams of psilocybin. The others received a placebo containing nicotinic acid, which produces a tingling sensation but no psychedelic effect. Neither guides nor students knew who had received the psychedelic and who the placebo. Nine subjects who had received psilocybin reported having had what they considered to be religious experi-

ences. Only one of those receiving the placebo made such a claim.

Leary, of course, had gathered much experimental material of his own. In the early 1960s, until he was forced to resign from Harvard, he and Richard Alpert had given psychedelics to a variety of people including psychologists, priests, students, and criminals. Their results indicated that when the setting was supportive but not spiritual, between 40 and 75 percent of psychedelic subjects reported intense, life-changing religious experiences; when the set and setting were supportive and spiritual, from 40 to 90 percent of the experiences were revelatory and mystico-religious.

Leary's attempts to organize a religion around the use of LSD or psilocybin took various external forms: the International Federation for Internal Freedom (IFIF), 1963; the Castalia Foundation, 1963–1966; and the League for Spiritual Discovery, 1966. The aim of this work was to provide conditions in which the state of *ecstasis,* or the expansion of consciousness, could be experienced. In an article entitled "Rationale of the Mexican Psychedelic Training Center," Leary, Alpert, and Ralph Metzner (in Bloom et al., 1964) described the psychedelic experience as a means of attaining *ecstasis* provided the set and the setting were appropriate.

Set and setting were important. In fact they could make the difference between an uplifting religious experience and a terrifying descent into a personal inferno. The authors also stressed the importance of preparation. The psychedelic experience, they said, was a tool, like a telescope or microscope, that could bring other space-time dimensions into focus. People had to be trained to use the tool, after which they would use it not once but whenever a situation arose that called for the examination of other dimensions of reality. The Mexican program was the first to provide a series of guided psychedelic sessions for prepared volunteer subjects. Subjects were encouraged to plan their own sessions. They might, at a certain time, arrange to listen to a particular reading, view an object that would open up a line of association, or hear a certain piece of music.

Special use was made by Leary's group of the Tibetan *Book of the Dead,* which was regarded not only as a guide for the dying but also as an aid to the living. It was "a manual for recognizing and utilizing altered states of consciousness and applying the ecstatic experience in the postsession life." To make the book more relevant to their subjects' psychedelic sessions Leary and company retranslated it from the scholarly style of W. Y. Evans-Wentz into "psychedelic English."

Leary confronted the problem of what constitutes a real religious experience and solved it to his own satisfaction: "The religious experience is the ecstatic, incontrovertibly certain, subjective discovery of answers to seven basic spiritual questions." All issues that did not involve the seven basic questions belonged, in Leary's opinion, to secular games. Liturgical practices, rituals, dogmas, and theological speculations could be, and too often were, completely divorced from spiritual experience.

The "seven basic spiritual questions" listed by Leary were the Power Question, the Life Question, the Human Being Question, the Awareness Question, the Ego Question, the Emotional Question, and the Escape Question. The list covered the entire field of scientific inquiry, from atomic physics to the highest levels of psychology. If science and religion addressed themselves to the same basic questions then what, Leary asked, was the distinction between the two disciplines? He answered by saying that science concerned itself with the measurement of energy processes and sequences of energy transformations; it answered the basic questions using objective, observed, public data. Religion, however, involved a systematic attempt to answer the same questions subjectively, in terms of direct personal experience.

It is interesting to compare Leary's definition of the religious experience with that given earlier by William James. James devoted two chapters in *The Varieties of Religious Experience* to that condition of being he called "saintliness." It was, he declared, "the collective name for the ripe fruits of religion." A group of spiritual emotions in the saintly character formed the habitual center of personal energy. Saintliness was the same in all the religions, and its features could easily be described. They involved

1. a feeling of being in a wider life than that of the world's selfish little interests and a direct conviction of the existence of an ideal power

2. a sense of the friendly continuity of this power with our life and a willing self-surrender to its control

3. a feeling of elation and freedom resulting from the escape from confining selfhood

4. a shifting of the center of emotions toward loving and harmonious affections; a move toward yes and away from no

These characteristics may strike an objective observer as being closer to the essence of religion than Leary's "seven basic spiritual questions," which are really scientific (concerned with knowing) rather than religious (concerned with being). The aim of the religious life is to raise the level of being of its practitioner. Expansion of consciousness is one of the signs of a raised level of being. Indifference to possessions, a capacity for impartial, objective love, indifference to physical discomfort, and a complete freedom from fear of death are other fruits of this raised level. Furthermore, the saintly character does not fluctuate. Its possessor is not saintly today and demonic tomorrow. There is a stability in such a character, an inner consistency, a permanent set of values. There is also an awareness of the presence of the power that some religions call God, and such awareness is a source of repose and confidence.

Of all the fruits of the religious life, the capacity for objective love, for compassion, is the most highly esteemed. The apostle Paul defined this all important emotion in a well-known passage: "Though I speak with the tongues of men and angels, and have not charity, I am become as sounding brass, or a tinkling cymbal" (*1 Cor.* 13:1). What would Paul have said about Leary's seven basic spiritual questions? "Though I . . . understand all mysteries, and all knowledge: and though I have all faith, so that I could remove mountains, and have not charity, I am nothing." Nor is Paul alone in extolling charity as the choicest fruit of the spiritual life. The concept of the *bodhisattva*, who regards with compassion all sentient beings, puts the same emphasis on charity as we see in Christian teachings.

In light of such considerations, it would seem reasonable to ask not whether psychedelic drugs help those who take them to answer Leary's seven questions, but whether they enable the drug taker to attain a permanently higher level of being according to the criteria listed by James. The most that can be said for the psychedelic experience is that sometimes it helps.

R. E. L. Masters and Jean Houston, in their book *The Varieties of Psychedelic Experience*, described the range of subjects' reactions to LSD. They were less naive and dogmatic than Leary and were careful to distinguish what they called "nature mysticism" from real religious experience. The important question was whether, as a result of the insights obtained during the psychedelic experience, the subject really underwent a change equivalent to a religious conversion. One of their subjects, a highly intelligent but devil-obsessed psychologist, did show behavioral changes of a positive character, which suggested that a permanent transformation had occurred. Many other subjects found the experience useful in that it revealed to them unsuspected heights and depths in themselves. On the whole, however, the psychedelic experience did not transport the subjects to a permanently higher level of awareness.

Richard Alpert, who worked closely with Leary at Harvard and later in Mexico and at Millbrook, New York, was also compelled finally to admit that the psychedelic experience led nowhere. He had certainly tried everything: LSD, psilocybin, mescaline, hashish. He had even, on one occasion, locked himself and five other people in a building for three weeks and taken 400 micrograms of LSD every four hours, a total of 2,400 micrograms a day. (One hundred micrograms is enough to produce a strong reaction in anyone unaccustomed to the drug.) "We were very high," said Alpert, describing the experience. But they walked out of the house at the end of three weeks, and within a few days severe depression set in, which was hardly surprising. The orgy of drug taking had left the participants so drained that it was surprising that they could function at all.

Alpert later went to India and found his guru in the foothills of the Himalayas. The guru amazed him by swallowing 915 micrograms of Alpert's "White Lightning," a special batch of high-quality LSD. That much LSD, taken by one unaccustomed to the drug, would constitute an enormous overdose, but the guru showed no reaction whatever. "All day long I'm there, and every now and then he twinkles at me and nothing—nothing happens! That was his answer to my question."

That demonstration of the power of mind over matter was enough for Alpert. He finally stopped trying to obtain results with psychedelics and took up a serious study of yoga. He returned to America transformed into Baba Ram Dass and wrote a book called *Remember: Be Here Now,* a very lively and honest account of his researches. In a section entitled "Psychedelics as an *Upaya*" (the Sanskrit term *upāya*

is generally translated as "skillful means") he conceded that psychedelics might help a person break out of an imprisoning model of reality created by his own mind. But no matter how high a person soared on the wings provided by such drugs, he would always come down, and coming down could bring despair.

How the Psychedelics Work

The psychedelic drugs, which range from simple chemical compounds to highly complex ones, have no single feature in common. The "anaesthetic revelation" so thoroughly explored by William James could be produced by substances as simple as nitrous oxide or ether. Details of molecular composition strongly affect psychedelic action, however. For example, cannabinol, a major component of the hemp resin, appears to produce no effect on the human psyche, but the closely related Δ-9–tetrahydrocannabinol is highly active. Lysergic acid diethylamide is the most powerful psychedelic presently known, but a very small change in the structure of this molecule is sufficient to render it inactive.

Aldous Huxley, whose experiences with mescaline I described earlier, was inclined to attribute the action of this drug to its effect on brain enzymes. Enzymes, he declared, regulate the supply of glucose to the brain cells. Mescaline inhibits the production of these enzymes and thus lowers the amount of glucose available to an organ that is in constant need of sugar. Slowed by its lack of sugar, the brain ceases to function effectively as a reducing valve, making it possible for the possessor of that brain to make contact with Mind at Large, a concept Huxley had borrowed from the Cambridge philosopher C. D. Broad.

Broad's theory suggested that the function of the brain and nervous system is eliminative rather than productive. Each person, said Broad, is capable at each moment of remembering all that has ever happened to him and of perceiving everything that is happening everywhere in the universe. The brain acts as a reducing valve to protect us from being overwhelmed and confused by a mass of useless and irrelevant knowledge. In consequence, although each of us is potentially Mind at Large, what we actually perceive is a mere fraction of what we could perceive. The brain's reducing valve cuts down to a mere trickle the profusion of Mind at Large, leaving the individual free to concentrate on the problem of how to stay alive on the surface of the planet.

Aldous Huxley suggested that in some people a kind of bypass circumvents the reducing valve or that temporary bypasses may be developed as a result of spiritual exercises, through hypnosis, or from the use of drugs. Through these bypasses human beings make contact with certain elements of Mind at Large outside of the carefully selected material that our individual minds regard as a complete picture of reality.

This theory is beyond the reach of science, for it postulates the existence of an entity (Mind at Large) that no physical instrument we possess can detect. But the assertion that mescaline acts by reducing the capacity of the brain to utilize glucose is not likely to be correct. More effective ways of reducing the glucose supply to the brain are known and were formerly employed in the treatment of schizophrenia. The chief of these methods is insulin shock treatment, which certainly cuts down the brain's sugar supply, resulting in convulsions and loss of consciousness by the patient. If Huxley's theory were correct, the schizophrenics who received this treatment should have experienced, before losing consciousness, the sort of effects that are produced by mescaline. There is no evidence that they did so.

To discover how the psychedelics work it would seem that we must postulate something other than oxygen starvation or glucose starvation of the brain. Oxygen starvation does produce strange effects on the brain, as is evident from the experiences of people who have been clinically dead but were later revived. (Their stories have been chronicled by such noted researchers as Elizabeth Kübler-Ross.) It seems probable that such experiences form the basis of the various visions described in the Tibetan *Book of the Dead*. It is also possible that yogins who have mastered *prāṇāyāma,* which allows them to reduce their oxygen intake, can experience after-death states without actually dying. It would be too simple, however, to assume that all the psychedelics operate by reducing the brain's oxygen consumption. The fact is that we really do not know how these substances produce their effects.

Legal, Social, and Spiritual Questions

The abuse of drugs is so widespread in the United States that calm discussion of the religious aspect of

certain drug experiences is next to impossible. The general public hysteria regarding drugs reaches a climax when the subject under discussion is the effect of drugs on the young. Young people, the argument goes, are innocent and must be protected. Laws are therefore passed making it a criminal offense to possess even such a relatively harmless weed as *Cannabis sativa.*

But it is exactly the young who are most likely to seek the psychedelic experience. There are several reasons for this. The young are often rebellious and attracted by forbidden fruit; they are enormously curious and want to explore all aspects of the world; finally, they often have religious impulses that are not satisfied by the standard forms of religion. These religious impulses arise from a deeply rooted craving to experience altered states of consciousness, a craving that becomes particularly powerful during adolescence. The modern teenager—rebellious, confused, and often defiant of authority—may feel particularly fascinated by drugs that offer, or seem to offer, new and strange experiences.

Some thinkers have imagined a society in which supervised psychedelic experience is provided those members, young and not so young, who seek to expand their awareness, but neither our own nor any other industrialized society has yet institutionalized such a practice. It was precisely this idea of the "guided trip" that underlay Leary's ill-starred efforts to found a new religion based on the psychedelic revelation. Given the hostility to drugs that prevails in American official circles, his attempts were bound to fail. He made that failure all the more inevitable by openly defying "the establishment" and taking every opportunity to provoke its wrath. Even two very cautious physicians, John W. Aiken and Louisa Aiken, were unable to win official permission to use peyote in their Church of the New Awakening. They argued that if Indian members of the Native American Church could legally use peyote for religious purposes, members of other races should enjoy the same right. But this logic was not accepted by the authorities.

Prohibition, however, has not prevented the use of psychedelics any more than it prevented the use of alcohol. The results of prohibitory legislation have been to ensure that those who do obtain these drugs pay outrageous prices, are often sold adulterated materials, and, because of lack of guidance and prevailing paranoia, often have bad trips. As long as alcohol and tobacco can be obtained legally, laws prohibiting the possession of substances such as marijuana and peyote will remain unenforceable.

The question that both legal and social prohibitions fail to confront is why some people want to use, or feel they need to use, psychedelic substances. To ask this question is to be open to the understanding that the problems lie not with drugs but with people. These problems are the result of a growing sense of futility that has affected our society. More and more occupations are taken over by automatic machinery and computerized robots. More and more people confront the fact that they will probably never find employment in a society dominated by automation. Under these circumstances, it is not surprising that millions experience what Paul Tillich in *The Courage to Be* called "the abyss of meaningless." To escape from that experience, they may stupefy themselves with alcohol, blunt their sensibilities with barbiturates or heroin, or attempt to get high with the aid of psychedelics.

Those who have experimented with psychedelic drugs and had what they consider to be authentic religious experiences are likely to fall into two groups. In the first are people who understand that the drugs act by using up certain vital energies of the body and that those energies must be replaced. For this reason, they will use drugs rarely and only under special conditions. They will also seek other, less destructive, ways of getting the same results, such as meditation or yoga postures. Sooner or later members of this group will probably abandon the use of psychedelics altogether.

In the second group are those who make the drug experience the center of their spiritual lives, failing to realize that using the drug is robbing them of strength and damaging their health. People in this group inevitably find themselves in trouble not because they have broken man-made laws but because they have broken the laws governing their own spiritual development. Inevitably, the psychedelic used becomes less and less effective and larger doses must be taken. Finally, the drug ceases to have any effect. But the drug user's reliance on his drug may have so weakened his will by that time that serious spiritual efforts become virtually impossible.

This is the main objection to the overuse of psychedelic drugs: they weaken the will, they substitute a dream world for the real world and a dream of religious experience for the real thing. But only personal experience with these drugs can bring this truth home to their votaries.

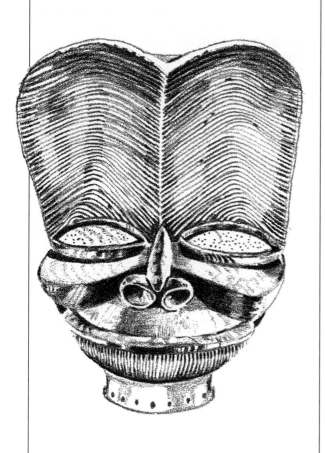

5

Ethnomedicine: Religion and Healing

If a single pervasive thought were to be singled out in this chapter, it would be the importance of culture in determining the etiology and treatment of disease and mental disorders. Just as humans have always suffered from disease, so too have we always responded to it, seeking ways to reduce its debilitating nature or, we hope, to banish it completely. All human societies have belief systems and practices that people turn to in order to identify disease and effect a cure. The integration of the study of these systems of beliefs and practices into the study of non-Western societies has created medical anthropology, the most recent addition to the discipline of anthropology (see Hahn 1995; Lindenbaum and Lock 1993; Mascie-Taylor 1993; Nichter 1992).

Explanations and cures of illnesses may be either natural or supernatural (a naturalistic response would not involve supernatural aid). As P. Stanley Yoder has clearly pointed out, one of the medical anthropologist's most important tasks is to distinguish between different types of causation and to understand the relationship between them, especially because "different types of causal explanations may be involved at different points during the process of diagnosis and

Bacham dance mask from Cameroun.

150

treatment, or may characteristically demand differing treatments" (1982: 15). Moreover, because the range and variability of medical beliefs and practices among the nonliterate peoples of the world is immense, there will be no easy explanation or simple generalization regarding causation and treatment of diseases. But always it will be possible to see the close relationship between medicine and religion, a cultural bonding that occurs in nonliterate, nonindustrialized cultures as well as in modern, technological cultures.

The importance of our understanding of ethnomedical systems is made clear by the fact that a great percentage of the non-Western world's population reside in areas that are not exposed to Western medical treatment. Primary among the concerns of such international groups as the World Health Organization is the role that improved health care can play in the socioeconomic development of Third World countries. The lack of implementation of modern medical care in these areas of the world is caused by a lack both of available funds and of information. Partly in response to the dearth of funding, some health planners have proposed that the most effective way to expand modern primary care would be for Western-trained practitioners to collaborate with traditional practitioners (Bichmann 1979: 175); however, lack of information is the greatest barrier to assessing the feasibility of such proposals in relation to national health goals and planning (Good 1977: 705). Because little substantive information concerning indigenous health care systems is available for non-Western countries, the identification and use of agents of change such as local curers to improve the quality of life in rural areas is extremely difficult.

It is noteworthy to point out also that intercultural contact seems to have caused an increase in both physical and psychological Western-based diseases among non-Western populations; the frustrations of not being able to cure these modern illnesses are liable to increase the use of traditional methods of healing. Other problems of contact also exist. Western-trained medical practitioners find little in traditional systems of health care they consider effective in either the physical or mental realms. On the other hand, modern medical treatment is often rejected by those in the culture. For example, in rural contemporary Kenya, modern medical technology is not changing the pervasive "ancestor spirit-sorcery theory" of disease causation that has traditionally been used to account for all major misfortunes (Kramer and Thomas 1982: 169): as late as 1969 there was still no indication among the rural Kamba of Kenya that modern medicine had made prominent inroads at the level of prevention, either in effecting behavioral change or in modifying etiological beliefs, despite their long exposure to Western techniques.

Determining why the ill choose to accept or reject a system of treatment not only would define who the people in the culture perceive as the proper healer but also would delineate their etiology of disease and their perception of appropriate treatment. What applied anthropologists are attempting to determine are the advantages and disadvantages of each of the health care systems—traditional and modern—in the eyes of the patients as well as the nature of the knowledge healers and their clients draw upon in the process of selecting treatment. Unfortunately, previous research in traditional medical systems has essentially ignored the studied people's own explanations of these criteria, criteria that ordinarily include both natural and supernatural explanations.

Knowledge of the naturalistic treatments and ethnopharmacological systems of non-Western societies is also important, for much of the pharmacopoeia administered by traditional healers does work. (Societies everywhere, including preliterate people, possess naturalistic explanations and treatments. Cures derived from hundreds of wild plants were used by the North American Indians, for example, and techniques for treating headaches and stomachaches, setting broken bones, bloodletting, lancing, cauterization, and other naturalistic skills are well known to the nonliterate world.) However, as the effectiveness of the traditional healer is dependent upon more than the use of proper chemical treatment, diagnosis is made not only at the empirical level but also at the psychological and social levels as well. In speaking of Africa, for example, Wolfgang Bichmann notes that illness does not mean so much an individual event but a disturbance of social relations (1979: 177), and M. F. Lofchie points out that "African medical research has much to contribute to Western medicine: its wholism, emphasis on treatment of the entire family as well as the 'ill' person, and its encyclopedic lore of information about the curative properties of items available in nature—all of these principles are now working their way into Western medical vocabulary" (1982: vii).

For years it was widely believed that only "civilized" people were subject to mental illness, whereas the preliterates of the world led a blissful life free of neuroses and psychoses. It did not take anthropology long to prove that Rousseau's Noble Savage was just as susceptible to the major disorders of the mind as was the individual coping with life in the so-called civilized societies of the world. Anthropologists have sought answers to such important questions as whether mental illness rates differ in preliterate and modern societies; whether styles and types of illnesses vary; and whether it is more difficult to adjust to life in modern cultures than in preliterate cultures. Anthropologists and others have shown, moreover, that traditional healers are particularly effective in the treatment of mental illness, and that their approaches to curing are beneficial to physical diseases as well. Not only are traditional healers' services readily available to the ill, for example, but their system of care is also nondisruptive to those in the culture, and the patient has the support of family members who are nearby or in actual attendance during the treatment. Beyond these advantages, and in contrast with the Western world, Third World countries frequently are much more accepting of those having mental illnesses. Sufferers of these disorders are often stigmatized in the West, and often attempt to hide their medical history.

A seven-year multicultural pilot study of severe mental illness by the World Health Organization reported in the magazine *Science '80* showed that relatively fast and complete recoveries from major psychoses are achieved in developing countries like Nigeria and India. In the United States and other Western countries, however, almost one-half of those who suffer psychotic breakdowns never recover. For example, whereas 58 percent of the Nigerians and 51 percent of the Indians studied had a single psychotic episode and were judged cured after treatment, the cure rate in the industrialized countries ranged from only 6 percent in Denmark to a high of 27 percent in China ("World Psychosis" 1980: 7). Certainly non-Western healing techniques are effective in the treatment of the mentally ill;

however, the treatment of physiological diseases cannot match that of the West. The fact that many non-Western pharmaceuticals may be effective in one society and not in another demonstrates the important relationship of beliefs and cures, in particular the interaction of the healer and the supernatural.

Throughout the world it is possible to place supernaturally caused illnesses into five categories: (1) sorcery, (2) breach of taboo, (3) intrusion of a disease object, (4) intrusion of a disease-causing spirit, and (5) loss of soul (Clements 1932: 252). It is important to note that these categories may not be recognized by certain societies. Indeed, it is a difficult task to determine the frequency and incidence of illnesses, especially mental illnesses, in non-Western, nonindustrialized countries. Native peoples may avoid seeking medical help from a modern health facility, for example; or, if they do seek treatment, there may be a question of accurate recordkeeping.

Anthropologists have correctly noted that the types of cures sought are based not only on the cause but also on the severity of the illness in terms of level of pain and difficulty of curing. Treatment based on cause and severity varies greatly; some non-Western groups maintain that most diseases are of natural origin whereas others blame the supernatural realm for the misfortunes.

It is apparent that anthropologists must understand the integration of ethnomedical systems with the other areas of culture if they are successfully to conduct comparative studies. Ethnomedical systems are deeply ingrained in the structure of societies, functioning in ways that create a positive atmosphere for health care. No longer can we view preliterate medical methods as inferior; indeed, Western society owes much to traditional medicine, not the least of which is the support given to the patient by the family and the community.

The selection of readings in this chapter for the most part deals with supernaturally caused diseases and mental illnesses and their etiology and treatment. Arthur Lehmann opens the chapter with an analysis of ethnomedicine among the Aka hunters and Ngando farmers. He stresses disease categories, disease etiology, treatment, and the role traditional healers (*ngangas*) play in interethnic contacts.

In the second article, Ari Kiev investigates psychotherapy in non-Western societies that have different patterns of food production. He demonstrates a relationship between technology and the complexity of ethnopsychological approaches by traditional healers.

Robert Bergman's article, "A School for Medicine Men," helps us see the similarities and dissimilarities between Navajo medicine men and Western-trained psychiatrists. Bergman also discusses the establishment of a school for Navajo medicine men.

In the next article, William Wedenoja focuses on the role of women as curers in the Balm yards of Jamaica; he keys especially on the relationship between the Balm healers and their patients.

Thomas Bass highlights the psychiatric approach of Thomas Adeoye Lambo, who startled the world of psychiatry by employing the techniques of traditional healers to successfully treat Nigerian patients having serious mental illnesses. Combining free association, group therapy, and behavior modification, Lambo achieved results that far exceeded those of Western therapists.

Claude Lévi-Strauss reminds us of the power of belief and faith in understanding certain psychophysiological mechanisms underlying death and illness caused by magic.

In the final article, Wayland D. Hand demonstrates that the use of folk medical magic and symbolism is not restricted to non-Western cultures. On the contrary, Hand's folkloric research illustrates that in the contemporary western United States, magical beliefs and the symbols that attend them are still popular and practiced in healing.

References

Bichmann, Wolfgang
 1979 "Primary Health Care and Traditional Medicine—Considering the Background of Changing Health Care Concepts in Africa." *Social Science and Medicine* 13B: 175–82.

Clements, Forrest E.
 1932 "Primitive Concepts of Disease." University of California *Publications in American Archaeology and Ethnology* 32 (2): 252.

Good, Charles M.
 1977 "Traditional Medicine: An Agenda for Medical Geography." *Social Science and Medicine* 11: 705–13.

Hahn, Robert A.
 1995 *Sickness and Healing: An Anthropological Perspective.* New Haven, Conn.: Yale University Press.

Kramer, Joyce, and Anthony Thomas
 1982 "The Modes of Maintaining Health in Ukambani, Kenya." In P. S. Yoder, ed., *African Health and Healing Systems: Proceedings of a Symposium,* pp. 159–98. Los Angeles: Crossroads Press, University of California.

Lindenbaum, Shirley, and Margaret Lock, eds.
 1993 *Knowledge, Power, and Practice: The Anthropology of Medicine and Everyday Life.* Berkeley: University of California Press.

Lofchie, M. F.
 1982 "Foreword." In P. Stanley Yoder, ed., *African Health and Healing Systems: Proceedings of a Symposium,* pp. vii–ix. Los Angeles: Crossroads Press, University of California.

Mascie-Taylor, C. G. N., ed.
 1993 *The Anthropology of Disease.* New York: Oxford University Press.

Nichter, Mark, ed.
 1992 *Anthropological Approaches to the Study of Ethnomedicine.* Philadelphia: Gordon and Breach.

"World Psychosis." *Science '80* 1 (6): 7.

Yoder, P. Stanley
 1982 "Issues in the Study of Ethnomedical Systems in Africa." In P. Stanley Yoder, ed., *African Health and Healing Systems: Proceedings of a Symposium,* pp. 1–20. Los Angeles: Crossroads Press, University of California.

Eyes of the *Ngangas:* Ethnomedicine and Power in Central African Republic

Arthur C. Lehmann

People of the Third World have a variety of therapies available for combating diseases, but because of cost, availability, and cultural bias, most rely on ethnomedical or traditional treatment rather than "biomedical" or Western therapies. Dr. Lehmann's field research focuses on the importance of ngangas *(traditional healers) as a source of primary health care for both the Aka Pygmy hunters and their horticultural neighbors, the Ngando of Central African Republic. Tracing the basis and locus of the* ngangas' *mystical diagnostic and healing powers, he shows that they are particularly effective with treatments for mental illness and, to an unknown extent, with herbal treatment of physical illnesses as well. The powers of the Aka* ngangas, *however, are also used to reduce the tensions between themselves and their patrons and to punish those Ngando who have caused the hunters harm. Lehmann points out the necessity of recognizing and treating the social as well as the biological aspects of illness and appeals to health care planners to establish counterpart systems that mobilize popular and biomedical specialists to improve primary health care in the Third World.*

ETHNOMEDICINE (ALSO REFERRED TO AS FOLK, traditional, or popular medicine) is the term used to describe the primary health care system of indigenous people whose medical expertise lies outside "biomedicine" the "modern" medicine of Western societies. Biomedicine does exist in the Third World, but it is unavailable to the masses of inhabitants for a number of reasons. Conversely, although popular medicine has largely been supplanted by biomedicine in the Western world, it still exists and is revived from time to time by waves of dissatisfaction with modern medicine and with the high cost of health care, by the health food movement, and by a variety of other reasons. The point is, all countries have pluralistic systems of health care, but for many members of society the combat against the diseases that have plagued mankind is restricted to the arena of popular medicine.

This is particularly true in the developing nations, such as those of the sub-Saharan regions of Africa, where over 80 percent of the population live in rural areas with a dearth of modern medical help (Bichmann 1979; Green 1980). Between 1984 and the present, I have made six field trips to one such rural area (the most recent in 1994), to study the primary health care practices of Aka Pygmy hunter-gatherers and their horticultural neighbors, the Ngando of Central African Republic (C.A.R.).

The Aka and the Ngando

Several groups of the Pygmies live in a broad strip of forested territory stretching east and west across the center of Equatorial Africa. The two largest societies are the Mbuti of the Inturi Forest of Zaire and the Aka, who live in the Southern Rainforest that extends from the Lobaye River in

This selection was written especially for this volume.

Central African Republic into the People's Republic of the Congo and into Cameroun (Cavalli-Sforza 1971). Like the Mbuti, the Aka are long-time residents of their region. It is on the edge of the Southern Rainforest in and near the village of Bagandu that the Aka Pygmies and the Ngando come into most frequent contact. The proximity, particularly during the dry season from December to April, allows for comparisons of health care systems that would be difficult otherwise, for the Aka move deep into the forest and are relatively inaccessible for a good portion of the year.

Since Turnbull described the symbiotic relationship between Mbuti Pygmies and villagers in Zaire (1965), questions remain as to why Pygmy hunters continue their association with their sedentary neighbors. Bahuchet's work shows that the relationship between the Aka and the Ngando of C.A.R. is one of voluntary mutual dependence in which both groups benefit; indeed, the Aka consider the villagers responsible for their well-being (1985: 549). Aka provide the Ngando with labor, meat, and forest materials while the Ngando pay the Aka with plantation foods, clothes, salt, cigarettes, axes and knives, alcohol, and infrequently, money.

This mutual dependence extends to the health care practices of both societies. Ngando patrons take seriously ill Aka to the dispensary for treatment; Aka consider this service a form of payment that may be withheld by the villagers as a type of punishment. On the other hand, Aka *ngangas* (traditional healers) are called upon to diagnose and treat Ngando illnesses. The powers believed to be held by the *ngangas* are impressive, and few, particularly rural residents, question these powers or the roles they play in everyday life in Central African Republic.

Eyes of the *Ngangas*

The people believe that the *ngangas* intervene on their behalf with the supernatural world to combat malevolent forces and also use herbal expertise to protect them from the myriad of tropical diseases. Elisabeth Motte (1980) has recorded an extensive list of medicines extracted by the *ngangas* from the environment to counter both natural and supernatural illnesses; 80 percent are derived from plants and the remaining 20 percent from animals and minerals.

Both Aka and Ngando *ngangas* acquire their power to diagnose and cure through an extensive apprenticeship ordinarily served under the direction of their fathers, who are practicing healers themselves. This system of inheritance is based on primogeniture, although other than first sons may be chosen to become *ngangas*. Although Ngando *ngangas* may be either male or female, the vast majority are males; all Aka *ngangas* are males. In the absence of the father or if a younger son has the calling to become a healer, he may study under an *nganga* outside the immediate family.

During my six trips to the field, *ngangas* permitted me to question them on their training and initiation into the craft; it became apparent that important consistencies existed. First, almost all male *ngangas* are first sons. Second, fathers expect first sons to become *ngangas;* as they said, "It is natural." Third, the apprenticeship continues from boyhood until the son is himself a *nganga,* at which time he trains his own son. Fourth, every *nganga* expresses firm belief in the powers of his teacher to cure and, it follows, in his own as well. As is the case with healers around the world, despite the trickery sometimes deemed necessary to convince clients of the effectiveness of the cure, the *ngangas* are convinced that their healing techniques will work unless interrupted by stronger powers. Fifth, every *nganga* interviewed maintained strongly that other *ngangas* who were either envious or have a destructive spirit can destroy or weaken the power of a healer, causing him to fail. Sixth, and last, the origin and locus of the *ngangas'* power is believed to be in their eyes.

Over and over I was told that during the final stages of initiation, the master *nganga* had vaccinated the initiate's eyes and placed "medicine" in the wound, thus giving the new *nganga* power to divine and effectively treat illnesses. At first I interpreted the term *vaccination* to mean simply the placement of "medicine" in the eyes, but I was wrong. Using a double-edged razor blade and sometimes a needle, the master *nganga* may cut his apprentice's lower eyelids, the exterior corners of the eyes, or below the eyes (although making marks below the eyes is now considered "antique" I was told); he concludes the ceremony by placing magical medicine in the cuts. At this moment, the student is no longer an apprentice; he has achieved the status of an *nganga* and the ability to diagnose illnesses with the newly acquired power of his eyes.

Not until my last field trip in 1994 did I witness a master *nganga* actually cut the whites of his apprentice's eyes. At the end of an hour-long interview with an *nganga,* which focused on my eliciting his concept of disease etiology in treatment of illness, I casually posed the question I had asked other *ngangas* many times before: "Do you vaccinate your apprentice's eyes?" The *nganga* beckoned his apprentice seated nearby, and, to my amazement, the apprentice immediately placed his head on the master's lap. I quickly retrieved my camcorder which I had just put away! The master removed a razor blade from a match box, spread the student's eyelids apart, deftly made five cuts on the whites of each eye, and squeezed the juice of a leaf (the "medicine") into the wounds. This astounding procedure performed on perhaps the most sensitive of all human parts took less than a total of three minutes and did not appear to cause the apprentice any degree of pain, albeit his eyes were red and his tears profuse.

During the career of an *nganga*, his eyes will be vaccinated many times, thus, it is believed, rejuvenating the power of the eyes to correctly diagnose illness and ensure proper therapy. It is clear that the multiple powers of *ngangas* to cure and to protect members of their band from both physical and mental illnesses as well as from a variety of types of supernatural attacks reside in their eyes.

It follows that the actual divinatory act involves a variety of techniques, particular to each *nganga*, that allows him to use his powers to "see" the cause of the illness and determine its treatment. Some burn a clear, rocklike amber resin called *paka* found deep in the rain forest, staring into the flames to learn the mystery of illness and the appropriate therapy. Some stare into the rays of the sun during diagnosis or gaze into small mirrors to unlock the secret powers of the ancestors in curing. Others concentrate on plates filled with water or large, brilliant chunks of glass. The most common but certainly the most incongruous method of acquiring a vision by both Aka and Ngando *ngangas* today is staring into a light bulb. These are simply stuck into the ground in front of the *nganga* or, as is the case among many village healers, the light bulb is floated in a glass of water during consultation. The appearance of a light bulb surfacing from an Aka *nganga*'s healing paraphernalia in the middle of a rain forest is, to say the least, unique. Western methods of divining—of knowing the unknown—were not, and to some degree are not now, significantly different from the techniques of the *ngangas*. Our ways of "seeing," involving gazing at and "reading" tea leaves, crystal balls, cards, palms, and stars, are still considered appropriate techniques by many.

Therapy Choices and Therapy Managers

A wide variety of therapies coexist in contemporary Africa, and the situation in the village of Bagandu is no exception. The major sources of treatment are Aka *ngangas*, Ngando *ngangas*, kinship therapy (family councils called to resolve illness-causing conflicts between kin), home remedies, Islamic healers (marabouts), and the local nurse at the government dispensary, who is called "doctor" by villagers and hunters alike. In addition, faith healers, herbalists, and local specialists (referred to as "fetishers") all attempt, in varying degrees, to treat mental or physical illness in Bagundu. Intermittently Westerners, such as missionaries, personnel from the U.S. Agency for International Development, and anthropologists, also treat physical ailments. Bagandu is a large village of approximately 3,400 inhabitants, however; most communities are much smaller and have little access to modern treatment. And, as Cavalli-Sforza has noted,

> If the chances of receiving Western medical help for Africans living in remote villages are very limited, those of Pygmies are practically nonexistent. They are even further removed from hospitals. African health agents usually do not treat Pygmies. Medical help comes exceptionally and almost always from rare visiting foreigners. (Cavalli-Sforza 1986: 421)

Residents of Bagandu are fortunate in having both a government dispensary and a pharmacy run by the Catholic church, but prescriptions are extremely costly relative to income, and ready cash is scarce. A more pressing problem is the availability of drugs. Frequently the "doctor" has only enough to treat the simplest ailments such as headaches and small cuts; he must refer thirty to forty patients daily to the Catholic pharmacy, which has more drugs than the dispensary but still is often unable to fill prescriptions for the most frequently prescribed drugs such as penicillin, medicine to counteract parasites, and antibiotic salves. Although the doctor does the best he can under these conditions, patients must often resort only to popular medical treatment —in spite of the fact that family members, the therapy managers, have assessed the illness as one best treated by biomedicine. In spite, too, of the regular unavailability of medicine, the doctor's diagnosis and advice is still sought out—"although many people will consent to go to the dispensary only after having exhausted the resources of traditional medicine" (Motte 1980: 311).

Popular, ethnomedical treatment is administered by kin, *ngangas* (among both the Aka and Ngando villagers), other specialists noted for treatment of specific maladies, and Islamic marabouts, who are recent immigrants from Chad. According to both Aka and Ngando informants, the heaviest burden for health care falls to these ethnomedical systems. Ngando commonly utilize home, kin remedies for minor illnesses, but almost 100 percent indicated that for more serious illnesses they consulted either the doctor or *ngangas* (Aka, Ngando, or both); to a lesser extent they visited specialists. The choice of treatment, made by the family therapy managers, rests not only on the cause and severity of the illness, but also on the availability of therapists expert in the disease or problem, their cost, and their proximity to the patient. Rarely do the residents of Bagandu seek the aid of the marabouts, for example, in part because of the relatively high cost of consultation. Clearly, both popular and biomedical explanations for illness play important roles in the maintenance of health among Bagandu villagers, although popular medicine is the most important therapy resource available. Popular medicine is especially vital for the Aka hunters, whose relative isolation and inferior status (in the eyes of the Ngando) have resulted in less opportunity for biomedical treatment. Yet even they seek out modern medicine for illnesses.

Whatever the system of treatment chosen, it is important to understand that "the management of illness and therapy by a set of close kin is a central aspect of the medical scene in central Africa. . . . The therapy managing group . . . exercises a brokerage function between the sufferer and the specialist" (Janzen 1978: 4). It is the kingroup that determines which therapy is to be used.

Explanations of Illness

The choice of therapy in Bagandu is determined by etiology and severity, as in the West. Unlike Western medicine, however, African ethnomedicine is not restricted to an etiology of only natural causation. Both the Aka and the Ngando spend a great deal of time, energy, and money (or other forms of payments) treating illnesses perceived as being the result of social and cultural imbalances, often described in supernatural terms. Aka and Ngando nosology has accommodated biomedicine without difficulty, but traditional etiology has not become less important to the members of these societies. Frequent supernatural explanations of illness by Aka and Ngando informants inevitably led me to the investigation of witchcraft, curses, spells, or the intervention of ancestors and nameless spirits, all of which were viewed as being responsible for poor health and misfortune. The Aka maintain, for example, that the fourth leading cause of death in Bagandu is witchcraft (diarrhea is the principal cause; measles, second, and convulsions, third [Hewlett 1986: 56]). During my research, it became apparent that a dual model of disease explanation exists among the Aka and Ngando: first, a naturalistic model that fits its Western biomedical counterpart well, and second, a supernaturalistic explanation.

Interviews with village and Pygmy *ngangas* indicated that their medical systems are not significantly different. Indeed, both groups agree that their respective categories of illness etiology are identical. Further, the categories are not mutually exclusive: an illness may be viewed as being natural, but it may be exacerbated by supernatural forces such as witchcraft and spells. Likewise, this phenomenon can be reversed: an illness episode may be caused by supernatural agents but progress into a form that is treatable through biomedical techniques. For example, my relatively educated and ambitious young field assistant, a villager, was cut on the lower leg by a piece of stone while working on a new addition to his house. The wound, eventually becoming infected, caused swelling throughout the leg and groin. As was the case in some of his children's illnesses, the explanation for the wound was witchcraft. It was clear to him that the witch was a neighbor who envied his possessions and his employment by a foreigner. Although the original cut was caused by a supernatural agent, the resulting infection fitted the biomedical model. Treatment by a single injection of penicillin quickly brought the infection under control, although my assistant believed that had the witch been stronger the medicine would not have worked. Here is a case in which, "in addition to the patient's physical signs and social relationships," the passage of time is also crucial to "the unfolding of therapeutic action" (Feierman 1985: 77). As the character of an illness changes with time as the illness runs its course, the therapy manager's decisions may change, because the perceived etiology can shift as a result of a variety of signs, such as a slow-healing wound or open conflict in the patient's social group (Janzen 1978: 9)

Studies on disease etiologies among select African societies (Bibeau 1979; Janzen 1978; Warren 1974) reported that most illnesses had natural causes, and this finding holds for the Ngando villagers as well. At first glance, these data would seem to reduce the importance of *ngangas* and of popular medicine generally, but it is necessary to recognize that *ngangas* treat both natural and supernatural illnesses utilizing both medical and mystical techniques. The question posed by Feierman, "Is popular medicine effective?" (1985: 5), is vital to the evaluation of *ngangas* as healers. Surely some traditional medicines used by these cures must in many cases work, and work regularly enough to earn the sustained support of the general public.

Illnesses of God and Illnesses of Man

Both the Ngando and Aka explanations for natural illnesses lack clarity. Some *ngangas* refer to them as "illnesses of God"; others simply identify them as "natural" ; and still others frequently use both classifications, regularly assigning each label to specific ailments. Hewlett maintains that the Aka sometimes labelled unknown maladies as illnesses of God (1986: personal communication). On the other hand, the Bakongo of neighboring Zaire defined illnesses of God as those "generally, mild conditions which respond readily to therapy when no particular disturbance exists in the immediate social relationships of the sufferer. . . . The notion of 'god' does not imply divine intervention or retribution but simply that the cause is an affliction in the order of things unrelated to human intentions" (Janzen 1978: 9).

Both Janzen's and Hewlett's data are accurate, but my field data show as well as that the explanations of natural illnesses among the Ngando and Aka not only refer to normal mild diseases and sometimes unknown ones but also to specific illnesses named by the *ngangas* and the residents of Bagandu. The confusion surrounding these mixed explanations of disease causation is an important topic for future ethnosemantic or other techniques of emic inquiry by ethnographers.

Residents of Bagandu and both Aka and Ngando *ngangas* categorized sickness caused by witchcraft, magic, curses, spells, and spirits as "illnesses of man." This is the second major disease category.

Witchcraft, for example, while not the main cause of death, is the most frequently named cause of illness in Bagandu. Informants in Bagandu cite the frequency of witchcraft accusations as proof of their viewpoint. Antisocial or troublesome neighbors are frequently accused of being witches and are jailed if the charge is proven. Maladies of all sorts, such as sterility among females, are also commonly attributed to the innate and malevolent power of witches. These types of explanations are not unusual in rural Africa. What is surprising are reports of new illnesses in the village caused by witches.

All Ngando informants claimed, furthermore, that the problem of witchcraft has not diminished over time; on the contrary, it has increased. The thinking is logical: because witchcraft is believed to be inherited, any increase in population is seen also as an inevitable increase in the number of witches in the village. Population figures in the region of the Southern Rainforest have increased somewhat in the past few decades despite epidemics such as measles; accordingly, the incidence of maladies attributed to witches has increased. One informant from Bagandu strongly insisted that witches are not only more numerous but also much more powerful today than before. Offiong (1983) reported a marked increase of witchcraft in Nigeria and adjacent states in West Africa, caused not by inflation of population but by the social strain precipitated by the frustration accompanying lack of achievement after the departure of colonial powers.

Insanity is not a major problem among the Ngando. When it does occur, it is believed to be caused by witchcraft, clan or social problems, evil spirits, and breaking taboos. Faith healers, marabouts, and *ngangas* are seen as effective in the treatment of mental illness due to witchcraft or other causes. The role of faith healers is particularly important in the lives of members of the Prophetical Christian Church in Bagandu. They have strong faith in the healing sessions and maintain that the therapy successfully treats the victims of spirits' attacks. Informants also claim the therapy lasts a long time.

The curse is a common method of venting anger in Bagandu, used by both male and female witches. Informants stated that women use curses more than men and that the subjects of their attacks are often males. The curses of witches are counted as being extremely dangerous in the intended victim. One villager accused the elderly of using the curse as a weapon most frequently. Spell-casting is also common in the area, and males often use spells as a method of seduction.

Most, if not all, residents of Bagandu use charms, portable "fetishes," and various types of magical objects placed in and around their houses for protection. Some of these objects are counter-magical: they simultaneously protect the intended victim and turn the danger away from the victim to the attackers. Counter-magic is not always immediate; results may take years to appear. Charms, fetishes, and other forms of protection are purchased from *ngangas,* marabouts, and other specialists such as herbalists. For example, the Aka and Ngando alike believe that wearing a mole's tooth on a bracelet is the most powerful protection from attacks by witches.

To a lesser extent, spirits are also believed to cause illness. It is problematic whether or not this source of illness deserves a separate category of disease causation. Bahuchet thinks not; rather, he holds that spirit-caused illnesses should be labeled illnesses of God (1986: personal communication). It is interesting to note that in addition to charms and other items put to use in Bagandu, residents supplicate ancestors for aid in times of difficulty. If the ancestors do not respond, and if the victim of the misfortune practices Christianity, he or she will seek the aid of God. Non-Christians and Christians alike commonly ask diviners the cause of their problem, after which they seek the aid of the proper specialist. Revenge for real or imagined attacks on oneself or on loved ones is common. One method is to point a claw of a mole at the wrongdoer. Ngando informants maintain the victim dies soon after. Simple possession of a claw, if discovered, means jail for the owner.

My initial survey of Aka and Ngando *ngangas* in 1984 brought out other origins of illness. Two *ngangas* in Bagandu specifically cited the devil, rather than unnamed evil spirits, as a cause for disease. The higher exposure of villagers to Christianity may account for this attribution: seven denominations are currently represented in the churches of Bagandu. Urban *ngangas* questioned in Bangui, the capital, stressed the use of poison as a cause of illness and death. Although poisonings do not figure prominently as a cause of death among the Aka and Ngando, it is common belief that *ngangas* and others do use poison.

Finally, while not a cause for illness, informants maintained that envious *ngangas* have the power to retard or halt the progress of a cure administered by another. All *ngangas* interviewed in 1984 and 1985 confirmed not only that they have the power to interrupt the healing process of a patient but also that they frequently invoke it. Interestingly, *ngangas* share this awesome power with witches, who are also believed by members of both societies to be able to spoil the "medicine" of healers. This kind of perception of the *ngangas'* power accounts, in part, for their dual character: primarily beneficial to the public, they can also be dangerous.

While the numerical differences in the frequency of physiologically and psychologically rooted illnesses in Bagandu are unknown, Ngando respondents in a small sample were able to list a number of supernaturally caused illnesses that are treatable by *ngangas,* but only a few naturally caused ones. Among the naturalistic illnesses were illnesses of the spleen; *katungba,* deformation of the back; and *Kongo,* "illness of the rainbow." According to Hewlett (1986: 53), *Kongo* causes paralysis of the legs (and sometimes of the arms) and death after the victim steps on a dangerous mushroom growing on a damp spot in the forest where a rainbow-colored snake has rested. Had the Ngando sample been more exhaustive, it is probable that the list of natural diseases would have been greater, although perhaps not as high as the twenty natural illnesses the *ngangas* said they could treat successfully. That impressive list includes malaria, hernia, diarrhea, stomach illness, pregnancy problems, dysentery, influenza, abscesses, general fatigue, traumas (snake bite, miscellaneous wounds, and poisoning), and general and specific bodily pain (spleen, liver, ribs, head, and uterus).

Powers of the *Ngangas*

The powers of the *ngangas* are not limited to controlling and defeating supernatural or natural diseases alone. In the village of Bagandu and in the adjacent Southern Rainforest where the Ngando and Aka hunters come into frequent contact, tensions exist due to the patron-client relationship, which by its very economic nature is negative. These tensions are magnified by ethnic animosity. Without the Akas' mystical power, their economic and social inferiority would result in an even more difficult relationship with the Ngando. Here the powers of the Pygmy *ngangas* play an important part in leveling, to bearable limits, the overshadowing dominance of the Ngando, and it is here that the *ngangas* demonstrate their leadership outside the realm of health care. Each Aka has some form of supernatural protection provided by the *nganga* of his camp to use while in the village. Still, the need exists for the extraordinary powers of the *nganga* himself for those moments of high tension when Aka are confronted by what they consider the most menacing segments of the village population: the police, the mayor, and adolescent males, all of whom, as perceived by the Aka, are dangerous to their personal safety while in the village.

In the summer of 1986, I began to study the attitudes of village patrons toward their Aka clients and, conversely, the attitudes of the so-called wayward servants (Turnbull's term for the Mbuti Pygmy of Zaire, 1965) toward the villagers. Participant observation and selective interviews of patrons, on the one hand, and of hunters, on the other, disclosed other important tangents of power of the Aka in general and of their *ngangas* in particular. First, the Aka often have visible sources of power such as scarification, cords worn on the wrist and neck, and bracelets strung with powerful charms for protection against village witches. These protective devices are provided the Aka by their *ngangas*. Second, and more powerful still, are the hidden powers of the Aka in general, bolstered by the specific powers of the *ngangas*. Although the villagers believe the hunters' power is strongest in the forest, and therefore weaker in the village setting, Aka power commands the respect of the farmers. Third, the villagers acknowledge the Aka expertise in the art of producing a variety of deadly poisons, such as *sepi*, which may be used to punish farmers capable of the most serious crimes against the Pygmies. The obvious functions of these means of protection and retribution, taken from the standpoint of the Aka, are positive. Clearly these powers reduce the tension of the Aka while in the village, but they also control behavior of villagers toward the hunters to some undefinable degree.

Villagers interpret the variety of punishments which the Aka are capable of meting out to wrongdoers as originating in their control of mystical or magical powers. Interestingly, even poisonings are viewed in this way by villagers because of the difficulty of proving that poison rather than mystical power caused illness or death. Although the use of poison is rare, it is used and the threat remains. Georges Guille-Escuret, a French ethnohistorian working in Bagandu in 1985, reported to me that prior to my arrival in the field that year three members of the same household had died on the same day. The head of the family had been accused of repeated thefts of game from the traps and from the camp of an Aka hunter. When confronted with the evidence—a shirt the villager had left at the scene of the thefts—the family rejected the demands of the hunter for compensation for the stolen meat. Soon thereafter, the thief, his wife, and his mother died on the same day. Villagers, who knew of the accusations of theft, interpreted the deaths as the result of poisoning or the mystical powers of the hunter.

Stories of Aka revenge are not uncommon, nor are the Akas' accusations of wrongdoing leveled against the villagers. To the Ngando farmers, the powers of the Aka *ngangas* include the ability to cause death through the use of fetishes, to cause illness to the culprit's eyes, and to direct lightning to strike the perpetrator. These and other impressive powers to punish are seen as real threats to villagers —but the power of the *ngangas* to cure is even more impressive.

Attempts in my research to delineate the strengths and weaknesses of the *ngangas* and other health care specialists discovered a number of qualities/characteristics widely held to be associated with each. First, each specialist is known for specific medical abilities; that is, Aka and Ngando *ngangas* recognize the therapeutic expertise of others in a variety of cures. A *nganga* from Bangui maintained that Aka *ngangas* were generally superior to the village healers in curing. This view is shared by a number of villagers interviewed, who maintained that the power of Aka *ngangas* is greater than that of their own specialists.

The Aka strongly agree with this view, and in a sense the Aka are more propertied in the realm of curing than are the villagers. There is no question that the Aka are better hunters. Despite the Ngandos' greater political and economic power in the area and the social superiority inherent in their patron status, the Ngando need the Aka. All these elements help balance the relationship between the two societies, although the supernatural and curative powers of Aka *ngangas* have not previously been considered to be ingredients in the so-called symbiotic relationship between Pygmy hunters and their horticultural neighbors.

Second, *ngangas* noted for their ability to cure particular illnesses are often called upon for treatment by other *ngangas* who have contracted the disease. Third, with one exception, all the *ngangas* interviewed agree that European drugs, particularly those contained in hypodermic syringes and in pills, are effective in the treatment of natural diseases. One dissenting informant from the capital disdained biomedicine altogether because, as he said, "White men don't believe in us." Fourth, of the fourteen Aka and Ngando *ngangas* interviewed in 1985, only five felt that it was possible for a *nganga* to work successfully with the local doctor (male nurse) who directed the dispensary in Bagandu. All five of these *ngangas* said that if such cooperation did come about, their special contribution would be the treatment of patients having illnesses of man, including mental illness resulting from witchcraft, from magical and spiritual attacks, and from breaking taboos. None of the *ngangas* interviewed had been summoned to work in concert with the doctor. Fifth, as a group of the *ngangas* held that biomedical practitioners are unable to successfully treat mental illnesses and other illnesses resulting from attacks of supernatural agents. In this the general population of the village agree. This is a vitally important reason for the sustained confidence in popular therapy in the region—a confidence that is further strengthened by the belief that the *ngangas* can treat natural illnesses as well. Sixth, the village doctor recognized that the *ngangas* and marabouts do have more success in the treatment of mental illnesses than he does. Although the doctor confided that he has called in a village *nganga* for consultation in a case of witchcraft, he also disclosed that upon frequent occasions he had to remedy the treatment administered by popular specialists for natural diseases. It is important to recognize that unlike biomedical specialists in the capital, the local doctor does appreciate the talents of traditional therapists who successfully practice ethnopsychiatry.

All respondents to this survey recognized the value of biomedicine in the community, and little variation in the types of cures the doctor could effect was brought out. No doubts were raised regarding the necessity of both biomedicine and popular therapy to the proper maintenance of public health. The

spheres of influence and expertise of both types of practitioners, while generally agreed upon by participants of the Ngando survey, did show some variation, but these were no more serious than our own estimates of the abilities of our physicians in the West. In short, all informants utilized both systems of therapy when necessary and if possible.

The continuation of supernatural explanations of illness by both the Ngando and the Aka results in part from tradition, in combination with their lack of knowledge of scientific disease etiology, and in part because of the hidden positive functions of such explanations. Accusations of witchcraft and the use of curses and malevolent magic function to express the anxiety, frustrations, and social disruptions in these societies. These are traditional explanations of disease, with more than a single focus, for they focus on both the physical illness and its sociological cause. "Witchcraft (and by extension other supernatural explanations for illness and disaster) provides an indispensable component in many philosophies of misfortune. It is the friend rather than the foe of mortality" (Lewis 1986: 16). Beyond this rationale, reliance upon practitioners of popular medicine assures the patient that medicine is available for treatment in the absence of Western drugs.

The Role of Ethnomedicine

Among the Aka and Ngando and elsewhere, systems of popular medicine have sustained African societies for centuries. The evolution of popular medicine has guaranteed its good fit to the cultures that have produced it; even as disruptive an element of the system as witchcraft can claim manifest and latent functions that contribute to social control and the promotion of proper behavior.

Unlike Western drug therapies, no quantifiable measure exists for the effectiveness of popular medicine. Good evidence from World Health Organization studies can be brought forth, however, to illustrate the relatively high percentage of success of psychotherapeutic treatment through ethnomedicine in the Third World compared to that achieved in the West. The results of my research in Bagandu also demonstrate the strong preference of villagers for popular medicine in cases involving mental illness and supernaturally caused mental problems. At the same time, the doctor is the preferred source of therapy for the many types of natural disease, while *ngangas* and other specialists still have the confidence of the public in treating other maladies, referred to as illnesses of man and some illnesses of God. Whatever the perceived etiology by kingroup therapy managers, both popular and biomedical therapists treat natural illnesses. It is in this realm of treatment that it is most important to ask, "What parts of popular medicine work?" rather than, "Does popular medicine work?" Because evidence has shown that psychotherapy is more successful in the hands of traditional curers, it is therefore most important to question the effectiveness of popular therapy in handling natural illnesses. Currently, the effectiveness of traditional drugs used for natural diseases is unknown; however, the continued support of popular therapists by both rural and urban Africans indicates a strength in the system. The effectiveness of the *ngangas* may be both psychological and pharmaceutical, and if the ecological niche does provide drugs that do cure natural illnesses, it is vital that these be determined and manufactured commercially in their countries of origin. If we can assume that some traditional drugs are effective, governments must utilize the expertise of healers in identifying these.

It is unrealistic to attempt to train popular therapists in all aspects of biomedicine, just as it is unrealistic to train biomedical specialists in the supernatural treatments applied by popular practitioners. However, neither type of therapist, nor the public, will benefit from the expertise of the other if they remain apart. The task is to make both more effective by incorporating the best of each into a counterpart system that focuses on a basic training of healers in biomedicine. This combination must certainly be a more logical and economic choice than attempting to supply biomedical specialists to every community in Central African Republic, a task too formidable for any country north or south of the Sahara. The significance of this proposal is magnified by the massive numbers for whom biomedicine is unavailable, those who must rely only upon ethnomedicine.

Even if available to all, biomedicine alone is not the final answer to disease control in the Third World. Hepburn succinctly presents strong arguments against total reliance upon the biomedical approach:

> Biomedicine is widely believed to be effective in the cure of sickness. A corollary of this is the belief that if adequate facilities could be provided in the Third World and "native" irrationalities and cultural obstacles could be overcome, the health problems of the people would largely be eliminated. However, this belief is not true, because the effectiveness of biomedicine is limited in three ways. First, many conditions within the accepted defining properties of biomedicine (i.e., physical diseases) cannot be treated effectively. Second, by concentrating on the purely physical, biomedicine simply cannot treat the social aspects of sickness (i.e., illness). Third, cures can only be achieved under favorable environmental and political conditions: if these are not present, biomedicine will be ineffective (1988: 68).

The problems facing societies in Africa are not new. These same issues faced Westerners in the past, and our partial solutions, under unbelievably better conditions, took immense time and effort to achieve. If primary health care in the non-Western world is to improve, the evolutionary process must be quickened by the utilization of existing popular medical systems as a counterpart of biomedicine, by the expansion of biomedical systems, and by the cooperation of international funding agencies with African policymakers, who themselves must erase their antagonism toward ethnomedicine.

The Psychotherapeutic Aspects of Primitive Medicine

Ari Kiev

The purpose of Ari Kiev's article is to explore various aspects of primitive medicine (that is, traditional healing) in order to achieve insight into the nature of psychotherapy. Kiev is primarily interested in discovering what particular attribute of the medicine man gives him the "power to cure" in the eyes of patients. Recognizing the great significance of subsistence patterns and technological development in the complexity of medical activities, Kiev examines three types of societies according to their primary method of food production. At the lowest level, where food gathering is the basic means of existence, there is little medical leadership. In the more complex fishing-hunting societies, healers have more prestige, and social influence is maintained by medical influence. But it is in agricultural societies, the highest level, where one finds all the features characteristic of modern psychotherapy. Kiev also concludes that the medical role seems to be related to the social organization and that, as societies become more complex, the healer increasingly shares the responsibility for success with the patient.

Reproduced by permission of the Society for Applied Anthropology from *Human Organization*, Spring 1962, 21 (1), pp. 25–29.

MEDICAL THINKERS IN WESTERN SOCIETY HAVE only recently come to recognize the importance of psychological and sociological factors in disease and treatment. In primitive societies, however, where the germ theory, antibiotics, and steroids have not as yet been introduced, the emotional, attitudinal, and interpersonal components of disease receive the chief emphasis. Primitive peoples have integrated their medical arts into the conceptual framework of their societies, and all members share the same theories of disease and treatment.

The purpose of this article is to examine certain aspects of primitive medicine in the hope of gaining some insight into the nature of psychotherapy. Following the suggestions of Ackerknecht (1942a) that much of the success of primitive medicine is attributable to the psychotherapeutic aspects of the witch doctor's role, the inquiry focuses on that aspect of the role which affords the witch doctor the "power to cure" in the eyes of his patients. As Frank (1959) has written:

> From the moment the prospective patient approaches psychotherapy until his treatment terminates he is confronted with cues and procedures which tend to impress him both with the importance of the procedure and its promise of relief. These heighten the therapist's potential influence over the patient and . . . probably have some therapeutic effects in themselves by mobilizing his favorable expectancies.

The expectation of cure seems as important in methods of primitive healing as in modern psychotherapy.

We have selected three types of society to examine, classifying each society according to the dominant means of food production: food gathering, fishing-hunting, or agricultural. The significance of food supply is great. With an abundance of it populations can flourish, specialized classes can develop, and societies can prosper and progress. The degree of technological development in dealing with problems relating to food seems to correlate well with the degree of societal development in other spheres. The aspect of the medical role which affords its possessor the "power to cure" seems also to be related to the degree of advancement and complexity of the society to which he belongs. Thus where there is little development of economic techniques and little specialization or division of labor, there should be similar evidences of minimal organization, technical development, and specialization in medical activities. Where surplus supplies are made possible through advanced technology, there should be some interrelationship between medical performance and the economic rewards of the social system.

Food-Gathering Societies

In food-gathering societies, medicine is dominated by magic. There is little systematic organization of theories and practices. Individuals gain power to deal with disease through special personal experiences with supernatural forces. Among the Australian Murngin the healer gains his power to cure through extraordinary experiences with two or three "soul children" (spirits of the dead) (Warner 1958). His magical rituals are exclusively owned and can only be exercised by him. For the Cheyenne a unique dream experience was necessary before a man could learn the special medical lore and language from an elder (Ackerknecht 1942b). Among the Shoshoni the shamans obtained their powers through dreams or by experiencing visions in special situations (Harris 1940). Likewise among the Southern Colorado Ute the unique endowments of the medicine men were attained through dream encounters with the supernatural (Opler 1940).

In these most-primitive societies the therapeutic prowess of the medicine men was due to the conviction of tribesmen that they had special power to cure. As the medicine men shared the same world view, they were able to exert influence partly because of their own belief in their magical powers. They also subscribed to prevalent notions of disease causation and in treatment utilized expected maneuvers. Among the Dobuans the diviner consistently selects disease-causing witches or sorcerers from those who have justified economic grievances against the sick person. Economic reparations suffice to pacify the injured and to repair the sick (Ackerknecht 1942b). The Dobuan diviner acts in accordance with the expectancies of his society and by virtue of his special powers exerts a therapeutic effect.

The close relationship between shaman and sick in terms of beliefs, expectancies, and shared values is demonstrated by Warner's observations on the Murngin (Warner 1958). Here the medicine men rely heavily on the power inherent in group pressure during ceremonials. Among the Murngin it is not only the supernatural power of the healer which is the effective vehicle of cure but also the impact of group attitudes reinforcing the therapist's position during cures. The medicine man in these simpler cultures does not develop his own theories and formulations about disease and cure. He relies on the beliefs of the group and his supernatural capacities in his work but functions as an ordinary citizen at all other times. Elaborate formulations seem to be unnecessary for the continuation of his practices, and since such work usually yields no extra prestige or remuneration in these barely subsisting societies and since there is little leisure time to pursue such intellectual pursuits, we find little evidence of any specifically medical theories among these groups.

Fishing-Hunting

In fishing-hunting societies the nature of the medical role changes. Increased control of environmental forces (particularly food sources) makes possible division of labor, specialization, and increased leisure time. There is greater emphasis on the qualifications for the medical role and a clearly outlined pattern for attaining this role. There is much elaboration of religious and medical beliefs by the medicine men, which ensures their security and strengthens their authority. Demonstrating clearly the manipulative and utilitarian aspects of this role in Eskimo society, Radin (1957) has written:

> In a society where murder is common phenomenon they are rarely murdered. Similarly in a society where women are scarce they have established and maintained the right to cohabit with all women. This unusual priority has come about through organization which has been associated with a complex religious theory and a spectacular shamanistic technique. Their system is designed to keep the contact with the supernatural exclusively in the hands of the angakok (shaman), and to manipulate and exploit the sense of fear of the ordinary man. Fear

seems to be the embracing focus of this religion—fear for the food supply or uncertainty of broken taboos and fear of dead and of malevolent ghosts. The shamans have combined the fear of economic insecurity with the magical formulas and taboos and with the fear of deceased human beings.

The Eskimo shaman attain this influence through special experiences involving genuine suffering from neurotic or epileptoid disorders, trance experiences, ordeals of physical and spiritual isolation away from the group, and adherence to special rituals and taboos while preparing for the assumption of the role. Such experiences are oftentimes sought after by non-neurotic individuals desirous of becoming medicine men. As Radin (1957) has pointed out:

> What was originally due to psychic necessity became the prescribed and mechanical formulae to be employed by anyone who desired to enter the priestly profession or for any successful approach to the supernatural.

The special experiences, status, and abilities of the medicine men in fishing-hunting economies is demonstrated by the Andaman Islanders (Radcliffe-Brown 1948). Here the *oko-jumu*, or medicine men, acquire power to communicate with the spirits, causing illness through "jungle meetings" with the spirits, dream experiences, fainting episodes, or epileptic fits. This supernatural endowment gives the *oko-jumu* the power to cure illness. Often medicine men circulate legends and lore about their derived power and therapeutic prowess, further bolstering their reputations. As a result they receive a good share of the game caught by tribesmen seeking their good will.

Where surplus economy allows for privileged roles the medicine men seem to have self-consciously recognized the value of maintaining power. Writing about Apache shamanistic technique, Opler (1936) has pointed out that the seasoned shaman is often reluctant to accept responsibility for the cure of serious organic disturbances:

> The seasoned shaman who eschews the incurables is usually quick to treat the less serious indispositions and solidify his reputation by rendering prompt relief. . . . The shaman will insist on the impossibility of curing one who is skeptical of the efficacy of the ceremony to be performed or unconvinced of the integrity of the practitioner.

In fishing-hunting societies special experiences were not always the sole criterion for assumption of the medical role. Thus among the Alkatchko Carriers of British Columbia the medicine men obtained only part of their power through visions (Goldman 1940). It was also necessary for the selected individual to be cured by another medicine man and complete a potlatch first. Here therapeutic power derived from actual achievement as well as special experience.

The enhanced social status acquired by the shamans contributed to their personal power and the efficacy of their technique. Privileged status reflected on the power of the individual who attained such status. The shaman among the Puyallup of Puget Sound lived in a bigger house than the other tribesmen and was treated deferentially by all (Smith 1940). Similarly among the Arapaho of Northern Wyoming the medicine men had vested interests in traditional religious forms and derived much material gain from the treatment of disease (Elkin 1940).

Agricultural

Agricultural techniques led to the development of larger and firmer social units. As the security and independence of the average man increased, the medicine man altered the methods used to maintain influence. Thus the prominent features of the medical role in agricultural societies are increased social organization, increased training, and systematization of techniques. There is increased competition, specialization, an emphasis on knowledge and heredity as qualifications for the role, and changes in the notions of disease causation.

Magic becomes increasingly less important. Less emphasis is placed on spirit causation, and illness more often is viewed as the outcome of the sick individual's own activities. Patient responsibility for success of treatment, which is intimately tied in with the medicine man's efforts to maintain status and control, is clearly illustrated by the Nandi of Kenya (Huntingford 1953). There the medicine man does not tolerate any suggestions that his predictions or medicines have failed. Failure of cure is attributed to the neglect of the patient to follow the specific instructions as to their use.

Specialization of medical roles is also prominent. Among the Chiga of Western Uganda homemade treatments such as poultices, blood-letting, or ingestion of herbs are tried first. If these fail the neighborhood specialist not infrequently tries the same cures.

Lastly, the expensive diviner with greater diagnostic and therapeutic ability to cure with complicated techniques of purification and sacrifice is consulted (Edel 1957).

Agricultural societies, in contrast to more primitive societies, make a clear-cut distinction between medicine and religion. Among the Mano of Liberia the first specialist to be consulted is usually an old woman or the local midwife, who is expected to know all the common remedies (Harley 1941). During the first stage of illness a priestess or head of a girl's initiation school might also be consulted. The next specialist would be a man of the medical guild. He might also be a priest of the boy's school. He would have access to the ancestral spirits but would not appeal to them directly except in a general way once a month for personal success. He would know remedies and procedures of a more magical nature calculated to reach evil influences causing the disease. Next would be a diviner to find out what person among the sick man's acquaintances might have cast a spell upon him. The guilty one might be able to do something about it by confessing and removing the spell. With increasing fear and uncertainty and lack of success there is an increased reliance on less empirical and more magical techniques. If death follows, a diviner would try to catch the guilty one by using a poison ordeal.

In many agricultural societies cure is attributed to the medicines rather than to the supernatural powers of the practitioners. Thus among the Fox of Iowa the power to cure was obtained through learning of medical techniques and through vision quests (Joffe 1940). Only intelligent children were taught the correct usage of herbs, and prestige was maintained by a broad knowledge of techniques. Ackerknecht (1942a), writing about the Thonga of South Africa, has commented:

> Medicine men are hereditary. . . . Sometimes the heritage of knowledge is small but a good medicine man tries to combine the activities not only of the diviner and therapist but also of the witchdoctor of the rain and the warm-magician-priest and thus gains a high social standing.

In Tahiti only the able-bodied and sure-footed who were free from personal defects were chosen as candidates for medical training. After a training period novitiates were required to pass examinations in order to graduate (Radin 1957). The Ashanti of West Africa required a three-year novitiate under a recognized master for those who received a call to be medicine men. In the first year, the novitiate must observe such strict taboos as not tapping palm wine, not setting fish traps, and refraining from sexual intercourse. If married he must leave his wife for the training period. During the second year elaborate fetishes are worn and ceremonial ablutions undertaken. In the final year, the candidate is taught water-gazing, divining, how to impregnate charms with various spirits, and other information and techniques for proper performance of the medical arts (Radin 1957).

Discussion

Examination of therapeutic factors in primitive medical roles reveals that it is only in the most advanced primitive societies (agricultural) that all the features characteristic of modern psychotherapy are found. In all societies examined, only some of the features delineated by Frank (1959) as characterizing the dynamics of the patient-doctor relationship are found. In all, the patient relies on the doctor to relieve distress, and favorable expectancies are reinforced by the setting of treatment and the technique of cure. In all, the medicine man has faith in the treatment method, faith in the patient's capacity to respond to the treatment, and adheres to a definite procedure, much as Western psychiatrists do.

All the features characteristic of the Western patient-psychiatrist relationship are found only in the primitive agricultural societies. Thus, among the Navaho, ambiguity is introduced and skillfully manipulated by the medicine man (Kluckhohn and Leighton 1947). The Navaho singer "conveys to patients that they know what is wrong with them but that they [the patients] must find out themselves," a situation which, according to Frank (1959) would heighten ambiguity, which heightens suggestibility and anxiety and increases the desire to please the therapist. This attitude compels patient participation, which, too, increases the likelihood to favorable therapeutic results.

Primitive therapies differ from modern psychiatry in the short-term nature of treatment. Therapeutic ceremonials are familiar to all. Faith in, and expectancy of relief from, the healer is established long before the patient seeks help. The tie-in of treatment with dominant values further increases therapeutic potential. In all societies examined, the medicine man, irrespective of his technical armamentarium, retained and utilized certain prestigious and influential notions about his person. In the most primitive societies, this quality is assigned by the group. In more advanced societies, the shaman cultivates this special quality himself. Coupled with the utilization of a special technique, it permits the medicine man to avoid entering into the intense emotional involvements characteristic of families and friends of the ill. He can remain "objective" and neutral and receive institutional support for this behavior. The support the medicine man receives from the community not only reinforces the patient's belief in the efficacy of the treatment but also minimizes the patient's fears about the medicine man's motives, which might be greater if the medical role was not community sanctioned. This orientation permits the patient to place greater trust in the medicine man as he does in the doctor in Western communities. By adhering to a socially acceptable standardized role, the medicine man gains the power of the role irrespective of personal qualities or abilities. Dissociation from the usual emotional reciprocities between human beings creates a psychological and perhaps therapeutic advantage for the person filling this medical role.

Conclusions

1. A survey of medical roles in a number of primitive societies suggests certain generalizations of interest to psychiatry. In contrast to the notion that all primitive medicines are fundamentally the same, examination reveals certain differences in medical systems which seem related to economic and technological development. In the most primitive societies, where food gathering is the basic means of food supply, there is little medical leadership, few privileges accorded to the medicine men, and little evidence of a systematized set of medical ideas. The medicine men assume their roles by virtue of extraordinary experiences with the supernatural forces believed to be responsible for illness.

In the fishing-hunting societies where medicine men obtain greater prestige and economic reward there is a deliberate attempt to maintain social influence by maintaining medical influence. More specific qualifications are devised for assumption of medical roles and there is a more elaborate systematization of medical theory. Where changes in economic structure have been introduced, as for example when the Fox of Iowa were moved on to reservations, the influence of the shaman declines and his therapeutic powers abate as well.

Agricultural societies place a greater emphasis on knowledge and acquire skills as qualifications for the medical roles. Medicine men are more often organized into medical societies, and one often finds specialization of functions and elaborate training programs.

2. The nature of the medical role seems related to the nature of the social organization. As economic differentiation becomes possible the shamans exert influences to provide themselves with surplus, special privileges, etc. Where the shamans have obtained valued wealth and prestige they utilize the social power inherent in such attainments in their medical work. The special power of the shaman is tied in with the dominant belief and value systems of his society. Where supernatural forces are deemed responsible for illness the shaman is the one who can contact the supernatural. Where successful cures are attributed to drugs his power is his "knowledge" of the drugs or herbs. The relationship between therapeutic effectiveness and social values has been demonstrated by Redlich and Hollingshead (1958) to exist in our society, where, for example, lower-class patients come to psychiatrists expecting pills and injections, not anticipating that psychotherapy entails talking.

3. With increasing complexity of society the medicine man increasingly shares the responsibility for treatment success with the patient. In food-gathering societies the shamans' success in treatment seems to be due to their belief and the patient's belief in their supernatural powers. In fishing-hunting societies the shaman increases his influence over the society and his patients through induction or perpetuation of fear among patients, through careful selection of curable patients and through much secrecy and exclusiveness about his techniques and medicines. In agricultural societies the shaman is less compelled to resort to sleight of hand. His power derives more from knowledge and skill and he derives security from medical organizations. He deliberately utilizes the guilt feelings of the sick and manipulates the extent of patient participation in treatment. He seems more aware of the relationship between taboo violation and the development of illness than in the more primitive societies. This is akin to modern Western notions ascribing psychiatric illness primarily to the interpersonal and intrapsychic conflicts of the patient.

A School for Medicine Men

Robert Bergman

The anthropological study of mental illness demonstrates that the types and frequency of mental disorders vary from one culture to another, as do the diagnosis and treatment of the illness. In this article Robert Bergman discusses a training school for Navajo medicine men founded by the Navajo themselves at Rough Rock, Arizona, a community on the Navajo reservation. As a non-Indian psychiatrist working for the Indian Health Service, the author volunteered his professional services to the fledgling school. Working side by side with the Navajo medicine men, or "singers," as they are called, Bergman analyzed the nature of Navajo curative ceremonies and their effects on patients. The clash of folk medicine and modern scientific medicine has received considerable attention by anthropologists, and reports of fear and grief felt by non-Western patients undergoing modern medical treatment are common. If preliterate patients and their curers are ignorant of the procedures and philosophies underlying modern medicine, so too are those trained in modern medicine ignorant of folk medicine and its accomplishments.

Reprinted from the *American Journal of Psychiatry,* vol. 130, no. 6 (1973), pp. 663–66, by permission of the author and the American Psychiatric Association. Copyright 1973 the American Psychiatric Association.

THIS PAPER IS AN ACCOUNT OF HOW A NAVAJO community set up its own medical school and how a non-Indian psychiatrist became involved in it. In order to understand what happened one must have some acquaintance with the nature of Navajo medicine. This subject has received an enormous amount of attention from anthropologists and other behavioral scientists. I will make no attempt here to review the extensive anthropologic literature except to recommend the great works of Haile (1950), Reichard (1938), and Kluckhohn and associates (1940, 1956, 1967 [see "References" in the Bibliography]). The psychiatric literature is less extensive. It includes the early article of Pfister (1932), which seems to me to be remarkably insightful and sound in spite of having been based on very little and quite secondhand evidence. The Leightons in 1941 described Navajo ceremonials beautifully and explained many of their beneficial elements. Sandner (1970) reported his work with Navajo medicine men to the APA three years ago. Almost everyone agrees that the ceremonies work.

Background

Navajo practitioners generally fall into three categories. The herbalists know a variety of medicinal plants, which are used primarily for symptomatic relief. The diagnosticians are shamans who work by inspiration. By one of several techniques, such as hand trembling, crystal gazing, or star gazing, they divine the nature and cause of an illness and make an appropriate referral to a member of the third and highest status group, the singers. The singers (I will use the terms "ceremonialist," "medicine man," and "singer" synonymously) do the only truly curative work, and it is a school to train them that I will be discussing.

Navajo nosology classes diseases by etiology; identical illnesses often have similar symptoms, but they need not. Note that psychiatric nosology is similar, e.g., depression is often characterized by insomnia, but sometimes the reverse can be true. A seriously oversimplified statement of Navajo etiology is that disease is caused by a disharmony with the universe, including the universe of other men. A singer restores this harmony by performing a ceremony proper to the case. Little or no reliance is placed on herbs or other medicines and, as is the case with psychiatry (at least from the psychoanalytic viewpoint), this absence of organic measures confers high status.

No one seems to know precisely how many ceremonies there are, but there are many. Important ones last five or nine nights and are difficult and elaborate to a degree approached among us physicians, I think, only by open heart surgery. The proper performance of a major sing requires the presence of the entire extended family and many other connections of the patient. The immediate family must feed all of these people for days. Many of the people present have important roles in the performance, such as chanting, public speaking, dancing in costume, leading group discussions, and many other prescribed activities of a more or less ritualized nature. For the singer himself the performance requires the letter-perfect performance of 50 to 100 hours of ritual chant (something approaching the recitation of the New Testament from memory), the production of several beautiful and ornate sand paintings, the recitation of the myth connected with the ceremony, and the management of a very large and difficult group process.

Non-Navajo explanations of why all this effort helps anyone tend to be rather offensive to the medicine men themselves, and *their* explanations, if they should feel like giving any, tend to be unsatisfying to us since they are based on the supernatural. The difference may not be as great as it appears, however. Traditional Navajos talk frequently in symbols: "We are glad you came from Washington to talk with us. There are many mountains between here and Washington," which translates as, "Communication with the federal government is difficult. We are glad you are making an effort to improve it." They also reject the notion that they are using figures of speech. They do not attach as much significance to the distinctions among different levels of reality as we do, and like some poets, they reject as stupid and destructive any attempt to translate their words into ordinary language. Though it seems to me that their myths and chants are symbols of human social-psychological forces and events, they would regard such a statement as silly and missing the point. Nevertheless, I will make a slight attempt in that direction.

The Rituals

For the past six years, I have been practicing psychiatry among the Navajo people. I have often referred patients to medicine men (who in turn occasionally refer patients to me). I have also often consulted medicine men, and patients have often told me about the medicine men's traditional cures and their feelings about these cures. It seems to me, although my knowledge of the sings is very limited, that the ceremony performed is almost always symbolically appropriate to the case. Pathologically prolonged grief reactions, for example, are almost always treated with a ceremony that removes the influence of the dead from the living and turns the patient's attention back toward life. "Treatment of a dream by a dream," Pfister called it.

It seems to me that the singers and we psychiatrists are the converse of one another with regard to our attitude toward ritual. To them ritual is the main focus: What is unvaryingly their practice from one case to another is at the center of their thought. Informal interaction with the patient and his family is considered important in an informal sort of way. This kind of interaction is not what is taught explicitly but only what is taught by the by. Our ritual, which I would argue is fairly elaborate, is not taught as the central part of psychiatry; rather, the more varying interaction is taught explicitly to psychiatry residents—ritual being taught by the by. In any event the singers do manage an intricate family interaction that, I think, has several important effects: (1) the patient is assured that his family cares for him by the tremendous effort being made; (2) the prolonged and intense contact makes it inevitable that conflicts are revealed and, if things are handled skillfully, resolved; and (3) a time of moratorium and turning point are established.

At the time I first heard of the medicine-man school in 1967, I was already quite convinced of the value of Navajo medicine. Aside from the cases I had seen, I was greatly influenced by my contact with a singer named Thomas Largewhiskers. Mr. Largewhiskers, who is now 100 years old, agreed to be my consultant and to teach me a little of what he knew. I first looked him up after seeing a formerly psychotic patient who attributed her remarkable and well-documented improvement to him. At the time of our first meeting I tried to explain what I do and said that I wanted to learn from him. He replied, "I don't know what you learned from books, but the most important thing I learned from my grandfathers was that there is a part of the mind that we don't really know about and that it is that part that is most important in whether we become sick or remain well." When he told me some of his life story it impressed me that he had become interested in being a singer when, as a young man, he had had an accident and the singer who took care of him explained that it had been unconsciously determined.

Mr. Largewhiskers and many other extremely old men are still practicing very actively. There is a growing demand for their services—growing because the population is increasing and their belief in traditional medicine is continuing. The trouble is that younger people are not becoming singers. The reasons behind the lack of students are largely economic. To learn to perform even one short ceremony takes at least a year of full-time effort. To learn a major ceremony takes much longer, and many medicine men know several. Since the end of the old herding economy, almost no one can afford to give up earning a living for such a long time. At the time of starting the school for medicine men Yazzie Begay, one of its founders, said "I have been acquainted with several medicine men who have recently died. They were not able to teach the ceremonies which they knew to their grandchildren or to anyone else. Today their sacred instruments and paraphernalia are sitting unused."

The School

The school is at Rough Rock, Ariz., a community near the center of the Navajo Reservation. It is part of the Rough Rock Demonstration School, the first community-controlled Indian school. The Demonstration School was started in 1965, when the Bureau of Indian Affairs (BIA) gave the buildings and equipment to a nonprofit corporation of Navajo leaders called Dine, Inc. Dine helped the Rough Rock chapter of the tribe set up and elect its own board of education (no one on the original board could speak English and all were ceremonialists) and then contracted with the board to operate an el-

ementary boarding school. BIA contributed funds that would have been equal to the budget of such a school if they had been operating it; funds also came from the Office of Economic Opportunity (OEO) and other sources. Soon after the school began operations in 1966, the people became convinced that their ideas really were taken seriously in its daily workings, and several local people suggested setting up the medicine-man school to the board. It was pointed out at a board meeting that white people have medical schools and give students scholarships to attend them and that what was needed most on the reservation were new medicine men. Therefore they felt Rough Rock should set up a school for singers and provide scholarships.

The idea was taken up enthusiastically by the board, and the details were worked out over the course of the next year. It was decided to alter the traditional method of teaching and learning sings as little as possible. (The old way is by apprenticeship and takes place in the teacher's home.) It was also decided that each medicine man would teach two apprentices of his own selection; that is, application for admission to the school would be made by trios consisting of a medicine man and two trainees. The school board would select among them on the basis of the medicine man's reputation, the trainees' apparent ability, and the importance of and threat of extinction to the ceremony that was proposed to be taught. The medicine men were to be paid a very modest salary and the trainees considerably less for their subsistence.

Obtaining Funds

Ever since the Demonstration School started, I had been going there once a month or more to consult with the guidance counselor and teachers. At one time the school administration, at the direction of the board, was preparing a project proposal in an attempt to obtain funds; I was asked to attend a meeting about the project, and here my support for the proposal was enlisted. This was the first of several project discussions in which I took part, and ultimately the board kindly included me in the proposal. It was decided that I should meet regularly with the trainees to discuss non-Navajo medicine, particularly psychiatry. I strongly suspect that my inclusion was a move to make the project look more reasonable to funding agencies.

I flatter myself that from time to time my colleagues in the school and the trainees have been glad to have me around, but I am sure that I have gained much more from this than they have. Before the project could materialize, however, we had to obtain funds.

The first proposal was made to OEO, which turned it down. The second proposal went to the Training and Special Projects Branch of the National Institute of Mental Health (NIMH). This one was accepted, although not, I suspect, without some trepidation. At the time of the site visit by NIMH it became apparent how many mountains there really were between Rough Rock and Bethesda, Md. First of all, the weather became very bad and the site visitors felt they were stranded in Albuquerque, which is 250 miles away from Rough Rock. Luckily the school board was able to go to Albuquerque, so we had a meeting. Two incidents seemed to me to epitomize the meeting. The first was a question from the visitors: "How can a project that supports the continuance of superstition promote mental health?" The reaction of the ceremonialist school board members was more restrained than I had expected. They answered at length, and I added my endorsement. The visitors seemed satisfied. Later one of them, in leafing through the documents, said, "The project director is to be full-time, and the salary listed here is $5000. Can that possibly be right?" When that question had been translated, Mr. John Dick, the director in question, who was a medicine man a former school board member, asked anxiously, "Is it too much?" I am very grateful that the project was funded, and I know that the board is also appreciative.

The Training Program

The work began in September 1969 and is still continuing. There are six medicine men and 12 trainees. Most of the original trainees are still in the program. One of the faculty members died during the first year and was replaced. The ceremonies being taught so far have been one and two nights in length, and almost all of the trainees have completed learning them. Soon they will be performing them for the first time. They will then go on to major ceremonies. Although the lessons (excluding the ones I teach) are conducted at various homes scattered over considerable territory in which there are no paved roads, Mr.

Dick as director maintains close supervision. He travels to each home and watches over the teaching and its results. As the trainees have progressed, he and other medicine men have tested them. My only criticism has been that Mr. Dick's supervision seems rather harsh at times. He has demanded continuous effort and has been very hard on some people whom he surprised when he thought they should be working and they weren't. Still, apart from minor professional jealousy, the group's morale seems high. The program has been well accepted, and there clearly will be a demand for the services of the graduates. Other communities are trying to start similar schools. Recently one of the medicine men had one of his students perform a sing over him.

My sessions are a full day every two weeks. Before I started holding them I met with the medicine men to describe what I intended to do and to ask their permission. To my great pleasure they not only agreed to my plans but said they would like to attend along with the trainees. Attendance has varied from time to time, but usually most of the trainees are present as well as three to five of the medicine men. During the first year I talked about somatic medicine, attempting to cover elements of anatomy, physiology, pathology, diagnosis, and treatment. I discovered that the entire group, including the trainees, had considerable knowledge of anatomy and some of physiology. The sessions were lively. The medicine men and the trainees enjoyed trying out stethoscopes, otoscopes, ophthalmoscopes, and blood-pressure cuffs. Microscope slides of blood smears and pathology specimens were also very popular. In return I was learning more about ceremonial practice, although not as much as I was to learn the next year when we began discussing psychology.

One of the high points of the first year was a visit that the group made to the Gallup Indian Medical Center. It was characteristic, I thought, that the two things the medicine men most enjoyed seeing at the hospital were an operation and a particularly good view of a sacred mountain peak from the windows of the psychiatric ward. They also had criticisms and suggestions. They were horrified by the pediatric ward because the children were so lonely. They kept asking, "Where are the parents?" They urged that better provision be made for parents to stay with their children. They also suggested that we build two hogans at the hospital for ceremonial purposes. They remarked that they all had performed brief ceremonies in the hospital but that they could do more in a real hogan. They said that the medical staff could see the patients during the sing and could go back and forth if necessary. Their suggestion still has not been followed, but I hope that it will be soon.

During the second year I began discussing psychiatry, and in this area there has been more of a two-sided interchange. We have spent much time on European and Navajo notions of the unconscious, a subject in which difficulties in translation have been great. Navajo metapsychology still largely eludes me, but it is clear that the medicine men know about the dynamic interpretation of errors and dreams and were pleased to discover that all of us followed the same custom with regard to them. We all, it turned out, spend our first waking moments in the morning contemplating and interpreting our dreams. One of the medicine men gave an example. He had dreamt about an automobile accident and said that that kind of a dream meant something serious was going on within him and that in order to prevent some disaster from happening to him, it was important to perform a chant about it.

There has been a good deal of case presentation on both sides, particularly, for some reason not clear to me, regarding returned Viet Nam veterans. My feeling of trust and closeness to this group ultimately became such that I presented my own case, describing some things that had led me to enter my analysis and something of the analysis itself. When I finished this rather long account, one of the singers asked me the name of my analyst and where he is now. When I told him, he said, "You were very lucky to find a man who could do so much for you. He must be a very intelligent person."

Another high point for me was demonstrating hypnosis. The group ordinarily looks half asleep—as seems to be the custom with medicine men in meetings. This was unnerving at first, until I found out from their questions and comments that they had been paying very close attention. When hypnosis was demonstrated, however, they were obviously wide awake, although at times I wondered if they were breathing. Working with a carefully prepared subject (I was unwilling to face failure before this audience), I demonstrated a number of depth tests, somnambulism, age regression, positive and negative hallucinations, and some posthypnotic suggestions. When I was done, one of the faculty members said, "I'm 82 years old, and I've seen white people all my life, but this is the first time that one of them has ever surprised me. I'm not surprised to see something like this happen because we do things like this, but I am surprised that a white man should know anything so worthwhile." They also pointed out the resemblance of hypnosis to hand trembling, a diagnostic procedure in which the shaman goes into a trance and his hand moves automatically and indicates the answers to important questions. After we had discussed the similarity, they asked that my subject, a young Navajo woman, diagnose something. I objected, saying that neither she nor I knew how to do this and that it was too serious a matter to play with. They insisted that we try, however, and finally we decided that a weather prediction was not too dangerous to attempt. They were particularly interested in the weather at that time because we were in the midst of an especially severe drought, and someone in the community had predicted that it would continue for another year. When my subject was in a deep trance, I instructed her to visualize the weather for the next six months. She predicted light rain within the week, followed by a dry spell of several months and finally by a good rainy season in late summer. I make no claim other than the truthful reporting of facts: She was precisely correct.

My involvement in this project has, of course, been extremely interesting to me. It is hard, however, to assess the effects of the project on the medicine men and on me. The medicine men say that they know better when and how to refer patients to the white doctors, and I think they feel more kindly toward us. In turn, I feel better able to understand my Navajo patients and know better when to refer them to medicine men. I have adopted some Navajo styles of thought, I think. I use hypnosis more than I used to. And one of my Navajo colleagues in the Indian Health Service Mental Health Program claims that I try to act like a medicine man all the time.

Mothering and the Practice of "Balm" in Jamaica

William Wedenoja

William Wedenoja has conducted field research in Jamaica since 1992 specializing in, among other interests, Afro-Jamaican religious cultism and folk healing. In this article he centers on the gender of healers, a subject almost totally neglected in anthropological literature. In particular, Wedenoja aims his research at women who practice Balm, an Afro-American folk healing tradition in Jamaica which, he maintains, brings about maternal transference, encourages patients' dependency and regression, and appears to be a ritualized extension of mothering. Traditional therapy in Jamaica can be complex at first glance, but the author makes a clear distinction among Balm healers, obeah men (sorcerers), and scientists (who provide their clients good luck charms), and demonstrates the relationship of these specialists to Myalist healing cults, Revivalism, and Pentecostalism.

Wedenoja explains the incompatibility of so-called biomedical (modern) practitioners with the majority of Jamaicans whose disease etiology is not restricted to Western explanations of illness, but includes ghosts (duppies), attacks by obeah men, fallen angels, demons, ancestor spirits, and the devil himself. The charismatic Mother Jones typifies Balm healers in Jamaica, and Wedenoja's description of her shows the importance of her strength and powers in primarily combating spiritual afflictions. The characterization of Mother Jones and others who practice Balm goes far in explaining why the author feels the feminine powers of women are vital to successful curing. Wedenoja's discussion of diagnostic divination ("concentration") is reminiscent of Lehmann's article, "Eyes of the Ngangas" in this chapter and suggests that healing, in all its forms, represents the strongest remnants of African culture in Jamaica.

Reprinted from Carol Shepherd McClain, ed., *Women as Healers, Cross-Cultural Perspectives* (New Brunswick and London, 1989), pp. 76–97, by permission.

. . .

JAMAICAN PEASANTS SHOW GREAT CONCERN FOR illness. It is a very common topic of discussion and a source of constant anxiety. There is, however, little understanding of the scientific theory of disease. Illnesses are blamed on drafts and exposure to cold temperature or imbalances of blood or bile in the body (M. F. Mitchell 1980: 28). They are also, perhaps more often, attributed to spiritual causes.

According to one Balm healer, the majority of illnesses are "chastisements" from God for "disobedience" to His ways. However, another said that "most sickness coming from nigromancy," which refers to Obeah (sorcery), and this is the most common belief. In the behavioral or perceived environment of Jamaican peasants, there are four types of malevolent spirits that can cause suffering: *duppies* (ghosts), fallen angels, demons, and the devil. In addition, ancestor spirits may punish their descendants. Jamaican peasants also worry that neighbors and relatives will turn, in envy or spite, to an *obeahman* (sorcerer), who has the supernatural power to manipulate spirits and use them to do harm.

The first resort in cases of illness is, of course, self-medication. Though Jamaica has a lengthy and extensive tradition of folk cures, it is dying out and rapidly being replaced by over-the-counter drugs. If an illness persists for several days, help may be sought from a private doctor or a government medical clinic, but there is widespread dissatisfaction with them. A sophisticated comparison of ninety-seven patients of healers and doctors in Jamaica by Long (1973: 217–32) showed that Balm healers are better liked, spend significantly more time with patients, and give more satisfying diagnoses than doctors.

The expense of a doctor's examination and prescription drugs is a serious drain on the financial resources of the average Jamaican, and seeing a doctor often involves significant travel and a long wait at the office. The greatest problem with the doctor-patient relationship, however, is communication, which is inhibited by cultural and class differences.

Doctors and patients normally come from separate subcultures of Jamaican society; they use different terms to describe symptoms and label diseases and they hold different beliefs about etiology and treatment. Consequently, a doctor may find it difficult to elicit diagnostically meaningful symptoms from a patient, and a patient may not understand a doctor's diagnosis or the purpose of prescribed medication. In addition, a patient may regard diagnostic inquiry as a sign of incompetence, because it is the custom of Balm healers to divine an illness before speaking with a patient. These factors undermine a patient's faith in a doctor and his expectation of successful treatment.

. . .

In general, rural Jamaicans are dissatisfied with the treatment they receive from doctors and have little faith in their effectiveness. Moreover, they believe doctors are incapable of dealing with illnesses of a "spiritual" nature. Therefore, many turn to religion and folk healers for relief.

A patient may consult an obeahman or a "scientist," but these magical practitioners are not generally viewed as healers. Obeahmen are widely feared for their power to curse others and control ghosts. People turn to scientists principally for good-luck charms like rings and bracelets, which are used to avoid accidents or to bring success.

Balm, which has been practiced for over one hundred years in Jamaica, is closely associated with an indigenous religious cult called Revival. Although Jamaicans regard Revivalism as a Christian faith, it is actually a syncretic, Afro-Christian religion that relies heavily on the intervention of spirits, often through dreams and "trance" states. Revival cults are descended from Myalist healing cults, which emerged in the late eighteenth century to counter Obeah (Wedenoja 1988). Many Revivalist ceremonies and practices are concerned with the prevention or alleviation of illness and misfortune, and about half of all Revival cults offer treatment for outsiders as well as members. Some Revivalists operate *balmyards* devoted entirely to the practice of healing. These healing centers employ Revivalist beliefs and practices but are not Revival cult centers.

. . .

Healing in Balmyards and Revival Cults

Jamaican peasant culture makes a distinction between the sacred and the profane, referred to indigenously as the "spiritual" and the "temporal." Revivalism is commonly called "the spiritual work" and Balm is often called "spiritual science," because they deal with spirits, treat spiritual afflictions, and rely on trance states. Although God is held to be the source of their healing power, the power is delivered to them through angels by means of the Holy Spirit. In contrast, Obeah is called "temporal science" because it can be learned and is not a gift. Moreover, Revivalists and balmists routinely rely on visions, dreams, precognition, glossolalia, and ceremonial possession trance, whereas the obeahman depends on magic and does not use altered states of consciousness.

The Balm healer is essentially a shaman, a person who has received—generally during a severe illness—a spiritual "calling to heal the nation" and the "spiritual gifts" of divination and healing. The balmist's power to heal is based on spirit mediumship; she works with angel familiars who advise her in diagnosis and treatment.

. . .

Patients are called out of a healing service, one at a time, to a shed where they are bathed in water that herbs have been boiled in. This bath is normally accompanied by the recitation of psalms. After being bathed, the patient is led to a private room for a consultation with the healer.

In order to diagnose an affliction, a Balm healer will perform a spiritual divination or "reading," which psychologically is an institutionalized form of empathy. There are several ways to read a patient, but in all cases symptoms are never elicited from the patient prior to a reading. The balmist must demonstrate her gift of healing by telling the patient what his or her problems are. One of the more common methods of divination is called "concentration": typically, the healer will gaze intently at a silver coin or a plant leaf in a glass of water until a "message" from an angel is received in her mind. Other forms of reading include interpreting the movement of the flame of a candle, reading a patient's tongue, card cutting, passing hands over the body of a patient, interpretation of dreams, and palm reading. Very powerful healers may be able to read patients simply by looking at them.

Balm healers deal with every conceivable form of human suffering except serious wounds and broken bones, but the most common complaint is pain in any part of the body. Another frequent problem is a vague syndrome called "bad feeling," which is generally characterized by sudden onset, "feeling out of self," losing self-control, feeling weak and fearful, profuse sweating, and fainting. Other popular problems include weakness, indigestion, headaches, and a feeling of "heaviness" or "beating" in the head. Every healer sees some cases of paralysis, blindness, crippled limbs, deafness, and dumbness. Mental disorders are almost always blamed on spirits, and they are frequently treated by healers. Patients also complain of problems in living such as excessive worry or "fretting," difficulties in raising children, and conflicts with family members, boyfriends, girlfriends, or spouses. Many patients believe that neighbors or relatives are trying to "kill" them—that is, using sorcery on them. Some are filled with hate and want to harm others supernaturally.

. . .

Balm healers specialize in spiritual afflictions. Although they usually provide or prescribe herbal remedies and common drugs, they also use rituals and magical items to counteract spiritual forces. Balmists routinely tell their patients to burn candles or frankincense and myrrh, recite prayers, and read psalms. They often anoint patients with lavender oil and perfumes or tell them to fast to "build up the spirit." Sometimes they will open and close a pair of scissors over the head of a patient to "cut"—that is, to exorcise—a spirit or use a padlock to "lock" a spirit.

A belief that conversion to Christianity and the living of a Christian life will protect one from Obeah and ghosts has been prevalent in Jamaica since the eighteenth century. Revivalism had its origin in antisorcery movements, and many of its ceremonies involve ritual combat with ghosts. . . .

Portrait of a Balm Healer

Ethnographic fieldwork is a fortuitous enterprise. By chance rather than by design, the hamlet I chose to live in had a very successful Revival cult led by a popular healer, who made me her "godson" on my first visit with her. During the following year and a half we spent a great deal of time together, and I came to know her as well as I have ever known anyone.

The Reverend Martha Jones, generally called "Mother" Jones (these are pseudonyms), is a stocky sixty-four-year-old black woman who stands about five feet five inches tall and weighs about 140 pounds. She lives with about thirty followers and children in a large house next to her church, which she founded in 1950.

Mother Jones was born in the community where she now lives, and spent her first twelve years there. Her father, who died in 1953, made his living as a painter and was also a leader in the local Missionary Alliance church, where she was baptized. She describes him as a quiet, strict, stern, sober, and hard-working man, who was close to her. Her mother, who died in 1937, was a housewife who gave birth to ten children, four of whom are still living. She too was quiet, strict, and home-loving.

Mother Jones was sickly throughout childhood and worried constantly about getting ill or hurt. She contracted malaria and typhoid fever, and lost her hair. Because she was their youngest child and so sickly, her parents were very protective, even keeping her from school, and gave her a great deal of attention.

At the age of twelve Mother Jones went to Kingston to live with an older sister, and she worked there as a maid for eighteen years. She married a black American sailor when she was twenty-two but never had any children. In her late twenties she had a number of "spiritual experiences"—epileptiform states and visions—and went to a Balm woman who told her she had a "spiritual gift."

Mother Jones moved to Washington, D.C., when she was thirty to work as a parlormaid for the British ambassador, but she became "crippled" during her first year there and received a vision telling her to return to Jamaica and start a healing ministry. After another year in Kingston, she and her husband moved to her home town and started a "work." Her husband, however, left in the following year, and she has not seen or heard from him since.

Mother Jones was ordained in the National Baptist church in 1960 and appointed "overseer" for four or five churches in the area. They eventually broke away, and she changed her membership to another American sect. Over the past twenty-five years, every moment of her life has been devoted to her church and healing. She once remarked to me, "my task is not an easy one, my time is not my own. I couldn't tell the day when I am able to rest my head on the pillow." Every Monday she holds a healing service and sees from ten to thirty patients. Throughout the week other patients come individually to her.

And her church holds a variety of services and classes almost every day or night of the week.

The people in her community have great respect for Mother Jones, and she has many devoted followers throughout the island and among Jamaican communities in England, Canada, and the United States. No one doubts her integrity and devotion. Everyone refers to her as "Mother" and relates to her as a mother. She shows concern not only for her patients and followers but for the entire community and society as well. She likes children and they are attracted to her. About twenty children live with her: some are ill or handicapped and others have been left with her for discipline or because their mothers are unable to care adequately for them.

Mother Jones says that people come to her for healing when a doctor fails to find anything wrong with them and they think it must be a spiritual, not a physical, problem. She sends her patients to a doctor if she thinks they need one and, for her protection, usually insists that they see a doctor before coming under her care; otherwise she could be liable for prosecution. She does not normally treat someone who is on medication, because "you can't mix the spiritual and the temporal."

Mother Jones tells her patients that "the Lord will help them and they will be healed just through faith, if they believe." But, she laments, "Some people want more. . . . They want something to take way with them. . . . They seem to think it is someone's bad intents. . . . They don't believe prayer and God will be able to keep them. . . . They feel they have to pay a lot of money . . . and get some superstitious something, or they are unsatisfied." Unlike some Jamaican healers, who blame many problems on Obeah and duppies and provide "guards" (protective amulets), Mother Jones often rebukes these patients by telling them "their thoughts are not right."

Mother Jones told me she wanted to be a preacher rather than a healer, but healing was the gift she received through the Holy Spirit. Although she says that spiritual healing is not a gift one can learn or teach, she does have pamphlets on gospel healing and an ancient book on anatomy, and she listens to radio talk shows on health problems.

One of Mother Jones's "spiritual gifts" is an ability to feel a patient's pain while she is "in the spirit." She also uses "concentration" to "read" a patient by staring at a glass of water with a leaf in it and asking the patient to drop a silver coin in "as a love offering" to an angel. Like most Balm healers, she does not ask patients to describe their symptoms, because she is supposed to be able to "read" them. But after giving a rather general diagnosis, she will question the patient and discuss the problem in detail before prescribing treatment.

All of the patients at a Monday healing service receive a glass of consecrated water and an herbal bath before seeing Mother Jones. In her private consultations with patients she often assigns them specific chapters of Scripture to read and gives them a "healing prayer" to wear next to the place of their illness. The latter is a sheet of "spirit writing," a propitiation to God written in cabalistic script while in a state of trance. She gives her patients "bush medicine" or herbs, prescriptions for vitamins and over-the-counter drugs, and offers advice on living. But she attributes her healing ability largely to her gift for spiritually absorbing a patient's suffering into her own body: "If you take their condition, you draw it off, the people goes free." She constantly complains about the suffering she bears for others, and says her gift might kill her if she entered a hospital.

A Healer's Personality

. . .

Mother Jones's roles as religious leader and healer appear to meet most of her personality needs well. They give her autonomy and dominance over others and gain her love, affection, and admiration. As a surrogate mother for many people, she can identify with her own mother, which gives her a strong sense of identity and relieves her of guilt. Healing provides her with a defense mechanism, undoing, which disguises her hostility toward others. It offers opportunities to criticize others and impose her strong sense of morality on those she dislikes. It is also, by means of projection, a way to satisfy her own need for nurturance. Mother Jones's ritual roles provide frequent and sanctioned outlets for her dissociative tendencies in the form of visions, trance, and ceremonial possession states. And her entire life is governed by such a narrow range of role expectations that she is seldom threatened and finds predictability and security in them. This restrictiveness is, however, something of a problem too: Mother Jones is always, in a sense, "on stage" and performing roles, which limits her personality and makes her lonely.

In order to have a successful balmyard or Revival cult, healing or leadership roles must be gratifying to patients and followers as well as to the healer or leader. I found several individuals who had a strong desire to become healers or leaders and had tried many times to establish a Balm practice or Revival cult, but had always failed to attract a clientele or devotees. They were not lacking in spiritual knowledge, but they did not meet the psychological needs of others. Given the renown and large following of Mother Jones, it is apparent that she not only meets her own needs but satisfies those of her patients and followers as well.

Mother Jones's characteristic optimism is encouraging to patients and raises their expectations for relief. Her sensitivity to the affective needs of others—that is, her warmth and concern—evokes feelings of love and security in her patients and allows her to establish rapport with a patient quickly. The psychological tests also show her to be a very creative and intuitive person, someone who thinks in a holistic manner and can easily make convincing interpretations of a case on the basis of a few clues.

Scheff (1975, 1979) has emphasized both the need for emotional arousal in therapy and the importance of group support if therapeutic change is to persist, and these elements are amply present in Mother Jones's practice. Her healing services employ drums and tambourines, singing and dancing, histrionic preaching, and ecstatic behavior, all of which is emotionally rousing. She holds periodic "Patient Tables," which are lengthy and ecstatic ceremonies, to honor former patients. And her patients often become involved in the regular cycle of ceremonies of her church, at which members are expected to "testify" often to their salvation or personal rebirth; normally, this involves declarations of the important influence of Mother Jones on their lives. The changes she instigates in her patients are then reinforced by her presence and by the support of other followers.

Women and Balm

. . .

This association of women with healing is not restricted to Balm and Revivalism. The medical system relies heavily on nurses and midwives, too. In rural areas, babies are delivered by government midwives, traditional *nanas,* or resident nurses at community clinics. The day-to-day operation of a rural hospital is managed almost entirely by the Matron and her nurses, with doctors serving mainly as surgeons and consultants. Obeahmen and scientists are, however, to my knowledge always men.

This sexual division of labor may be due, in part, to considerations of wealth and prestige. The practice of Obeah or Science is reputedly very remunerative and a source of great influence. But the practice of Balm, though it may bring one honor and respect, usually offers little in the way of income or formal prestige and power. As in most societies, men monopolize public positions of wealth and power and leave the less lucrative positions to women.

The association of men with sorcery and women with healing may also be based on cultural stereotypes about the sexes. In interviews and TAT responses, men are generally depicted as violent, troublesome, unreliable, untrustworthy, sexually aggressive, deceitful, and exploitative. Obeahmen are feared because they work in secret, with malicious ghosts (duppies), and cause harm or misfortune. Women, in contrast, are portrayed as peaceful, benevolent, nurturing, caring, responsible, and trustworthy. Correspondingly, Balm and Revivalism are benign institutions; their purpose is to counteract Obeah and malicious ghosts or provide protection from them. Thus we have a simple semiotic equation of Obeah with men, aggression, harm, and evil, on the one hand, and Balm and Revivalism with women, protection, helping, and good, on the other.

Mothering and Balm

. . .

The relationship between Balm healers and patients is a ritualized version of the mother-child relationship, and this is openly recognized in Jamaican culture. Healers are referred to as "mothers" and they are expected to play a maternal role. They are idealized as supermothers and adopted as surrogate mothers. Moreover, healers often refer to patients as their "children."

Familial idioms are used extensively in Revivalism, and they are not merely metaphors. Cultists behave according to the familial roles associated with their positions. The social organization of Revival cults strongly reflects the mother-centered pattern of the family in Jamaica, and one of the attractions of Revival cults is that they are fictive family groups.

The "Mother" is usually the central figure in a cult, and everything revolves around her. The "Armor Bearer," Mother Jones's "right hand," is in charge of the day-to-day activities of the cult, a role resembling that of the eldest daughter in a large family. Other women are referred to as "sisters." Some of the younger sisters, who are known as the "workers," serve the Armor Bearer much as younger daughters work under the eldest daughter in a family.

In general, women have instrumental roles that involve a great deal of work but little recognition, whereas men are given expressive roles that have prestige but little responsibility. The "Father" or "Daddy" is sometimes the dominant but more often a removed but respected figure. Many of the men are deacons, and they seem to play the role of uncles. The pastor of Mother Jones's church, who was raised by Mother Jones, is a handsome and charming young public health inspector. His official duties are to preach sermons and perform weddings and funerals, but he also fills the familial role, common in Jamaican families, of a favorite son who is admired by all. Other men are referred to as "brothers." Mother Jones always called me "my son," and her followers referred to me as "Brother Bill."

Mother Jones is a mother not just to her patients and followers but to the entire community. She is its moral standard and conscience and, more generally, a symbol of the love, affection, and devotion of mothers. There is a great respect for mothers in Jamaica, and the mother-child tie is the strongest bond in the society. Children are often reluctant to leave home and mother when they reach adulthood, and the most traumatic event in the life cycle is the death of one's mother. Mothers have almost total responsibility for their children; the role of fathers is largely limited to punishment for severe offenses. In addition, mothers delegate many domestic tasks and child-care responsibilities to their daughters, while sons are free to roam and play. The needs of rural children are therefore met largely by women.

The cultural patterning of the healer-patient relationship on the mother-child bond encourages maternal transference, regression, and the development of a dependency relationship. This can give the Balm healer a great deal of influence over her patients, because it makes them more receptive and suggestible. Moreover, the mother-child bond prob-

ably has some effect on all other relationships, because it is usually the first and most influential relationship in life. Maternal transference can thus provide the healer with an opportunity to make some rather fundamental changes in the personality and behavior of her patients.

Maternal dependency can be very supportive for patients. The healer, as a surrogate mother, consoles them, looks after them, and takes control when things go wrong. She gives them attention, affection, nurturance, encouragement, and offers them direction and purpose. Through attachment to her, they can regain a childlike sense of protection and security.

Western therapists would regard the dependency aspect of the healer-patient relationship in Balm as a problem, but it is not seen as one in Jamaica. Jamaicans are very sociable and they do not place much value on independence and self-reliance. Dependency is not condemned or discouraged.

. . .

Illness and Emotional Needs

. . .

Jamaican Balm exemplifies what I believe to be a basic principle of psychological anthropology, that every culture produces a unique set of personality needs and conflicts and develops institutionalized means for their satisfaction or resolution. Balm is not simply a traditional medical system but also, and perhaps more importantly, a source of psychological support. The psychological processes involved in Balm are not just techniques that facilitate healing but ends in themselves. Patients come to healers not only to be cured of illnesses but to gratify affective needs as well.

One of the dominant concerns of Jamaicans is "love." Many older people remarked to me that Jamaicans were once very "loving," but they are too "selfish" today. The plague of violence that Kingston has experienced over the past two decades is generally blamed on lack of love. Church sermons often dwell on social disorder, and Christian love is put forward as the salvation of society. "Peace and love" and the need for brotherly love and unity are central themes in popular music and in the ideology of the messianic cult of Rastafarianism. Mother Jones is of the opinion that most illnesses are due to "stress" in general and "lack of love" in particular. She says Jamaicans are not close, they fear each other, and they cannot give love to others. So she offers them her love, and tries to teach them to love others, to "make them whole."

What Jamaicans mean by "love" is closeness, caring, and concern for others—unity, sharing, and cooperation. Family ties are strong, and they want community relations to be close and friendly as well. Although there has probably been some erosion of *gemeinschaft* and a weakening of kin ties over the past few decades, I cannot agree with Mother Jones that Jamaicans are unloving. They are at least as "loving" as Americans, but they have a much stronger need for affiliation and place a higher value on interpersonal relations (Jones and Zoppel 1979; Phillips 1973). "Love" is a cultural focus, part of the Jamaican ethos, and one of the principal functions of Balm and Revivalism is to gratify that need.

Women and Healing

As Spiro (1978: xvi–xvii) has noted, "The practitioner of anthropology as 'science,' placing the local setting in a theoretical context, is concerned with the local as a variant of—and therefore a means for understanding—the universal." According to my analysis, the relationship between healers and patients in Balm is modeled on the mother-child relationship, a very strong bond in Jamaican society, and the mothering behavior of maternal figures such as Mother Jones provides emotional support for distressed and demoralized individuals. To what extent can this interpretation be generalized to other cultures?

A pioneering article by Carl Rogers (1957) identified congruence (genuineness and personality integration), unconditional positive regard (warm acceptance and nonpossessive caring), and accurate empathy as personal qualities that a healer must communicate to a patient if psychotherapeutic change is to take place. Additional research has indicated that effective healers are also intelligent, responsible, creative, sincere, energetic, warm, tolerant, respectful, supportive, self-confident, keenly attentive, benign, concerned, reassuring, firm, persuasive, encouraging, credible, sensitive, gentle, and trustworthy (J. D. Frank 1974; Lambert, Shapiro, and

Bergin 1986). It should be noted, however, that these conclusions are based on research on American psychotherapists and thus the characteristics may not be universal.

Many of the personal qualities noted above seem to apply to women more than men. Women are said to be more empathic and have more positive feelings about being close to others, to be more cooperative and altruistic, to share more, to be more accommodative and interested in social relationships, to be more vocal, personal, and superior at nonverbal communication (G. Mitchell 1981), "more sensitive to social cues and to the needs of others" (Draper, quoted in Quinn 1977: 198), and more nurturant or kind and supportive to others (Martin and Voorhies 1975). In a study of kibbutz children, Spiro (1979: 93) found that girls showed more "integrative behavior"—aid, assistance, sharing and cooperation—than boys, and regularly consoled victims of aggression.

These claims about universal differences in adult male and female "styles" of behavior have apparently not been put to the test of a systematic cross-cultural study. However, there are excellent data on children aged three through eleven from the Six Cultures Study (Whiting and Whiting 1975), which found that girls are more intimate-dependent (touch and seek help) and nurturant (offer help and support) and that boys are more aggressive (assault, insult, horseplay) and dominant-dependent (seek dominance and attention).

Characteristics associated with women seem to be closely related to their role as mothers. Although this may reflect an innate predisposition to bond with and nurture infants (Rossi 1977), it can also be adequately explained by socialization practices. Women have the main responsibility for child care in every society, and they are prepared for that role in childhood. A well-known cross-cultural survey on sex differences in socialization concluded that there is "a widespread pattern of greater pressure toward nurturance, obedience, and responsibility in girls, and toward self-reliance and achievement striving in boys" (Barry, Bacon, and Child 1957: 332).

There is a close correspondence between the personal qualities of effective healers and women, and it seems to be due to strong similarities between the roles of healing and mothering. According to Kakar (1982: 59), many psychotherapists claim that "the 'feminine' powers of nurturance, warmth, concern, intuitive understanding, and relatedness . . . are essential in every healing encounter and for the success of the healing process."

If "feminine powers" are essential for healing, then women should, on average, be more effective at it than men. In fact, a review of research on the sex of psychotherapists concluded that "there appear to be some demonstrable trends, under certain circumstances, toward greater patient satisfaction or benefit from psychotherapy with female therapists and no studies showing such trends with male therapists" (Mogul 1982: 1–3).

It might also be reasonable to expect that the majority of healers in the world are, as in Jamaica, women. However, a cross-cultural survey of seventy-three societies by Whyte (1978) found that male shamans were more numerous or powerful in 54 percent; female shamans were more numerous or powerful in only 10 percent. This finding does not necessarily disprove the hypothesis that women generally make better healers. Personal qualities are only one factor in recruitment to a healing role and social, political, and economic factors can be important too. Given what we know about sexual inequality, it would not be surprising to find that women occupy healing roles when these roles are low in prestige or income, while men come to monopolize them when healing is high in prestige or income. It would be worthwhile to conduct a more extensive cross-cultural survey on the sex of healers in a study that would broaden the subject from shamans to include other types of healers and would attempt to identify social conditions associated with a preponderance of male or female healers.

Although "feminine powers" such as nurturance, warmth, and concern may, as Kakar suggests, be necessary for effective healing, they are probably not sufficient. Healers also seem to be firm and often domineering. For example, Raymond Prince (personal communication) notes that Nigerian healers, who are almost all male, are "abrupt, authoritarian, and sometimes punitive in their relations with patients, particularly psychotic ones."

It is probably more accurate to say that the personal qualities of effective healers are androgynous. Mother Jones is not only warm, empathic, caring, sensitive, and supportive with her patients but also firm, assertive, and domineering. Male shamans often dress in female clothing and assume female roles (Halifax 1979: 24). I noticed that the husky voice of a Jamaican male healer changed to a high pitch when he entered a trance to treat his patients, and he became warmer and more empathic as well. Torrey (1972: 103) described a male healer in Ethiopia as having a fatherly relationship with his patients and an "underlying warmth . . . partly masked by an authoritarian manner."

The personal qualities of an effective healer may vary with the degree of involvement of men and women in child care in a society. However, the maternal element of healing is probably more constant than the paternal element, because women are always heavily involved in child care and there is much greater variation in the involvement of men. The emphasis on mothering in Balm is a reflection of the strong degree of maternal dependency in Jamaican society, which is encouraged by a high rate of father-absence and a general lack of involvement of men in child rearing. In addition, the androgynous character of Jamaican healers seems to be due to the fact that Jamaican mothers often have to play maternal and paternal roles in child care and family life.

Healing relationship may also vary with, and reflect, the style of parenting in a society. Jamaican mothers tend to be very domineering, restrictive, nagging, scolding, punitive, directive, and even dictatorial with their children. I observed a popular Balm healer who matched this description when I was asked to drive two patients to a balmyard. She was very abrasive and publicly scolded her patients, and I was quite surprised to hear my companions extolling her on our journey home. When I asked them if they would like her for a mother, they enthusiastically replied that she would be splendid.

Traditional African Psychotherapy: An Interview with Thomas Adeoye Lambo

Thomas Bass

Dr. Thomas Adeoye Lambo startled the world with the results of his pioneering work on traditional African psychiatry (ethnopsychiatry). Under the direction of Professor Lambo, a seven-year World Health Organization (WHO) study demonstrated that in terms of the rate of actual cures, Western psychiatric practices were far less successful than those used by traditional African curers and those used in other Third World countries included in the project.

This interview by Thomas Bass highlights successful techniques of African ethnopsychiatry that are absent in Western treatment of the mentally ill, and illustrates that Lambo's incorporation of traditional psychotherapeutic methods is a blend of biology, culture, and social psychology. One key factor in achieving success in treating Africans suffering from schizophrenia, for example, is the tremendous social support given patients by placing them in a village setting much like that of their own homes, a kind of support usually unavailable to mentally ill patients in the West. Other factors in traditional African psychotherapy include the patient's faith in the healer's knowledge of herbal medicine, the healer's power to call on the spirit world for assistance in effecting a cure, and the healer's deep knowledge of the stresses current in the patient's social setting. This eclectic approach to the treatment of mental illness is a lesson for Western psychiatry, but one that may be impossible for Western industrial societies to emulate. Lambo himself projects that as African cultures change, becoming industrialized and detribalized, the approaches he applied in the WHO study may no longer be successful.

Reprinted from *Reinventing the Future* (Reading, Massachusetts: Addison Wesley, 1994.) © Thomas A. Bass, pp. 69–86, by permission of the author.

SAVAGES ARE HAPPY. THEY LAUGH AND DANCE and forget their problems in the blink of an eye. Or so said the missionaries who first penetrated into the interior of Africa. It took an African psychiatrist—the continent's first—to explode this myth of the happy savage.

When Thomas Adeoye Lambo looked into the villages of his native Nigeria, he found plenty of psychotics and schizophrenics. In fact, the per capita incidence of mental illness in Africa is the same as in New York City. But Africans treat crazy people as part of everyday life, and this high tolerance for aberrant behavior is what made the *un*happy savages invisible to Western eyes.

Lambo also discovered that African village life with its strong tribal and familial bonds, has therapeutic benefits of its own. Employing what he calls "methodological syncretism," the fusion of Western and traditional ideas, he began incorporating family members and villagers into his patients' psychiatric cures.

The missionaries had made another mistake in dismissing Africa's traditional healers as "witch doctors." Lambo found them employing many of the same psychiatric techniques he had learned at the University of London. Centuries before Freud, traditional healers invented the "talking cure," free association, group therapy, and behavioral modification. They also had an extensive pharmacopoeia of herbal and psychotropic drugs.

"Their psychotropic sessions were vastly superior to ours," says Lambo. "They showed us we hadn't got it right." He borrowed liberally from these traditional healers while developing his village-based cure for mental illness. Faster, more effective, and one-fifth the price of a Western cure, Lambo's model has since been adopted by sixty countries throughout the Third World.

One of more than 30 children fathered by a Yoruba chief with 12 wives, Thomas Adeoye Lambo was born in Abeokuta, Nigeria, in 1923. His early missionary schooling included lighting bonfires on Sunday to burn up statues and masks seized from neighboring villages. He studied medicine at Birmingham University and went on to advanced degrees at London University's Institute of Psychiatry.

In the first of several famous research projects, Lambo was hired by the Nigerian government to study mental illness and nervous breakdowns among his fellow African students in England. Touring the wards, he discovered that sick Africans, in spite of their Ph.D.'s and Saville Row suits, cast their delusions in terms of witchcraft and juju. Lambo already suspected that only an indigenous African psychiatry could deal with the African psyche.

Returning to Nigeria in 1950, he was appointed director of the Aro Hospital for Nervous Diseases, Africa's first mental hospital. Lambo's British wife, while waiting for the buildings to be finished, suggested he billet his patients in neighboring villages. This gave Lambo his original idea for deviating from psychiatric orthodoxy. Colonial administrators looked aghast at his next experiment. Using his own money, Lambo hired a dozen traditional healers to practice alongside his regular clinical staff. For twelve years he filmed and analyzed these "witch doctors" at work. "The major factor in their success was the incorporation of the family into their psychotherapeutic sessions, something that psychiatry in Vienna and London had totally failed to do."

Along with his experiments in traditional medicine and village-based psychotherapy, Lambo began studying the psychological effects of modernization in postcolonial Africa. Depression, anxiety, and other neuroses are the price paid for social change. In its "malignant" form, this anxiety spawns secret societies devoted to ritual murder.

After founding the modern practice of psychiatry in Africa, Lambo ascended into the ranks of the continent's few internationally known scholars. He became head of the department of psychiatry, dean of the medical school, and vice chancellor of the University of Ibadan. In 1971 he left Africa to work at the World Health Organization in Geneva, emerging by 1975 as WHO's Deputy Director-General. Now retired and living in Nigeria, the grand old man of African science still travels the world advising everyone from popes to presidents.

Bass: What's your opinion of the term "witch doctor?"

Lambo: It's a derogatory term coined by missionaries. When I went to mission school, every Sunday we were sent into the villages and told to collect all the idols and carved objects that now fetch millions of dollars at Christie's auction house. We'd pile them in the middle of the village and burn them. This was part of our mission to convert the savages to Christianity. But just as there's no one single religion, so too there's no one single way to practice medicine. I could call quite a number of modern physicians "witch doctors," such as the ones who do "exploratory" surgery so they can hand you a heavy bill.

Bass: Are some traditional healers better than others?

Lambo: Of course. Some are generalists, while others specialize in treating blindness or mental illness. They may be powerful in one area, like herbalism, but they usually employ other methods as well, like the Ifa oracles. The Ifa spirit is a powerful thing. It's super-mathematical. You throw sixteen palm nuts from hand to hand, while marking the message of the deity in a sand-covered Ifa tray. These marks relate to one of two hundred fifty-six verses in the Odu, or Ifa oracular system. After twenty or thirty minutes of calculating, the Ifa spirit begins talking to the patient, telling him what's wrong with him.

Bass: How do the oracles work?

Lambo: When I first began watching traditional healers talk to the Ifa spirit, I tried to be skeptical. Did they cheat? I don't think so. How accurate is it? I think it's fairly accurate. Probability and chance play a great part in medicine. We "real" doctors are often blamed for what we had to do and praised for what we didn't do. The fact of the matter is that your guess is as good as mine. But what's important is whether or not the patient believes you. When the patient and psychiatrist agree, you have positive transference. If the patient is skeptical about what you're saying, the transference is negative, and you might as well send him somewhere else.

Bass: What was your family like?

Lambo: My father was paramount chief in the ancient town of Abeokuta. He had twelve wives and well over thirty children. But my "family" is even larger than this. In Africa, especially among the Yorubas, a child has no one single father. Your mother's brother is also your father. Psychodynamically, this substitution is a good thing. It allows for extended care and a choice of role models. My grandmother carried me on her back for many years and gave me her own breast to suckle. There was nothing in it, but it kept me quiet! I actually spent my early years thinking she was my real mother. We lived in a large compound, and even today there are people there whose relationships are so ill defined that I can't trace them. Only in the big city do we use the word "cousin," so everyone is known as your brother or sister.

My father was a farmer of kola nuts and cocoa. My mother was a cloth trader who ran a big shop employing quite a number of people. Nigerian women in those days had tremendous economic power, and even today there is hardly a market in West Africa where you won't find Yoruba women traders. My "brother" Joseph Lambo—he is actually my cousin, although he gets upset with me when I call him that—is a traditional healer. Even back in grade school he was interested in herbalism, which he practiced on all of us. But now that he's famous, he wouldn't do it for free!

Bass: Does he have magical powers?

Lambo: Traditional healers tend to think that everything is supernatural. Africans on the whole still believe this. When confronting our destiny and unknown forces in the world, we are essentially a religious people. If my cousin is going to cure you with the leaves of a particular tree, he'll visit the tree early in the morning, chanting incantations and invoking the spirit of the tree. He also uses a great deal of psychotherapy. He looks into the coals of a fire to analyze your dreams and makes startling observations. "Did you ever do such and such?" "Why yes! How did you know?" He sacrifices chickens and goats and uses their blood to wash a man's head. These sacrifices and ritual expiations to the spirits are important to the cure. Psychotherapy takes many forms.

Bass: Why do you call this psychotherapy?

Lambo: Because I am a psychiatrist and psychiatrists don't do any more than this, even in New York City. In fact, they do less because they have no time for you. Traditional healers spend a lot of time talking to their patients, getting medical histories. They hold psychotherapeutic sessions, either jointly or in groups, where they analyze dreams, dance, or perform ritual sacrifices. They burn incense and commune with spirits. They go into the patient's home and place fetish objects in the corners to ward off evil spirits.

Unfortunately, the modern economy has made many traditional healers into money grubbers. But the ones I employed at Aro were serious people, and they were poor. At the end of his cure, a patient might give them some yams, a couple of chickens, or a goat. They weren't in it for the money. Their knowledge was passed from father to son in a seven-year apprenticeship. No one called himself a therapist just because he'd spent three years getting a B.Sc. degree.

Bass: How effective are they?

Lambo: At Aro we taped everything they did for nine years, and we found their techniques to be remarkably effective. For both human and scientific reasons, I wanted to provide alternatives to Western medicine, which is not the only way to a cure. Patients coming to the hospital were asked whether they wanted to use Western or traditional methods. So the two developed along parallel lines, like the Chinese system.

Bass: When did traditional healers start working at the hospital?

Lambo: They never worked at the hospital. In fact, the colonial government officially disassociated itself from my work. They sent me a letter saying, "We have just built the most modern psychiatric hospital in Africa. What are you doing hiring witch doctors? If one of your schizophrenics goes and kills someone, His Majesty's government will take no responsibility."

Bass: Aro was the first psychiatric hospital in West Africa?

Lambo: It was the first psychiatric hospital in the whole of Africa. There were asylums for locking up the insane but no treatment centers whatsoever. All the nurses and occupational therapists I hired were Europeans, because it took years before Africans were trained to assume these positions. People still come to Aro from as far away as Tanzania and Botswana for a degree in psychiatry.

Bass: Why did you decide to lodge some patients in the neighboring villages?

Lambo: I'm restless. I'm willing to take risks. I wanted to prove that psychotic patients aren't any more violent than normal humans. Their violence is caused by the way you look at them. You expect them to be violent, so even before they do anything, you tie them down. But for forty years now the Aro village program has worked. I used my own money to set up the experiment, and it proved my point quite conclusively.

Bass: Where did you get the idea of a village cure for mental illness?

Lambo: From my wife, who is an historian and educator. We met at the University of London. She has tremendous empathy, and I am very lucky that I married someone who shares almost everything I stand for. When we arrived at Aro, the hospital hadn't been built yet, and the government told me to supervise the project. "You're not the administrative type who is going to be happy sitting down at a desk for three or four years," she said. "It will drive you crazy."

"You are quite right," I replied. In the evenings after work we would drive our Volkswagen into different villages I was curious to see. One night I got out of the car to speak to a group of people. When I got back in, my wife *said, "They love you. They know about your work at the hospital. Why don't you ask them if you can billet patients here until Aro is built?" So that's how it started, although of course we kept using the villages even after the hospital was built.*

Bass: When did you notice that village life itself had therapeutic benefits?

Lambo: Long before the hospital started to function. The nurses were sent out into the villages at nine in the morning to make their rounds. By eleven they were back reporting to me on what was happening. Then I went out to have my "ward rounds" in the villages. "What happened yesterday, Mama?" I would ask someone. "My son is much better," she would say. "He went for a long walk and came back exhausted. He slept very well, and he's no longer talking in his sleep." We began documenting thousands of similar case histories.

Bass: How did you decide whether to put a patient in the hospital or the village?

Lambo: I'd put one schizophrenic or psychotic in the hospital and one in the village, at random. I insisted that those going to the village be accompanied by their relatives. The others went into the hospital alone, just like in New York or Chicago. I wanted to prove that the village cure would be faster, better, with fewer relapses. Rehabilitation would be smoother, because the patients were accompanied by their parents. Even during psychotherapy, the mother or aunt would sit with us. This meant that when the patient was discharged, there was no special follow-up to explain to the parent what was being done.

Bass: What kind of psychotherapy did the village patients receive?

Lambo: Some was planned, some spontaneous. This included talking to normal villagers. Communication is important. You don't want to isolate patients by locking them up. This leads to convulsions and heavy reliance on psychotropic drugs. These drugs were just coming onto the market in great variety and abundance when I started working at Aro. But I thought the most important thing was interaction with normal human beings.

Bass: How did the villagers treat their crazy guests?

Lambo: I billeted patients in the homes of people who showed the greatest tolerance for these pre-literate, or illiterate, patients. Even today Africans are tremendously tolerant of what Westerners call "deviant" behavior. One reason why the myth of the "happy savage" developed is that no one noticed the unhappiness in African villages, where psychotics and schizophrenics are treated as part of everyday life. This made it very difficult for us to diagnose the general level of mental illness in Africa.

Bass: How did the village health care system work?

Lambo: We paid five shillings a night for each patient and another five for each relative. In addition, the villages were given electricity and piped water to improve hygiene. The people living there were farmers, fishermen, and small traders. At first they were afraid I was going to put into their homes schizophrenics and depressives who would endanger their families. It took a year and a half of negotiations to set up the experiment, but finally we got everyone solidly behind the project, so much so that new patients could be taken into the villages at midnight and people would open their doors to them. During the twelve years I was there, not a single incident took place.

Bass: Which worked better, the villages or the hospital?

Lambo: Unless they chose to be treated by a traditional healer, patients in both the villages and the hospital had planned therapy, injections of psychotropic drugs, electroshock, and so on. The only difference lay in the social dynamics. Those in the hospital couldn't talk to anyone but their psychotic neighbor, while those in the villages, after getting their shots of thorazine, could go sit in the market and talk to anyone they wanted. The village cure was qualitatively better. Even people who didn't recover totally were able to function on their own. They were less dependent on psychiatrists and nurses. They showed significantly lower rates of recidivism. There were also economic benefits. The village cure cost one-fifth of a hospital stay.

Bass: What other benefits come from a village health care system?

Lambo: Psychotics don't regress to the bottom of the heap, as I saw in the big hospitals in London. People buried away in the depths of the hospital could no longer put on their socks and shoes. But you don't get this regression to the infantile stage in people who are maintaining social contact. Locking up patients for twenty or thirty years costs the government a hell of a lot of money. It's in everybody's interest to get these people out and productive as quickly as possible.

Bass: Are the villages still functioning?

Lambo: At a low level. People have told me my experiment worked only because Nigeria at the time was in a pre-industrial stage of development. Once a country is industrialized—people living in nuclear families in city apartments, moving here and there at the whim of their employers—it becomes difficult to tie yourself down caring for relatives. Eighty percent of Africa is still rural, but maybe as soon as the next generation it will be detribalized and industrialized. The hypothesis I tested so successfully at Aro may not survive these developments.

Bass: What did your Western doctors and traditional healers learn from each other?

Lambo: I introduced into Africa this particular form of methodological syncretism. I arranged the marriage of traditional and Western cultures. The traditional healers themselves are now using tranquilizers, thorazine, and other psychotropic drugs, combined with psychotherapy, ritual killing, and the interpretation of dreams. They're even giving antibiotics in cases where patients have pneumonia or chest infections. I've been able to persuade them that only in extreme cases should they restrain their patients. They're becoming more modernized. They realize they can syncretize both approaches. Just as there is no one religion—there are many religions—so, too, is there no one medicine. There are many medicines.

Bass: What are the psychological benefits of ritual sacrifice?

Lambo: I once treated a Cambridge-educated judge who ran his car off the road on his way to court. He was only slightly injured, but badly shaken when they brought him to me at the University of Ibadan. I examined him and gave him tranquilizers so he could rest. A few weeks later he came to see me. "How is your recovery going?" I asked.

"Tom, to be perfectly honest," he said, "I think this was a case of juju." By juju, he meant black magic. "I had a vision in which I saw my grandfather. He told me that in order to break the spell I should sacrifice a goat. Not believing in such things, I told my parents to sacrifice the goat, and you know what? Since then I've been right as rain!"

This shows that in spite of our sophistication, our Cambridge degrees and Western ways, there remains down in the soul a belief in the metaphysical and the supernatural. This was why he was so agitated when I first saw him, but he couldn't tell me.

Bass: What other experiences have you had with ritual sacrifice?

Lambo: I've seen hundreds of cases like this. The Nigerian government employed me to lead a team of researchers studying mental breakdowns among Nigerian students in England. There were twelve of us, anthropologists, sociologists, psychologists, and psychiatrists like myself. We went to every major hospital in the country. What interested me was the fact that people—despite their M.A.s and Ph.D.s—cast their delusions in terms of their African culture. They believed some sort of psychic ray or beam had come from Nigeria, from their mother's uncle or whomever, opposing their wish to become a lawyer or doctor. Some of them had been in England for years, but in spite of their long exposure to Western civilization, when they became ill they fell back on their culture.

Bass: Have you ever practiced ritual sacrifice?

Lambo: Never. It's not that I don't believe in it, it's just that I've never prescribed it to anyone.

Bass: How does sacrifice work, psychodynamically?

Lambo: I don't know. How does acupuncture work? I can't tell you, but it does. If you believe in it, you feel relieved. And don't forget that the native healers prescribing sacrifice are powerful, charismatic men.

Bass: Is human sacrifice still practiced in Africa?

Lambo: I'm told in the markets one can still buy human heads. There's no doubt human sacrifice was practiced as recently as ten years ago. Certain tribes in remote parts of Africa may still practice it. The oracle or some other voice tells you that the blood of a human must be sacrificed, otherwise the community will be wiped out by famine or another malevolent force. Men also kill to enhance their sense of maleness and potency. This resembles being thrown into the bush to fight lions as a test of manhood. If you come back alive, you're a big man.

Bass: You coined the term "malignant anxiety." What does it mean?

Lambo: It describes the psychic state of people like the Leopard Men, a condition of excruciating, impulsive anxiety that is action oriented. Once it has seized you in its grip, you have to do something about it—rip out the heart of an animal or kill someone. The phenomenon is similar to running amok in Southeast Asian cultures.

The person becomes deadly unstable and restless. He perspires tremendously. When you hold him down and ask, "What's wrong?" he replies, "I don't know! I don't know!" People say the spirits have possessed him. Men in this condition have been brought to me. I've given them sedatives and sent them home after they've slept for two days. But in other cases, when they have been taken to hospitals where the condition wasn't recognized, they have gone out and done serious injury.

Bass: How does mental illness in Africa differ from that in New York City?

Lambo: In Africa it's pure. If you're dealing with schizophrenia, it's schizophrenia pure and simple. In the West, schizophrenia will have multiple manifestations, and these manifestations will be masked. Africans recover more quickly and permanently than the other people we studied. This is because of the tremendous social support they receive in their villages. Illness in Africa is not individual, it's communal; psychotherapy is built into everyone's everyday interactions.

Bass: Does Africa have forms of mental illness not found in Europe?

Lambo: My colleagues thought the Yoruba tended to get manic without being depressive. But I told them this wasn't true. It was only from their Western perspective that the African looked manic. While the European is withdrawn, quiet, a cornered type of person, the African is so excitable that he's almost normally manic.

Bass: Is hysteria more prevalent in Africa?

Lambo: Yes, but we use the term "hysteria" because there is no other word for it. In the evening an entire village will be crying and wailing as goats are killed for a burial ceremony, but by morning everyone is back to laughing and joking. Do we call this hysteria and talk of "dualism in the African personality," or is it really just tribal life? We need new words. Our psychiatric terminology is culture-bound, and the culture it's bound to is not our own. I prefer to describe these phenomena as "pseudo-hysteria." They resemble hysteria, but they are not hysteria. They are actually acute manifestations of grief.

Bass: What do you mean when you say that Africans display "herd solidarity?"

Lambo: Sometimes whole villages would hire a truck and arrive outside the gates of the Aro hospital at four o'clock in the morning. One night I counted sixty-four people in three huge lorries. They might been been on the road for days, travelling up to seven hundred miles. The patient would be bound in ropes, suffering from schizophrenia or another form of psychosis. But if he were the son of a chief or the chief himself, the whole village would come in solidarity.

I took case histories from all these people, the patient's mother, his wives, cousins, uncles, and so on. How did his sickness first manifest itself? How long has he been acting strange? This wasn't just Mrs. Smith telling the psychiatrist about the odd behavior of her husband. This was the whole village recounting months of observations. Although I haven't been there for years, I understand people are still driving hundreds of miles from every part of Nigeria to get to "Lambo's hospital."

Bass: What are the drawbacks of tribalism?

Lambo: It is supposed to be a balance wheel, but in practice it is a locked brake. Herd solidarity provides tremendous social support, but at the same time you have to obey its rules by not marrying outside the tribe and so on. Tribalism is a profoundly conservative influence.

Bass: Will tribalism survive in modern Africa?

Lambo: It won't vanish, but it will be transformed. New social support mechanisms will take its place. Africa has many valuable things that the Western powers have lost.

That's why I shout, "Don't throw out the baby with the bath water!" Look to your own culture. Learn from it. Develop your own models for living."

Bass: Is the spirit world of the ancestors still a real force in Africa?

Lambo: Tremendously so, and I hope it will go on for a long time. The ancestors support you. You go to their graves when faced with making an important decision. The mechanism is similar to confession in the Roman Catholic church. If you have nowhere to go, if you are alone in the world, you internalize your guilt, and the only way out is to commit suicide.

In Africa the atmosphere is still charged with supernaturalism. Even people who have got their Ph.D.s in England can fall back on their culture. When I was in Geneva, someone came into my office and said, "Tom, they're after me. So and so is using juju on me." This man wanted to get the Ministry of Health, and the other man didn't want him to. Within three days of becoming minister, the man was found dead in his chair, maybe because of a heart attack, maybe not. The other man was offered the chance to succeed him, but he would only take the job if the chair was destroyed. In Africa the gods are still alive.

Bass: How can Africa avoid the psychological problems of development?

Lambo: We have not prepared people for social change. For example, Nigeria woke up one day and said it wanted to build a big cement factory in a rural area. No one thought about the young men of the villages who would have to work there. None of them was trained to get up at seven o'clock in the morning. Time is timeless in Africa. After doing a two-year study financed by the Ford Foundation, I found the young men becoming progressively more confused, depressed, anxious. Absenteeism was climbing sky high. Building something overnight had caused tremendous psychoneuroses.

Very little could be done about the problem. I told the government and the bwanas in the factory, "Look, you've done the wrong thing. It's not enough just to clear the land and build a factory. You started this operation without giving the slightest thought to training the people who would have to work in it."

Bass: Are you pessimistic or optimistic about the future?

Lambo: Africans are resilient and courageous. Like a soccer ball kicked against the wall, they keep coming back at you. Europeans are fragile, while Africans are more agile, both physically and mentally. This is why we will absolutely survive. But you know, there is no culture in the world free of neuroses.

The Sorcerer and His Magic

Claude Lévi-Strauss

Claude Lévi-Strauss, the leading exponent of the French structural school of anthropology, here analyzes the elements of the "shamanistic complex" and demonstrates by example their reliance on one another. The overall effectiveness of the sorcerer's treatment relies on the integration of his own belief in the effectiveness of his powers, the patient's belief in therapy, and the support of and faith in the shaman and his herbal and supernatural powers by members of society. An important component of the success or failure of shamans is directly related to the powerful elements of suggestion that pervade the interaction of shamans with patients and society. The marked difference between the confidence, indeed omnipotence, of the shaman, on the one hand, and the anxiety of the patient and his family, on the other, is important to the cure. So too is the sorcerer's secret knowledge of formulas, incantations, and other methods of control over supernatural agents who work at his command to help effect the cure. The final element in suggestion is the homogeneous belief system of the members of the patient's society, who reify and validate the power of the sorcerer. All these elements aid the sorcerer and demonstrate a marked difference between Western and non-Western treatment of psychophysical ailments.

SINCE THE PIONEERING WORK OF CANNON, WE understand more clearly the psycho-physiological mechanisms underlying the instances reported from many parts of the world of death by exorcism and the casting of spells. An individual who is aware that he is the object of sorcery is thoroughly convinced that he is doomed according to the most solemn traditions of his group. His friends and relatives share this certainty. From then on the community withdraws. Standing aloof from the accursed, it treats him not only as though he were already dead but as though he were a source of danger to the entire group. On every occasion and by every action, the social body suggests death to the unfortunate victim, who no longer hopes to escape what he considers to be his ineluctable fate. Shortly thereafter, sacred rites are held to dispatch him to the realm of shadows. First brutally torn from all of his family and social ties and excluded from all functions and activities through which he experienced self-awareness, then banished by the same forces from the world of the living, the victim yields to the combined effect of intense terror, the sudden total withdrawal of the multiple reference systems provided by the support of the group, and, finally, to the group's decisive reversal in proclaiming him —once a living man, with rights and obligations —dead and an object of fear, ritual, and taboo. Physical integrity cannot withstand the dissolution of the social personality.

How are these complex phenomena expressed on the physiological level? Cannon showed that fear, like rage, is associated with a particularly intense activity of the sympathetic nervous system. This activity is ordinarily useful, involving organic modifications which enable the individual to adapt himself to a new situation. But if the individual cannot avail himself of any instinctive or acquired response to an extraordinary situation (or to one which he conceives of as such), the activity of the sympathetic nervous system becomes intensified and disorganized; it may, sometimes within a few hours, lead to a decrease in the volume of blood and a concomitant drop in blood pressure, which result in irreparable damage to the circulatory organs. The rejection of food and drink, frequent among patients in the throes of intense anxiety, precipitates this process; dehydration acts as a stimulus to the sympathetic nervous system, and the decrease in blood volume is accentuated by the growing permeability of the capillary vessels. These hypotheses were confirmed by the study of several cases of trauma resulting from bombings, battle shock, and even surgical operations; death results, yet the autopsy reveals no lesions.

There is, therefore, no reason to doubt the efficacy of certain magical practices. But at the same time we see that the efficacy of magic implies a belief in magic. The latter has three complementary aspects: first, the sorcerer's belief in the effectiveness of his techniques; second, the patient's or victim's belief in the sorcerer's power; and, finally, the faith and expectations of the group, which constantly act as a sort of gravitational field within which the relationship between sorcerer and bewitched is located and defined. Obviously, none of the three parties is capable of forming a clear picture of the sympathetic nervous system's activity or of the disturbances which Cannon called homeostatic. When the sorcerer claims to suck out of the patient's body a foreign object whose presence would explain the illness and produces a stone which he had previously hidden in his mouth, how does he justify this procedure in his own eyes? How can an innocent person accused of sorcery prove his innocence if the accusation is unanimous—since the magical situation is a consensual phenomenon? And, finally, how much credulity and how much skepticism are involved in the attitude of the group toward those in whom it recognizes extraordinary powers, to whom it accords corresponding privileges, but from whom it also requires adequate satisfaction? Let us begin by examining this last point.

It was in September, 1938. For several weeks we had been camping with a small band of Nambicuara Indians near the headwaters of the Tapajoz, in those desolate savannas of central Brazil where the natives wander during the greater part of the year, collecting seeds and wild fruits, hunting small mammals, insects, and reptiles, and whatever else might prevent them from dying of starvation. Thirty of them were camped together there, quite by chance. They were grouped in families under frail lean-tos of branches, which give scant protection from the scorching sun, nocturnal chill, rain, and wind. Like most bands, this one had both a secular chief and a sorcerer; the latter's daily activities—hunting, fishing, and handicrafts—were in no way different from those of the other men of the group. He was a robust man, about forty-five years old, and a *bon vivant*.

One evening, however, he did not return to camp at the usual time. Night fell and fires were lit; the natives were visibly worried. Countless perils lurk in the bush: torrential rivers, the somewhat improbable danger of encountering a large wild beast—jaguar or anteater—or, more readily pictured by the Nambicuara, an apparently harmless animal which is the incarnation of an evil spirit of the waters or forest. And above all, each night for the past week we had seen mysterious campfires, which sometimes approached and sometimes receded from our own. Any unknown band is always potentially hostile. After a two-hour wait, the natives were convinced that their companion had been killed in ambush and, while his two young wives and his son wept noisily in mourning for their dead husband and father, the other natives discussed the tragic consequences, foreshadowed by the disappearance of their sorcerer.

Toward ten that evening, the anguished anticipation of imminent disaster, the lamentations in which the other women began to join, and the agitation of the men had created an intolerable atmosphere, and we decided to reconnoiter with several natives who had remained relatively calm. We had not gone two hundred yards when we stumbled upon a motionless figure. It was our man, crouching silently, shivering in the chilly night air, disheveled and without his belt, necklaces, and arm-bands (the Nambicuara wear nothing else). He allowed us to lead him back to the camp site without resistance, but only after long exhortations by his group and pleading by his family was he persuaded to talk. Finally, bit by bit, we extracted the details of his story. A thunderstorm, the first of the season, had burst during the afternoon, and the thunder had carried him off to a site several miles distant, which he named, and then, after stripping him completely, had brought him back to the spot where we found him. Everyone went off to sleep commenting on the event. The next day the thunder victim had recovered his joviality and, what is more, all his ornaments. This last detail did not appear to surprise anyone, and life resumed its normal course.

A few days later, however, another version of these prodigious events began to be circulated by certain natives. We must note that this band was actually composed of individuals of different origins and had been fused into a new social entity as a result of unknown circumstances. One of the groups had been decimated by an epidemic several years before and was no longer sufficiently large to lead an independent life; the other had seceded from its original tribe and found itself in the same straits. When and under what circumstances the two groups met and decided to unite their efforts, we could not discover. The secular leader of the new band came from one group and the sorcerer, or religious leader, from the other. The fusion was obviously recent, for no marriage had yet taken place between the two groups when we met them, although the children of one were usually betrothed to the children of the other; each group had retained its own dialect, and their members could communicate only through two or three bilingual natives.

This is the rumor that was spread. There was good reason to suppose that the unknown bands crossing the savanna belonged to the tribe of the seceded group of which the sorcerer was a member. The sorcerer, impinging on the functions of his colleague the political chief, had doubtless wanted to contact his former tribesmen, perhaps to ask to return to the fold, or to provoke an attack upon his new companions, or perhaps even to reassure them of the friendly intentions of the latter. In any case, the sorcerer had needed a pretext for his absence, and his kidnapping by thunder and its subsequent staging were invented toward this end. It was, of course, the natives of the other group who spread this interpretation, which they secretly believed and which filled them with apprehension. But the official version was never publicly disputed, and until we left, shortly after the incident, it remained ostensibly accepted by all.

Although the skeptics had analyzed the sorcerer's motives with great psychological finesse and political acumen, they would have been greatly astonished had someone suggested (quite plausibly) that the incident was a hoax which cast doubt upon the sorcerer's good faith and competence. He had

probably not flown on the wings of thunder to the Rio Ananaz and had only staged an act. But these things might have happened, they had certainly happened in other circumstances, and they belonged to the realm of real experience. Certainly the sorcerer maintains an intimate relationship with the forces of the supernatural. The idea that in a particular case he had used his power to conceal a secular activity belongs to the realm of conjecture and provides an opportunity for critical judgment. The important point is that these two possibilities were not mutually exclusive; no more than are, for us, the alternate interpretations of war as the dying gasp of national independence or as the result of the schemes of munitions manufacturers. The two explanations are logically incompatible, but we admit that one or the other may be true; since they are equally plausible, we easily make the transition from one to the other, depending on the occasion and the moment. Many people have both explanations in the back of their minds.

Whatever their true origin, these divergent interpretations come from individual consciousness not as the result of objective analysis but rather as complementary ideas resulting from hazy and unelaborated attitudes which have an experiential character for each of us. These experiences, however, remain intellectually diffuse and emotionally intolerable unless they incorporate one or another of the patterns present in the group's culture. The assimilation of such patterns is the only means of objectivizing subjective states, of formulating inexpressible feelings, and of integrating inarticulated experiences into a system.

These mechanisms become clearer in the light of some observations made many years ago among the Zuni of New Mexico by an admirable fieldworker, M. C. Stevenson. A twelve-year-old girl was stricken with a nervous seizure directly after an adolescent boy had seized her hands. The youth was accused of sorcery and dragged before the court of the Bow priesthood. For an hour he denied having any knowledge of occult power, but this defense proved futile. Because the crime of sorcery was at that time still punished by death among the Zuni, the accused changed his tactics. He improvised a tale explaining the circumstances by which he had been initiated into sorcery. He said he had received two substances from his teachers, one which drove girls insane and another which cured them. This point constituted an ingenious precaution against later developments. Having been ordered to produce his medicines, he went home under guard and came back with two roots, which he proceeded to use in a complicated ritual. He simulated a trance after taking one of the drugs, and after taking the other he pretended to return to his normal state. Then he administered the remedy to the sick girl and declared her cured. The session was adjourned until the following day, but during the night the alleged sorcerer escaped. He was soon captured, and the girl's family set itself up as a court and continued the trial. Faced with the reluctance of his new judges to accept his first story, the boy then invented a new one. He told them that all his relatives and ancestors had been witches and that he had received marvelous powers from them. He claimed that he could assume the form of a cat, fill his mouth with cactus needles, and kill his victims—two infants, three girls, and two boys—by shooting the needles into them. These feats, he claimed, were due to the magical powers of certain plumes which were used to change him and his family into shapes other than human. This last detail was a tactical error, for the judges called upon him to produce the plumes as proof of his new story. He gave various excuses which were rejected one after another, and he was forced to take his judges to his house. He began by declaring that the plumes were secreted in a wall that he could not destroy. He commanded to go to work. After breaking down a section of the wall and carefully examining the plaster, he tried to excuse himself by declaring that the plumes had been hidden two years before and that he could not remember their exact location. Forced to search again, he tried another wall, and after another hour's work, an old plume appeared in the plaster. He grabbed it eagerly and presented it to his prosecutors as the magic device of which he had spoken. He was then made to explain the details of its use. Finally, dragged into the public plaza, he had to repeat his entire story (to which he added a wealth of new detail). He finished it with a pathetic speech in which he lamented the loss of his supernatural power. Thus reassured, his listeners agreed to free him.

This narrative, which we unfortunately had to abridge and strip of all its psychological nuances, is still instructive in many respects. First of all, we see that the boy tried for witchcraft, for which he risks the death penalty, wins his acquittal not by denying but by admitting his alleged crime. Moreover, he furthers his cause by presenting successive versions, each richer in detail (and thus, in theory, more persuasive of guilt) than the preceding one. The debate does not proceed, as do debates among us, by accusations and denials, but rather by allegations and specifications. The judges do not expect the accused to challenge their theory, much less to refute the facts. Rather, they require him to validate a system of which they possess only a fragment; he must reconstruct it as a whole in an appropriate way. As the field-worker noted in relation to a phase of the trial, "The warriors had become so absorbed by their interest in the narrative of the boy that they seemed entirely to have forgotten the cause of his appearance before them." And when the magic plume was finally uncovered, the author remarks with great insight, "There was consternation among the warriors, who exclaimed in one voice: 'What does this mean?' Now they felt assured that the youth had spoken the truth." Consternation, and not triumph at finding a tangible proof of the crime—for the judges had sought to bear witness to the reality of the system which had made the crime possible (by validating its objective basis through an appropriate emotional expression), rather than simply to punish a crime. By his confession, the defendant is transformed into a witness for the prosecution, with the participation (and even the complicity) of his judges. Through the defendant, witchcraft and the ideas associated with it cease to exist as a diffuse complex of poorly formulated sentiments and representations and become embodied in real experience. The defendant, who serves as a witness, gives the group the satisfaction of truth, which is infinitely greater and richer than the satisfaction of justice that would have been achieved by his execution. And finally, by his ingenious defense which makes his hearers progressively aware of the vitality offered by his corroboration of their system (especially since the choice is not between this system and another, but between the magical system and no system at all—that is, chaos), the youth, who at first was a threat to the physical security of his group, became the guardian of its spiritual coherence.

But is his defense merely ingenious? Everything leads us to believe that after groping for a subterfuge, the defendant participates with sincerity and—the word is not too strong—fervor in the drama enacted between him and his judges. He is proclaimed a sorcerer; since sorcerers do exist, he might well be one. And how would he know beforehand the signs which might reveal his calling to him? Perhaps the signs are there, present in this ordeal and in the convulsions of the little girl brought before the court. For the boy, too, the coherence of the system and the role assigned to him in preserving it are values no less essential than the personal security which he risks in the venture. Thus we see him, with a mixture of cunning and good faith, progressively construct the impersonation which is thrust upon him—chiefly by drawing on his knowledge and his memories, improvising somewhat, but above all living his role and seeking through his manipulations and the ritual he builds from bits and pieces, the experience of a calling which is, at least theoretically, open to all. At the end of the adventure, what remains of his earlier hoaxes? To what extent has the hero become the dupe of his own impersonation? What is more, has he not truly become a sorcerer? We are told that in his final confession, "The longer the boy talked the more absorbed he became in his subject. . . . At times his face became radiant with satisfaction at his power over his listeners." The girl recovers after he performs his curing ritual. The boy's experiences during the extraordinary ordeal become elaborated and structured. Little more is needed than for the innocent boy finally to confess to the possession of supernatural powers that are already recognized by the group.

We must consider at greater length another especially valuable document, which until now seems to have been valued solely for its linguistic interest. I refer to a fragment of the autobiography of a Kwakiutl Indian from the Vancouver region of Canada, obtained by Franz Boas.

Quesalid (for this was the name he received when he became a sorcerer) did not believe in the power of the sorcerers—or, more accurately, shamans, since this is a better term for their specific type of activity in certain regions of the world. Driven by curiosity about their tricks and by the desire to expose them, he began to associate with the shamans until one of them offered to make him a member of their group. Quesalid did not wait to be asked twice, and his narrative recounts the details of his first lessons, a curious mixture of pantomime, prestidigi-

tation, and empirical knowledge, including the art of simulating fainting and nervous fits, the learning of sacred songs, the technique for inducing vomiting, rather precise notions of auscultation and obstetrics, and the use of "dreamers," that is, spies who listen to private conversations and secretly convey to the shaman bits of information concerning the origins and symptoms of the ills suffered by different people. Above all, he learned the *ars magna* of one of the shamanistic schools of the Northwest Coast: The shaman hides a little tuft of down in the corner of his mouth, and he throws it up, covered with blood, at the proper moment—after having bitten his tongue or made his gums bleed—and solemnly presents it to his patient and the onlookers as the pathological foreign body extracted as a result of his sucking and manipulations.

His worst suspicions confirmed, Quesalid wanted to continue his inquiry. But he was no longer free. His apprenticeship among the shamans began to be noised about, and one day he was summoned by the family of a sick person who had dreamed of Quesalid as his healer. This first treatment (for which he received no payment, any more than he did for those which followed, since he had not completed the required four years of apprenticeship) was an outstanding success. Although Quesalid came to be known from that moment on as a "great shaman," he did not lose his critical faculties. He interpreted his success in psychological terms—it was successful "because he [the sick person] believed strongly in his dream about me." A more complex adventure made him, in his own words, "hesitant and thinking about many things." Here he encountered several varieties of a "false supernatural," and was led to conclude that some forms were less false than others—those, of course, in which he had a personal stake and whose system he was, at the same time, surreptitiously building up in his mind. A summary of the adventure follows.

While visiting the neighboring Koskimo Indians, Quesalid attends a curing ceremony of his illustrious colleagues of the other tribe. To his great astonishment he observes a difference in their technique. Instead of spitting out the illness in the form of a "bloody worm" (the concealed down), the Koskimo shamans merely spit a little saliva into their hands, and they dare to claim that this is "the sickness." What is the value of this method? What is the theory behind it? In order to find out "the strength of the shamans, whether it was real or whether they only pretended to be shamans" like his fellow tribesmen, Quesalid requests and obtains permission to try his method in an instance where the Koskimo method has failed. The sick woman then declares herself cured.

And here our hero vacillates for the first time. Though he had few illusions about his own technique, he has now found one which is more false, more mystifying, and more dishonest than his own. For he at least gives his clients something. He presents them with their sickness in a visible and tangible form, while his foreign colleagues show nothing at all and only claim to have captured the sickness. Moreover, Quesalid's method gets results, while the other is futile. Thus our hero grapples with a problem which perhaps has its parallel in the development of modern science. Two systems which we know to be inadequate present (with respect to each other) a differential validity, from both a logical and an empirical perspective. From which frame of reference shall we judge them? On the level of fact, where they merge, or on their own level, where they take on different values, both theoretically and empirically?

Meanwhile, the Koskimo shamans, "ashamed" and discredited before their tribesmen, are also plunged into doubt. Their colleague has produced, in the form of a material object, the illness which they had always considered as spiritual in nature and had thus never dreamed of rendering visible. They send Quesalid an emissary to invite him to a secret meeting in a cave. Quesalid goes and his foreign colleagues expound their system to him: "Every sickness is a man: boils and swellings, and itch and scabs, and pimples and coughs and consumption and scrofula; and also this, stricture of the bladder and stomach aches. . . . As soon as we get the soul of the sickness which is a man, then dies the sickness which is a man. Its body just disappears in our insides." If this theory is correct, what is there to show? And why, when Quesalid operates, does "the sickness stick to his hand"? But Quesalid takes refuge behind professional rules which forbid him to teach before completing four years of apprenticeship, and refuses to speak. He maintains his silence even when the Koskimo shamans send him their allegedly virgin daughters to try to seduce him and discover his secret.

Thereupon Quesalid returns to his village at Fort Rupert. He learns that the most reputed shaman of a neighboring clan, worried about Quesalid's growing renown, has challenged all his colleagues, inviting them to compete with him in curing several patients. Quesalid comes to the contest and observes the cures of his elder. Like the Koskimo, this shaman does not show the illness. He simply incorporates an invisible object, "what he called the sickness" into his head-ring, made of bark, or into his bird-shaped ritual rattle. These objects can hang suspended in mid-air, owing to the power of the illness which "bites" the house-posts or the shaman's hand. The usual drama unfolds. Quesalid is asked to intervene in cases judged hopeless by his predecessor, and he triumphs with his technique of the bloody worm.

Here we come to the truly pathetic part of the story. The old shaman, ashamed and despairing because of the ill-repute into which he has fallen and by the collapse of his therapeutic technique, sends his daughter to Quesalid to beg him for an interview. The latter finds his colleague sitting under a tree and the old shaman begins thus: "It won't be bad what we say to each other, friend, but only I wish you to try and save my life for me, so that I may not die of shame, for I am a plaything of our people on account of what you did last night. I pray you to have mercy and tell me what stuck on the palm of your hand last night. Was it the true sickness or was it only made up? For I beg you have mercy and tell me about the way you did it so that I can imitate you. Pity me, friend."

Silent at first, Quesalid begins by calling for explanations about the feats of the head-ring and the rattle. His colleague shows him the nail hidden in the head-ring which he can press at right angles into the post, and the way in which he tucks the head of his rattle between his finger joints to make it look as if the bird were hanging by its beak from his hand. He himself probably does nothing but lie and fake, simulating shamanism for material gain, for he admits of being "covetous for the property of the sick men." He knows that shamans cannot catch souls, "for . . . we all own a soul"; so he resorts to using tallow and pretends that "it is a soul . . . that white thing . . . sitting on my hand." The daughter then adds her entreaties to those of her father: "Do have mercy that he may live." But Quesalid remains silent. That very night, following this tragic conversation, the shaman disappears with his entire family, heartsick and feared by the community, who think that he may be tempted to take revenge. Needless fears: He returned a year later, but both he and his daughter had gone mad. Three years later, he died.

And Quesalid, rich in secrets, pursued his career, exposing the impostors and full of contempt for the profession. "Only one shaman was seen by me, who sucked at a sick man and I never found out whether he was a real shaman or only made up. Only for this reason I believe that he is a shaman; he does not allow those who are made well to pay him. I truly never once saw him laugh." Thus his original attitude has changed considerably. The radical negativism of the free thinker has given way to more moderate feelings. Real shamans do exist. And what about him? At the end of the narrative we cannot tell, but it is evident that he carries on his craft conscientiously, takes pride in his achievements, and warmly defends the technique of the bloody down against all rival schools. He seems to have completely lost sight of the fallaciousness of the technique which he had so disparaged at the beginning.

We see that the psychology of the sorcerer is not simple. In order to analyze it, we shall first examine the case of the old shaman who begs his young rival to tell him the truth—whether the illness glued in the palm of his hand like a sticky red worm is real or made up—and who goes mad when he receives no answer. Before the tragedy, he was fully convinced of two things—first, that pathological conditions have a cause which may be discovered and second, that a system of interpretation in which personal inventiveness is important structures the phases of the illness, from the diagnosis to the cure. This fabulation of a reality unknown in itself—a fabulation consisting of procedures and representations—is founded on a threefold experience: first, that of the shaman himself, who, if his calling is a true one (and even if it is not, simply by virtue of his practicing it), undergoes specific states of a psychosomatic nature; second, that of the sick person, who may or may not experience an improvement of his condition; and, finally, that of the public, who also participate in the cure, experiencing an enthusiasm and an intellectual and emotional satisfaction which produce collective support, which in turn inaugurates a new cycle.

These three elements of what we might call the "shamanistic complex" cannot be separated. But they are clustered around two poles, one formed by the intimate experience of the shaman and the other by group consensus. There is no reason to doubt that sorcerers, or at least the more sincere among them,

believe in their calling and that this belief is founded on the experiencing of specific states. The hardships and privations which they undergo would often be sufficient in themselves to provoke these states, even if we refuse to admit them as proof of a serious and fervent calling. But there is also linguistic evidence which, because it is indirect, is more convincing. In the Wintu dialect of California, there are five verbal classes which correspond to knowledge by sight, by bodily experience, by inference, by reasoning, and by hearsay. All five make up the category of knowledge as opposed to conjecture, which is differently expressed. Curiously enough, relationships with the supernatural world are expressed by means of the modes of knowledge—by bodily impression (that is, the most intuitive kind of experience), by inference, and by reasoning. Thus the native who becomes a shaman after a spiritual crisis conceives of his state grammatically, as a consequence to be inferred from the fact—formulated as real experience—that he has received divine guidance. From the latter he concludes deductively that he must have been on a journey to the beyond, at the end of which he found himself—again, an immediate experience—once more among his people.

The experiences of the sick person represent the least important aspect of the system, except for the fact that a patient successfully treated by a shaman is in an especially good position to become a shaman in his own right, as we see today in the case of psychoanalysis. In any event, we must remember that the shaman does not completely lack empirical knowledge and experimental techniques, which may in part explain his success. Furthermore, disorders of the type currently termed psychosomatic, which constitute a large part of the illnesses prevalent in societies with a low degree of security, probably often yield to psychotherapy. At any rate, it seems probable that medicine men, like their civilized colleagues, cure at least some of the cases they treat and that without this relative success magical practices could not have been so widely diffused in time and space. But this point is not fundamental; it is subordinate to the other two. Quesalid did not become a great shaman because he cured his patients; he cured his patients because he had become a great shaman. Thus we have reached the other—that is, the collective—pole of our system.

The true reason for the defeat of Quesalid's rivals must then be sought in the attitude of the group rather than in the pattern of the rivals' successes and failures. The rivals themselves emphasize this when they confess their shame at having become the laughingstock of the group; this is a social sentiment *par excellence*. Failure is secondary, and we see in all their statements that they consider it a function of another phenomenon, which is the disappearance of the *social consensus*, recreated at their expense around another practitioner and another system of curing. Consequently, the fundamental problem revolves around the relationship between the individual and the group, or, more accurately, the relationship between a specific category of individuals and specific expectations of the group.

In treating his patient the shaman also offers his audience a performance. What is this performance? Risking a rash generalization on the basis of a few observations, we shall say that it always involves the shaman's enactment of the "call," or the initial crisis which brought him the revelation of his condition. But we must not be deceived by the word *performance*. The shaman does not limit himself to reproducing or miming certain events. He actually relives them in all their vividness, originality, and violence. And since he returns to his normal state at the end of the séance, we may say, borrowing a key term from psychoanalysis, that he *abreacts*. In psychoanalysis, abreaction refers to the decisive moment in the treatment when the patient intensively relives the initial situation from which his disturbance stems, before he ultimately overcomes it. In this sense, the shaman is a professional abreactor.

We have set forth elsewhere the theoretical hypotheses that might be formulated in order for us to accept the idea that the type of abreaction specific to each shaman—or, at any rate, to each shamanistic school—might symbolically induce an abreaction of his own disturbance in each patient. In any case, if the relationship is that between the shaman and the group, we must also state the question from another point of view—that of the relationship between normal and pathological thinking. From any non-scientific perspective (and here we can exclude no society), pathological and normal thought processes are complementary rather than opposed. In a universe which it strives to understand but whose dynamics it cannot fully control, normal thought continually seeks the meaning of things which refuse to reveal their significance. So-called patho-

logical thought, on the other hand, overflows with emotional interpretations and overtones, in order to supplement an otherwise deficient reality. For normal thinking there exists something which cannot be empirically verified and is, therefore, "claimable." For pathological thinking there exist experiences without object, or something "available." We might borrow from linguistics and say that so-called normal thought always suffers from a deficit of meaning, whereas so-called pathological thought (in at least some of its manifestations) disposes of a plethora of meaning. Through collective participation in shamanistic curing, a balance is established between these two complementary situations. Normal thought cannot fathom the problem of illness, and so the group calls upon the neurotic to furnish a wealth of emotion heretofore lacking a focus.

An equilibrium is reached between what might be called supply and demand on the psychic level—but only on two conditions. First, a structure must be elaborated and continually modified through the interaction of group tradition and individual invention. This structure is a system of oppositions and correlations, integrating all the elements of a total situation, in which sorcerer, patient, and audience, as well as representations and procedures, all play their parts. Furthermore, the public must participate in the abreaction, to a certain extent at least, along with the patient and the sorcerer. It is this vital experience of a universe of symbolic effusions which the patient, because he is ill, and the sorcerer, because he is neurotic—in other words, both having types of experience which cannot otherwise be integrated—allow the public to glimpse as "fireworks" from a safe distance. In the absence of any experimental control, which is indeed unnecessary, it is this experience alone, and its relative richness in each case, which makes possible a choice between several systems and elicits adherence to a particular school or practitioner.

In contrast with scientific explanation, the problem here is not to attribute confused and disorganized states, emotions, or representations to an objective cause, but rather to articulate them into a whole or system. The system is valid precisely to the extent that it allows the coalescence or precipitation of these diffuse states, whose discontinuity also makes them painful. To the conscious mind, this last phenomenon constitutes an original experience which cannot be grasped from without. Because of their complementary disorders, the sorcerer-patient dyad incarnates for the group, in vivid and concrete fashion, an antagonism that is inherent in all thought but that normally remains vague and imprecise. The patient is all passivity and self-alienation, just as inexpressibility is the disease of the mind. The sorcerer is activity and self-projection, just as affectivity is the source of symbolism. The cure interrelates these opposite poles, facilitating the transition from one to the other, and demonstrates, within a total experience, the coherence of the psychic universe, itself a projection of the social universe.

Thus it is necessary to extend the notion of abreaction by examining the meanings it acquires in psychotherapies other than psychoanalysis, although the latter deserves the credit for rediscovering and insisting upon its fundamental validity. It may be objected that in psychoanalysis there is only one abreaction, the patient's, rather than three. We are not so sure of this. It is true that in the shamanistic cure the sorcerer speaks and abreacts *for* the silent patient, while in psychoanalysis it is the patient who talks and abreacts *against* the listening therapist. But the therapist's abreaction, while not concomitant with the patient's, is nonetheless required, since he must be analyzed before he himself can become an analyst. It is more difficult to define the role ascribed to the group by each technique. Magic readapts the group predefined problems through the patient, while psychoanalysis readapts the patient to the group by means of the solutions reached. But the distressing trend which, for several years, has tended to transform the psychoanalytic system from a body of scientific hypotheses that are experimentally verifiable in certain specific and limited cases into a kind of diffuse mythology interpenetrating the consciousness of the group, could rapidly bring about a parallelism. (This group consciousness is an objective phenomenon, which the psychologist expresses through a subjective tendency to extend to normal thought a system of interpretations conceived for pathological thought and to apply to facts of collective psychology a method adapted solely to the study of individual psychology.) When this happens—and perhaps it already has in certain countries—the value of the system will no longer be based upon real cures from which certain individuals can benefit, but on the sense of security that the group receives from the myth underlying the cure and from the popular system upon which the group's universe is reconstructed.

Even at the present time, the comparison between psychoanalysis and older and more widespread psychological therapies can encourage the former to re-examine its principles and methods. By continuously expanding the recruitment of its patients, who began as clearly characterized abnormal individuals and gradually become representative of the group, psychoanalysis, transforms its treatments into conversions. For only a patient can emerge cured; an unstable or maladjusted individual can only be persuaded. A considerable danger thus arises: The treatment (unbeknown to the therapist, naturally), far from leading to the resolution of a specific disturbance within its own context, is reduced to the reorganization of the patient's universe in terms of psychoanalytic interpretations. This means that we would finally arrive at precisely that situation which furnishes the point of departure as well as theoretical validity of the magico-social system that we have analyzed.

If this analysis is correct, we must see magical behavior as the response to a situation which is revealed to the mind through emotional manifestations, but whose essence is intellectual. For only the history of the symbolic function can allow us to understand the intellectual condition of man, in which the universe is never charged with sufficient meaning and in which the mind always has more meanings available than there are objects to which to relate them. Torn between these two systems of reference—the signifying and the signified—man asks magical thinking to provide him with a new system of reference, within which the thus-far contradictory elements can be integrated. But we know that this system is built at the expense of the progress of knowledge, which would have required us to retain only one of the two previous systems and to refine it to the point where it absorbed the other. This point is still far off. We must not permit the individual, whether normal or neurotic, to repeat this collective misadventure. The study of the mentally sick individual has shown us that all persons are more or less oriented toward contradictory systems and suffer from the resulting conflict; but the fact that a certain form of integration is possible and effective practically is not enough to make it true, or to make us certain that the adaptation thus achieved does not constitute an absolute regression in relation to the previous conflict situation.

The reabsorption of a deviant specific synthesis, through its integration with the normal syntheses, into a general but arbitrary synthesis (aside from critical cases where action is required) would represent a loss on all fronts. A body of elementary hypotheses can have a certain instrumental value for the practitioner without necessarily being recognized, in theoretical analysis, as the final image of reality and without necessarily linking the patient and the therapist in a kind of mystical communion which does not have the same meaning for both parties and which only ends by reducing the treatment to a fabulation.

In the final analysis we could only expect this fabulation to be a language, whose function is to provide a socially authorized translation of phenomena whose deeper nature would become once again equally impenetrable to the group, the patient, and the healer.

Folk Medical Magic and Symbolism in the West

Wayland D. Hand

In this selection, folklorist Wayland Hand turns to the United States to give us several fascinating examples of magical medicine and folk medical symbolism. In Utah, there are those who believe walnuts are good for diseases of the brain (because the meat of the nut looks like the brain), whereas in other Western states some people wear a red string around the neck to stop a nosebleed. In California, Arkansas, and Oklahoma, children with chickenpox may be taken to a chicken coop in order to let chickens fly over them and thus effect a cure. These and dozens of other magical beliefs from the western United States are discussed in this article, which will help the reader to realize that folk medical magic and symbolism are not just part of a system of quaint beliefs and practices from Africa, New Guinea, or aboriginal Australia but continue to be well known and practiced in the contemporary United States.

Reprinted from Austin and Alfa Fife and Henry H. Glassie, eds., *Forms upon the Frontier*. Utah State University, Monograph Series, XVI, no. 2 (April 1969), pp. 103–18. By permission of the publisher. The article's citations, originally numbered footnotes, have been interpolated into the text in this volume for consistency of presentation.

THE COLLECTING OF FOLK MEDICINE IN THE WEST has not been under way long enough to permit anything approaching a full survey of the causes and cures of disease and matters having to do with the medical aspects of the life cycle, particularly with birth and death. Even so, there is at hand a sufficiently representative body of medical folklore to constitute at least an adumbration of the kinds of material that still await the hand of the collector in the sprawling country beyond the Mississippi (Anderson 1968; Fife 1957; Hand 1971; Lathrop 1961). It is my purpose here to concentrate on the more neglected areas of folk medical study in the West, namely magical medicine and folk medical symbolism as it derives from elementary forms of magic.

In putting this paper together, I have drawn on archival material for California and other western states that has been accumulating from student collectanea for the past fifteen or twenty years in the Archive of California and Western Folklore at the University of California at Los Angeles. Systematic collecting in Utah, also through students, has been undertaken by my colleague at the University of Utah, Professor Anthon S. Cannon, who is collaborating with me in the preparation of the Utah volume tributary of the Dictionary of American Popular Beliefs and Superstitions. The extensive Austin and Alta Fife collections, made in Moab, Utah, in 1953, have also been at my disposal. To the heavy unpublished material from California and Utah have been added much lighter samplings from other western states, but the footnotes to this paper contain a backup of published material from older parts of the country, particularly from the eastern seaboard and the South. (In the main, these references are found in the notes to the entries from the Brown Collection.) For the purposes of defining the West, I am including all states west of the Mississippi, including Minnesota, when it has served my purposes to do so. In taking only unpublished material to illustrate magical folk medicine I have sought to show field collectors that it is still possible to collect magical medical lore in the West in addition to turning up accounts of the use of plant and animal samples, the preparation and administration of various kinds of medicines, teas, and tonics, the application of different sorts of dressings and poultices, and resort to manipulative therapy of one kind and another.

Homeopathic principles of medicine are well known, and are based on analogic magic, wherein it is assumed that external similarity rests on what would seem to be an apparent internal connection and a basic inner unity and dependence (Bakker 1960; *Dictionnaire encyclopedique des sciences medicales* 1881; *Handwortenbuch* 1927–1942; Jungbauer 1934; Wuttke 1900). Under this premise, cures are undertaken on the theory that similar things are cured by similar means, as set forth in the celebrated Latin phrase, *similia similibus curantur* (Bonser 1963; Mogk 1906).

Although these notions were known in antiquity, it remained for later medical practitioners such as the Italian physician Jean Baptiste Porta to state these principles of unity in terms that were more specific. Porta, among other things, enunciated the "doctrine of signatures," whereby the efficacy of a plant for the cure of a certain malady could be assessed in terms of its shape, its color, its appendages, and the essences secreted as they related to the diseased part or the impeded function (*Dictionnaire encyclopedique* 1881). These simple preliminary observations on magic and symbolism, then, will prepare us for assorted folk medical notions that involve homeopathy which are still to be found in the West.

Similarity of shape is seen in a Utah belief, supported by seven texts from different parts of Salt Lake County, that walnuts are good for diseases of the brain, one informant declaring that the efficacy rested in the fact that "the meat of the nut looks like the brain, and the shell resembles the skull." Also from Salt Lake County comes a variation on the doctrine of signatures affecting shape and relative position, namely, the belief that the tops of plants should be used to cure diseases of the head, while the roots of plants should be utilized for maladies of the legs.

Kissing a pain better is an age-old custom of the nursery employed by mothers to assure children that the pain will go away. The kissing of a person's thumb when he stubs his toe, rests on an extension of the principles of analogy stated above, and is made necessary by the fact that a person is actually unable to kiss his own toe. Examples of this whimsical notion come from California, one entry being possibly of ultimate Polish provenience. The other allusion comes from Helena, Montana.

The use of appropriate colors to combat disease is seen in the following examples from western states: in Missouri, South Dakota, Washington, and Utah, a nosebleed is stanched by wearing either a red string, red yarn, a red handkerchief, or a red necklace about the neck (Brown 1952–64; Fife 1957; Hand 1961–64; Neal 1955). Two additional items from Utah prescribe carrying the red yarn or red string in one's pocket.

A Salt Lake doctor reports having heard many times in his practice that yellow jaundice should be treated with yellow drugs, on the theory that "yellow rids yellow" (*Journal of American Folklore* 1944). A variation on this general prescription, also from Salt Lake, is the hanging of a carrot in the basement, which is supposed to absorb the jaundice as the carrot dries up (Neal 1955). Scarlet fever was treated in Utah by wrapping the patients up in scarlet blankets, and doctoring them with medicine scarlet or red in color.

The curing of frostbite and other conditions brought on by cold are treated in their own terms in Minnesota, where frozen members are treated with snow; in Kansas, where frostbitten ears are likewise rubbed with snow; and in Utah, where chilblains are combatted by the same agent that caused them, namely, snow (Brown 1952–64; Lathrop 1961). In Los Angeles, for example, it is recommended that one swim in the ocean to combat a cold. In heat therapy, on the contrary, an old lady in Moab, Utah, reported to be a witch, cured burns by holding the wound over heat until it supposedly drew the heat out of the burn (Brown 1952–64; Fife 1957). In Ogden, Utah, in an entry dating back to 1885, it was recommended that a hot stone be placed on the head of a person suffering from fever. This application supposedly caused the fever to leave.

The almost classical cure of a disease by the agent causing it, is seen in the well-known example of curing the bite of a mad dog by "the hair of the dog that bit you" (Brown 1952–64; Hendricks 1966). Three recent California examples and one from Oregon dating from 1915, attest to this old folk medical belief and practice, as do a spate of examples from Utah, including a prescription from Park City (1930) to the effect that the mad dog be killed immediately so that the person bitten would not go insane. Two other Utah items employ this same primitive logic, one recommending the eating of a snake that has inflicted a bite, and the other, from Provo about 1900, merely dictating that the snake's head should be bitten off (Brown 1952–64).

The taking of children to chicken coops to let the chickens fly over them is reported from Arkansas and Oklahoma and is found also in two entries from California, one of which indicates that "when the chickens fly over the kids, they take the pox away" (Brown 1952–64; Hendricks 1966). In parts of California as widely separated as San Luis Obispo, Ojai, and Los Angeles, the eating of poison oak is supposed to convey a lasting immunity against skin poisoning by this plant.

Space precludes a treatment of the sympathetic principles related to the marking of unborn children, a situation, or course, in which contagious magic as well as homeopathic principles come into play (Brown 1952–64). I shall cite but a single example from the unpublished Fife collection: "during the pregnancy the father or some close relative had an accident . . . and the child was born with a mark resembling the injury the father had." Here, you see, the child's most immediate connection, namely, the mother, is not mentioned at all. One might think of this as a secondary situation on which the analogy rests. Even so, a purely external event is magically communicated to the child by its mother.

The following four items—none related to each other—have in common only the sympathetic enlistment of a similar response, or the avoidance of an act that will induce a similar reaction. In Moab, Utah, for example, in order to get a child to fall asleep, it was prescribed that the person holding the child must herself yawn. In a California belief that probably came from Russia before 1900 it was feared that if a person swallowed string he would tie up his intestines. Another Utah example, and one involving contagious magic also, indicates that if a person carries the crutches of someone with a broken arm

or leg, he or she too will be the next to break a limb. A New Mexico belief that if one has boils, and a menstruating woman comes into the room, the boils will get worse, rests on the notion that one ailing person can influence another adversely. It does not matter that the respective maladies have nothing whatsoever in common.

The ancient notion of treating the weapon that has inflicted a wound (*Handwortenbuch* 1927–42), raised to a doctrine and widely advertised by Sir Kenelm Digby in 17th-century England, is seen in the West by the fact that lard or turpentine is put on a rusty nail after it has inflicted a puncture wound. Treatments of this kind are reported from Missouri and Oklahoma, and from three different parts of Utah. The Salt Lake version is summed up in a neat prescription: "Treat the weapon that made the wound" (Brown 1952–64).

Contrary measures, or a sort of reverse magic, are seen in the notion, for example, that playing with fire or matches will induce bed-wetting. Reports of this folk belief come from Utah, North Dakota, and New Mexico, the last-named instance stemming from the Latin-American tradition (Brown 1952–64). It must be noted that the principle of reversal, or *contraria contrariis* (*Handwortenbuch* 1927–42; Jungbauer 1934) as seen here, represents the cause of this noisome frailty in young children. Cures are seen in the combatting of a cold with hot drinks of various kinds, sweating, etc., etc. These are so common that I have not listed them. An unusual cure for sore throat —perhaps a bit of whimsy—involves reverse magic so extraordinary that one is tempted hardly to take it seriously. This cure from New Mexico prescribes rubbing Vicks Vaporub into the rectum to cure a sore throat.

Contagious magic opens up an even wider range of unusual folk medical beliefs and practices than those we have considered under homeopathic magic. All of these rest on the fundamental assumption that things once conjoined remain magically connected, even though dissevered (Frazer 1911–15). In folk medicine the law of contact, and of contagion, almost invariably has to do with the magical divestment of disease, whereby the malady is passed off wholly, or in a part which still represents the whole. This is a corollary of contagious magic known under the Latin formulation *pars pro toto* (Jungbaurer 1934). In the ensuing discussions we shall see various manifestations of contagious magic. Intermingled will also be some symbolic cures not resting on actual contact. In handling material of this kind, one must bear in mind that contagious magic, as well as homeopathic magic, are part of the broader category of sympathetic magic.

Let us begin with the transference of disease (see Hand 1965). The cure of venereal diseases by transmitting the malady to a virgin, as found elsewhere in the United States, but not widely, is reported from Oakland and Hanford, California, for gonorrhea. A less sensational kind of transference is recommended from Montana for the cure of a cold, simply by passing it on to another person, and making a scapegoat of him. The transference of warts either to a willing or an unwary host is one of the commonplaces of magical transference of disease (Brown 1952–64; Fife 1957; Stout 1936). This is usually done outright by "sale." In various examples from Iowa, Nebraska, New Mexico, Utah, and California, the buyer usually pays a small sum of money, for instance, a penny, for each wart, or a dime. Contagious principles are not at work here (Brown 1952–64; McKinney 1952; Stout 1936), except where the owner of the wart himself makes the sale, and pays out his own money to be freed of the wart. Under these circumstances the buyer, as in a California example, must bury the money to avoid getting the wart himself. Equally common with an outright sale is the use of a penny as a so-called *Zwischenträger*, or an intermediate agent (Hand 1965). Once rubbed on the wart, and hence impregnated with part of it, the coin may be thrown away, buried, or sold, as is seen in various practices from Iowa, North Dakota, Washington, Idaho, Utah, and California (Brown 1952–64). A common way of wishing the wart onto others is to cast it off in such a way that it will be picked up by another person, who is thus sure to contract the wart (Brown 1952–64). This traffic is seen in a riddance cure from Salt Lake (Hand 1965). A unique cure from Iowa, dating from 1902, and involving a reversal, is seen in the following prescription: "Pick out a special dime and rub it over the wart, and give it to the person with the wart. As soon as the dime is spent the wart will disappear. The dime is kept with the patient's other money so it cannot be distinguished." Warts may be transferred to another person merely by his counting them, or by placing as many pebbles in a candy bag, or other kind of container, as there are warts. The bag is then left in some likely place to be picked up by an inquisitive person (Brown 1952–64). Utah, Idaho, and California examples do not involve rubbing the wart to impregnate the pebbles, but an instance from Vernal, Utah, runs true to the more traditional form, wherein stones, peas, and beans are rubbed on the warts and then disposed of in a roadway. Even so, the picking up of the new host objects is not recorded in this last-named instance. The use of a transient in the ritual of divestment is seen in a California prescription from Hollywood, wherein the itinerant person counts the warts, writes them (the number?) on the inside of his hatband, and then magically takes the warts with him when he leaves town.

Aid of the dead in disposing of warts and other excrescences, and maladies of all kinds, is known in the United States, but this practice is no longer as common as it once was. From the western area of the country under survey, however I have only two or three good examples, and two of these are from California. A friend of mine in Canoga Park, California, who had a goiter was once waiting for a green light at a intersection, when an unknown woman walked up and said: "Lady, if you place your hand on a dead person's throat, your goiter will go away" (Hand, n.d.). The other item is a less striking variant of this well-known cure for goiter. As late as 1960 there is a report from Salt Lake City that a dead hand touched to a cancer will cure it (Black 1935). In another Utah cure involving the dead, or objects connected with the dead, it was believed in Helper years ago that the cutting of a wart with a razor used to shave a dead person would cause the wart to disappear. Two other wart cures, both reported from California, involve traffic with the corpse. "When a corpse (in a funeral procession) goes by," the entry reads, "flick your wart, and say, 'Corpse take my wart with you.' Then forget about it, and the wart will soon be gone." The other instance reveals the common practice of rubbing the wart with a rag, but instead of burying the rag in the usual way, it is placed in the coffin with the dead person. When the rag rots, the wart will be gone.

Communicating disease to animals and thus ridding oneself of the malady is a prominent form of magical divestment of sickness (Hand 1965). This transfer is accomplished by contact with the animal, usually a dog or a cat, in sleeping or in other kinds of contact. In the classical sense of magical transference, however, as I have discussed it elsewhere (Hand 1965), the animal manifestly contracts the disease, and often dies as a result. Three Utah examples, the earliest from Grantsville, about 1880, display this cardinal feature. The Grantsville item reads: "Three hairs taken from the cross of an ass will cure whooping cough, but the ass will die." A cure for this same disease is reported from Salt Lake in 1928: "Tie a hairy caterpillar in a bag around a child's neck. As the insect dies, the whooping cough will vanish" (Black 1883; *Folklore* 1913; *Notes and Queries* 1903). The sacrificial role of the caterpillar, of course, is envisioned as part of the cure, and actually is thought to insure its success. The final Utah example, which was recorded in Salt Lake in 1953, is equally illuminating, and bears out the traditional pattern of eventual death to the creature to whom the disease has been communicated. "To cure warts, impale a frog on a stick and rub the warts on the frog. They will disappear as the frog dies" (Brown 1952–64). In less drastic kinds of transference to animals, rheumatic diseases are cured by contact with the animal, usually a dog or a cat, in sleeping or in other kinds of contact. (Brown 1952–64). Sleeping with a cat at the foot of the bed is recommended in Nebraska, and a dog is thought to accomplish the same purpose in California. It is claimed in this same California entry that a cat sleeping with you will result in your contracting arthritis from the cat. The wearing of a cat's fur on one's skin is recommended in Utah for the cure of pneumonia and consumption, and in California and Nebraska the fur of both cats and dogs is recommended for rheumatism (Brown 1952–64; Hendricks 1966). Merely keeping a Mexican Chihuahua dog in the house will ward off asthma, it is claimed in two entries from the Los Angeles area (Hendricks 1966). In an item from Murray, Utah, it is believed that sleeping on a bear rug will cure backache. In a very rare item from California, but possibly referable to Michigan, the cure of tuberculosis by sleeping in the hay with horses is recommended. Riddance of stone bruises by contact with a frog according to Oklahoma belief, and the loss of a wart in California by touching a frog are reported, while in Utah it is recommended to let a horny toad

crawl on the victim's bare skin so he can carry off the rheumatism (Brown 1952–64). In the same way, a snake wrapped around the neck will take the goiter with it when it disengages itself and crawls away, according to a Colorado belief (Black 1935).

Chickens are used to consume grains of barley after the barley has been rubbed on the wart. In this way, both by symbolic and contagious principles, the fowl takes the wart as it ingests the kernel of barley. This belief and practice is reported from Oklahoma, but the observance is widely reported wherever standard collections of folk medicine have been made (Brown 1952–64). Another item from Oklahoma, far more inscrutable than the first, recommends a cure for night blindness wherein a chicken is made to jump over the sleeping victim. No explanation is given, nor can I offer one.

In folk medicine swallows figure importantly in maladies of the eye, and there is an interesting Utah belief in the ability of this bird to help in restoring sight. The first time you hear the swallow in the spring, it is said, if you go to a stream or fountain and wash your eyes, at the same time making a silent prayer, the swallows will carry away all your eye troubles. A brutal ritual in contagious magic is reported from California, wherein a congenitally blind person must secure a frog, gouge its eyes out, return the frog to the water alive, and then place the animal's eyeballs on his own neck, in order to regain his eyesight.

Oral contact with animals, or breathing their expired breath, is a category of folk medical therapy found in the area under survey, even though the tradition is not well known (Hand 1968a). Kissing a donkey for the relief of toothache is reported from California and Utah, and having a full-bred stallion blow its breath in the face of the victim of whooping cough, is also reported from California (Brown 1952–64; Hand 1968b), although this cure ultimately comes from West Virginia. Spitting into the mouth of a frog is supposed to cure one of asthma, as reported in an instance from California. From the same state a recommended cure of whooping cough is to have the child cough into the mouth of a live fish (Brown 1952–64; Hand 1968a). In Utah, as three Salt Lake entries attest, toads are credited with being able to suck the poison of cancer from the system. One other magical cure involving the passage of air into the respiratory tract of the patient is the well-known cure of thrush by having a posthumous child breathe into the mouth of a baby with thrush, as is reported in a case from Bakersfield, California (Brown 1952–64; Hand 1968a).

A curious connection between headache and discarded hair combings that eventually are used in birds' nests is found in some California items, two of which stem from Louisiana and Georgia before the turn of the century (Brown 1952–64). Loss of hair is also reported from the misappropriation of a person's hair for nest building, as is seen in two Los Angeles county entries. Here, of course, harm to the hair, even though it is no longer connected with the person, results in harm to the person himself.

Transference of diseases to trees, generally rare in America, is found in only two reports. In Utah, around 1918, warts were transferred to an aspen tree by means of a piece of bacon. According to the classical requirements of such a transfer, the warts were thought to "grow on the tree and vanish from you," as the report states. Transference of diseases to trees by "plugging," "nailing," "wedging," and kindred means is more common in my sampling than communication to trees by means of strings, rubbing against the tree, and the like (Hand 1966; *Handwörtenbuch* 1927–42), but, once more, it must be remembered that records of the practice in the western part of the country are scanty. In Missouri before the turn of the century, the victim probed a wart with a pin until it bled, and then stuck the pin into the tree (Brown 1952–64). Instead of the tree's getting the wart, as in normal procedures of this kind, it was supposed to be passed on the first person who touched the pin. A more typical example of this general kind of transference, and one which I have called "wedging," is seen in a Utah example collected in Salt Lake as late as 1959: "Rub your warts with a piece of bacon, and then put the bacon in the slit of a tree. The warts will grow on the tree as knobs." To cure chills and fever in California, an "X" mark was cut in a persimmon tree, but details are lacking as to how the magical transfer took place. The incisions were made on different sides of the tree according to the seasons, as follows: summer: south; fall: west; winter: north; spring: east. In a wart cure reported from Los Angeles, a lock of the victim's hair is placed in the natural cleft of a tree, and he is supposed never to return to it. At best this is a

secondary contagion, since the hair apparently was not brought into contact with the wart. Another California account of plugging runs truer to form: "To cure asthma cut a square from the door facing where the person gasped for breath. Take out a chunk of wood, cut a lock of hair off the person, and place it back in the hole; then cover it up with a chunk of wood" (Hand 1966).

Magical "plugging" of diseases is frequently confused with magically outgrowing a disease by a procedure of "measuring." A good example of this confusion is contained in a curative ritual reported as a memorat from Tarzana, California. "To cure a child of asthma, stand he or she (sic) against a doorjamb and drill a hole just above the head. Put a hank of hair in the hole and plug. After the child has grown above the hole he or she will never have asthma again." In another cure of asthma, a prescription recorded in North Hollywood, a lock of the child's hair is cut and placed in the window sill. When the child grows as high as where the hair was placed, he will have outgrown the disease. Measuring a wart with a pine needle in Spanish Fork, Utah, and then burying it, seems to emphasize the magic of burial and decay more than that of measurement (Brown 1952–64). This would be true, too, of course, for all counting rituals having to do with warts, in which the string or thread is ultimately buried, there to await rotting and the magical disappearance of the warts.

The accounts at my disposal of "notching" as a magical folk medical practice are inadequate to convey this complicated ritual, which involves, in its various manifestations, not only notching as a measurement (Brown 1952–64), but also as a means of counting warts, and the like, and in some cases it also involves elements of plugging. A South Dakota entry, dating from World War I, simply involved notching a piece of wood and throwing it away to get rid of a wart. A more detailed procedure is indicated in a practice reported from Moab, Utah, in 1953, but referable to a much earlier date, wherein a notch was cut in a stick for every wart, and then some other person made to bury the stick. When the stick decayed, it was thought that the warts would be gone.

"Passing through," or "pulling through," as this symbolic curing ritual is known, is little reported from the western part of the United States, and it is also rapidly becoming a thing of the past elsewhere in America. A good example that fits the usual description of this healing ritual is an item from San Diego, California. If a child gets a rupture, to heal it one has to find a young living willow, or any other young suitable tree, cut it lengthwise at the time of the full moon, and then pass the child through the willow. Tie the two parts together, and as the tree grows together, so will the rupture heal together (Hand 1968b). The Utah examples fill out the picture a bit. In Southern Utah about 1920, for example, a person suffering from blackheads was made to creep on hands and knees under a bramble bush three times with the sun (clockwise) in order to be cured. In Logan, it was claimed as recently as 1938 that a child's cough could be cured by passing him three times underneath the belly of a horse. In enquiring for old medical practices of this sort, including such additional practices as pulling people through waterworn holes in stones, through rungs of ladders, and the like, one should not fail to mention the ailments for which these passing-through rituals are most often employed, namely, rupture, fits, whooping cough, rheumatism, rickets, epilepsy, and even boils. Blackheads, mentioned above, I should regard as being exceptional.

The circumscribing of an area within which the disease must remain, or an area within which the cure will be carried out, is one of the rarities of magical medicine. For this purpose rings or other ring-shaped objects are used, or string and thread are also pressed into service. In Moab, Utah, for example, some people wear lead around their necks, tied with buckskin, to keep mumps from "going down." For this same purpose a sock was tied around the neck in Centerville, Utah, in 1920, and a plain string as late as 1955 in Morgan County of the same state (Brown 1952–64). A Utah physician had encountered in his practice the custom of tying string around an infected area to confine the malady to that spot. It

was stated that this was to "keep the spirit from going deeper into the body." Los Angeles public health nurses, for example, frequently find ribbons or strings around the abdomens of pregnant Mexican women who wear them to protect the unborn child from harm and fairy influences of all kinds. Ringworm is circumscribed in New Mexico by placing a gold ring on it, drawing a circle around the ring, and then wearing the ring until the rash disappears (Brown 1952–64). In Los Angeles, for the same malady, one should spit on a golden thimble, place it on the affected spot, and turn it three times. This should be done by the light of the moon (Brown 1952–64).

Spitting as a means of divestment is seen in California and Utah cures for sideache, wherein the sufferer spits on a rock and either throws it away, or he spits under a stone, which he then replaces (Brown 1952–64). This is an aspect of burial of disease, it would seem. A more magical cure involves going to a crossroads at night and spitting to rid oneself of a sty (Thomas and Thomas 1920), as reported in a Utah item a few years ago. According to the belief, the sty will be gone by morning.

I am sorry that lack of space precludes my doing more with such relatively common magical practices as getting rid of warts by burial, measurement, notching, floating away, and the like. Likewise, curing rheumatism by various kinds of absorptive measures has had short shrift, and I have said nothing at all about the supposed magnetic and galvanic cures of this dread disease. These are subjects for independent treatment (Brown 1952–64), as is also the widespread use of various kinds of amulets in folk medical practice, including the still popular buckeye and the whole nutmeg pierced and suspended on a string around the throat. Verbal magic, finally, is also widely used in folk medicine, but this subject, too, must await a later discussion.

6

Witchcraft and Sorcery

All societies recognize the frailness of the human condition; wherever pain, illness, injury, and unjustness exist, so too do culturally prescribed explanations. In many parts of the world, where opportunities for formal education are limited to an elite whose numbers are small, although their economic and political power may be considerable, explanations of events and phenomena are still rooted deeply in traditional interpretations passed from generation to generation by word of mouth. In rural Africa, for example, where between 70 and 90 percent of the population is not covered by public health services (Shehu 1975: 29), mental and physical illness are often accounted for in terms of a formidable array of supernatural sources, including witchcraft, sorcery, magic, curses, spirits, or a combination of these. The point is that, whether explanations for illness are "scientific" or "mystical," all societies must have explanations for crises. Mental and physical illness cannot be permitted to go unchecked.

In preliterate societies, a vast number of daily crises are attributed to witchcraft, particularly in sub-Saharan Africa, where the highest level of belief in witchcraft exists today. Here witchcraft explanations are logical, indeed, some say indispensable. In short, witchcraft is an integral part of traditional African belief systems, as are sorcery

Devil mask from the Tyrol.

and magic, and it is considered by many anthropologists to be essential to African religions.

Lucy Mair, a British social anthropologist and a leading authority on African witchcraft, points out that the belief in witchcraft is universal. Around the world, greed and sexual motifs are commonly associated with witches, as is the "nightmare" witch that prowls at night and is distinguished from the everyday witch by nocturnal habits (1969: 36–37). Women are more often labeled witches than men, and societies frequently associate particular types of personalities with individuals who they feel have the highest probability of becoming witches. According to Mair (1969: 43), many of the qualities associated with being a poor neighbor, such as unsociability, isolation, stinginess, unfriendliness, and moroseness, are the same qualities ascribed to the everyday witch. Nothing compares in terms of sheer evil, however, to the nightmare witch, whose hatred of the most basic tenets of human decency earns it a special place of infamy.

Witches, wherever they exist, are the antithesis of proper behavior. Their antisocial acts, moreover, are uncontrollable. A final commonality of witch beliefs is that their powers are innate, unlike those of the sorcerer, whose powers are learned; the witch inherits the power for evil or is given the power by God.

To the beginning student in anthropology, witchcraft surely must appear to affect a society negatively; a careful analysis of belief systems demonstrates more positive than negative functions, however. In his analysis of the functions of witchcraft among the Navaho, Clyde Kluckhohn evaluated the belief more positively than negatively in terms of economic and social control and the psychological states of a group (1967; Kluckhohn and Leighton 1962). Beliefs in witchcraft act to level economic differences, for example. Among the Navaho, the rich are believed to have gained their wealth by secret supernatural techniques. In such cases, the only way to quell this kind of rumor is through a variety of forms of generosity that may take the form of redistribution of wealth among relatives and friends (Kluckhohn and Leighton 1962: 247). In his later work, Kluckhohn demonstrated that witchcraft beliefs help reinforce social values. For example, the belief that uncared-for elderly will turn into witches demands that the Navaho treat the aged

with proper care. The worry that the death of a close relative may cast suspicion of witchcraft on survivors, particularly siblings, also reinforces their social values regarding obligations to kin. Ironically, because leaders are thought to be witches, people were hesitant to be disobedient for fear of supernatural retribution (1967: 113).

Kluckhohn maintained that at the psychological level witchcraft was an outlet for hostility because frustrated individuals used witches, rather than relatives or neighbors, as scapegoats. Anxiety and neglect could also be accommodated through commonly held witchcraft beliefs, for people showing symptoms of witchcraft-caused illnesses, usually those neglected or of low status, would reaffirm their importance to kinsmen and the group at the public curing ceremonies (1967: 83–84).

The terms *witchcraft* and *sorcery* are often used interchangeably to mean any kind of evil magic; however, E. E. Evans-Pritchard's (1937) analysis of Azande witchcraft and sorcery resulted in a distinction between the two terms that is accepted by most anthropologists today. Generally speaking, a sorcerer intentionally seeks to bring about harm. Sorcerers have learned how to cast spells and use certain formulas and objects to inflict evil. The sorcerer's methods are real, not psychic like those of the witch. Sorcery is conscious and an acquired skill, whereas witchcraft is unconscious and innate. Contrary to witchcraft, sorcery is not always antisocial or illegitimate and occurs with a higher frequency than does witchcraft.

Interestingly, some scholars believe that witchcraft does not, in truth, exist despite the strong beliefs of those in the culture. Witchcraft, they argue, exists only in the minds of the people, whereas sorcery is proven by the presence of paraphernalia, medicines, and the identification of sorcerer specialists in the community. The point is, however, that witchcraft serves so many functions it is hard to believe its importance can be whittled away by the difficulties involved in trying to prove its existence or in distinguishing it from sorcery. Everywhere there is social conflict: People become angry, get insulted, or perhaps become jealous of someone's success; it is during such uncomfortable times that witches may be found at fault and sorcerers may be called upon for help.

When someone in North American culture thinks of witches and witchcraft, the usual association is with early modern European witchcraft and the Salem trials in New England in 1692. Yet, these European-based witch beliefs, including the Salem case, were quite different from those of the preliterate societies in which witchcraft occurs, where it functions as an everyday, socially acceptable way of managing tension, explaining the otherwise unexplainable, leveling disparities in wealth and status, and resolving social conflict. In contrast, early modern European witchcraft was a response to the strains of a time of profound change, marked by immense political and religious conflict. Although witch beliefs had been a feature of European culture since the Dark Ages, the Church managed to keep the situation under control until the turmoil of the sixteenth and seventeenth centuries, when the practice of labeling Church heretics as witches became popular and the witchhunt craze became a terrifying fact of history. Naturally, the Salem witchhunt of 1692 is of the greatest interest to Americans, but Salem's 200 arrests and 19 executions pale in comparison with the approximately 500,000 people who were executed in Europe during the fifteenth, sixteenth, and seventeenth centuries after having been convicted of witchcraft. By the end of this period, the witchcraze was coming to an end. "Cartesian and scientific thought had no room for witchcraft; ecclesiastical and civil authorities agreed that witch prosecutions had got out of hand; and European society was settling down to two centuries (1700–1900) of relative peace and prosperity" (Russell 1987: 196).

Ethnographic reports on witchcraft and sorcery dominate the literature, but other forces of evil are also responsible for much unjust suffering. One such power, but certainly not the only one, is the evil eye—widely known in the Middle East, parts of Europe, Central America, and Africa, areas characterized by Islamic and Judeo-Christian as well as so-called pagan religious traditions. The evil eye was believed to be a voluntary power brought about by the malicious nature of the possessor, on the one hand, or an involuntary but still dangerous, uncontrolled power, on the other. Strangers, dwarfs, old women, certain types of animals, menstruating women, and people with one eye have been often viewed as being particularly dangerous. Children

and farm animals, the most precious of one's possessions, were thought most vulnerable to the evil eye, which could cause various disasters to occur immediately or in the future, particularly by asserting control over the victim. A variety of protective measures have been prescribed to ward off the evil eye. Glass evil eyes and various shaped metal amulets, for example, are sold to tourists and residents alike in modern Greece. Plants, certain avoidance actions, colors, and magical words and gestures have also at different times and places been felt to be effective against the evil eye.

In addition to the evil eye, anguish can be created by malicious ghosts, spirit possession, attacks by enemy shamans, curses of the envious, and the spells of evil magicians and other specialists who have learned how to manipulate power to harm others. Each of these causes harms and creates fear in a community and as such is an index of social strain; however, each may also function positively by allowing individuals to blame supernatural agencies rather than kinsmen and neighbors for illness or misfortunes that befall them.

In societies where no other explanations are available or satisfactory, belief in witchcraft and sorcery still accounts for the occurrence of disease, death, injustice, and other unpleasant and tragic events. In the lead article of this chapter, James Brain employs a cross-cultural approach to witchcraft, emphasizing the near-universal image of woman as witch, and presents his theory that the mobility of nomadic societies, such as hunter-gatherers, accounts for the absence of witchcraft among those groups and its presence among the hunter's sedentary horticultural neighbors.

In the second article, Phillips Stevens Jr. explores various social, clinical, and judicial implications of witchcraft beliefs in contemporary Western urban communities.

In the third article, Naomi McPherson investigates sorcery and concepts of deviance among the Kabana of West New Britain. She shows the Kabana to be quite unusual in that for them, unlike most other groups, the practice of sorcery is not always considered evil and may, under certain conditions, function positively in their society.

Harry Eastwell updates previous research on "voodoo deaths," arguing that some Australian aborigine deaths by magic or sorcery, resembling classic cases of "voodoo death," may be more accurately diagnosed as orthodox medical conditions.

The final article is written by Loretta Orion, a member of a modern-day neopagan movement, Wicca. In the article, Orion describes and interprets several elements of a Wiccan Yule celebration.

References

Evans-Pritchard, E. E.
  1937 *Witchcraft, Oracles and Magic Among the Azandi.* Oxford: Clarendon Press.

Kluckhohn, Clyde
  1967 *Navaho Witchcraft.* Boston: Beacon Press (first published, 1944).

Kluckhohn, Clyde and Dorothea Leighton
  1962 *The Navaho.* Cambridge, Mass.: Harvard University Press (first published, 1946).

Mair, Lucy
  1969 *Witchcraft.* New York: McGraw-Hill.

Russell, Jeffrey Burton
  1987 "Witchcraft," in Mircea Eliade, ed., *The Encyclopedia of Religion,* pp. 415–23. New York: Macmillan.

Shehu, U.
  1975 *Health Care in Rural Areas.* AFRO Technical Papers, No. 10.

An Anthropological Perspective on the Witchcraze

James L. Brain

At first glance it would appear impossible that an anthropological investigation of the European witchcraze, so far removed from contemporary America, could shed light on current attitudes toward gender. In this article, however, James L. Brain demonstrates that the idea of the witch is closely related to the subversion of male authority, a reversal of patriarchal authority that Saint Paul asserted was divinely ordered. The denigration of women in European thought can, in part, be traced to Aristotle who saw women's souls and bodies as being inferior. Weaknesses such as these, it was thought, predisposed women to be witches. Close on the heels of this came the idea of ritual pollution of men by women, female emissions being further evidence of women's inferiority.

The image of women as witches is widespread, but it was not until witchcraft was linked to the Devil that it was considered heresy, a crime punishable by death. It is not difficult to link these historical attitudes toward women with the present. In fact, Brain maintains that "the witchcraze ended, but misogyny and gynophobia are still alive and well at the end of the twentieth century."

In addition to the issue of gender and witchcraft, Brain addresses the question of why witches are believed to exist in some societies and not others. Here the author's "mobility theory," based on the nomadic lifestyle of hunter-gatherers, offers a provocative explanation for the absence of witchcraft among these peoples but its presence among sedentary horticultural societies.

Reprinted from Jean R. Brink, Allison P. Coudert, and Maryanne C. Horowitz, eds., *The Politics of Gender in Early Modern Europe* (Kirksville, Mo.: Sixteenth Century Journal Publishers, Inc.), pp. 15–27. By permission of the publisher. The article's citations, originally numbered footnotes, have been interpolated into the text in this volume for consistency of presentation.

OUR UNDERSTANDING OF HISTORICAL ATTITUDES toward gender may be illuminated by a comparative cross-cultural approach to witchcraft. Two issues are especially important: the reason for the near universality of the image of woman as witch, and the idea that geographic and spatial mobility may be an important and overlooked factor in the absence of witchcraft accusations and in the decline of their frequency.

The Image of the Witch

Anthropological and historical evidence shows that the specific details of beliefs about witches and their behavior will vary according to the concerns of a particular society. There are, however, two universal constants about witch beliefs that cut across cultures: witches represent people's deepest fears about themselves and society, and they represent a reversal of all that is considered normal behavior in a particular society. This has been documented for small-scale societies (Wilson 1951; Mair 1969), but the situation in Europe needs to be examined. Norman Cohn discusses the European witchcraze in terms of "collective fantasies," "obsessive fears," and "unacknowledged desires" in the minds of sixteenth- and seventeenth-century men and women (Cohn 1975: 258–63). Margaret Murray and, to a certain extent, Carlo Ginzburg locate the origins of European witchcraft beliefs in pre-Christian religions (Ginzburg 1983; Murray 1931/1970).

It would be unfortunate if we were to revive Murray's hypothesis. The beliefs about witches can be explained without reference to pre-Christian religions, if we assume that witch-like behavior is a simple reversal of normal and socially accepted behavior. In Catholic Europe, the Church demanded attendance at mass in the daytime on Sundays; the predominant color there was white. By reversing this, one can easily predict that witches will celebrate their own sabbath at night, and that black will be the predominant color in their community or congregation—hence the term "black mass." Reversal also predicts that whatever ritual or service is performed will be a reversal of the Christian mass—the recitation of prayers backwards, the reversed cross, and worship of some form of Antichrist. The Church demanded acceptance of the doctrine of the Trinity, in which subliminally one can perceive that Mary is made pregnant by her own son in the shape of the Holy Ghost; the reversal of this doctrine makes profane incest an attribute of witches. If there was a sacred act of ritual cannibalism in Holy Communion, then witches could be expected to take part in some blasphemous form of cannibalism. The belief in Jesus' conquest of death and decay manifested itself in the idea that the bodies of saints do not decay at death; in witch beliefs, this finds its reversal in the belief in vampires that do not decay. If heterosexuality is the extolled norm, then homosexuality will be seen as witch-like, and if chastity is the ultimate condition of holiness then obviously one should expect witches to engage in sexual orgies.

This point can be carried even further: if patriarchal authority is divinely ordained, as Saint Paul insisted, then any attempt by women to subvert or to assume that authority can be seen as an illicit reversal and hence as witch-like behavior. The first example of the subversion of divine authority, of course, is attributed to Eve in her disobedience. Both Protestants and Catholics were concerned with issues of authority and women. Martin de Castañega's treatise on superstition and witchcraft (1529) answers the question of why women are more prone to be witches than men thus: "The first reason is because Christ forbade them to administer the sacraments and therefore the devil gives them the authority to do it with his execrations" (Darst 1979: 298–322). Here we see not only the reversal of normal, i.e., God-given authority, but also the idea of the administration of blasphemous, heretical sacraments. Additional reversals occur in his explanations of how and why witches, like angels and Christ, can fly; how and why they, like Christ can walk on water; and how and why they, like Christ and the devil, can become invisible or change their shape (Darst 1979: 306). In the pattern of inheritance D. H. Darst records another reversal. Instead of passing on inheritance

from father to son, witches inherit their discipleship to the devil from mother to daughter, from aunt to niece, or from grandmother to granddaughter.

To the issue of authority, feminist anthropological scholarship offers very cogent insights (Rosaldo 1974: 1–42). Authority is always legitimate; power may be, but often is not. Where women are denied authority, they inevitably seek their ends by the manipulation of the power they possess: by denying sex, food or nurture; by failing to perform household tasks, by outright disobedience, or by passive resistance in the form of sulking, scolding, and gossiping. All of these possibilities subvert legitimate male authority and can, therefore, be seen as evidence of witchcraft. One can conceive of a sliding scale: the less authority—or responsibility—women possess, the more manipulation of power will occur, and vice versa. Thus we can confidently expect to find the paradox that women are often extremely powerful in societies in which they are denied any authority; in these social organizations they develop strategies to attain their ends outside the legitimate parameters of authority.

This paradigm has great relevance to women in Renaissance Europe in terms of the generation of misogyny. As Lamphere demonstrates, the image of women in patrilineal and patrilocal societies is invariably negative: women are believed to be deceitful, untrustworthy and manipulative (Lamphere 1974: 97–112). This negative image is a direct result of marriage practices: the men are all related by blood; the women, because of rules of clan exogamy, are all strangers both to the men and to each other. In a large extended family, the men will have the solidarity of kinship; the women will lack any solidarity. In such societies the only possible way for a woman to achieve her goals is for her to manipulate those who possess legitimate authority—her husband and her sons. Lamphere contrasts this inevitably negative image of women with the very positive image enjoyed by Navajo women. In that matrilineal society marriage is often matrilocal, so that it is the husband who moves to his wife's family. Here he is the one surrounded by strangers and must depend on his wife to negotiate concessions for him. Under these circumstances women are viewed as competent managers and good negotiators. This shows that the locality of marriage is crucial in determining the image of women. While it is true that in northern European societies bilateral descent was the norm, most marriages probably have demanded that women move to join their husbands. If manipulation of power is the only available route a woman can follow to achieve her ends then inevitably her image will be that of a manipulative bitch—as the *Malleus Maleficarum* makes abundantly clear.

There is little doubt that a contributing factor to the denigration of women in European thought was the legacy of Aristotle by way, particularly, of Augustine. "Conceiving of the soul as possessing nutritive, sensitive or appetitive and reasonable faculties, Aristotle saw women's souls as deficient in all three aspects, but especially in the faculty of reason" (Robertson n.d.). Acceptance of this idea leads inexorably to the dicta of the *Malleus* about the predisposition of women to be witches because of their manifold weaknesses (Question 4) (Kramer and Sprenger 1971).

Not only was the woman's soul seen as inferior; her body was too. "In Aristotelian and Galenic terms, woman is less fully developed than man. Because of lack of heat in germination, her sexual organs have remained internal, she is incomplete, colder and moister in dominant humors. She has less body heat and thus less courage, liberality, moral strength" (Robertson n.d.). That these ideas may appear absurd to us has to be tempered by their legacy and persistence in more recent times. Darwin believed that women were less evolved than men because of their childlike skins and softness (Dykstra 1986: 167–73), and the Freudian doctrine of penis-envy surely owes something to them.

The denigration of the body leads into another area germane to the witch stereotype and one that has been much explored by anthropology. The question of ritual pollution is used widely to "prove" that women are inferior, and doubtless has much to do with latter-day disputes about the ordination of women. All bodily emissions are considered polluting or, in our modern idiom, disgusting. Among others, Mary Douglas seeks an explanation for this attitude (Douglas 1966). In her opinion, all such substances are considered threatening because they are liminal, because they have "traversed the boundary of the body" and are thus of the body but yet not of the body, and thus do not fit our standard categories. While I do not dispute this point, I have argued elsewhere that what makes these substances so deeply threatening is that they remind us of death (Brain 1977b: 371–84). It is no coincidence that they

are often sought for and used in magic intended to bring about the death of the victim. Of course, both men and women produce polluting emissions, but only women menstruate, give birth messily, and lactate. Customarily women take care of small babies who, like animals, are uncontrolled in their excretions, and the association with babies makes women additionally polluting. The issue of pollution throws additional light on why midwives were disproportionately often accused of witchcraft. Because they assisted at birth, they inevitably became contaminated with polluting substances. It should also be recalled that midwives traditionally laid out the dead and were contaminated by death, the ultimate pollutant.

Women's very physiology therefore makes them appear more polluted and polluting than men. Even in regard to the sexual act itself, a man can more easily be cleansed since his genitals are external and can be readily washed. A woman cannot be so readily cleansed, since her own polluting bodily fluids have been augmented by the deposition of the man's semen. Pollution alone would not make a witch, yet the *Malleus* makes clear that pollution is a primary aspect of sexuality. Sexuality is allied to temptation, and the Devil is the great tempter. Nowhere is this more powerfully demonstrated than through the medium of lust for women—"though the devil tempted Eve to sin, yet Eve seduced Adam" (*Malleus:* Part 1, Question 6).

Although the *Malleus* is obsessive in its misogyny and loathing of sex, it seems to deal only indirectly with one sexual matter—the nature of semen. Literary references of the Shakespearian period show that this was a subject that exercised men's minds. In some ways, this belief is still widely held as part of folk beliefs even today in the United States. The basic assumption of this belief is that marrow and semen are the same substance; the skull is the largest bone in the body and the brain is its marrow. Therefore any emission of semen depletes a man's life force and intelligence. "As the main storehouse of bone marrow, the brain is the source of semen, via the spinal cord. The supply is limited. . . . Loss of manhood, power, and ultimate life itself results from the 'spending' of the life force, which is a finite capital" (La Barre 1984: 130). Francis Bacon wrote in 1626 that "The skull has Braines, as a kind of Marrow, within it"; and even Leonardo da Vinci apparently believed in a duct connecting the brain to the penis via the spinal cord (La Barre 1984: 115–18). Understanding the belief that semen and marrow were one and the same gives point to the many references in literature to the danger of expending a man's marrow. If we grasp this unfounded fear, we can well understand yet another aspect of the witch image: that of the succubus and its terrifyingly debilitating potential.

Claude Lévi-Strauss suggested that the primary pair of oppositions is that of nature versus culture (Leach 1970: 35). Sherry B. Ortner claims that universally women are perceived as being, if not *part of* nature, at least as *closer to* nature than men, who are perceived as the generators of culture (Ortner 1974: 67–87). This position has been challenged (McCormack and Strathern 1980), but it is convincing. It generates the following sets of oppositions (always unequal in value):

> Nature—Culture
> Women—Men
> Darkness—Light
> Left—Right
> Disorder—Order
> Death—Life.

It is significant that in many languages the word for left is synonymous with female and right with male (Brain 1977a: 180–92). One should note that "right" as in side or hand and "right" as in correct or "the right to" are not merely homonymous. The same is true of "droit" or "recht." Perceptually, witches are always believed to do and to be everything that is the reverse of normal and right. Similarly, all the other characteristics in the left column are applicable to the witch stereotype.

The link between women and nature suggested by Ortner was hardly an unfamiliar one in Renaissance Europe. Bacon in particular took the view that the mission of science was the subjugation of nature. Moreover, he participated in the "rhetoric that conjoins the domination of nature with the insistent image of nature as female" (Fox-Keller 1983: 116).

That the image of witch as woman (or vice versa) is extremely widespread in the world is beyond doubt. Elsewhere in the world, and in Europe before the association of witchcraft with heresy, witchcraft was considered bad but of minor importance. During the witchcraze a new doctrine emerged that linked witchcraft with devil worship and hence with heresy. This change in doctrine made the image of woman as witch lethal to women. The change did not occur in a vacuum, and there are many powerful reasons why the witchcraze occurred. The witchcraze ended, but misogyny and gynophobia are still alive and well at the end of the twentieth century.

Mobility as a Factor in the Nonexistence or Decline of Witchcraft Beliefs

Examining non-Western small-scale societies, one discovers a rather startling fact. Societies with the simplest technologies of all—hunter-gatherers such as the San of the Kalahari, the Mbuti pygmies of the Ituri Forest, and the Hadza of northwest Tanzania—are quite unconcerned about witchcraft and do not think that it occurs in their societies (Marshall 1962: 221–52; Turnbull 1968: 132–37; Woodburn 1968: 49–55). They do, however, impute it to their sedentary agricultural neighbors (Turnbull 1961: 228; Woodburn 1982a: 431–51; Lee 1976: 127–29). When they themselves are forced into a sedentary way of life, "witchcraft fears are rampant" (Woodburn 1982b: 187–210). Why fears of witchcraft are unimportant to such peoples is described by several authors. Of the San peoples, L. Marshall writes, "the composition of a band is fluid—marriage takes individuals from one band to another, and whole families move from one band to another; bands split and disband completely" (Marshall 1976: 180). Similarly, Richard Lee notes that "hunters have a great deal of latitude to vote with their feet, to walk out of an unpleasant situation" (Lee 1972: 182). In J. Woodburn's description of conflict resolution in these societies lies the key to the absence of witchcraft beliefs. When conflict arises, people move, giving an ecological reason. Thus, "they solve disputes simply by refusing to acknowledge them" (Woodburn 1968: 156; 1979: 244–60).

It is significant that all these African hunter-gatherers possess negligible property and practice bilateral descent. The situation is very different in societies that practice unilineal descent. In his essay, Meyer Fortes suggests that unilineal descent is characteristic of societies in which property rights are acknowledged (Fortes 1953: 17–41). Such societies invariably subscribe to a belief in sorcery or witch-craft or both. Unlike their African counterparts, Australian hunter-gatherers practice unilineal descent. They claim ownership over totemic sites and believe in evil magic, as evidenced by accounts of "bone-pointing" (Thomas 1906; Spencer and Gillen 1904: 462–63; Spencer and Gillen 1899/1938: 533; Elkin 1938: 203–205; Meggitt 1962: 139, 176). All the accounts emphasize, however, that only men are involved; that the practice is thought to be rare. It is also believed that "the professional worker of magic is always to be found in another tribe" (Elkin 1938: 203). Woodburn suggests that the crucial factor that differentiates African from Australian hunter-gatherers is "the relatively tight control which men exercise over women" among the Australians (Woodburn 1979: 258). This point has relevance to the European witchcraze. It is also important that Woodburn describes the African hunter-gatherers as having an "immediate return system" of econom-ics, whereas the Australians, more like sedentary peoples, have "delayed return systems" (Woodburn 1982a: 258). A comparable people, the Ona (or Selk'nam) of Tierra del Fuego, are a hunting-gathering people. Anne Chapman describes them as inegalitarian, oppressive to women (unlike the African hunter-gatherers). They put an "emphasis on patrilineality, and patrilocality [and] the preemi-nence of territoriality" (Chapman 1984: 63). Like the Australians, they change campsites frequently; like them they believe in sorcerers; like them they claim that sorcerers belong to another tribe (Bridges 1949: 213, 373).

If we turn to the nomadic pastoral peoples, we should, according to my hypothesis, find a situation similar to that found among the Australians and the Ona/Selk'nam, since all pastoralists practice patri-lineal descent, and own property, but move fairly frequently. This proves to be the case. There is no mention of witchcraft among the Fulani (Peuls) of the Sahel region of West Africa (Stenning 1959, 1965), while among the pastoral Somali "magic, witchcraft and sorcery play a small part" (Lewis 1965). The same is true of the Turkana and Dodos of Northern Kenya (Gulliver and Gulliver 1953: 86), and the Karamojong of Northern Uganda (Dyson-Hudson 1966: 40), where "in theory, witches are never found in one's own settlement but always in a different group from one's own" (Gulliver and Gul-liver 1953: 49). The closely related Jie, their neigh-

bors, have adopted a partially sedentary mode of ex-istence. They diagnose witchcraft as the cause for a sequence of misfortunes, and their "normal proce-dure [then] is to move to a new homestead to avoid the evil influence" (Gulliver 1955: 104). Similarly, the nomadic pastoral Maasai of Kenya and Tanzania be-lieve that one can learn the techniques of sorcery, but "they have no conventional category of superna-tional 'witches' . . . and they often make fun of their Bantu neighbors who they know do possess such be-liefs" (Jacobs 1985). Their linguistically and ethni-cally similar sedentary neighbors, the Arusha (il Arusa), on the other hand, are very concerned about witchcraft (Gulliver 1963: 21). The same holds true for the closely related agricultural Nandi and Kip-sigis in Kenya (Peristiany 1939: 94–95; Langley 1979: 10, 62), and for the related Lango and Teso of Uganda (Driberg 1923: 241ff; Lawrence 1957: 182; Gulliver and Gulliver 1953: 26). The ethnically dif-ferent, click-speaking Sandawe, not far away, who were probably formerly hunter-gatherers, now prac-tice agriculture. Predictably, G. W. B. Huntingford says of them that "witchcraft is prevalent and illness and death are attributed either to it or to the anger of ancestral spirits" (Huntingford 1953: 137–38).

The ethnographic data show that in societies with total mobility and little attachment to property and with consequently little development of hierarchy and authority, there are no fears about witchcraft. Where there is considerable mobility but some at-tachment to property—often expressed by the pres-ence of unilineal descent—we can expect to find a belief that witchcraft exists. The assumption is, how-ever, that it is located in some other group and can easily be avoided by the move of a homestead. As dwellings are temporary huts in a thorn corral or something similar, this is not considered a particu-larly serious matter. When we turn to the sedentary peoples of the non-industrial world, however, we can expect always to find beliefs in witchcraft. The details of the beliefs may vary, but, as I have already mentioned, there is a remarkable consistency about aspects of the beliefs.

At the same time, it is manifest that particular forms of social organization or socio-political situa-tions can generate more or less acute fears of witch-craft. Siegfried Frederick Nadel shows convincingly that two peoples that are almost identical ethnically, linguistically, and culturally can demonstrate radi-cally different attitudes to witchcraft (Nadel 1952:

18–29). One society was rife with fears and accusations; the other had none. The only difference between the two societies is that the former has three age grades; the latter six. To move into the next higher grade, men had to forego the privileges of the age group they were relinquishing. Where there are six grades this presents no problem; where there are only three, suspicions and accusations proliferate between the young men and those in the middle grade—who are understandably reluctant to assume the mantle of old age and to eschew sexual activity and other privileges. Comparably, J. C. Mitchell shows that even in the circumstances of a modern tobacco estate in Zimbabwe (then Rhodesia), relatively well-educated permanent staff members constantly suspected their colleagues of evil magic directed against them (Mitchell 1965: 196). Uneducated casual laborers on the same estate who in their home areas might well have been anxious about witchcraft, were quite unconcerned during their temporary sojourn on the estate. The more highly educated workers were in constant contact with one another and were always in competition for the favors of the white management.

. . . That virtually everywhere people believed in witchcraft from time immemorial until the eighteenth century is well established (Trevor-Roper 1969: 91). Why, then, was there the enormous surge of accusations during the Renaissance period? And why did the craze draw to a close? As Thomas notes of the decline in belief and the acceptance of a more rational viewpoint, "the ultimate origins of this faith in unaided human capacity remain mysterious." Thomas accepts that "the decline of magic coincided with a marked improvement in the extent to which the environment became amenable to control" (Thomas 1971: 650, 663). Better food supplies and conditions of health, the cessation of plague (Midelfort 1972: 194), better communications and banking services, insurance, better fire-fighting—all these factors undoubtedly contributed to a greater sense of security. While it is true that the human impulse to seek scapegoats remains with us in the twentieth century, we have, in the main, abandoned the idea of personal malice as a cause for misfortune. In contemporary small-scale societies this personal view of misfortune persists, as numerous anthropological studies show.

It is quite clear to anyone who has worked in countries where there is still a general belief in witchcraft that education alone, even at university level, does not destroy the belief. It is quite easy to graft a theory of witchcraft onto a scientific theory of causation such as the germ theory (Offiong 1985: 107–24), and thus to assume that even a microorganism can attack one person rather than another because some person used evil magic. Moreover, most rational scientific observers would admit that psychological factors are important in reducing immunity. The reality of psychosomatic afflictions, however, is rather different from imputing each misfortune to the malevolence of one's kin or neighbors. If we look at the history of Europe it is only too evident that education per se was not the major reason for the waning of the craze; indeed, as Joseph Klaits notes, "the educated were in the forefront of the witch hunts" (Klaits 1985: 1–2). The rebirth of ideas after the medieval period should, one would think, have signalled the end of belief, yet Trevor-Roper observes, "There can be no doubt that the witchcraze grew, and grew terribly, after the Renaissance" (Trevor-Roper 1969: 91).

The skeptics who had the courage to challenge the prevailing orthodoxy about witches did not dispute the existence of witchcraft. Not to believe in witches was often seen as tantamount to being an atheist, as Sir Thomas Browne pointed out (Browne 1964: 29). What Weyer and Scot in the sixteenth century objected to was the injustice of accusing the wrong people. Bekker in the seventeenth century based his challenge on a fundamentalist piece of theology: if the devil on his fall from heaven was locked up in hell, how then could he be involved with witches here on earth (Trevor-Roper 1969: 174).

Precisely what caused the change from the relatively benign attitude toward witches in the Middle Ages to the hysterical attitude characteristic of the *Malleus Maleficarum* (Midelfort 1972: 193–94) is the subject of an ongoing debate. Cross-cultural study may contribute to our understanding of what caused the end of the witchcraze. One reason may be the only conceivable aspect that our social organization shares with that of the African hunter-gatherers: our mobility.

Humanity is by its nature a mass of contradictions. Impulses for conformity war with those for individualism. Tension develops and somehow has to be resolved. Where it is possible physically to remove oneself from those with whom one is in conflict, the tension disappears. Where this is not possible and where it is socially unacceptable to admit to tension arising from feelings of hate toward close kin, spouses, affines or neighbors, the human imagination seems to build up a whole edifice of fantasy about witches based on childish fears and imaginings. This holds especially true for societies where childrearing practices are harsh. While the details of beliefs may vary according to cultural prescription, the broad outlines are remarkably similar world-wide. They retain their fascination even in our skeptical, secular world, as Bruno Bettelheim has reminded us (Bettelheim 1977).

It is Thomas's contention that the surge in witchcraft accusations in the late sixteenth and early seventeenth centuries was not generated by any fundamental change in folk beliefs, but by a change in the structure of society. He speaks of the "increasingly individualistic forms of behavior which accompanied the economic changes" (Thomas 1971: 561). Cross-culturally one might draw a parallel with present-day Africa, where scholars have universally reported the widespread belief that the practice of evil magic has proliferated (Middleton and Winter 1963: 25). In Europe the change was from a feudal society with its well-understood certitudes about class and status; in Africa from a tribal form of social organization in which status was largely ascribed to the emerging societies, in which status can be achieved through education, wage employment, cash-cropping, entrepreneurial, political and religious activities; class divisions have begun to appear and become institutionalized (Gluckman 1965).

During the sixteenth and seventeenth centuries there was enormous social, political, economic, and religious ferment in Europe. This led initially to feelings of deep insecurity in all these arenas of human activity, exacerbated by the Copernican revolution; it also led to unrivaled opportunities for the acquisition of wealth, power, and social status. All this activity generated great divisions in society, as well as powerful emotions such as envy, jealousy, hostility, self-questioning, and guilt. This is entirely consistent with the large number of witchcraft accusations in the Tudor and early Stuart period. A similar phenomenon—though not on quite so lethal a scale—is taking place in Africa today. . . .

. . .

Some Implications of Urban Witchcraft Beliefs

Phillips Stevens, Jr.

*In this selection Phillips Stevens explores various
social, clinical, and judicial implications of witchcraft
beliefs in contemporary urban communities. He
expresses dismay at the failure of modern communities
to recognize sorcery and witchcraft as social problems
and observes that it is the misunderstanding of such
phenomena, rather than the actual beliefs, that proves
to be disruptive to society. Students will need to
look carefully at Stevens's important distinction
between sorcery and witchcraft, a key element in
understanding American popular sentiment toward
"witchcraft." Reminding the reader that there is a
common agreement among many researchers that
charges of witchcraft increase with the intensity of
social stress, Stevens examines the relationships
between witchcraft and stress caused by urban life,
especially stress experienced by recent arrivals
from rural or different cultural backgrounds (the
"culturally marginal"). Drawing on data from specific
hexing cases in western New York and Ontario,
Stevens also discusses the clinical and judicial
implications of the problem.*

Reprinted from *New York Folklore,* vol. 8, nos. 3–4 (Winter 1982), pp. 29–42, by permission of the New York Folklore Society and the editor of *New York Folklore.* The article's citations, originally numbered footnotes, have been interpolated into the text in this volume for consistency of presentation.

BELIEFS IN PHENOMENA VARIOUSLY TERMED
"witchcraft" are timeless and universal, found at
all stages of recorded human history and in all societies, and at all levels of society, today. They
have become a popular topic in the U.S., but they
are generally either dismissed as "superstition,"
relegated to "the occult," or wrapped up in fantasy; or they are condemned and suppressed—as
they have been for centuries—by organized religion. It is, therefore, not generally appreciated
that they are very real, very serious, and immediate, for a great many people; indeed, those who
profess *not* to believe in witchcraft constitute a
tiny minority of the world's peoples. And such
skeptics are acting from individual, not cultural,
convictions. This paper demonstrates and discusses some social, clinical, and judicial implications of witchcraft beliefs in urban communities
today. The extent of such beliefs in well-
established cultural communities is seldom recognized by social researchers, because victims of
hexing have access to anti-witchcraft and curative
agencies. But for recent migrants and others who
are not well integrated into urban social networks, witchcraft beliefs can have unfortunate
implications. General observations are illustrated
by data from specific cases of hexing encountered
in western New York and southern Ontario.

Sorcery and Witchcraft as Social Problems

Witchcraft beliefs persist—indeed, as we shall see,
they can intensify—within contemporary urban
populations, but they receive little sympathetic attention by academic, clinical, judicial, theological,
or popular agencies. This is especially unfortunate when it is recognized that *sorcery and witchcraft are social problems.* They are not addressed to,
nor do they invoke, any "supernatural" agency,

nor do they fall within modern popular categories of the "paranormal" or "occult." There are, to be sure, within all religious traditions, mythological explanations of the origins of evil, including accounts of Faustian alliances between mortals desirous of temporal wealth and power and supernatural beings who use such people as their terrestrial agents. But such traditions themselves assert that once such powers, be they mystical (witchcraft) or magical (sorcery), are implanted in human society they are transmitted socially (or congenitally) to subsequent generations. Witchcraft and sorcery are social problems, conceived by and perpetrated within society, and it is through social agencies that relief from them is obtained.

Such beliefs are extremely widespread and deeply rooted, particularly within the American urban environment where they can develop urgent implications. But they tend to remain covert, for two principal reasons: (1) within specific cultural populations anti-witchcraft and curative mechanisms operate and are available to persons who are well integrated into such socio-cultural networks, and such mechanisms are adequate during times when the degree of social stress remains within generally tolerable limits; and (2) little sympathy for such belief systems is to be found within "mainstream" institutions, to which the traditional cultural populations are ultimately subordinate.

Paradoxically, it is often the general misunderstanding of such beliefs, rather than the beliefs themselves, which is the more divisive or disruptive to society. People in whose lives sorcery and witchcraft are real and active but who are not sufficiently integrated into a cultural system to avail themselves of effective anti-witchcraft mechanisms, and who at the same time perceive little sympathy within mainstream institutions, may be left frustrated, victimized, psychologically damaged, or perhaps even victims of "the Voodoo Death" syndrome (Cannon 1942, 1957).

And adding to the general misunderstanding and resultant callous treatment of the problem is the lack of consensus on meanings of terms applied to what may be related or totally distinct phenomena. Anthropologists are generally—though by no means universally—agreed that *sorcery* is evil magic, involving the learned use of objects or words and believed to operate according to the classic principles of sympathy elucidated in 1890 by Sir James George Frazer in *The Golden Bough*, whereas *witchcraft* is the belief in an evil extra-somatic ("psychic" or "mystical") power vested in certain individuals which operates without recourse to magic. But American popular sentiment, being largely heir to Christian attitudes developed during the Middle Ages, still subsumes under "witchcraft," sorcery, any association with Satan, and all those nefarious traffickings and dabblings condemned in Deuteronomy (18:10–12). Hence, for example, a lecture titled "Sorcery, Witchcraft, and Inter-Personal Conflict" which I was scheduled to present to a local suburban teachers' conference was cancelled at the last minute because some influential members of the school board objected to having such topics discussed among the teachers of their children. And members of Wicca and other "neo-pagan" organizations have experienced some difficulties simply because they call themselves witches, even though Margot Adler (*Drawing Down the Moon*) and a few other representatives of "The Craft" have publicly denied any recognition of Satan (or Christ), or practice of evil, and have delineated the principal tenets of their religion through various widely available media.

What is meant by "witchcraft" in this paper, unless otherwise specified, is sorcery, the most common referent of the term today. Sorcery is evil sympathetic magic, the manipulation of objects and/or the uttering of words with intent to bring about that which is symbolically communicated or enacted in the rite. Sorcery works according to Frazer's "law of sympathy": things or actions which resemble others, either extant or expected, can have a causal relationship with those other things or actions. The "resemblance" is most commonly symbolic, and symbols are culturally assigned, often to material things or verbal utterances which have no intrinsic resemblance to that which is desired. Their meanings—often no more than the perpetrator's general malice toward the recipient of the hex—are culturally understood. The victim's own psychology, strengthened by the beliefs in the efficacy of magic held by those close to him, does the rest. He may either assign the cause of a real or perceived misfortune to the alleged hex, or he may experience genuine physical discomfort after "knowing" that he has been hexed. A "cure" is effected by reversing that psychology; i.e., convincing the victim and, of course, his supportive social network, that the magical act has been nullified, or counteracted (Prince 1982; Tivnan 1979).

This, really, is all the researcher needs to know about the way sorcery works. Theoretically, magic in primitive society operates according to a fairly sophisticated set of ideas about the way the cosmos works, constituting what might be called "primitive physics," involving the actions of natural forces and the notion that the speed, efficiency, and direction of these forces can be influenced by sympathetic human action. Increasing speed and/or efficiency of the forces along their pre-determined paths is the theoretical premise underlying good magic; slowing or stopping or altering the direction of the forces is the basis for evil magic, or sorcery. This latter action is dangerous. Although the skilled sorcerer is presumed to be able to control the deflected forces, he can err; and no one knows what havoc might result by thus tampering with the natural order of things —and this partly accounts for the fact that sorcery is a clandestine activity. The fact of the sorcerer's selfish or malicious intent, making his activities antisocial, accounts for its illegality. These underlying theoretical premises probably cannot be elucidated by most urban folk today, but understanding them as they obtain within the traditional cultures from which most urban dwellers are derived strengthens my earlier observation that sorcery is a *social* problem. If left alone, the forces of nature will operate in smooth, systemic order. The natural order is good. Social magic aims to help it along, to make it somehow better. Sorcery, conducted solely by people, invoking no supernatural intermediary, disrupts the natural order.

Witchcraft, in its historical and ethnological sense, is less common on the American urban scene, but variants of it are nevertheless strong among certain American Indian groups, and peoples of Mediterranean, Eastern European, and Latin American derivation. "Evil Eye" beliefs are among the most common of such variants. Witchcraft is the belief in an evil, extra-somatic power, often involuntary, originally of supernatural origin either evil (as the witches of medieval Europe were agents of Satan) or as a good power corrupted by the people to whom it was entrusted, as is often the case in African mythology. The power enables the bearer to change form or to project malign direction into an-

other body which becomes his *alter ego,* to fly, and to influence the natural order directly, without magical means. The power develops only in some people, but why them and not others is not known; therefore, under certain conditions almost anyone might be suspect. Patterns of suspicion in "normal" times are accurately predictable by the social researcher who has a good understanding of the social system (Gluckman 1944). Such suspicions most commonly follow patterns of tension or conflict.

This elaboration has been included here because of the general misunderstanding of these phenomena among the public and among social researchers. Any researcher working for long in an urban setting is bound to encounter some variation of them, although without some preparation he may not recognize it, or its social or cultural significance. But the point of this paper is not to discuss what witchcraft is, but rather to emphasize that not only does it persist in the urban environment, but in some cases it can increase in intensity; and it can develop implications for which mainstream social institutions are unprepared, and about which there is little or no discussion in the literature.

The Stress of Urban Life

The fundamental premise upon which this paper is based is now accepted as axiomatic among investigators of witchcraft: that allegations of witchcraft increase with intensity of social stress (Seelye 1956). To this I will add some others, which I hope will be accepted, for now, without evidence of testing by scientific method. These are: (1) that life in a multicultural urban environment is stressful; (2) that the stress of urban life is great for recent arrivals from a rural background; (3) that stress is compounded when the cultural background of such immigrants differs from that of the "mainstream"; and (4) that the nature of rural-urban or trans-cultural migration causes disruption to the point of fragmentation of traditional cultural systems, intensifying to a critical point the degree of stress experienced by some. The results of such stress can most often be identified as culture shock, the symptoms of which might include regression to and embracing with neurotic fervor selected elements of belief from the culture left behind (Furnham and Bochner 1982; Oberg 1960). In such a state, a person who has ascribed his misfortune to the evil influence of others projected by means of witchcraft, and cannot obtain treatment satisfactory within his cultural framework, can suffer severe psychological damage; at worst, he can fall victim to the syndrome of "Voodoo Death" (Eastwell 1982; Lex 1974; Lester 1972; Richter 1957). My fourth premise needs some elaboration before we can go further.

Most recent immigrants to the city could be described as "culturally marginal." Only partially acculturated, they have brought with them some beliefs and values from their traditional culture, but certain needs which developed there cannot be accommodated in their new surroundings. They are neither fully of the old nor fully integrated into the new. Most find supportive networks in cultural communities (unfortunately termed "ethnic neighborhoods") established by older migrants which help their adjustment. But kinship and other social ties retained or newly established are tenuous; urban life, primarily because the only medium of exchange is money, has a way of sharply limiting and inexorably reducing traditional forms of social networks. Some newcomers are therefore unwelcome, for hard practical reasons, even though there exists a cultural community into which they might seem to assimilate easily. In most cultural communities complete cultural systems are operative, which include voluntary associations and institutions for the satisfaction of most basic cultural needs. Specifically, stress-reduction mechanisms like anti-witchcraft and curative agencies are available. For some migrants, however, access to these services is not available. To take a recent, though extreme, example: hospitals in Dade County, Florida, in 1981 and 1982 encountered a staggering number of cases of hexing among Caribbean, particularly Haitian, "boat people," some serious, for which their clinicians were woefully unprepared (*New York Times* 1981). Such recent arrivals come with the reality of witchcraft, exacerbated by economic deprivation and culture shock. One both preys upon and feeds the other. Uneducated, unemployed, separated from traditional support groups and unable to assimilate, the immigrants become victims of an intensifying vicious cycle of disorientation, fear, and helplessness.

I have been involved with several such cases. None has been nearly as severe as those recently encountered among Caribbean refugees, but the histories of most of them show remarkably similar patterns, and they will serve to illustrate the general principles I have discussed above. They also have implications for which neither the social researcher, nor mainstream clinicians, nor members of the judiciary, are prepared. In the remainder of this paper I shall discuss some of these cases and their significance. Space will not permit lengthy detailing of the cases nor full analyses of their implications, which is just as well because, as will become clear, they raise problems for which the available data offer no easy resolutions. But they are problems which have previously unrecognized implications for transcultural research and understanding.

A number of persons in western New York and southern Ontario who have believed themselves victims of hexing personally contacted me for help, following my commentary on the subject of witchcraft in various television and radio interviews and newspaper articles. To deal with these cases I developed a method which I have called, without much novelty, "anthropological intervention." In some cases my method has had positive clinical implications, as conventional psychotherapy had been unsuccessful. In 1978 and 1979 I became peripherally involved with the celebrated Gail Trait murder case, because a belief in witchcraft was initially alleged to have influenced the defendant's behavior. This case revealed that beliefs in witchcraft could have complicated and potentially serious judicial implications for which most clinical and legal practitioners, and anthropologists, are unprepared.

Clinical Implications

I was aware of one general guidebook to cross-cultural counseling (Pedersen 1976) and another has recently appeared (Sue 1981), but for guidance specific to witchcraft cases one can only attempt to glean from the few and disparate case studies published in specific professional journals (Cappannari *et al.* 1975; Galvin and Ludwig 1961; Golden 1977; Johns Hopkins 1967; Leininger 1973; Lewis 1977; Michaelson 1972; Raybin 1970; Snell 1967; Tinling 1967; Warner 1977; Wintrob 1973). My method of approach involved two basic premises, both based in sound anthropology. My primary operating premise was that there exists a profound risk in attempting to interpret belief systems engendered in and structured by one cultural framework, through models of "reality" and principles of etiology developed from the perspective of another. In cases of attributions of the causes of physiological or psychological ailments to the practice of sorcery, at least since Senter's 1947 advice to the psychiatric profession (Senter 1947), it has been increasingly widely recognized that the most effective treatment is that worked within a framework that is culturally familiar to the patient, if such treatment can begin early enough—that is, before any serious and debilitating pathological syndrome has developed. I would add the strong caveat that any thought of converting the patient to an alternate mode of "reality" ought to be postponed during the treatment process, which should also include a substantial period of monitoring during recovery.

The basis for my secondary operating premise was that there are only two ways to deal effectively with the power of a hex: (1) to have it voluntarily withdrawn by the perpetrator, or (2) to nullify it, deflect it, or return it directly to its source by countermagic. In either case, of course, the patient must be satisfied of the efficacy of the method. I was not prepared to attempt either of these two methods, and the nature of most of my cases made seeking the aid of a folk practitioner inadvisable. My clients were first attracted to me principally because they had limited or no access to, or unhappy experiences with, folk practitioners; and they respected me during therapy because I was able knowledgeably and objectively to explain the principles of magic, on the one hand in general terms in a public context, then individually and specifically. So I was able to adopt a third approach: to attempt to convince the client that the hex was ineffectual, either because it had atrophied and lost its power, or that it had been implied but never actually activated in the first place; and whatever symptoms the client was experiencing at the time of consultation with me could be effectively treated by conventional medical means including, if indicated, psychotherapy.

I have selected three cases for presentation, in summary form, here. They represent the range of efficacy of my method, from dramatically successful to discouragingly ineffective. The second case necessitated the enlistment of sympathetic psychiatric assistance. The third case was complicated by manifestations of severe psychosis, which made anthropological intervention premature.

Mrs. B.

She was a black Barbadian woman who had left Bridgetown in 1969 at the age of 17 to work as a nursemaid for a family in Ontario. After 17 months she moved to Toronto to live with a girlfriend and to take a clerical job. For the next two years, and after her marriage in 1973 to a Jamaican factory worker, she experienced a great variety of unpleasant emotional and physical symptoms, specifically and increasingly centering upon problems in her genital area which made sexual activity uncomfortable for both partners. Consultations with physicians and psychiatrists gave only temporary relief, and she and her husband concluded that she had been hexed by a jilted boyfriend in Bridgetown. With the cause of her problems thus identified to her satisfaction, she clung to and elaborated upon it with consuming intensity. She recalled her farewell party when he had given her something strange-tasting to drink, and she retrieved letters from relatives which mentioned inquiries he had made about her. Strongest of all was her recollection that he had asked to keep a pair of her underpants, "so that he could still feel close to me"; she became convinced that he still kept this item and was using it to work sorcery against her. This belief explained, in classic principles of contagious sympathetic magic, all of her sexual problems. Her former lover did not want her "to make it" with any other man.

When she came to me in February 1977, Mrs. B. had sought the help of folk practitioners, by proxy, in Brooklyn, "Long Island," and "California," who had confirmed her suspicions of sorcery. She had experienced real gynecological problems, including a blocked Fallopian tube and an ovarian cyst; these further strengthened her conviction that her former boyfriend wanted not only to spoil her sex life, but to render her barren as well.

I asked for time to consult "a learned doctor at a great university" who had much experience with her sort of case. I was able subsequently to convince her that if her boyfriend had hexed her, the spells had long since weakened and died; he could not still be "working" with her underpants because his current steady girlfriend (Mrs. B. had informed me of her) would not tolerate this; he could not possibly have placed spells on her ovaries or Fallopian tubes because this sort of detailed knowledge of the internal female anatomy was beyond his understanding as a primary school leaver; and that she should trust her gynecologist. She had successful surgery, she and her husband entered marital therapy together, and in February 1978 she telephoned to announce that she was pregnant.

Mrs. H.

This was an American black woman, raised in rural Alabama, who moved to Buffalo with her husband in 1952, when she was 20. She had four grown children when she and her husband separated, in 1966. Thereafter she experienced a number of work-related physiological and psychological problems, and consulted a physician who prescribed medication, but her problems recurred.

At some point during this period she read a novel which involved "voodoo" and hexing, and she began to read extensively on witchcraft in the public library. She analyzed segments of her own history, and after a time she concluded that she was being bewitched. She had suspected fellow workers in the plant where she was employed, recalling certain suspicious glances, conversations abruptly terminated when she approached, positions on the production line changed for no good reason. She had similarly suspected neighbors, relatives, members of her church. She had finally settled on her estranged husband as the evil-doer. She recalled vignettes of her past: that from their childhood her children had "acted up" during the full moon, their favorite pet had been a black cat, she had difficulty persuading them to attend Sunday school. Her husband had not been willing to support her wishes that the children receive a Christian education, and he himself had been reluctant to attend church with her. He had been "out" one or two evenings per week; he did not smell of alcohol when he returned, but he would not say where he had been. She recalled, now with suspicion, many peculiarities in his behavior, and in certain incidents following their separation she found stronger indications that he was working evil magic against her. She remem-

bered that sometimes his support checks arrived in envelopes that were stained in ways that should not occur during routine postal handling. Sometimes after he had been to her house to fix something she noticed traces of strange dust in doorways, on stairs, and in the kitchen and bathroom. Once a light bulb he had replaced had been smeared with "a brown substance" that gave off a noxious smoke shortly after it had been switched on.

She came to me after seeing a television show on which I had been interviewed in January 1977 (the same show Mrs. B. had seen). She was quite determined and explicit about what she wanted from me. Her husband had placed various hexes on her which were causing headaches, dizziness, and sleeplessness, so that she would inevitably have to quit whatever job she had. She wanted the hexes removed and, if possible, re-directed at him.

Mrs. H. was an intelligent and well-read woman. She was convinced that local spiritualists and "two-headed doctors" were quacks. She had a reverential respect for "scientific method," to which I was able to appeal. I pointed out that hexing was only one possible explanation for her physical problems and for the incidents she had interpreted as evidence of hexing; there were others, and these others were far more likely. Furthermore, the indications were that if evil magic was at work, and if her husband was the perpetrator, he was very inefficient at root work; from her readings she herself knew of far more effective methods which he could have used. Any spells he might have placed on her by his methods were so weak as to have been extremely short-lived. I was able to recommend her to a psychiatrist of a West African nationality whom I had apprised of our relationship and my approach, and she entered into reluctant, although eventually successful, therapy with him.

Mrs. P.

A third, and the least successful of all my cases, involved a Polish woman of 60 in Lackawanna, who contacted me in November 1977 after having read a Halloween newspaper interview. She was married to a steelworker of Czechoslovak background who was bedridden from an industrial accident in the mid-1960s. Her first husband lived in Houston. Mrs. P. had constructed a confused chronology of events since her recollection of an incident in the early 1960s when her first husband reappeared one day accompanied by a strange little man who cast the Evil Eye upon her. Her second husband's accident, the death of a brother-in-law in an auto accident, and a host of other misfortunes including her own deteriorating sense of control and physical well-being, were all attributable to that incident. Her relatives abhorred discussion of "the evil" that possessed her, and associated with her only infrequently. A "faith-healer" gave her an envelope of white powder for $300, and was untraceable thereafter. A psychiatrist whom she had contacted earlier assured me that she was severely psychotic and needed urgent therapy; my methods might be effective after she had regained some mental stability. I arranged an appointment with a Polish-speaking psychiatrist with whom I had consulted; but she refused to meet with him, and as I had informed her that I would not attempt to cure her by magical means, which was what she wanted, I had to give up her case.

Mrs. B's entry into Canada was eased by her close association with the family who had befriended her and her family in Barbados. Her problems began when she left her Canadian hosts. Most of her early symptoms were ascribable to a severe case of culture shock, which disoriented her to the point that when an explanation which had validity within her traditional cultural background was offered, she grasped and clung to it with neurotic intensity. It might be said that her beliefs in witchcraft served a positive function for her. All her energies now focused on this, and with her husband's patient support she found stability in this apparently regressive and dysfunctional belief system. Her early symptoms, many of which were very unpleasant, cleared up, and when the case came to me I had only her belief in her former boyfriend's hex to deal with.

Although she had been an urban dweller for 25 years, Mrs. H. was also isolated, probably due to problems in her own personality, from social and cultural networks in the black community. During the earlier years she maintained stability through familial relationships. Her problems developed, and intensified, following her separation from her family. She regressed to and focused upon a belief system which had been very real in the rural Alabama environment of her childhood, but her pride in her intelligence made her distrustful of traditional healers. For apparently similar personality reasons, Mrs. P. was isolated from effective culturally-supportive social networks. She found some stability in clinging to a belief which was culturally relevant to her and her husband's eastern European backgrounds, but which was substantiated in an incident which was quite clearly the product of her own neurotic fantasies. She did attempt to seek relief through what she considered to be traditional means, but she was victimized, and her psychosis intensified.

Each of these three women had sought clinical help through "mainstream" agencies and each had been dissatisfied. The traditional cultural beliefs to which they regressed held that magic could be countered by magic, and provided no preparation for the lengthy analysis required of conventional psychological therapy. Similarly, the medical position on the clinical implications of hexing is generally intolerant.

The three cases discussed above are those of persons whose cultural backgrounds differ from that of mainstream institutions and who are not well integrated into traditional networks; I have called them "marginal" and have focused my discussion upon them. It should not, however, be assumed that magical or supernatural explanations for misfortunes are unique to such persons. Two of my cases involved white middle-class persons who had become convinced that Satan was influencing their lives. Both had high school diplomas. One completed junior college, the other, secretarial school. The first, a 37-year-old Roman Catholic of Italian ancestry, was unaware that his own parish priests were potentially good sources of counsel. The other, a Protestant woman, aged 28, of German descent, had been diagnosed as chronic paranoid schizophrenic. (She claimed to have received 11 such diagnoses! I was able to confirm that at least five doctors had treated her for this disease, since her early teens.) She was obliged to stop by a neighborhood clinic weekly to receive medication, but she claimed never to have been informed that her auditory hallucinations, which she identified as Satanic voices, were experiences typical of this syndrome. Clearly, these people's ascriptions of their problems to the work of the devil derives from their own cultural heritage, and such ascriptions were not made hastily, but long after symptoms developed and efforts at obtaining satisfactory treatment had been made.

Such cases receive notice when they are associated with bizarre, violent, or criminal behavior (*New Haven Register* 1981); but persons who believe themselves so afflicted are surely more numerous than is generally recognized. And, reflective of the growing acceptability of "supernatural" or "occult" explanations at all levels of society, such cases are very probably increasing. Most of them are very probably amenable to patient sympathetic treatment of the sort I utilized for my clients, in which the collection of case histories includes eliciting data on cultural beliefs, and in which the nature of those beliefs helps to structure the specific therapeutic approach taken.

Judicial Implications

The fact that this whole business could have legal implications came to me quite suddenly on July 18, 1978, when I was telephoned in Washington, D.C., by a reporter from a Buffalo newspaper. The paper's headlines the day before had suggested, "'Voodoo Curse' May be Linked to 4 Stabbings" (*Buffalo Evening News*). Mrs. Gail Trait had methodically butchered her four children with kitchen cutlery the evening of the 16th, and a police lieutenant had reported that "family members had told him Mrs. Trait thought she was under a voodoo curse." The reporter had hoped to build a story on witchcraft-related crimes, stimulated by an article in a Rochester paper on July 14, which was headlined, "'Witchcraft' Called a Reason for Fatal Firebombing. Police Say Family Believed a Spell Was Cast" (*Times-Union*). The story was not pursued and the witchcraft element was played down in the press thereafter, and Mrs. Trait was remanded for psychiatric examination.

She was incarcerated for a year, during which time she received anti-psychotic medication, and was interviewed extensively by three court-appointed psychiatrists. The reports of all three doctors show clearly that Mrs. Trait was quite obsessed with ideas of sorcery, "voodoo," "roots," and demon possession. Two reports saw her as psychotic and not responsible for her behavior at the time of the crime, and diagnosed chronic paranoid schizophre-

nia. Mrs. Trait was judged competent to stand trial, and her case came to court in the late summer of 1979. In August a representative of the Erie County District Attorney's office telephoned me, saying that his office feared that Mrs. Trait's defense counsel would bring up the alleged "voodoo hex," and they wanted to be prepared. "How widespread is this voodoo business?" and "Is there anything to it?" were among his questions. But Mrs. Trait's trial progressed with no mention of witchcraft, and in spite of the pre-trial psychiatric testimony, it concluded in the Spring of 1980 with a finding of guilty of eight counts of murder.

The Trait case raises some very disturbing questions, for which neither the psychiatric nor, certainly, the legal professions are prepared. Since seventeenth-century New England courts denied the admissibility of "spectral evidence," there have been few precedents for defense of criminal acts based on beliefs in the supernatural. I have found no reported modern cases in this country in which beliefs in witchcraft formed the basis for a defense (Lewis 1958; Williams 1949, 1961). In retrospect, it is just as well that such a defense was not pursued in the Trait case. Mrs. Trait's ultimate fate, specifically the nature of her institutionalization, would probably not have been different; but a complicated anthropological and legal dilemma would certainly have developed.

Many of my clients were culturally marginal people. All had been at least partially acculturated, and had fallen back on explanations recovered from their cultural heritage after sporadic efforts at achieving relief through other means had failed. But after having focused on their cultural explanations, such persons receive little sympathy from either acculturated *or* traditional friends; relatives may not want to get involved, probably for reasons, unspoken, of fear of contagion; and doctors use Western methods and tend to dismiss such beliefs as superstitions, infantile regressions, or paranoid fantasies. Such people may become desperate in their obsession, and become vulnerable to fraudulent—and expensive—promises of magical cures, as in the case of Mrs. P. Or they may resort to criminal acts. Gail Trait was possessed by evil, she told her psychiatrists, and she dispatched her children to God to save them from similar possession.

It is such people that the practitioner of "anthropological intervention" is best able to help, although, as my data show, he may be of some help to people who are well integrated in a cultural system. But in attempting to provide such help, certain unforeseen problems may develop, problems with complicated and far-reaching implications. The clinical implications are becoming more widely recognized. Judicial implications, however, are potentially so complicated as to require careful thought and detailed examination of resources which are not available at the time of this writing. But given contemporary urban social problems, and the directions of popular sentiment, it seems to me that mainstream practitioners *and* social researchers must be far more amenable to the recognition of the nature and strength of cultural beliefs and of their validity within the cultural traditions which generate them.

Sorcery and Concepts of Deviance among the Kabana, West New Britain

Naomi M. McPherson

Most beginning students of comparative religion picture sorcerers as practitioners of evil with few, if any, positive functions in their societies. As is the case of Jamaican obeahmen described by Wedenoja (see Chapter 5), sorcerers are to be feared. Contrary to this general view, Naomi McPherson's data demonstrate that depending on the circumstances that initiate the attack, sorcery may or may not be considered by the Kabana as a criminal act. She writes (Anthropologica, *vol. 33, no. 1–2, 1991, p. 127):*

> *For the Kabana of New Britain, deviant behavior is essentially the advancement of self-interest untempered by self-regulation such that the individual infringes on the ability of others to pursue their own self-interest. Social labeling is applied to deviant behaviors, but no permanent stigma attaches to individuals. Reactions to deviance include shame, gossip and ridicule, proceedings before the village magistrate, and sorcery. The performance of sorcery, a major cause of death, is a complex and ambiguous event, insofar as a sorcerer's threat may both inhibit deviance and mediate conflict, but the actual enactment of the threat is itself a deviant act. In cases where a victim's illness is attributed to sorcery, a moot may be held to discern the motives of sorcery and identify the sorcerer. In a particular case, which is examined at length here, failure clearly to identify the sorcerer was followed by the victim's death.*

Deaths resulting from sorcery are always classified as "bad deaths" by the Kabana, and bring up the question of the veracity of so-called voodoo death discussed by Harry Eastwell later in Chapter 6.

Reprinted with permission from *Anthropologica*, vol. 33, no. 1–2, 1991, pp. 127–43.

IN THE STUDY OF WHAT WE NOW RECOGNIZE AS "deviance" in Pacific societies, the work of Malinowski is central. Vincent considers his treatment of sorcery, in particular, to be "pathbreaking." In the Trobriands, sorcery was *both* a criminal practice and a method of administering justice. Which it was in any particular case depended on who was practising it on whom and when he was doing it. On the one hand, sorcery was

> the main criminal agency (Malinowski 1926: 85); on the other, the Trobriand chief used sorcery to punish offenders.... Thus he concluded that where there was no *formal* code or administration of justice, it was very difficult to draw a line between the "quasi-legal" and the "quasi-criminal." (Vincent 1990: 165–166)

The line was usually drawn in some public arena.

In this early view, sorcery may be either deviance per se, or it may be the *control* of deviance. This treatment is compatible with the labelling theory of deviance that has developed since Malinowski wrote, especially in its focus on reactions to deviance rather than deviance itself. Indeed, the earliest statement of labelling theory by Becker (1963: 10–11) included a lengthy citation of one of Malinowski's cases from *Crime and Custom in Savage Society* (Malinowski 1967). Becker used this quote to differentiate between the relatively common commission of an act and the rare adjudication of the same act as *deviant by virtue of the reaction to it.*

In this paper, a similar analysis is applied to the Kabana of West New Britain, Papua New Guinea. Labelling theory is used to call attention to the multiple levels of political negotiation that go into a decision about whether an act of sorcery is—or is not—deviant. In the process, the analysis leads us to an examination of the organizational complexity of labelling. In order to provide context for the analysis, I begin with a discussion of Kabana morality and then move to a discussion of lower, "pre-sorcery" levels of social control among the Kabana, and, finally, I examine Kabana notions of sorcery as a social sanction. With this background established, the paper then moves to an extended analysis of a particular case of alleged sorcery and the political negotiation that took place, when villagers tried to decide whether the sorcery was deviance or had been used as a means to *control* deviance. The case is a provocative and rich one, because the outcome of the negotiation was indeterminate. The line between sorcery as deviance and sorcery as control of deviance could not be drawn, and the case entered Kabana history as backdrop for some dispute that would arise later.

Kabana Morality

Among the Kabana of West New Britain, Papua New Guinea, the framework of ideal social values and morals is grounded in concepts of human nature and the obligations inherent in the structure of human relations. It is this ethic of morality which provides a guide for individual action, and against which actions are judged. In this non-literate society, where the locus of individual experience is social, relations among individuals and groups do not exist in the abstract but always and only in connection with someone or something else. Given the extensive and overlapping network of Kabana social relations, there is an equally extensive range of behaviour that can be perceived as deviant to some degree and can elicit varying degrees of response from a particular audience. What constitutes deviant behaviour thus depends on whether relevant others perceive a certain act as a threat to the basic tenets of Kabana social life, that is, to the moral obligations which structure human relations.

Offended persons may select from a hierarchy of responses of increasing complexity to restore and restructure their interpersonal relations. Ultimately, social conformity derives from a fundamental principle of reciprocal self-interest which is based upon two related concepts: self-regulation and self-help. Self-regulation entails that all individuals are deemed to be in control of their own existence and, therefore, are accountable to, and responsible for, others. Self-help is the principle whereby individuals who perceive their rights to have been infringed upon may rightfully take retaliatory action against those who have infringed upon them (cf. Lawrence 1984: 161). The interrelated concepts of self-help and self-regulation are, in turn, based on the Kabana belief in personal autonomy, that is, that all individuals have the freedom to empower their existence as a basic human right. For the Kabana, deviant behaviour is essentially the advancement of self-interest untempered by self-regulation such that the individual infringes on the ability of others to pursue their own self-interest.

The Kabana label behaviour but not individuals as deviant, and the imposition of negative sanctions in no way implies an intent to permanently discriminate against or stigmatize an offender. The aim of any sanction is to provide the culprit with the opportunity for expiation thereby limiting the consequences of the transgression to that single event. There is no intentional discrimination against, and no stigma applied to, offenders, for to stigmatize persons is to set aside and mark them permanently as incorrigibly different, thus denying them the opportunity to redress the imbalance in social relations caused by their offenses. By not allowing a person to rectify wrongful behaviour, others arbitrarily rescind that individual's personal autonomy, integrity and right to self-help, thus effectively reducing the individual to a non-social (and, therefore, non-human) being. To label an individual permanently as deviant is to place him or her outside the pale of human relations as a social pariah. Ultimately, such action is tantamount to a death sentence, because in societies of this nature, no one can exist outside the context of social relations. The only options left to the stigmatized individual would be exile or suicide (cf. Counts and Counts 1984; Lawrence 1984: 132).

Most reactions to deviance occur at the level of personal relations, though they may involve whole families. On occasion, however, reactions to deviance can be escalated to levels that involve multiple families within villages, and may even include whole villages. Sorcery events also involve their own levels of organization and styles of political negotiation.

After briefly delineating the range of responses to lower levels of deviance, I focus on a traditional village "court" proceeding which was convened in reaction to a particular sorcery event. Sorcery is the most pervasive and powerful regulatory device that the Kabana have for dealing with deviant behaviour. The practice of sorcery is not unambiguously right or wrong. As a negative sanction, sorcery is a legitimate form of social control, both an expected and accepted consequence of a breach of morality. Since sorcery is always potentially lethal, however, any act of sorcery, regardless of the circumstances, can be construed as a deviant act and thus be subject to negative social sanctions itself. The case history presented here demonstrates how the community reacted to the ambiguous nature of sorcery, when they attempted to determine whether or not one woman's imminent death by sorcery was a legitimate form of social control or a case of homicide, which, in turn, would require control.

Lower Levels of Social Control

All Kabana relationships are face-to-face relations and everyone is known to, and knows about, everyone else. Anonymity is impossible and no behaviour, albeit good, bad or indifferent, goes undiscovered. For the most part, a perceived breach of the ideal of reciprocal self-interest is couched in terms of positive criticism. Someone who ignores the rules of reciprocity is advised or reminded of the potentially negative consequences that could be experienced as a result of the impropriety. For example, a youth who avoids assisting his kin in cutting and hauling trees to make a garden fence may be criticized for his laziness and warned that when he needs the aid of these same kin in some venture of his own, such as the amassing of his bride-wealth, help may not be forthcoming. Continued failure to observe proper behaviour reduces a person's chances for success in other desired achievements, and, since it is in their own best interests to do so, most people adjust their behaviour in response to the pressure exerted on them to conform.

The Kabana do not equate simple non-conformity with deviance. Idiosyncratic personality types are marked, for example, by teasing or nicknaming. They may become the butt of jokes, be lampooned, criticized or otherwise disparaged, but there is no stigma imposed on them. When a person is recognized as having social or physical disabilities, others compensate for the idiosyncratic personality by lowering their expectations. Acknowledging individual differences defines the attributes of individuals who comprise a relationship, but the relationship itself remains unaffected, operating according to the level of expectations of all involved. Within the framework of lowered expectations, the idiosyncratic personality is recognized but not stigmatized in the sense of being negatively stereotyped or marginalized.

Shaming, gossip and ridicule are extremely effective means of sanctioning deviant behaviour. The power of shame as an overt negative sanction derives from the discomfort of "an intrusion of one's private self into public awareness and the reciprocal invasion of the self by public scrutiny" (Jorgensen 1983–84: 123). Shaming and gossip expose the inadequacies of the individual and exert pressure on the target to behave according to commonly held values and to repair the imbalance in social relations. The balance between public and private, self and other, is restored through a process of negotiations and settled when the culprit presents a gift of wealth to those who have gossiped about or shamed the victim. The gift of wealth both relieves the culprit of the sense of shame and obliges the recipients to curtail their slander or risk censure themselves for perpetuating a situation that has been resolved satisfactorily.

At a higher level of response, theft, physical violence and adultery often result in the perpetrator being brought before the village magistrate by the injured party. More often than not, in communities of this type, "the culprit is condemned on the basis of ideal social values even by those who have been guilty of the same offense in the past" (Lawrence 1984: 132). Again, since the Kabana label only behaviour, not individuals, as deviant, any sanction imposed by the public court allows the culprit the opportunity for expiation and limits the consequences of the transgression to a single event. Once reparation is made, usually in the form of a compensation payment, the incident is forgiven, although rarely forgotten, and the culprit resumes his or her usual place in the community. There is no intentional discrimination against, and no permanent stigma applied to the offender.

For the Kabana, observation of the moral obligations that structure and organize normal relations can be, ultimately, a life-and-death matter. Persons who survive to an extreme old age are by definition those persons who have lived a morally correct life. Death from old age is a good death (cf. Counts and Counts 1976–77), a death which is the result of, and performs closure on, a socially correct and moral life span. The Kabana observe, however, that human nature being what it is, very few people survive to the culturally defined life span that culminates in a good death. With few exceptions, most people die a bad death as victims of sorcery (see Scaletta 1985).

Sorcery as Social Sanction and as Deviance

Sorcery can be defined as a form of esoteric knowledge bestowing personal power which the adept can use willfully to realize desired ends. While not everyone could or would acquire the knowledge and skill to become a sorcerer, all have access to sorcery as a mode of self-help by purchasing the services of a known sorcerer. Awareness of the fact that others can choose to exercise their right to self-help through sorcery serves to define sorcery as the primary deterrent to deviant behaviour. Victims of sorcery are assumed to be persons who have violated social mores and values thereby infringing on the rights of others. Because sorcery is notoriously difficult to control once unleashed, both the decision to sorcerize and the execution of that decision should result from corporate deliberation and follow certain other procedural rules. The injured party should discuss any intention to instigate redressive action in the form of sorcery with his or her kin. If one's kin are not in agreement with such measures, the whole matter is dropped or deferred. If there is sufficient agreement to warrant action, however, usually because others have complaints against the intended victim or because the offence is such that sorcery is the only appropriate form of punishment, then the services of a sorcerer are solicited. Sorcery is a male prerogative acquired through apprenticeship and arranged in the *lum,* "men's house." Once the sorcerer has been approached and all the details have been worked out, the sorcerer and his clients exchange equal lengths of the most highly valued category of shell-money, *bula misi.* This exchange of wealth "buys" both the sorcerer's services and the silence and complicity of those employing him. Since the men's house is a semi-public domain, there is no question that the business of soliciting a sorcerer has been witnessed by other men in or near the building, and the whole episode becomes a topic for discreet gossip, a public secret, and moves into a wider area of involvement.

The sorcerer's role may also be construed as that of a mediator hired to resolve a conflict between two parties. Acting on behalf of his client, the sorcerer leaves a "calling card" (Zelenietz 1981: 105) which alerts the recipient that some action on his or her part has offended another party, thus jeopardizing their relationship. The calling cards of Kabana sorcerers can take a number of forms: a large basket, of the type only sorcerers carry, lodged in the rafters of the victim's house; a gutted frog pinioned on the footpath the victim travels to the gardens; a bundle of croton leaves tied in a particular way and placed conspicuously where the victim will find it, and so on.

Kabana sorcerers also send calling cards in the form of ensorcelled stones that they throw onto or into the victim's house. The stone called *pamododonga* carries a form of sorcery that causes the victim to become ill for an indefinite period or time. It is generally assumed that, during the illness, victims will examine their consciences, review their actions and deduce for themselves the nature of their transgressions. They can then take steps to rectify the situation by approaching those with whom they are in conflict and trying to negotiate a resolution to the difficulty. If a resolution is reached, they pay the sorcerer to rescind his spell. If they are unable to identify the locus of conflict, the sorcerer might approach them, inform them why they have been ill, remove the spell and restore health. It is more common, however, because sorcery is a non-confrontational social act, for spells to be removed as stealthily as they were applied. Then, a second stone, *angual,* is thrown on the victim's house. Sorcery of this type puts transgressors on notice that they should discover the source of the conflict and repair the rift in their relationships, before they develop into open confrontation.

Although sorcery is an expected negative sanction for breach of expected behaviour, the actual implementation of sorcery as a form of self-help is, in itself, a deviant act. Evidence of sorcery indicates that someone has succeeded in a private act of collusion. When sorcery is suspected, "the contradiction between autonomy and control is flagrantly exposed and every villager is witness to his or her own vulnerability" (Weiner 1976: 223). Sorcery takes away from the victim all that the Kabana define as human rights: the right to self-help, personal autonomy and control over one's existence. To be a victim of sorcery is to be threatened with death, for one's "personal autonomy has collapsed" (Weiner 1976: 219). It is for this reason that death by sorcery is a bad death. It is a bad death not just because of the manner in which it occurred, but also because of the manner in which it was incurred. Death by sorcery entails a negative judgment upon the behaviour of the victim by relevant others, but does not allow the culprit to amend the situation in his or her own best interests. Personal autonomy is negated and the target becomes a victim of the power that others wield in pursuit of their own self-interest. Death by sorcery is a moral issue, and those who practise it are themselves subject to public disapprobation: "Individual power, the cause of all death, demands the display of group power" (Weiner 1976: 226).

A Case of Sorcery

Jean had been seriously ill for three months. During this time, attempts to cure her had proved fruitless. Treatments at the local hospital and by local healers, and the attempts of a sorcerer-curer to heal her by extracting foreign substances from her body were all ineffective. From the beginning of her illness, Jean was convinced that she had been sorcerized, a conviction reinforced when all attempts to cure her failed. Only the sorcerer who inflicts the spell has the correct formula for rescinding it and restoring the victim to health. As her illness progressed, Jean became more and more incapacitated. She became a non-participant in the myriad conceptual and social minutiae that make life worth living. As an invalid, her social interactions were essentially passive. She was dependent on others to care for her, and she resented being powerless, the victim of someone's ill-will. There was no question in anyone's mind, least of all Jean's, that she was dying. Her family refused, however, to open the magic bundle containing her vital essence, *tautau,* and kept it in contact with her body to prevent her death. The final indignity, from Jean's perspective, was that she was denied the right to take control of the situation and end her own life. (See Scaletta 1985 for a detailed discussion of these events.)

Given that illness or death caused by sorcery are the result of specifically inflicted punishment for a breach of socially expected behaviour on the part of the victim (or her family), Jean's condition created a climate of heightened awareness of a variety of social relations. Relations between Jean and other individuals, between her family and other family groups, between her hamlet and the other three hamlets in the village, and between her village as a unit and other villages, particularly the two villages where the majority of her cognatic kin lived, were all minutely scrutinized. There was constant re-evaluation and discussion of past events, interpersonal and intergroup interactions, in order to determine why, and by whom, she was sorcerized. Jean's personal crisis as an individual escalated to the level of an inter-village social crisis.

Jean added to the escalating tensions by making specific charges of sorcery against three men in the village. She accused Ken, her deceased husband's brother. His motive, she said, was revenge: Ken and his kin group were avenging the death of their brother by attacking his wife. The second man she accused was Lari. She had no specific reason for accusing him, except that he had renown as a powerful sorcerer, and was, at the time, under suspicion by everybody in the area as the individual responsible for the current drought. She argued that if Lari would create hardship in the whole area in his efforts to destroy a rival, then it was reasonable that he should attack her for no motive other than that it was in the nature of his disposition to do so. The third man she accused was Tomi, her sister's husband. Tomi was obsessively jealous of his wife and resented the time she spent in Jean's company. By eliminating her, Jean reasoned, Tomi was eliminating a major competitor for his wife's affection.

In all these accusations, Jean portrayed herself as an innocent victim. At no time did she name anyone who may have had reason to resort to sorcery in retaliation for some misdeed on her part. In proclaiming her innocence, she was implying that sorcery was being practised arbitrarily and, therefore, that everyone was vulnerable unless it could be stopped. Jean's steady decline, the general unease generated by the active presence of sorcery in their midst, the increasing strain between her cognatic and affinal kin and the intervillage tensions arising from Jean's accusations coalesced one morning with the arrival of a delegation of Jean's male kin from her natal village. They came both to express their anger that someone was "killing" their sister and to demand that a meeting be convened to "break the talk," to expose and punish the sorcerer.

Breaking the Talk

To "break the talk" means to cut through the multitude of conjecture and gossip about why a person has been sorcerized and by whom. When the "talk is broken," it is exposed to public scrutiny so that its veracity can be analyzed and a logical sequence of events leading up to the illness or death can be reconstructed. When the nature of the victim's offence has been determined, thereby identifying those who had reason to sorcerize her, witnesses can either refute or confirm the charges of culpability. The meeting to "break the talk" also provides a forum where persons who are associated with the illness or death, because of past disputes with the victim, can proclaim their innocence and clear their names, thereby avoiding the possibility that they might be sorcerized by the victim's avenging kin group. Ideally, this procedure culminates in a solid case of circumstantial evidence identifying the protagonists in the conflict, and leaves no doubt as to who caused the victim to become ill or to die. Any doubt as to the identity of the sorcerer is dispelled when those who witnessed the meeting between the sorcerer and the persons who employed him produce the length of shell-money they were given to "buy" their silence. Ultimately, the "talk is broken" when the silence surrounding the act of collusion is broken, thus publicly exposing those who participated in the decision to sorcerize.

A meeting to "break the talk" is a highly charged public confrontation and represents the most complex level of the adjudication of deviance in Kabana culture. At such meetings in the past, it is said, the end came with a fight and the killing of the exposed sorcerer. The sorcerer's death was considered compensation for the death of the victim, and obviated (in theory, if not always in practice) the need for retributive sorcery by balancing the losses on both sides of the conflict. The death of the sorcerer was a public statement to those who sought control over others that homicidal sorcery was an amoral act so heinous that death was the only appropriate social response.

On the day of the meeting, all the adult males from the four concerned villages convened in the plaza in front of the "men's house." There were no women (except myself) or children visibly present. It was dangerous for them to be there. The meeting lasted for five hours, during which the discussion ranged widely. Several young men professed their lack of knowledge of sorcery, and called on their senior male relatives to attest to the fact that they had not instructed them in the ways and means of sorcery. Another man acknowledged that he had disputed with Jean and her sister over the ownership of

certain sago palms, but said they had settled the problem, and that the altercation could not, therefore, be construed as a motive for sorcery on his part. Much of the meeting proceeded in this manner, the underlying premise being that unchallenged, public denials of guilt or involvement are sufficient to prove innocence. The most important contributions came from the three men specifically accused by Jean, and from Jean's brother.

The three accused took the opportunity to refute Jean's charges against them. Tomi, Jean's sister's husband, stated that he did not and could not know sorcery because he was associated with women (a consequence of his jealous obsession with his wife). This was common knowledge, he went on, for did not everyone refer to him as "first woman"? Sorcery is the business of men, and a man who spends his time with women would not have occasion to learn the art. Even if he did, his powers would be diminished by his contact with females, who are "different" (Tok Pisin: *narapela kain*) from men. It was true, he admitted, that he had tried to purchase rain magic (a form of sorcery) from an old man in another village, but he had been refused. Tomi had given valid reasons why he could not know sorcery, and why, even if he did have some skill as a sorcerer, this skill would be minimal. He had admitted to being in the company of a sorcerer, given reasons for being there and revealed the outcome of the meeting, thus forestalling any misconstruction of his behaviour by others who might have witnessed the meeting. No one challenged what he had to say.

Ken, Jean's husband's brother, also denied her accusations against him. He pointed out that when she first became ill, she had come to him on her own initiative and asked him to use his skills to cure her. He had assumed she was suffering from the effects of "bad blood," a problem peculiar to post-menopausal women. He had prepared the appropriate cure, which proved ineffective. Because of this and her worsening condition, she became fearful and accused him of sorcerizing rather than curing her. He also noted that she, and perhaps other members of her family, thought he might have attacked her in revenge for the death of his brother, Jean's husband. He denied the credibility of such speculations on the grounds that he was a member of the Catholic Church which forbade the practice of sorcery. He further denied the fact of sorcery, saying that sickness and death were not caused by human actors, but by God, as divine punishment for sins committed. Jean was dying, he concluded, because God was punishing her as a sinner.

The third man accused by Jean was Lari. As the person considered responsible for the drought and a self-acknowledged sorcerer, Lari defended himself on both counts. He argued that no one could claim they had actually seen him practising weather magic. Even though he had all the paraphernalia, which he then produced for all to see, without eyewitnesses, all the talk about him was nothing but air, insubstantial and without truth value. Did people think, he demanded, that he or a member of his family would be so "insane" (Kabana: *mangamanga*) as to attack this woman and run the risk of retaliation from her kin? They must look to the woman herself, he admonished, for the origin of her problem. From the time of their ancestors, he continued, there were two reasons why females were attacked by sorcery. They were sorcerized for being foul-tempered, malicious gossips, and for repulsing the sexual advances of males, or conversely, for engaging in illicit love affairs. (The seeming paradox of this situation is more apparent than real, but a detailed discussion is beyond the scope of the task at hand.)

Lari's point here was to prompt people to examine Jean's behaviour rather than continuing to look for wrongdoing on the part of others. He was, in effect, both denying the validity of the scenario that Jean had created in which she played the role of innocent victim, and situating the whole episode within the accepted explanatory framework—people are sorcerized for breach of social norms. It then came out that during the weeks of Jean's illness, there had been a great deal of discussion about her reputation for maligning others, particularly two senior women who were highly respected. There was also talk of her affair with a married man who was also a person of some renown. It was further reported that she had accepted a proposal of marriage, and the shell money that accompanied it, from a man in the Kove district. She had later reneged on her promise to marry him, claiming that she wanted to remain a widow and live near her children, but had failed to return the shell money. The rejected man thus had motive—the loss of his shell money, not the broken promise—and the wherewithal to attack her, the Kove being notorious sorcerers. All agreed that any one of the foregoing was a likely origin of her illness and, if so, that (1) she had gotten

only what she deserved, and (2) that, if the sorcery originated with the Kove man, her chances of recovery were slim because no one knew either the Kove techniques, or, consequently, the specific counter spell to effect a cure.

Discussion turned to the possibility that Jean was part of a long-standing vendetta to eliminate all the members of her family. In the past five years, sorcery had claimed the lives of Jean's father, her 20–year-old son, a classificatory son and her eldest son's wife. Everyone knew that her father had died of *mosi* "privately owned designs." Without permission or payment, he had used the traditional totemic designs of another kin group on a set of spirit masks of his own group. Death by sorcery was the expected and accepted response to such a serious crime; hence, there had been no "talk" or retaliation, and the incident was closed. Perhaps, however, the issue was not closed, and Jean was the most recent casualty of the offended group's unrequited anger for her father's transgression against them.

These observations focussed attention on indigenous ancestral laws, and Lari began a forceful harangue about the loss of traditional customs. In the past, he began, this meeting would have taken place inside the men's house, not in the open plaza. Now the men's house stood abandoned, and young men no longer gathered there to learn from their elders. Now men slept, not in the men's house, but with their wives and children in the women's houses. Even the practice of sorcery was no longer done according to tradition. In the time of their grandfathers, sorcery was always undertaken by two or three men with the sanction of their kin group. With these several people involved, it was possible to "break the talk," discover who worked the sorcery and why, and thus permit resolution of the situation. This was no longer possible because sorcery was being practised on an individual basis, making it impossible to expose and control the practice of sorcery.

Jean's elder brother Karl, located at the outer perimeter of the assembly, had stood quietly throughout the foregoing, awaiting his opportunity to speak. When he had everyone's attention, he began by reprimanding people for listening to Jean's accusations. The ravings of a sick person should not be given credibility. Such talk is *mangamanga*, "hysterical," and based on fear. He went on to point out that those who brought up his father's death by sorcery were wrong to revive this incident, for it implied that he, or a member of his family, had avenged their father's death and that Jean's illness was retaliation for that second death. When their father died, he and his brothers had "put on the grass skirt" worn by women. Metaphorically, he was arguing that they had become like women, and thus did not know or engage in sorcery. The death of their father had nothing to do with his sister's dying, and such talk must cease, he emphasized, so that old animosities were not revived. He reiterated that they must look to Jean's own behaviour as the cause of her dying, and, having nicely set the mood, he went on to elaborate what, in his opinion, that behaviour might have been.

Some years before, Jean and her husband had contracted a marriage between one of their sons and the daughter of Rio and Sandra, a couple who have considerable prestige in the area. During a ceremonial feast at another village, Jean's son had an affair with another woman. The young people were discovered, and, when confronted with the options of either paying fines to "buy their shame," or with getting married, the two said they wished to be married. With this public declaration of intent, they were married *de facto,* and the betrothal previously arranged by the young man's parents was nullified.

When the jilted girl's parents heard this, they were furious and confronted Jean and her husband. While venting her anger, the girl's mother assumed the stylistic stance associated with throwing spears during battle, and called down the name of her personal protective spirit upon Jean's head, an effective and sometimes deadly curse. She berated Jean for breaking the marriage contract, thereby shaming both her and her daughter. Jean claimed she had nothing to do with the situation, and had heard of her son's behaviour and marriage only after the fact.

Two days after this confrontation, Jean sat on some wood shavings on her verandah, and, several days later, her legs became swollen. It was assumed that Jean had been sorcerized by the offended parents through the medium of wood shavings. She was treated by a curer familiar with that type of sorcery, and the condition was removed. It now appeared that the sorcery had not been neutralized, but had lain dormant in her body these past years, and was only now manifesting itself as her current illness.

Karl's speech was extremely effective. He had discredited Jean's accusations against others as the ravings of a sick and frightened person, thus soothing the anxieties of the accused; he had denied that her illness was a continuation of the conflict that resulted in their father's death, thus avoiding the possibility of old animosities resurfacing, and he had described a specific breach of moral obligation—the breaking of a marriage contract. At the same time, he had left it an open question whether or not Jean was responsible for the breach. (Everybody knew that nowadays children made up their own minds about whom they would or would not marry.) His suggestion that specific, known events and individuals might be responsible for Jean's illness helped defuse the tensions that had built up around people's fears that sorcery was being practised arbitrarily. The individuals implicated had been away from the village for the past year, living in urban centres, and so were not on hand to give their interpretation or to defend themselves. No one else present hurried to defend them either, possibly because one of them was already considered responsible for other recent, and unresolved, sorcery related incidents. At the conclusion of his speech, the meeting was brought to a close. Karl had provided an acceptable explanatory framework for Jean's condition, thus redressing the "threat of disorderliness" that a motiveless death implies (Zelenietz 1981: 9). The consensus was, however, that the meeting had not been totally satisfactory. They had been unable to "break the talk" and prove conclusively the validity of the reconstruction. No one had come forth to bear witness against the sorcerer whose behaviour threatened Jean's life and the moral infrastructure of social order. Because the situation was not totally resolved, there was little hope that Jean could be cured.

Three weeks later, Jean died. When the funeral rites and period of mourning were finished, life in the village reverted to the status quo ante; the crisis created by Jean's dying and death might never have occurred. When I inquired of my informants what steps, if any, would be taken to avenge her death or punish the sorcerer, I was advised that we ought not to discuss such matters. Others might hear of our talk, assume we are plotting vengeance and take steps to protect themselves by striking first; we could be sorcerized. Circumstances surrounding her death are not forgotten. The entire experience will be woven into the fabric of ongoing personal and social relations where it will affect people's motives and behaviour in the future.

Conclusion

This analysis of sorcery and deviant behaviour in Kabana society shows that the generic processes noted in labelling theory can be applied to the cross-cultural study of deviance, even in a society in which deviants are not specifically "labelled." Certain kinds of behaviour, under certain conditions, are reacted to as deviant in Kabana society, and there are rules about what constitutes a socially acceptable response to deviant behaviour. The Kabana data show that, regardless of the level of community involvement, the reaction to deviant behaviour does not result in the typing of individuals as permanently deviant, or in the differentiation of people into groups defined as "normals" and "deviants." Given the egalitarian ideology and lack of stratification in Kabana society, the creation of a class of deviants is unlikely, and, in Kabana terms, philosophically untenable. Rather, deviance is a highly negotiated, highly complex phenomenon which occurs in an interpersonal network. Sorcery is an interesting case in point. While it is inherently neither deviant nor a normative sanction for the social control of deviance, it may be negotiated as *either* according to the specifics of any particular case. It may begin with individual relations and end there; it may rise to the familial level and end there or escalate to even more complex levels before it is publicly mooted. In the moot, sorcery may be judged to be a device for the legitimate control of deviance, deviance in and of itself, or the problem of what it is may prove to be insoluble. *Whatever* the outcome,

the case remains in the cultural memory of the groups involved and forms part of relevant knowledge that will be brought to bear in subsequent cases of sorcery or other trouble.

Afterword

The events described above took place in early 1983. When I returned to the village in 1985, one of the first pieces of news that I was given was that Ken, Jean's husband's brother, had been ill for some months and was currently at the local health clinic for medical treatment. The public explanation for his illness was that he "had no blood" (acute anaemia, possibly leukaemia?); the *very* private explanation was that he had been sorcerized. In response to my queries about who had sorcerized him and why, people referred to the case of Jean and her accusations against her brother-in-law. I was also advised not to pursue this matter with "certain other people," lest those people infer that my inquiries were informed by the (malicious) speculation of the people who spent time with me, thus placing them at risk. It was clear that Ken's lingering illness was linked to Jean's death by sorcery, but people preferred not to make this connection a matter of public record or public moot. The feeling was that, if ignored, the attacks and counterattacks of sorcery would cease, and order and well-being would prevail. I respected these views and did not pursue the matter further. Ken died in 1986 after a prolonged and painful dying process.

Voodoo Death and the Mechanism for Dispatch of the Dying in East Arnhem, Australia

Harry D. Eastwell

Among the Murngin of Australia, if a person commits a particularly heinous act—incest, for example—a possible response may be punishment by sorcery. The perpetrator may have a supernatural curse leveled at him and as a result shortly sicken or die. Cases of illness or death caused by witchcraft or sorcery are common in the ethnographic literature, with many documented accounts coming from aboriginal Australia. Several terms have been applied to this phenomenon— psychosomatic, magical, psychogenic—but voodoo death *appears to be the most popular usage. In a classic article, Walter Cannon (1942) reasoned in physiological terms that a victim of sorcery may experience fear to the extent that he or she will die from the prolonged shock. W. Lloyd Warner (1958) believed a person who fell victim to a sorcerer's witchcraft could become ill or die because the community withdrew its support from the already "half-dead" person. Although Cannon's and Warner's theories on the subject have prevailed over the years, Harry D. Eastwell, a senior lecturer in psychiatry at the University of Queensland, Australia, provides in this article a much-needed update. Professor Eastwell does not deny the role of sorcery in "voodoo deaths"; rather, he takes issue with explanations that place the mechanism of the illness or death on "psycho-physiological reactions." It is Eastwell's belief that sorcery-induced phenomena such as those described in this article are more accurately diagnosable as orthodox medical conditions— specifically, dehydration by confiscation of fluids. With this explanation, Eastwell believes much of the mystique of voodoo death will fade.*

Reproduced by permission of the American Anthropological Association from the *American Anthropologist,* vol. 84, no. 1 (March 1982), pp. 5–17. Not for further reproduction.

PIONEER ARNHEM ANTHROPOLOGIST W. LLOYD Warner, working with the "Murngin" people in and around Milingimbi Mission in 1926–29, thought that social practices involving direct suggestion caused certain deaths. In *A Black Civilization* he describes this sequence:

> The attitude is taken that the man is "half-dead" and will shortly die. The effect on a suggestible individual . . . is sufficient to set up certain psychophysiological reactions which tend to destroy him. Pressure is then applied through the mortuary rites which perform the function of attempting to remove him from the society of the living to that of the dead, further destroying his desire to live and frequently bringing about his ultimate death. (1958: 9)

Together with other sections of Warner's account, this statement is regarded by Landy (1975) as a most useful description of the involvement of the social system in voodoo death which it helps define. Another early Arnhem anthropologist, Donald Thompson, also believed that suggestion could kill. He records: "to the individual the prediction of death is sufficient ultimately to bring it to pass" (1939: 20).

The term "voodoo death" is time-hallowed, although Yap (1974) prefers "thanatomania," but also uses "psychosomatic" or "magical," and Lex (1974) uses "death by suggestion" but considers "psychocultural" as more appropriate. "Psychogenic" is also used, as by Lewis (1977). By implying a nonphysical cause, all these terms beg the question as to the mode of death, which characteristically occurs among native peoples after putative sorcery, from taboo violation, or while anticipating avengers. Barber (1961) notes the scarcity of satisfactorily documented case material, and Lewis comments that "it would require very special circumstances to be able to provide such information" (1977: 136). He concludes that most reports are anecdotal, not having been observed first-hand. Thus it has always been difficult to study actual cases scientifically, and this problem may become more acute in the future. Because medical services are now within call, to observe in Australia today is to intervene.

It is the nature of Warner's "psycho-physiological reaction," the mechanism of death, which is under debate. The classic contribution is by physiologist W. B. Cannon (1942), who uses Warner's descriptions. Cannon's concussions are summarized by ethnopsychiatrist P. M. Yap, who defines voodoo death as "progressive psychophysiological disorganization with surgical shock from terror in catastrophic situations" (1974: 95), thus dispelling any ambiguity lingering around the term. Yap here follows Cannon in implicating dysfunction of the autonomic nervous system, translating this concept as "surgical shock," which is a well-known clinical entity associated with many conditions other than surgery, and which is often terminal. The autonomic nervous system adjusts the body to emotional stimuli, of which hearing the prediction of one's own imminent demise is an extreme example. Other forceful proponents of an autonomic cause are Richter (1957) and Lex (1974). Lewis stresses the inconclusive aspect of this work of Cannon, Richter, and Lex: "[this] area of the subject is uncertain, holding a morbid fascination to find if it is true or not" (1977: 111).

Alternatively, the psychology of voodoo death is stressed by other authors, without specifying precisely the bodily mode of death. Thus Engel (1971) coined the term "giving up—given up complex" for the mental state involved. Lester (1972) describes it as hopelessness or helplessness, reinforced by social process. Another school of thought rejects the whole concept of psychogenic death. Barber (1961) favors physical illness or poison, but admits the possibility of terminal dehydration. Clune (1973), in a short comment unsupported by cases, also believes that poisoning is the mechanism, but this is criticized by Yap (1977), who regards it unlikely to be used by relatively unsophisticated peoples. Medical anthropologist G. Lewis is also skeptical: "Is it really the case

that healthy people have died in a day, or three days, because they know they were victims of sorcery? Who has seen this happen with his own eyes? Is there no explanation for it but sorcery?" (1977: 111). In the face of discord and questioning, Yap (1977) appeals for concrete findings from ethnologists and medical field-workers that can be appraised critically.

Deaths in Times of Transition

Local Whites refer to this region with no roads to the outside world as "a backwater within a backwater," but White imperialism is nevertheless pervasive. In the northeast there is a small mining community, Nhulunbuy, where the hotel acts as a magnet for Aboriginal men on drinking sprees. The administration of the area is from the state capital, Darwin (population 50,000), 650 km. west of Nhulunbuy. Here the White coroner records and scrutinizes the details of each death. The Aboriginal population centers around five ex-mission settlements and one government settlement, each with 500 to 1,000 people. More traditional life styles are preserved in the 30 or so small outstations in the bush (populations from about 30 to 70). These are on clan territory and are an Aboriginal reaction to White encroachments. The total Aboriginal population is approximately 6,000.

Materially, White technology drastically changes death practices. Bush vehicles and aircraft now transport corpses and are then ritually decontaminated. At one settlement there are two mobile freezers, one for each moiety, so the corpse can be preserved in the deceased's house while distant relatives forgather (Reid 1979), some of them hiring aircraft for the journey. Above all, the behavior of relatives and health caretakers around the dying person is an amalgam of custom and intruding modern medical interventions, the latter increasingly carried out by trained Aboriginal health workers. White nurse practitioners organize small clinics at centers of over 200 people, and the Flying Doctor makes routine visits. The missionary pastor commonly sits on the sand with the dying patients. The juxtaposition of cultures makes the events under discussion more outstandingly incongruous and more difficult to describe with the minimum of bias.

Method

Since 1969 I have collected data during visits that were primarily for the purpose of conducting psychiatric clinics among the people. During the years 1970–76, I spent six weeks in the field; in other years I made two visits of two weeks each. The data were compiled from patients' medical records kept at the bush hospitals and outstation clinics, and from 15 Aboriginal health workers: 12 females and 3 males who were mostly in their 30s. All came from different clans: they were selected widely to gain community acceptance for their unsupervised work at night and weekends when, among other tasks, they attend the dying. They were not particularly acculturated, and most were not Christians. I have known many of them for a couple of years, some for a decade. All found these topics about death highly distasteful. All female informants were questioned in groups of two or three. Five spoke of the deaths of close relatives in the recent past. All responses were in Aboriginal English, and where relevant, these are recorded verbatim. Older male informants were deliberately not sought out for two reasons: they found the topics even more disagreeable, regarding the discussion as personally ominous, and the language problem was greater.

The Sorcery Syndrome: A Forerunner of Voodoo Death?

The third most common "psychiatric" syndrome in East Arnhem is a gross fear state. Fear of death from sorcery is the dominant symptom, with intense agitation and restlessness, gross sleeplessness and increased vigilance at night, terror, sweating, and other physiological accompaniments of fear. Many patients attempt to arm themselves with guns, knives, or spears, or to flee to the protection of Whites. Illusory misperceptions are common, such as hearing malefactors prowling outside their huts. The syndrome is similar whether or not sorcery has actually been performed; it is the belief of the patient and the patient's kin that establishes the diagnosis. It is treated pragmatically using tranquilizing drugs, with or without referral to traditional healers. Commonly, the syndrome exists for some weeks before diagnosis and treatment; because sorcery is suspected, it is not immediately referred for Western treatment. The syndrome understandably refuses to fit readily into Western classificatory molds. I treated 39 such East Arnhem patients between 1969 and 1980; all but 1 were men. The syndrome is a reaction to specific life events that conform to the ethnographic situation preceding classical voodoo death, as listed in Table 1. Most commonly, the evidence for sorcery is the sudden death of a clan relative, where all clan members regard themselves endangered by sorcery; when one patient recovers, another clan member may show the same symptoms. Three patients showed the overwhelming extent of their fear by an unusual autonomic reaction—marked protrusion of the eyeballs with widely dilated pupils. All these patients can be considered prime risks for voodoo death because of the ethnographic precipitants and because of the extreme autonomic reaction (Table 1).

Only two patients died; their cases will be considered individually. The first died three months after the onset of his symptoms. He was 27 years old in 1973, and his father was accused of a mistake in a ceremony. His family moved to Numbulwar to minimize the sorcery risk. The son feared retribution, becoming so tremulous that he could not place tranquilizing tablets in his mouth and his pupils were widely dilated from autonomic activity. He died in the company of his parents, an Aboriginal health worker, and his tribal practitioner, in a panic attack with froth issuing from his mouth, similar to the description of one of Cannon's cases. A chest radiograph one month before death was normal. Arguments for the reality of voodoo death are not advanced in this case, because the patient suffered from a syndrome of psychosexual infantilism with a hormonal basis, with sex characteristics very poorly developed. This may have predisposed him to sudden death under stress, possibly because of abnormality of the adrenal glands, which mediate responses to stress as well as male sexual characteristics.

The second fatality was a 20–year-old Numbulwar man, newly married to an attractive girl. Within months of his marriage in 1979 he began losing weight and became impotent. He was dismayed when his wife began consorting with a rival who

Table 1   EVIDENCE OF SORCERY

Life Event Precipitating Fear-of-Sorcery Syndrome	Number of Patients
Sudden death of close clan relative	8
Serious illness of close clan relative	5
Disputes over acquisition of second or third wives	5
Promiscuity with married women	5
Life-threatening accident to patient (motor vehicle, electric shock, lightning strike)	3
Dispute with wife's lover	2
Promiscuity by sons	1
Murder of opponent in interclan spear fight	1
Unwitting desecration of ceremony ground	1
Ceremonial "mistakes" by father	1
Severe physical illness	1
Tribal healers accused of causing deaths	2
Unknown (precipitants not investigated)	4
	39

had been interested in her in the past but who had not negotiated successfully for her. The patient was more dismayed when his parents, seeking to explain his obvious physical decline, asserted that his rival was ensorcelling his beer. When referred for treatment, he was a well-developed case of the syndrome described above, convinced that nothing could save him. At this time, medical tests at the settlement clinic suggested an alternative explanation for his physical decline: kidney function was failing. He was transported by Flying Doctor aircraft to Darwin for treatment in a fully equipped hospital, where the diagnosis was chronic nephritis and treatment involved correcting the imbalance of chemicals in his body by intravenous therapy, with tubes inserted into veins, mouth, and bladder. In his frightened state he misinterpreted these tubes into and out of his body, fearing that his vital essence was draining away through them, a recurrent Aboriginal fear in this situation. He escaped from the hospital, bor-

rowed air fare, and returned home to the care of his parents who were already making plans to avenge his death. Here his kidney failure was complicated by heart failure, and he died one month after the initial diagnosis. (The young wife remarried the rival after the unseemly lapse of only four months. Thereupon the patient's uncles, who lived on a large island off the coast, hired an aircraft to mount a revenge expedition to Numbulwar. The new husband was wounded but escaped with his life, and the uncles retired with honor, reboarded their aircraft, and headed back home.)

In these 39 syndrome cases both patient and relatives expected death, but when it did occur it was explainable by orthodox Western medicine. These data cannot be used to argue that terror can never cause death, but its rarity here poses significant questions. It implies we may have adopted the native belief system too readily and unquestioningly in accepting sorcery as a sufficient cause. Fear states such as this

Arnhem example are widely distributed among native peoples. The Latin American variant, *susto*, meaning "fright," is mentioned by Rubel (1964) as not being associated with dramatic death. Despite Lewis's familiarity with sorcery cases during his two years in New Guinea, he also found the absence of dramatic deaths noteworthy: "I did not witness illnesses or deaths more devastating and intrinsically mysterious than illnesses and deaths I had seen in English hospitals" (1977: 112). As Western medical services extend into regions where voodoo deaths were reported, so the possibility diminishes of detecting a death in which psychosocial factors operate to the exclusion of physical causes. The two cases already described would serve as good models of voodoo death if the physical substratum remained undisclosed. From his study of historical and ethnographic sources, Ellenberger (1965) elaborates the concept of psychogenic death into rapid and slow varieties. The above cases conform to his rapid variety and to his Australo-Melanesian type which is characterized by paralyzing fear. This is contrasted with his Polynesian type, in which the emotion of shame is predominant.

Voodoo Death Averted

To establish the cause of voodoo death in bodily terms, a series of victims should be examined just prior to death. Cannon recommends a set of simple but valuable observations to test the validity of his theory, for example: "The pulse towards the end would be rapid and thready. The skin would be cool and moist" (1942: 180). That such observations are not available attests to the difficulty of examining even isolated cases. In practical terms of fieldwork, once the sequence is set in motion, the major difficulty in making observations is lack of preexisting rapport with the relatives who must tolerate the intrusion and potential intervention of the observer. The voodoo death sequence of Warner where "all the members of the society act in a manner exactly opposite to the ordinary" (1958: 9) was interrupted in the following two cases.

G., an unmarried mother aged 24, lived in a tribally oriented outstation 30 km. from Milingimbi. She refused marriage to a tribal elder as his third wife, and there was speculation, even expectation, that he

would retaliate with sorcery because he had paid the bride price, which could not now be repaid. In 1974, her mother, an attractive widow, decided to remarry, threatening to end G.'s notably dependent relationship with her. G. was supported by her mother's welfare payments, which would cease when she remarried. G. responded to these twin threats of losing mother and losing financial support with a series of dramatic hysterical trances, treated first by a tribal practitioner. These trances were misinterpreted by her relatives as evidence of sorcery from her spurned husband. After one trance, they responded by commencing the ancestral songs, withdrawing from her, and restricting her water. This was an effort to salvage her soul, which would then be available to animate later generations of her clan, as Warner describes. Hearing of these events, the White nurse at Milingimbi demanded that G. be brought to her clinic. After two days G. was carried in, close to death from dehydration, with a fungal growth in her mouth from the drying up of salivary flow. At that time she was anuric (experiencing kidney failure from severe dehydration), a state akin to Yap's "surgical shock." She was beyond help in the bush and was flown to the Darwin Hospital, 450 km. away, against the wishes of relatives who acted as if she were dead already and so should remain near clan territory. In the hospital she was still anuric, clear evidence of dehydration, despite intravenous fluids given in the bush. After lengthy resuscitation in hospital, hysterical blindness remained, easily interpreted as reaction to her recent victim status. I examined the patient in the hospital and took her full history later from her mother at Milingimbi. Her sight recovered in four months and she is presently quite well. It is clear that had this patient died, the mode of death would have been dehydration.

M. of Yirrkala was 35 years old in 1972 when he suffered a radiographically demonstrated artery occlusion to the brain (the basis of a severe stroke). This occurred while he was dancing in a ceremony, clear evidence of sorcery. A year later I found him lying in the sun, socially isolated, with chanting relatives withdrawn to the shade of a nearby hut. Against the wishes of relatives, but at his own request, he was removed by air to Darwin Hospital 650 km. away. He drank copiously before boarding the plane. In the hospital I treated him with major tranquilizing drugs. After a good recovery he chose not to return to Yirrkala for one year for fear of further "singing" (his own word). For him this was a year of lonely existence in Darwin, so he relented and returned to his clan. He died at his clan outstation one month later but the circumstances are unknown. The precipitant of the previous mortification is known in this case: his stroke induced disinhibited behavior in which he made sexual advances to his caretaker, a classificatory mother.

The death of M. of Milingimbi (born 1929, died 1955) is recounted here, not because of relevance to the dehydration hypothesis, but because it provides additional information about the relatives' reactions, necessary for the presentation of a more complete model of the voodoo death sequence. The information comes from her medical file and from the White nurse who was in attendance. Three weeks before death, relatives began chanting her clan songs, wailing in grief, and withdrawing from her, saying that she was "dead," the sequence described by Warner. She attended the clinic daily in an agitated state, spending most of her time in the company of White nurses, a most unAboriginal behavior, which is otherwise observed only in the fear state described above. She was not immediately diagnosed as pregnant but she went into labor and delivered a small, stillborn baby of perhaps 24 weeks gestation. She remained in postpartum care because of grossly disturbed behavior unrelated to any signs of fever, in which she screamed repeatedly and attacked White staff. Then three days postpartum, a fever of 39°C was recorded and she died with copious frothing of saliva and mucus. Her relatives then arranged burial within hours, while her body was still warm, with no chanting or rites. Her brother asked the White linguist to write to absent relatives giving the time of death as three weeks previously, the time when the chanting and wailing was heard. From the Aboriginal viewpoint, the cause of death was sorcery by a cowife, using the patient's urine patch. From the Western viewpoint, the sudden rise of temperature preceding death is typical of a well-known complication of childbirth, abnormal blood clots in the lung, which occurs with greatest frequency two to four days postpartum, as here, and with a temperature of the order recorded. This does not imply that psychosomatic factors were completely absent. The

case is included as "voodoo death averted" because her death in the manner described probably preempted the usual voodoo death sequence with terminal dehydration had she returned to her relatives.

A model for mortification in voodoo death can now be presented. The relatives and victim conclude that sorcery-induced death is inevitable. The relatives withdraw, wailing in grief, and the songs begin. The victim is socially dead and fluid is withheld. After death there is no wailing and burial takes place promptly, for fear of the victim's trickster spirit, the *mokwuy*.

The Psychosocial Sequence for the Dispatch of the Dying

The predeath events surrounding certain old, enfeebled patients are described in this section. The majority of the patients have diagnosable medical conditions that sooner of later will cause death. All are regarded by relatives as loosely integrating body and soul. It is the concern for timely salvage of the soul that precipitates the sequence. Because of the difficulty of recording a series of voodoo deaths, it is proposed to argue by analogy, with the inference that if the mode of expediting bodily dying can be established in these cases, then it is likely that the same holds for voodoo death. The conclusion is that dehydration from confiscation of fluids is the common factor and the ultimate cause of death. The components of the sequence follow.

Beginning the Funeral Rites

Health-worker informants are adamant that chanting is requested by the dying person. H., a Rembarrnga woman, says: "Sick person asks his sons to start that singing." This is not always so, as Warner implies, because in the two cases cited previously where voodoo death was averted, and in the one following, the victims were not expecting the songs to begin and it was against their wishes, but they were powerless to prevent the sequence from continuing. These cases conform closely to the situation that Warner and Cannon discuss. Some local Whites mistakenly believe that the rites themselves are meant to hasten death, as mentioned by Reid (1979). That the rites alone are not a major factor is shown by the large number of patients who recover after the chants are begun, as Reid also notes. These recovering patients sometimes dismiss their mourners with some vexation, a comment on the power ascribed to the sequence, of which the songs are harbingers.

J. (born 1925, died 1976) was a man from the Arnhem bush. He underwent lengthy hospital stays in Darwin for leprosy, which became complicated by failure of major organs. When nothing more could be done, hospital authorities discharged him on November 29 to his clan outstation where it was expected he would live for a few weeks or months. He himself anticipated renewing associations with brothers, sons, ex-wives, and seeing for the last time places in the bush of significance to him (so stated to hospital staff). Relatives hired a small plane to take him to the nearest airstrip, Ramangining. He alighted unassisted from the plane to confront a situation he was totally unprepared for. As witnessed by resident anthropologist J. P. Reser, his clansmen were chanting his ancestral songs, and they remained at a distance from the plane. This is an example of Warner's "looking at the man as one already dead" (1958: 241). J. was conveyed back by truck to his outstation, where he died within three days, on December 2.

The Acquiescence of the Dying

"The victim on his part reciprocates this feeling" (that his proper position is in the world of the dead) (Warner 1958: 242). Once the mortification gains momentum, when the body is regarded as weakly animated by the spirit of a guiding forefather, the patient develops a fatalistic acceptance of death. Health worker H. comments that her grandmother said emphatically in the vernacular, "This is time for me to die." Many patients are still capable of walking for nourishment if they so desired, but medical aid is rejected from this point on, and death occurs within days. Engel's complex of "giving up—given up" applies to this psychological state rather better than Lester's "hopelessness or helplessness." The ideology of clanship in Arnhem includes the concept of recycling the individual soul through future generations of the clan. This implies a quality of timelessness to individual life which aids the acceptance of death. Terminal patients often show great relief once the rites have begun, as White nurses comment.

The components of this psychological sequence are summed up by the senior nurse discussing death at Yirrkala in 1972, of a woman I examined.

> Maku was an old widow, probably in her late 50s. After a vertebra collapsed (probably from tuberculosis) she was hospitalized for bedrest. We did not think she would die. One morning an old man appeared and said he dreamt she was going to die. He brought singers and dancers who began outside but she was left alone in the room. From that time she was not given water and we were asked not to help her. The health workers did what the old man ordered. Her tongue was misshapen from thirst and she died the next day. There was running water in the hospital room but she made no attempt to reach it, although she could have if she tried.

This sequence was encountered again in a death at Galiwinku in 1978. G. was born in the bush around 1930 and became the second of four wives, with five grown children. When infection supervened on her chronic lung disease she became bedridden but was not considered moribund. She was moved on her blanket into the open where she remained day and night, until her death three days later. To the local missionary she said: "This is time for me to die." Relatives requested the White nurse to discontinue antibiotic injections. Twenty people were sitting in the shade 5 m. away. While she was still alert, one of her sons delivered a large bolt of red cloth in which her body was to be wrapped. This was ceremoniously placed beside her on the blanket. At this time the songs were begun and all fluid was withdrawn for her last two days. The cause of her death was listed as dehydration, not chest infection.

These three cases show an element of isolation by the relatives which brings them closely into line with the voodoo death sequence. This factor with its negation of lifelong social bonds must suggest strongly to the dying person the role he or she is expected to play.

The Death Mechanism: Dehydration by Confiscation of Fluids

With the establishment of this mechanism, much of the mystique of voodoo death will fade, at least for Arnhem. In this permaheat region which is 12° south latitude, where day temperatures below 27°C occur only once or twice a year, deaths were observed to take place 24 to 36 hours after total restriction of fluids. The deaths range from a desirable euthanasia where the sequence prevents prolonged dying, to an occasional avoidable death. In this circumstance the term "senilicide" is appropriate, signifying active intervention by the relatives in the confiscation of fluids. Jones and Horne (1972) believe that dehydration is the cause of similar deaths in the Australian Western Desert, but their case material, gathered from White nurses, is not given in detail. Two Melanesian voodoo deaths from dehydration are recorded in the literature (Barber 1961; Simon et al. 1961). Cannon quotes his medical correspondent W. E. Roth of Queensland, Australia, who says of the victim: ". . . he will actually lie down to die . . . even at the expense of refusing food and succor within his reach" (1942: 172). Other commentators record the refusal of food without specifically mentioning fluid: Gelfand's reliable African account is an example (1957: 539), as is Elkin's Arnhem case of 1956 (1977: 153). Cannon himself mentions of the victim: "In his terror he refuses both food and drink, a fact which many observers have noted . . ." (1942: 176), and he quotes a Spanish Civil War death from "malignant anxiety" in which "The lack of food appears to have attended lack of water for the urine was concentrated . . ." (1942: 180).

In Arnhem, the health workers are explicit that fluid is actually confiscated. Health worker H. states, "We take that water away from him—no need for water or food. We just don't give food or water." P., a Burada clanswoman living in Gailiwinku: "The relatives say no more water." Male health worker D. of the Warramirri at Galiwinku: "If real close up finish, take water away so spirit goes." M., a Djapu woman at Yirrkala: "We take the water and food from the sick one." They reveal that it is a common practice which can be discussed openly.

Deaths at Two Settlements

Recent deaths at the compact settlement of Millingimbi, population 700, are well documented for two reasons. First, the nurse practitioner has been resident for nearly 30 years; she knows all the aged, and personally ministers to them at their deaths. Second,

because Aboriginal houses have no refrigeration to store milk drinks, a system of distributing them to the dying has been arranged. When a container is used, it is returned to the clinic where it is refilled and sent back to the patient again. Thus the regularity of refilling gives some check on probable fluid intake. Between 1978 and mid-1980 there were eight deaths of patients over the age of 50, with terminal dehydration observed in seven, and brief case descriptions of these follow.

L., female, was born about 1915 and led a healthy life until an episode of heart failure developed, which would normally respond to therapy allowing a prolongation of life. The Flying Doctor was hopeful of recovery but finally annotated her medical file: "I cannot be held responsible if relatives refuse to give my patient food or fluid." The last note in her file reads: "Not eating or drinking. Deceased."

D., female, was born about 1926. She suffered from the common obstructive airways disease, not necessarily fatal. Toward the end of her life she lived in the household of her son, a traditional healer. She was befriended by White staff members for many years. One of them, a graduate teacher, had this to say of her last illness: "Her relatives became upset when I gave fluids and her son threatened to knock me down. Later she herself became negativistic and refused water. She died of thirst." White concern had been increased by the patient's role in caring for an eight-year-old waif not directly related to her.

M., male, was born about 1922. He was a traditional painter on bark, which brought him an adequate income. Eventually he developed severe heart failure, which required hospital treatment away from his home, but which he refused. The senior nurse commented: "He would have died anyhow, but he was not given water for his last 24 hours." This was the most prompt death in the series, and one which was unquestionably a desirable euthanasia.

D., male, born about 1892, showed great tenacity for life, recovering from repeated chest infections. He was a sought-after informant as one of the last men to remember the annual visits of Indonesian traders to this coast. Warner mentions him by name. He was mentally alert up to his final year when senility supervened. The senior nurse commented on his mode of death: "His mouth was so dry, and the milk container left unused in the same room."

M., male, born about 1917, suffered from lung cancer. He died within days of receiving news of the death of his favorite son. The file reads: "Sept. 12: Told about son's death, deteriorating. Sept. 13: Fluid intake—minimal oral. Has not passed urine. Sept. 14: Died." The psychological aspect of "giving up—given up" was particularly prominent.

D., female, born about 1911, is mentioned in Warner as the femme fatale of the day. She later became a respected traditional healer. She suffered from obstructive airways disease but her last days were marked by temporary recovery when fluids were given by nurses. The file reads: "Aug. 28. More alert. Taking drinks when offered. Aug. 30. Flying Doctor orders intravenous fluids. 2 litres given. Sept 2. Refused fluids. Sept. 7 Died." Initially ambivalent about the prospect of death, she later became resigned and succumbed when additional relatives gathered.

D., male, born around 1900. Warner mentions him as embarking on a political career in which he acquired eight wives. Five of these were sitting at a respectful distance from him in his dying days. His physical disease was prostate cancer. "May 16: No fever. Given only very small amounts of fluid. May 18: Very little water. May 20: No fever. Died." The aspect of euthanasia with the prevention of suffering was paramount in his case. Three hundred people attended his funeral, with burial five days after death.

The Darwin coroner's conclusions are quoted for the following two deaths in 1978 at the remote Lake Evella settlement of 300 people. The first was D., male, born about 1915, who was in unskilled employment until his final illness, which was a potentially treatable heart ailment. The coroner recorded this finding: "He continued to refuse food and would drink only sips of water. He deteriorated rapidly and deceased." The second was M., female, born about 1920. She was reported to the nurse as suffering from diarrhea, but no evidence for this could be found. The coroner concluded: "While her condition improved she became reluctant to eat and drink and refused further medical treatment. Her condition stabilized but due to her refusal to eat or drink she gradually wasted away, deceasing June 19th." The coroner's findings were more detailed than usual for tribal deaths for the following reason.

The only White nurse at this outpost became alarmed when he observed the confiscation of fluids from patients whom he judged capable of recovery. He gave sufficient evidence in writing to enable the coroner to absolve him from responsibility in these deaths.

Ritual Nullification of the Thirst Drive

According to Yap (1977), voodoo death takes place too rapidly to be due to dehydration, but he refers no case material. The most rapid death reported here is that of M. from Milingimbi, 1978, when death took place in 24 hours in the absence of any fluid intake. Lex (1974) concedes that dehydration may sometimes be a factor, but she takes the view that autonomic dysfunction prevents the victim swallowing fluid or absorbing it. The evidence of the health workers is that fluid is actively withheld to expedite dying, and this also applied to the two cases in which voodoo death was averted. This confiscation of fluids explains the observed dehydration more parsimoniously; Lex's hypothesis regarding difficulty in swallowing is not a major factor, but in terminal dehydration it is true that water cannot be absorbed without aggravating the imbalance of minerals and salts in the body fluids. Among these people there is the cultural rationalization that the mortified individual is animated only by the spirit of the forefather, which does not require fluid: "It is then too late for food or drink." This ideology explains why some relatives actively promote dehydration while others passively allow it to occur. A unitary hypothesis for voodoo death is not proposed: what is proposed is that psychological factors are secondary to the basic physical process of dehydration, but both are involved. The continuing concept of voodoo death as caused by suggestion, that is, by the victim's belief in sorcery and the conviction of the victim's own demise, speaks to total involvement in his or her assumptive world. The notion of the psychological causation has persisted because "it would seem to show such final and tragic evidence of true belief" (Lewis 1977: 139).

The social behavior of beginning the obsequies while the patient-victim is alert defines the role of the dying person and prescribes the person's behavior. The ancestral songs in which he or she silently participates become self-referential, and the induced mental state of "giving up—given up" is sufficient to suppress the physiological drive for fluid. It allows dehydration its final action and prevents active efforts to obtain fluid. In this fatalistic state of mind the person truly regards death as a rite of passage and is oriented to the next world. Significantly, as the health workers say, it is a "water world and has spirits in it," in the depths of the clan waterhole. As Warner says, "[he] returns to his totemic well, and the circle is complete" (1958: 5).

Wicca, a Way of Working

Loretta Orion

In 1986, Loretta Orion was initiated into the Minoan Sisterhood, one of a cluster of witch covens practicing various forms of Gerald Gardner's Wicca. Gardner, an Englishman who was born in 1884, is given credit for launching the modern neopagan witch movement, or Wicca. In this article, Orion introduces the reader to the Minoan Sisterhood's Yule celebration, in which she participated. Orion provides a description and interpretation of its several ceremonial elements: the creation of sacred space, invocation of divinities and elementals, raising energy, drawing down, magical work (or play), the ceremony of cakes and wine, and the feast. Jeffrey Burton Russell, a respected scholar of witchcraft, believes that modern witchcraft is a naïve, genial nature religion. He writes (Encyclopedia of Religion, *vol. 15, 1987, p. 318*):

> *The tenets of witchcraft as it has evolved include a reverence for nature expressed in the worship of a fertility goddess and (sometimes) a god; a restrained hedonism that advocates indulgence in sexual pleasures so long as such indulgence hurts no one; the practice of group magic aimed (usually) at healing or other positive ends; colorful rituals; and release from guilt and sexual inhibitions. It rejects diabolism and even belief in the Devil on the grounds that the existence of the Devil is a Christian, not a pagan, doctrine. It offers a sense of the feminine principle in the godhead, a principle almost entirely forgotten in the masculine symbolism of the great monotheistic religions. And its eclectic paganism promotes a sense of the variety and diversity of the godhead.*

After reading this selection, readers will find it instructive to read the article entitled "Occult Beliefs" by Barry Singer and Victor Benassi in Chapter 10.

Reprinted by permission of Waveland Press, Inc. from Loretta Orion, *Never Again the Burning Times: Paganism Revived* (Prospect Heights, IL: Waveland Press, Inc.), 1995. All rights reserved.

MANY WITCHES SAY WITCHCRAFT IS "A WAY OF working" with the flexible nature of the world. Although it is etymologically incorrect, many of them believe that the word "witch" is derived from *weik,* meaning willow. Nonetheless, the witches make the word the basis for an apt metaphor: the craft is one of bending and shaping reality like a flexible branch of willow. Like the early Wiccans, present-day witches try to effect enchantments and healings by the use of a technology (magic) that is founded in the premises of nature religion.

The Book of Shadows prescribes a ritual for creating sacred space, "a fit abode for the gods to enter in"; however, I have seen that there is an unstated purpose: creation of a sacred *work space.* In fact, the basic ritual serves as template for the creative process, as we shall see in my interpretation of the Minoan Sisterhood's Yule celebration in which I participated on the winter solstice of 1986, about two months after I had been initiated into the first of three "degrees," or levels of expertise.

The Minoan Sisterhood

The Minoan Sisterhood is one of a cluster of covens that practice various modifications of Gardner's Wicca. All of the covens were descended from one that was formed by individuals —whose identities I prefer not to disclose—who brought Gardner's Wicca to America after being initiated in England by one of Gardner's high priestesses.

Carol Bulzone, the high priestess who initiated me, and a young man named Ed Buczynski organized two covens, the Minoan Sisterhood and Brotherhood, that deviated somewhat from Gardner's Wicca. Carol and Eddie wanted to create a coven exclusively for female witches, and another exclusively for males. They believe that the male/female polarity exists in every individual and can be activated in rituals performed in covens consisting of members who are all of the same gender. Thirteen-member-covens are ideal, but the Minoan covens and most others in America operate effectively with fewer members. Although the Minoan Sisterhood coven was created for lesbian women, all but two or three of the eleven members were heterosexual at the time I was an active member. Creativity was a common thread in the lives of these women. Three of the members are actresses, three are dancers, one is a photographer, another is an artist's model. I never learned the occupations of two of the women. As we will see later, my artworks served as proof of my aptitude for the craft of witchcraft. Largely because of that, I was accepted in the role of anthropologist.

The exclusive female membership necessitates modifications of Gardner's two rituals, drawing down the moon and the great rite, a ceremonial *hieros gamos,* that I shall presently describe. There are various other ways in which the Minoan Sisterhood differs from Gardner's witchcraft. The Sisterhood has its own Book of Shadows that deviates from Gardner's in its reliance on a myth motif derived from Crete . . . . After I was initiated, I was given two Books of Shadows, one supposedly a copy of copies of Gardner's original, the other a copy of the one created by Carol and Eddie for the Minoan Sisterhood.

Yule Celebration in a Minoan-Gardnerian Coven

On the evening of the solstice in the winter of 1986, the Minoan Sisterhood gathered in the back room of the occult supply store, Enchantments, in the East Village in New York City to celebrate Yule. This was one of the rare occasions when a male witch was present at a meeting of the sisterhood: The young man, whom I shall call Raven to protect his true identity, was invited to represent the sun god whose rebirth is celebrated at Yule.

As soon as the last customer left the shop and the iron gates were pulled closed and locked, the preparations for the ceremony began. The witches emptied the back room of its few pieces of furniture. Lexa, the *kore* of the coven—second in command to the high priestess—mopped the floor with a cinnamon-scented concoction called "Yule" that was

created according to a recipe in the grimoire. With this humble "purification," the coven members transformed a tiny room that ordinarily served as an office and consultation room for psychic readings into a temple.

The coven members built an altar in the center of the floor out of several crates of merchandise covered with a satin cloth. Magical implements, including an iron caldron and all of the tools of the craft . . . were arranged on the altar. A wooden wheel, with eight spokes—one for each sabbath—represented the turning wheel of the year. It was placed among the usual altar furnishings that include small statues of the goddess and the god.

On this occasion the image of the god was wrapped in a black cloth to symbolize his invisibility following the sacrifice or harvest that had been reenacted on the autumnal equinox. Candles were lit in each cardinal direction to mark the boundaries of a circle, nine feet in diameter, within which the ceremony would take place.

Generally the witches prepare themselves to enter sacred space by bathing in salt-water. In the shop the witches made do with a symbolic purification of anointing each of their pulse points with the musky "Minoan" oil. Most, but not all of the witches, removed their clothing. Many of them sang along with recorded music while they made their preparations and drifted into place in the circle around the altar. Then silence.

Creating Sacred Space

Everyone stood around the altar at the center of the circle when the high priestess took her athame between her palms to begin to create and consecrate a sacred space. Making magical signs with the athame and speaking blessings, the high priestess purified and blessed the substances on the altar representing the four "elements": salt for earth; incense for air; candle flame for fire; and water. Taking up the long sword from the altar she "cast," or drew, a circle approximately nine feet in diameter, and inside of it she placed a candle at the four cardinal directions, pointing the sword down while walking clockwise (*deosil*) around the circumference of the circle. All movement in the circle must be clockwise to be in harmony with the sun's apparent path. Deosil motion creates; anti-clockwise (*widdershins*) movement is used to banish or destroy.

After drawing the circle, the priestess purified and reinforced the circle with each of the elements by walking its perimeter four times: once with the candle, then sprinkling salt, then water, and finally creating a trail of incense smoke. As she distributed the elements, Carol "consecrated" the circle. She forcefully declared, while visualizing, that the circle she had drawn would serve as a boundary and as a container for the energy that the witches would raise and release from their bodies to imbue their magic with power.

This operation is called the creation and consecration of the circle. The sacred space is more accurately conceived of as a completely enclosed sphere; the circle merely marks the place where it intersects the ground.

The circle is said to exist "between the worlds," that is, between the world of humans and that of the gods, and between the realms of form and idea. It marks a boundary, or *limen,* between structures of time and space, between ordinary reality and the sacred time (infinity). The sacred space serves as both a work space for magic and a temple for worship and symbolizes the relationship between microcosm and macrocosm that merge inside the circle.

In a ceremony deriving from alchemy, the existing form of matter was reduced to the elements air, fire, water and earth (solid matter). In the course of the ritual, these raw materials of earthly existence would be reassembled in a new form, according to the design of the witches. Between the worlds, form is thought to be fluid and susceptible to refashioning when new relationships among its fundamental building blocks, the four elements, are established.

Humans also constitute a synthesis of the four elements. The more balanced the synthesis, the more highly developed the individual. Reaching such a balance is an important goal of the "work" of witchcraft. The most significant product of the craft is the physical, mental and spiritual self.

The creation of the circle serves as a psychological cue that informs the witches that a former state of being has been broken apart; the world of ideas and matter awaits restructuring by the witches' magic.

Invocation of Divinities and Elementals

After the sacred work space was prepared, the high priestess called out to the "guardians of the watchtowers" of the four directions, the "mighty ones," and the "lords" of the spirits of the elements (elementals) to alert them that magic was to be worked and invite them to protect the space and witness the rite.

"Elementals," generally thought by the witches to be invisible spirits of the elements, take their place at the low end of the Wiccan hierarchy of sentient entities believed to populate the supernatural universe. The elementals animate fundamental categories of existence: salamanders/fire, ondines/water, sylphs/air, and gnomes/earth. Each of these is associated with a cardinal direction: air with the east; fire with the south; water with the west; earth with the north.

The ultimate manifestation of divinity is generally conceptualized by the Neopagans as the life force or energy that permeates and sustains the universe. As it manifests itself through matter, this divine force polarizes as the opposites represented by the masculine and feminine principles symbolized by the goddess and god.

Each attribute of divinity is symbolized as an archetypal image of gods, or spirits, clothed in mythic form and reflecting spiritual reality. Each conveys to the worshipper that aspect of divinity that she or he is trying to access during a particular religious ritual, magical working, or mystical experience: Venus for love, perhaps, or Mercury for ease of communication.

The elemental forces of the natural world, although symbolized as creatures of the "Land of Faerie"—sylphs, salamanders, ondines, and gnomes —are also imagined as psychic potentials: air as intellect; fire representing passion; waters, the emotions; and Earth, solid physical matter. In a theological sense, they represent a four-part subdivision of the cosmos.

When the witches invoke the divinities and elementals they ask for the permission, approval, and assistance of the universe and the spiritual beings inhabiting—or symbolizing—it. The "threefold law" expresses the awareness of adverse repercussions of creating badly: whatever one puts out into the universe is believed to return three-fold in kind to the creator. Magic, like art, is successful to the extent that it expresses something greater or more universal than the individual artist. The witches attempt to ensure that their creations will be beneficial not only for themselves in their limited sphere of existence but in the broadest possible sense for the universe—

all time and space—within which they locate themselves as eternal beings.

Raising Energy

Next, the witches "raised" energy from their bodies to fill the circle by dancing and chanting the names of the goddess of the Earth and the dying and resurrecting god: "Isis, Astarte, Diana, Hecate . . . Pan, Woden, Baphomet, Osiris . . . ," after which—flushed and slightly breathless—everyone sat around the altar.

Energy is, to the witches, a valuable resource, a concrete substance that can be molded, directed, and projected over long distances. Human vitality—which the witches possess and the gods, mighty ones, and spirits do not—is the force of life that witches see as moving and changing the physical as well as emotional contours of reality.

Generally the next part of the ritual is the "drawing down of the moon," in which the priest draws the essence of the goddess and/or the moon into the high priestess to induce a mild possession state.

Drawing Down

As I have come to understand it, the drawing down ceremony bridges the gap between form (human) and idea (divinity); it is an invitation for inspiration. The witches assume the role of Demiurge in their rituals. They strive to "be as the gods" so that they can assume the prerogative of the gods: creation. Like artists seeking inspiration from the "muses," witches "draw down" divine inspiration from their gods, and like artists, they offer their bodies as vehicles of expression for these sacred influences. In other words, the witch as creator attempts to transcend the individual ego in order to express a sacred or more universal force.

The yielding of an artist, priestess, or priest to such an inspiration resembles collaboration more than the submission of a worshipper to the care of a protecting deity. The celebrant *invites* the influence of divine force. No matter how compelling the vision, one who has mastered the craft remains in control. In this reciprocal relationship the human may—or may not—give voice or substance to the inspiration, and in that way, serve the deity.

In the Minoan Sisterhood, the high priestess generally "draws down" the mother goddess and the supernatural powers associated with the moon into the kore. But this evening the sun god's rebirth was being accomplished, and his influence would be drawn down. She oriented the coveners by retelling the story: At this point on the turning wheel of the year, the great goddess, queen of the moon and Earth and sea, gives birth to the golden-haired son who illuminates the world. The son/sun will increase in strength and influence—the cause of joy and celebration—until his manhood and the sun's peak of influence is reached on the midsummer solstice.

. . .

The Magical Work, or Play

Generally, "magic is worked"—that is, collective spell-working for some practical purpose—on the new and full moons; while Sabbaths, such as Yule, are reserved for worship, games, and celebration. The spinning Yule wheel is an exception, or combination. Each person developed in her or his mind a clear image of something they wished to accomplish, or help to accomplish, with magic. They carved words or symbols of that wish on a white candle with a boline. Each witch lit and fixed her or his carved candle onto the hub of the Yule with melted wax. When all the candles were positioned, the high priestess set the wheel spinning on the altar. As it spun faster and faster, the candle flames blurred together into a ring of fire, the visible circuit of a vortex of energy.

All the while, each witch concentrated on her or his wish, visualizing it accomplished. The witches generated more vital energy adding it to the vortex, by running and dancing around the altar singing the chant, "Listen to the Lord and Lady, in the Moonlight . . . ." The singing speeded up until I could no longer sustain the vision of my wish without jumbling the words of the chant or stumbling over my own feet. The witches continued to laugh and sing while the wheel spun faster and faster, weaving energy into their visualizations. Soon everyone collapsed in laughter.

After a few minutes of rest, the witches rose and danced around the circle to "raise the cone of power" (generate more energy). As the dancers sang and spun around the circle, they visualized energy flowing from their bodies to the center of the circle, where it theoretically spirals upward into a cone. When the high priestess sensed that the group's collective energy had reached its climax, she gave the signal for everyone to release the cone of power. With that image in their minds, and with the force of their wills, the witches projected the cone of power into the world beyond the sacred space of the circle to accomplish the purposes they had visualized and inscribed on the candles. Having released energy from their bodies in loud, howling screams the witches dropped exhausted to the floor.

The Ceremony of Cakes and Wine

In Gardnerian covens the high priest and priestess perform "the great rite," a hieros gamos. In this sacred sexual union opposites are combined—male and female; sky and earth; gods and humans; eternity and periodicity, to name a few—for the purpose of generating energy and a state of grace, the witches say. The great rite is seldom performed in the ritual circle, and on the few occasions that it is done, the coven members generally leave the priestess and priest to enact the rite in private (Farrar 1983).

In the Minoan Sisterhood's Yule celebration, the more common symbolic great rite, "the ceremony of cakes and wine," was enacted: Raven held the chalice filled with homemade wassail. Into this vessel, that represented the receptive womb and the formative forces operative in the universe, Carol plunged the blade of her athame, that represented the phallus and projectile forces. While doing so she spoke of the blessings that result from the conjunction of the male and female polarities. Following that, cakes were blessed by touching them with the moistened dagger. The wine and cakes consecrated in this ritual are shared by coven members and the gods, who receive portions as libations.

As is the case in the alchemists' operations of purification, the witches' ritual divides the world first into four parts or elements that must later be distilled into one pair of opposites. In the great rite, actual or symbolic, the opposing terms of this opposition are conjoined to create a new synthesis, an idea that was expressed particularly clearly by an American witch in this poem:

Blessed be the darkness, the vast expansion the all encompassing, all surrounding womb of space.
Blessed be the light, the penetrating point the all focusing, all aligning core of creation.
Blessed be the blade that divided the darkness from light, thus generating duality, And from duality is all substance formed.
Blessed be the vessel, wherein the divided may unite.

Several strata of mythic motifs are evident in the great rite. The literal hieros gamos is an obvious example of agricultural rites of sympathetic magic intended to induce fertility of crops and herds. Superimposed on the plant model is that of the hieros gamos practiced in the hieratic city-state. In these societies a priestess who represented the Earth entered into sexual union with a king or his substitute who represented the sky. The sexual conjunction brought together the worlds of gods and humans.

The symbolic great rite, the ceremony of cakes and wine, is also reminiscent of the quest for the Holy Grail. The witches' chalice has associations with the Celtic caldron of rebirth, a distinctly feminine symbol. The dagger serves the witches as a representative of the sword that the knight, Galahad, of King Arthur's Round Table withdrew from a stone in a more recent version of the Myth of the Caldron in which it becomes the Holy Grail filled with Christ's blood. The more universal impulse to bring human society into life-generating harmony with the cosmos is expressed in the ceremony of cakes and wine through the more "local"—in terms of time and space—idea of the Arthurian grail legend.

The great rite, symbolic or actual, is the heart of the creative act. The phallus conjoined with the womb may bring human birth; the intellect—symbolized by the dagger—stirs, carves, and shapes the four elements contained in the chalice, cauldron, or other vessel. All opposites are brought into conjunction. Inspiration of the gods is combined with the will and talent of the craftsperson to give new form to the vital energy raised and released from the witches' bodies. The elements that were torn asunder and scattered in the consecration of the circle are forged into new relationships in the chalice that symbolizes the womb. The great rite or the symbolic ceremony of cakes and wine is the moment of creation, the *magic*.

The Feast

The wassail and cakes that had been consecrated in the ceremony of cakes and wine were passed so that each person might make a libation to the gods and taste the cakes and wine. Offerings were put into the libation bowl, whose contents would later nourish the garden behind the shop.

In the traditional feast of cakes and wine, a multitude of complementary opposites are brought into conjunction: cakes nourish the physical body and wine quickens the spirit. Liquid wine symbolizes the fluidity of energy, the probabilities and possibilities of the future, the—as yet—uncreated world.

Michael Thorne, a Gardnerian high priest, explained the magic of manipulating energy by resorting to the analogy of a lemon cake: it is easier to influence physical manifestation of the future while it is in the process of developing just as it is easier to introduce lemon flavoring into a cake while it is still in the form of batter, rather than after it is already baked. The "batter" in the chalice is whipped with the athame. The wine represents the fluidity of sacred time and space; the more solid cake symbolizes the apparent solidity of physical form and the concrete structure of ordinary reality that is about to be reentered. The celebrants were theoretically transformed by the magic; the world and the self were recreated.

Following the ceremony of cakes and wine, the high priestess gave thanks and said farewell to the spirits, the mighty ones and the guardians of the watchtowers in the four cardinal directions. The threshold of sacred and ordinary time and space was considered dissolved when the high priestess declared that the circle was "opened." The festive mood intensified as the secular feast began in earnest: more food was spread out and gifts were exchanged.

"Magic is hungry work," the witches say. According to neuro-physiologist Barbara Lex (1977), rituals (that involve chanting, dancing, and inhalation of incense) stimulate both the sympathetic and parasympathetic autonomic nervous system. During periods of sympathetic activation accompanied by heightened activity, such as ecstatic dancing, circulation is diverted away from the internal organs to the skeletal muscles and the appetite is suppressed. The rebound parasympathetic response is restorative. Circulation is returned to the viscera, and a relaxed mood is accompanied by an increased appetite.

One of the purposes of the feast that concludes all Wiccan ceremonies is "grounding." After the exertion of creativity—physical, mental, and spiritual—the body requires replenishment. Nourishment gives the body weight and substance. After a period of communion with the sacred realm, food reorients awareness to the mundane world. Feasting brings one back "down to earth."

7

Demons, Exorcism, Divination, and Magic

Demons, spirits, ancestors, and gods all exist as realities in the human mind and possess the power to harm and harass the living. Good and evil are counter-balanced in every society through a variety of rituals and other forms of protection; yet this balance is inevitably broken by human weaknesses and transgressions that invite the evil nature of supernatural agents. The malicious acts of these agents inflict pain and anguish on the innocent as well as on those deserving of punishment. Although all supernaturals can possess an individual and cause an unending variety of harm, the most commonly known agent of possession is the demon. Demons may aid their human consorts from time to time, but generally they are seen as being responsible for diseases, injuries, or a myriad of major and minor personal and group disasters. More powerful than mere humans, they are also generally believed to be less powerful than gods and ancestral spirits (Collins 1978: 195).

Possession by demons is ordinarily considered dangerous, but this is not always the case. For the

Tsham mask from Tibet.

Aymara Indians of Bolivia, for example, possession results in serious consequences for the victims and their community whereas among the Haitians it is actively sought at voodoo ceremonies in order to obtain the supernatural knowledge of the spirits. The acceptance or the actual seeking out of beneficent spirits and situating them in a medium where they can be called upon when needed is termed "adorcism" by L. DeHeusch (1971). I. M. Lewis distinguishes between "central possession cults" and "peripheral possession cults." In the former, spirits such as ancestors most commonly possess men and sustain the moral order of society. In the latter, women and others having lesser status are possessed by malevolent spirits; possession of this type is often considered an illness and damages the social fabric of the group (1989). Haitians, however, conceive of both good and evil spirits, and all fear possession by the latter. "Possession, then, is a broad term referring to an integration of spirit and matter, force or power and corporeal reality, in a cosmos where the boundaries between an individual and her environment are acknowledged to be permeable, flexibly drawn, or at least negotiable" (Boddy 1994: 407).

The functions of possession commonly go unnoticed, overshadowed as they are by the dramatic expressive actions of the possessed and those in attendance. Stanley and Ruth Freed (1964: 71) showed that spirit possession in a north Indian village functioned primarily to relieve the individual's intropsychic tensions while simultaneously giving the victim the attention and sympathy of relatives and friends. The possession itself and its overt demonstration was only a vehicle for these functions. Even rules designed to avoid demons, such as the *jinns* of Islamic countries, can promote individual self-discipline and propriety in behavior, both, as William Howells has pointed out, desirable qualities (1962: 202). The prohibitions promoted to avoid *jinns* do direct behavior toward socially approved goals, but despite these positive functions, the fact remains that demons cause suffering and pain to members of both Western and non-Western societies and every society is forced to cope with their devious nature.

Exorcism—the driving away of evil spirits such as demons by chanting, praying, commanding, or other ritual means—occurs throughout the world and is invoked when an evil spirit has caused illness by entering a person's body. (A belief in exorcism assumes a related belief in the power of ritual to move an evil spirit from one place to another.) Although the idea that foreign objects can enter the body and cause illness has been widespread, it was especially prevalent among American Indians, where curers, shamans, and sometimes a specialist known as a "sucking doctor," had the ability to remove these materials by such techniques as rubbing and kneading the patient's body, gesturing over the diseased area, or directly sucking out the evil object. Shamans, because of the "trick" aspect of their rituals, are especially well versed in the intricacies of exorcism as a means of removal of disease-causing objects. Typically, a sleight-of-hand maneuver is used to show the patient that the harmful substance has been removed.

Howells (1962: 92–94) has described several techniques used around the world for exorcising evil spirits and diseases: using sweat-baths, cathartics, or emetics to flush out the offending spirits; trephining; manipulating and massaging the body; sucking out the disease objects; scraping or sponging the illness off the body; reciting magical spells, coaxing, or singing songs to lure the spirit away; tempting the spirit to evacuate the body by laying out a sumptuous meal for it; keeping the patient uncomfortable, sometimes by administering beatings, so the spirit will be discontented with the body and want to depart; building a fire under the patient to make it uncomfortably warm for the spirit; placing foul-smelling, overripe fruit near the patient; and scandalizing the demon by having the patient's naked wife jump over the patient.

There is considerable evidence to support the belief that trephination among pre-Columbian Peruvians was a supernatural-based method of exorcism. A technique of skull surgery, trephining involved cutting a hole in the skull with a type of small saw or knife known as a trephine. Although the primary reason for the procedure was generally believed to be the physical easing of pressure on the brain, the supernatural reasons for the practice cannot be overlooked.

Until the recent popularity of movies, television shows, and novels about possession by demons, the American public was largely unaware that exorcism has been practiced throughout the history of

Western religions. Somewhat alarming to many Americans was the realization that the Catholic church continued to approve exorcisms in twentieth-century America. The following seventeenth-century conjuration was recited by priests in order to exorcise evil spirits from troubled houses. The words may be different, as are the names for the supernatural beings referred to, but the intent of the conjuration is identical to incantations uttered by religious specialists in preliterate societies during exorcism rites for similar purposes:

> I adjure thee, O serpent of old, by the Judge of the living and the dead; by the Creator of the world who hath power to cast into hell, that thou depart forthwith from this house. He that commands thee, accursed demon, is He that commanded the winds and the sea and the storm. He that commands thee, is He that ordered thee to be hurled down from the height of heaven into the lower parts of the earth. He that commands thee is He that bade thee depart from Him. Hearken, then, Satan, and fear. Get thee gone, vanquished and cowed, when thou art bidden in the name of our Lord Jesus Christ who will come to judge the living and the dead and all the world by fire. Amen. (Crehan 1970: 873)

William James saw religion as the belief in an unseen order. If one important aspect of religion is helping believers to come to know that unknown, it follows that divination is important to religion. Divination means learning about the future or about things that may be hidden. Although the word itself may be traced to "divinity," which indicates its relationship to gods, the practice of divination belongs as much to magic as it does to religion proper. From the earliest times, human beings have wanted to know about such climatic changes as drought and heavy rainfall. Without scientific information to help predict natural events, early humans looked for "signs" in the flight of birds, or the entrails of small animals, or perhaps the positions of coals in a fire or pebbles in a stream. To this day the methods of divination in the world's cultures are far too varied and numerous to mention here. However, John Collins (1978: 56–58), following a classification scheme conceived by H. J. Rose, has listed ten basic varieties of divination techniques:

1. *Dreams,* probably the most prevalent form of divination, with the dream's meaning either obvious or requiring analysis.

2. *Presentiments,* a more personal type of divination in which an individual develops a feeling, or presentiment, about something.

3. *Body actions,* such as sneezing, twitching, and hiccupping, which may be interpreted as predictions of rainfall, good or bad luck, drought, or some other particular event.

4. *Ordeals,* painful and often life-threatening tests that a person suspected of guilt may be forced to undergo, such as dipping a hand into hot oil, swallowing poison, or having a red-hot knife blade pressed against some part of the body. Although the ordeal is usually used to help resolve conflict situations, the likelihood that an innocent person may be found guilty is potentially as great as "divining" the actual guilty individual.

5. *Possession* by spirits, enabling the diviner better to reveal the future by discovering hidden knowledge.

6. *Necromancy,* similar to possession, a technique of seeking "signs" from spirits of the dead, or perhaps by close observation of a corpse.

7. *Animal types,* a form of divination in which knowledge is derived either from the observation of living animals or from the inspection of the entrails of dead animals.

8. *Mechanical types,* a form of divination (the most comprehensive category of all) that involves seeking answers by manipulating an innumerable number of objects (for example, a sandal flipped in the air may be interpreted as meaning yes if it lands on its sole, no if on the straps).

9. *Nature types,* in which answers are determined by looking for signs in nature (for example, a particular pattern of mushrooms in the ground, the way leaves tumble from a tree, astrological signs such as the position of the stars and moon).

10. *Miscellaneous divination,* a large category including divination techniques that do not fit into the previous types (for example, death always strikes in threes).

Until recently controversy has surrounded the definition of magic and religion by anthropologists. Only in the last few years have they come close to agreement that the dichotomy is a false one or that, if a dichotomy does exist, its ramifications are not significant to the study of the practitioners of each. Both magic and religion deal directly with the supernatural, and our understanding of the cultural applications of each provides deeper insights into the worldview of the people practicing them.

Magic is usually divided into types, depending on the techniques involved. For example, Sir James Frazer distinguished "imitative magic," in which the magician believes that the desired result could be achieved by imitation, from "contagious magic," in which materials or substances once in contact with the intended victim are used in the magical attack. Other scholars would include "sympathetic magic," a form of magic in which items associated with or symbolic of the intended victim are used to identify and carry out the spell. Obviously, sympathetic magic contains elements of both imitative and contagious magic.

These forms of magic, still in use today, have been important methods of reducing anxiety regarding problems that exceeded the ability of people to understand and control them, especially because of a lack of technological expertise. Divination, special formulas and incantations, spells and curses, all are considered magical, and all can be used for good or evil. Because these activities are learned, they should be differentiated from witchcraft, which is considered innate and, most believe, uncontrollable.

It is logical to assume that non-Western reliance on explanations of events in terms of magic, sorcery, and witchcraft is a natural outcome of a lack of scientific training. But it is equally important to note that Westerners also rely on religious beliefs, with faith playing a strong role in determining actions and behaviors in our daily lives. Our ethnocentrism still blinds us to the similarities between ourselves and our fellow humans in the underdeveloped regions of the world. The great questions concerning the human condition are asked by all peoples, and despite the disparate levels of technology our sameness is demonstrated by the universality of religion.

In the first article of this chapter, June Nash describes the relationship of Bolivian miners with the Devil and other spirits residing in the mines.

E. Mansell Pattison's article is concerned with the widespread renewal of social interest in the supernatural, mystical, magical, and "irrational" in contemporary Western society. The article is a good choice for this chapter because of its focus on exorcism, demonology, and possession.

Using Africa as an example, Lucy Mair discusses divination, a worldwide mystical technique for acquiring knowledge—about past, present, or future events—that is unobtainable using ordinary explanatory methods. E. E. Evans-Pritchard describes the Zande poison oracle *benge* and the beliefs surrounding its usage. The Bronislaw Malinowski essay is a classic analysis of the distinction preliterate people make between magic and science. In the last article, George Gmelch cleverly applies Malinowski's ideas on magic and science to modern baseball.

References

Boddy, Janice
 1994 "Spirit Possession Revisited: Beyond Instrumentality." *Annual Reviews in Anthropology* 23: 407–34.

Collins, John J.
 1978 *Primitive Religion.* Totowa, N.J.: Littlefield, Adams and Co.

Crehan, J. H.
 1970 "Exorcism." In Richard Cavendish, ed., *Man, Myth and Magic*, Vol. 7, pp. 869–73. London: BPCC/Phoebus Publishing.

DeHeusch, L.
 1971 *Why Marry Her? Society and Symbolic Structures.* Translated by J. Lloyd. Cambridge: Cambridge University Press.

Freed, Stanley A., and Ruth S. Freed
 1964 "Spirit Possession as Illness in a North Indian Village." *Ethnology* 3: 152–71.

Howells, William
 1962 *The Heathens.* Garden City, N.Y.: Doubleday.

Lewis, I. M.
 1989 *Ecstatic Religion: A Study of Spirit Possession and Shamanism*, 2nd ed. London: Routledge.

Devils, Witches, and Sudden Death

June Nash

In this article, June Nash describes the dangerous and frightening workaday world of Bolivian tin miners as they ply their trade one-half mile deep in the high Andean plateau of Bolivia. In this fearful world they have found a spiritual ally in the Devil, or Tio (uncle). Because Tio controls the mines, revealing veins of ore at his whim, the miners must venerate him. In addition to the omnipresent images of Tio, there are other spirits in the shafts: Awiche, a positive force who can temper the evil of Tio, and Virida, a consort of Tio who has the power to make men lose their minds. Shortly after Professor Nash visited the mines, three workers were killed in a mine explosion, thus necessitating the holding of a k'araku, a ceremonial banquet of sacrificed animals. During the ceremony, Tio is offered coca and alcohol and is recognized as the true owner of the mine (the ch'alla ceremony). Nash's article is a poignant reminder of the power of the Devil and of the rituals that the miners have constructed to turn his destructive power into the positive force of increasing the ore yield and providing a safer place to work.

Reprinted with permission from *Natural History*, vol. 81, no. 3. Copyright © 1972 the American Museum of Natural History.

TIN MINERS IN THE HIGH ANDEAN PLATEAU OF Bolivia earn less than a dollar a day when, to use their phrase, they "bury themselves alive in the bowels of the earth." The mine shafts—as much as two miles long and half a mile deep—penetrate hills that have been exploited for more than 450 years. The miners descend to the work areas in open hauls; some stand on the roof and cling to the swaying cable as the winch lowers them deep into the mine.

Once they reach their working level, there is always the fear of rockslides as they drill the face of the mine, of landslides when they set off the dynamite, of gas when they enter unfrequented areas. And added to their fear of the accidents that have killed or maimed so many of their workmates is their economic insecurity. Like Wall Street brokers they watch international price quotations on tin, because a difference of a few cents can mean layoffs, loss of bonuses, a cut in contract prices—even a change of government.

Working in the narrow chimneys and corridors of the mine, breathing the dust- and silicate-filled air, their bodies numbed by the vibration of the drilling machines and the din of dynamite blasts, the tin miners have found an ally in the devil, or Tio (uncle), as he is affectionately known. Myths relate the devil to his pre-Christian counterpart Huari, the powerful ogre who owns the treasures of the hills. In Oruro, a 13,800-foot-high mining center in the western Andes of Bolivia, all the miners know the legend of Huari, who persuaded the simple farmers of the Uru Uru tribe to leave their work in the fields and enter the caves to find the riches he had in store. The farmers, supported by their ill-gained wealth from the mines, turned from a virtuous life of tilling the soil and praying to the sun god Inti to a life of drinking and midnight revels. The community would have died, the legend relates, if an Inca maiden, Nusta, had not descended from the sky and taught the people to live in harmony and industry.

Despite four centuries of proselyting, Catholic priests have failed to wipe out belief in the legend, but the principal characters have merged with Catholic deities. Nusta is identified with the Virgin of the Mineshaft, and is represented as the vision that appeared miraculously to an unemployed miner.

The miners believe that Huari lives on in the hills where the mines are located, and they venerate him in the form of the devil, or Tio. They believe he controls the rich veins of ore, revealing them only to those who give him offerings. If they offend the Tio or slight him by failing to give him offerings, he will withhold the rich veins or cause an accident.

Miners make images of the Tio and set them up in the main corridors of each mine level, in niches cut into the walls for the workers to rest. The image of the Tio varies in appearance according to the fancy of the miner who makes him, but his body is always shaped from ore. The hands, face, horns, and legs are sculptured with clay from the mine. Bright pieces of metal or burned-out bulbs from the miners' electric torches are stuck in the eye sockets. Teeth are made of glass or crystal sharpened "like nails," and the mouth is open, gluttonous and ready to receive offerings. Sometimes the plaster of Paris masks worn by the devil dancers at Carnival are used for the head. Some Tios wear embroidered vests, flamboyant capes, and miners' boots. The figure of a bull, which helps miners in contract with the devil by digging out the ore with its horns, occasionally accompanies the image, or there may be *chinas,* female temptresses who are the devil's consorts.

The Tio is a figure of power: he has what everyone wants, in excess. Coca remains lie in his greedy mouth. His hands are stretched out, grasping the bottles of alcohol he is offered. His nose is burned black by the cigarettes he smokes down to the nub. If a Tio is knocked out of his niche by an extra charge of dynamite and survives, the miners consider him to be more powerful than others.

Another spirit present in the mines but rarely represented in images is the Awiche, or old woman. Although some miners deny she is the Pachamama, the earth goddess worshiped by farmers, they relate to her in the same way. Many of the miners greet her when they enter the mine, saying, "Good-day, old woman. Don't let anything happen to me today!" They ask her to intercede with the Tio when they feel in danger; when they leave the mine safely, they thank her for their life.

Quite the opposite kind of feminine image, the Viuda, or widow, appears to miners who have been drinking *chicha,* a fermented corn liquor. Miners who have seen the Viuda describe her as a young and beautiful *chola,* or urbanized Indian, who makes men lose their minds—and sometimes their paychecks. She, too, is a consort of the devil and recruits men to make contracts with him, deluding them with promises of wealth.

When I started working in Oruro during the summer of 1969, the men told me about the *ch'alla,* a ceremonial offering of cigarettes, coca, and alcohol to the Tio. One man described it as follows:

"We make the *ch'alla* in the working areas within the mine. My partner and I do it together every Friday, but on the first Friday of the month we do it with the other workers on our level. We bring in banners, confetti, and paper streamers. First we put a cigarette in the mouth of the Tio and light it. After this we scatter alcohol on the ground for the Pachamama, then give some to the Tio. Next we take out our coca and begin to chew, and we also smoke. We serve liquor from the bottles each of us brings in. We light the Tio's cigarette, saying 'Tio, help us in our work. Don't let any accidents happen.' We do not kneel before him as we would before a saint, because that would be sacrilegious.

"Then everyone begins to get drunk. We begin to talk about our work, about the sacrifices that we make. When this is finished, we wind the streamers around the neck of the Tio. We prepare our *mesas* [tables of offerings that include sugar cakes, llama embryos, colored wool, rice, and candy balls].

"After some time we say, 'Let's go.' Some have to carry out those who are drunk. We go to where we change our clothes, and when we come out we again make the offering of liquor, banners, and we wrap the streamers around each others' necks. From there on, each one does what he pleases."

I thought I would never be able to participate in a *ch'alla* because the mine managers told me the men didn't like to have women inside the mine, let alone join them in their most sacred rites. Finally a friend high in the governmental bureaucracy gave me permission to go into the mine. Once down on the lowest level of San José mine, 340 meters below the ground, I asked my guide if I could stay with one of the work crews rather than tour the galleries as most visitors did. He was relieved to leave me and get back to work. The men let me try their machines so that I could get a sense of what it was like to hold a 160-pound machine vibrating in a yardwide tunnel, or to use a mechanical shovel in a gallery where the temperature was 100 °F.

They told me of some of their frustrations—not getting enough air pumped in to make the machines work at more than 20 percent efficiency and constant breakdowns of machinery, which slowed them up on their contract.

At noon I refused the superintendent's invitation to eat lunch at level 0. Each of the men gave me a bit of his soup or some "seconds," solid food consisting of noodles, potatoes, rice, and spicy meat, which their wives prepare and send down in the elevators.

At the end of the shift all the men in the work group gathered at the Tio's niche in the large corridor. It was the first Friday of the month and the gang leader, Lino Pino, pulled out a bottle of fruit juice and liquor, which his wife had prepared, and each of the men brought out his plastic bag with coca. Lino led the men in offering a cigarette to the Tio, lighting it, and then shaking the liquor on the ground and calling for life, "Hallalla! Hallalla!"

We sat on lumps of ore along the rail lines and Lino's helper served us, in order of seating, from a little tin cup. I was not given any priority, nor was I forgotten in the rounds. One of the men gave me coca from his supply and I received with two hands, as I had been taught in the rituals above-ground. I chewed enough to make my cheek feel numb, as though I had had an injection of novocaine for dental work. The men told me that coca was their gift from the Pachamama, who took pity on them in their work.

As Lino offered liquor to the Tio, he asked him to "produce" more mineral and make it "ripen," as though it were a crop. These rituals are a continuation of agricultural ceremonies still practiced by the farmers in the area. The miners themselves are the sons or grandsons of the landless farmers who were recruited when the gold and silver mines were reopened for tin production after the turn of the century.

A month after I visited level 340, three miners died in an explosion there when a charge of dynamite fell down a chute to their work site and exploded. Two of the men died in the mine; the third died a few days later in the hospital. When the accident occurred, all the men rushed to the elevators to help or to stare in fascinated horror as the dead and injured were brought up to level 0. They carried the bodies of their dead comrades to the social center where they washed the charred faces, trying to lessen the horror for the women who were coming. When the women came into the social center where the bodies were laid out, they screamed and stamped their feet, the horror of seeing their husbands or neighbors sweeping through their bodies.

The entire community came to sit in at the wake, eating and drinking in the feasting that took place before the coffins of their dead comrades. The meal seemed to confirm the need to go on living as well as the right to live.

Although the accident had not occurred in the same corridor I had been in, it was at the same level. Shortly after that, when a student who worked with me requested permission to visit the mine, the manager told her that the men were hinting that the accident had happened because the gringa (any foreign-born, fair-haired person, in this case myself) had been inside. She was refused permission. I was disturbed by what might happen to my relations with the people of the community, but even more concerned that I had added to their sense of living in a hostile world where anything new was a threat.

The miners were in a state of uneasiness and tension the rest of that month, July. They said the Tio was "eating them" because he hadn't had an offering of food. The dead men were all young, and the Tio prefers the juicy flesh and blood of the young, not the tired blood of the sick older workers. He wanted a k'araku, a ceremonial banquet of sacrificed animals.

There had not been any scheduled k'arakus since the army put the mines under military control in 1965. During the first half of the century, when the "tin barons"—Patiño, Hochschild, and Arayamao—owned the mines, the administrators and even some of the owners, especially Patiño, who had risen from the ranks, would join with the men in sacrificing animals to the Tio and in the drinking and dancing that followed. After nationalization of the mines in 1952, the rituals continued. In fact, some of the miners complained that they were done in excess of the Tio's needs. One said that going into the mine after the revolution was like walking into a saloon.

Following military control, however, the miners had held the ritual only once in San José, after two men had died while working their shift. Now the Tio had again shown he was hungry by eating the three miners who had died in the accident. The miners were determined to offer him food in a *k'araku*.

At 11:30 P.M. on the eve of the devil's month, I went to the mine with Doris Widerkehr, a student, and Eduardo Ibañez, a Bolivian artist. I was somewhat concerned about how we would be received after what the manager of the mine had said, but all the men seemed glad we had come. As we sat at the entry to the main shaft waiting for the *yatiris,* shamans who had been contracted for the ceremony, the miners offered us *chicha* and cocktails of fruit juice and alcohol.

When I asked one of the men why they had prepared the ritual and what it meant, his answer was:

"We are having the *k'araku* because a man can't die just like that. We invited the administrators, but none of them have come. This is because only the workers feel the death of their comrades.

"We invite the Pachamama, the Tio, and God to eat the llamas that we will sacrifice. With faith we give coca and alcohol to the Tio. We are more believers in God here than in Germany or the United States because there the workers have lost their soul. We do not have earthquakes because of our faith before God. We hold the crucifix to our breast. We have more confidence before God."

Most miners reject the claim that belief in the Tio is pagan sacrilege. They feel that no contradiction exists, since time and place for offerings to the devil are clearly defined and separated from Christian ritual.

At 11:00 P.M. two white llamas contributed by the administration were brought into level 0 in a company truck. The miners had already adorned the pair, a male and a female, with colored paper streamers and the bright wool earrings with which farmers decorate their flocks.

The four *yatiris* contracted for did not appear, but two others who happened to be staying at the house of a miner were brought in to perform the ceremony. As soon as they arrived, the miners took the llamas into the elevator. The male was on the right and the female to his left, "just the same as a marriage ceremony," one miner commented. Looking at the couple adorned with bright streamers and confetti, there was the feeling of a wedding.

Two men entered the elevator with the llamas and eight more climbed on top to go down to level 340. They were commissioned to take charge of the ritual. All the workers of 340 entered to participate in the ceremony below and about 50 men gathered at level 0 to drink.

At level 340 the workers guided the *yatiris* to the spot where the accident had occurred. There they cast liquor from a bottle and called upon the Tio, the Awiche, and God to protect the men from further accidents—naming all the levels in the mine, the various work sites, the different veins of ore, the elevator shaft, and the winch, repeating each name three times and asking the Tio not to eat any more workers and to give them more veins to work. The miners removed their helmets during this ritual. It ended with the plea for life, "Hallalla, hallalla, hallalla." Two bottles of liquor were sprinkled on the face of the rock and in the various work places.

The *yatiris* then instructed the men to approach the llamas with their arms behind their backs so that the animals would not know who held the knife that would kill them. They were also told to beg pardon for the sacrifice and to kiss the llamas farewell. One miner, noting what appeared to be a tear falling from the female's eye, cried and tried to comfort her. As the men moved around the llamas in a circle, the *yatiris* called on the Malkus (eagle gods), the Awiche, the Pachamama, and finally the Tiyulas (Tios of the mines), asking for their care.

The female llama was the first to be sacrificed. She struggled and had to be held down by two men as they cut her jugular vein. When they disemboweled her, the men discovered that she was pregnant, to which they attributed the strength of her resistance. Her blood was caught in a white basin.

When the heart of the dying llama had pumped out its blood, the *yatiri* made an incision and removed it, using both his hands, a sign of respect when receiving an offering. He put the still palpitating heart in the basin with the blood and covered it with a white cloth on which the miners placed *k'oa*—an offering made up of herbs, coca, wool, and sweets—and small bottles of alcohol and wine.

The man in charge of the ceremony went with five aides to the site of the principal Tio in the main corridor. There they removed a piece of ore from the image's left side, creating a hole into which they put the heart, the blood, and the other offerings. They stood in a circle, their heads bent, and asked for safety and that there be no more accidents. In low voices, they prayed in Quechua.

When this commission returned, the *yatiris* proceeded to sacrifice the male llama. Again they asked the Tio for life and good ore in all the levels of the mine, and that there be no accidents. They took the heart, blood, *k'oa,* and bottles of alcohol and wine to another isolated gallery and buried it for the Tio in a place that would not be disturbed. There they prayed, "filled with faith," as one commented; then returned to the place of the sacrifice. The *yatiris* sprinkled the remaining blood on the veins of ore.

By their absorption and fervid murmuring of prayers, both young and old miners revealed the same faith and devotion. Many of them wept, thinking of the accident and their dead companions. During the ritual drinking was forbidden.

On the following day those men charged with responsibility for the ritual came to prepare the meat. They brought the two carcasses to the baker, who seasoned them and cooked them in large ovens. The men returned at about 1:15 P.M. to distribute the meat. With the meat, they served *chicha*. Some sprinkled *chicha* on the ground for the Pachamama, saying "Hallalla," before drinking.

The bones were burned to ashes, which were then offered to the Tio. The mine entrance was locked shut and left undisturbed for 24 hours. Some remarked that it should be closed for three days, but the company did not want to lose that much time.

During the *k'araku* the miners recognize the Tio as the true owner of the mine. "All the mineral that comes out from the interior of the mine is the 'crop' of the devil and whether one likes it or not, we have to invite the Tio to drink and eat so that the flow of metal will continue," said a young miner who studied evenings at the University of Oruro.

All the workers felt that the failure of the administrators to come to the *k'araku* indicated not only their lack of concern with the lives of the men but also their disregard of the need to raise productivity in the mine.

When the Tio appears uninvited, the miners fear that they have only a short time to live. Miners who have seen apparitions say the Tio looks like a gringo —tall, red-faced, with fair hair and beard, and wearing a cowboy hat. This description hardly resembles the images sculptured by the miners, but it does fit the foreign technicians and administrators who administered the mines in the time of the tin barons. To the Indian workers, drawn from the highland and Cochabamba farming areas, the Tio is a strange and exotic figure, ruthless, gluttonous, powerful, and arbitrary in his use of that power, but nonetheless attractive, someone to get close to in order to share that power. I was beginning to wonder if the reason I was accepted with such good humor by the miners, despite their rule against women in the mines, was

because they thought I shared some of these characteristics and was a match for the devil.

Sickness or death in the family can force a man in desperation to make a contract with the devil. If his companions become aware of it, the contract is destroyed and with it his life.

The miners feel that they need the protection of a group when they confront the Tio. In the *ch'alla* and the *k'araku* they convert the power of the Tio into socially useful production. In effect, the rituals are ways of getting the genie back into the bottle after he has done his miracles. Security of the group then depends upon respect toward the sacrificial offering, as shown by the following incident told me by the head of a work gang after the *k'araku*:

"I know of a man who had a vein of ore near where the bones of the sacrificial llama were buried. Without advising me, he made a hole with his drill and put the dynamite in. He knew very well that the bones were there. On the following day, it cost him his life. While he was drilling, a stone fell and cut his head off.

"We had to change the bones with a ceremony. We brought in a good shaman who charged us B$500 [about $40], we hired the best orchestra, and we sang and danced in the new location where we laid the bones. We did not work in that corridor for three days, and we spent all the time in the *ch'alla*."

Often the miners are frightened nearly to death in the mine. A rock falls on the spot they have just left, a man falls in a shaft and is saved by hitting soft clay at the bottom, a tunnel caves in the moment after a man leaves it—these are incidents in a day's work that I have heard men say can start a *haperk'a*, or fear, that can take their lives.

A shaman may have to be called in to bring back the spirit that the Tio has seized. In one curing, a frightened miner was told to wear the clothing he had on when the Tio seized his spirit and to enter and give a service to the Tio at the same spot where he was frightened. The shaman himself asked the Tio to cure his patient, flattering him, "Now you have shown your power, give back his spirit."

The fear may result in sexual impotency. At one of the mines, Siglo XX, when there is full production, a dynamite blast goes off every five minutes in a section called Block Haven. The air is filled with smoke and the miners describe it as an inferno. Working under such tension, a shattering blast may unnerve them. Some react with an erection, followed by sexual debilitation. Mad with rage and fear, some miners have been known to seize a knife, the same knife they use to cut the dynamite leads, and castrate themselves. When I visited Block Haven, I noticed that the Tio on this level had a huge erection, about a foot long on a mansized figure. The workers said that when they find themselves in a state of impotency they go to the Tio for help. By exemplifying what they want in the Tio, they seek to repair the psychic damage caused by fear.

After feasting on the meat of the llamas and listening to stories of the Tio, I left the mine. The men thanked me for coming. I could not express the gratitude I felt for restoring my confidence in continuing the study.

Shortly thereafter I met Lino Pino returning from a fiesta for a miraculous saint in a nearby village. He asked me if I would be *madrina* at his daughter's forthcoming confirmation, and when I agreed, his wife offered me a tin cup with the delicious cocktail she always prepares for her husband on the days of the *ch'alla,* and we all had a round of drinks.

Later, when I knelt at the altar rail with Lino and his daughter as we received the wafer and the wine, flesh and blood of another sacrifice victim, I sensed the unity in the miners' beliefs. The miraculous Virgin looked down on us from her marbelized, neon-lit niche, her jewelled finger held out in benediction. She was adequate for that scene, but in the mine they needed someone who could respond to their needs on the job.

In the rituals of the *ch'alla* and the *k'araku* the power of the Tio to destroy is transformed into the socially useful functions of increasing mineral yield and giving peace of mind to the workers. Confronted alone, the Tio, like Banquo's ghost makes a man unable to produce or even to go on living. Properly controlled by the group, the Tio promises fertility, potency, and productivity to the miners. Robbed of this faith, they often lose the faith to continue drilling after repeated failure to find a vein, or to continue living when the rewards of work are so meager. Knowing that the devil is on your side makes it possible to continue working in the hell that is the mines.

Psychosocial Interpretations of Exorcism

E. Mansell Pattison

E. Mansell Pattison, a professor of psychiatry and human behavior, begins this article with an examination of the contemporary interest in demonology and exorcism in Western society. Agreeing with Claude Lévi-Strauss, Pattison observes that primitive ideas of reality result in a more coherent and cohesive model of the world than do Western scientific explanations. He traces the present renewal of interest in demonology and exorcism in contemporary scientific cultures to certain social situations that support an oppressive social structure. Pattison believes modern psychiatry's failure to provide meaning and understanding of reality has caused people to abandon the psychoanalyst in favor of the exorcist. The author demonstrates how modern psychoanalytic psychotherapy is like exorcism, discusses the differences between "scientific healers" and "folk healers," and analyzes the implications for psychotherapeutic practice.

Reprinted from the *Journal of Operational Psychiatry*, vol. 8, no. 2 (1977), pp. 5–19, by permission of the author and the University of Missouri-Columbia, Department of Psychiatry. The article's citations, originally numbered footnotes, have been interpolated into the text in this volume for consistency of presentation.

"The power of magic defeats the demons of scientific technology" (advertisement for the movie *Wizards*, 1977).

THIS PAPER IS CONCERNED WITH THE WIDE-spread renewal of social interest in the supernatural, mystical, magical, and "irrational" in contemporary western society. This is reflected in the rapid shift among young people from the iconoclastic social activism of the 1960s toward an internal personal quest for peace and meaning in the 1970s. This latter quest is seen in the popularity of non-conventional religiosity, mystical experience, and eastern philosophies. The tip of the iceberg of this social revolution of consciousness is our manifest fascination with demonology and exorcism.

Corollary to society in general, the mental health professions have begun to closely examine the beliefs and practices of indigenous healers. Therefore, my inquiry begins with the general social phenomenon and leads into a comparative examination of "scientific healers" versus "folk healers" and the implications for psychotherapeutic practice.

Naturalistic Versus Supernaturalistic Systems

Our western views of health and illness, cause and effect, reality and fantasy are, of course, the product of an evolving construction and explanation of reality, in large part determined by the empirical rationalism of experimental science, its adoption by medicine, and thence to psychiatry. The western mode of thought and its construction of reality has often been the measure against which all other cultural constructions of reality were assessed while so-called primitive cultures were considered to be unrealistic, irrational, simplistic, and naive. From this point of view, it seems absurd that sophisticated western people should evince interest, much less belief, in magical, mystical, and metaphysical ideas that western culture has long since given up for more realistic views and explanations of the world. In particular the belief in demons, possession, and exorcism seems especially atavistic.

What the western mind does not see, is that western science and its construction of reality is terribly fragmented. The naturalistic system of the world of the west, rooted in the empirical rationalism of latter day humanism, provides proximate and limited explanations of isolated fragments of human life. It fails to provide western mankind with a cohesive picture of human life. Further, without ontological grounding it does not provide a rationale, nor purpose, nor meaning to life. The optimistic world view of 19th-century scientific humanism has become the 20th-century world view of cynicism, despair, existential ennui and a cosmos of the absurd.

Sartre states the dilemma of modern western man succinctly:

> The existentialist . . . thinks it very distressing that God does not exist, because all possibility of finding values in a heaven of ideas disappears along with him. . . . Everything is permissible if God does not exist, and as a result man is forlorn, because neither within him nor without does he find anything to cling to. . . . We find no values or commands to turn to which legitimize our conduct. So, in the right realm of values, we have no excuse behind us, nor justification before us. We are alone, with no excuses (1959).

Or consider the conclusion of psychoanalyst Allen Wheelis:

> At the beginning of the modern age science did, indeed, promise certainty. It does no longer. Where we now retain the conviction of certainty we do so on our own presumption, while the advancing edge of science warns that absolute truth is a fiction, is a longing of the heart, and not to be had by man. . . . Our designations of evil are as fallible now as they were ten thousand years ago; we simply are better armed now to act on our fallible vision (1971).

My point is that the superiority of western consciousness and the western construction of reality as a mode of existence has failed to be demonstrated. That western empirical technology has achieved greater creature comforts and longevity of life is in-

disputable, but what of the quality, meaning, and value of life?

These considerations only briefly intimate the conclusion that in the west we have entered a new age of irrationalism. Yet at the same time, we continue to misinterpret other world views of reality.

As Lévi-Strauss (1966) has demonstrated so well in *The Savage Mind,* so-called primitive constructions of reality provide a much more coherent, cohesive, and explanatory model of the world and human behavior than does the western scientific construction of the cosmos. Science does not provide a very comprehensive description and explanation of human behavior. *The Savage Mind* had an explanation and intervention for everything.

Foster (1976) has compared naturalistic versus supernaturalistic systems of thought about health and illness. He finds that naturalistic systems (western) view misfortune and illness in atomistic terms. Disease is unrelated to other misfortune, religion and magic are unrelated to illness; and the principal curers lack supernatural or magical powers, for their function is solely an instrumental technical task performance. On the other hand, supernaturalistic systems integrate the totality of all life events. Illness, religion, and magic are inseparable. The most powerful curers are astute diagnosticians who employ both technical and symbolic means of therapeusis.

Early students of supernaturalistic systems of healing such as Ackerknecht and Rivers emphasized the particular magical beliefs and rituals of shamans and other folk healers; thus they overlooked the complex integrated view of nature and mankind, and the complex refined distinctions that were made between different kinds of misfortunes, their causes, and cures.

Loudon comments:

> This reduces the study of health and disease to studies of witchcraft, sorcery, magic, and in general curative or socially readjustive ritual practices, with herbalist and empirically rational treatment and prophylaxis as residual categories (1976).

In brief, supernaturalistic systems encompass the totality of life, which integrates man and nature. Careful ethnographic studies of folk healers reveal a complex and sophisticated description of reality, in which there is indeed differentiation between accidents, distortions of natural process such as malformed fetus, hazards such as snakebites, psychosomatic disorders, and existential disorders of impaired human relations. Similarly, within the supernaturalistic system there are a range of interventions practiced by a variety of healers with skills suitable to the curing of the misfortune.

In sum, I have attempted to illustrate that the distinction between the naturalistic and the supernaturalistic is not so wide a gulf as we might suppose. Our rationalistic culture is absurd and irrational while the supernaturalistic cultures possess a sophisticated, coherent construction of reality, with attendant differentiated diagnostic and therapeutic concepts. The fundamental difference may lie rather in our differing construction of what reality is.

Demonology as Part of Supernaturalism

Beliefs in demonology, possession, and exorcism can be adequately interpreted only within the framework of supernaturalistic systems. Anthropologist Erika Bourguignon (1973) has organized the variety of trance behaviors and associated beliefs into convenient chart form, as shown in Figure 1. As illustrated, the same phenomena can be explained in either naturalistic or supernaturalistic systems. And also evident is that demon possession is only one sub-type of many concepts of man and spirits.

Abundant ethnographic data have shown that although there may be widespread tacit acceptance and private belief in demonology, the actual practice of witchcraft and experience of possession states is limited. That is, the particular emergence of demon possession and exorcism can be shown to relate to rather particular socio-cultural milieux. The general conclusion is that the eruption of demonology is coincident with social situations where there is an oppressive social structure, a loss of trust in the efficacy of social institutions, and a seeming inability to cope with the evils of the social structure. In this situation, then, we see the personification of social evil in evil demons, and a displaced social protest in the form of accusations of witchcraft and personal experiences of possession. Being possessed of social evil is personified, while accused, accuser, and exorcist act out the symbolization of the social dilemma in safely displaced form, since active social protest and reform seem impossible.

For example, Bourguignon finds the distribution of demonic possession in folk societies to be correlated with conditions of social oppression and stagnation (1968). Wijesinghe et al. (1976) report a high incidence of possession in a low status subcommunity of Sri Lanka; and Carstairs and Kapur note that in an Indian community it was in the most oppressed case that they found possession (1976).

Socio-cultural studies have thus emphasized the social dynamics that produce demonology. Yet at the same time we must account for the psychological dimensions which have played such a large part in typical psychiatric interpretations of demonology.

Freud (1961) stated the classic psychological formulation: "The states of possession correspond to our neuroses. . . . The demons are bad and reprehensible wishes." But this interpretation reduces demonology to nothing but individual neurosis, and may lead to the conclusion that the actors in the drama of demonology are dealing with individual neuroses.

In contrast the eminent medical historian George Rosen observes:

> Witch hunting expresses a dis-ease of society, and is related to a social context. . . . To be sure, some individuals involved in witch trials were mentally and emotionally disordered. Most of those involved were not. In part, their reactions were learned, in part, they conformed because of fear-producing pressures (1968).

Similarly the historian Russell concludes:

> But it will not do to assume that the witches were on the whole mentally ill. They were responding to human needs more universal than those of individual fantasy: universal enough to be described in terms of myth. . . . The phenomenon of witchcraft, whether we are talking about the persecutors or the witches, was the result of fear, expressed in supernatural terms in a society that thought in supernatural terms, and repressed by a society that was intolerant of spiritual dissent. In most respects a variety, or at least an outgrowth, of heresy, witchcraft was one manifestation of alienation (1972).

We cannot gainsay that the belief and practice of demonology was not and is not a defensive and adaptive psychological maneuver. But from the viewpoint of culture this is not neurosis. As Spiro (1965) says: "There is a third category of defense mechanisms—culturally constituted defenses—

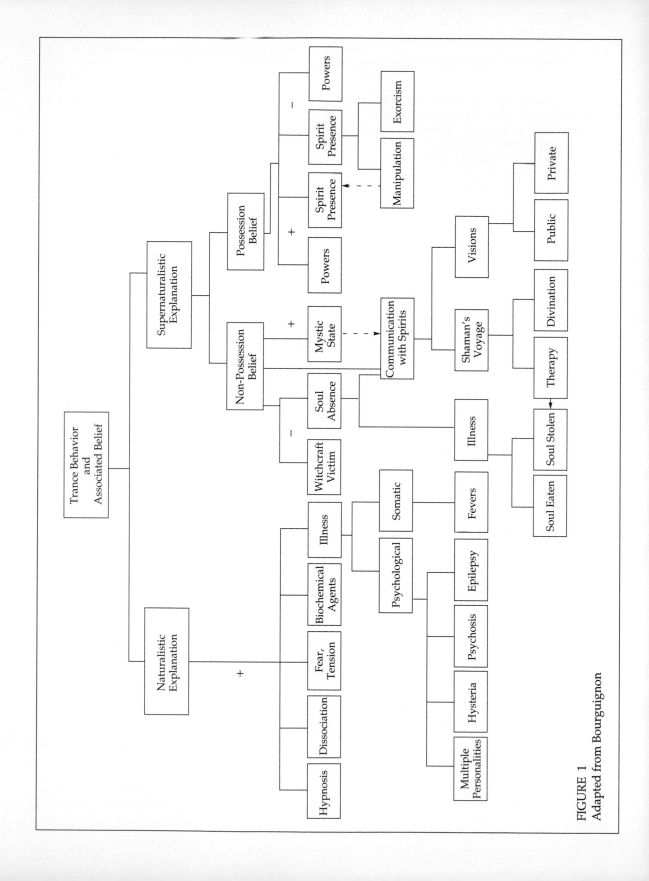

FIGURE 1
Adapted from Bourguignon

which are not only not disruptive of, but rather serve to perpetuate, the socio-cultural system."

Robert LeVine (1973) has pointedly synthesized the issue by describing a *psychosocial* interpretation of demonology. That is, within the general culture of belief there will be degrees of potential, for more or less individuals, to act out the beliefs of demonology. And where the general belief of demonology is culturally no longer a modal belief, only those with specific psychological propensities (i.e., neurotic) are likely to use such beliefs in their ego defense.

With this summary at hand, we can now see that Freud and other psychiatric observers could readily reduce demonology to nothing but neurosis, for they were observing persons acting out beliefs not modal to the culture. But where demonology is modal, we must look beyond neurosis for our understanding.

Contemporary Demonology

With an understanding of the social conditions which give rise to demonology, it is possible to see that contemporary social conditions are ripe in the western world for the re-emergence of supernaturalistic belief systems, and even demonology. Society has been perceived as oppressive, trust in social institutions has disintegrated, social protest has been realistically dangerous, and a mood of helpless impotence has emerged. New hope, new meaning, and new purpose can be seen in the myriad of supernaturalistic systems now gaining devotees. So it should not surprise us that the evil society should again be personified and symbolized in demonology.

In his analysis of medieval demonology the Spanish anthropologist Baroja notes that western rationalism ousted the belief in witchcraft from its place in the collective consciousness of man, to survive only in the marginal circles of cranks and neurotics. Yet he finds us coming full circle with the breakdown of rationalism:

We are in a better position nowadays to appreciate the feelings of the people involved, who discovered one day that they had a devilish power in them, or were subject to the devilish power of a close enemy who had lived near them for years, watching and hating. For ours is no period of calm, with an optimistic view of public morality and religious philosophy and beliefs. It is an age of existentialism and an existentialist way of life, which leads man to break down the barriers and conventions and face up to his own angst (1964).

Following along the existential consciousness of our day is the stark sense of alienated and singular responsibility for everything. Historian Judith Neaman finds it not surprising that psychiatry is becoming more biological just at the time when our society is becoming more metaphysical. She recalls that in every culture hyper-rationalism has been followed by a renewal of supernaturalism. For with the rationalism and ultimately the existentialism comes too much responsibility—too much to bear. Psychiatry brought man from outer reality into himself and only himself, and left man there. Neaman concludes:

The legacy of the Middle Ages was the increasing interiorization of the self and a concomitant increase in responsibility for human action. These ideas were consummated in the twentieth century belief that we are responsible not only for our own actions but also for our own guilts, fears, and obsessions. The fantasy of the 1970s has been a wish to return to an age of exorcism (1975).

Bourguignon (1968) similarly finds: "There is a wish to find alternative ways of living; and thus not only modify the society, but to modify the self."

Thus, we see that rather than unexpected, it is most consonant with history that supernaturalism and demonology should again appear in our time. The nadir of scientific psychiatry offers least to western man in terms of meaning, and people turn from the psychoanalyst to the exorcist.

Psychoanalytic Demonology

The demons out there that possessed us, have been gradually deanthropomorphized. Healing which was exorcism of the personal spirit became gradually more an exorcism of bad thoughts and feelings. Pattison et al. (1973) found that modern seekers of faith healing seek a spiritual cure of the self, which is but a step from the final abstraction of evil into pure thought in Christian Science, where evil, misfortune and illness exist only in thought and have no reality.

But demonology has been resurrected in new form in the object relations theory of psychoanalysis. Possession is not to be left behind, but only redefined. We are possessed of good and bad objects— ego introjects. So we find twentieth century demonology interpreted by Fairbairn thusly:

> It is to the realm of these bad objects . . . that the ultimate origin of all psychopathological developments is to be traced; for it may be said of all psychoneurotic and psychotic patients that, if a True Mass is being celebrated in the chancel, a Black Mass is being celebrated in the crypt. It becomes evident, accordingly, that the psychotherapist is the true successor to the exorcist, and that he is concerned, not only with the "forgiveness of sins," but also with "the casting out of devils" (1954).

From the same object-relations theory, Henderson concludes that the therapist is not successor to the exorcist, just different in technique:

> The religious view of emotional pain contains an important if imperfect truth which has been too long disregarded. The psychotherapist differs from the exorcist not so much in theory, although his terminology is different, but in his belief that the therapeutic process to be effective is apt to require a more painstaking process to dissolve the persecuting forces (1976).

This quote is interesting from several points of view, which all reflect typical western cultural biased assumptions. One, that the supernatural description of possession is less accurate than the naturalistic. Two, that folk healers are less painstaking than psychoanalysts. Three, that psychotherapy, western style, is more efficacious than folk healing. These assumptions are clearly challenged in the volumes cited in the bibliography; here I wish only to highlight the above assumptions, which lead to the next issue.

Modes of Relations Between Scientific and Folk Healers

In our time it has become fashionable to talk about providing psychotherapy to ethnic and minority groups, the poor and the working class, and the application of western psychotherapy to other cultures. But the limits of application of western style psychotherapy have yet to be clearly determined. Up to this point most of such interest has led to the notion of developing working relations between scientific psychotherapists and indigenous folk healers. Again what those working relations should or can consist of, remains vaguely defined. I propose that there are three current modes of working relations.

The first mode is *cooperation*. This mode is frequently found in developing countries where western psychiatrists establish friendly cooperative relations with native healers. Each retains his own assumptive world view, provides treatment within separate spheres of action, and transfers or triages mutual clients between each other. Carstairs and Kapur (1976) and Kiev (1972) have documented many examples of this type.

The second mode is *syncretistic*. That is, there is an attempt to functionally use indigenous healers as part of the psychiatric mental health care system. This mode functionally fuses two worlds of existence that have no necessarily logical relation. In this view the indigenous healer becomes coopted as a new style mental health "para-professional."

The third mode is *collaborative*. Here I have in mind a working relationship that involves sharing and participating in two worlds of consciousness and action.

In some cases documented by Carstairs and Kapur (1976) western psychotherapists have gradually given up western psychiatry and become healers within the folk tradition. It is hard to live in two worlds! Even to begin to move into collaborative modes requires real immersion into nonwestern modes of existence. Jilek and Jilek describe their efforts:

> We found it is possible to bridge the cultural gap by first making oneself known to the people through participation in the activities of the non-western community. We strove to inform ourselves on the belief system, myths, rituals, social customs and organizations; we attended feasts, social, religious and political functions, seeking discussion with leading community figures and traditional healers (1974).

In sum, I suggest that the popular enthusiasm to "work with the natives" does not do justice to the profound differences in consciousness and construction of reality involved. It would appear that we are just beginning to appreciate the culture-boundedness of our western psychiatric thinking.

A Case Study

To illustrate some issues raised thus far, the following case from my own experience highlights the psychological meaning of possession and the function of exorcism from a comparative therapeutic view.

This experience occurred during a period when I served as the psychiatric consultant to the public Health Service Clinic serving the Yakima Indian reservation. The Yakima are located on several thousand acres of farming and lumbering land in central Washington amidst the rich agricultural Yakima valley. As on many Indian reservations, these Indian people live in close proximity to white western culture. Although they have relatively good economic resources, life on the reservation is isolated from the world in which it is located. The reservation culture is in the midst of cultural disintegration. The "long hair" Indians cling to the traditional Yakima mores, while their middle-aged children flounder in bewilderment, not part of the white culture, not part of the Indian. Meanwhile the grandchildren attend the local white schools and watch television in the homes of their grandparents. Here in the middle of two cultures we find our case.

Upon arrival at the reservation one snowy December morning, the young public health doctor grabbed me for an emergency consultation. He had been called to the home of an Indian family the previous night to see an adolescent girl. The family stated that she was crying, frightened, incoherent, running around the house in a state of panic. He reported that upon arrival at the home he found the girl incoherent, babbling, agitated, muttering about ghosts and stated that she was afraid of dying. He gave her an intramuscular injection of chlorpromazine which calmed her down, and she went to sleep. He made a diagnosis of acute schizophrenic psychosis. Since I was due to arrive the next day, he requested that the family bring the girl to the clinic for my evaluation and recommendation for further treatment.

Precisely at the appointed time, the mother and daughter appeared. I had worked on the reservation for several years at this time, and was known to the Indian people. I had found good rapport and little difficulty in establishing working relationships with my Indian clientele. But this was a different situation from my usual clinical consultations. Both mother and daughter were sullen, guarded, withdrawn. The girl was a pretty, well developed, adolescent, thirteen years old. She was dressed like a typical high school girl. But she hunched herself over, eyes downcast, speaking in barely audible tones. With great difficulty and much patience her story was told.

The problems began the prior August when Mary (her pseudonym) had gone off to a week-long summer camp for Indian girls, sponsored by the local O.E.O. program. One night, as children are wont to do at a summer camp, after lights were out and the counselors were in bed, Mary and several of her girl friends went sneaking out of their cabin to frolic in the moonlight among the tall fir trees. As they ran about in the moonlight they looked up in the trees and saw human figures. These ghost-like figures drifted down from the trees, and the girls recognized them as their tribal ancestors. The girls talked to the ghosts and the ghosts talked to the girls. But after a few minutes the girls became frightened, ran back to their cabin, jumped into bed, and hid under their covers.

All seemed safe now. Except for Mary. A ghost followed her into the cabin, jumped on her as she lay in bed, and tried to choke her. She fought and struggled against the ghost, she gasped for breath, she screamed for help. The counselors came running into the cabin, but they could not calm her. Mary was sure the ghosts would kill her, she sobbed and screamed. Finally, the counselors bundled her up in a car and drove back home to the local hospital. When seen in the emergency room she was still in an agitated state and was given an intramuscular tranquilizer shot before being taken home to her parents.

The stage was set, and the pattern from then on to December was rather routine. Mary would go off to high school everyday with ratted hair and teenie-bopper clothes. She would participate in her daily high school activities like any teenager. She was on the honor roll, was a cheerleader, and a student body officer. But when she came home a different Mary appeared. She combed her hair into long Indian braids. She put on long-skirted traditional Indian clothes, and wandered about the house as if in a daze. She would see ghosts at the window and cry out in startled fright. She went walking in the fields and saw blood on the ground. She thought the ghosts had killed one of her girl friends. She thought the ghosts would attack and kill her younger brothers and sisters. She would become so frightened and worried that at times she would cry, and scream, and run around the house. At times the parents could not calm her, and they would take her to the hospital for a shot to calm her down. But the next morning she would always get up and go to school like a normal adolescent girl.

The mother and the girl had no explanation for this behavior. They were bewildered. The mother turned to me and asked what I, as a psychiatrist, thought of this behavior. Was her daughter crazy? What I observed was a withdrawn sullen girl. But she spoke in a coherent manner; she was logical and realistic in her conversation with me. I stated that I did not know what this all meant, but perhaps the mother might have some ideas.

The mother said she had heard that psychiatrists did not believe in religion. Did I believe in religion? I told her that I thought religion was very important in the lives of people. Did I believe that she had been healed? I told her that many people experience healing, and that she too might have had a healing experience. She smiled, relaxed and leaned toward me. Look at my face! Do you see any scars? No, I don't. Well, my father healed me. Do you believe that? Yes. Well he was a witchdoctor; he used to care for the whole tribe. And when I was a girl I fell in a fire and burned my face. And he made a pack of mud with his spittle, and anointed my face and said his prayers. And said I would be healed and have no scars. He said I would have a beautiful face. Do you think he was right? Is my face beautiful? Yes.

The mother was satisfied. She sat back. Then she tensed up again. Doctor? Yes? Should I say this? Maybe I shouldn't. I've never talked about this before. My daughter doesn't know about this. I've never told her. Well. You see, my father, the witchdoctor, he told me that his powers would be passed on when he died. But not to his children, not to me. His powers would be passed on to his grandchil-

dren. And the oldest, this daughter, this girl, would have his powers.

By this time my thoughts about the clinical situation had been stirred. Do you think that Mary's experience has something to do with your father? Oh yes, she answered. But we don't talk about those things anymore, because, you know, we're Presbyterians now, and people don't believe in witchcraft anymore. But what if they did, I asked. How would you handle something like this?

The mother was now animated, and the daughter was listening intently. Well, we knew what to do. You see, in the old times, when someone was going to be given the powers of the spirits, was to be given the gifts of the witchdoctor, you had to struggle with the spirits. You had to prove you could rule them. Well, what would you do? I asked. Oh, there's nothing we can do. If this were the old times we would just open the door and let Mary wander out of the house at night. And she would go out and meet the spirits. And she would have to fight with them. And then she would come back with the powers . . . or maybe we would just find her out there after a few days, but that's the way it happens. . . .

I see, Well, what do you think about this now? Since this is not the old days, what do you think might be the best way to help Mary now?

Well, you know doctor, I've been thinking about that. You can't really practice much as a witchdoctor these days. It might be better if Mary were a Presbyterian and didn't accept the gift her grandfather left her.

Well, how would you work that out?

You see, doctor, we have to get rid of the spirits. We have to tell them that Mary doesn't want to fight with them. And then they'll go away and leave her alone. And she'll be O.K.

H'm. Well what do you have to do?

Oh, I don't know how to do that.

Who does?

Oh, Grandma does. She and some of the other old women know the ceremony. We all have to get together. And we would dress Mary up in the ceremonial dress, and we have to have prayers, and offerings, and we would anoint her, and say the prayers. . . .

Lest I leave the reader in suspense, at the end of one of the most fascinating experiences in my professional life, I reached an agreement with Mary and her mother. We agreed that it was not appropriate for Mary to attempt to achieve the mantle of power her grandfather had bequeathed her. That would be looking backward. So we agreed that Mary should renounce the legacy and look forward to becoming part of the modern world. The mother agreed to call the grandmother and see if she and the other tribal women could conduct a ritual of exorcism that night. I would return in one month. They agreed to see me again at that time.

Now it was January. With some trepidation I awaited their arrival. They came early! They were delighted to see me. I was a great doctor. They had followed my advice. The ceremony of exorcism had been conducted. It had been successful. Mary was healed.

Indeed, since that night of exorcism, the strange behavior had disappeared. The mother was happy, Mary was happy, I was happy. Because of my ongoing contact with this tribe, I had the opportunity to follow this family for many months thereafter. Mary remained healthy and happy. No more was she bothered. In contrast to her mien that first cold snowy December morning, when I saw her thereafter she was bright and bouncy, talkative and enthusiastic, like any other energetic adolescent girl beginning to become a woman.

Some Religious Observations

As I listened to this story, I thought of an Old Testament story that was almost identical, and I thought of the universality of human experience.

In the following passage, we read of Jacob wrestling with the angel of the Lord, in order to obtain power over the spirits:

> And Jacob was left alone; and there wrestled a man with him until the breaking of the day. And when he saw that he prevailed not against him, he touched the hollow of his thigh; and the hollow of Jacob's thigh was out of joint, as he wrestled with him. And he said, Let me go, for the day breaketh. And he said, I will not let thee go, except thou bless me. And he said unto him, What is thy name? And he said, Jacob. And he said, Thy name shall be called no more Jacob, but Israel: for as a prince hast thou power with God and with men, and hast prevailed.... And Jacob called the name of the place

> Peniel: for I have seen God face to face, and my life is preserved . . . and he halted upon his thigh. (Genesis 32:24–31)

What is remarkable is that over a span of perhaps six thousand years and over three continents we find the same interpretation. The man gains power over spirits by fighting with the spirits. If man wins, he then has special powers, he can command the spirits. He is a shaman, a healer, a witchdoctor. But it is a dangerous business, for to acquire the special powers requires a mortal combat. Jacob won, but he was crippled for life. And as for Mary, she feared her own death, or that of her siblings, if they got in the way of the combat.

In this case, we have the reenactment of an age-old saga: man in quest of power over the forces of his life.

Some Psychodynamic Observations

Although we have limited clinical material, we may rough out the following possible interpretations. The mother presents herself as the favored daughter of her father. Father heals her, using his spittle (semen?). Mother continues to frame her acceptability as a person around her external appearance, her beauty, her sexuality. She asks for acceptance as a desirable object from the therapist (father symbol). Daughter Mary appears on the scene at the time of adolescence as a maturing woman, hence competitor to mother. Mother does not give approval to daughter to become a sexually mature woman, for that poses a threat to mother. Mary projects the disapproving mother into the hallucinatory ghost object who would kill her. But also the projected forbidden object is the father figure who lies upon her in bed—the incestuous father. Mary wanders in the field and finds blood in the fields (menstrual blood?) where her girl friend was killed. . . . the sibling competitive rivalry between mother and daughter is projected onto the fear of Mary's siblings being killed by the spirits.

The conflict is resolved. The mother is reaffirmed in her role as woman. She in turn, in concert with her own mother, participates in a symbolic ritual which gives daughter, mother, granddaughter the sanction and approval to mature, to grow up, to become a sexually mature woman. Daughter Mary is no longer a competitive rival, seeking to gain the exclusive rights and affections of the witchdoctor grandfather (oedipal father). So mother can now allow daughter Mary to become a woman in her own right. Result: daughter no longer acts out the mother-daughter conflict.

A Trans-Cultural Perspective

Our observations are in concert with the work of Melford Spiro who has shown how one can look at various possession states and methods of healing from both the western psychodynamic perspective and from the cultural perspective of the indigenous healer. It is of note that, in Spiro's work on possession, the most common conflict was sexual conflict. Spiro notes that the dissociative state of possession deals with the fear of retaliation, which is certainly true in this case (1967).

But given the fact that we deal with a dissociative state, can we consider this an abnormal state? Here we have an instance in which the particular psychodynamic of family life was acted out in a pattern provided by the culture. Within the culture set, the behavioral pattern exhibited by Mary was not unusual nor unexpected. In fact, she acted out the cultural norm.

In this instance we can note that the diagnosis of acute schizophrenia is understandable, but inappropriate. However, the family itself was caught in an interesting and pathetic cultural bind. If they had been living within the traditional Indian culture, they would have followed the prescribed patterns of response. We may assume that the deviant behavior would have been appropriately resolved. However, the family was caught between two cultures, between two belief systems. And so the family was immobilized. The behavior of the patient, Mary, was congruent with the belief system of the old culture, while the treatment of the hospitals was congruent with the new belief system.

What provided a significant intervention in this impasse was a sanction by a scientific professional psychotherapist to an indigenous cultural healer. And that collaborative support enabled this natural system to function and to restore a person to function.

A psychodynamic interpretation of this case intervention might include the possibility of a "transference cure." In this instance the mother experiences reaffirmation of her beauty, her wholeness, her person, from the psychiatrist (witchdoctor-transferential father). She need not feel threatened by her daughter's emerging sexuality, for mother is still the favored one. Then too, the psychiatrist (transference father symbol) enlists the aid of mother (herself now the successful oedipal competitor) to help daughter grow up. And this is allowed because daughter will not be stronger than mother.

Although these psychodynamic speculations may be appropriate and accurate, I do not think that one can conclude that this explains the total interaction.

In my opinion, these psychoanalytic motifs may indicate why this particular intervention was so rapidly catalytic of a therapeutic resolution. The psychodynamic cards were stacked in my favor.

On the other hand, the family had sought medical treatment on many occasions before they came to see me. The medical interventions could have been given the same symbolic ascriptions, which I propose were ascribed to me. And the failure of medical treatment, or the knowledge of the tribal beliefs could have resulted in the family going ahead and conducting the exorcism ceremonies. Yet they have not ostensibly even thought about exorcism.

If this family were fully participant in the western thought world of the psychiatrist, then I would have considered a typical family therapy model of intervention. But this family was not in my thought world—it only looked like they were thinking and living within the western scientific tradition of medicine. Indeed, they themselves were only conscious of their western world thought and beliefs. Whether one can consider this solely an intrapsychic repression is an interesting problem. My own inclination is to conclude that this family had a higher than usual level of repressive defense structures. But also that idiosyncratic family style was reinforced by the transitional Indian culture in which they live, in which repression of the "old" belief systems is built into the experiential world of living on the reservation.

I seriously doubt that a scientific style psychotherapy intervention would have been of any value at all. Not that one cannot conduct rather typical psychotherapy with Indians living on the reservation. For I did conduct a great deal of straightforward psychodynamic interpretive psychotherapy. But the problem of Mary and her mother was embedded in the traditional Indian belief system. I think that psychotherapy with either Mary or her mother around other issues might have been possible and appropriate within the western scientific frame of thought. But with the acting out of the problem within the framework of the traditional Indian belief system, in order to conduct a scientific psychotherapy, one would have to translate the whole problem from one belief system to another belief system.

The alternative which I followed was to take the traditional Indian belief system for real. To accept the interpretation of cause and effect within that system for real also, and to support an intervention within that system that would indeed be real.

Healing Symbols and the Future

It has long been recognized that there are many similarities if not identities between the western psychotherapist and the folk healer. Jerome Frank (1973) has elegantly summarized the non-specific *extrinsic* factors common to all psychotherapeutic healers while Prince has recently reviewed evidence for the fact that there are common *intrinsic* self-healing factors in the client, which any healer may catalyze. Thus, there may be common extrinsic and intrinsic factors in psychotherapy regardless of the particular cultural context, language, or belief system. Thus, it might seem that moving across cultural systems of belief would be relatively simple, if one could make the necessary translations and understand the idioms.

But I propose that the matter of therapeutic healing is more profound than just the extrinsic factors of healing alluded to above. We see clearly in the healing rituals of folk healers a right symbolization. What we do not see so clearly is that western psychotherapy is also a healing ritual with its own symbols.

Symbols are vital aspects of our existence. As Rollo May notes:

> The symbol draws together and unites experience. It bridges the inescapable antinomies of life— conscious and unconscious, reason and emotion, individual and society, history and the present. . . . A symbol is real and efficacious only to those who commit themselves to it.

It is noteworthy that in folk society, anthropologists such as Turner (1969) and Lévi-Strauss (1966), have shown that the healing rituals symbolize not only personal conflict and resolution, but at the same time mirror the cultural conflict and its resolu-

tion. The symbols of the rituals unite the person and his culture. The client and the healer both communicate effectively through the symbolic modes which are given them in their culture.

Now Perry London (1964) has pointed out that all psychotherapies have three common elements: (1) a theory of the nature of man, (2) a superordinate moral code, (3) healing techniques which symbolically evoke a healing transformation in accord with the first two elements.

In this light I suggest that western modes of psychotherapy are extremely limited to a small segment of our current society—at least as widely practiced. Henri Ellenberger (1970) notes the subcultural consciousness within which psychotherapy has been symbolized:

> By the end of the nineteenth century the upper classes could no longer be content with the existing method of hypnotic and suggestive therapy and demanded a new, nonauthoritarian psychotherapy that would explain to the patient what was going on in his own mind.

And again:

> One had to find a psychotherapy for educated people; it would be a non-authoritarian method, which would keep personal liberty intact, explain to the patient what was going on in his own mind, and guarantee that all the methods employed acting only through his own psyche.

Furthermore, it is widely recognized that the linguistic verbal content of psychotherapy may not be the most pertinent aspect of therapy, but rather there is a therapeutic transaction that symbolizes rationalistic construction of reality for "psychotherapeutic man." I find it interesting that the most recent symbolic-linguistic study of psychotherapy is aptly titled "The Structure of Magic."

In his history of psychotherapy, Jan Ehrenwald (1976) begins with the magical encounter (which is symbolization) and leads us finally to encounter groups (which, too, is symbolization). Is the history of psychotherapy then not linear but circular?

Returning to Ellenberger, he concludes his magnum opus aware of the fact that the history and evolution of psychotherapy may be circular, for he says:

> The dynamic psychotherapist is thus dealing . . . with psychic realities. . . . But what exactly are psychic realities? . . . there are many kinds of psychic

realities, and they often are contradictory and incompatible with each other, though endowed with the same character of certainty for those who are working with them. . . . The coexistence of two mutually incompatible approaches to the cognition of the human psyche shocks the scientist's yearning for unity (1970).

Western psychoanalytic psychotherapy, I submit, has emerged as a healing ritual, based upon a particular western rationalistic, deterministic, and empiricist image of man. It has its own existentialist morality. And its therapeutic technique symbolizes this modern reality. Martin Grotjahn, the eminent psychoanalyst grasps this latter point well in his most recent book, "The Voice of the Symbol." Therein Grotjahn describes psychoanalytic technique as fundamentally a process for symbolizing reality:

> He seeks the outline of the future in which "free creative symbol integration" will fulfill the only demand, the only duty which man has to life: to live to the fullest capacity of his potential, to experience life with all his courage, to become literate in terms of understanding himself and to integrate his unconscious with his intelligence (1976).

The problem inherent in Grotjahn's description of psychoanalytic symbolizing is his assumption that Freud was the first to discover a method for understanding the symbol and the unconscious and thereby create a symbolizing therapy that integrates conscious man with unconscious realities of his socio-cultural development.

I suggest that the same discovery and process of integrating symbolization can be found in the therapies of indigenous folk healers. I believe the ethnographic evidence indicates that we have sold the folk healers short. We have interpreted their therapies solely as simple-minded magic rituals whereas the potency and efficacy of their therapies may be every bit as efficacious with their culture as psychoanalytic therapy is in our culture. And perhaps with the same failures, as well!

In turn, there seems to be an almost romantic fascination with folk healers today. But belief in supernatural demonology and exorcism is not an unmixed blessing, even if supernatural rites of exorcism may be effective. For the particular forms of supernaturalism that become distilled as witchcraft and demonology contain a virulent disguise of the social ills of the society, and invite the acting out of personalized destructiveness.

Thus, Geoffrey Parrinder concludes:

> Belief in witchcraft is one of the great fears from which mankind has suffered. It has taken its toll literally in blood. . . . Witchcraft must be symbolic. It is a belief which helps to interpret and canalize the disease of society . . . (witchcraft beliefs) resolve certain conflicts or problems: but I did not say that this is a good solution. The aggression invited by witchcraft beliefs is as harmful as anything a society can produce in the way of disruptive practices; the relief offered by witch-hunting and witch-punishing is no more than temporary and their capacity to allay anxieties no more illusory: for if witchcraft beliefs resolve certain fears and tensions, they also produce others . . . the kind of remedy which both becomes a drug and poisons the system (1958).

The personalization of social evil into demonology is the transformation to be avoided, not supernaturalism.

Paul Pruyser (1968) states it well: "The great question is: if illusions are needed, how can we have those that are capable of correction, and how can we have those that will not deteriorate into delusions." Similarly, Becker says: "If men live in myths and not absolutes, there is nothing we can do or say about that. But we can argue for nondestructive myths" (1973).

It is appropriate now, to examine the future of psychoanalytic western psychotherapy, both in relation to other folk healing systems and unto itself.

First, I have alluded to the data which allow us to conclude that psychoanalytic psychotherapy is part of a mythic system of western man, that its view of man, its morality, and its symbolizing techniques are relevant and efficacious only within the symbolizing mythic culture out of which it has developed. Therefore, we face a major task of reevaluating the structure and future of the interface between this symbolizing psychotherapy and other cultural views of man and the attendant symbolizing therapies of those cultures. Even within western culture there are widely divergent sub-cultures, such as the various religious associations of America for whom the psychoanalytic construction of reality is by no means easily made relevant. I only make passing note of the many modifications of psychotherapy underway today in America to provide effective therapeutic services to other than the educated well-to-do intelligentsia of America.

Second, let us turn to the future of psychoanalytic psychotherapy itself. As we have seen, psychoanalysis and its derivative dynamic therapies are an integral part of the scientific epoch of western civilization—the time of the humanistic rational man.

As noted herein, we live in the twilight of the scientific age—we have moved on to the age of existential man. Accordingly, it is not surprising that there is widespread disillusionment with the psychoanalytic model of man.

S. K. Pande (1968), a non-western psychiatrist, observes how the western cosmology created "deficits in the Western way of life . . . negative psychological implications . . . and Western psychotherapy, especially the psychoanalytic model, as a symbolic and substantive undertaking to correct them." But the psychoanalytic model becomes increasingly irrelevant as a symbolically effective force as it addresses a vanishing breed of humanistic rational men. Indeed irrational man, or at least existential man, is creating a new view of man, a new morality, and therefore new symbolizing therapeutic techniques, as represented in the existential psychotherapies, the humanistic psychotherapies, and direct experiential encounters of sundry form.

In all of this we are gradually becoming aware of the fact that the ontological underpinnings of any psychotherapy is critical to its relevance, acceptance, and efficacy. Psychotherapy in the western world is indeed a supernaturalistic system, that parades itself as a naturalistic system. Consider the trenchant observations of Ernest Becker:

> Often psychotherapy seems to promise the moon: a more constant joy, delight, celebration of life, perfect love, and perfect freedom . . . psychotherapists are caught up in modern culture and forced to be part of it. Commercial industrialism promised western man a paradise on earth, . . . that replaced the paradise in heaven of Christian myth. And now psychology must replace them both with the myth of paradise through self-knowledge. This is the promise of psychology, and for the most part psychotherapists are obliged to live it and embody it (1973).

At issue is the fact that over history and centuries of time, folk healers, the psychotherapists of societies and culture were unabashedly part of the supernaturalistic system. Thus, they moved easily between the treatment of accident, illness, misfortune, interpersonal conflict and existential malaise.

But as Ellenberger (1970) has so nicely illustrated, the historical development of western psychotherapy has led it to a fragmented, isolated, and naturalistic position within society. The crisis of modern psychiatry is reflected in the fact that medical science cannot provide a belief system to live by, nor can psychiatry as a branch of medicine. Thus, we see a return of "psychiatry to medicine"—as a limited enterprise. Meanwhile, the psychotherapeutic side of psychiatry has been increasingly vulnerable to competing systems and persons each offering discipleship.

The problem is this: that the *atomization* and *particularization* of misfortune in western society leads to the *fragmentation* of healing. We have a seeming paradox. We see that psychotherapeutic healing deeply involves ideology, belief, and symbolization of reality. Yet in western society we have attempted to create a non-ideological, belief-free psychotherapy. I suggest that psychotherapy in the west has survived thus far because it has been based on a covert belief system. As we have unmasked that covert belief system, psychotherapists are now making unabashed pitches for their method of psychotherapy, which is a belief system.

Again Becker pertinently observes:

> Now there are only three ways, I think, that psychology itself can become an adequate belief system. One of them is to be a creative genius as a psychologist and to use psychology as the immorality vehicle for oneself—as Freud and subsequent psychoanalysts have done. Another is to use the language and concepts of psychotherapy in much of one's waking life, so that it becomes a lived belief system . . . this is one of the reasons that psychotherapy has moved away from the Freudian intellectual model to the new experiential model. . . . The third and final way is merely an extension and sophistication of this. It is to take psychology and deepen it with religious and metaphysical associations so that it becomes actually a religious belief system with some breadth and depth. At the same time, the psychotherapist himself beams out the steady quiet power of transference and becomes the guru-figure of religion (1973).

In conclusion, the symbolizing power of psychoanalytic psychotherapy is waning as the society out of which it sprang changes. I suggest that psychoanalytic psychotherapy is a supernaturalistic system of belief. (In this case the God and cosmos of science.) But its ontological grounding, its fundamental commitment to humanistic rational man, its method of experimental empiricism, is melting away. We can see the truth pointed out some time ago by the French anthropologist Lévi-Strauss, that the psychoanalyst and the shaman are structurally the same. Both engage in powerful rituals that are symbolizing exercises of their culture. *Both are exorcists.*

My interpretation of all the foregoing data is that the reemergence of demonology and exorcism in our current society is symptomatic of an ontological crisis in western society. Psychoanalytic psychotherapy is losing its symbolic power because the society no longer strongly invests in the symbols of a scientific cosmos. And where the symbols have lost their power, the accompanying techniques become vapid. Accordingly, we see the search for a new cosmos, a new symbolic integration of life, and new healers invested with therapeutic powers because they participate in the new symbolization. One solution is regressive, a return to the ancient forms and symbols of demonology. Another solution, that of a scientific psychotherapy has been tried and is failing because of loss of its symbolic community and the erosion of its ontology. I propose that the future may produce psychotherapies that are much more explicit in their ontology; that there will be a delineation of the limited goals of treatment that can be offered by psychiatry as a universal science; that the more overarching existential problematics of life may well be addressed within a diversity of socio-culturally specific psychotherapeutics, which are part of specific supernaturalistic communities.

It appears to me that western psychotherapy has engaged in the self illusion that we offer a culture-free, value free, ideology-free cure, under the universal rubric of mental health. But as philosopher Joseph Margolis acutely observes:

> Psychotherapy, then, is primarily concerned with a technical goal, the preservation and restoration of mental health; nevertheless its own development leads it, inevitably, to take up the role of moral legislator (1966).

Thus, it may be that we are on the edge of a new interpretation of psychotherapy. The notion of a scientific psychotherapy may be a chimera. The challenge for tomorrow is to explore the relationship between universalistic dimensions of psychotherapy which are naturalistic and particularistic dimensions of psychotherapy that must be supernaturalistic, naturalistic.

Summary

This study started with an exploration of the current social interest in demonology and exorcism in western society. We have seen that beliefs in demonology are part of a larger supernaturalistic cosmology. However, acting out of demonology beliefs occurs only in times where there is social oppression and loss of social integration. Modern demonology can be seen to be part of the social repudiation of the scientific determinism of rational man, coincident with the rise of existential irrationalism. The practice of exorcism is but one example of the powerful use of symbolic transformations in healing rituals. Seen in terms of symbolic actions, psychoanalytic psychotherapy is also a practice of exorcism. This leads us then to examine the symbolic systems of society that incorporate both the client and the healer. It is seen that western psychotherapy is just as much a part of its culture as other healing systems. We close with an eye to the future, can there be a psychotherapy that is not supernaturalistic?

Divination

Lucy Mair

Because the future is largely unknowable, human beings everywhere regard it with a degree of healthy concern or downright fear. Indeed, much of modern science is appreciated because of its attempts to predict future events. But even science is repeatedly reminded of the difficulties inherent in trying to foresee the future; witness the problems of correctly forecasting earthquakes, floods, economic cycles, and the like.

Divination, a worldwide practice, is a mystical technique for acquiring knowledge about past, present, or future events that is unobtainable using ordinary explanatory methods. Rituals of divination are vast and varied and typically involve the use of oracles, omens, and ordeals. Oracles require the performance of an experiment to determine the unknown, whereas omens need only simple observation, usually of some natural phenomena such as movement of heavenly bodies, flights of birds, schools of fish, or any of hundreds of other signs or guides. Ordeals are trials by divination, whereby the accused person's body becomes the determinant of the unknown.

In this article Lucy Mair examines various types of divination used by several African populations. She ends the article by asking if people who consult diviners really believe in their mystical power. Her answer is that people in distress rely on the nearest help available, and although there may be some doubts regarding the skill of some diviners, there are no doubts about the phenomenon of divination itself.

Although Professor Mair refers throughout the article to African diviners as "witchdoctors," anthropologists today prefer the terms shamans, curers, healers, *and* traditional doctors.

Lucy Mair was a British anthropologist who taught at the London School of Economics and several other universities in Great Britain and the United States.

Reprinted from *Witchcraft* (George Wiedenfeld & Nicolson, 1969), pp. 76–101, by permission of the publisher.

SINCE WITCHCRAFT IS BY DEFINITION AN ACTIVity that cannot be detected by everyday means, it must be tracked down by the actions of people, or the manipulation of objects, believed to have mystical power to reveal secrets. The general term for processes of this kind is divination, "the endeavor to obtain information about things future, or otherwise removed from ordinary perception, by consulting informants other than human." They can be divided into three main classes. Objects such as the Zande rubbing-board, which answer questions automatically, are usually referred to as oracles. In anthropological literature the word divination is commonly used for more complicated objects, the behaviour of which has to be interpreted by an expert who manipulates them. Both these processes have been called "mechanical divination." In the third type, hidden knowledge is revealed by men or women believed to have special powers, speaking as the mediums of spirits or otherwise in a condition of heightened excitement. Some diviners, though not all, are believed to have been called to their vocation by a supernatural experience. Most mediums are persons believed to have been summoned to the service of the spirit on whose behalf they speak by some kind of psychological disturbance. But it is possible to become a "witch-doctor" simply by receiving appropriate instruction and ritual treatment from already qualified practitioners. This is the method recognized by the Zande.

The Zande witch-doctor, like his Zulu counterpart, is physician, magician, and diviner, and the word that describes his mystical activities cannot be used of his everyday medical ones. He must be taught his profession by a qualified practitioner and must undergo a ritual of initiation; fathers may teach their sons, but anyone may learn the secrets of the craft for a fee. These consist in knowledge of the properties of plants, particularly those which are held to give the power of divining, and of the tricks by which the doctors purport to remove alien substances from the bodies of their patients. But a part of the training of a witch-doctor consists in actually eating a sufficient quantity of the divining medicines. These are said to give the diviner *mangu,* the same word that is used for the witchcraft substance that he purports to detect in others. There is a close parallel here with the defensive pythons that the Nyakyusa headman acquires by drinking magical potions and employs to combat the pythons of witches. But some practitioners prefer to use a different word, one which refers only to the medicines that give the divining power, and others say that if any diviner is actually a witch, this is because he happens to have been born with witchcraft substance before he ate anti-witchcraft medicine.

Zande divination is a public event, indeed the most interesting event of village life. A séance is held at the house of some man who has a problem troubling him, and it may be combined with the initiation of a new recruit to the profession. All doctors who are within convenient distance attend, perhaps half a dozen; it was said, in about 1930, that their numbers were increasing too fast and that their skill was decreasing in proportion. Any person present may put a question to any one of them. The occasion is one of great excitement, generated by drumming and singing. The diviners dance, shaking hand-bells and making a clatter with wooden bells round their waists and bunches of rattling seeds round their arms and legs. After a concerted opening performance, individuals dance in reply to questions put to them. The dancing is supposed to activate the medicines which give the answer to the man who has eaten them; he dances until he is breathless and exhausted, then recovers himself and speaks. As Evans-Pritchard remarks, while he may be thinking what to answer all the time he is dancing, this is clearly not a matter purely of detached reasoning. What the practitioners themselves interpret as the activity of the medicines they have eaten that morning is the effect of the general rhythmic noise and exhausting movement; as they describe what happens, the medicines suddenly make the diviner's heart beat faster at the thought of a particular name, and this is the name of the witch. But he does not openly denounce the witch; he speaks in hints which will mean more to the man consulting him than to the rest of the audience, and leaves his client to draw his own conclusions. As Evans-Pritchard reminds us, he believes in the dangers of witchcraft as firmly as any

of his clients, and he does not wish to expose himself to the revenge of somebody he has accused, which could be directed against him at a time when he was not protected by his anti-witchcraft medicines. He is an everyday member of the community, not a specialist called in from outside who does not have to live with consequences of his diagnosis.

Evans-Pritchard's study of the witch-doctor's place in Zande society is the best possible corrective to the notion of the "dreaded witch-doctor." In Zande eyes he is not the only, or the most reliable, detector of witches; a man who has consulted a witch-doctor checks his answers by reference to one of the oracles which are believed to be more reliable because they operate automatically. But he is "a special agent summoned from time to time with a general commission to ferret out witch-activities in the neighborhood and to protect people against them." In the heightened atmosphere of a séance he is an impressive and perhaps even alarming figure, particularly in view of the Zande theory of witchcraft as something innate of which its possessor may not even be aware. Anyone at a séance may find that he is denounced as a witch, and although names are rarely named, in Evans-Pritchard's view people are always afraid that they will be. Moreover, he was present on one occasion where this did happen; the accused person, however, was not struck with terror but got up and threatened to knife the diviner, who then danced again and gave a different answer— and later said in private that the accused man's behavior was an admission of guilt.

But in everyday life he has as much prestige, and no more, than that enjoyed in Europe by a consultant physician outside his hospital. He has special knowledge which others lack, but these others are well aware of the jealousies and quarrels between different specialists, and regard them with amusement. A witch-doctor of high repute is consulted by the princes and nobles who command the greatest respect in Zande society, and this gives him a certain prestige; but it is the prestige of a favored employee, like that of some musicians in the eighteenth century. But those who do not attain eminence in their profession are objects neither of admiration nor of dread, and indeed are often said to be charlatans, though there is no Zande who rejects entirely the belief in the witch-doctor's powers, and there cannot be as long as all Zande are convinced of the reality of witchcraft. Moreover, they do not spend all their time practicing their profession; most of the time they are farming their fields or hunting in the bush like their neighbours.

It is a peculiarity of the Zande witch-doctors that they claim to derive their power of divination solely from the medicines they eat, and thus to speak in their own name and not in that of some spirit which is making them its mouthpiece. The Zande are un-usual in assuming that witchcraft is responsible for all their troubles, and not considering the just anger of some spiritual being as a possible alternative. More commonly diviners who do not rely on me-chanical means are believed to speak in the name of some spirit by which they are possessed, and this spirit is expected to identify one among various pos-sible sources of the trouble about which the diviner is consulted.

Spirit Mediums

The Nyoro, in the west of Uganda, consult men who they believe are possessed by spirits (called *mbandwa*) and reveal secret matters as their mouth-pieces. Nyoro traditional religion was built around such spirits. They bore the names of ancient kings of a mythical dynasty that is supposed to have founded the kingdom and then mysteriously disap-peared. Different lineages were under the guardian-ship of different spirits, and each had a medium through which the *mbandwa* could communicate with the living by "mounting into his (or her) head." In recent years great numbers of new *mbandwa* have appeared, just as the minor spirits are said to have multiplied in Ghana. The new *mbandwa*, who are distinguished from the old by being called "black," are not the guardian spirits of particular lineages; their mediums are persons much more like the Zande witch-doctors, who will identify the source of mystical sickness for a fee. Beattie holds, as do many of those who have studied contemporary ways of detecting witchcraft and sorcery in Africa, that this increase is a response to the increase of anxiety among African populations which find themselves disoriented by the changes that have been thrust on them, first by colonial rule and mission teaching, and now by their own westernized rulers. It would be difficult to measure or compare the quantity of anxiety in African societies at different times, but an indisputable fact is that today very many Africans earn cash incomes and can pay to consult spirit mediums. Indeed, Beattie offers this also as an ex-planation of the proliferation of new *mbandwa*. A large number of the questions put to these mediums are aimed at identifying sorcerers. Nyoro believe that the new "black" *mbandwa* themselves practice sorcery, both by sending their tutelary spirits to af-flict others, and by hiring out their knowledge to kill the enemies of people who consult them. The rem-edy for affliction by a *mbandwa* is to become a mem-ber of his cult, and to be initiated into the cult a person must pay a fee to the medium who organizes the initiation; this is a field in which the opportuni-ties for exploitation are clear.

It is obvious that there is more room for flexibility in this kind of divination than there is where the be-havior of an inanimate object is held to give a yes-or-no answer. Intermediate between these methods is that in which the diviner interprets the behavior of an inanimate object. But it is essential to any of these processes that the possible answers are limited by the ideas that present themselves to the consultant. The medium may be expected to guess what is trou-bling his client; but he guesses within a recognized range of likely troubles, and the answer he gives may be far from explicit. If he diagnoses witchcraft as the cause he may still stop short of identifying the witch. Thus a Tswana diviner might say, "The wife of an older brother has bewitched you," or "Your trouble comes from the righteous anger of an older kinsman," and a Ghanaian medium may simply ad-vise someone to move out of reach of a witch who is harming him.

Oracle Operators

A person who is in trouble or concerned about the possibility of trouble in the future may either oper-ate an oracle for himself, as has been described in the case of the Zande, or consult a specialist. Privately-operated oracles must work on yes-or-no principles, since the ability to read the meaning of a combina-tion of symbols calls for special knowledge. The Zande rubbing-board and termite oracles give straightforward answers to simple questions, but when poison [*benge*] is administered to chickens the most elaborate care is taken to check the results. A question is put twice over (two chickens are used), and unless the same answer is given at each test the oracle is held to be inconclusive. Then the same question is put in negative form.

The Zande do not conceive this as a simple mechanical test, but believe that the poison is in some mysterious way considering the problem while it is in the body of the chicken. Hence they do not administer it to fully-grown birds because, they say, such birds die too quickly, before the poison has had a chance to consider its answer. The administration of the poison and the questioning of the oracle—that is the poison, making its answer known by the reaction of the chicken—are held to call for considerable skill, and there may be three persons present at a consultation, whom Evans-Pritchard calls the consultant, the operator and the questioner. The consultant is the man who wants to know the answer, and who provides the poison and the chickens, the operator is the one who makes the chicken swallow the poison, and the questioner addresses the poison, often at some length, say for five or ten minutes at a time. One man may play all three roles but most prefer to rely on friends whose skill they respect. But the skill is not that of a closed profession; it is a matter of intelligence and practice. The operator needs to know how much poison to give, how to jerk the chicken about to "stir up the poison," and when it is time to throw it on the ground and see whether it dies or lives. The questioner must know how to put the questions so that the oracle understands them clearly, since, although it is addressed at such length, the actual matter it is called on to decide must be capable of a clear positive or negative answer. If several people take part in a consultation they agree on the question before it starts. This does not always take so crude a form as "Is X responsible for my sickness?" Rather the oracle might be asked "Does the sickness come from my own homestead or that of my wife's parents?" When the answer is received the consultant might either ask a more specific question, or go to the homestead held responsible and entreat its members as a body to withdraw the anger to which the sickness was ascribed.

As can be seen from this account, an oracle does not necessarily give an unambiguous answer, even when the method of consulting it seems designed to secure one. In this case, since the consultant frames the questions, it would seem that he may prefer to avoid naming possible enemies. When it is for a diviner to give the answer he may avoid the final con-

clusion in much the same way by saying "The sickness comes from your father's brothers" or some other category of relatives.

Consultation of a supposedly automatic oracle whose answers nevertheless need interpretation is on the border of professional divination, in which the operator rather than the objects he manipulates is expected to give the answer the consultant is seeking. But not many processes of private divination are as elaborate as the consultation of *benge*. A number have been described from the Lugbara. The most widely used is the rubbing-stick, which operates on the same principle as the Zande rubbing-board. A twist of grass is rubbed up and down against a piece of cane while names are "placed before it"—the names of persons, living or dead, who may be responsible for the trouble about which the oracle is consulted; obviously the operator himself chooses the names. The right name is indicated when the grass sticks. Another way of operating the rubbing-stick, used by the Nyoro, is for the operator to wet the stick and simply run his finger and thumb up and down it.

Lugbara use other oracles to confirm the answer given by the rubbing-stick, since neither it nor any other is assumed to be infallible. Or rather it is assumed that an oracle may be dishonest. People do not say that oracles make mistakes but that they "tell lies," and that the chances that an answer from the rubbing-stick may be true or false are about equal. But it is always the oracle, and not the operator, that is supposed to be dishonest. The further oracles need not be operated by the same man whose rubbing-stick gave the first answer. They are all held to work independently of human manipulation and therefore to be more reliable.

The owner of a rubbing-stick oracle which has a reputation for "telling lies" is held to be shamed by its behavior rather than to be himself to blame. But he has to interpret what his oracle has "said," and here there is room for differences in skill between one operator and another. The skill is held to be given by God, who conveys to a man in a dream that he has it. Only older men practice as rubbing-stick operators. Elders of lineages—the only holders of authority in Lugbara—often have their own rubbing-stick, but an elder does not become a professional operator of oracles. Such men are very often the younger brothers of elders. A man in that position cannot hope to attain independent authority, since an elder must be succeeded by his son, but he can gain influence and reputation as an oracle operator. Others with this skill are men who are feared as suspected witches. The confirmatory oracles may be operated by anyone who owns them; they do not require a supernatural authorization.

Diviners

A different method is employed by the Yombe of the Zambia-Malawi border. They, like many other peoples, regard it as a necessary part of mortuary ritual to discover by divination who is responsible for the death. To do so they send a man to hunt a duiker (a small antelope), and see whether he kills a male or a female. If the former, the death comes from the man's own kin, if the latter from his wife's. The questioning is repeated, each time offering two alternatives. This is a long-drawn-out process, involving a series of expeditions in pursuit of animals that are nowadays very scarce, and it may be given up before a clear answer is reached. This is particularly likely to happen if the answers point towards the people responsible for making the enquiry.

We may describe as a diviner someone who does not purport to be speaking with the voice of a spirit, but who goes beyond the simple oracle operator in that he interprets the answer that is supposed to be given by the behaviour of the mechanical objects he uses. Oracle operators no doubt do this to some extent, but the essence of divination in this sense is that the process used allows for much greater complexity of interpretation. A very common African method consists in throwing a number of objects on the ground and seeing how they fall. If the objects are all alike—cowrie shells or pieces of leather, for example—the answer to the question depends on which way up they are. But many diviners have a collection of different objects each of which has a symbolic meaning, or many possible meanings, and the answer they give is arrived at by seeing how these objects lie in relation to one another. The interpretations given by such diviners resemble those offered in telling fortunes by playing-cards, the favourite method of divination in Europe from the fifteenth century.

The commonest Nyoro method is to drop a number of cowrie shells on the ground after whispering an address to them, and to see which way up, and in what kind of pattern, they have fallen. In his address the diviner reminds the shells that he is an authoritative practitioner, using the skill that has come to him from his forefathers, and may also adjure them to give a true answer. There are a number of standard interpretations of a very general nature. If the cowries, which have had the top of the shell sliced off so that they will be flat, fall with the sliced-off side upwards, the prognosis is good; if one falls on another, someone will die; if they are scattered, someone is going on a journey, and if three or more are in a line he will return safely. But none of these indications by itself tells the victim of misfortune what has caused his trouble; and it is Beattie's opinion that when it comes to ascribing responsibility each diviner makes his own interpretation of the answers given by the shells to questions prompted by his own knowledge of the circumstances or by what his client tells him.

This kind of divination can also be used for the more specific purpose of assigning responsibility for a death, by mentioning names one after the other in the same way as with the rubbing-board. This is the popular method among the Shona in Rhodesia, and it is done there in the presence of persons among whom whoever is suspected is likely to be included.

The Ndembu of Angola and western Zambia regard as the most reliable of their many methods of divination the tossing of objects in a basket so that they form a heap at one side, and then seeing which are on top. In their case the objects are all different, and each has its meaning. Turner, who worked in the Ndembu area of Zambia from 1950–4, has analyzed the symbolism of the objects used, and the metaphors in the vocabulary of divination, basing his conclusions on statements made to him by diviners whom he knew. The divinatory objects are shaken up in a winnowing-basket, which is said to sift truth from falsehood as winnowing sifts grain from chaff. Turner was given meanings for twenty-eight objects used as symbols, but he has only discussed the more important ones. All diviners do not have identical collections; most have twenty to thirty objects.

These include, first, small figures of human beings and one of an *ilomba* snake, the human-headed serpent that is believed to be a sorcerer's familiar. A group of three, man, woman and child, fastened together, are called "the elders," and may be nominated by the diviner to stand for some body of kinsmen concerned in the affairs of the clients—the chief and his kin, the village headman and his kin, or a lineage related to one client. A piece of red clay means a grudge, a piece of white clay innocence. If "the elders" are on top of the heap with the red clay, the people they represent have a grudge which may have led one of them to attack by sorcery the person on whose behalf the consultation is being held. If they are on top with white clay, the group they represent are innocent.

A figure representing a man in the posture of mourning indicates whether a sickness about which the diviner is consulted will be fatal or not, according as it appears on top of the heap of objects or is concealed by others. But this figure, called Katwambimbi, also stands for a double-dealer who instigates others to kill by sorcery, falsely telling someone that another is seeking to bewitch him.

The very hard and long-lasting stone of a local fruit, which is slow to ripen, stands for "a long time" and, among other things, for bewitching by means of the *ilomba* familiar, which is believed to cause a long sickness as the snake invisibly swallows its victim from the feet up. A small wooden model of a drum, associated with the drumming ritual to cure a person of possession by spirits, shows that a sick person for whom the divination is being conducted has been afflicted by a spirit and not by a human enemy.

Among the human figures is one representing a folklore character who vacillates, cannot make up his mind, will not commit himself or acts inconsistently. If this figure comes to the top of the heap something has gone wrong; no clear answer can be given. This can be blamed on the interference of witchcraft.

Although Ndembu diviners speak in their own persons when practicing their art, they are not held to have acquired it merely by instruction. As is common in the case of mediums, a man learns that he is destined to become a diviner through a visitation of affliction from a spirit, here known as Kayong'u. As this was described to Turner by one who had experienced it, he suffered physical and not mental illness. But the ritual of Kayong'u, which was performed to cure the illness, and did do so, included the experience of possession by the spirit, manifested in bouts of trembling, and it is said to be in a recurrence of this trembling, sent by the spirit, that the diviner shakes his basket of symbols. Kayong'u also sends him a pricking sensation which, a diviner said, "tells him to look closely." The presence of Kayong'u in

his body is supposed to be shown by a kind of asthmatic breathing or grunting.

Yet the Ndembu diviner is in full possession of his faculties, and there is no question of Kayong'u inspiring his speech. He is to find out where his clients have come from, on whose behalf, and the nature of their trouble. It is a characteristic of Ndembu consultations that they are not made by a single individual either on his own behalf or on that of one of his dependents, as is much more common. How many people make up the party will depend upon the seriousness of the trouble and the importance of the sufferer. The death of a leading man is the most serious matter of all, and in such a case all sections of the area in which he was important will be represented. If a village headman has died or is sick, someone should go to the diviner from each of the two or three sublineages making up the village, as well as a representative of people living there in virtue of affinal relationships.

While shaking his basket and putting questions supposedly to it the diviner is in fact, at each stage, narrowing down a field which is already limited by circumstances. He must find what they want to know, but here too the field is limited, as Turner points out; nearly all consultations concern "death, illness, reproductive trouble or misfortune at hunting." If the matter is a death he will ask questions— expecting the answer "yes"—about the nature and duration of the illness. Then he will identify the dead person's name. Again, Ndembu names fall into a limited number of categories by their meaning, and he begins by asking "Does the name belong to the earth, to the trees, to the water, to insects, to animals, to fishes" going on to the sub-classes within these categories and finally to the name itself. This is the method of all guessing games. Even in countries where everyone plays these games, some people seem to have an uncanny skill at them, and in a culture where they are not an everyday pastime, skill in quickly reaching the right answer makes an enormous impression. He then finds in the same way the village of victim or sufferer. This must be within a limited area, since the people will probably have come on foot and are not likely to have travelled for many days. Then he must find the relationship of kinship or affinity to the victim of each of the consultants. "He might say," said one informant, "You are the dead person's older brother. This one is your youngest brother, but this one here is your brother-in-law." As a diviner put it, he finds out "through Kayong'u" and "by asking questions and by mentioning things one after the other." By this time he is in a field where his general knowledge of local gossip and of typical sources of enmity come to his aid. Now he must reveal the "grudge" that has caused the death or sickness, by the position of the red clay in his basket in relation to the human figures; he may make the "elders" stand for one or other subdivision in the village and see whether "the grudge" attaches itself to them.

The significance of the presence at the consultation of members of all sections of the village is that all may know the source of the grudge that has injured their village-mate. It is the task of the Ndembu diviner—as it is not that of many others—to assign guilt, and he does so by marking one of the consultants with red clay on his forehead and the rest with white. As will be made clearer in a later chapter, accused persons and their kin rarely accept such a judgment with meekness, and it is said of Ndembu diviners, who are more specific in their accusations than many others, that at the end of a consultation they must depart in haste for fear of violence.

Somewhat similar is the process of divination of the Pondo in the Cape Province of South Africa. Here too several people will visit a diviner together, and here the diviner is supposed to indicate where they come from and what their trouble is, simply by making statements. After each statement the consultants must clap their hands and say "We agree," but the diviner has to judge from the volume of applause whether the agreement is genuine. Also there is a phrase, translatable as "Put it behind you," which is used to indicate genuine agreement that a fact has been established and need not be further inquired into. The Pondo diviner, like the Ndembu one, receives his first payment at the point when the facts of the situation have been elicited. But the Pondo diviner may fail in this task, whereupon the consultants go to another; it is of course possible that this may happen among the Ndembu too. If he succeeds, however, he goes on to divine the source of the trouble in the same way, judging from the manner of the stereotyped answer whether his analysis is acceptable. Like the Tswana diviner, he does not mention names but refers to categories of kin. In Monica Wilson's opinion, those who consult him have already made up their own minds who is responsible for the trouble, and, if their view is not upheld, will seek another diviner. But Turner says that in the consultation of an Ndembu diviner there are always conflicting suspicions; and this must surely be so, since each of those present is seeking to direct suspicion away from himself and his close kin.

Some very elaborate types of divination are characteristic of West Africa. One which was observed among the Dogon people of Mali (former French Sudan) has been described by the late Marcel Griaule and Denise Paulme. Here the oracular answer is believed to be given by a jackal, the animal which the Dogon believe to be the most cunning of all, the only one who could deceive God. Certain spots are treated as sacred to the jackal, and at such a place a diviner traces out in the sand a diagram which includes every factor that seems relevant to the problem brought to him. The basic diagram is a rectangle divided into sections for the sky, the earth and the underworld—God, man and the dead—and the diviner adds marks to represent elements specific to the question about which he is being consulted. These latter are drawn in such a way that their meaning is not obvious; hence the consultant cannot offer his own interpretation as an alternative to the diviner's. The drawing is left overnight, and groundnuts are laid around it to attract the animal. The answer to the question is given by the prints left by the jackal as they are interpreted by the diviner when he comes back in the morning. The traces of other creatures, such as land crabs or spiders, are used in the same way in the Ivory Coast, Nigeria and the Cameroons.

Since we are dealing not with physical treatments but with grave accusations against persons, the need for an answer that will satisfy public opinion, even if it must be only a majority opinion, is clear, and one of the purposes of the diviner's questioning is to elicit this opinion. It is obviously easier to do this with the flexible methods of the Ndembu basket-diviner than with an object which is supposed to give an unequivocal yes or no. Yet where such an object is used in public, as in the Shona "throwing of bones," the problem has to be faced. One way of dealing with it is described in one of the court records published by Crawford. It is the evidence of one of two men, *A* and *G*, accused of consulting a diviner, which is an offense in Rhodesian law. *A*'s brother had died and he asked *G* to go with "all his people" to the diviner to find the cause. This is in accordance with the Shona rule that all suspects, or at least the heads of their families, must be present at the divination. The bones were thrown, first for all the spirits who might have slain the man in anger, then for the members of *A*'s homestead. Then "The doctor said, 'Yes, the person died in your kraal' [i.e., the cause of his death was there]. I asked if he meant that I was responsible. The doctor replied that he meant one of my people." A man *S* was identified; the doctor was asked to repeat the throw, and it gave the same result. Then *G* asked if this man was the witch and was told no, his wife. At this "I asked the doctor if he was telling lies. I said 'She is a small person and could not find medicine to kill.'" This seems to be a case where, to avoid making an accusation that would evidently have given offense, the diviner named somebody whom no one suspected. The consultants went away, outwardly satisfied, but took no action against the woman.

But the result of an unpopular answer can often be annulled by consulting another diviner, as it can in the case of personal consultations by using another oracle.

All African peoples have stories of the rivalries and jealousies between diviners, and there is nothing surprising in this, since it is a characteristic of most skilled professions. Evans-Pritchard describes how, during the Zande witch-doctors' dance, one will aim at another a kick which is supposed to shoot a piece of bone into his body and make him ill; the other will twist round to dodge the missile, and later return one of his own. They can discomfit their rivals in other ways too. When Evans-Pritchard travelled in the Congo with Kamanga, his servant whom he had had instructed in witch-doctoring, the latter's presence was resented by the leading local ex-

pert. They engaged in a long dance of rivalry, in which Kamanga triumphed when his magic missiles caused the other man's hat and leg ornaments to fall off. More often it is said, without elaboration, that diviners injure one another by sorcery. Pondo diviners use special medicines for protection against envious rivals.

Many writers on this subject have asked whether all those who consult diviners believe in their mystical powers. The answer is in some ways analogous to that which might be given to a similar question about medical practitioners. Some people assume that the doctor must be right; a few say that all doctors are quacks; many become critical of their own medical man if they dislike his diagnosis or treatment. But people in distress must be able to think there is somebody somewhere who can help them, and the greater the distress the readier they are to rely on the nearest help that is available.

Though there may be scepticism about the skill of particular diviners, there can be none about divination as such as long as there is no doubt of the existence of witches and sorcerers. Zande witch-doctors learn the technique of appearing to extract harmful substances from their patients' bodies. It is not to be supposed that there are no laymen who suspect that this is a deception. But however many individuals may be discredited—and few are publicly discredited—the faith that reliable diviners exist if only one can find them remains unshaken. Travelled men who have lived in cities will assert that, although they have never found a reliable diviner in the place where they live, they know of one in a city a hundred miles away.

Consulting the Poison Oracle among the Azande

E. E. Evans-Pritchard

If one important aspect of religion is helping believers to come to know the unknown, it follows that divination is important to religion. Divination means learning about the future or about things that may be hidden. Although the word itself may be traced to "divinity," which indicates its relationship to gods, the practice of divination belongs as much to magic as it does to religion proper. In this selection, E. E. Evans-Pritchard describes the Zande poison oracle benge, *a substance related to strychnine, and the myriad sociocultural beliefs surrounding its usage. Anthropological literature has long confirmed the great importance of divination to the Azande; it is a practice that cuts across every aspect of their culture. Azande diviners frequently divine with rubbing boards and termite sticks, but for the most important decisions they consult* benge *by "reading" its effect on chickens. Control over the poison oracle by older men assures them power over young men and all women. More importantly, control of* benge *in all legal cases provides Zande princes with enormous power. Indeed, the entire legal system of the Zande rests with divination-based decisions.*

The late Evans-Pritchard is recognized for his extensive and outstanding anthropological work in Africa, notably in the Sudan, Congo, Ethiopia, and Kenya. He was the author of several scholarly books and articles on African cultures as well as theories of religion.

Reprinted in excerpted form from E. E. Evans-Pritchard, "Consulting the Poison Oracle," in *Witchcraft, Oracles and Magic Among the Azande* (Oxford: Clarendon Press, 1937), Part III, Chapter 3, by permission of Oxford University Press.

THE USUAL PLACE FOR A CONSULTATION IS ON the edge of cultivations far removed from homesteads. Any place in the bush screened by high grasses and brushwood is suitable. Or they may choose the corner of a clearing at the edge of the bush where crops will later be sown, since this is not so damp as in the bush itself. The object in going so far is to ensure secrecy, to avoid pollution by people who have not observed the taboos, and to escape witchcraft, which is less likely to corrupt the oracle in the bush than in a homestead.

Oracle poison is useless unless a man possesses fowls upon which to test it, for the oracle speaks through fowls. In every Zande household there is a fowl house, and fowls are kept mainly with the object of subjecting them to oracular tests. As a rule they are only killed for food (and then only cocks or old hens) when an important visitor comes to the homestead, perhaps a prince's son or perhaps a father-in-law. Eggs are not eaten but are left to hens to hatch out. Generally a Zande, unless he is a wealthy man, will not possess more than half a dozen grown fowls at the most, and many people possess none at all or perhaps a single hen which someone has given to them.

Small chickens, only two or three days old, may be used for the poison oracle, but Azande prefer them older. However, one sees fowls of all sizes at oracle consultations, from tiny chickens to half-grown cockerels and pullets. When it is possible to tell the sex of fowls Azande use only cockerels, unless they have none and a consultation is necessary at once. The hens are spared for breeding purposes. Generally a man tells one of his younger sons to catch the fowls the night before a séance. Otherwise they catch them when the door of the fowl house is opened shortly after sunrise, but it is better to catch them and put them in a basket at night when they are roosting.

Old men say that fully grown birds ought not to be used in oracle consultations because they are too susceptible to the poison and have a habit of dying straight away before the poison has had time to consider the matter placed before it or even to hear a full statement of the problem. On the other hand a chicken remains for a long time under the influence of the poison before it recovers or expires, so that the oracle has time to hear all the relevant details concerning the problem placed before it and to give a well-considered judgment.

Any male may take part in the proceedings. However, the oracle is costly, and the questions put to it concern adult occupations. Therefore boys are only present when they operate the oracle. Normally these are boys who are observing taboos of mourning for the death of a relative. Adults also consider that it would be very unwise to allow any boys other than these to come near their poison because boys cannot be relied upon to observe the taboos on meats and vegetables.

An unmarried man will seldom be present at a séance. If he has any problems his father or uncle can act on his behalf. Moreover, only a married householder is wealthy enough to possess fowls and to acquire poison and has the experience to conduct a séance properly. Senior men also say that youths are generally engaged in some illicit love affair and would probably pollute the poison if they came near it. It is particularly the province of married men with households of their own to consult the poison oracle and no occupation gives them greater pleasure. It is not merely that they are able to solve their personal problems; but also they are dealing with matters of public importance, witchcraft, sorcery, and adultery, in which their names will be associated as witnesses of the oracle's decisions. A middle-aged Zande is happy when he has some poison and a few fowls and the company of one or two trusted friends of his own age, and he can sit down to a long séance to discover all about the infidelities of his wives, his health and the health of his children, his marriage plans, his hunting and agricultural prospects, the advisability of changing his homestead, and so forth.

Poor men who do not possess poison or fowls but who are compelled for one reason or another to consult the oracle will persuade a kinsman, blood-brother, relative-in-law, or prince's deputy to consult it on their behalf. This is one of the main duties of social relationships.

Control over the poison oracle by the older men gives them great power over their juniors and it is one of the main sources of their prestige. It is possible for the older men to place the names of the youths before the poison oracle and on its declarations to bring accusations of adultery against them. Moreover, a man who is not able to afford poison is not a fully independent householder, since he is unable to initiate any important undertaking and is dependent on the good will of others to inform him about everything that concerns his health and welfare. In their dealings with youths older men are backed always by the authority of the oracle on any question that concerns their juniors, who have no means of directly consulting it themselves.

Women are debarred not only from operating the poison oracle but from having anything to do with it. They are not expected even to speak of it, and a man who mentions the oracle in the presence of women uses some circumlocutory expression. When a man is going to consult the poison oracle he says to his wife that he is going to look at his cultivations or makes a similar excuse. She understands well enough what he is going to do but says nothing.

The poison oracle is a male prerogative and is one of the principal mechanisms of male control and an expression of sex antagonism. For men say that women are capable of any deceit to defy a husband and please a lover, but men at least have the advantage that their oracle poison will reveal secret embraces. If it were not for the oracle it would be of little use to pay bridewealth, for the most jealous watch will not prevent a woman from committing adultery if she has a mind to do so. And what woman has not? The only thing which women fear is the poison oracle; for if they can escape the eyes of men they cannot escape the eyes of the oracle. Hence it is said that women hate the oracle, and that if a woman finds some of the poison in the bush she will destroy its power by urinating on it. I once asked a Zande why he so carefully collected the leaves used in operating the oracle and threw them some distance away from the bush, and he replied that it was to prevent women from finding them and polluting them, for if they pollute the leaves then the poison which has been removed to its hiding place will lose its power.

Occasionally very old women of good social position have been known to operate the poison oracle, or at least to consult it. A well-known character of the present day, the mother of Prince Ngere, consults the poison oracle, but such persons are rare exceptions and are always august persons.

When we consider to what extent social life is regulated by the poison oracle we shall at once appreciate how great an advantage men have over women in their ability to use it, and how being cut off from the main means of establishing contact with the mystical forces that so deeply affect human welfare degrades woman's position in Zande society. I have little hesitation in affirming that the customary exclusion of women from any dealings with the poison oracle is the most evident symptom of their inferior social position and means of maintaining it.

Great experience is necessary to conduct a séance in the correct manner and to know how to interpret the findings of the oracle. One must know how many doses of poison to administer, whether the oracle is working properly, in what order to take the questions, whether to put them in a positive or negative form, how long a fowl is to be held between the toes or in the hand while a question is being put to the oracle, when it ought to be jerked to stir up the poison, and when it is time to throw it on the ground for final inspection. One must know how to observe not only whether the fowl lives or dies, but also the exact manner in which the poison affects it, for while it is under the influence of the oracle its every movement is significant to the experienced eye. Also one must know the phraseology of address in order to put the questions clearly to the oracle without error or ambiguity, and this is no easy task when a single question may be asked in a harangue lasting as long as five or ten minutes.

Everyone knows what happens at a consultation of the poison oracle. Even women are aware of the procedure. But not every man is proficient in the art, though most adults can prepare and question the oracle if necessary. Those who as boys have often prepared the poison for their fathers and uncles, and who are members of families which frequent the court and constantly consult the oracle, are the most competent. When I have asked boys whether they can prepare the poison and administer it to fowls they have often replied that they are ignorant of the art. Some men are very expert at questioning the oracle, and those who wish to consult it like to be accompanied by such a man.

Any man who is invited by the owner of the oracle poison may attend the séance, but he will be expected to keep clear of the oracle if he has had relations with his wife or eaten any of the prohibited foods within the last few days. It is imperative that the man who actually prepares the poison shall have observed these taboos, and for this reason the owner of the poison, referred to in this account as the owner, generally asks a boy or man who is under taboos of mourning to operate the oracle, since there can be no doubt that he has kept the taboos, because they are the same for mourning as for oracles. Such a man is always employed when as in a case of sudden sickness, it is necessary to consult the oracle without warning so that there is no time for a man to prepare himself by observation of taboos. I shall refer to the man or boy who actually prepares the poison and administers it to fowls as the "operator." When I speak of the "questioner" I refer to the man who sits opposite to the oracle and addresses it and calls upon it for judgments. As he sits a few feet from the oracle he ought also to have observed all the taboos. It is possible for a man to be owner, operator, and questioner at the same time by conducting the consultation of the oracle by himself, but this rarely, if ever, occurs. Usually there is no difficulty in obtaining the services of an operator, since a man knows which of his neighbors are observing the taboos associated with death and vengeance. One of his companions who has not eaten tabooed food or had sexual relations with women for a day or two before the consultation acts as questioner. If a man is unclean he can address the oracle from a distance. It is better to take these precautions because contact of an unclean person with the oracle is certain to destroy its potency, and even the close proximity of an unclean person may have this result.

The owner does not pay the operator and questioner for their services. The questioner is almost invariably either the owner himself or one of his friends who also wishes to put questions to the oracle and has brought fowls with him for the purpose. It is usual to reward the operator, if he is an adult, by giving him a fowl during the séance so that he can place one of his own problems before the oracle. Since he is generally a man who wears a girdle of mourning and vengeance he will often ask the oracle when the vengeance magic is going to strike its victim.

To guard against pollution a man generally hides his poison in the thatched roof of a hut, on the inner side, if possible, in a hut which women do not use, but this is not essential, for a woman does not know that there is poison hidden in the roof and is unlikely to come into contact with it. The owner of the poison must have kept the taboos if he wishes to take it down from the roof himself, and if he is unclean he will bring the man or boy who is to operate the oracle into the hut and indicate to him at a distance where the poison is hidden in the thatch. So good a hiding place is the thatched roof of a hut for a small packet of poison that it is often difficult for its owner himself to find it. No one may smoke hemp in a hut which lodges oracle poison. However, there is always a danger of pollution and of witchcraft if the poison is kept in a homestead, and some men prefer to hide it in a hole in a tree in the bush, or even to build a small shelter and to lay it on the ground beneath. This shelter is far removed from human dwellings, and were a man to come across it in the bush he would not disturb it lest it cover some kind of lethal medicine. It is very improbable that witchcraft will discover oracle poison hidden in the bush. I have never seen oracle poison under a shelter in the bush, but I was told that it is frequently housed in this manner.

Oracle poison when not in use is kept wrapped in leaves, and at the end of a séance used poison is placed in a separate leaf-wrapping from unused poison. The poison may be used two or three times and sometimes fresh poison is added to it to make it more potent. When its action shows that it has lost its strength they throw it away.

Special care is taken to protect a prince's oracle poison from witchcraft and pollution because a prince's oracles reveal matters of tribal importance, judge criminal and civil cases, and determine whether vengeance has been exacted for death. A prince has two or three official operators who supervise his poison oracle. These men must be thoroughly reliable since the fate of their master and the purity of law are in their hands. If they break a taboo the whole legal system may become corrupted and the innocent be judged guilty and the guilty be judged innocent. Moreover, a prince is at frequent pains to discover witchcraft or sorcery among his wives and retainers which might do him an injury, so that his life is endangered if the oracle is not working properly.

. . .

Control of the poison oracle in all legal cases gave the princes enormous power. No death or adultery could be legally avenged without a verdict from their oracles, so that the court was the sole medium of legal action and the king or his representative the sole source of law. Although the procedure was a mystical one it was carried out in the king's name and he was vested with judicial authority as completely as if a more common-sense system of justice had obtained.

Azande are very secretive about oracle séances and wish no one to be present when they are inquiring about private matters unless he is a trusted friend. They do not tell any one except trusted friends that they are going to consult the oracle, and they say nothing about the consultation on their return. It frequently happens when a man is about to set out from his homestead to the place of the oracle that he is visited by someone whom he does not wish to acquaint with his business. He does not tell the unwelcome visitor that he must hurry off to consult the oracle, but uses any pretext to get rid of him, and prefers to abandon the consultation rather than confess his intentions.

After this short introduction I will describe the manner in which poison is administered to fowls. The operator goes ahead of the rest of the party in order to prepare for the test. He takes with him a small gourdful of water. He clears a space by treading down the grasses. Afterwards he scrapes a hole in the earth into which he places a large leaf as a basin for the oracle poison. From *bingba* grass he fashions a small brush to administer the poison, and from leaves he makes a filter to pour the liquid poison into the beaks of the fowls; and from other leaves he makes a cup to transfer water from the gourd to the poison when it needs to be moistened. Finally, he tears off some branches of nearby shrubs and extracts their bast to be used as cord for attaching to the legs of fowls which have survived the test so that they can be easily retrieved from the grass when the business of the day is finished. The operator does not moisten the poison till the rest of the party arrive.

There may be only one man or there may be several who have questions to put to the oracle. Each brings his fowls with him in an open-wove basket. As it has been agreed beforehand where the oracle consultation is to take place they know where to foregather. As each person arrives he hands over his basket of fowls to the operator who places it on the ground near him. A man who is used to acting as questioner sits opposite to it, a few feet away if he has observed the taboos, but several yards away if he has not observed them. Other men who have not kept the taboos remain at a greater distance.

When every one is seated they discuss in low tones whose fowl they will take first and how the question shall be framed. Meanwhile the operator pours some water from the gourd at his side into his leaf cup and from the cup on to the poison, which then effervesces. He mixes the poison and water with his finger tips into a paste of the right consistency and, when instructed by the questioner, takes one of the fowls and draws down its wings over its legs and pins them between and under his toes. He is seated with the fowl facing him. He takes his grass brush, twirls it round in the poison, and folds it in the leaf filter. He holds open the beak of the fowl and tips the end of the filter into it and squeezes the filter so that the liquid runs out of the paste into the throat of the fowl. He bobs the head of the fowl up and down to compel it to swallow the poison.

At this point the questioner, having previously been instructed by the owner of the fowl on the facts which he is to put before the oracle, commences to address the poison inside the fowl. He continues to address it for about a couple of minutes, when a second dose of poison is usually administered. If it is a very small chicken two doses will suffice, but a larger fowl will receive three doses, and I have known a fowl to receive a fourth dose, but never more than four. The questioner does not cease his address to the oracle, but puts his questions again and again in different forms, though always with the same refrain, "If such is the case, poison oracle kill the fowl," or "If such is the case, poison oracle spare the fowl." From time to time he interrupts his flow of oratory to give a technical order to the operator. He may tell him to give the fowl another dose of poison or to jerk it between his toes by raising and lowering his foot (this stirs up the poison inside the fowl). When the last dose of poison has been administered and he has further addressed it, he tells the operator to raise the fowl. The operator takes it in his hand and, holding its legs between his fingers so that it faces him, gives it an occasional jerk backwards and forwards. The questioner redoubles his oratory as though the verdict depended upon his forensic efforts, and if the fowl is not already dead he then, after a further bout of oratory, tells the operator to

put it on the ground. He continues to address the poison inside the fowl while they watch its movements on the ground.

The poison affects fowls in many ways. Occasionally it kills them immediately after the first dose, while they are still on the ground. This seldom happens, for normally a fowl is not seriously affected till it is removed from the ground and jerked backwards and forwards in the hand. Then, if it is going to die, it goes through spasmodic stretchings of the body and closing of the wings and vomits. After several such spasms it vomits and expires in a final seizure. Some fowls appear quite unaffected by the poison, and when, after being jerked backwards and forwards for a while, they are flung to the ground peck around unconcernedly. Those fowls which are unaffected by the poison generally excrete as soon as they are put to earth. Some fowls appear little affected by the poison till put to earth, when they suddenly collapse and die.

One generally knows what the verdict is going to be after the fowl has been held in the hand for a couple of minutes. If it appears certain to recover the operator ties bast to its leg and throws it to the ground. If it appears certain to die he does not trouble to tie bast to its leg, but lays it on the earth to die. Often when a fowl has died they draw its corpse in a semicircle round the poison to show it to the poison. They then cut off a wing to use as evidence and cover the body with grass. Those fowls which survive are taken home and let loose. A fowl is never used twice on the same day.

. . .

The main duty of the questioner is to see that the oracle fully understands the question put to it and is acquainted with all facts relevant to the problem it is asked to solve. They address it with all the care for detail that one observes in court cases before a prince. This means beginning a long way back and noting over a considerable period of time every detail which might elucidate the case, linking up facts into a consistent picture of events, and the marshalling of arguments, as Azande can so brilliantly do, into a logical and closely knit web of sequences and interrelations of facts and inference. Also the questioner is careful to mention to the oracle again and again the name of the man who is consulting it, and he points him out to the oracle with his outstretched arm. He mentions also the name of his father, perhaps the name of his clan, and the name of the place where he resides, and he gives similar details of other people mentioned in the address.

An address consists usually of alternate directions. The first sentences outline the question in terms demanding an affirmative answer and end with the command, "Poison oracle kill the fowl." The next sentences outline the question in terms demanding a negative answer and end with the command, "Poison oracle spare the fowl." The consulter then takes up the question again in terms asking an affirmative answer; and so on. If a bystander considers that a relevant point has been left out he interrupts the questioner, who then makes this point.

The questioner has a switch in his hand, and while questioning the oracle beats the ground, as he sits cross-legged, in front of it. He continues to beat the ground till the end of his address. Often he will gesticulate as he makes his points, in the same manner as a man making a case in court. He sometimes plucks grass and shows it to the poison and, after explaining that there is something he does not wish it to consider, throws it behind him. Thus he tells the oracle that he does not wish it to consider the question of witchcraft but only of sorcery. Witchcraft is *wingi*, something irrelevant, and he casts it behind him.

. . .

While the fowl is undergoing its ordeal men are attentive to their behavior. A man must tighten and spread out his bark-cloth loin-covering lest he expose his genitals, as when he is sitting in the presence of a prince or parent-in-law. Men speak in a low voice as they do in the presence of superiors. Indeed, all conversation is avoided unless it directly concerns the procedure of consultation. If anyone desires to leave before the proceedings are finished he takes a leaf and spits on it and places it where he has been sitting. I have seen a man who rose for a few moments only to catch a fowl which had escaped from its basket place a blade of grass on the stone upon which he had been sitting. Spears must be laid on the ground and not planted upright in the presence of the poison oracle. Azande are very serious during a séance, for they are asking questions of vital importance to their lives and happiness.

Rational Mastery by Man of His Surroundings

Bronislaw Malinowski

Rare is the anthropology course that sometime during the semester is not directed to the thought and writings of Bronislaw Malinowski (1884–1942). This world-famous Polish anthropologist was trained in mathematics, but shifted his interests to anthropology after reading Sir James Frazer's The Golden Bough. *Malinowski's fieldwork in the Trobriand Islands of Melanesia influenced the direction of anthropology as an academic discipline. He is recognized as the founder of functionalism, an anthropological approach to the study of culture that believes each institution in a society fulfills a definite function in the maintenance of human needs. His major works include* Crime and Customs in Savage Society *(1926),* The Sexual Life of Savages *(1929), and* Coral Gardens and Their Magic *(1935). Malinowski was professor of anthropology at the University of London from 1927 until his death in 1942.*

In this classic article Malinowski asks two important questions: Do preliterate people have any rational mastery of their surroundings; and can primitive knowledge be regarded as a beginning or rudimentary type of science, or is it merely a crude hodgepodge devoid of logic and accuracy? Although the use of the word savage *by the author is considered a pejorative by anthropologists today, in Malinowski's time it was commonplace.*

Reprinted from *Magic, Science and Religion* (New York: Doubleday, 1955), pp. 25–35, by permission of the Society for Promoting Christian Knowledge.

THE PROBLEM OF PRIMITIVE KNOWLEDGE HAS been singularly neglected by anthropology. Studies on savage psychology were exclusively confined to early religion, magic, and mythology. Only recently the work of several English, German, and French writers, notably the daring and brilliant speculations of Professor Lévy-Bruhl, gave an impetus to the student's interest in what the savage does in his more sober moods. The results were startling indeed: Professor Lévy-Bruhl tells us, to put it in a nutshell, that primitive man has no sober moods at all, that he is hopelessly and completely immersed in a mystical frame of mind. Incapable of dispassionate and consistent observation, devoid of the power of abstraction, hampered by "a decided aversion towards reasoning," he is unable to draw any benefit from experience, to construct or comprehend even the most elementary laws of nature. "For minds thus orientated there is no fact purely physical." Nor can there exist for them any clear idea of substance and attribute, cause and effect, identity and contradiction. Their outlook is that of confused superstition, "prelogical," made of mystic "participations" and "exclusions." I have here summarized a body of opinion, of which the brilliant French sociologist is the most decided and the most competent spokesman, but which numbers besides, many anthropologists and philosophers of renown.

But there are dissenting voices. When a scholar and anthropologist of the measure of Professor J. L. Myres entitles an article in *Notes and Queries* "Natural Science," and when we read there that the savage's "knowledge based on observation is distinct and accurate," we must surely pause before accepting primitive man's irrationality as a dogma. Another highly competent writer, Dr. A. A. Goldenweiser, speaking about primitive "discoveries, inventions and improvements"—

which could hardly be attributed to any preempirical or prelogical mind—affirms that "it would be unwise to ascribe to the primitive mechanic merely a passive part in the origination of inventions. Many a happy thought must have crossed his mind, nor was he wholly unfamiliar with the thrill that comes from an idea effective in action." Here we see the savage endowed with an attitude of mind wholly akin to that of a modern man of science!

To bridge over the wide gap between the two extreme opinions current on the subject of primitive man's reason, it will be best to resolve the problem into two questions.

First, has the savage any rational outlook, any rational mastery of his surroundings, or is he, as M. Lévy-Bruhl and his school maintain, entirely "mystical"? The answer will be that every primitive community is in possession of a considerable store of knowledge, based on experience and fashioned by reason.

The second question then opens: Can this primitive knowledge be regarded as a rudimentary form of science or is it, on the contrary, radically different, a crude body of practical and technical abilities, rules of thumb and rules of art having no theoretical value? This second question, epistemological rather than belonging to the study of man, will be barely touched upon at the end of this section and a tentative answer only will be given.

In dealing with the first question, we shall have to examine the "profane" side of life, the arts, crafts and economic pursuits, and we shall attempt to disentangle in it a type of behavior, clearly marked off from magic and religion, based on empirical knowledge and on the confidence in logic. We shall try to find whether the lines of such behavior are defined by traditional rules, known, perhaps even discussed sometimes, and tested. We shall have to inquire whether the sociological setting of the rational and empirical behavior differs from that of ritual and cult. Above all we shall ask, do the natives distinguish the two domains and keep them apart, or is the field of knowledge constantly swamped by superstition, ritualism, magic or religion?

Since in the matter under discussion there is an appalling lack of relevant and reliable observations, I shall have largely to draw upon my own material, most unpublished, collected during a few years' field work among the Melanesian and Papuo-Melanesian tribes of Eastern New Guinea and the surrounding archipelagoes. As the Melanesians are reputed, however, to be specially magic-ridden, they will furnish an acid test of the existence of empirical and rational knowledge among savages living in the age of polished stone.

These natives, and I am speaking mainly of the Melanesians who inhabit the coral atolls to the N.E. of the main island, the Trobriand Archipelago and the adjoining groups, are expert fishermen, industrious manufacturers and traders, but they rely mainly on gardening for their subsistence. With the most rudimentary implements, a pointed digging-stick and a small axe, they are able to raise crops sufficient to maintain a dense population and even yielding a surplus, which in olden days was allowed to rot unconsumed, and which at present is exported to feed plantation hands. The success in their agriculture depends—besides the excellent natural conditions with which they are favored—upon their extensive knowledge of the classes of the soil, of the various cultivated plants, of the mutual adaptation of these two factors, and, last not least, upon their knowledge of the importance of accurate and hard work. They have to select the soil and the seedlings, they have appropriately to fix the times for clearing and burning the scrub, for planting and weeding, for training the vines of the yam plants. In all this they are guided by a clear knowledge of weather and seasons, plants and pests, soil and tubers, and by a conviction that this knowledge is true and reliable, that it can be counted upon and must be scrupulously obeyed.

Yet mixed with all their activities there is to be found magic, a series of rites performed every year over the gardens in rigorous sequence and order. Since the leadership in garden work is in the hands of the magician, and since ritual and practical work are intimately associated, a superficial observer might be led to assume that the mystic and the rational behavior are mixed up, that their effects are not distinguished by the natives and not distinguishable in scientific analysis. Is this so really?

Magic is undoubtedly regarded by the natives as absolutely indispensable to the welfare of the gardens. What would happen without it no one can exactly tell, for no native garden has ever been made without its ritual, in spite of some thirty years of European rule and missionary influence and well over a century's contact with white traders. But certainly various kinds of disaster, blight, unseasonable droughts, rains, bush-pigs and locusts would destroy the unhallowed garden made without magic.

Does this mean, however, that the natives attribute all the good results to magic? Certainly not. If you were to suggest to a native that he should make his garden mainly by magic and scamp his work, he would simply smile on your simplicity. He knows as well as you do that there are natural conditions and causes, and by his observations he knows also that he is able to control these natural forces by mental and physical effort. His knowledge is limited, no doubt, but as far as it goes it is sound and proof against mysticism. If the fences are broken down, if the seed is destroyed or has been dried or washed away, he will have recourse not to magic, but to work, guided by knowledge and reason. His experience has taught him also, on the other hand, that in spite of all his forethought and beyond all his efforts there are agencies and forces which one year bestow unwonted and unearned benefits of fertility, making everything run smooth and well, rain and sun appear at the right moment, noxious insects remain in abeyance, the harvest yields a superabundant crop; and another year again the same agencies bring ill luck and bad chance, pursue him from beginning till end and thwart all his most strenuous efforts and his best-founded knowledge. To control these influences and these only he employs magic.

Thus there is a clear-cut division: there is first the well-known set of conditions, the natural course of growth, as well as the ordinary pests and dangers to be warded off by fencing and weeding. On the other hand there is the domain of the unaccountable and adverse influences, as well as the great unearned increment of fortunate coincidence. The first conditions are coped with by knowledge and work, the second by magic.

This line of division can also be traced in the social setting of work and ritual respectively. Though the garden magician is, as a rule, also the leader in practical activities, these two functions are kept strictly apart. Every magical ceremony has its distinctive name, its appropriate time and its place in the scheme of work, and it stands out of the ordinary course of activities completely. Some of them are ceremonial and have to be attended by the whole community, all are public in that it is known when they are going to happen and anyone can attend them. They are performed on selected plots within the gardens and on a special corner of this plot. Work is always tabooed on such occasions, sometimes only while the ceremony lasts, sometimes for a day or two. In his lay character the leader and magician directs the work, fixes the dates for starting, harangues and exhorts slack or careless gardeners. But the two roles never overlap or interfere: they are always clear, and any native will inform you without hesitation whether the man acts as magician or as leader in garden work.

What has been said about gardens can be paralleled from any one of the many other activities in which work and magic run side by side without ever mixing. Thus in canoe building empirical knowledge of material, of technology, and of certain principles of stability and hydrodynamics, function in company and close association with magic, each yet uncontaminated by the other.

For example, they understand perfectly well that the wider the span of the outrigger the greater the stability yet the smaller the resistance against strain. They can clearly explain why they have to give this span a certain traditional width, measured in fractions of the length of the dugout. They can also explain, in rudimentary but clearly mechanical terms, how they have to behave in a sudden gale, why the outrigger must be always on the weather side, why the one type of canoe can and the other cannot beat. They have, in fact, a whole system of principles of sailing, embodied in a complex and rich terminology, traditionally handed on and obeyed as rationally and consistently as is modern science by modern sailors. How could they sail otherwise under eminently dangerous conditions in their frail primitive craft?

But even with all their systematic knowledge, methodically applied, they are still at the mercy of powerful and incalculable tides, sudden gales during the monsoon season and unknown reefs. And here comes in their magic, performed over the canoe during its construction, carried out at the beginning and in the course of expeditions and resorted to in moments of real danger. If the modern seaman, entrenched in science and reason, provided with all sorts of safety appliances, sailing on steel-built steamers, if even he has a singular tendency to superstition—which does not rob him of his knowledge or reason, nor make him altogether prelogical —can we wonder that his savage colleague, under much more precarious conditions, holds fast to the safety and comfort of magic?

An interesting and crucial test is provided by fishing in the Trobriand Islands and its magic. While in the villages on the inner lagoon fishing is done in an easy and absolutely reliable manner by the method of poisoning, yielding abundant results without danger and uncertainty, there are on the shores of the open sea dangerous modes of fishing and also certain types in which the yield greatly varies according to whether shoals of fish appear beforehand or not. It is most significant that in the lagoon fishing, where man can rely completely upon his knowledge and skill, magic does not exist, while in the open-sea fishing, full of danger and uncertainty, there is extensive magical ritual to secure safety and good results.

Again, in warfare the natives know that strength, courage, and agility play a decisive part. Yet here also they practice magic to master the elements of chance and luck.

Nowhere is the duality of natural and supernatural causes divided by a line so thin and intricate, yet, if carefully followed up, so well marked, decisive, and instructive, as in the two most fateful forces of human destiny: health and death. Health to the Melanesians is a natural state of affairs and, unless tampered with, the human body will remain in perfect order. But the natives know perfectly well that there are natural means which can affect health and even destroy the body. Poisons, wounds, burns, falls are known to cause disablement or death in a natural way. And this is not a matter of private opinion of this or that individual, but it is laid down in traditional lore and even in belief, for there are considered to be different ways to the nether world for those who died by sorcery and those who met "natural" death. Again, it is recognized that cold, heat, overstrain, too much sun, overeating can all cause minor aliments, which are treated by natural remedies such as massage, steaming, warming at a fire and certain potions. Old age is known to lead to bodily decay and the explanation is given by the natives that very old people grow weak, their esophagus closes up, and therefore they must die.

But besides these natural causes there is the enormous domain of sorcery and by far the most cases of illness and death are ascribed to this. The line of distinction between sorcery and the other causes is clear in theory and in most cases of practice, but it must be realized that it is subject to what could be called the personal perspective. That is, the more closely a case has to do with the person who considers it, the less will it be "natural," the more "magical." Thus a very old man, whose pending death will be considered natural by the other members of the community, will be afraid only of sorcery and never think of his natural fate. A fairly sick person will diagnose sorcery in his own case, while all the others might speak of too much betel nut or overeating or some other indulgence.

But who of us really believes that his own bodily infirmities and the approaching death is a purely natural occurrence, just an insignificant event in the infinite chain of causes? To the most rational civilized men health, disease, the threat of death, float in a hazy emotional mist, which seems to become denser and more impenetrable as the fateful forms approach. It is indeed astonishing that "savages" can achieve such a sober, dispassionate outlook in these matters as they actually do.

Thus in his relation to nature and destiny, whether he tries to exploit the first or to dodge the second, primitive man recognized both the natural and the supernatural forces and agencies, and he tries to use them both for his benefit. Whenever he has been taught by experience that effort guided by knowledge is of some avail, he never spares the one or ignores the other. He knows that a plant cannot grow by magic alone, or a canoe sail or float without being properly constructed and managed, or a fight be won without skill and daring. He never relies on magic alone, while, on the contrary, he sometimes dispenses with it completely, as in fire-making and in a number of crafts and pursuits. But he clings to it, whenever he has to recognize the impotence of his knowledge and of his rational technique.

I have given my reasons why in this argument I had to rely principally on the material collected in the classical land of magic, Melanesia. But the facts discussed are so fundamental, the conclusions drawn of such a general nature, that it will be easy to check them on any modern detailed ethnographic record. Comparing agricultural work and magic, the building of canoes, the art of healing by magic and by natural remedies, the ideas about the causes of death in other regions, the universal validity of what has been established here could easily be proved. Only, since no observations have methodically been made with reference to the problem of primitive knowledge, the data from other writers could be gleaned only piecemeal and their testimony though clear would be indirect.

I have chosen to face the question of primitive man's rational knowledge directly: watching him at his principal occupations, seeing him pass from work to magic and back again, entering into his mind, listening to his opinions. The whole problem might have been approached through the avenue of language, but this would have led us too far into questions of logic, semasiology, and theory of primitive languages. Words which serve to express general ideas such as *existence, substance,* and *attribute, cause* and *effect,* the *fundamental* and the *secondary;* words and expressions used in complicated pursuits like sailing, construction, measuring and checking; numerals and quantitative descriptions, correct and detailed classifications of natural phenomena, plants and animals—all this would lead us exactly to the same conclusion: that primitive man can observe and think, and that he possesses, embodied in his language, systems of methodical though rudimentary knowledge.

Similar conclusions could be drawn from an examination of those mental schemes and physical contrivances which could be described as diagrams or formulas. Methods of indicating the main points of the compass, arrangements of stars into constellations, co-ordination of these with the seasons, naming of moons in the year, of quarters in the moon— all these accomplishments are known to the simplest savages. Also they are all able to draw diagrammatic maps in the sand or dust, indicate arrangements by placing small stones, shells, or sticks on the ground, plan expeditions or raids on such rudimentary charts. By co-ordinating space and time they are able to arrange big tribal gatherings and to combine vast tribal movements over extensive areas. The use of leaves, notched sticks, and similar aids to memory is well known and seems to be almost universal. All such "diagrams" are means of reducing a complex and unwieldly bit of reality to a simple and handy form. They give man a relatively easy mental control over it. As such are they not—in a very rudimentary form no doubt—fundamentally akin to developed scientific formulas and "models," which are also simple and handy paraphrases of a complex or abstract reality, giving the civilized physicist mental control over it?

This brings us to the second question: Can we regard primitive knowledge, which, as we found, is both empirical and rational, as a rudimentary stage of science, or is it not at all related to it? If by science be understood a body of rules and conceptions, based on experience and derived from it by logical inference, embodied in material achievements and in a fixed form of tradition and carried on by some sort of social organization—then there is no doubt that even the lowest savage communities have the beginning of science, however rudimentary.

Most epistemologists would not, however, be satisfied with such a "minimum definition" of science, for it might apply to the rules of an art or craft as well. They would maintain that the rules of science must be laid down explicitly, open to control by experiment and critique by reason. They must not only be rules of practical behavior, but theoretical laws of knowledge. Even accepting this stricture, however, there is hardly any doubt that many of the principles of savage knowledge are scientific in this sense. The native shipwright knows not only practically of buoyancy, leverage, equilibrium, he has to obey these laws not only on water, but while making the canoe he must have the principles in his mind. He instructs his helpers in them. He gives them the traditional rules, and in a crude and simple manner, using his hands, pieces of wood, and a limited technical vocabulary, he explains some general laws of hydrodynamics and equilibrium. Science is not detached from the craft, that is certainly true, it is only a means to an end, it is crude, rudimentary, and inchoate, but with all that it is the matrix from which the higher developments must have sprung.

If we applied another criterion yet, that of the really scientific attitude, the disinterested search for knowledge and for the understanding of causes and reasons, the answer would certainly not be in a direct negative. There is, of course, no widespread thirst for knowledge in a savage community, new things such as European topics bore them frankly and their whole interest is largely encompassed by the traditional world of their culture. But within this there is both the antiquarian mind passionately interested in myths, stories, details of customs, pedigrees, and ancient happenings, and there is also to be found the naturalist, patient and painstaking in his observations, capable of generalization and of connecting long chains of events in the life of animals, and in the marine world or in the jungle. It is enough to realize how much European naturalists have often learned from their savage colleagues to appreciate this interest found in the native for nature. There is finally among the primitives, as every field worker well knows, the sociologist, the ideal informant, capable with marvelous accuracy and insight to give the *raison d'être*, the function and the organization of many a simpler institution in his tribe.

Science, of course, does not exist in any uncivilized community as a driving power, criticizing, renewing, constructing. Science is never consciously made. But on this criterion, neither is there law, nor religion, nor government among savages.

Baseball Magic

George Gmelch

In the preceding article, Malinowski observed that in the Trobriand Islands magic did not occur when the natives fished in the safe lagoons but when they ventured out into the open seas: Then the danger and uncertainty caused them to perform extensive magical rituals. In the following article, anthropologist George Gmelch demonstrates that America's favorite pastime is an excellent place to put the test to Malinowski's hypothesis about magic. Anyone who has watched baseball, either at a ballpark or in front of a television set, is aware of some of the more obvious rituals performed by the players; but Gmelch, drawing upon his previous experience as a professional baseball player, provides an insider's view of the rituals, taboos, and fetishes involved in the sport. (The following is a 1999 revision of Gmelch's original article.)

ON EACH PITCHING DAY FOR THE FIRST THREE months of a winning season, Dennis Grossini, a pitcher on a Detroit Tiger farm team, arose from bed at exactly 10:00 A.M. At 1:00 P.M. he went to the nearest restaurant for two glasses of iced tea and a tunafish sandwich. Although the afternoon was free, he changed into the sweatshirt and supporter he wore during his last winning game, and one hour before the game he chewed a wad of Beech-Nut chewing tobacco. After each pitch during the game he touched the letters on his uniform and straightened his cap after each ball. Before the start of each inning he replaced the pitcher's rosin bag next to the spot where it was the inning before. And after every inning in which he gave up a run, he washed his hands.

When asked which part of the ritual was most important, he said, "You can't really tell what's most important so it all becomes important. I'd be afraid to change anything. As long as I'm winning, I do everything the same."

Trobriand Islanders, according to anthropologist Bronislaw Malinowski, felt the same way about their fishing magic. Among the Trobrianders, fishing took two forms: in the *inner lagoon* where fish were plentiful and there was little danger, and on the *open sea* where fishing was dangerous and yields varied widely. Malinowski found that magic was not used in lagoon fishing, where men could rely solely on their knowledge and skill. But when fishing on the open sea, Trobrianders used a great deal of magical ritual to ensure safety and increase their catch.

Baseball, America's national pastime, is an arena in which players behave remarkably like Malinowski's Trobriand fishermen. To professional ballplayers, baseball is more than just a game. It is an occupation. Since their livelihoods depend on how well they perform, many use magic to try to control the chance that is built into baseball. There are three essential activities of the game—pitching, hitting, and fielding. In the first two, chance can play a surprisingly important role. The pitcher is the player least able to control

Revised from the original article that appeared in *Transaction*, vol. 8, no. 8 (1971), pp. 39–41, 54. Reprinted by permission of the author.

the outcome of his own efforts. He may feel great and have good stuff warming up in the bullpen and then get into the game and not have it. He may make a bad pitch and see the batter miss it for a strike out or see it hit hard but right into the hands of a fielder for an out. His best pitch may be blooped for a base hit. He may limit the opposing team to just a few hits yet lose the game, or he may give up a dozen hits but still win. And the good and bad luck don't always average out over the course of a season. Some pitchers end the season with poor won-lost records but good earned run averages, and vice versa. For instance, this past season (1998) Andy Benes gave up over one run per game more than his teammate Omar Daal but had a better won-lost record. Benes went 14-13, while Daal was only 8-12. Both pitched for the same team—the Arizona Diamondbacks—which meant they had the same fielders behind them. Regardless of how well a pitcher performs, on every outing he depends not only on his own skill, but also upon the proficiency of his teammates, the ineptitude of the opposition, and luck.

Hitting, which Hall of Famer Ted Williams called the single most difficult task in the world of sports, is also full of risk and uncertainty. Unless it's a home run, no matter how well the batter hits the ball, fate determines whether it will go into a waiting glove, whistle past a fielder's diving stab, or find a gap in the outfield. The uncertainty is compounded by the low success rate of hitting: the average hitter gets only one hit in every four trips to the plate, while the very best hitters average only one hit every three trips. Fielding, as we will return to later, is the one part of baseball where chance does not play much of a role.

How does the risk and uncertainty in pitching and hitting affect players? What do they do to introduce some control over the outcomes of their performance? These are questions that I first became interested in many years ago as both a ballplayer and an anthropology student. I'd devoted much of my youth to baseball and played professionally as first baseman in the Detroit Tiger organization in the 1960s. It was shortly after the end of one baseball season that I took an anthropology course called "Magic, Religion, and Witchcraft." As my professor described the magic practiced by a tribe in Papua New Guinea, it occurred to me that what these so-called primitive people did wasn't all that different

from what my teammates and I had done to give ourselves luck and confidence in baseball.

The most common way players attempt to reduce chance and their feelings of uncertainty is to develop and follow a daily routine. By routine I mean a course of action that is regularly followed. Florida Marlins coach Rich Donnelly talked about the routines of his ballplayers:

> They're like trained animals. They come out here [to the ballpark] and everything has to be the same, they don't like anything that knocks them off their routine. Just look at the dugout and you'll see every guy sitting in the same spot every night. It's amazing, everybody in the same spot. And don't you dare take someone's seat. If a guy comes up from the minors and sits here, they'll say, 'Hey, Jim sits here, find another seat.' You watch the pitcher warm up and he'll do the same thing every time. And when you go on the road its the same way. You got a routine and you adhere to it and you don't want anybody knocking you off it.

Routines are comforting; they bring order into a world in which players have little control. And sometimes practical elements in routines produce tangible benefits, such as helping the player to concentrate. But a lot of what players do often goes beyond mere routine and is what anthropologists define as *ritual*—prescribed behaviors in which there is no empirical connection between the means (e.g., tapping home plate three times) and the desired end (e.g., getting a base hit). Because there is no real connection between the two, rituals are not rational. Similar to rituals are the nonrational beliefs that form the basis of taboos and fetishes which players also use to reduce chance and bring luck to their side. But first let's look closer at the ballplayers' rituals.

Rituals

Most rituals are personal, that is, they're performed as individuals rather than as a team or group. Most are done in an unemotional manner, in much the same way as players apply pine tar to their bats to improve the grip or dab eye black on their upper cheeks to reduce the sun's glare. Baseball rituals are infinitely varied. A ballplayer may ritualize any activity—eating, dressing, driving to the ballpark—that he considers important or somehow linked to good performance. For example, White Sox pitcher

Jason Bere listens to the same song on his Walkman on the days he is to pitch. Tampa's Wade Boggs eats chicken before every game (that's 162 meals of chicken per year), and he has been doing that for twelve years. Jim Leyritz eats turkey, and Dennis Grossini tunafish. Infielder Julio Gotay always played with a cheese sandwich in his back pocket (he had a big appetite, so there might also have been a measure of practicality here). San Francisco Giants pitcher Ron Bryant added a new stick of bubble gum to the collection in his bulging back pocket after each game he won. Jim Ohms put another penny in the pouch of his supporter after each win. Clanging against the hard plastic genital cup, the pennies made an audible sound as he ran the bases toward the end of a winning season.

Many hitters go through a series of preparatory rituals before stepping into the batter's box. These include tugging on their caps, touching their uniform letters or medallions, crossing themselves, tapping or bouncing the bat on the plate, or swinging the weighted warm-up bat a prescribed number of times. Red Sox shortstop Nomar Garciaparra tightens his batting gloves and pounds the toes of his shoes into the earth several times before each pitch. Mike Hargrove, former Cleveland Indian first baseman, had a dozen elements in his batting ritual, from grabbing his belt to pushing his helmet down tight. And after each pitch he would step out of the batter's box and repeat the entire sequence, believing that his batting ritual helped him regain his concentration. His ritual sequence was so time-consuming that he was known as the "human rain delay."

Latin Americans draw upon rituals from their Catholic religion. Some make the sign of the cross or bless themselves before every at bat, and a few like the Rangers' Pudge Rodriguez do so before every pitch. Some, like Juan Gonzalez, wear very visible religious medallions around their neck, while others wear them discretely inside their undershirts.

One ritual associated with hitting is tagging a base when leaving and returning to the dugout between innings. Some players don't "feel right" unless they tag a specific base on each trip between the dugout and the field. Dave Jaeger added some complexity to his ritual by tagging third base on his way to the dugout only after the third, sixth, and ninth innings. Baseball fans observe a lot of ritual behavior —such as tagging bases, pitchers tugging their caps or touching the rosin bag after each bad pitch, smoothing the dirt on the mound before each new batter or inning—never realizing the importance of these actions to the player. One ritual that many fans do recognize, and one that is a favorite of TV cameramen, is the "rally cap"—players in the dugout folding their caps and wearing them bill up in hopes of sparking a rally.

Most rituals grow out of exceptionally good performances. When a player does well, he seldom attributes his success to skill alone. He knows that his skills were essentially the same the night before. What was different about today that explains his three hits? He decides to repeat what he did today in an attempt to bring more good luck. And so he attributes his success, in part, to a food he ate, not having shaved, or just about any behavior out of the ordinary. By repeating that behavior, he seeks to gain control over his performance. Outfielder John White explained how one of his rituals started:

> I was jogging out to centerfield after the National Anthem when I picked up a scrap of paper. I got some good hits that night, and I guess I decided that the paper had something to do with it. The next night I picked up a gum wrapper and had another good night at the plate. . . . I've been picking up paper every night since.

One of Mike Saccocia's rituals concerned food, "I got three hits one night after eating at Long John Silver's. After that when we'd pull into town, my first question would be, 'Do you have a Long John Silver's?'" Like most players, White and Saccocia abandoned their rituals and looked for new ones when they stopped hitting.

Because starting pitchers play once every four days, they perform their rituals less frequently than do hitters. But their rituals are just as important to them, perhaps more so. A starting pitcher cannot make up for a poor performance the following day like other players can. And having to wait three days to redeem oneself can be miserable. Moreover, the team's performance depends more on the pitcher than on any other player. Considering the pressures to do well, it is not surprising that pitchers' rituals are often more complex than those of hitters. Mike Griffin begins his ritual a full day before he pitches by washing his hair. The next day, although he does not consider himself superstitious, he eats bacon for lunch. When Griffin dresses for the game he puts on his clothes in the same order, making certain he puts the slightly longer of his two stirrup socks on his right leg. "I just wouldn't feel right mentally if I did it the other way around," he explains. He always wears the same shirt under his uniform on the day he pitches. During the game he takes off his cap after each pitch, and between innings he sits in the same place on the dugout bench. He, too, believes his rituals provide a sense of order that reduces his anxiety about pitching.

Some pitchers involve their wives or girlfriends in their rituals. One wife reported that her husband insisted that she wash her hair each day he was to pitch. In her memoirs, Danielle Torrez reported that one "rule" she learned as a baseball wife was "to support your husband's superstitions, whether you believe in them or not. I joined the player's wives who ate ice cream in the sixth inning or tacos in the fifth, or who attended games in a pink sweater, a tan scarf, or a floppy hat" (Torrez 1983).

When in a slump, most players make a deliberate effort to change their rituals and routines in an attempt to shake off their bad luck. One player tried taking different routes to the ballpark; several players reported trying different combinations of tagging and not tagging particular bases in an attempt to find a successful combination. I knew one manager who would rattle the bat bin when his players weren't hitting, as if the bats were in a stupor and could be aroused by a good shaking. Similarly, I have seen hitters rub their hands along the handles of the bats protruding from the bin in hopes of picking up some power or luck from bats that are getting hits for their owners. Some players switch from wearing their contact lenses to glasses. In his book, Brett Mandel described how his Pioneer League team, the Ogden Raptors, tried to break a losing streak by using a new formation for their pre-game stretching (Mandel 1997).

Taboo

Taboos are the opposite of rituals. The word *taboo* comes from a Polynesian term meaning prohibition. Breaking a taboo, players believe, leads to undesirable consequences or bad luck. Most players observe at least a few taboos, such as never stepping on the foul lines. One teammate of mine would never watch a movie on a game day, despite the fact that we played nearly every day from April to September. Another teammate refused to read anything before a game because he believed it weakened his batting eye.

Many taboos take place off the field, out of public view. On the day a pitcher is scheduled to start, he is likely to avoid activities he believes will sap his strength and detract from his effectiveness. Some pitchers avoid eating certain foods; others will not shave on the day of a game and won't shave as long as they are winning. Early one season Oakland's Dave Stewart had six consecutive victories and a beard by the time he lost. Ex-St. Louis Cardinal Al Hrabosky took this taboo to extremes. Samson-like, he refused to cut his hair or beard during the entire season, which was part of the basis for his nickname the "Mad Hungarian."

Taboos usually grow out of exceptionally poor performances, which players, in search of a reason, attribute to a particular behavior. During my first season of pro ball, I ate pancakes before a game in which I struck out four times. A few weeks later I had another terrible game, again after eating pancakes. The result was a pancake taboo: I never again ate pancakes during the season. White Sox pitcher Jason Bere has a taboo that makes more sense in dietary terms: After eating a meatball sandwich and not pitching well, he swore them off for good.

While most taboos are idiosyncratic, there are a few that all ballplayers hold and that do not develop out of individual experience or misfortune. These form part of the culture of baseball; some are learned as early as Little League. Mentioning a no-hitter while one is in progress is a well-known example. It is believed that if a pitcher hears the words *no-hitter*, the spell accounting for this hard-to-achieve feat will be broken and the no-hitter lost. This taboo is also observed by many sports broadcasters, who use various linguistic subterfuges to inform their listeners that the pitcher has not given up a hit, never saying "no-hitter."

Fetishes

Fetishes are material objects believed to embody "supernatural" power (i.e., luck) that can aid or protect the owner. Such charms are standard equipment for some ballplayers. These include a wide assortment of objects from coins, chains, and crucifixes to a favorite baseball hat. In the words of Jim Snyder, "When you are going good you take notice of what you are doing. I still use my glove from college. It's kind of beat up but it's got 40 wins in it, so I still use it. I use my professional glove in practice and my college glove in games." The fetishized object may be a new possession or something a player found that happens to coincide with the start of a streak and that he holds responsible for his good fortune. While playing in the Pacific Coast League, Alan Foster forgot his baseball shoes on a road trip and borrowed a pair from a teammate. That night he pitched a no-hitter, which he attributed to the shoes. Afterwards he bought them from his teammate and they became a fetish. Expo farmhand Mark LaRosa's rock has a very different origin and use:

> I found it on the field in Elmira after I had gotten bombed [pitched poorly]. It's unusual, perfectly round, and it caught my attention. I keep it to remind me of how important it is to concentrate. When I am going well I look at the rock and remember to keep my focus. It reminds me of what can happen when I lose my concentration.

For one season Marge Schott, owner of the Cincinnati Reds, insisted that her field manager rub her St. Bernard "Schotzie" for good luck before each game. When the Reds were on the road, Schott would sometimes send a bag of the dog's hair to the field manager's hotel room.

During World War II American soldiers used fetishes in much the same way. Social psychologist Samuel Stouffer and his colleagues found that in the face of great danger and uncertainty, soldiers developed magical practices, particularly the use of protective amulets and good luck charms (crosses, Bibles, rabbits' feet, medals) and jealously guarded articles of clothing they associated with past experiences of escape from danger (Stouffer 1965). Stouffer also found that pre-battle preparations were carried out in fixed "ritual" order, much as ballplayers and certain other athletes prepare for a game.

Uniform numbers have special significance for some players who request their lucky number. Since the choice is usually limited, they try to at least get a uniform that contains their lucky number, such as 14, 24, 34, or 44 for the player whose lucky number is 4. Oddly enough, there is no consensus about the effect of wearing number 13. Some players will not wear it, others will, and a few request it. Number preferences emerge in different ways. A young player may request the number of a former star, hoping that—through what anthropologists call *imitative* magic—it will bring him the same success. Or he may request a number he associates with good luck. Vida Blue changed his uniform number from 35 to 14, the number he wore as a high school quarterback. When 14 did not produce better pitching performance, he switched back to 35. Larry Walker has a fixation with the number 3. Besides wearing 33, he takes three practice swings before stepping into the batter's box and sets his alarm for three minutes past the hour (Thrift and Shapiro 1990). Fans in ballparks all across America rise from their seats for the seventh inning stretch before the home club comes to bat because the number 7 is "lucky."

Clothing, both the choice and the order in which they are put on, combine elements of both ritual and fetish. Some players put on their uniform in a ritualized order. Expos farmhand Jim Austin always puts on his left sleeve, left pants leg, and left shoe before the right. Most players, however, single out one or two lucky articles or quirks of dress. After hitting two home runs in a game, for example, infielder Jim Davenport discovered that he had missed a buttonhole while dressing for the game. For the remainder of his career he left the same button undone. For Brian Hunter the focus is shoes, "I have a pair of high tops and a pair of low tops. Whichever shoes don't get a hit that game, I switch to the other pair." At the time of our interview, he was struggling at the plate and switching shoes almost every day. For Birmingham Baron pitcher Bo Kennedy the arrangement of the different pairs of baseball shoes in his locker is critical:

> I tell the clubbies [clubhouse boys] when you hang stuff in my locker don't touch my shoes. If you bump them move them back. I want the Pony's in front, the turfs to the right, and I want them nice and neat with each pair touching each other. . . . Everyone on the team knows not to mess with my shoes.

During streaks—hitting or winning—players may wear the same clothes day after day. Once I changed sweatshirts midway through the game for seven consecutive nights to keep a hitting streak going. Clothing rituals, however, can become impractical. Catcher Matt Allen was wearing a long-sleeve turtleneck on a cool evening in the New York-Penn League when he had a three-hit game. "I kept wearing the shirt and had a good week," he explained. "Then the weather got hot as hell, 85 degrees and muggy, but I would not take that shirt off.

I wore it for another ten days—catching—and people thought I was crazy." Also taking a ritual to the extreme, Leo Durocher, managing the Brooklyn Dodgers to a pennant in 1941, is said to have spent three and a half weeks in the same gray slacks, blue coat, and knitted blue tie. During a 16-game winning streak, the 1954 New York Giants wore the same clothes in each game and refused to let them be cleaned for fear that their good fortune might be washed away with the dirt.

Losing often produces the opposite effect. Several Oakland A's players, for example, went out and bought new street clothes in an attempt to break a 14-game losing streak. When I recently joined the Birmingham Barons for a road trip, outfielder Scott Tedder was in a slump. He changed batting gloves daily and had already gone through a dozen pairs trying to find one that would change his luck and get him some hits.

Baseball's superstitions, like most everything else, change over time. Many of the rituals and beliefs of early baseball are no longer observed. In the 1920s and 1930s sportswriters reported that a player who tripped en route to the field would often retrace his steps and carefully walk over the stumbling block for "insurance." A century ago players spent time on and off the field intently looking for items that would bring them luck. To find a hairpin on the street, for example, assured a batter of hitting safely in that day's game. Today few women wear hairpins —a good reason the belief has died out. To catch sight of a white horse or a wagon-load of barrels were also good omens. In 1904 the manager of the New York Giants, John McGraw, hired a driver and a team of white horses to drive past the Polo Grounds around the time his players were arriving at the ballpark. He knew that if his players saw white horses, they'd have more confidence and that could only help them during the game. Belief in the power of white horses survived in a few backwaters until the 1960s. A gray-haired manager of a team I played for in Quebec would drive around the countryside before important games and during the playoffs looking for a white horse. When he was successful, he'd announce it to everyone in the clubhouse before the game.

One belief that appears to have died out recently is a taboo about crossed bats. Some of my Latino teammates in the 1960s took it seriously. I can still recall one Dominican player becoming agitated when another player tossed a bat from the batting cage and it landed on top of his bat. He believed that the top bat might steal hits from the lower one. In his view, bats contained a finite number of hits, a sort of baseball "image of limited good." It was once commonly believed that once the hits in a bat were used up, no amount of good hitting would produce any more. Hall of Famer Honus Wagner believed each bat contained only one hundred hits. Regardless of the quality of the bat, he would discard it after its hundredth hit. This belief would have little relevance today, in the era of light bats with thin handles —so thin that the typical modern bat is lucky to survive a dozen hits without being broken. Other superstitions about bats do survive, however. Hitters on the Class A Asheville Tourists would not let pitchers touch or swing their bats, not even to warm up. The poor-hitting pitchers were said to pollute or weaken the bats.

Uncertainty and Magic

The best evidence that players turn to rituals, taboos, and fetishes to control chance and uncertainty is found in their uneven application. They are associated mainly with pitching and hitting—the activities with the highest degree of chance—and not fielding. I met only one player who had any ritual in connection with fielding, and he was an error-prone shortstop. Unlike hitting and pitching, a fielder has almost complete control over the outcome of his performance. Once a ball has been hit in his direction, no one can intervene and ruin his chances of catching it for an out (except in the unlikely event of two fielders colliding). Compared with the pitcher or the hitter, the fielder has little to worry about. He knows that in better than 9.7 times out of 10 he will execute his task flawlessly. With odds like that there is little need for ritual. Clearly, the ritual behavior of American ballplayers is not unlike that of the Trobriand Islanders studied by Malinowski many years ago (1948). In professional baseball, fielding is the equivalent of the inner lagoon while hitting and pitching are like the open sea.

While Malinowski helps us understand how ballplayers and other people respond to chance and uncertainty, behavioral psychologist B. F. Skinner sheds light on why personal rituals get established in the first place (Skinner 1938, 1953). With a few grains of seed Skinner could get pigeons to do anything he wanted. He merely waited for the desired behavior (e.g., pecking) and then rewarded it with some food. Skinner then decided to see what would happen if pigeons were rewarded with food pellets regularly, every fifteen seconds, regardless of what they did. He found that the birds associate the arrival of the food with a particular action, such as tucking their head under a wing or walking in clockwise circles. About ten seconds after the arrival of the last pellet, a bird would begin doing whatever it associated with getting the food and keep doing it until the next pellet arrived. In short, the pigeons behaved as if their actions made the food appear. They learned to associate particular behaviors with the reward of being given seed.

Ballplayers also associate a reward—successful performance—with prior behavior. If a player touches his crucifix and then gets a hit, he may decide the gesture was responsible for his good fortune and touch his crucifix the next time he comes to the plate. If he gets another hit, the chances are good that he will touch his crucifix each time he bats. Unlike pigeons, however, most ballplayers are quicker to change their rituals once they no longer seem to work. Skinner found that once a pigeon associated one of its actions with the arrival of food or water, only sporadic rewards were needed to keep the ritual going. One pigeon, apparently believing that hopping from side to side caused pellets to fall into its feeding cup, hopped ten thousand times without a single pellet appearing before finally giving up. But, then, hasn't Wade Boggs continued to eat chicken, through slumps and good times, before every game for the past dozen years? Obviously the rituals and superstitions of baseball do not make a pitch travel faster or a batted ball locate gaps between the fielders, nor do Trobriand rituals calm the seas or bring fish. What both do, however, is give their practitioners a sense of control, and with that, confidence. And we all know how important that is.

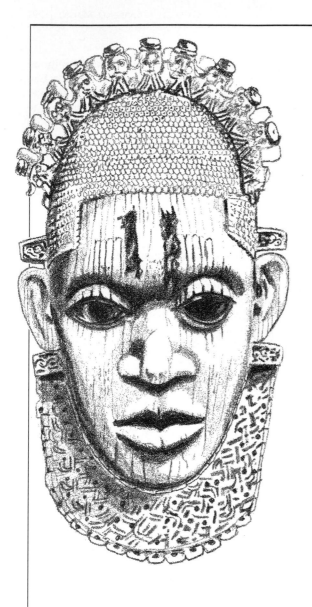

8

Ghosts, Souls, and Ancestors: Power of the Dead

Religions universally promise believers that there is life after death. Although the worship of ancestors is not universal, a belief in the immortality of the dead occurs in all cultures. There is variation among cultures in the degree of interaction between the living and the dead, however, as well as in the intensity and concern a people may have for the deceased. Eskimos are never free of anxieties about ghosts, whereas Pueblo Indians are seldom bothered by them; the Plains Indians of North America constructed elaborate ghost beliefs, whereas the Siriono of South America, although believing in ghosts, paid little attention to them.

Perhaps humans have some basic need that causes us to believe in ghosts and to worship ancestors: to seek verification that although the mortal body may die, the soul survives after death. The nineteenth-century sociologist Herbert Spencer speculated that the beginnings of religion were in ancestor worship—the need for the living to continue an emotional relationship with their dead relatives. A major problem with Spencer's argument is that many societies at the hunting-and-gathering level do not practice ancestor worship. The Arunta of Australia, for

Ivory pendant mask from Benin, Nigeria.

example, worshipped their totemic plants and animals, but not their human ancestors. This objection to Spencer's belief notwithstanding, ancestor worship does remind the living of a vital continuing link between the living and the dead. "Ritually, the most important category of animistic beings was the ancestors of the band, village, and clan or other kinship groups whose members believed they were bonded by common descent" (Harris 1989: 399).

One writer has pointed out that two major attitudes are widely held about the dead: that they have either left the society or remain as active members (Malefijt 1968: 156–59). In societies that separate the dead from the living social group, any possibility of the dead returning is regarded as undesirable because they could disrupt the social order and the daily routine of life. In such cultures, Annemarie de Waal Malefijt believes, the dead are likely to be greatly feared, and an elaborate belief system—a cult of the dead—is constructed and practiced in order to separate them from the living. The primary function of cults of the dead is to aid the survivors in overcoming the grief they may feel about the dead. Such cults are not found in societies where the dead are seen as active members of the group; instead, funeral ceremonies are undertaken with the hope the deceased will return to society in their new status. These beliefs, according to Malefijt, result in the development of ancestor cults instead of cults of the dead. S. C. Humphreys's *Comparative Perspective on Death* (1981) sets out the great variety of belief concerning the fate of the dead as does M. Bloch and J. Parry's work, *Death and the Regeneration of Life* (1982).

Ancestor cults and the ritual that surrounds them may also be seen as an elaboration of cults of the dead. The Bantu of Africa, for example, outline distinct ancestral deities for each lineage and clan. All of these ancestral gods are gods to their living relatives, but not to individuals who belong to other kinship organizations. Further elaboration of Bantu ancestor worship may be seen in Bantu beliefs about the supernatural beings believed to head their royal clans. Gods of such royal clans are worshipped by the entire kingdom, not just the royal clan itself.

The study of ancestor worship conducted by American and British anthropologists has emphasized the connection between the identity and behavioral characteristics of the dead, on one hand,

and the distribution and nature of their authority in both domestic and political domains of the society, on the other (Bradbury 1966: 127). Although the belief in ghosts of ancestors is universal, the functions ancestors play vary greatly among societies. It is also clear that variations in ancestor worship are directly related to social structure and that this relationship is not based on mere common religious interests alone: Rather, the structure of the kin group and the relationships of those within it serve as the model of ancestor worship (Bradbury 1966: 128). Among the Sisala of Ghana, for example, only a select number of Sisala elders, based on their particular status and power within the group, can effectively communicate with the ghosts of ancestors (Mendonsa 1976: 63–64). In many other parts of the non-Western world, non-elder ritual specialists, such as heads of households, are responsible for contacting the ancestors. A cross-cultural study of fifty societies found that where important decisions are made by the kin group, ancestor worship is a high probability (Swanson 1964: 97–108).

Many, but certainly not all, non-Western societies believe ancestors play a strong and positive role in the security and prosperity of their group, and anthropological data offer many of these kinds of examples. It is important, however, to recognize that ancestors are but one of several categories of spirits whose actions directly affect society. John S. Mbiti's study of East and Central Africa shows that the status of spirits may change through time. Ancestor spirits, the "living dead," are those whose memory still exists in the minds of their kin and who are primarily beneficial to the surviving relatives. When the living dead are forgotten in the memory of their group and dropped from the genealogy as a result of the passing of time (four or five generations), they are believed to be transformed into "nameless spirits," non-ancestors, characterized as malicious vehicles for misfortune of all kinds (1970). In keeping with Mbiti's model, the Lugbara of Uganda recognize two types of dead. The first group, simply called "ancestors," comprises nameless, all deceased relatives; these are secondary in importance to the recently deceased, called "ancestor spirits" or "ghosts," who can be invoked by the living to cause misfortune to befall those whose acts threaten the solidarity of the kin group (Middleton 1971: 488).

Clearly spirits, ghosts, and ancestors are often given unique statuses in the afterlife and are viewed as having different functions and effects on the living. In many respects the relationship of fear and responsibility of elders toward ancestors is mirrored by the son-father relationship among the living. The ancestral world in many cases is an extension or model of the real world. The supernatural status of the ancestors exhibits major differences, for although one can argue to a point with an elder, no one questions the wisdom and authority of an ancestor.

The power of the dead is an important aspect of religion and social control. If, for example, a Lugbara man threatened the solidarity of the clan or lineage in any of a number of ways, the elder may invoke ghosts to punish the troublemaker (Middleton 1971: 488–92). Without doubt this veneration of the ancestors and the fear of their power functions importantly to help control many societies. Interestingly, ancestor worship also contributes to the conservative nature of those cultures where it is practiced. Typically, dead ancestors do not smile on any kind of change in the cultures of their living relatives. Because ghosts are capable of severely punishing an earthly mortal desirous of change, the force for conformity is strong.

Not all societies assign power to ancestors. In many cultures, North America included, a high god (monotheism) or gods (polytheism) exert authority over the living, punishing those who violate religious tenets, rules that often are duplicated in civil law and serve as the bases of appropriate social behavior. In these groups ancestor cults and worship of the deceased are not found, although the spiritual nature of ancestors and belief in the afterlife persevere.

Among people where the deceased are believed to take an active role in society, the living are understandably concerned with the welfare of ancestors. Customs are established to assure the comfort of the dead in their life after death. Most commonly, rituals carried out at funerals, burials, and in some cases reburial or cremation, ensure that loved ones arrive safely at what the living believe is the proper abode of the dead. The care taken in preparing the deceased for the afterlife is an important reinforcement of the society's customs and an expression of unity among its members. Participation helps ensure that the same care can be expected to be given at the time of one's own death. Beyond this motiva-

tion, however, the power to rain down misfortunes is a major reason for carefully following customs surrounding the preparation, interment, and propitiation of the dead. No one wants to be subjected to supernatural punishment by vengeful and angry ghosts.

To most people in Western culture the word *ghost* brings forth an image of a disembodied spirit of a dead person swooping through dark halls, hovering frighteningly over a grave, or perhaps roaming aimlessly through damp woods. Typically, the ghost is observed wearing white sheets—an image that undoubtedly arises from the shroud or winding sheet used to wrap the corpse for its placement in the grave. There is a wide variety of shapes available to would-be ghosts, however. Some are transparent; some are lifelike apparitions of their former selves; others appear with horribly gaunt, empty faces, devoid of eyes and lips. Not all ghosts take a human or even vaguely human shape: Horses frequently appear in phantom form, as do dogs and large birds, and ghost lore is full of accounts of ghost trains, stagecoaches, and, of course, such phantom ships as the Flying Dutchman.

Very few cultures do not support the idea of a separate spirit world—a land of the dead. It is to this other world that souls will travel and, once there, will rest in eternal peace. At some point in history, however, the notion arose that not all souls deserved an easy trip to a blissful spiritual world. Murder victims, miscreants, and evil people, for example, might become ghosts doomed to wander the earthly world. Inadequate funerals also might give rise to restless ghosts, thus explaining the attention paid by cultures everywhere to meticulously preparing and dressing the corpse for burial, and to placing gifts, food, and weapons in the grave or at the gravesite to enhance the spirit's journey to the place of eternal rest.

In the first article of this chapter, Shirley Lindenbaum explores the problem of why some New Guinea societies show little interest in ghosts and sorcery whereas others seem preoccupied with both. The granting of the first gun permits to another New Guinea group and the resulting formation of a cult is the subject of the article by William Mitchell. Mitchell shows how the cult's belief in vengeful spirits helps them understand why they sometimes experience unsuccessful hunting. In the third selection, Paul Barber vividly illustrates the fear with which eighteenth-century Europeans regarded vampires.

Karen McCarthy Brown examines the practice of Voodoo in Haiti, pointing out that despite the distorted popular version we see all too frequently in the mass media, it is a legitimate religious practice of 80 to 90 percent of Haitians. Gino Del Guercio's article, "The Secrets of Haiti's Living Dead," serves as a companion piece to Brown's more broadly based discussion of Voodoo. Del Guercio recounts the research of Wade Davis, who believes that zombies do exist in Haiti but are actually "the living drugged" rather than "the living dead." William Booth, in the next article, counters this conclusion by claiming that Davis ignored contrary evidence and generally used poor scientific methods (dubbed by Booth "voodoo science"). In the final selection, Peter Metcalf compares American and Berawan funeral rites. As Metcalf learned to see Berawan funerary customs as natural, American treatment of the dead began to seem exotic.

References

Bloch, M., and J. Parry, eds.
1982 *Death and Regeneration of Life.* Cambridge: Cambridge University Press.

Bradbury, R. E.
1966 "Fathers, Elders, and Ghosts in Edo Religion." In Michael Banton, ed., *Anthropological Approaches to the Supernatural*, pp. 127–53. London: Tavistock.

Harris, Marvin
1989 *Our Kind.* New York: Harper and Row.

Humphreys, S. C.
1981 *Comparative Perspectives on Death.* New York: Academic Press.

Malefijt, Annemarie de Waal
1968 *Religion and Culture: An Introduction to Anthropology of Religion.* New York: Macmillan.

Mbiti, John S.
1970 *African Religions and Philosophies.* Garden City, N.Y.: Doubleday.

Mendonsa, Eugene L.
1976 "Elders, Office-Holders and Ancestors among the Sisala of Northern Ghana." *Africa* 46: 57–64.

Middleton, John
1971 "The Cult of the Dead: Ancestors and Ghosts." In William A. Lessa and Evon Z. Vogt, eds., *Reader in Comparative Religion: An Anthropological Approach*, 3rd ed., pp. 488–92. New York: Harper and Row.

Swanson, Guy A.
1964 *The Birth of the Gods.* Ann Arbor: University of Michigan Press.

Sorcerers, Ghosts, and Polluting Women: An Analysis of Religious Belief and Population Control

Shirley Lindenbaum

Concentrating on three important components of New Guinean culture, Shirley Lindenbaum here analyzes the roles that sorcery, ancestral ghosts, and female pollution play in maintaining social structural integrity. Emphasis on varying ecological conditions led her to the construction of a continuum in which groups could be located and compared in terms of the relative importance they placed on these elements. Taking a structural-functional approach, her data and the resulting model clarify why some groups differ so radically in their beliefs surrounding incest, adultery, chastity, and the relative importance of witches, sorcerers, and ghosts, in enforcing the institutionalization of male-female relationships and reproduction.

Reprinted from *Ethnology*, vol. 11 (1972), pp. 241–53, by permission of the author and the Department of Anthropology, University of Pittsburgh.

THE PROBLEM OF WHY SOME NEW GUINEA societies evince little interest in sorcery while others seem preoccupied with sorcery as an explanation for disease and death has been examined in recent publications (Hogbin 1958; Lawrence and Meggitt 1965; Lindenbaum 1971). Analyses have focused on the structural features of society. It has been suggested that sorcery accusations are a necessary means of easing tension between individuals who lack the security of membership in solidarity groups. Sorcery also acts as a mechanism whereby permanently settled descent groups maintain their identity in the absence of wars for economic aggrandizement (Lawrence and Meggitt 1965; 17). It has been noted that these theories do not account for the absence of a great interest in sorcery among the Mae Enga and the Ngaing, and it was suggested that these peoples have an alternate means of challenging aggression through warfare and ceremonial exchange (Lawrence and Meggitt 1965: 18). This paper continues the discussion, but relates the presence of sorcery to ecological variables. The polluting woman is also seen to inhabit a particular form of social and material environment; an examination of the interaction of the two accounts for her presence.

Enga and Fore

Two societies in the Highlands of New Guinea illustrate the variations which exist at each end of the range; the Enga in the West and the Fore in the East. It has been noted that Enga, for instance, believe misfortune and death to be the result of attacks by malicious ghosts of the dead rather than by living sorcerers. Enga, moreover, do not simply fear ghosts in general; they fear male ancestral ghosts. As the degree of danger is judged more serious—such as the death of a socially important victim or an epidemic of illness—Enga turn from appeasing particular domestic ghosts to the placation of all the ancestral ghosts of a clan. There is, as Meggitt (1965b: 131) points out, an isomorphism of the structures of the lineage system and the religious system. A hierarchical order runs through them both.

Fore beliefs about the etiology of disease also reflect structural features of their society. Fore use the idea of sorcerers rather than of ancestral ghosts to define the boundaries of their social groups and to maintain their internal cohesion. The composition of South Fore political groups provides the bases for mutual mistrust. The political unit of widest span, the parish, is an aggregate of people residing on a defined territory. Parish membership is not based on common descent; rather, the parish may be described as a temporary coalition of factions united by a common desire for security and defense. The parish section is similarly a residential rather than a genealogical unit. The smallest parish subdivision, the "people of a place," is based on genealogical criteria, although the permitted adoption of outsiders disqualifies it as a strictly unilineal group. The social system at all levels is thus characterized by flexibility and expediency. Every parish includes immigrants who have fled conflict in their original parish. Newcomers are readily incorporated, given gardening land, and if necessary are bound to their new co-residents by ties of fictional kinship. The ambiguity felt about the loyalty of people with ties to an outside parish is expressed in sorcery beliefs and activities. Sorcery is thus a political institution peculiarly suited to the organizational problems of South Fore society. Fore do not enjoy the comfort of genealogical unity, and sorcery discussions are endemic (Lindenbaum 1971).

I wish to argue here that the choice between ancestral ghosts or sorcerers as an explanation for death from disease may be ecologically determined. If disease is considered to result from the anger of ancestors, the society in which such a religious belief is held is one in which there is population pressure on scarce resources. The implication is that members of the society regard disease sent by one's own former kinsmen as an acceptable form of population control. Enga typify this position. Enga land is scarce, and the relative scarcity of arable land is a significant determinant of the rigidity of lineage structure in the society. Enga religion is also one in which agnatic ghosts are believed to control the fertility of the land and the people (Meggitt 1965b: 105–31). Disease and death are attributed to angry ghosts. This philosophical viewpoint appears to be a Malthusian acceptance of the realities of the Enga man-land ratio.

Fore, on the other hand, do not hold such beliefs. They have ample land for a small population. Their problems are not focused on restricting the access of outsiders to group resources. The opposite is the case—how to maintain group strength in the face of aggressive neighbors. South Fore groups readily admit newcomers and provide them with fertile land. Fore view illness and death as an attack by jealous enemy sorcerers who not only endanger the viability of small groups, but who may be attempting to wipe out the entire society. The presence of *kuru,* a fatal neurological disorder which mainly kills women, gives rise to realistic fears for survival, expressed in terms of the assault of particularly malignant sorcerers.

Illness and Death

The hypothesis may be illustrated by examining the behavior provoked by illness and death in Enga and Fore societies. Meggitt (1965b: 113) describes Enga response to the illness and death of an adult man. The victim's brothers or sons kill a pig and give its essence to the ghost they think is causing the misfortune, distributing the meat to both maternal and paternal kinsmen. If the sick man does not recover, his agnates consult a diviner to locate the identity of the angered ghost, and again kill pigs to propitiate the ghost. If the victim is an important person, all the men of his patrilineage, with pigs contributed by subclan and even parallel subclan members, may perform a ritual to placate the ancestral ghosts of a clan. The clan fertility stones are rubbed with pig grease. If the patient then dies, his relatives mourn briefly and publicly. Close relatives of the deceased slice their ear lobes or cut off finger joints. For the next two or three weeks the immediate family members do not tend their pigs or gardens. They subsequently return to everyday life after holding a feast.

The Enga response thus appears to be controlled and orderly. The source of attack is assumed to come from within the group itself—not a disrupting idea for Enga. It is assumed that an invisible agnatic ghost attacks the internal agnatic spirit of the victim, and at the same time injures the victim's maternally acquired flesh and vitality. Both paternal and maternal kinsmen are thus offered pork in compensation for their loss. Enga attempt to avert the loss of an important man by ceremonial treatment of the clan fertility stones, but the death itself elicits only a brief, public mourning period. The family's loss of a productive member is indicated by injury to body extremities, an important mutilation of the domestic group but not of the body of the lineage. The family group, in a realistic acknowledgment of its decreased size, does not attempt to increase its food production for the following two or three weeks. Meggitt (1965a: 187) also notes that the deaths of women and children are rarely the subject of inquiry.

Fore response to illness and death is markedly more excited. Sorcery accusations arise over the severe illness or death of any adult male or female. Most sorcery accusations occur between men residing in different parish groups. The location of a sorcery challenge thus indicates the extent of mutual distrust felt by allies and neighbors; if an accusation occurs within parish borders, it signals the possibility of incipient political fission. Sorcery challenges are therefore socially disruptive, particularly as the sorcerer is assumed to be within a close range. In the past, sorcery challenges led to fighting and migration; now charges and countercharges are adjudicated in indigenous courts and cases heard by the Administration.

Fore do not accept severe illness with equanimity. Much day-to-day behavior is concerned with preventing a sorcerer from acquiring the material he needs for attack. Men, women, and children make use of deep pit latrines for feces and food scraps. They also hide hair cuttings and nail parings. Women, in particular, scrupulously eliminate menstrual blood, the emissions from childbirth, and an infant's umbilical cord; that is, they conceal evidence of their fertility in response to the high incidence of *kuru*, a sex-biased disease. Fore use the image of the human body to make symbolic statements about the body politic (Douglas 1966). They monitor substances entering and issuing from the body; the small South Fore groups fear population decline resulting from social intermingling. South Fore both protect the body's boundaries and police the borders of their social groups (Lindenbaum 1972).

When an adult falls ill, Fore resort to a variety of cures, part of which involves a divination test to reveal the identity of the sorcerer. Opossum meat, an environmental mediator, is used as an oracle to screen suspected groups, and after many tests the malicious actor is finally identified. Relatives of the victim try to persuade or threaten the sorcerer to reverse his actions, to remove his hidden sorcery materials, and to allow the patient to recover. This acrimonious political activity, in the case of *kuru* victims, may last for a year or more. The victim's supporting group, her husband, and his kinsmen and friends, are also involved in expensive, time-consuming visits to foreign curers who live outside Fore territory.

At this point the patient may die. In the past, most deceased persons were eaten. Rules of the cannibal consumption of dead bodies are somewhat undefined because cannibalism was a relatively late custom in Fore society and has been forbidden since the mid 1950s. In general, however, body parts were distributed along the same lines as were traditional death payments in pork and valuables—large payments to matrilateral kinsmen and smaller payments to age-mates and classificatory brothers and friends. That is, kinship cannibalism among the Fore appears to underline the recognition of responsibility for loss to those who generated the body and to those who see themselves as its equivalents.

Little ideology was associated with the consumption of dead bodies. If the body was buried, the Fore say "the ground ate him"; that is, bodies fertilize the ground. Dismemberment of a corpse for consumption was carried out in a kinsman's garden. The association between cannibalism and fertility has also been noted by Berndt (1962: 271). Kinship cannibalism among the Fore suggests that a society in biological decline may attempt regeneration by eating itself. A wife expects to eat her husband's buttocks and penis (Berndt 1962: 273). It may be significant that South Fore society has a marked imbalance in the sex ratio; *kuru* decimates adult women, and women were in the main the cannibals. In contrast, cannibalism is repugnant to the Enga (Meggitt 1965b: 120). Cannibalism does occur, according to Enga, among demons who inhabit the inhospitable forest. Some demons with an appetite for human flesh eat solitary bush travelers; others appear as snakes to abduct men from the men's houses, or as sexually appealing women whose false promises of wealth lead to property dissipation and dementia (Meggitt 1965b: 122). For Enga, fertility and cannibalism present the same kinds of danger.

The responses to epidemic illness in Enga and Fore societies are markedly different. If Enga are troubled by an increase in the death rate of children or important men, or by an increase in the incidence of disease, they turn their attention to clan ghosts. The same response is elicited by a sudden rise in the death rate of pigs, or by a clan-wide crop failure, resources on which man depends (Meggitt 1965b: 114). To deal with this threat, they perform rituals which require peace to be observed among neighboring clans. During part of the rituals, a bachelor and a spinster sit on the roof of a cult house which protects the clan stones. The ancestral ghosts are believed to have temporarily removed their potency from men and land, withdrawing into the stones. Each clansman is offered a fragment of pork fat bespelled in the presence of the ancestral ghosts. Married men may eat it; bachelors may only smell the fat. Black opossums, used in another part of the ritual, are offered to the oldest men of the clan, but some refuse to eat, fearing it may hasten their deaths. For a month or two following the rituals, clansmen should not copulate or prepare new gardens; such activities would, it is said, "antagonize the ancestors." The cult house may be left to disintegrate, or neighboring clans may be invited to destroy it. This contest to destroy the cult house generates much ill will against the triumphant clan, which boasts its superiority (Meggitt 1965b: 114–20).

The rituals may be interpreted as a cultural mechanism by which Enga accept a population or a subsistence loss. The performance of the rituals requires a truce amongst warring clans, a regulation which precludes further depletion of numbers. Although the purpose of the rituals is ostensibly to restore the good humor of ancestral ghosts so that they will cease meting out punishment in the form of illness and death, the central actors are persons whose generative powers are recognized to be temporarily inactive—bachelors and spinsters—as are the generative powers of the clan stones. Nor does the impetus of the ritual seem to suggest great renewal of fertility. Indeed, Meggitt (1965b: 118) comments that

"the propitiatory rituals . . . are not thought to be immediately efficacious . . . it is assumed that revitalization of the clan and its land may take some time." Ritual symbolism seems to have more to do with death, and a recognition of temporary stasis, than with renewed fertility. Some old men are afraid to eat the large black opossums which may propel them beyond life to join the body of ancestors. For one or two months following the rituals there is a ban on copulation and new gardening of which the ancestors might disapprove—an indication that there will be no new additions to society and no provision for them.

In similar rituals held by Western Enga, ceremonies surround the clan pool (Meggitt 1965b: 118–19). Again the theme is a separation of men and women, the use of a pair of bachelors as central actors, and a temporary ban on copulation and gardening. The young boys selected to participate in the clan pool rituals are moreover considered inducted into the bachelors' association, which prescribes prolonged avoidance of contact with women.

Thus the response to epidemic illness or unusual loss of life and resources results in ceremonies which do not emphasize fertility, or symbolize creative behavior. Rather, the depletion of clan membership is publicly accepted in a number of ceremonies whose content emphasizes instead the spacing of men and women, the importance of men whose sexual capacities are socially constrained, and an acceptable stasis in the relationship between men and land. Enga clans appear to repair damaged relationships with the ghosts of their ancestors lest they decline in relation to similar groups. The clan which successfully demolishes the cult house—a symbol of withdrawn fertility—threatens others with its suggestion of superiority and imbalance.

Fore response to illness is another matter. Fore rituals concern protection and unity; groups close their ranks against the sorcerer. Annual ceremonies are observed for the safety of children and pregnant women. Infants and future mothers eat special foods, and receive a share of the feast before other women and all men. The ceremonies are held if there is news of infant illness in surrounding areas, or at the beginning of the dry season, presumably a time of increased sickness. During the early 1960s, the South Fore responded dramatically to the high incidence of *kuru* among the population. From November, 1962, to March, 1963, mass meetings took place almost daily throughout the entire region. Men from hostile parishes faced each other in compact opposing groups and demanded an end to *kuru* sorcery and the mending of the male-female sex imbalance. Reputed sorcerers made public confessions of their past activities; men sought to purge themselves of ill feeling in a context of beneficial ritual forces at a time when mutual suspicion and hostility were disrupting social life. To the often expressed fears of extinction through the loss of the reproductive capacity of the women was now added the fear of internal disorder so great that society itself was felt to be endangered. Persuasive orators gave moral discourses on good behavior and appealed to those sorcerers who had not come forward to relinquish all future activities. The meetings had a formal, ritual quality in seating arrangement, orderly speechmaking, and food distribution. Sometimes they culminated in peacemaking rituals that signaled an end to hostile action. Men clapped hands and poured water on *kuru* victims—symbolic actions common to ceremonies calling for a truce between enemies, whether warriors or sorcerers.

Ritual emerged as a device by which the society attempted to create an illusion of unity. Orators recalled a golden past of supposedly less divisive times when their ancestors were not troubled by *kuru*. Men, they said, must halt their present intergroup strife and realize that they are one people. They named little-known all-inclusive groups to which they said they belonged. The meetings sought to redefine and enlarge the moral boundaries of the assembled groups. To survive the epidemic, the Fore thus offered the fiction of a united community.

Sorcerers, the Fore noted, had plainly exceeded the concept of self-limitation that men recognize in wartime. In the past, peace ceremonies were arranged when the toll of deaths met a certain limit of propriety. Fore accused sorcerers of aiming to eliminate all women, of perpetrating a crime against society, a breach of the natural order. Women of the host group were present to listen to the discussion, sometimes angrily taking part. At some meetings, borrowing symbolism from recent mission exposure, men pledged their commitment to the future by washing their right hands in soapy water and raising the purged hand for all to see. They promised thenceforth, to forego sorcery.

The Fore image of society, then, is that of a body under attack. Illness, like warfare, endangers the vi-

ability of small groups whose cohesion is constitutionally unsound. Fore therefore attempt to enlarge their moral boundaries to avert further loss. Debates emphasize renewal, a new order, a society without sorcerers.

For the Enga, interpretation of disease as a form of ghost attack is an acknowledgment that the attack is coming from within one's own political group. It is internal and invisible, and not subject to identification in living human form. A population or resource reduction caused by the ancestors is socially acceptable; they are assumed to have the proper balance in mind. On the other hand, when Fore interpret disease as a consequence of attack by sorcerers they assume that aggression is coming from known living enemies outside the viable political units. It is unacceptable, and the ritual underlines this. The choice between the two interpretations is related to the man-resource ratio.

Sorcery is therefore a political instrument whereby antagonistic political groups recognize and adjust to a competitive advance or decline in strength. In societies where sorcery is an overwhelming issue—Tangu (Burridge 1960: 122), Dobu (Fortune 1963: 312), and Fore—epidemic disease has created alarming population problems. Sorcerers in these societies not only kill people; they are also wife stealers. Men are in competition for the sexual productivity of the women. Sorcerers are thus predators of the scarcest resource. This throws into relief other New Guinea societies where sorcery is not a central issue, but where the predominant theme is fear of women and their powers of contamination. The concept of female pollution in the latter societies would therefore appear to be a cultural regulator impressing on men their need to keep distant from the women.

Female Pollution

In a paper on female pollution in New Guinea, Meggitt (1964) outlined a complex of social attitudes and practices characteristic of certain parts of the Highlands. Meggitt (1964: 219) pointed out, without suggesting any causal sequence, that certain attitudes and practices clustered together.

> We might expect, therefore to find the notion of female pollution emphasized in societies where affinal groups are seen—for whatever reason—as inimical to one's own group, but absent or of little

significance where marriages usually occur between friendly groups. Moreover, as a logical extension of this argument, associations devoted to male purification, seclusion, or initiation should be more sharply defined among the former. Finally, it follows that where male-female hostility exists in societies of the second category—those favouring inter-marriage among friendly groups—it will differ markedly from that of the first category.

He defined a regional variation in the phenomenon, noting two main kinds of intersexual conflict or opposition, the "Mae type" and the "Kuma type," reflecting the Western and Central Highlands social arrangements. The Mae reflect the anxiety of prudes to protect themselves from contamination by women, the Kuma the aggressive determination of lechers to assert control over recalcitrant women (Meggitt 1964: 21). In addition, Meggitt noted that Eastern Highlands societies appear to display both sets of characteristics simultaneously or in parallel form.

The argument pursued here would add causality to the analysis. The idea of female pollution is used as a cultural whip in societies where available resources are endangered by further population increase. Pollution is of less concern (Eastern Highlands) or absent (Central Highlands) where population expansion is not an environmental threat and is generally desired. Fear of pollution is a form of ideological birth control. Fear of female contamination thus declines with the introduction of new technologies and food sources.

Enga, Kaulong, and Sengseng are New Guinea societies with the most acute fear of female pollution yet recorded (Meggitt 1964; Goodale and Chowning 1971). Enga pressure on resources and pollution fears are well documented (Meggitt 1965a, 1965b), fears that lead to male postponement of marriage and to conflict over the need for heirs (Meggitt 1964: 210). Kaulong and Sengseng, neighboring societies in the Passismanua Census Division of Southwest New Britain, also live in a taxing environment, one subject to rapid flooding. Shifting taro cultivation is a major subsistence activity, while "at least 60% of the food consumed comes from the forest" (Goodale and Chowning 1971: 3). The "lack of any strong demarcation of sex roles in basic subsistence," noted as an unusual feature of New Guinea societies, suggests the need for an equal labor contribution by both men and women. Fear of female pollution and

male avoidance of marriage are "one of the most distinctive aspects of Passismanua culture" (Goodale and Chowning 1971: 6). Kaulong and Sengseng males, like Enga, marry late. Some avoid sexual union until their 60s, and permanent bachelors are allowed a place of prestige in society. Until Mission and Administration interference, widows were strangled and buried 24 hours after the death of their husbands, thus seriously limiting their reproductive years. Kaulong and Sengseng manifest no strong desire for heirs, and practice infanticide. Belief in the contaminating powers of women, together with certain socially accepted behavioral manipulations, appears to have resulted in an effective cultural barrier to human reproduction. The population density of two to three persons per square mile is reported to have been held constant for many generations (Goodale and Chowning 1971: 2).

In Enga, Kaulong, and Sengseng societies the cultural sanctions against sexual congress are expressed in biological terms. An Enga husband refrains from frequent copulation, equating the loss of semen with a depletion of male vitality. Overindulgence will "dull his mind and leave his body permanently exhausted and withered" (Meggitt 1964: 210). The Enga bachelor, who should remain chaste, is kept from socially disapproved sexual congress by the belief that contact with a menstruating woman "will, in the absence of countermagic sicken a man and cause persistent vomiting, turn his blood black, corrupt his vital juices so that his skin darkens and wrinkles as his flesh wastes, permanently dull his wits, and eventually lead to a slow decline and death" (Meggitt 1964: 207). That is, socially approved sexual congress within marriage is a biological danger; sexual contact outside the severe limits imposed by society leads to premature withering of the society.

Kaulong and Sengseng similarly resort to threats of biological disaster to enforce behavioral compliance. Shortly after her husband's death, a widow should be strangled by a close male kinsman—her son, brother, or father (Goodale and Chowning 1971: 8). The widow goads the reluctant murderer by suggesting that his restraint is based on a desire to copulate with her (Goodale: personal communication). This is not only a taunt of incest, but also an open reference to sex which is an affront in this prudish culture. The feeling of guilt is sufficient to force the murderer's hand. Enga, Kaulong, and Sengseng thus appear to be telling us their problems. For

Enga, to contemplate nonapproved sexual activity leads to the dispatch of the actor. Kaulong and Sengseng males face a similar threat to their health; in addition, a male who fails to carry out a socially approved execution is contemplating an improper addition to society.

People are also telling us something of their problems by the way they mix or separate sex and the staple crop. Enga men, with magic to protect them from female pollution, copulate with their wives in the bush. Moreover, a husband "should not enter his gardens on the day he copulates, lest the female secretions adhering to him blight his crops" (Meggitt 1964: 210). Nor should he attempt to cook meat on that day, for it would spoil. In addition, Enga believe the menstrual blood destroys the *Acorus calamus* plants men use for wealth, pig, and war magic. Enga thus fear that increased female fertility would upset the delicate balance between men and their resources. Fore males, in contrast, purchase love magic to enchant the women they desire, and they copulate in the gardens.

Initiation

Initiation and bachelor associations also differ markedly in the Eastern and Western Highlands. The theme of Enga initiation rites concerns the shielding of males "from femininity, sexuality and impurity" (Meggitt 1964: 123). The men's behavior is prudish; they refrain from looking at each other's sexually provocative body areas and keep their conversations free of reference to sex or natural functions. Boys enter the bachelor associations when they are fifteen or sixteen, and remain members until marriage at a modal age of 25 to 27 (Meggitt 1965a: 86). The rituals require bathing to purify the youths from female influence, and ceremonies to keep alive the *Acorus* plants, the joint heritage of the subclan. A bachelor who breaks the sex rules prescribing chastity endangers not only his own health but also the welfare of the bachelors of the entire subclan. The iris plant would consequently die. Subclan members then beat the wayward youth and demand from him pig compensation "for the injury he has done them." The subclan thus exerts strong sanctions against unregulated additions to its size.

Courtship ceremonies in Enga society are "drearily proper gatherings," unlike the licentious functions in other parts of the Highlands, and girls attend with their chaperones (Meggitt 1964: 212).

The playful culmination, where girls seize favored bachelors, is "not a betrothal" but a sign of willingness to pursue future acquaintance. The bachelors use the left hand to touch the penis throughout the unmarried period, thus keeping it from the fertilizing dangers of the right hand which has had contact with women (Meggitt 1964: 223–24). The bachelors themselves, the purificatory rituals, and the bog-iris leaves are all referred to as *sanggai*, "that which is hidden." That which is hidden would seem to be the penis, a fact recognized by the frustrated women who exert no restraint on public reference to sex, and taunt men about the smallness of their penises (Meggitt 1964: 210, 214).

The stress throughout the ceremonies is on male chastity and the aggregation of clan groups. The rituals culminate in a potentially explosive period, as the bachelors in each clan group shout mutually aggressive and boastful songs at other clans. Their earlier songs indicate the problems and ultimate dangers in Enga society; they tell of the shortage of the bog-iris plants for the many bachelors of the clan, and their dreams of territorial conquest (Meggitt 1964: 215).

Fore initiation is another matter. The ceremonies emphasize fertility and stress the rapid maturity of the youths. Rituals center on symbolic and imitative biological reproduction. In place of the bog-iris, which must be protected by the chastity of the bachelors, Fore men in seclusion reveal a pair of flutes, one male and one female. For men the flutes are a symbol of their virility, but the women refer to them as "flute-women" or co-wives (Berndt 1962: 70). Like the flutes, age-mates in Fore society are ideally pictured as matched pairs, men with an interest in the same women. The two must protect each other in life and are pledged to avenge each other's death. They are sexual confidants, and each has the right to inherit the other's widow (Lindenbaum and Glasse 1969).

The flutes are thus potent symbols of fertility, and during rituals are rubbed with pig blood, as are the male and female participants. Pig blood is also splashed on the earth. The ritual also requires that the youths undergo forced nose-bleeding, an imitative menstruation (Berndt 1962: 65–73, 104), believed to strengthen them and hasten maturity. Moreover, the same nose-bleeding ritual is performed for girls to strengthen them after menstruation and childbirth and before marriage (Berndt 1962: 106). This illuminates the danger men fear most. It seems that women represent two different kinds of danger in the Eastern and Western Highlands. Enga men fear women for the dangers of excess fertility. Fore men fear sexual inadequacy in the face of aggressively demanding females. Fore fear for their powers of reproduction; men and women alike must protect and increase their fertility with rituals which celebrate the physiological events of menstruation and childbirth (Berndt 1962: 105). Male-female relationships in the Eastern Highlands express complementarity rather than conflict (cf. Newman 1964: 265–66).

The tone of Fore society would shock the Enga. Male initiation ceremonies include men dressed as women, enacting scenes of copulation as a lesson on the dangers of adultery (Berndt 1962: 103). Female initiation presents women dressed as men, causing vaginal bleeding with mock coitus (Berndt 1962: 106). Fore women's songs, predictably, do not include frustrated reference to penises the size of tiny mushrooms (Meggitt 1964: 214) but extol the irresistible attraction of the penis-flutes (Berndt 1962: 70). Erotic farces are also frequently enacted, dramatizing incidents from myth or everyday life (Berndt 1962: 148).

Fore boys undergo initiation at a tender age (Berndt 1962: 106 photo) and continue until past adolescence. Participation in the rituals, however, does not rule out sexual adventure. Rather the ceremonies stimulate an interest in sex and carry the message that society awards prestige to the sexually active male. Moral rules during initiation stress protection of the political unit by aggressive behavior in both war and sex (Berndt 1962: 110), while negative lessons deal emphatically with stealing property and adultery, thefts which endanger internal solidarity. The negative lessons are hardly effective, for adultery is a common source of conflict. Berndt (1962: 328–80) records 107 indigenous court hearings among Fore and their neighbors. Most cases concern adultery, and there was no case of homicide. Punishment in one adultery case required the forced re-enactment of the crime by the adulterous pair, after which the husband received a compensation payment and also kept his wife. In contrast, Enga beat adulterous wives and then transfer them to the adulterer in return for a compensation payment of pigs, a scarce resource.

Although Fore may talk about female pollution, they lack the Enga sense of horror. Premarital and extra-marital affairs abound, and Fore are cavalier in their approach to incest. Faced with a shortage of women, South Fore redefine classificatory sisters as marriageable partners; the new wife's father then becomes a mother's brother, and her brothers the husband's cross-cousins (Glasse 1969: 29–30).

Conclusion

Gross differences thus emerge in the relationship of men to women throughout New Guinea. It may be possible to construct a continuum whereby Enga, Kaulong, and Sengseng typify societies in which the man-resource ratio is unusually high, giving rise to a certain cultural complex. Here death from disease is accepted as the punishment of ancestral spirits, pollution ideas limit the meeting of men and women during their fertile years, and there is an emphasis on male chastity. Other cultural features also seem to cluster at this end of the spectrum: a severe attitude towards incest and a view that adulterers are no great threat. Cannibalism in these societies is considered repulsive to the living, but may occur among ogres and other inhabitants of the pantheon.

At the other end of the spectrum are societies where population increase is desired—Fore, Daribi, Tangu, Dobu, Bena-Bena, and Orokaiva. Here disease is interpreted as an external attack by sorcerers, pollution ideas are not strenuously used to curb the access of men to women, the incest rule may be loosely observed, adultery is the serious theft of a scarce resource, and cannibalism may be present as a form of symbolic self-generation.

Few societies are found at these extremes. Kyaka, for instance, who are neighbors of the Enga but with a lower population density, have a cultural complex that includes malicious ghosts of the dead, together with a fertility goddess and more emphasis on sorcery (Bulmer 1965: 132–61). It is suggested that witches appear in the middle of the continuum, where population densities rise, altering the ratio of people to resources. Witches are not connected with the important survival issues but are concerned with the lesser dangers of infant mortality, small property less, and constitutional conflicts. Important survival issues are left to gods or to sorcerers.

A New Weapon Stirs Up Old Ghosts

William E. Mitchell

*In the following article, William E. Mitchell describes
the Wape shotgun cult, a belief and behavioral system
that sprang up in New Guinea after the introduction
of guns to the area in the late 1940s and early 1950s.
Mitchell tells how Wape villagers pool their money to
collectively purchase a shotgun and then select a
candidate from within their ranks to take the firearm
test administered by officials. If the applicant is
successful, a permit is issued, and the individual must
agree to shoot game for his village. Of special interest
for this chapter is the role of ancestral ghosts in the
system. Among the Wape, the dead are believed not
only to protect the living from harm but also to supply
them with meat and punish anyone who may have
wronged them. Thus, a dead male relative becomes an
invaluable aide to the hunter. The author shows how
the cult's belief in vengeful spirits helps them
understand why they sometimes experience
unsuccessful hunting.*

Reprinted with permission from *Natural History,* vol. 82,
no. 10 (December 1973), pp. 75–84. Copyright © 1973
the American Museum of Natural History.

WHEN, IN 1947, THE FRANCISCAN FRIARS WENT
to live among the nearly 10,000 Wape people of
New Guinea, the principal native weapons were
bone daggers and the bow and arrow. Even then,
game was scarce in the heavily populated mountains where the Wape live, and the killing of a
wild pig or a cassowary, New Guinea's major
game animals, was an important village event.
The Wape live in the western part of the Sepik
River Basin. Their small villages lie along the narrow ridges of the Torricelli Mountains, above the
sago palm swamps where women process palm
pith, the Wape staff of life.

Today the Wape hunter's principal weapon is
still the bow and arrow and game is even scarcer.
This is partially the result of a new addition to the
hunter's armory—the prosaic shotgun—which
has had a profound moral impact on Wape village
life.

The first guns were brought into this area in
the late 1940s and early 1950s by missionaries,
traders, and Australian government officials. Although natives were not permitted to own guns,
they could use them if employed by a white man
to shoot game for his table. This was a very prestigious job.

In 1960, government regulations were changed
to permit natives to purchase singleshot shotguns.
At first only a few Wape men, living in villages
close to the government station and helpful to
government officials, were granted gun permits.
Eventually more permits were issued, but today,
in hopes of preserving the remaining game, one
permit is issued for every 100 people.

Within ten years of the granting of the first gun
permits, a belief and behavioral system had
evolved around the shotgun. It was based on traditional Wape hunting lore but had distinctive
elaborations stemming from native perceptions of
the teachings of government officials and missionaries. For descriptive purposes I call this system of formalized beliefs and ritual the "Wape

shotgun cult." It is one of several Wape ceremonial cults, but the only one originating after contact with Europeans. Although the specific practices of the shotgun cult vary from village to village, the underlying beliefs are the same.

In creating the shotgun cult the Wape faced the challenge of adapting an introduced implement to their culture. Unlike steel axes and knives, which replaced stone adzes and bamboo knives, the shotgun has never replaced the bow and arrow. The shotgun is a scarce and expensive machine. This, together with the European sanctions imposed upon its introduction, places it in a unique position, both symbolically and behaviorally, among the Wape.

The cult is a conservative institution. It breaks no new cognitive ground by challenging established Wape concepts. Instead it merges traditional hunting concepts with European moral teachings to create a coherent system. The cult upholds traditional beliefs, accepts European authority, and most important, provides an explanation for unsuccessful hunting.

In 1970, my family and I arrived in Lumi, a small mountain settlement, which is the government's subdistrict headquarters in the middle of Wapeland. For the next year and a half, we lived in the village of Taute, near Lumi. There my wife and I studied Wape culture.

Taute, which has a population of 220, is reached by narrow foot trails, root strewn and muddy, passing through the dense, damp forest. The low houses —made of sago palm stems and roofed with sago thatch—are scattered about in the sandy plaza and among the coconut palms and breadfruit trees along the ridge. Towering poinsettias, red and pink hibiscus, and multicolored shrubs contrast with the encircling forest's greens and browns. A few small latrines perch on the steep slopes, concessions to Western concepts of hygiene. In the morning, flocks of screeching cockatoos glide below the ridge through the rising mists. When the breadfruit trees are bearing, giant fruit bats flop across the sky at dusk.

Since the mid-1950s the Franciscan friars have maintained off and on, a religious school in Taute. There, Wape boys are instructed by a native catechist in Catholicism, simple arithmetic, and Melanesian Pidgin. A priest from Lumi visits the village several times a year, and the villagers, Catholic and heathen alike, are proud of their affiliation with the Francis-

cans and staunchly loyal to them. But their Catholicism is nominal and superficial—a scant and brittle frosting that does not mask their own religious beliefs, which dominate everyday life.

The ethos of Wape society is oriented around sacred curing rituals. Whereas some Sepik cultures aggressively center their ceremonial life around headhunting and the raising of sturdy and brave children, the Wape defensively center theirs in the ritual appeasement of malevolent ghosts and forest demons, who they believe cause sickness. Most men belong to one of the demon-curing cults where, once initiated as priests, they are responsible for producing the often elaborate curing ceremonies for exorcising the demon from the afflicted.

The little money that exists among the Wape is earned primarily by the men, who work as two-year contract laborers on the coastal and island copra plantations. Because of the lack of money to buy canned meats, the scarcity of game, and the paucity of fish in the mountain streams, the protein intake of the Wape is exceedingly low. The most common meal is sago dumplings and boiled leaves. Malnutrition is common among youngsters, and physical development is generally retarded. According to studies by Dr. Lyn Wark, a medical missionary who has worked widely among the Wape, the average birth weight of the Wape baby is the lowest recorded in the world. Correspondingly, secondary sex characteristics are delayed. For example, the mean age for the onset of menses is over eighteen years.

Before contact with Westerners, Wape men were naked and the women wore short string skirts. Today most men wear shorts and the women wear skirts purchased from Lumi's four small stores. To appear in a semblance of European dress, however meager or worn, is a matter of pride and modesty to both sexes. "Savages" do not wear clothes, but white men and those who have been enlightened by white men do. In this sense, the Wape's Western-style dress represents an identification with the politically and materially powerful white man. The identification is with power; it is an ego-enhancing maneuver that permits the Wape to live with dignity, even though they are subservient to Western rule and influence. The tendency of the Wape to identify with, and incorporate, the alien when it serves to preserve their culture will help us to understand how they have woven diverse cultural strands into the creation of the shotgun cult.

From the first day I arrived in Taute, the men repeatedly made two urgent requests of me. One was to open a store in the village, saving them the difficult walk into Lumi; the other was to buy a shotgun to help them kill game. This was the least, they seemed to indicate, a fair-minded and, in Wape terms, obviously rich neighbor should do. One of the hardest things the anthropologists in the field must learn is to say "no" to deserving people. To be stingy is almost to be un-American, but we had come half-way around the world to learn about the Wape way of life, not to introduce stores and shotguns that would alter the established trading and hunting patterns.

After several months the people of the major Taute hamlets, Kafiere, where we lived, and Mifu, a ten-minute walk away, each decided to buy a group-owned shotgun. The investment was a sizable forty-two Australian dollars; forty dollars for the gun, and two dollars for the gun permit. Each hamlet made a volunteer collection from its members and I, as a fellow villager, contributed to both guns. A week later the villagers purchased the guns from one of the Lumi stores, and I began to learn about the shotgun's ritual and moral importance to the Wape. The villagers were already familiar with the significance of the shotgun for they had purchased one several years before. The cult ended, however, when the gun broke.

The shotgun, like Melanesian Pidgin, is associated by the Wape with Europeans and modernity. Not surprisingly, Pidgin is favored for shotgun parlance. The licensed gunman is not only called *sutboi* ("shootboy") but also *laman* ("law man"), the latter a term that connotes his official tie to European law and government as perceived by the villagers.

When a candidate for a gun permit appears before the government official in Lumi, he is examined orally on the use of firearms, then given an unloaded shotgun and tested on his handling knowledge. Under the direct and questioning gaze of the examining official, candidates sometimes become flustered. One inadvertently aimed the gun first toward the wife of the assistant district commissioner and then toward a group of observers. His examination ended ignominiously on the spot.

If the candidate passes the test and the examining official approves of his character, he is then lectured on the use of the gun: only the candidate can fire it, he must willingly shoot game for his fellow vil-

lagers, and the gun must be used exclusively for hunting. He is strongly warned that if any of these rules are broken or if there is trouble in the village, he will lose the gun and the permit and will be imprisoned.

The candidate's friends and the inevitable audience are present for the lecture. Here, as in many spheres of native life, the official's power is absolute, and the Wape know this from long experience. Guns have been confiscated or destroyed without reimbursement and gunmen have been jailed.

The official's charge to the candidate is willingly accepted. Henceforth, he will never leave the village without carrying his gun. He is now a *laman*, and he has the gun and permit, printed entirely in English, to prove it.

The government official's strong sanctions against village quarrels are motivated by his fear that the gun might be used in a dispute among villagers. The sanctions are further upheld by the missionaries' and catechists' sermons against quarreling and wrongdoing as they attempt to teach the Christian doctrine of brotherly love. The message the villagers receive is this: To keep the white man's gun, they must follow the white man's rules. This the Wape do, not in servile submission, but with some pride because the presence of the gun and the public focus on morality mark the village as progressive and modern. The licensed gunman, therefore, is not only the guardian of the gun but of village morality as well.

Rain or shine, he is expected to go into the forest without compensation to hunt for his fellow villagers, who give him cartridges with some personal identifying mark upon them. After a gunman makes a kill, the owner of the cartridge receives the game and distributes it according to his economic obligations to others. But the gunman, like the bow and arrow hunter, is forbidden to eat from the kill; to do so would jeopardize further successful hunting.

In the hamlet of Kafiere, the clan that had contributed the most money toward the gun and on whose lands the most game was to be found appointed Auwe as gunman. But Auwe's wife, Naiasu, was initially against his selection. Her previous husband, Semer, now dead several years, had been Kafiere's first *sutboi* and she argued that the heavy hunting responsibilities of a *sutboi* took too much time, forcing him to neglect his own gardening and hunting obligations.

When Auwe first requested a gun permit he was turned away. The villagers believed that the ghost of Naiasu's dead husband, Semer, had followed Auwe to Lumi and influenced the examining official against him. Semer's ghost was acting to fulfill Naiasu's wish that her young son, now Auwe's stepson, would have a stepfather who was always available. This was the first of many stories I was to hear about the relationship between ghosts and the gun. When Auwe returned to Lumi for a second try, he passed the examination and was given the official permit.

The hamlet now had its own gun and hunting could begin in earnest. The first step was an annunciation feast called, in Pidgin, a *kapti* ("cup of tea"). Its purpose was to inform the villagers' dead ancestors about the new gun. This was important because ancestral ghosts roam the forest land of their lineage, protecting it from intruders and driving game to their hunting descendants. The hunter's most important hunting aide is his dead male relatives, to whom he prays for game upon entering his hunting lands. The dead remain active in the affairs of the living by protecting them from harm, providing them with meat, and punishing those who have wronged them.

The small sacrificial feast was held in front of Auwe's house. Placing the upright gun on a makeshift table in the midst of the food, Auwe rubbed it with sacred ginger. One of Auwe's elderly clansmen, standing and facing his land, called out to his ancestors by name and told them about the new gun. He implored them to send wild pigs and cassowaries to Auwe.

Several men spoke of the new morality that was to accompany hunting with a gun. The villagers should not argue or quarrel among themselves; problems must be settled quietly and without bitterness; malicious gossip and stealing were forbidden. If these rules were not obeyed, Auwe would not find game.

In traditional Wape culture there is no feast analogous to the *kapti*. Indeed, there are no general community-wide feasts. The *kapti* is apparently modeled on a European social gathering.

For the remainder of my stay in Taute, I followed closely the fortunes of the Taute guns and of guns in nearby villages as well. All seemed to be faced with the same two problems: game was rarely seen; and when seen, was rarely killed. Considering that a cartridge belongs to a villager, not the gunman, how was this economic loss handled? This presented a most intriguing and novel problem for there were no analogs to this type of predicament within the traditional culture. By Wape standards, the pecuniary implications of such a loss, although but a few Australian shillings, could not graciously be ignored by the loser. At the very least the loss had to be explained even if the money for the cartridges could not be retrieved.

Now I understood the concern about the ancestral ghosts. If the hunter shot and missed, the owner of the fired shells was being punished by being denied meat. Either he or a close family member had quarreled or wronged another person whose ghost-relative was securing revenge by causing the hunter to miss. This, then, was the functional meaning of the proscription against quarreling. By avoiding disputes, the villagers were trying to prevent the intervention of ancestral ghosts in human affairs. In a peaceful village without quarrels, the gunman could hunt undisturbed by vengeful ghosts chasing away game or misrouting costly shells.

Although a number of factors in European culture have influenced the shotgun cult, the cult's basic premise of a positive correlation between quarreling and bad hunting is derived directly from traditional Wape culture. In bow and arrow hunting, an individual who feels he was not given his fair share of a hunter's kill may punish the hunter by gossiping about him or quarreling openly with him. The aggrieved person's ancestral ghosts revenge the slight by chasing the game away from the offending hunter or misdirecting his arrows. But this is a private affair between the hunter and the angered person; their quarrel has no influence upon the hunting of others. And it is rare for an issue other than distribution of game to cause a ghost to hinder a bowman's success. The hunter's prowess is restored only when the angered person performs a brief supplication rite over the hunter.

This, then, is the conceptual basis for the tie between quarreling and bad hunting. Originally relevant only to bow and arrow hunting, it was then broadened to accommodate the government's pronouncements about the shotgun and keeping the village peace. And it applies perfectly to the special circumstances of shotgun hunting. Because the shotgun is community owned and many villagers buy cartridges for it, the villagers are identified with both the gun and the gunman. As a proxy hunter for the villagers, the gunman is potentially subject to the ghostly sanctions resulting from their collective wrongs. Thus gun hunting, unlike bow and arrow hunting, is a community affair and the community-wide taboo against quarrels and personal transgressions is the only effective way to prevent spiteful ghosts from wrecking the hunt.

No village, however, even if populated by people as disciplined and well behaved as the Wape, can constantly live in the state of pious peace considered necessary for continuous good gun hunting. When the hunting is poor, the gunman must discover the quarrels and wrongs within the village. After having identified the individuals whose ancestral ghosts are sabotaging the hunting, the gunman must also see to it that they implore the ghosts to stop. Embarrassed by the public disclosure, they will quickly comply.

The common method for detecting points of friction within the village is to bring the villagers together for a special meeting. The gunman will then document in detail his misfortunes and call on the villagers to find out what is ruining the hunting. If confessions of wrongdoing are not forthcoming, questioning accusations result. The meeting, beginning in Pidgin, moves into Wape as the discussion becomes more complex and voluble. It may last up to three hours; but even if there is no resolution, it always ends amiably—at least on the surface. For it is important to create no new antagonisms.

The other technique for locating the source of the hunting problem is to call in a professional clairvoyant. As the villagers must pay for his services, he is usually consulted only after a series of unsuccessful meetings. Clairvoyants have replaced the shamans, who were outlawed by the government and the mission because they practiced sorcery and ritual murders. The Wape do not consider a clairvoyant a sorcerer; he is a man with second sight who is experienced in discovering and treating the hidden causes of intractable problems. As such, shotguns are among his best patients.

Mewau, a clairvoyant from a neighboring village, held a "shotgun clinic" in Taute to examine the Mifu and Kafiere guns. For about an hour he examined the two guns and questioned the villagers. Then he declared the reasons for their misfortune.

Kapul, a dead Mifu shaman, was preventing the Mifu gun from killing game because a close relative of the gunman had allegedly stolen valuables from Kapul's daughter. Because of the family ties between the gunman and the thief, Kapul's ghost was punishing the gunman.

The Kafiere gun, Mewau declared, was not able to find game because a widow in the village felt that her dead husband's clan had not previously distributed game to her in a fair way. By interfering with the Kafiere gun, her husband's ghost was punishing his clan for the neglect of his family.

Once the source of trouble is named, there are several possible types of remedial ritual depending upon the seriousness of the situation. For example, the circumstances surrounding the naming of the husband's ghost were considered serious, and a *kapti* was held to placate him. Another, simpler ritual involves the preparation of taro soup, which the gunman consumes. But the simplest, commonest remedial rite is the supplication ritual without sacrificial food offerings, a ritual in which I became involved.

Mifu's gunman had shot a pig with one of his own cartridges but did not give me the small portion due me as a part owner of the gun. Partly as a test to see if my ancestors counted for anything in Taute and partly because I did not want to let this calculated slight go unchallenged, I, in typical Wape fashion, said nothing to the gunman but gossiped discreetly about his selfishness. The gunman continued to hunt but had no further success. When his bad luck persisted, a meeting was called to find out the reason. The gunman asked me if I was angry because I had not been given my portion of the pig. When I acknowledged my anger, he handed the shotgun to me and I dutifully spoke out to my ancestors to stop turning the game away from the gun.

But the gunman still had no success in the hunt, and the villagers decided there were other wrongs as well. The search for the offending ghosts continued. Eventually the villagers became so discouraged with the Mifu gun that they stopped giving cartridges to the gunman. The consensus was that a major undetected wrong existed in the hamlet, and until it was uncovered and the guilty ghost called off, hunting with the gun was senseless and extravagant. Thus the propriety of a remedial rite is established if there is success on the next hunt. The system is completely empirical: if no game is seen or if seen, is not killed, then the search for the wrong must continue.

Wape people are generally even tempered, and their villages, in contrast to many in New Guinea, strike the newcomer as almost serene. But the social impact of the guns at this time was pervasive, and life in Taute literally revolved around the guns and their hunting fortunes. Whereas the villagers previously had kept to their own affairs, they now became embroiled in meeting after meeting, seeking out transgressions, quarrels, and wrongdoing. As the gunman continued to have bad luck, his efforts to discover the cause became more zealous. A certain amount of polarization resulted: the gunman accused the villagers, the men accused the women, and the adults accused the young people of hiding their wrongs. And a few who had lost many cartridges wondered if the *sutboi* was keeping the game for himself. But no one ever suggested that he was an inexperienced shotgun hunter. The gunman was generally considered to be blameless; in fact, the more game he missed, the more self-righteous he became and the more miscreant the villagers.

Six months of poor hunting had gone by; the villagers felt that the only recourse left to them was to bring a bush demon named *mani* into the village from the jungle for a festival. The *mani*'s small stone heart is kept enshrined in a rustic altar in a corner of Kafiere's ceremonial house and after a kill the animal's blood is smeared upon it. The *mani* will reward the village with further kills only if he is fed with blood. *Mani* is the only spirit, other than ghosts, who can cause both good and bad hunting depending upon the way he is treated. Soon after the shotgun arrived in Taute, the gunman and some other men left their homes to sleep in the men's ceremonial house to keep *mani*'s stone heart warm. They thought *mani*, in appreciation, would send game to the gunman.

When little game was killed, the villagers decided on the hunting festival. In a special house outside of the village, men constructed the great conical mask that depicts *mani*. For several weeks they worked to cover the mask's frame with the spathes of sago palm fronds painted with designs traditional to *mani*. Finally, a priest of the *mani* cult, wearing a 20-foot-high mask festooned with feathers and leaves, pranced into the village to the thunderous beat of wooden drums.

For the next week and a half men from other villages who wished us well came and joined in the all-night singing of the *mani* song cycle. In the morning, if the weather was clear, *mani* led the bow and arrow hunters and the gunman to the edge of the village and sent them on their way to hunting success. But in spite of the careful attentions the villagers directed toward *mani*, he rewarded them with only one wild pig. The villagers became openly discouraged, then annoyed. Finally the hunters, disgusted and weary from numerous long futile hunts, and other men, their shoulders sore and bloody from constantly carrying the heavy mask around the plaza, decided that *mani* was simply taking advantage of them; all of their hard work was for nothing. Disgusted, they decided to send *mani* back to his home in the forest.

One late afternoon the *mani* appeared in the plaza but he did not prance. He walked slowly around the plaza, stopping at each house to throw ashes over himself with his single bark cloth arm. The villagers said he was in mourning because he had to leave by dusk and would miss the company of men. Silently the people watched the once gay and graceful *mani* lumber out of the village. The men and boys followed him into the forest. Then the gunman split open the mask, to insure the spirit's exit and eventual return to his forest home, and hurled it over the edge of the cliff into the bush below.

A few months after the *mani* hunting festival, the shotgun cult as I had known it in Taute ceased to function. All but one of the able young men of the hamlet of Kafiere went off to work on a coastal plantation for two years. With no young men, the ceremonial activities of the hunting and curing cults were suspended and the fault-finding meetings halted until their return. The drama and excitement of the previous months had vanished with the men.

The Real Vampire

Paul Barber

Tales of the undead in eighteenth-century Europe were preeminent in establishing the folklore of the vampire, a figure whose bloodlust struck stark terror into the hearts of believers of that day. Images of evil of such magnitude die hard. Bram Stoker's novel introduced the horrors of vampiric attack to the rest of the world through the character of Count Dracula, later immortalized on the American screen in the 1930s by Bela Lugosi. But to many eighteenth-century Europeans, vampires were not fictional; they were real and accounted for deaths due to contagion in a world that had no theory of communicable disease. Paul Barber's forensic evidence provides a physiological basis for the belief that the dead could return from the grave, for Europeans then believed that any corpse having what they considered an abnormal or peculiar condition was most certainly a vampire. But the sociological explanations for the existence of vampires and the techniques for protecting themselves from them are equally provocative. One protective measure was the act of consuming the blood of a vampire, thereby invoking the elementary concept of "similia similiis curantur" (similar things are cured by similar things), a rationale commonly found in folklore.

Personal characteristics attributed to those with the potential to become vampires are amazing, like the characteristics of those accused of witchcraft today—for example, in Africa. Like the witches of Africa, vampires of Europe had the ability to leave the body and attack their victims unseen, and like witches, vampires were responsible for a wide variety of everyday, rather pedestrian misfortunes. Clearly the human propensity to create monstrous mental images such as vampires, responsible for misfortunes of such an extreme caliber as death, was and is common and functions as an explanation of the unexplainable. The negative effects on society, however, of the dysfunctional aspects of fear and accusation resulting from these mystical types of explanations cannot be discounted.

Reprinted with permission from *Natural History* (October 1990), pp. 74–82. Copyright © 1990 the American Museum of Natural History.

I saw the Count lying within the box upon the earth, some of which the rude falling from the cart had scattered over him. He was deathly pale, just like a waxen image, and the red eyes glared with the horrible vindictive look which I knew too well. . . .

The eyes saw the sinking sun, and the look of hate in them turned to triumph.

But, on the instant, came the sweep and flash of Jonathan's great knife. I shrieked as I saw it shear through the throat; whilst at the same moment Mr. Morris's bowie knife plunged into the heart.

It was like a miracle; but before our very eyes, and almost in the drawing of a breath, the whole body crumbled into dust and passed from our sight.

—Bram Stoker, *Dracula*

IF A TYPICAL VAMPIRE OF FOLKLORE WERE TO come to your house this Halloween, you might open the door to encounter a plump Slavic fellow with long fingernails and a stubbly beard, his mouth and left eye open, his face ruddy and swollen. He would wear informal attire—a linen shroud—and he would look for all the world like a disheveled peasant.

If you did not recognize him, it would be because you expected to see—as would most people today—a tall, elegant gentleman in a black cloak. But that would be the vampire of fiction—the count, the villain of Bram Stoker's novel and countless modern movies, based more or less on Vlad Tepes, a figure in Romanian history who was a prince, not a count; ruled in Walachia, not Transylvania; and was never viewed by the local populace as a vampire. Nor would he be recognized as one, bearing so little resemblance to the original Slavic revenant (one who returns from the dead)—the one actually called *upir* or *vampir*. But in folklore, the undead are seemingly everywhere in the world, in a variety of disparate cultures. They are people who, having died before their time, are believed to return to life to bring death to their friends and neighbors.

We know the European version of the vampire best and have a number of eyewitness accounts telling of the "killing" of bodies believed to be vampires. When we read these reports carefully and compare their findings with what is now known about forensic pathology, we can see why people believed that corpses came to life and returned to wreak havoc on the local population.

Europeans of the early 1700s showed a great deal of interest in the subject of the vampire. According to the *Oxford English Dictionary,* the word itself entered the English language in 1734, at a time when many books were being written on the subject, especially in Germany.

One reason for all the excitement was the Treaty of Passarowitz (1718), by which parts of Serbia and Walachia were turned over to Austria. The occupying forces, which remained there until 1739, began to notice, and file reports on, a peculiar local practice: exhuming bodies and "killing" them. Literate outsiders began to attend such exhumations. The vampire craze was an early "media event," in which educated Europeans became aware of practices that were by no means of recent origin.

In the early 1730s, a group of Austrian medical officers were sent to the Serbian village of Medvegia to investigate some very strange accounts. A number of people in the village had died recently, and the villagers blamed the deaths on vampires. The first of these vampires, they said, had been a man named Arnold Paole, who had died some years before (by falling off a hay wagon) and had come back to haunt the living.

To the villagers, Paole's vampirism was clear: When they dug up his corpse, "they found that he was quite complete and undecayed, and that fresh blood had flowed from his eyes, nose, mouth, and ears; that the shirt, the covering, and the coffin were completely bloody; that the old nails on his hands and feet, along with the skin, had fallen off, and that new ones had grown; and since they saw from this that he was a true vampire, they drove a stake through his heart, according to their custom, whereby he gave an audible groan and bled copiously."

This new offensive by the vampires—the one that drew the medical officers to Medvegia—included an attack on a woman named Stanacka, who "lay down to sleep fifteen days ago, fresh and healthy, but at midnight she started up out of her sleep with a terrible cry, fearful and trembling, and complained that she had been throttled by the son of a Haiduk by the name of Milloe, who had died nine weeks earlier, whereupon she had experienced a great pain in the chest and became worse hour by hour, until finally she died on the third day."

In their report, *Visum et Repertum* (Seen and Discovered), the officers told not only what they had heard from the villagers but also, in admirable clinical detail, what they themselves had seen when they exhumed and dissected the bodies of the supposed victims of the vampire. Of one corpse, the authors observed, "After the opening of the body there was found in the *cavitate pectoris* a quantity of fresh extravascular blood. The *vasa* [vessels] of the *arteriae* and *venae,* like the *ventriculis cordis,* were not, as is usual, filled with coagulated blood, and the whole *viscera,* that is, the *pulmo* [lung], *hepar* [liver], *stomachus, lien* [spleen], *et intestina* were quite fresh as they would be in a healthy person." But while baffled by the events, the medical officers did not venture opinions as to their meaning.

Modern scholars generally disregard such accounts—and we have many of them—because they invariably contain "facts" that are not believable, such as the claim that the dead Arnold Paole, exhumed forty days after his burial, groaned when a stake was driven into him. If that is untrue—and it surely seems self-evident that it must be untrue—then the rest of the account seems suspect.

Yet these stories invariably contain detail that could only be known by someone who had exhumed a decomposing body. The flaking away of the skin described in the account of Arnold Paole is a phenomenon that forensic pathologists refer to as "skin slippage." Also, pathologists say that it is no surprise that Paole's "nails had fallen away," for that too is a normal event. (The Egyptians knew this and dealt with it either by tying the nails onto the mummified corpse or by attaching them with little golden thimbles.) The reference to "new nails" is presumably the interpretation of the glossy nail bed underneath the old nails.

Such observations are inconvenient if the vampire lore is considered as something made up out of whole cloth. But since the exhumations actually took place, then the question must be, how did our sources come to the conclusions they came to? That issue is obscured by two centuries of fictional vampires, who are much better known than the folkloric variety. A few distinctions are in order.

The folklore of the vampire comes from peasant cultures across most of Europe. As it happens, the best evidence of actual exhumations is from Eastern Europe, where the Eastern Orthodox church showed a greater tolerance for pagan traditions than the Catholic church in Western Europe.

The fictional vampire, owing to the massive influence of Bram Stoker's *Dracula,* moved away from its humble origin. (Imagine Count Dracula—in formal evening wear—undergoing his first death by falling off a hay wagon.)

Most fiction shows only one means of achieving the state of vampirism: people become vampires by being bitten by one. Typically, the vampire looms over the victim dramatically, then bites into the neck to suck blood. When vampires and revenants in European folklore suck blood—and many do not—they bite their victims somewhere on the thorax. Among the Kashubes, a Slavic people of northern Europe, vampires chose the area of the left breast; among the Russians, they left a small wound in the area of the heart; and in Danzing (now Gdansk), they bit the victim's nipples.

People commonly believed that those who were different, unpopular, or great sinners returned from the dead. Accounts from Russia tell of people who were unearthed merely because while alive they were alcoholics. A more universal category is the suicide. Partly because of their potential for returning from the dead or for drawing their nearest and dearest into the grave after them, suicides were refused burial in churchyards.

One author lists the categories of revenants by disposition as "the godless [people of different faiths are included], evildoers, suicides, sorcerers, witches, and werewolves; among the Bulgarians the group is expanded by robbers, highwaymen, arsonists, prostitutes, deceitful and treacherous barmaids and other dishonorable people."

A very common belief, reported not only from Eastern Europe but also from China, holds that a person may become a revenant when an animal jumps over him. In Romania there is a belief that a bat can transform a corpse into a vampire by flying over it. This circumstance deserves remark if only because of its rarity, for as important as bats are in the fiction of vampires, they are generally unimportant in the folklore. Bats came into vampire fiction

by a circuitous route: the vampire bat of Central and South America was named after the vampire of folklore, because it sucks (or rather laps up) blood after biting its victim. The bat was then assimilated into the fiction: the modern (fictional) vampire is apt to transform himself into a bat and fly off to seek his victims.

Potential revenants could often be identified at birth, usually by some defect, as when (among the Poles of Upper Silesia and the Kashubes) a child was born with teeth or a split lower lip or features viewed as somehow bestial—for example, hair or a taillike extension of the spine. A child born with a red caul, or amniotic membrane, covering its head was regarded as a potential vampire.

The color red is related to the undead. Decomposing corpses often acquire a ruddy color, and this was generally taken for evidence of vampirism. Thus, the folkloric vampire is never pale, as one would expect of a corpse; his face is commonly described as florid or of a healthy color or dark, and this may be attributed to his habit of drinking blood. (The Serbians, referring to a redfaced, hard-drinking man, assert that he is "blood red as a vampire.")

In various parts of Europe, vampires, or revenants, were held responsible for any number of untoward events. They tipped over Gypsy caravans in Serbia, made loud noises on the frozen sod roofs of houses in Iceland (supposedly by beating their heels against them), caused epidemics, cast spells on crops, brought on rain and hail, and made cows go dry. All these activities attributed to vampires do occur: storms and scourges come and go, crops don't always thrive, cows do go dry. Indeed, the vampire's crimes are persistently "real-life" events. The issue often is not whether an event occurred but why it was attributed to the machinations of the vampire, an often invisible villain.

Bodies continue to be active long after death, but we moderns distinguish between two types of activity: that which we bring about by our will (in life) and that which is caused by other entities, such as microorganisms (in death). Because we regard only the former as "our" activity, the body's posthumous movements, changes in dimension, or the like are not real for us, since we do not will them. For the most part, however, our ancestors made no such distinction. To them, if after death the body changed in color, moved, bled, and so on (as it does), then it continued to experience a kind of life. Our view of death has made it difficult for us to understand earlier views, which are often quite pragmatic.

Much of what a corpse "does" results from misunderstood processes of decomposition. Only in detective novels does this process proceed at a predictable rate. So when a body that had seemingly failed to decompose came to the attention of the populace, theories explaining the apparent anomaly were likely to spring into being. (Note that when a saint's body failed to decompose it was a miracle, but when the body of an unpopular person failed to decompose it was because he was a vampire.) But while those who exhumed the bodies of suspected vampires invariably noted what they believed was the lack of decomposition, they almost always presented evidence that the body really was decomposing. In the literature, I have so far found only two instances of exhumations that failed to yield a "vampire." (With so many options, the body almost certainly will do something unexpected, hence scary, such as showing blood at the lips.) Our natural bias, then as now, is for the dramatic and the exotic, so that an exhumation that did not yield a vampire could be expected to be an early dropout from the folklore and hence the literature.

But however mythical the vampire was, the corpses that were taken for vampires were very real. And many of the mysteries of vampire lore clear up when we examine the legal and medical evidence surrounding these exhumations. "Not without astonishment," says an observer at the exhumation of a Serbian vampire in 1725, "I saw some fresh blood in his mouth, which, according to the common observation, he had sucked from the people killed by him." Similarly, in *Visum et Repertum,* we are told that the people exhuming one body were surprised by a "plumpness" they asserted had come to the corpse in the grave. Our sources deduced a cause-and-effect relationship from these two observations. The vampire was larger than he was because he was full to bursting with the fresh blood of his victims.

The observations are clinically accurate: as a corpse decomposes, it normally bloats (from the gases given off by decomposition), while the pressure from the bloating causes blood from the lungs to emerge at the mouth. The blood is real, it just didn't come from "victims" of the deceased.

But how was it that Arnold Paole, exhumed forty days after his death, groaned when his exhumers drove a stake into him? The peasants of Medvegia

assumed that if the corpse groaned, it must still be alive. But a corpse does emit sounds, even when it is only moved, let alone if a stake were driven into it. This is because the compression of the chest cavity forces air past the glottis, causing a sound similar in quality and origin to the groan or cry of a living person. Pathologists shown such accounts point out that a corpse that did not emit such sounds when a stake was driven into it would be unusual.

To vampire killers who are digging up a corpse, anything unexpected is taken for evidence of vampirism. Calmet, an eighteenth-century French ecclesiastic, described people digging up corpses "to see if they can find any of the usual marks which leads them to conjecture that they are the parties who molest the living, as the mobility and suppleness of the limbs, the fluidity of the blood, and the flesh remaining uncorrupted." A vampire, in other words, is a corpse that lacks rigor mortis, has fluid blood, and has not decomposed. As it happens, these distinctions do not narrow the field very much: Rigor mortis is a temporary condition, liquid blood is not at all unusual in a corpse (hence the "copious bleeding" mentioned in the account of Arnold Paole), and burial slows down decomposition drastically (by a factor of eight, according to a standard textbook on forensic pathology). This being the case, exhumations often yielded a corpse that nicely fit the local model of what a vampire was.

None of this explains yet another phenomenon of the vampire lore—the attack itself. To get to his victim, the vampire is often said to emerge at night from a tiny hole in the grave, in a form that is invisible to most people (sorcerers have made a good living tracking down and killing such vampires). The modern reader may reject out of hand the hypothesis that a dead man, visible or not, crawled out of his grave and attacked the young woman Stanacka as related in *Visum et Repertum.* Yet in other respects, these accounts have been quite accurate.

Note the sequence of events: Stanacka is asleep, the attack takes place, and she wakes up. Since Stanacka was asleep during the attack, we can only conclude that we are looking at a culturally conditioned interpretation of a nightmare—a real event with a fanciful interpretation.

The vampire does have two forms: one of them the body in the grave; the other—and this is the mobile one—the image, or "double," which here appears as a dream. While we interpret this as an event that takes place within the mind of the dreamer, in nonliterate cultures the dream is more commonly viewed as either an invasion by the spirits of whatever is dreamed about (and these can include the dead) or evidence that the dreamer's soul is taking a nocturnal journey.

In many cultures, the soul is only rather casually attached to its body, as is demonstrated by its habit of leaving the body entirely during sleep or unconsciousness or death. The changes that occur during such conditions—the lack of responsiveness, the cessation or slowing of breathing and pulse—are attributed to the soul's departure. When the soul is identified with the image of the body, it may make periodic forays into the minds of others when they dream. The image is the essence of the person, and its presence in the mind of another is evidence that body and soul are separated. Thus, one reason that the dead are believed to live on is that their image can appear in people's dreams and memories even after death. For this reason some cultures consider it unwise to awaken someone suddenly: he may be dreaming, and his soul may not have a chance to return before he awakens, in which case he will die. In European folklore, the dream was viewed as a visit from the person dreamed about. (The vampire is not the only personification of the dream: the Slavic *mora* is a living being whose soul goes out of the body at night, leaving it as if dead. The *mora* first puts men to sleep, and then frightens them with dreams, chokes them, and sucks their blood. Etymologically, *mora* is cognate with the *mare* of nightmare, with German *Mahr,* and with the second syllable of the French *cauchemar.*)

When Stanacka claimed she was attacked by Milloe, she was neither lying nor even making an especially startling accusation. Her subsequent death (probably from some form of epidemic disease; others in the village were dying too) was sufficient proof to her friends and relatives that she had in fact been attacked by a dead man, just as she had said.

This is why our sources tell us seemingly contradictory facts about the vampire. His body does not have to leave the grave to attack the living, yet the evidence of the attack—the blood he has sucked from his victims—is to be seen on the body. At one and the same time he can be both in the grave in his physical form and out of it in his spirit form. Like the fictional vampire, the vampire of folklore must

remain in his grave part of the time—during the day —but with few exceptions, folkloric vampires do not travel far from their home towns.

And while the fictional vampire disintegrates once staked, the folkloric vampire can prove much more troublesome. One account tells that "in order to free themselves from this plague, the people dug the body up, drove a consecrated nail into its head and a stake through its heart. Nonetheless, that did not help: the murdered man came back each night." In many of these cases, vampires were cremated as well as staked.

In Eastern Europe the fear of being killed by a vampire was quite real, and the people devised ways to protect themselves from attacks. One of the sources of protection was the blood of the supposed vampire, which was baked in bread, painted on the potential victim, or even mixed with brandy and drunk. (According to *Visum et Repertum,* Arnold Paole had once smeared himself with the blood of a vampire—that is, a corpse—for protection.) The rationale behind this is a common one in folklore, expressed in the saying "similia similiis curantur" (similar things are cured by similar things). Even so, it is a bit of a shock to find that our best evidence suggests that it was the human beings who drank the blood of the "vampires," and not the other way around.

Perhaps foremost among the reasons for the urgency with which vampires were sought—and found—was sheer terror. To understand its intensity we need only recall the realities that faced our informants. Around them people were dying in clusters, by agencies that they did not understand. As they were well aware, death could be extremely contagious: if a neighbor died, they might be next. They were afraid of nothing less than death itself. For among many cultures it was death that was thought to be passed around, not viruses and bacteria. Contagion was meaningful and deliberate, and its patterns were based on values and vendettas, not on genetic predisposition or the domestic accommodations of the plague-spreading rat fleas. Death came from the dead who, through jealousy, anger, or longing, sought to bring the living into their realm. And to prevent this, the living attempted to neutralize or propitiate the dead until the dead became powerless —not only when they stopped entering dreams but also when their bodies stopped changing and were reduced to inert bones. This whole phenomenon is hard for us to understand because although death is as inescapable today as it was then, we no longer personify its causes.

In recent history, the closest parallel to this situation may be seen in the AIDS epidemic, which has caused a great deal of fear, even panic, among people who, for the time being at least, know little about the nature of the disease. In California, for instance, there was an attempt to pass a law requiring the quarantine of AIDS victims. Doubtless the fear will die down if we gain control over the disease—but what would it be like to live in a civilization in which all diseases were just as mysterious? Presumably one would learn—as was done in Europe in past centuries—to shun the dead as potential bearers of death.

Voodoo

Karen McCarthy Brown

It is likely that no other topic in this book is as misunderstood as Voodoo. Movies, television, and novels have been merciless in delivering to the public a highly distorted picture of what is a legitimate religious practice of 80 to 90 percent of the people of Haiti. In this article, Karen McCarthy Brown explains that Voodoo, or Vodou according to Haitian Creole orthography, is an African-based, Catholic-influenced religion. She also points out the differences between urban and rural Voodoo and discusses African and Roman Catholic influence in the development of the religion. In addition, Brown discusses Voodoo spirits, Voodoo ceremonies, and the relationship of magic to Voodoo. The article concludes with some comments on the massive emigration of Haitians, mostly to Miami, New York, or Montreal, where Voodoo ceremonies are carried on in storefronts, rented rooms, and apartments.

"Voodoo" by Karen McCarthy Brown. Reprinted with permission of Macmillan Reference USA, a Division of Simon & Schuster, from *The Encyclopedia of Religion*, Mircea Eliade, Editor-in-Chief, Vol. 15, pp. 296–301. Copyright © 1987 by Macmillan Publishing Company.

VOODOO, OR *VODOU* (ACCORDING TO OFFICIAL Haitian Creole orthography), is a misleading but common term for the religious practices of 80 to 90 percent of the people of Haiti. A mountainous, poverty-stricken, largely agricultural country of approximately six million people, Haiti has a land area of 10,700 square miles that covers the western third of the island of Hispaniola, which it shares with the Dominican Republic. The term *voodoo* (or *hoodoo*, a derivative) is also used, mostly in a derogatory sense, to refer to systems of sorcery and magic or to specific spells, or charms, emanating from such systems, which are for the most part practiced by the descendants of the African slaves brought to the Western Hemisphere.

Outsiders have given the name *Voodoo* to the traditional religious practices of Haiti; only recently, and still to a very limited extent, have Haitians come to use the term as others do. The word can be traced to *vodu* ("spirit" or "deity") in the language of the Fon peoples of Dahomey (present-day Benin). In contemporary Haiti, *vodou* refers to one ritual style or dance among many in the traditional religious system. Haitians prefer a verb to identify their religion: they speak of "serving the spirits."

Sensationalized novels and films, as well as spurious travelers' accounts, have painted a highly distorted picture of Haitian religion. It has been incorrectly depicted as magic and sorcery that involves uncontrolled orgiastic behavior and even cannibalism. These distortions are undoubtedly attributable to racism and to the fear that the Haitian slave revolution sparked in predominantly white nations. Haiti achieved independence in 1804, thus becoming a black republic in the Western Hemisphere at a time when the colonial economy was still heavily dependent on slave labor.

Voodoo is an African-based, Catholic-influenced religion that serves three (not always clearly distinguished) categories of spiritual beings: *lemò*, *lemistè*, and *lemarasa* (respectively, "the dead," "the mysteries," and "the sacred twins").

While certain Voodoo prayers and invocations preserve fragments of West African languages, Haitian Creole is the primary language of Voodoo. Creole (*Kreyol* in the orthographical system employed in this article) is the first and only language of 80 percent of contemporary Haitians; it has a grammatical structure influenced by West African languages and a largely French vocabulary.

Although many individuals and families regularly serve the Voodoo spirits without recourse to religious professionals, Voodoo does have a loosely organized priesthood, open to both men and women. The male priest is called *oungan* and the female, *manbo*. There are many different types of Voodoo ritual, including individual acts of piety, such as the lighting of candles for particular spirits, and large feasts, sometimes of several days' duration, which include animal sacrifice as part of a meal offered to the spirits. Energetic drumming, singing, and dancing accompany the more elaborate rituals. In the countryside, rituals often take place outdoors on family land that has been set aside for the spirits. On this land there is often a small cult house, which houses the Voodoo altars. In the cities, most rituals occur in the *ounfò* ("temple"). Urban altars are maintained in *jèvo,* small rooms usually off the *peristil,* which is the central dancing and ritualizing space of the temple.

The goal of Voodoo drumming, singing, and dancing is to *chofe,* that is, to "heat up," the situation sufficiently to bring on possession by the spirits. As a particular spirit is summoned, a devotee enters a trance and becomes that spirit's *chwal* ("horse"), thus providing the means for direct communication between human beings and the spirits. The spirit is said to ride the *chwal.* Using that person's body and voice, the spirit sings, dances, and eats with the people and offers them advice and chastisement. The people, in turn, offer the spirit a wide variety of gifts and acts of obeisance whose goal is to placate the spirit and ensure his or her continuing protection.

There are marked differences in Voodoo as it is practiced throughout Haiti, but the single most important distinction is that between urban and rural Voodoo. The great majority of Haiti is agricultural, and the manner in which peasants serve the spirits is determined by questions of land tenure and ancestral inheritance. Urban Voodoo is not tied to the land, but the family connection persists in another form. Urban temple communities become substitutes for the extended families of the countryside. The priests are called "papa" and "mama"; the initiates, who are called "children of the house," refer to one another as "brother" and "sister." In general, urban Voodoo is more institutionalized and more elaborate than its rural counterpart.

African Influence

Haiti's slave population was largely built up in the eighteenth century, a period in which Haiti supplied a large percentage of the sugar consumed in Western Europe. Voodoo was born on the sugar plantations out of the interaction among slaves who brought with them a wide variety of African religious traditions. But, due to inadequate records, little is known about this formative period in Voodoo's history. There are, however, indications that Voodoo played a key role in the organization of the slave revolt (Leyburn 1941), as it apparently did in the downfall of President Jean-Claude Duvalier in February 1986.

Three African groups appear to have had the strongest influence on Voodoo: the Yoruba of present-day Nigeria, the Fon of Dahomey (present-day Benin), and the Kongo of what are now Zaire and Angola. Many of the names of Voodoo spirits are easily traceable to their African counterparts; however, in the context of Haiti's social and economic history, these spirits have undergone change. For example, Ogun among the Yoruba is a spirit of ironsmithing and other activities associated with metal, such as hunting, warfare, and modern technology. Neither hunting nor modern technology plays a significant role in the lives of Haitians. Haiti does, however, have a long and complex military history; thus the Haitian spirit Ogou is a soldier whose rituals, iconography, and possession-performance explore both the constructive and destructive uses of military power, as well as its analogues within human relations—anger, self-assertion, and willfulness.

Africa itself is a powerful concept in Voodoo. Haitians speak of Gine ("Guinea") both as their ancestral home, the continent of Africa, and as the watery subterranean home of the Voodoo spirits. Calling a spirit *frangine* (lit., "frank Guinea," i.e., truly African) is a way of indicating that the spirit is good, ancient, and proper. The manner in which an individual or a group serves the spirits may also be called *frangine,* with similar connotations of approval and propriety.

Roman Catholic Influence

The French slaveholders were Catholic, and baptism was mandatory for slaves. Many have argued that slaves used a veneer of Catholicism to hide their traditional religious practices from the authorities. While Catholicism may well have functioned in this utilitarian way for slaves on the plantations, it is also true that the religious of West Africa, from which Voodoo was derived, have a long tradition of syncretism. Whatever else Catholicism represented in the slave world, it was most likely also seen as a means to expand Voodoo's ritual vocabulary and iconography. Catholicism has had the greatest influence on the traditional religion of Haiti at the level of rite and image, rather than theology. This influence works in two ways. First, those who serve the spirits call themselves Catholic, attend Mass, go to confession, and undergo baptism and first communion, and, because these Catholic rituals are at times integral parts of certain larger Voodoo rites, they are often directed to follow them by the Voodoo spirits. Second, Catholic prayers, rites, images, and saints' names are integrated into the ritualizing in Voodoo temples and cult houses. An active figure in Voodoo is the *pretsavan* ("bush priest"), who achieves his title by knowing the proper, often Latin, form of Catholic prayers. Though neither a Catholic nor a Voodoo priest, he is called into the Voodoo temple when the ritualizing has a significant Catholic dimension.

Over the years, a system of parallels has been developed between the Voodoo spirits and the Catholic saints. For example, Dambala, the ancient and venerable snake deity of the Fon peoples, is worshiped in Haiti both as Dambala and as Saint Patrick, who is pictured in the popular Catholic chromolithograph with snakes clustered around his feet. In addition, the Catholic liturgical calendar dominates in much Voodoo ritualizing. Thus the Voodoo spirit Ogou is honored on 25 July, the feast day of his Catholic counterpart, Saint James the Elder.

Bondye, the "Good God," is identified with the Christian God and is said to be the highest, indeed the only, god. The spirits are said to have been an-gels in Lucifer's army whom God sent out of heaven and down to Gine. Although the spirits may exhibit capricious behavior, they are in no sense evil. Rather, they are seen as intermediaries between the people and the high god, a role identical to the one played by the so-called lower deities in the religions of the Yoruba and Fon. Bondye is remote and unknowable. Although evoked daily in ordinary speech (almost all plans are made with the disclaimer "if God wills"), Bondye's intervention is not sought for most of life's problems. That is the work of the spirits.

The Catholic church of Haiti has sometimes participated in the persecution of those who follow Voodoo. However, the last "antisuperstition campaign" was in the 1940s, and currently there is an uneasy peace between Voodoo and the Catholic church. Until quite recently, the Catholic clergy routinely preached against serving the spirits, and those who served routinely remarked, "That is the way priests talk." Most Catholic events have a simultaneous Voodoo dimension that the Catholic church for the most part ignores. Since Catholicism is the official religion of Haiti and the church has been to some extent state-controlled, the degree to which Voodoo has been tolerated, or even encouraged has been at least partly a function of politics. For instance, Haitian presidents Dumarsais Estime (1946–1950) and François Duvalier (1957–1971) were known for their sympathy with Voodoo.

Voodoo Spirits

The Voodoo spirits are known by various names: *lwa* (from a Yoruba word for "spirit" or "mystery"), *sint* ("saints"), *mistè* ("mysteries"), *envizil* ("invisibles"), and, more rarely, *zanj* ("angels"). In the countryside, the spirits are grouped into *nanchon* ("nations"). Although no longer recognized as such by Haitians, the names of the Voodoo spirit nations almost all refer to places and peoples in Africa. For example, there are *nanchon* known as Rada (after the Dahomean principality Allada), Wangol (Angola), Mondon (Mandingo), Ibo, and Nago (the Dahomean name for the Ketu Yoruba and Kongo). In rural Voodoo, a person inherits responsibilities to one or more of these *nanchon* through maternal and paternal kin. Familial connections to the land, where the *lwa* are said to reside in trees, springs and wells, also determine which spirits are served.

In urban Voodoo, two *nanchon,* the Rada and the Petro, have emerged as dominant largely by absorbing other *nanchon.* Rada and Petro spirits contrast sharply in temperament and domain. The Rada spirits are *dous* ("sweet") and known for their wisdom and benevolence. The Petro spirits were probably named for the Spanish Voodoo priest Dom Petro; they show a marked Kongo influence and are considered *cho* ("hot"), and their power is stressed. Each spirit group has drum rhythms, dances, and food preferences that correspond to its identifying characteristics. For example, Dambala, the gentle Rada snake spirit, is said to love *orja,* a syrup made from almonds and sugar. His worshipers perform a sinuous spine-rippling dance called *yanvalou.* By contrast, the Petro rhythm, played for such rum-drinking spirits as Dom Petro and Tijan Petro, is energetic and pounding, and the accompanying dance is characterized by rapid shoulder movements.

The Voodoo View of the Person

In Voodoo teachings the human being is composed of various parts: the body, that is, the gross physical part of the person, which perishes after death, and from two to four souls, of which the most widely acknowledged are the *gro bonanj* and the *ti bonanj.* The *gro bonanj* ("big guardian angel") is roughly equivalent to consciousness or personality. When a person dies the *gro bonanj* survives, and immediately after death it is most vulnerable to capture and misuse by sorcerers. During possession, it is the *gro bonanj* that is displaced by the spirit and sent to wander away from the body, as it does routinely during sleep. The *ti bonanj* ("little guardian angel") may be thought of as the conscience or the spiritual energy reserve of a living person and, at times, as the ghost of a dead person. Each person is said to have one spirit who is the *mèt-tet* ("master of the head"). The *mèt-tet* is the major protector and central spirit served by that person, and it is that spirit that corresponds to the *gro bonanj.* Because the *gro bonanj* is the soul that endures after death and because it is connected to a particular *lwa,* a person who venerates the ancestors inherits the service of particular spirits. In addition to the master of the head, each person has a small number of other *lwa* with whom there is a special protective connection. There is a rough parallel between the characters of the spirits and those of the people who serve them. Thus the language of Voodoo is also a language for categorizing and analyzing the behavior of groups and individuals. For example, when an individual, family, or temple is described as worshiping in a mode that is *Rada net,* ("straight *Rada*"), a great deal is also being said about how that person or group functions socially.

Voodoo and the Dead

In both urban and rural Haiti, cemeteries are major ritual centers. The first male buried in any cemetery is known as the Baron. Baron's wife is Gran Brijit, a name given to the first female buried in a cemetery. Every cemetery has a cross either in the center or at the gate. The cross is known as the *kwa Baron* ("Baron's cross"), and this is the ritualizing center of the cemetery. Lighted candles and food offerings are placed at the foot of Baron's cross. In addition, many rituals for healing, love, or luck that are performed in the rural cult houses or the urban temples are not considered complete until the physical remnants of the "work" are deposited at crossroads or at Baron's cross, which is itself a kind of crossroads marking the intersection of the land of the living and the land of the dead.

Haitians make a distinction between *lemò* ("the dead") and *lemistè* ("the mysteries"). Within Voodoo, there are rituals and offerings for particular family dead; however, if these ancestral spirits are seen as strong and effective, they can, with time, become *mistè.* The group of spirits known as the *gèdè* are not ancestral spirits but *mistè,* and their leader is the well-known Baron Samdi, or Baron Saturday. In and around Port-au-Prince, the capital of Haiti and its largest city, the *gèdè* are the object of elaborate ritualizing in the cemeteries and Voodoo temples during the season of the Catholic Feast of All Souls, or Halloween.

The *gèdè* are not only spirits of death but also patrons of human sexuality, protectors of children, and irrepressible social satirists. Dances for *gèdè* tend to be boisterous affairs, and new *gèdè* spirits appear every year. The satirical, and often explicitly sexual, humor of the *gèdè* levels social pretense. Appearing as auto mechanics, doctors, government bureaucrats, Protestant missionaries, and so forth, the *gèdè* use humor to deal with new social roles and to question alienating social hierarchies.

Voodoo Ceremonies

In rural Voodoo, the ideal is to serve the spirits as simply as possible because simplicity of ritual is said to reflect real power and the true African way of doing things (Larose 1977). In practice, rural ritualizing tends to follow the fortunes of the extended families. Bad times are said to be due to the displeasure of the family spirits. When it is thought to be no longer possible to satisfy the spirits with small conciliatory offerings, the family will hold a large drumming and dancing feast that includes animal sacrifice.

Urban Voodoo, by contrast, has a more routine ritualizing calendar, and events tend to be larger and more elaborate. Ceremonies in honor of major spirits take place annually on or around the feast days of their Catholic counterparts and usually include sacrifice of an appropriate animal—most frequently a chicken, a goat, or a cow. A wide variety of ceremonies meet specific individual and community needs: for example, healing rites, dedications of new temples and new ritual regalia, and spirit marriages in which a devotee "marries" a spirit of the opposite sex and pledges to exercise sexual restraint one night each week in order to receive that spirit in dreams. There is also a cycle of initiation rituals that has both public segments and segments reserved for initiates. The latter include the *kanzo* rituals, which mark the first stage of initiation, and those in which the adept takes the *asson,* the beaded gourd rattle that is the symbol of the Voodoo priesthood. Certain rituals performed during the initiation cycle, such as the *brule zen* ("burning of the pots") and the *chire ayzan* ("shredding of the palm leaf") may also be used in other ritual contexts. Death rituals include the *desounen,* in which the *gro bonanj* is removed from the corpse and sent under the waters, and the *rele mò nan dlo* ("calling the dead up from the waters") a ritual that can occur any time after a period of a year and a day from the date of death. Good-luck baths are administered during the Christmas and New Year season. Many of the rituals of urban Voodoo are performed in rural Haiti as well.

Annual pilgrimages draw thousands of urban and rural followers of Voodoo. The focal point of events, which are at once Catholic and Voodoo, is usually a Catholic church situated near some striking feature of the natural landscape that is believed to be sacred to the Voodoo spirits. The two largest pilgrimages are one held for Ezili Dantò (Our Lady of Mount Carmel) in mid-July in the little town of Saut d'Eau, named for its spectacular waterfall, and one held for Ogou (Saint James the Elder) in the latter part of July in the northern town of Plain du Nord, where a shallow pool adjacent to the Catholic church is sacred to Ogou.

Voodoo and Magic

Serge Larose (1977) has demonstrated that magic is not only a stereotypic label that outsiders have applied to Voodoo, but also a differential term internal to the religion. Thus an in-group among the followers of Voodoo identifies its own ritualizing as "African" while labeling the work of the out-group as *maji* ("magic"). Generally speaking, this perspective provides a helpful means of grasping the concept of magic within Voodoo. There are, however, those individuals who, in their search for power and wealth, have self-consciously identified themselves with traditions of what Haitians would call the "work of the left hand." This includes people who deal in *pwen achte* ("purchased points"), which means spirits or powers that have been bought rather than inherited, and people who deal in *zombi.* A *zombi* may be either the disembodied soul of a dead person whose powers are used for magical purposes, or a soulless body that has been raised from the grave to do drone labor in the fields. Also included in the category of the left hand are secret societies known by such names as Champwel, Zobop, and Bizango. These powerful groups are magic not for personal gain but to enforce social sanctions. Wade Davis (1985) claims that *zombi* laborers are created by judgments of tribunals of secret societies against virulently antisocial persons.

The "work of the left hand" should not be confused with more ordinary Voodoo ritualizing that also has a magical flavor, such as divination, herbal healing, and the manufacture of charms for love or luck, or for the protection of the home, land, or person. Much of the work of Voodoo priests is at the level of individual client-practitioner interactions. Theirs is a healing system that treats problems of love, health, family, and work. Unless a problem is understood as coming from God, in which case the Voodoo priest can do nothing, the priest will treat it as one caused by a spirit or by a disruption in human relationships, including relations with the dead. Generally speaking, cures come through a ritual adjustment of relational systems.

Voodoo in the Haitian Diaspora

Drought and soil erosion, poverty, high urban unemployment, and political oppression in Haiti have led to massive emigration in the last three decades. Voodoo has moved along with the Haitians who have come to the major urban centers of North America in search of better life. In Miami, New York, and Montreal, the cities with the greatest concentrations of Haitian immigrants, Voodoo ceremonies are carried on in storefronts, rented rooms, and high-rise apartments. North American rituals are often truncated versions of their Haitian counterparts. There may be no drums, and the only animals sacrificed may be chickens. However, it is possible to consult a *manbo* or *oungan* in these immigrant communities with ease, and the full repertoire of rituals is found there in one form or another. Even the pilgrimages are duplicated. On 16 July, rather than going to the mountain town of Saut d'Eau to honor Ezili Dantò, New York Haitians take the subway to the Italian-American Church of Our Lady of Mount Carmel in the Bronx.

The Secrets of Haiti's Living Dead

Gino del Guercio

Recounting the experience of Wade Davis, author of The Serpent and the Rainbow, *Gino del Guercio points out Davis's startling discovery that zombies do indeed exist in Haiti; however, rather than being "the living dead," they are actually the "living drugged." Haitian secret societies use the threat of zombification to control deviant activity, and for the rural population, this punishment is regarded as more severe than death. The secret was unlocked by enthnobotanist Davis, who recognized that the symptoms brought on by fish poisoning in Japan were identical to those experienced by victims of so-called zombification in Haiti. Davis shows that zombies cannot be dismissed as folklore, nor are they the living dead. It is important to note here that serious controversy continues to surround the Davis thesis. William Booth's review article "Voodoo Science," which follows, cites scholars who question the findings of Davis.*

Reprinted from *Harvard Magazine,* January-February 1986, pp. 31–37. Copyright © 1986 *Harvard Magazine.* Reprinted by permission.

FIVE YEARS AGO, A MAN WALKED INTO L'ESTÈRE, a village in central Haiti, approached a peasant woman named Angelina Narcisse, and identified himself as her brother Clairvius. If he had not introduced himself using a boyhood nickname and mentioned facts only intimate family members knew, she would not have believed him. Because, eighteen years earlier, Angelina had stood in a small cemetery north of her village and watched as her brother Clairvius was buried.

The man told Angelina he remembered that night well. He knew when he was lowered into his grave, because he was fully conscious, although he could not speak or move. As the earth was thrown over his coffin, he felt as if he were floating over the grave. The scar on his right cheek, he said, was caused by a nail driven through his casket.

The night he was buried, he told Angelina, a voodoo priest raised him from the grave. He was beaten with a sisal whip and carried off to a sugar plantation in northern Haiti where, with other zombies, he was forced to work as a slave. Only with the death of the zombie master were they able to escape, and Narcisse eventually returned home.

Legend has it that zombies are the living dead, raised from their graves and animated by malevolent voodoo sorcerers, usually for some evil purpose. Most Haitians believe in zombies, and Narcisse's claim is not unique. At about the time he reappeared, in 1980, two women turned up in other villages saying they were zombies. In the same year, in northern Haiti, the local peasants claimed to have found a group of zombies wandering aimlessly in the fields.

But Narcisse's case was different in one crucial respect; it was documented. His death had been recorded by doctors at the American-directed Schweitzer Hospital in Deschapelles. On April 30, 1962, hospital records show, Narcisse walked into the hospital's emergency room spitting up blood.

He was feverish and full of aches. His doctors could not diagnose his illness, and his symptoms grew steadily worse. Three days after he entered the hospital, according to the records, he died. The attending physicians, an American among them, signed his death certificate. His body was placed in cold storage for twenty hours, and then he was buried. He said he remembered hearing his doctors pronounce him dead while his sister wept at his bedside.

At the Centre de Psychiatrie et Neurologie in Port-au-Prince, Dr. Lamarque Douyon, a Haitian-born Canadian-trained psychiatrist, has been systematically investigating all reports of zombies since 1961. Though convinced zombies were real, he had been unable to find a scientific explanation for the phenomenon. He did not believe zombies were people raised from the dead, but that did not make them any less interesting. He speculated that victims were only made to *look* dead, probably by means of a drug that dramatically slowed metabolism. The victim was buried, dug up within a few hours, and somehow reawakened.

The Narcisse case provided Douyon with evidence strong enough to warrant a request for assistance from colleagues in New York. Douyon wanted to find an ethnobotanist, a traditional-medicines expert, who could track down the zombie potion he was sure existed. Aware of the medical potential of a drug that could dramatically lower metabolism, a group organized by the late Dr. Nathan Kline—a New York psychiatrist and pioneer in the field of psychopharmacology—raised the funds necessary to send someone to investigate.

The search for that someone led to the Harvard Botanical Museum, one of the world's foremost institutes of ethnobiology. Its director, Richard Evans Schultes, Jeffrey professor of biology, had spent thirteen years in the tropics studying native medicines. Some of this best-known work is the investigation of curare, the substance used by the nomadic people of the Amazon to poison their darts. Refined into a powerful muscle relaxant called D-tubocurarine, it is now an essential component of the anesthesia used during almost all surgery.

Schultes would have been a natural for the Haitian investigation, but he was too busy. He recommended another Harvard ethnobotanist for the assignment, Wade Davis, a 28–year-old Canadian pursuing a doctorate in biology.

Davis grew up in the tall pine forests of British Columbia and entered Harvard in 1971, influenced by a *Life* magazine story on the student strike of 1969. Before Harvard, the only Americans he had known were draft dodgers, who seemed very exotic. "I used to fight forest fires with them," Davis says. "Like everybody else, I thought America was where it was at. And I wanted to go to Harvard because of that *Life* article. When I got there, I realized it wasn't quite what I had in mind."

Davis took a course from Schultes, and when he decided to go to South America to study plants, he approached his professor for guidance. "He was an extraordinary figure," Davis remembers. "He was a man who had done it all. He had lived alone for years in the Amazon." Schultes sent Davis to the rain forest with two letters of introduction and two pieces of advice: wear a pith helmet and try ayahuasca, a powerful hallucinogenic wine. During that expedition and others, Davis proved himself an "outstanding field man," says his mentor. Now, in early 1982, Schultes called him into his office and asked if he had plans for spring break.

"I always took to Schultes's assignments like a plant takes to water," says Davis, tall and blond, with inquisitive blue eyes. "Whatever Shultes told me to do, I did. His letters of introduction opened up a whole world." This time the world was Haiti.

Davis knew nothing about the Caribbean island —and nothing about African traditions, which serves as Haiti's cultural basis. He certainly did not believe in zombies. "I thought it was a lark," he says now.

Davis landed in Haiti a week after his conversation with Schultes, armed with a hypothesis about how the zombie drug—if it existed—might be made. Setting out to explore, he discovered a country materially impoverished, but rich in culture and mystery. He was impressed by the cohesion of Haitian society; he found none of the crime, social disorder, and rampant drug and alcohol abuse so common in many of the other Caribbean islands. The cultural wealth and cohesion, he believes, spring from the country's turbulent history.

During the French occupation of the late eighteenth century, 370,000 African-born slaves were imported to Haiti between 1780 and 1790. In 1791, the black population launched one of the few successful slave revolts in history, forming secret societies and overcoming first the French plantation owners and then a detachment of troops from Napoleon's army, sent to quell the revolt. For the next hundred years Haiti was the only independent black republic in the Caribbean, populated by people who did not forget their African heritage. "You can almost argue that Haiti is more African than Africa," Davis says. "When the west coast of Africa was being disrupted by colonialism and the slave trade, Haiti was essentially left alone. The amalgam of beliefs in Haiti is unique, but it's very, very African."

Davis discovered that the vast majority of Haitian peasants practice voodoo, a sophisticated religion with African roots. Says Davis, "It was immediately obvious that the stereotypes of voodoo weren't true. Going around the countryside, I found clues to a whole complex social world." Vodounists believe they communicate directly with, indeed are often possessed by, the many spirits who populate the everyday world. Vodoun society is a system of education, law, and medicine; it embodies a code of ethics that regulates social behavior. In rural areas, secret vodoun societies, much like those found on the west coast of Africa, are as much or more in control of everyday life as the Haitian government.

Although most outsiders dismissed the zombie phenomenon as folklore, some early investigators, convinced of its reality, tried to find a scientific explanation. The few who sought a zombie drug failed. Nathan Kline, who helped finance Davis's expedition, had searched unsuccessfully, as had Lamarque Douyon, the Haitian psychiatrist. Zora Neale Hurston, an American black woman, may have come closest. An anthropological pioneer, she went to Haiti in the thirties, studied vodoun society, and wrote a book on the subject, *Tell My Horse,* first published in 1938. She knew about the secret societies and was convinced zombies were real, but if a powder existed, she too failed to obtain it.

Davis obtained a sample in a few weeks.

He arrived in Haiti with the names of several contacts. A BBC reporter familiar with the Narcisse case had suggested he talk with Marcel Pierre. Pierre owned the Eagle Bar, a bordello in the city of Saint Marc. He was also a voodoo sorcerer and had supplied the BBC with a physiologically active powder of unknown ingredients. Davis found him willing to negotiate. He told Pierre he was a representative of "powerful but anonymous interests in New York," willing to pay generously for the priest's services,

provided no questions were asked. Pierre agreed to be helpful for what Davis will only say was a "sizable sum." Davis spent a day watching Pierre gather the ingredients—including human bones—and grind them together with mortar and pestle. However, from his knowledge of poison, Davis knew immediately that nothing in the formula could produce the powerful effects of zombification.

Three weeks later, Davis went back to the Eagle Bar, where he found Pierre sitting with three associates. Davis challenged him. He called him a charlatan. Enraged, the priest gave him a second vial, claiming that this was the real poison. Davis pretended to pour the powder into his palm and rub it into his skin. "You're a dead man," Pierre told him, and he might have been, because this powder proved to be genuine. But, as the substance had not actually touched him, Davis was able to maintain his bravado, and Pierre was impressed. He agreed to make the poison and show Davis how it was done.

The powder, which Davis keeps in a small vial, looks like dry black dirt. It contains parts of toads, sea worms, lizards, tarantulas, and human bones. (To obtain the last ingredient, he and Pierre unearthed a child's grave on a nocturnal trip to the cemetery.) The poison is rubbed into the victim's skin. Within hours he begins to feel nauseated and has difficulty breathing. A pins-and-needles sensation afflicts his arms and legs, then progresses to the whole body. The subject becomes paralyzed; his lips turn blue for lack of oxygen. Quickly—sometimes within six hours—his metabolism is lowered to a level almost indistinguishable from death.

As Davis discovered, making the poison is an inexact science. Ingredients varied in the five samples he eventually acquired, although the active agents were always the same. And the poison came with no guarantee. Davis speculates that sometimes instead of merely paralyzing the victim, the compound kills him. Sometimes the victim suffocates in the coffin before he can be resurrected. But clearly the potion works well enough to make zombies more than a figment of Haitian imagination.

Analysis of the powder produced another surprise. "When I went down to Haiti originally," says Davis, "my hypothesis was that the formula would contain *concombre zombi,* the 'zombie's cucumber,' which is a *Datura* plant. I thought somehow *Datura* was used in putting people down." *Datura* is a powerful psychoactive plant, found in West Africa as well as other tropical areas and used there in ritual as well as criminal activities. Davis had found *Datura* growing in Haiti. Its popular name suggested the plant was used in creating zombies.

But, says Davis, "there were a lot of problems with the *Datura* hypothesis. Partly it was a question of how the drug was administered. *Datura* would create a stupor in huge doses, but it just wouldn't produce the kind of immmobility that was key. These people had to appear dead, and there aren't many drugs that will do that."

One of the ingredients Pierre included in the second formula was a dried fish, a species of puffer or blowfish, common to most parts of the world. It gets its name from its ability to fill itself with water and swell to several times its normal size when threatened by predators. Many of these fish contain a powerful poison known as tetrodotoxin. One of the most powerful nonprotein poisons known to man, tetrodotoxin turned up in every sample of zombie powder that Davis acquired.

Numerous well-documented accounts of puffer fish poisoning exist, but the most famous accounts come from the Orient, where *fugu* fish, a species of puffer, is considered a delicacy. In Japan, special chefs are licensed to prepare *fugu*. The chef removes enough poison to make the fish nonlethal, yet enough remains to create exhilarating physiological effects—tingles up and down the spine, mild prickling of the tongue and lips, euphoria. Several dozen Japanese die each year, having bitten off more than they should have.

"When I got hold of the formula and saw it was the *fugu* fish, that suddenly threw open the whole Japanese literature," says Davis. Case histories of *fugu* poisoning read like accounts of zombification. Victims remain conscious but unable to speak or move. A man who had "died" after eating *fugu* recovered seven days later in the morgue. Several summers ago, another Japanese poisoned by *fugu* revived after he was nailed into his coffin. "Almost all of Narcisse's symptoms correlated. Even strange things such as the fact that he said he was conscious and could hear himself pronounced dead. Stuff that I thought had to be magic, that seemed crazy. But, in fact, that is what people who get *fugu*-fish poisoning experience."

Davis was certain he had solved the mystery. But far from being the end of his investigation, identifying the poison was, in fact, its starting point. "The

drug alone didn't make zombies," he explains. "Japanese victims of puffer-fish poisoning don't become zombies, they become poison victims. All the drug could do was set someone up for a whole series of psychological pressures that would be rooted in the culture. I wanted to know why zombification was going on," he says.

He sought a cultural answer, an explanation rooted in the structure and beliefs of Haitian society. Was zombification simply a random criminal activity? He thought not. He had discovered that Clairvius Narcisse and "Ti Femme," a second victim he interviewed, were village pariahs. Ti Femme was regarded as a thief. Narcisse had abandoned his children and deprived his brother of land that was rightfully his. Equally suggestive, Narcisse claimed that his aggrieved brother had sold him to a *bokor*, a voodoo priest who dealt in black magic; he made cryptic reference to having been tried and found guilty by the "masters of the land."

Gathering poisons from various parts of the country, Davis had come into direct contact with the vodoun secret societies. Returning to the anthropological literature on Haiti and pursuing his contacts with informants, Davis came to understand the social matrix within which zombies were created.

Davis's investigations uncovered the importance of the secret societies. These groups trace their origins to the bands of escaped slaves that organized the revolt against the French in the late eighteenth century. Open to both men and women, the societies control specific territories of the country. Their meetings take place at night, and in many rural parts of Haiti the drums and wild celebrations that characterized the gatherings can be heard for miles.

Davis believes the secret societies are responsible for policing their communities, and the threat of zombification is one way they maintain order. Says Davis, "Zombification has a material basis, but it also has a societal logic." To the uninitiated, the practice may appear a random criminal activity, but in rural vodoun society, it is exactly the opposite—a sanction imposed by recognized authorities, a form of capital punishment. For rural Haitians, zombification is an even more severe punishment than death, because it deprives the subject of his most valued possessions: his free will and independence.

The vodounists believe that when a person dies, his spirit splits into several different parts. If a priest is powerful enough, the spiritual aspect that controls a person's character and individuality, known as *ti bon ange,* the "good little angel," can be captured and the corporeal aspect, deprived of its will, held as a slave.

From studying the medical literature on tetrodotoxin poisoning, Davis discovered that if a victim survives the first few hours of the poisoning, he is likely to recover fully from the ordeal. The subject simply revives spontaneously. But zombies remain without will, in a trance-like state, a condition vodounists attribute to the power of the priest. Davis thinks it possible that the psychological trauma of zombification may be augmented by *Datura* or some other drug; he thinks zombies may be fed a *Datura* paste that accentuates their disorientation. Still, he puts the material basis of zombification in perspective: "Tetrodotoxin and *Datura* are only templates on which cultural forces and beliefs may be amplified a thousand times."

Davis has not been able to discover how prevalent zombification is in Haiti. "How many zombies there are is not the question," he says. He compares it to capital punishment in the United States: "It doesn't really matter how many people are electrocuted, as long as it's a possibility." As a sanction in Haiti, the fear is not of zombies, it's of becoming one.

Davis attributes his success in solving the zombie mystery to his approach. He went to Haiti with an open mind and immersed himself in the culture. "My intuition unhindered by biases served me well," he says. "I didn't make any judgments." He combined this attitude with what he had learned earlier from his experiences in the Amazon. "Schultes's lesson is to go and live with the Indians as an Indian." Davis was able to participate in the vodoun society to a surprising degree, eventually even penetrating one of the Bizango societies and dancing in their nocturnal rituals. His appreciation of Haitian culture is apparent. "Everybody asks me how did a white person get this information? To ask the question means you don't understand Haitians —they don't judge you by the color of your skin."

As a result of the exotic nature of his discoveries, Davis has gained certain notoriety. He plans to complete his dissertation soon, but he has already finished writing a popular account of his adventures. To be published in January by Simon and Schuster, it is called *The Serpent and the Rainbow,* after the serpent that vodounists believe created the earth and the rainbow spirit it married. Film rights have already been optioned; in October Davis went back to Haiti with a screenwriter. But Davis takes the notoriety in stride. "All this attention is funny," he says. "For years, not just me, but all Schultes's students have had extraordinary adventures in the line of work. The adventure is not the end point, it's just along the way of getting the data. At the Botanical Museum, Schultes created a world unto itself. We didn't think we were doing anything above the ordinary. I still don't think we do. And you know," he adds, "the Haiti episode does not begin to compare to what others have accomplished—particularly Schultes himself."

Voodoo Science

William Booth

In the prior article, Gino Del Guercio discussed the hypothesis put forward by botanist Wade Davis that the so-called zombies do exist in Haiti and that zombification is the result of administering to the victim a powerful poison extracted from the puffer fish.

Here William Booth challenges Davis's zombie theory and claims that crucial evidence that did not support the theory was ignored. Charges ranging from accusations of outright fraud to bad science have been leveled at Davis. Focusing on the key ingredient of "zombie powder" (tetrodotoxin), Davis maintained that the administration of a precise amount of the drug would cause the victim to fall into a deathlike state. But clouding the idea of precise dosages is Davis's statement that some Haitians are psychologically or culturally predisposed to becoming zombies whereas others are not. As a further complication, the ingredients in drugs manufactured by folk pharmacologists (in this case the "bokors," voodoo sorcerers) are nearly impossible to replicate. Despite this, Davis asserted that there is good pharmacological evidence for zombification, and the critical chemical is the poison tetrodotoxin. His detractors say there is simply no data to support this theory, calling Davis's experiments "voodoo science."

For many, the major question remaining is, Do zombies really exist? For others, it is whether the scientific method has been followed in this research. Whatever the questions, the mystery of the zombies remains just that.

Reprinted from *Science*, vol. 240, no. 4850, April 15, 1988, pp. 274–77. Copyright 1988 American Association for the Advancement of Science. Reprinted by permission.

A YOUNG BOTANIST FROM HARVARD UNIVERSITY named Wade Davis claims to have discovered a pharmacological explanation for zombies, the "living dead" of Haitian folklore. But his detractors say his assertions are bunk and his methods are unscientific.

The lingering controversy has been sparked in part by the collision of two different worlds of research. In the first world, the intrepid ethnobotanist Davis goes down to the troubled island nation of Haiti. His mission: discover how zombies are made. What Davis found was "a surrealistic landscape" and a country "full of spirits." Armed with cash but scant knowledge of Haitian Creole, Davis immersed himself in the secret societies of the voodoo religion. With sorcerers as paid informants, Davis participated in the preparation of several batches of "zombie powder," and witnessed the exhumation of the corpse of a child from a rural graveyard at night. When Davis emerged from his trials in Haiti, he reported having found the pharmacological underpinning for the zombie phenomenon. Fame and fortune followed.

This romantic world has collided with another world, a less glamorous place of mass spectrometers, gas chromatography, and mouse bioassays, where a group of toxicologists and pharmacologists familiar with the work of Davis are crying foul. Leading the charge is C. Y. Kao of State University of New York Downstate Medical Center in Brooklyn, who has aggressively challenged Davis at every turn. Kao does not mince words: "I actually feel this is an issue of fraud in science." One of Kao's comrades in the dispute, Bo Holmstedt of the Karolinksa Institute in Stockholm, is more restrained: "It is not deliberate fraud. It is withholding negative data. It is simply bad science."

The controversy involves the role of a powerful poison called tetrodotoxin in the creation of zombies. Davis' critics say there is either no tetrodotoxin or little in the samples of zombie powder brought back by Davis to support his hypothesis. But there is more to it than that. The pharmacologists are accusing Davis of not playing by the rules by suppressing information that fails to bolster his case, while playing up a number of unconfirmed experiments that are repeatedly cited in his work as "personal communications." Some of the critics seem especially irked because Davis sought out their assistance but allegedly refuses to listen when told his conclusions are not supported by the evidence. "I feel like I've been taken for a ride," says Kao.

The story is complicated by the popular accounts of Davis and the sensational nature of his work. Predictably, there has been a flurry of articles and television programs, for who does not enjoy a good story about zombies now and then? Davis also wrote a popular book in 1985 called *The Serpent and the Rainbow* and then sold the rights to Hollywood, which recently released a rather lurid movie under the same title. Another book about zombies—this time a scholarly treatment based almost entirely on Davis' Harvard dissertation—is scheduled for release in May by the University of North Carolina Press. All of this attention has certainly created bad feelings, with pronouncements from both sides becoming increasingly invidious. David says that Kao and others are victims of "old-fashioned jealousy."

The story begins in 1982, when Davis was introduced to the late Nathan Kline, then director of the Rockland State Research Institute in New York. Kline, a pioneer in the use of tranquilizers, wanted Davis to go to Haiti to search for a mysterious powder reputedly used to make zombies. Despite 30 years of work in Haiti, Kline had never succeeded in securing such a sample.

When Davis met Kline, the older man was particularly excited about zombies because he and a colleague in Haiti believed that for the first time they had found a verifiable case, a man named Clairvius Narcisse, who returned to his village after an 18-year absence, claiming to have been made a zombie and sold into slavery. Narcisse has since become quite famous as the object of documentaries by the BBC and ABC. Narcisse's account, though highly intriguing, is far from watertight. Davis himself says that Narcisse had received so much attention by the time he arrived that the case was hard to evaluate. Other anthropologists with years of experience in Haiti discount the reality of zombies. "You hear stories all the time, but you can never actually find a zombie," says Leslie Desmangles of Trinity College in Hartford,

Connecticut, a Haitian who has studied the religions of his homeland for the past 15 years.

Davis made several trips to Haiti between 1982 and 1984, collecting a total of eight samples of zombie powder from several voodoo sorcerers, or "bokors" as they are called. Most of the powders contained a variety of ingredients. Some included the fresh remains of a human cadaver, as well as stinging nettles, noxious toads, and one or more species of puffer fish found in Haitian waters. It was the fish that interested Davis, since puffer fish are known to sometimes contain the potent tetrodotoxin. Tetrodotoxin blocks the sodium channels between nerve endings and can cause paralysis and death. Davis says he paid about $300 for each sample, an enormous sum of money in Haiti, which is one of the poorest countries in the Western Hemisphere.

According to the hypothesis touted by Davis, the process of "zombification" works something like this: A victim is administered a powder that contains among other things the dried and pulverized remains of puffer fish, whose livers and reproductive organs may contain tetrodotoxin. At a dosage containing a precise amount of tetrodotoxin, Davis maintains that a victim of zombie powder poisoning could lapse into a state of such low metabolic activity that he might appear clinically dead. This poor soul would then be buried alive, only to be rescued hours later by a sorcerer who digs up the victim, feeds him an hallucinogenic paste, and then sells his newly minted zombie into slavery, often to sugar plantations.

As Davis points out, not all victims of tetrodotoxin poisoning would become zombies. A psychological or cultural predisposition is essential. One has to live in Haiti and believe in zombies to actually become one. It is what Davis calls the "set and setting" of the experience. For example, says Davis, a person who goes into the woods with the purpose of eating hallucinogenic mushrooms usually enjoys his experience. But the person who eats the mushrooms by mistake is often rushed to the emergency room, thinking himself a victim of poisoning.

Upon return to the United States after his first trip to Haiti in 1982, Davis provided several samples of zombie powder to Leon Roizin, a pathologist from Columbia Presbyterian Hospital in New York City who has been studying the effects of drugs on the central nervous system for 40 years. As a personal favor to his "old friend" Kline, Roizin agreed to test the crude mixtures on several rats and one rhesus monkey. He administered the zombie powder by rubbing an extract onto the shaved bellies of the rats or by injecting a solution into peritoneal tissue. What happened next was very intriguing. According to the account cited as a personal communication from Roizin to Davis, some rats "appeared comatose and showed no response at all to external stimuli. The electroencephalograph continued to monitor central nervous system activity, and the hearts were not affected. Certain rats remained immobilized for 24 hours and then recovered with no apparent sign of injury." A somewhat similar response was observed in the monkey.

Roizin is upset that the results of this preliminary experiment have been circulated by Davis. "I am very embarrassed," says Roizin, who maintains that he was promised by Kline that the powders would be thoroughly analyzed and that the initial experiment was "just among friends" to see if there was any biological activity. The experiment was never repeated by Roizin and has never been published. Roizin returned all trace of the powders and today refuses to have anything to do with Davis. "Whether someone added some kind of drug, I don't know. How do I know that something was not added to that material?" says Roizin, who reports that he has produced catatonia and immobility in lab animals with other compounds, such as various neuroleptics, analgesics, and hallucinogens.

An experiment like Roizin's, however, was attempted again. In 1984, Davis and John Hartung, a Harvard anthropologist turned medical researcher at SUNY's Downstate Medical Center in Brooklyn, encouraged rats to ingest zombie powder by mixing it with peanut butter. They also rubbed the powder on the rats' shaved bellies and injected powder in solution into the peritoneal cavities of mice and rats. "We failed completely," says Hartung. The animals did not become immobilized, let alone protozombies. Reports Hartung: "It is my suspicion that there was no tetrodotoxin in the samples we tested."

The experiment has never been published, and unlike Roizin's results, is not cited as a "personal communication" by Davis. Hartung defends the silence, stating that "absence of evidence is not evidence of absence." It is a refrain repeated often by Davis and one that drives his critics to distraction. "What does that mean? The burden of proof is no longer on the scientist? Does it mean I can say any-thing I want and then tell my critics it is up to them to prove me wrong," says John Moore, a physiologist at Duke University Medical Center in Durham who relayed Kao's charges to the University of North Carolina Press, publishers of Davis' new book.

Evidence that tetrodotoxin plays a central role in the initial phase of the zombification process has proved to be something of a moving target. No one disputes the observation by Davis that bokors add pulverized puffer fish to their zombie powders. What they dispute is the role of tetrodotoxin in transforming victims into the living dead. In Davis' first paper on the topic in 1983, he reported in the *Journal of Ethnopharmacology* that "the poisons which I collected during my first two expeditions to Haiti are currently being analyzed at the Karolinska Institute in Stockholm and at the University of Lausanne, Switzerland." Then Davis details the "initial experiments" of Roizin and suggests that "3.5 grams of crude poison might put a 73-kilogram human into a comatose, catalyptic state (Roizin, personal communication)." Davis concludes: "These preliminary laboratory results, together with what we know from the field and from the biomedical literature suggest strongly that there is an ethnopharmacological basis to the zombie phenomenon."

In his 1986 Ph.D. dissertation at Harvard, entitled "The ethnobiology of the Haitian zombie," Davis reported the details of Roizin's experiment, yet failed to note his own work with Hartung. As for further proof that tetrodotoxin helps make zombies, Davis wrote: "Laboratory tests have shown both the presence of tetrodotoxin in the samples, and have indicated that the powders when applied topically to rats and monkeys are biologically active." The citation is Davis' 1983 paper in *Journal of Ethnopharmacology,* which contains no evidence for the presence of tetrodotoxin. It also implies that tetrodotoxin was present in all of the samples, which is incorrect. To date, tetrodotoxin has only been found in one sample.

In his latest book, *Passage of Darkness: The Ethnobiology of the Haitian Zombie,* Davis again cites Roizin. In a footnote, Davis adds that "three distinct analytical techniques provided unequivocal evidence that tetrodotoxin is present in [one] sample." The citation is a personal communication from Laurent Rivier at the University of Lausanne.

Tracking the analysis of the various powders is an equally tricky business. The only published data appear in a letter to the journal *Taxicon* from Kao and Takeshi Yasumoto of the Tohoku University in Sendai, Japan. A well-known authority on tetrodotoxin, Kao received two samples of zombie powder from Davis in 1984. Initially very excited about the research, Kao did some preliminary assays on mice and found no biological activity, so he sent the samples to Yasumoto, who had developed an automated tetrodotoxin analyzer based on high-performance liquid chromatography (HPLC), a method which separates chemical components out of a solution. Kao says that he called upon Yasumoto for help because Yasumoto has been involved in testing the stomach contents of victims of fugu fish poisoning in Japan, where gourmands occasionally eat improperly prepared fugu, a species similar to the puffer fish identified by Davis as ingredients in zombie powder. (Normally fugu should contain only enough tetrodotoxin to give diners tingling lips and a sense of mild euphoria, though sometimes the chef makes a tragic mistake.) Using his HPLC machine and mouse bioassay, Yasumoto found less than 1.1 micrograms of tetrodotoxin per gram of crude material in one sample. In the other sample, they found far less. Kao and Yasumoto called the amounts "insignificant traces." They wrote: "From these results it can be concluded that the widely circulated claim in the lay press to the effect that tetrodotoxin is the causal agent in the initial zombification process is without factual foundation."

At Lausanne, Rivier eventually received six samples of powder from Davis. In letters written in 1983 and 1985, Rivier informed Davis that little or no tetrodotoxin could be found. "I am rather disappointed by these results," Rivier wrote. In 1986, Rivier sent portions of all six samples to Michel Lazdunski, director of the Center for Biochemistry at the University of Nice in France. Using a competitive binding assay that involved radiolabeled tetrodotoxin and the sodium channels of rat brain membranes, Lazdunski's laboratory found 64 nanograms of tetrodotoxin per gram of zombie powder in only one of the six samples. A nanogram is one billionth of a gram. As even Hartung says, "If you asked me to drink 64 nanograms of tetrodotoxin, I would. It's not enough to do anything to a human."

Rivier recently told *Science* that he himself has now found between 5 and 20 micrograms of tetrodotoxin per gram of powder in one sample.

What could possibly account for three laboratories finding such wildly different amounts of tet-

rodotoxin in the same sample? Rivier attributes the difference to the powder itself, which is both heterogeneous and very alkaline. Kao, in fact, maintains that the powder is so alkaline that tetrodotoxin would be "decomposed irreversibly into pharmacologically inactive products." The *p*H of the samples often exceeds 10, even after the powder is mixed with a buffered solvent. Yet Rivier and Davis contend that *p*H does not express itself in a dry powder. Says Rivier: "The fact that we have found after 3 years tetrodotoxin in powder kept at room temperature means that the powder itself is able to conserve tetrodotoxin for a long time." For his part, Davis reports that the bokors advised him to rub the powder onto the skin of his victim or place the powder in his shoes or to sprinkle the powder on the ground and whisper the victim's name. "The bokors never suggest that you put the powder in solution," says Davis.

Tetrodotoxin can cause an array of symptoms in lab animals, from wobbly legs to death. Blood pressure may drop and stay quite low. There is shallow breathing and wide paralysis. Without the aid of a respirator, Kao says, the animal usually dies. In cases of tetrodotoxin poisoning in humans, Bruce Halstead of the World Life Research Institute of Colton, California, reports that victims also suffer from decreased blood pressure. In Halstead's *Poisonous and Venomous Marine Animals of the World,* he states: "The muscles of the extremities become paralyzed and the patient is unable to move. As the end approaches the eyes of the victim become glassy. The victim may be comatose but in most cases retains consciousness, and the mental facilities remain acute until shortly before death."

In Japan, cases of fugu fish poisoning are not uncommon. About 100 people a year die from the delicacy. From the Japanese scientific literature and from newspaper accounts, Davis cites several cases of fugu fish poisoning where a victim lingers at the brink of death, but recovers. Says Kao: "If it happens, it is a very, very rare event."

The amount of tetrodotoxin necessary to produce the pharmacological effects that Davis attributes to zombification is unclear. Kao reports that 10 micrograms of pure tetrodotoxin per kilogram of body weight produces a lethal dose in 50% of the lab animals tested. According to the report from Lazdunski's laboratory in Nice, at 64 nanograms of tetrodotoxin per gram of crude poison, a bokor would have to administer 10 kilograms of powder to his victim to produce a lethal dose in 50% of his victims. Of course, the bokors are not trying to kill their victims, only to place them into a state resembling death. Using Rivier's latest figures, a bokor might only have to administer about 70 grams of poison or less. Kao reluctantly concedes that this "is getting into the ballpark of feasibility."

And it is through this window of feasibility that Davis presents his case. "It could well be that my hypothesis is in need of work or is incorrect, but it is not fraudulent," says Davis, who adds that because his critics approach his research as pharmacologists or toxicologists, they fail to appreciate the cultural context. The bokors can always rationalize their failures, says Davis. If a bokor overdoes it and kills a victim "too completely," no one is the wiser. It is a call from God. *Mort bon dieu.* While if a bokor fails to produce a state of near death, he can always try again. Davis notes: "The zombie powders are not manufactured by Merck Sharp & Dohme." Also, the puffer fish may harbor varying amounts of tetrodotoxin depending on the season and its sex.

Says Davis: "I've never maintained there is some kind of assembly line producing zombies in Haiti." He admits that it is, at best, a rare event. "I'm not even saying that it is happening today," says Davis.

Davis does indeed have his supporters. Harvard professor Richard Evans Schultes, the grand old man of ethnobotany, calls his former student "a solid anthropologist and a good botanist and a very good field man with a promising future." As for Davis' hypothesis linking zombies to tetrodotoxin, Schultes says he did not scrutinize that aspect of the dissertation. "I don't know anything about the pharmacology of all this," says Schultes. Indeed, there were no pharmacologists or toxicologists on Davis' dissertation committee.

Irven DeVore, an anthropologist at Harvard who was on the committee, considers the Davis hypothesis "interesting but unproven." Like Schultes, DeVore judged the research as a work of anthropology, not pharmacology. "Red flags did not go up in my mind," says DeVore. "But if Davis has gone well beyond his data, he should have his wrist slapped."

As for paying for samples, this is a gray area. Anthropologists and field biologists often give mirrors, clothing, and sometimes cash to native people in exchange for information or assistance. Davis says that

since Haitians are expected to pay for zombie powders, why shouldn't he?

The exhumation of the corpse, however, raises more troubling questions. Holmstedt calls the act "disgusting." Kao correctly points out that Davis did not just witness a grave-robbing, he commissioned it by paying a bokor to make zombie powder for him. The exhumation, though, does not bother Schultes: "I think they exhume people all the time. I don't see any problem there." Mark Plotkin, an ethnobotanist at the World Wildlife Fund and a former student of Schultes, says that Davis did not pay the bokor to exhume corpses; he paid for zombie powder.

DeVore, however, says that Kao might have a point. "I think the issue is whether Davis paid someone to do something he never does, or rarely does, or paid him to do something he routinely does," says DeVore. "There is a difference."

Says Timothy Plowman, an ethnobotanist at the Field Museum in Chicago: "We're expected to participate in a lot of weird things in the field that we wouldn't do back home." DeVore adds that "anthropologists are forever witnessing something illegal." In his own research on the bushmen of the Kalahari, for example, DeVore says that "there is elephant poaching going on all around us."

Davis defends his actions in Haiti, saying that he simply played the role of participant-observer. In his interviews, Davis often mentions that his work has helped elevate voodoo from a folk cult to a legitimate religion in the minds of outsiders. Some of Davis' critics are not so sure. "Davis complains about the popular accounts of zombies, but here he has contributed to the very same thing," says Holmstedt. Desmangles of Trinity College says that the film made from Davis' book, complete with snakes crawling out of a zombie's mouth, "has taken us back 100 years."

For now, at least, the mystery of the zombies remains unsolved, despite all the noise and attention. For Davis, the zombie research might be over. It will at least have to wait until he finishes two other book projects that are occupying his time these days in Vancouver. Though Davis may make another trip to Haiti, he says he does not plan on becoming a "zombiologist." Says Davis: "My purpose was not to generate absolute truths." Kao agrees with that.

Death Be Not Strange

Peter A. Metcalf

In this article, Peter A. Metcalf compares American and Berawan funeral and mortuary rites and shows why Western practices so shocked the Berawan. To the Berawan, we trap the deceased in a suspended condition between life and death, producing evil, not beneficent spirits. "For the Berawan, America is a land carpeted with potential zombies." Metcalf's fieldwork not only explains the fate of the Berawan dead and demonstrates their beliefs to be as coherent and reasonable as any but also draws attention to the exotic nature of American funerary practices. His comparison reminds us that our level of ethnocentrism both leads us to view the beliefs of others as illogical and sometimes reprehensible and causes us to ignore our own death rituals and practices.

THE POPULAR VIEW OF ANTHROPOLOGY IS THAT it is concerned with faraway places, strange peoples, and odd customs. This notion was neatly captured by a nineteenth-century wit who described the field as "the pursuit of the exotic by the eccentric." In recent decades many anthropologists have tried to shake this image. They see the exotic as dangerously close to the sensational and, therefore, a threat to the respectability of a serious academic discipline. They argue that anthropology has solid theoretical bases, and that some anthropologists routinely work in cities right here in America. And they are right. Nevertheless, anthropologists are as much involved with the exotic as ever, and I think that this concern actually works to scholarship's advantage.

This continuing involvement is a result of the characteristic *modus operandi* of anthropologists. First, we seek out the exotic, in the sense of something originating in another country or something "strikingly or excitingly different," as my *Webster's* puts it. Second, we try to fit this alien item—culture trait, custom, piece of behavior—into its social and cultural context, thereby reducing it to a logical, sensible, even necessary element. Having done that, we feel that we can understand why people do or say or think something instead of being divorced from them by what they say, think, or do.

Sir James Frazer, whose classic study of primitive religions *The Golden Bough,* was first published in 1890, provides an excellent example of the eccentric in pursuit of the exotic. For him, the process of reducing the mysterious to the commonplace was the very hallmark of scientific progress. Like many anthropologists of his time, Frazer assumed that some societies were superior and others inferior, and that anthropology's main task was to describe how the latter had evolved into the former. To Frazer, Europe's technological achievements were proof of social, intellectual, and moral superiority. The dominance of the West represented the triumph of science, which in Frazer's evolutionary schema, superseded even the most rational of world religions. Science's clear light was to shine far and wide, driving superstition, the supernatural, and even God himself back into shadows and dimly lit corners.

But Frazer might have found a second aspect of the anthropological *modus operandi* less to his taste. In the course of making sense of someone else's behavior or ideas, we frequently begin to observe our own customs from a new angle. Indeed, this reflexive objectivity is often acclaimed as one of the great advantages of our methods and cited as a major justification for the long, expensive physical and psychic journeys that we make, seeking out societies far removed from our own cultural traditions. Less often remarked upon, however, is that the exotic possesses its own reflexive quality. As we learn to think of other people's ways as natural, we simultaneously begin to see our own as strange. In this sense, anthropologists import the exotic, and that, I suppose, puts us on the side of the angels.

An incident that occurred about four years ago during my fieldwork in north-central Borneo brought home to me the depth and subtlety of anthropologists' involvement with the exotic. I was working with the Berawan, a small tribe comprising four communities, each made up of several hundred people living in a massive wooden longhouse. The four longhouses stand beside the great rivers that are the only routes into the interior of Borneo. Berawan communities live on fish and on rice planted in clearings cut anew in the rain forest each year. In the late nineteenth century, which was a stormy period of tribal warfare, each longhouse was a fortress as well as a home, and the Berawan look back with pride on the military traditions of that era.

Among the things that interested me about the Berawan were their funeral rites, which involve what anthropologists call "secondary burial," although the Berawan do not usually bury the dead at all. Full rites consist of four stages: the first and third involve ritual preparation of the corpse; the second and fourth make up steps in storage of the remains. The first stage, lasting two to ten days, consists of rites performed immediately after death. During the second stage, the bereaved family stores the corpse in the longhouse or on a simple platform in the graveyard. This storage lasts at least eight months and sometimes for several years if the close kin cannot immediately afford to complete the expensive final stages. Third, if the corpse has been in the graveyard, the family brings it back to the longhouse, where it is kept for six to ten days, while the family lavishly entertains guests who have been summoned from far and wide. Finally, the remains are removed to a final resting place, an impressively proportioned mausoleum.

Within this four-part plan, details of the corpse's treatment vary considerably. During the first storage stage, the family may place the corpse in a large earthenware jar or in a massive coffin hewn from a single tree trunk. For secondary storage, the family may use a valuable glazed jar or the coffin left over from the first stage. During the third-stage rites, the family may take out the bones of the deceased and clean them. As the corpse decomposes, its secretions may be collected in a special vessel. Some neighbors of the Berawan reportedly consume liquids of decomposition mixed with rice—a variety of endocannibalism.

For anthropologists, this intimate interaction with the corpse is certainly exotic. For Americans not professionally trained in the niceties of cultural relativism, Berawan burial is no doubt disgusting: keeping corpses around the house, shuttling them between the graveyard and the longhouse, storing them above ground instead of burying them, manipulating the bones, and, to Western eyes, paying macabre attention to the process of decay itself. My Berawan informants were aware that some phases of their ritual bothered Europeans. They soon learned, moreover, that I had a lot of questions about their funerals. One of the pleasures of working in Borneo is that people soon begin to cross-examine their interviewer. They are as curious about the stranger as he or she is about them. So before long, they began to quiz me about the death ways of my country.

On one memorable occasion, during a lull in ritual activity, I responded to one of these questions by outlining American embalming practices—the treatment of the corpse with preservative fluids and its display in an open coffin. I was well into my story, concentrating on finding the right words to describe this unfamiliar topic, when I became aware that a sudden silence had fallen over my audience. They asked a number of hesitant questions just to be sure that they had understood me correctly and drew away from me in disgust when they found that they had. So shocked were they that I had to backtrack rapidly and change my story. The topic was never broached again.

At the time, I did not understand why American embalming practices had so unnerved the Berawan. Now, having thought about the meaning of Berawan death rituals, I think that I do understand.

The death rituals of central Borneo early attracted the interest of explorers and ethnologists. In 1907, Robert Hertz, a young student of French sociologist Emile Durkheim, wrote an essay about these rites that has become a classic. Never having set foot in Borneo, Hertz relied on the accounts of travelers. Had he not been killed during the First World War, he might well have undertaken firsthand research himself. Nevertheless, his analysis is still routinely cited in discussions and comparisons of funeral customs. Yet, oddly, Hertz's central thesis has received very little attention. Hertz hypothesized that peoples who practice secondary burial have certain beliefs about the afterlife, namely, that the fate of the body provides a model for the fate of the soul.

Since Hertz did not know of the Berawan, they provided me with an appropriate test case for his hypothesis. I collected data on everything related to Berawan death rites: the people involved, mourning practices, related rituals, myths and beliefs, and so on. I also pressed my informants for interpretations of rituals. All the material I accumulated revealed a consistent set of ideas very similar to those described by Hertz. The Berawan believe that after death the soul is divorced from the body and cannot reanimate the already decaying corpse. However, the soul cannot enter the land of the dead because it is not yet a perfect spirit. To become one of the truly dead, it must undergo a metamorphosis. As the body rots away to leave dry bones, so the soul is transformed slowly into spirit form. As the corpse is formless and repulsive until putrefaction is completed, so the soul is homeless. It lurks miserably on the fringes of human habitation and, in its discomfort, may affect the living with illness. The third stage of the mortuary sequence, which Hertz called the "great feast," marks the end of this miserable period. The soul finally passes to the land of the dead, and the mortal remains of the deceased join those of its ancestors in the tomb.

But before this happy conclusion is reached, the hovering soul is feared because it may cause more death. Even more dread surrounds the body itself, caused not by the process of rotting, for that releases the soul of the deceased from the bonds of the flesh, but by the possibility that some malignant spirit of nonhuman origin will succeed in reanimating the corpse. Should this occur, the result will be a monster of nightmarish mien, invulnerable to the weapons of men, since it is already dead.

I once witnessed an incident that dramatically demonstrated how real is the Berawan fear of reanimated corpses. Toward sunset, a group of mourners and guests were chatting casually beside a coffin that was being displayed on the longhouse veranda in preparation for primary storage. Suddenly there was a tapping sound, apparently from inside the coffin. The noise could have come from the house timbers, contracting in the cool of the evening, but the people present saw a different explanation. After a moment of shock, the women fled, carrying their children. Some panic-stricken men grabbed up what weapons were handy, while others tied up the coffin lid with yet more bands of rattan. Calm was not restored until later in the evening when a shaman investigated and declared that nothing was amiss.

We can now see why American mortuary practices so shock the Berawan. By delaying the decomposition of corpses, we commit a most unnatural act. First, we seem to be trying to trap our nearest and dearest in the unhappiest condition possible, neither alive nor in the radiant land of the dead. Second, and even more perverse and terrifying, we keep an army of undecomposed corpses, each and every one subject to reanimation by a host of evil spirits. For the Berawan, America is a land carpeted with potential zombies.

After a couple of years of field work, and an application of the ideas of Hertz and others, I can offer a relatively full account of Berawan death ways: what they express about Berawan notions of life and death; how they are manipulated by influential men in their struggles for power; how they relate to their sense of identity, art forms, and oral history. Meanwhile, I have also explored the literature on American death ways—and have found it wanting. For the most part, it is restricted to consideration of psychological variables—how people react to death, either the possibility of their own or that of close relatives and friends. None of these studies begins to explain why American funerals are the way they are; why they differ from British funerals, for instance.

Jessica Mitford, author of *The American Way of Death,* tried to explain the form that American funerals take by arguing that they are a product of the death industry's political power. But Mitford's theory does not explain the tacit support that Americans give to this institution, why successive immigrant groups have adopted it, or why reform movements have failed.

I have tried to relate American practices to popular ideas about the nature of a fulfilling life and a proper death. Despite these intellectual efforts, I am left with a prickly sense of estrangement. For, in fact, I had spared my Berawan friends the more gruesome details of embalming: replacement of the blood with perfumed formaldehyde and other chemicals; removal of the soft organs of the chest and abdomen via a long hollow needle attached to a vacuum pump; injection of inert materials. I did not mention the American undertaker's elaborate restorative techniques: the stitching up of mutilated corpses, plumping out of emaciated corpses with extra injections of waxes, or careful cosmetic care of hands and face. Nor did I tell the Berawan about the padded coffins, grave clothes ranging in style from business suits to negligees, and other funeral paraphernalia. Had I explained all this, their shock might have been transformed into curiosity, and they might have reversed our roles of social scientist and informant.

In the meantime, something of their reaction has rubbed off on me. I have reduced the celebrated mortuary rites of remote and mysterious Borneo to a kind of workaday straightforwardness, only to be struck by the exotic character of an institution in our very midst.

9

Old and New Religions: The Search for Salvation

Anthropologists have long studied cultural stability and change and agree that all cultures have continuous change, although the rate of change can vary dramatically. Whereas American society has an unmatched cultural dynamism, other cultures change so gradually as to appear static. The types and rates of cultural changes are functions of many factors originating from within the society itself or from external pressures and influences.

> Internal conditions affecting the rate of change include the relative degree of cultural receptivity to new ideas, the amount of freedom of inquiry and competition, the degree of cultural elaboration, the population size and density, the presence of innovators and inventors, and—perhaps most important—the degree of harmony between cultural and social values. Among the external conditions affecting culture change, the degree of contact with other groups is the outstanding factor. (Malefijt 1968: 329)

What anthropologists have discovered is that religious change occurs for the same reasons as

Protective mask from the Sepik River region, New Guinea.

general culture change and, as is the case with change generally, religious change is both continuous and universal.

One of the most dramatic classes of change, and one that has strong religious content, is what Anthony F. C. Wallace termed "revitalization movements": "a deliberate, organized, conscious effort by members of society to construct a more satisfying culture" (1956: 265). Wallace (1956) outlined several major types of revitalization movements that are clearly religious in nature. It is important to recognize that these kinds of cultural change phenomena are not mutually exclusive; several may be at work within a single society at any one time, all simultaneously contributing to change in the cultural gestalt. Nativistic and revivalistic movements are often combined, but also there are cases in which these types of changes in a single society are accompanied by messianic and millenarian movements as well. All revitalization movements have in common a reactionary character; all are the result of real or imagined conditions that create a demand for change.

Wallace's categories and definitions have been broadly accepted. Nativistic movements are characterized by a strong emphasis on the elimination of alien persons, customs, values, and material from the "mazeway," which Wallace defined as the mental image an individual has of the society and its culture, as well as of his own body and its behavior regularities, in order to act in ways to reduce stress at all levels of the system. Revivalistic movements emphasize the readoption of customs, values, and even aspects of nature in the mazeway of previous generations. Cargo cults emphasize the importation of alien values, customs and material into the mazeway, these being expected to arrive, metaphorically, as a ship's cargo. Vitalistic movements also emphasize the importation of alien elements into the mazeway, although not via a cargo mechanism. Millenarian movements emphasize changes in the mazeway through an apocalyptic world transformation engineered by the supernatural. Messianic movements emphasize the actual participation of a divine savior in human flesh in bringing about desired changes in the mazeway (1956: 267). (This categorization of revitalization movements, however, is only one of many schemes used by ethnographers, and as John Collins has noted, "any such scheme, basically, is merely a device to initiate thought and comparison" [1978: 137]).

The religious nature of revitalization in the non-Western world, particularly in Melanesia, is made clear not only by the expectation of a messiah and the millennium in some of the movements but also by the very structure of movement phenomena, in which prophets play an indispensable role. I. C. Jarvie maintains that the religious character of these movements may be explained by the fact that traditional institutions are not able to adopt and respond to social changes, and that the only new organizational system offered these societies by European colonialists is Christianity. Melanesians, for example, have learned more about organization from religion than from any other foreign institution, and it is logical for them to mold revitalization movements in religious form in order to accommodate, indeed combat, the impact of European society (1970: 412–13).

Revitalization in the broad sense of bringing new vigor and happiness to society is certainly not restricted to traditional groups or to the religious realm. Edward Sapir (1924), for example, spoke of cultures "genuine" and "spurious": In the former, individuals felt well integrated into their culture, and in the latter they experienced alienation from the mainstream of society. Examples of attempts to change Western cultures abound. Political and economic conditions have frequently moved modern prophets to seek power to change, sometimes radically, the institutional structure and goals of society.

Throughout the readings in this chapter, reference is frequently made to churches, cults, and sects. These are terms that have been used in the anthropology and sociology of religion to describe particular types of religious organization. Typically, the word *church* is applied to the larger community's view of the acceptable type of religious organization, whereas the term *sect* is used to refer to a protest group. Sects are generally small, express defiance of the world, or sometimes withdrawal from the world. Sect members are strict believers who usually experience some sort of conversion experience before becoming members. Bryan Wilson (1959, 1961) has described four different types of sects based on their ideologies: (1) the conversionist sect is hopeful of converting others; (2) the adventist sect anticipates a drastic divine intervention; (3) the introversionist sect is very pious and eager to develop its inner spirituality; and (4) the gnostic sect possesses esoteric religious knowledge. The word *cult* is not as clearly defined as sect and church, and appears to refer to a more casual, loosely organized group. Cults seem to have a fluctuating membership whose allegiance can be shared with other religious organizations. (It is well to remember, however, that the terms *church, sect,* and *cult* are best seen as scholarly descriptions of ideal, theoretical concepts). Of the three, *cult* has taken on such a perjorative character that the term is almost useless (Barkun 1994: 43).

During the last decade, this country has witnessed an immense growth in the number of religious groups. The Children of God, Hare Krishna, the followers of Bhagwan Shree Rajneesh, the Maharaj Ji's Divine Light Mission, and, the largest and most controversial group of all, the Reverend Sun Myung Moon's Unification Church, are a few examples of groups that have attracted thousands disenchanted with traditional religious organizations. The history of the world is replete with examples of new religious groups springing to life as spiritually dissatisfied people seek alternatives to traditional religious organizations.

What is the appeal of these movements? What social forces underlie the development and rapid growth of religious movements? Many sociological and psychological analyses have attempted to answer these important questions (see especially Glock and Stark 1965; Eister 1972; Zaretsky and Leone 1974; Talmon 1969). Briefly, these studies draw a picture of people who have become attracted to new movements because of such lures as love, security, acceptance, and improved personal status. Unstable and rapidly changing social and political situations in contemporary technological countries also provide a rich seedbed for the emergence and blossoming of religious movements.

Charles Y. Glock (1964) has listed five types of deprivation that may result in the establishment of a new sect or that may lead individuals to join one: (1) *economic deprivation,* which is suffered by people who make less money, have fewer material goods, and are financially beholden to others; (2) *organismic deprivation,* which applies to those who may exhibit physical, mental, and nutritional problems; (3) *ethical deprivation,* which grows out of a perceived discrepancy between the real and the ideal; (4) *psychic deprivation,* which can result in the search for meaning and new values (and which is related to the search for closure and simplicity); and (5) *social deprivation,* which results from a society's valuation of some individuals and their attributes over others. Established religions have tremendous staying power, and "it is certainly premature to conclude that religions as forces in the world and as forces in individual lives are a thing of the past" (Reynolds and Tanner 1994: 44). This is not to say that the so-called great faiths (such as Islam, Christianity, and Judaism) do not lose followers; they do. "It seems to be mainly in the northwest of Europe, in Scandinavia, and in parts of the United States that religion remains in the doldrums" (Reynolds and Tanner 1994: 44).

The articles in this chapter have been selected to demonstrate how religion can help people living in cultures undergoing sudden and disruptive social change. The selections also show the wide extent of ritual used by religious groups in their quest and deep longing for holiness. First, Anthony F. C. Wallace analyzes the phenomenon of revitalization movements and their role in a society's attempts to construct a more satisfying culture. In the second article, Alice Kehoe discusses the Ghost Dance religion. Next, Peter Worsley points out that throughout history people who have felt themselves to be oppressed and deceived have always been ready to pour their hopes and fears into a belief in a coming golden age. Worsley's article describes a cargo cult, a revitalization movement among the peoples of New Guinea and adjacent islands.

William F. Lewis provides an ethnographic account of three urban Rastafarians living in Kingston, Jamaica. Mary Lee Daugherty discusses serpent-handlers in West Virginia, who base their particular religious practice on the Gospel of Mark: "they shall speak with new tongues; they shall take up serpents." In the final article, Elizabeth Puttick examines the counter-culture of the 1960s and its influence on several new religious movements of the time.

References

Barkun, Michael
   1994 "Reflections After Waco: Millennialists and the State." In James R. Lewis, ed., *From the Ashes: Making Sense of Waco,* pp. 41–49. Lanham, Maryland: Rowman and Littlefield.

Collins, John J.
   1978 *Primitive Religion.* Totowa, N.J.: Rowman and Littlefield.

Eister, Allen
 1972 "An Outline of a Structural Theory of Cults." *Journal for the Scientific Study of Religion* 11: 319–33.

Glock, Charles Y.
 1964 "The Role of Deprivation in the Origin and Evolution of Religious Groups." In R. Lee and M. E. Marty, eds., *Religion and Social Conflict*. New York: Oxford University Press.

Glock, Charles, Y., and Rodney Stark
 1965 *Religion and Society in Tension*. Chicago: Rand McNally.

Jarvie, I. C.
 1970 "Cargo Cults." In Richard Cavendish, ed., *Man, Myth and Magic*, pp. 409–12. New York: Marshall Cavendish.

Malefijt, Annemarie de Waal
 1968 *Religion and Culture: An Introduction to Anthropology of Religion*. New York: Macmillan.

Reynolds, Vernon, and Ralph Tanner
 1994 *The Social Ecology of Religion*. New York: Oxford University Press.

Sapir, E.
 1924 "Culture, Genuine and Spurious." *American Journal of Sociology* 29: 401–29.

Talmon, Yonina
 1969 "Pursuit of the Millennium: The Relation Between Religious and Social Change." In Norman Birnbaum and Gertrude Lenzer, eds., *Sociology and Religion: A Book of Readings*. Englewood Cliffs, N.J.: Prentice-Hall.

Wallace, A. F. C.
 1956 "Revitalization Movements." *American Anthropologist* 58: 264–81.

Wilson, Bryan R.
 1959 "Role Conflicts and Status Contradictions of the Pentecostal Minister." *American Journal of Sociology* 64: 494–504.
 1961 *Sects and Society: A Sociological Study of the Elim Tabernacle, Christian Science, and Christadelphians*. Berkeley: University of California Press.

Zaretsky, Irving S., and Mark P. Leone, eds.
 1974 *Religious Movements in Contemporary America*. Princeton, N.J.: Princeton University Press.

Revitalization Movements

Anthony F. C. Wallace

Anthony Wallace's article shows how people use religious principles to cope with a cultural crisis that has prevented them from achieving a more satisfying culture. Revitalization movements have been witnessed frequently in diverse geographic regions, and each displays variation of expression that may be explained by the culturally specific conditions under which they are formed. As a social process, they have the goal of reconstituting a way of life that has been destroyed for one reason or another.

Wallace helps us understand the phenomenon of revitalization by describing five overlapping but distinct stages. A revitalization movement, unlike cultural evolution and historical change, is a relatively abrupt culture change that frequently completes itself in the span of a few short years. Wallace also discusses "mazeway synthesis" and "hysterical conversion," two psychological mechanisms that are of the utmost importance in any type of culture change.

Anthony F. C. Wallace is a distinguished anthropologist whose wide research interests have resulted in many significant publications.

Reprinted from Anthony F. C. Wallace, *Culture and Personality*, 2nd ed. (New York: Random House, 1970), pp. 188–99, by permission of the publisher.

DURING PERIODS OF STABLE MOVING EQUILIBrium, the sociocultural system is subject to mild but measurable oscillations in degree of organization. From time to time, however, most societies undergo more violent fluctuations in this regard. Such fluctuation is of peculiar importance in culture change because it often culminates in relatively sudden change in cultural *Gestalt*. We refer, here, to revitalization movements, which we define as deliberate and organized attempts by some members of a society to construct a more satisfying culture by rapid acceptance of a pattern of multiple innovations (Wallace 1956b; Mead 1956).

The severe disorganization of a sociocultural system may be caused by the impact of any one or combination of a variety of forces that push the system beyond the limits of equilibrium. Some of these forces are climatic or faunal changes, which destroy the economic basis of its existence; epidemic disease, which grossly alters the population structure; wars, which exhaust the society's resources of manpower or result in defeat or invasion; internal conflict among interest groups, which results in extreme disadvantage for at least one group; and, very commonly, a position of perceived subordination and inferiority with respect to an adjacent society. The latter, by the use of more or less coercion (or even no coercion at all, as in situations where the mere example set by the dominant society raises too-high levels of aspiration), brings about uncoordinated cultural changes. Under conditions of disorganization, the system, from the standpoint of at least some of its members, is unable to make possible the reliable satisfaction of certain values that are held to be essential to continued well-being and self-respect. The mazeway of a culturally disillusioned person, accordingly, is an image of a world that is unpredictable, or barren in its simplicity, or both, and is apt to contain severe identity conflict. His mood (depending on the precise nature of the disorganization) will be one of panic-stricken anxiety, shame, guilt, depression, or apathy.

An example of the kind of disorganization to which we refer is given by the two thousand or so Seneca Indians of New York at the close of the eighteenth century. Among these people, a supreme value attached to the conception of the absolutely free and autonomous individual, unconstrained by and indifferent to his own and alien others' pain and hardship. This individual was capable of free indulgence of emotional impulses but, in crisis, freely subordinated his own wishes to the needs of his community. Among the men, especially, this ego-ideal was central in personality organization. Men defined the roles of hunting, of warfare, and of statesmanship as the conditions of achievement of this value; thus the stereotypes of "the good hunter," "the brave warrior," and "the forest statesman" were the images of masculine success. But the forty-three years from 1754, when the French and Indian War began, to 1797, when the Seneca sold their last hunting grounds and became largely confined to tiny, isolated reservations, brought with them changes in their situation that made achievement of these ideals virtually impossible. The good hunter could no longer hunt: the game was scarce, and it was almost suicidally dangerous to stray far from the reservation among the numerous hostile white men. The brave warrior could no longer fight, being undersupplied, abandoned by his allies, and his women and children threatened by growing military might of the United States. The forest statesman was an object of contempt, and this disillusionment was perhaps more shattering than the rest. The Iroquois chiefs, for nearly a century, had been able to play off British and French, then Americans and British, against one another, extorting supplies and guarantees of territorial immunity from both sides. They had maintained an extensive system of alliances and hegemonies among surrounding tribal groups. Suddenly they were shorn of their power. White men no longer spoke of the League of the Iroquois with respect; their western Indian dependents and allies regarded them as cowards for having made peace with the Americans.

The initial Seneca response to the progress of sociocultural disorganization was quasipathological: many became drunkards; the fear of witches increased; squabbling factions were unable to achieve a common policy. But a revitalization movement developed in 1799, based on the religious revelations reported by one of the disillusioned forest statesmen, one Handsome Lake, who preached a code of patterned religious and cultural reform. The drinking of whiskey was proscribed; witchcraft was to be stamped out; various outmoded rituals and prevalent sins were to be abandoned. In addition, various syncretic cultural reforms, amounting to a reorientation of the socioeconomic system, were to be undertaken, including the adoption of agriculture (hitherto a feminine calling) by the men, and the focusing of kinship responsibilities within the nuclear family (rather than in the clan and lineage). The general acceptance of Handsome Lake's Code, within a few years, wrought seemingly miraculous changes. A group of sober, devout, partly literate, and technologically up-to-date farming communities suddenly replaced the demoralized slums in the wilderness (Wallace 1970).

Such dramatic transformations are, as a matter of historical fact, very common in human history, and probably have been the medium of as much culture change as the slower equilibrium processes. Furthermore, because they compress into such a short space of time such extensive changes in pattern, they are somewhat easier to record than the quiet serial changes during periods of equilibrium. In general, revitalization processes share a common process structure that can be conceptualized as a pattern of temporally overlapping, but functionally distinct, stages:

I. *Steady State.* This is a period of moving equilibrium of the kind discussed in the preceding section. Culture change occurs during the steady state, but is of the relatively slow and chainlike kind. Stress levels vary among interest groups, and there is some oscillation in organization level, but disorganization and stress remain within limits tolerable to most individuals. Occasional incidents of intolerable stress may stimulate a limited "correction" of the system, but some incidence of individual ill-health and criminality are accepted as a price society must pay.

II. *The Period of Increased Individual Stress.* The sociocultural system is being "pushed" progressively out of equilibrium by the forces described earlier: climatic and biotic change, epidemic disease, war and conquest, social subordination, acculturation, internally generated decay, and so forth. Increasingly large numbers of individuals are placed under what is to them intolerable stress by the failure of the system to accommodate the satisfaction of their needs. Anomie and disillusionment become widespread, as the culture is perceived to be disorganized and inadequate; crime and illness increase sharply in frequency as individualistic asocial responses. But the situation is still generally defined as one of fluctuation within the steady state.

III. *The Period of Cultural Distortion.* Some members of the society attempt, piecemeal and ineffectively, to restore personal equilibrium by adopting socially dysfunctional expedients. Alcoholism, venality in public officials, the "black market," breaches of sexual and kinship mores, hoarding, gambling for gain, "scapegoating," and similar behaviors that, in the preceding period, were still defined as individual deviances, in effect become institutionalized efforts to circumvent the evil effects of "the system." Interest groups, losing confidence in the advantages of maintaining mutually acceptable interrelationships, may resort to violence in order to coerce others into unilaterally advantageous behavior. Because of the malcoordination of cultural changes during this period, they are rarely able to reduce the impact of the forces that have pushed the society out of equilibrium, and in fact lead to a continuous decline in organization.

IV. *The Period of Revitalization.* Once severe cultural distortion has occurred, the society can with difficulty return to steady state without the institution of a revitalization process. Without revitalization, indeed, the society is apt to disintegrate as a system: the population will either die off, splinter into autonomous groups, or be absorbed into another, more stable, society. Revitalization depends on the successful completion of the following functions:

1. Formulation of a code. An individual, or a group of individuals, constructs a new, utopian image of sociocultural organization. This model is a blueprint of an ideal society or "goal culture." Contrasted with the goal culture is the existing culture, which is presented as inadequate or evil in certain respects. Connecting the existing culture and the goal culture is a transfer culture: a system of operations that, if faithfully carried out, will transform the existing culture into the goal culture. Failure to institute the transfer operations will, according to the code, result in either the perpetuation of the existing misery or the ultimate destruction of the society (if not of the whole world). Not infrequently in primitive societies the code, or the core of it, is formulated by one individual in the course of a hallucinatory revelation; such prophetic experiences are apt to launch religiously oriented movements, since the source of the revelation is apt to be regarded as a supernatural being. Nonhallucinatory formulations usually are found in politically oriented movements. In either case, the formulation of the code constitutes a reformulation of the author's own mazeway and often brings to him a renewed confidence in the future and a remission of the complaints he experienced before. It may be suggested that such mazeway resynthesis processes are merely extreme forms of the reorganizing dream processes that seem to be associated with REM (rapid-eye-movement) sleep, which are necessary to normal health.

2. Communication. The formulators of the code preach the code to other people in an evangelistic spirit. The aim of the communication is to make converts. The code is offered as the means of spiritual salvation for the individual and of cultural salvation for the society. Promises of benefit to the target population need not be immediate or materialistic, for the basis of the code's appeal is the attractiveness of identification with a more highly organized system, with all that this implies in the way of self-respect. Indeed, in view of the extensiveness of the changes in values often implicit in such codes, appeal to currently held values would often be pointless. Religious codes offer spiritual salvation, identification with God, elect status; political codes offer honor, fame, the respect of society for sacrifices made in its interest. But refusal to accept the code is usually defined as placing the listener in immediate spiritual, as well as material, peril with respect to his existing values. In small societies, the target population may be the entire community; but in more complex societies, the message may be aimed only at certain groups deemed eligible for participation in the transfer and goal cultures.

3. Organization. The code attracts converts. The motivations that are satisfied by conversion, and the psychodynamics of the conversion experience itself, are likely to be highly diverse, ranging from the mazeway resynthesis characteristic of the prophet,

and the hysterical conviction of the "true believer," to the calculating expediency of the opportunist. As the group of converts expands, it differentiates into two parts: a set of disciples and a set of mass followers. The disciples increasingly become the executive organization, responsible for administering the evangelistic program, protecting the formulator, combatting heresy, and so on. In this role, the disciples increasingly become full-time specialists in the work of the movement. The tri-cornered relationship between the formulators, the disciples, and the mass followers is given an authoritarian structure, even without the formalities of older organizations, by the charismatic quality of the formulator's image. The formulator is regarded as a man to whom, from a supernatural being or from some other source of wisdom unavailable to the mass, a superior knowledge and authority has been vouchsafed that justifies his claim to unquestioned belief and obedience from his followers.

In the modern world, with the advantages of rapid transportation and ready communication, the simple charismatic model of cult organization is not always adequate to describe many social and religious movements. In such programs as Pentecostalism, Black Power, and the New Left, there is typically a considerable number of local or special issue groups loosely joined in what Luther Gerlach has called an "acephalous, segmentary, reticulate organization" (1968). Each segment may be, in effect, a separate revitalization organization of the simple kind described above; the individual groups differ in details of code, in emotional style, in appeal to different social classes; and, since the movement as a whole has no single leader, it is relatively immune to repression, the collapse of one or several segments in no way invalidating the whole. This type of movement organization is singularly well adapted to predatory expansion; but it may eventually full under the domination of one cult or party (as was the case, for instance, in Germany when the SS took over the fragmented Nazi party, which in turn was heir to a large number of nationalist groups, and as is the case when a Communist party apparatus assumes control of a revolutionary popular front).

4. Adaptation. Because the movement is a revolutionary organization (however benevolent and humane the ultimate values to which it subscribes), it threatens the interests of any group that obtains advantage, or believes it obtains advantage, from

maintaining or only moderately reforming the status quo. Furthermore, the code is never complete; new inadequacies are constantly being found in the existing culture, and new inconsistencies, predicative failures, and ambiguities discovered in the code itself (some of the latter being pointed out by the opposition). The response of the code formulators and disciples is to rework the code, and, if necessary, to defend the movement by political and diplomatic maneuver, and, ultimately, by force. The general tendency is for codes to harden gradually, and for the tone of the movement to become increasingly nativistic and hostile both toward nonparticipating fellow members of society, who will ultimately be defined as "traitors," and toward "national enemies."

True revolutions, as distinguished from mere coups d'état, which change personnel without changing the structure, require that the revitalization movement of which they are the instrument add to its code a morality sanctioning subversion or even violence. The leadership must also be sophisticated in its knowledge of how to mobilize an increasingly large part of the population to their side, and of how to interfere with the mobilization of the population by the establishment. The student of such processes can do no better than to turn to the works of contemporary practitioners such as Che Guevara and Mao Tse Tung for authoritative explications and examples of the revolutionary aspect of revitalization.

5. Cultural transformation. If the movement is able to capture both the adherence of a substantial proportion of a local population and, in complex societies, of the functionally crucial apparatus (such as power and communications networks, water supply, transport systems, and military establishment), the transfer culture and, in some cases, the goal culture itself, can be put into operation. The revitalization, if successful, will be attended by the drastic decline of the quasi-pathological individual symptoms of anomie and by the disappearance of the cultural distortions. For such a revitalization to be accomplished, however, the movement must be able to maintain its boundaries from outside invasion, must be able to obtain internal social conformity without destructive coercion, and must have a successful economic system.

6. Routinization. If the preceding functions are satisfactorily completed, the functional reasons for

the movement's existence as an innovative force disappear. The transfer culture, if not the goal culture, is operating of necessity with the participation of a large proportion of the community. Although the movement's leaders may resist the realization of the fact, the movement's function shifts from the role of innovation to the role of maintenance. If the movement was heavily religious in orientation, its legacy is a cult or church that preserves and reworks the code, and maintains, through ritual and myth, the public awareness of the history and values that brought forth the new culture. If the movement was primarily political, its organization is routinized into various stable decision-making and morale-and-order-maintaining functions (such as administrative offices, police, and military bodies). Charisma can, to a degree, be routinized, but its intensity diminishes as its functional necessity becomes, with increasing obviousness, outmoded.

V. *The New Steady State.* With the routinization of the movement, a new steady state may be said to exist. Steady-state processes of culture change continue; many of them are in areas where the movement has made further change likely. In particular, changes in the value structure of the culture may lay the basis for long-continuing changes (such as the train of economic and technological consequences of the dissemination of the Protestant ethic after the Protestant Reformation). Thus in addition to the changes that the movement accomplishes during its active phase, it may control the direction of the subsequent equilibrium processes by shifting the values that define the cultural focus. The record of the movement itself, over time, gradually is subject to distortion, and eventually is enshrined in myths and rituals which elevate the events that occurred, and persons who acted, into quasi- or literally divine status.

Two psychological mechanisms seem to be of peculiar importance in the revitalization process: mazeway resynthesis (Wallace 1956a) and hysterical conversion. The resynthesis is most dramatically exemplified in the career of the prophet who formulates a new religious code during a hallucinatory trance. Typically, such persons, after suffering increasing depreciation of self-esteem as the result of their inadequacy to achieve the culturally ideal standards, reach a point of either physical or drug-induced exhaustion, during which a resynthesis of values and beliefs occurs. The resynthesis is, like other innovations, a recombination of preexisting configurations; the uniqueness of this particular process is the suddenness of conviction, the trance-like state of the subject, and the emotionally central nature of the subject matter. There is some reason to suspect that such dramatic resyntheses depend on a special biochemical milieu, accompanying the "stage of exhaustion" of the stress (in Selye's sense) syndrome, or on a similar milieu induced by drugs. But comparable resyntheses are, of course, sometimes accomplished more slowly, without the catalytic aid of extreme stress or drugs. This kind of resynthesis produces, apparently, a permanent alteration of mazeway: the new stable cognitive configuration, is, as it were, constructed out of the materials of earlier configurations, which, once rearranged, cannot readily reassemble into the older forms.

The hysterical conversion is more typical of the mass follower who is repeatedly subjected to suggestion by a charismatic leader and an excited crowd. The convert of this type may, during conversion display various dissociative behaviors (rage, speaking in tongues, rolling on the ground, weeping, and so on). After conversion, his overt behavior may be in complete conformity with the code to which he has been exposed. But his behavior has changed not because of a radical resynthesis, but because of the adoption under suggestion of an additional social personality which temporarily replaces, but does not destroy, the earlier. He remains, in a sense, a case of multiple personality and is liable, if removed from reinforcing symbols, to lapse into an earlier social personality. The participant in the lynch mob or in the camp meeting revival is a familiar example of this type of convert. But persons can be maintained in this state of hysterical conversion for months or years, if the "trance" is continuously maintained by the symbolic environment (flags, statues, portraits, songs, and so on) and continuous suggestions (speeches, rallies, and so on). The most familiar contemporary example is the German under Hitler who participated in the Nazi genocide program, but reverted to *Gemütlichkeit* when the war ended. The difference between the resynthesized person and the converted one does not lie in the nature of the codes to which they subscribe (they may be the same), but in the blandness and readiness of the hysterical convert to revert, as compared to the almost paranoid intensity and stability of the resynthesized prophet. A successful movement, by virtue of its ability to maintain suggestion continuously for years, is able to hold the hysterical convert indefinitely, or even to work a real resynthesis by repeatedly forcing him, after hysterical conversion, to reexamine his older values and beliefs and to work through to valid resynthesis, sometimes under considerable stress. The Chinese Communists, for instance, apparently have become disillusioned by hysterical conversions and have used various techniques, some coercive and some not, but all commonly lumped together as "brain-washing" in Western literature, to induce valid resynthesis. The aim of these communist techniques, like those of the established religions, is, literally, to produce a "new man."

It is impossible to exaggerate the importance of these two psychological processes for culture change, for they make possible the rapid substitution of a new cultural *Gestalt* for an old, and thus the rapid cultural transformation of whole populations. Without this mechanism, the cultural transformation of the 600,000,000 people of China by the Communists could not have occurred; nor the Communist-led revitalization and expansion of the USSR; nor the American Revolution; nor the Protestant Reformation; nor the rise and spread of Christianity, Mohammedanism, and Buddhism. In the written historical record, revitalization movements begin with Ikhnaton's ultimately disastrous attempt to establish a new, monotheistic religion in Egypt; they are found, continent by continent, in the history of all human societies, occurring with frequency proportional to the pressures to which the society is subjected. For small tribal societies, in chronically extreme situations, movements may develop every ten or fifteen years; in stable complex cultures, the rate of a societywide movement may be one every two or three hundred years.

In view of the frequency and geographical diversity of revitalization movements it can be expected that their content will be extremely varied, corresponding to the diversity of situational contexts and cultural backgrounds in which they develop. Major culture areas are, over extended periods of time, associated with particular types: New Guinea and Melanesia, during the latter part of the nineteenth and the twentieth centuries, have been the home of the well-known "cargo cults." The most prominent feature of these cults is the expectation that the ancestors soon will arrive in a steamship, bearing a cargo of the white man's goods, and will lead a nativistic revolution culminating in the ejection of European masters. The Indians of the eastern half of South America for centuries after the conquest set off on migrations for the *terre sans mal* where a utopian way of life, free of Spaniards and Portuguese, would be found; North American Indians of the eighteenth and nineteenth centuries were prone to revivalistic movements such as the Ghost Dance, whose adherents believed that appropriate ritual and the abandonment of the sins of the white man would bring a return of the golden age before contact; South Africa has been the home of the hundreds of small, enthusiastic, separatist churches that have broken free of the missionary organizations. As might be expected, a congruence evidently exists between the cultural *Anlage* and the content of movement, which, together with processes of direct and stimulus diffusion, accounts for the tendency for movements to fall into areal types (Burridge 1960).

The Ghost Dance Religion

Alice Beck Kehoe

During the late 1860s, a Northern Paiute Indian named Wodziwob ("white hair") experienced several visions telling him to create the Ghost Dance religion. By following Wodziwob's vision-revealed instructions, the day would be hastened when White men would disappear, dead Indians would live again, and the old Indian way of life would return. The movement experienced early success and quickly expanded from the Great Basin area into California and Oregon, but eventually faltered. In 1889, years after Wodziwob's religion had died, a second and more extensive Ghost Dance movement began, this time led by another Paiute Indian, Jack Wilson, or in the Paiute language, Wovoka ("the woodcutter"). In this selection Alice Kehoe describes Wovoka's early life with David Wilson, an Anglo rancher, and his family; as well as his preaching as a young adult and his 1889 vision that resulted in his becoming a prophet. Kehoe believes that the Ghost Dance religion was a complete religion and that its basic message, though aimed primarily at Indians, was applicable to all people of goodwill. Wovoka's gospel was especially appealing to the Indians, who in 1889 were suffering from persecution by the Whites, epidemics, loss of their economic resources and lands, and continuing attempts to eradicate their customs and beliefs. The Ghost Dance religion spread to the tribes of the Northwest, eventually reaching the plains from Oklahoma to Canada. The religion came to a violent end for the Sioux in late December 1890, with the killing of 370 Indians at Wounded Knee.

NEW YEAR'S DAY, 1892. NEVADA.

A wagon jounces over a maze of cattle trails crisscrossing a snowy valley floor. In the wagon, James Mooney, from the Smithsonian Institution in faraway Washington, D.C., is looking for the Indian messiah, Wovoka, blamed for riling up the Sioux, nearly three hundred of whom now lie buried by Wounded Knee Creek in South Dakota. The men in the wagon see a man with a gun over his shoulder walking in the distance.

"I believe that's Jack now!" exclaims one of Mooney's guides. "Jack Wilson," he calls to the messiah, whose Paiute name is Wovoka. Mooney's other guide, Charley Sheep, Wovoka's uncle, shouts to his nephew in the Paiute language. The hunter comes over to the wagon.

"I saw that he was a young man," Mooney recorded, "a dark full-blood, compactly built, and taller than the Paiute generally, being nearly 6 feet in height. He was well dressed in white man's clothes, with the broad-brimmed white felt hat common in the west, secured on his head by means of a beaded ribbon under the chin. . . . He wore a good pair of boots. His hair was cut off square on a line below the base of the ears, after the manner of his tribe. His countenance was open and expressive of firmness and decision" (Mooney [1896] 1973:768–769).

That evening, James Mooney formally interviewed Jack Wilson in his home, a circular lodge ten feet in diameter, built of bundles of tule reeds tied to a pole frame. In the middle of the lodge, a bright fire of sagebrush stalks sent sparks flying out of the wide smoke hole. Several other Paiutes were with Jack, his wife, baby, and little son when Mooney arrived with a guide and an interpreter. Mooney noticed that although all the Paiutes dressed in "white man's" clothes, they preferred to live in traditional wickiups. Only Paiute baskets furnished Jack Wilson's home; no beds, no storage trunks, no pots or pans, nothing of alien manufacture except the hunting gun and knife lay in the wickiup, though the family could have bought the invaders' goods. Jack had steady employment as a ranch laborer, and from his wages he could have constructed a cabin and lived in it, sitting on chairs and eating bread and beef from metal utensils. Instead, Jack and Mary, his wife, wanted to follow the ways of their people as well as they could in a valley overrun with Euro-American settlement. The couple hunted, fished, and gathered pine nuts and other seeds and wild plants. They practiced their Paiute religion rather than the Presbyterian Christianity Jack's employer insisted on teaching them. Mooney was forced to bring a Euro-American settler, Edward Dyer, to interpret for him because Jack would speak only his native Paiute, though he had some familiarity with English. This was Mason Valley, in the heart of Paiute territory, and for Jack and Mary it was still Paiute.

Jack Wilson told Mooney that he had been born four years before the well-remembered battle between Paiutes and American invaders at Pyramid Lake. The battle had been touched off by miners seizing two Paiute women. The men of the Paiute community managed to rescue the two women. No harm was done to the miners, but they claimed they were victims of an "Indian outrage," raised a large party of their fellows, and set off to massacre the Paiutes. Expecting trouble, the Paiute men ambushed the mob of miners at a narrow pass, and although armed mostly with only bows and arrows, killed nearly fifty of the mob, routing the rest and saving the families in the Indian camp. Jack Wilson's father, Tavibo, was a leader of the Paiute community at that time. He was recognized as spiritually blessed—gifted and trained to communicate with invisible powers. By means of this gift, carefully cultivated, Tavibo was said to be able to control the weather.

Tavibo left the community when his son Wovoka was in his early teens, and the boy was taken on by David Wilson, a Euro-American rancher with sons of his own close in age to the Paiute youth. Though employed as a ranch hand, Wovoka was strongly encouraged to join the Wilson family in daily prayers and Bible reading, and Jack, as he came to be called, became good friends with the Wilson boys. Through these years with the Wilsons, Jack's loyalty to, and pride in, his own Paiute people never wavered. When he was about twenty, he married a Paiute

woman who shared his commitment to the Paiute way of life. With his wages from the ranch, Jack and Mary bought the hunting gun and ammunition, good-quality "white man's" clothes, and ornaments suited to their dignity as a respected younger couple in the Mason Valley community.

As a young adult, Jack Wilson began to develop a reputation as a weather doctor like his father. Paiute believe that a young person lacks the maturity and inner strength to function as a spiritual agent, but Jack was showing the self-discipline, sound judgment, and concern for others that marked Indians gifted as doctors in the native tradition. Jack led the circle dances through which Paiute opened themselves to spiritual influence. Moving always along the path of the sun—clockwise to the left—men, women, and children joined hands in a symbol of the community's living through the circle of the days. As they danced they listened to Jack Wilson's songs celebrating the Almighty and Its wondrous manifestations: the mountains, the clouds, snow, stars, trees, antelope. Between dances, the people sat at Jack's feet, listening to him preach faith in universal love.

The climax of Jack's personal growth came during a dramatic total eclipse of the sun on January 1, 1889. He was lying in his wickiup very ill with a fever. Paiute around him saw the sky darkening although it was midday. Some monstrous force was overcoming the sun! People shot off guns at the apparition, they yelled, some wailed as at a death. Jack Wilson felt himself losing consciousness. It seemed to him he was taken up to heaven and brought before God. God gave him a message to the people of earth, a gospel of peace and right living. Then he and the sun regained their normal life.

Jack Wilson was now a prophet. Tall, handsome, with a commanding presence, Jack already was respected for his weather control power. (The unusual snow blanketing Mason Valley when James Mooney visited was said to be Jack's doing.) Confidence in his God-given mission further enhanced Jack Wilson's reputation. Indians came from other districts to hear him, and even Mormon settlers in Nevada joined his audiences. To carry out his mission, Jack Wilson went to the regional Indian agency at Pyramid Lake and asked one of the employees to prepare and mail a letter to the President of the United States, explaining the Paiute doctor's holy mission and suggesting that if the United States government would send him a small regular salary, he would convey God's message to all the people of Nevada and, into the bargain, make it rain whenever they wished. The agency employee never sent the letter. It was agency policy to "silently ignore" Indians' efforts toward "notoriety." The agent would not even deign to meet the prophet.

Jack Wilson did not need the support of officials. His deep sincerity and utter conviction of his mission quickly persuaded every open-minded hearer of its importance. Indians came on pilgrimages to Mason Valley, some out of curiosity, others seeking guidance and healing in that time of afflictions besetting their peoples. Mormons came too, debating whether Jack Wilson was the fulfillment of a prophecy of their founder, Joseph Smith, Jr., that the Messiah would appear in human form in 1890. Jack Wilson himself consistently explained that he was *a* messiah *like* Jesus but not the Christ of the Christians. Both Indians and Euro-Americans tended to ignore Jack's protestations and to identify him as "the Christ." Word spread that the Son of God was preaching in western Nevada.

Throughout 1889 and 1890, railroads carried delegates from a number of Indian nations east of the Rockies to investigate the messiah in Mason Valley. Visitors found ceremonial grounds maintained beside the Paiute settlements, flat cleared areas with low willow-frame shelters around the open dancing space. Paiutes gathered periodically to dance and pray for four days and nights, ending on the fifth morning shaking their blankets and shawls to symbolize driving out evil. In Mason Valley itself, Jack Wilson would attend the dances, repeating his holy message and, from time to time, trembling and passing into a trance to confirm the revelations. Delegates from other reservations were sent back home with tokens of Jack Wilson's holy power: bricks of ground red ocher dug from Mount Grant south of Mason Valley, the Mount Sinai of Northern Paiute religion; the strikingly marked feathers of the magpie; pine nuts, the "daily bread" of the Paiutes; and robes of woven strips of rabbit fur, the Paiutes' traditional covering. James Mooney's respectful interest in the prophet's teachings earned him the privilege of carrying such tokens to his friends on the Cheyenne and Arapaho reservations east of the mountains.

Jack Wilson told Mooney that when "the sun died" that winter day in 1889 and, dying with it, he was taken up to heaven,

he saw God, with all the people who had died long ago engaged in their oldtime sports and occupations, all happy and forever young. It was a pleasant land and full of game. After showing him all, God told him he must go back and tell his people they must be good and love one another, have no quarreling, and live in peace with the whites; that they must work, and not lie or steal; that they must put away all the old practices that savored of war; that if they faithfully obeyed his instructions they would at last be reunited with their friends in this other world, where there would be no more death or sickness or old age. He was then given the dance which he was commanded to bring back to his people. By performing this dance at intervals, for five consecutive days each time, they would secure this happiness to themselves and hasten the event. Finally God gave him control over the elements so that he could make it rain or snow or be dry at will, and appointed him his deputy to take charge of affairs in the west, while "Governor Harrison" [President of the United States at the time] would attend to matters in the east, and he, God, would look after the world above. He then returned to earth and began to preach as he was directed, convincing the people by exercising the wonderful powers that had been given him. (Mooney [1896] 1973:771–772)

Before Mooney's visit, Jack Wilson had repeated his gospel, in August 1891, to a literate young Arapaho man who had journeyed with other Arapaho and Cheyenne to discover the truth about this fabled messiah. Jack instructed his visitors, according to the Arapaho's notes:

When you get home you make dance, and will give you the same. . . . He likes you folk, you give him good, many things, he heart been sitting feel good. After you get home, will give good cloud, and give you chance to make you feel good. and he give you good spirit. and he give you all a good paint. . . .

Grandfather said when he die never no cry. no hurt anybody. no fight, good behave always, it will give you satisfaction, this young man, he is a good Father and mother, dont tell no white man. Jueses [Jesus?] was on ground, he just like cloud. Everybody is alive agin, I dont know when they will [be] here, may be this fall or in spring.

Everybody never get sick, be young again,— (if young fellow no sick any more,) work for white men never trouble with him until you leave, when it shake the earth dont be afraid no harm any body.

You make dance for six weeks night, and put you foot [food?] in dance to eat for every body and wash in the water. that is all to tell, I am in to you. and you will received a good words from him some time, Dont tell lie. (Mooney [1896] 1973:780–781)

Seeing the red ocher paint, the magpie feathers, the pine nuts, and the rabbit skin robes from the messiah, his Arapaho friends shared this message with James Mooney. Jack Wilson himself had trusted this white man. Thanks to this Arapaho document, we know that Jack Wilson himself obeyed his injunction, "Dont tell lie": he had confided to the Smithsonian anthropologist the same gospel he brought to his Indian disciples.

"A clean, honest life" is the core of Jack Wilson's guidance, summed up seventy years later by a Dakota Sioux who had grown up in the Ghost Dance religion. The circling dance of the congregations following Jack Wilson's gospel symbolized the ingathering of all people in the embrace of Our Father, God, and in his earthly deputy Jack Wilson. As the people move in harmony in the dance around the path of the sun, leftward, so they must live and work in harmony. Jack Wilson was convinced that if every Indian would dance this belief, the great expression of faith and love would sweep evil from the earth, renewing its goodness in every form, from youth and health to abundant food.

This was a complete religion. It had a transcendental origin in the prophet's visit to God, and a continuing power rooted in the eternal Father. Its message of earthly renewal was universalistic, although Jack Wilson felt it was useless to preach it to those Euro-Americans who were heedlessly persecuting the Indian peoples. That Jack shared his gospel with those non-Indians who came to him as pilgrims demonstrates that it was basically applicable to all people of goodwill. The gospel outlined personal behavior and provided the means to unite individuals into congregations to help one another. Its principal ceremony, the circling dance, pleased and satisfied the senses of the participants, and through the trances easily induced during the long ritual, it offered opportunities to experience profound emotional catharsis. Men and women, persons of all ages and capabilities, were welcomed into a faith of hope for the future, consolation and

assistance in the present, and honor to the Indians who had passed into the afterlife. It was a marvelous message for people suffering, as the Indians of the West were in 1889, terrible epidemics; loss of their lands, their economic resources, and their political autonomy; malnourishment and wretched housing; and a campaign of cultural genocide aimed at eradicating their languages, their customs, and their beliefs.

Jack Wilson's religion was immediately taken up by his own people, the Northern Paiute, by other Paiute groups, by the Utes, the Shoshoni, and the Washo in western Nevada. It was carried westward across the Sierra Nevada and espoused by many of the Indians of California. To the south, the religion was accepted by the western Arizona Mohave, Cohonino, and Pai, but not by most other peoples of the American Southwest. East of the Rockies, the religion spread through the Shoshoni and Arapaho in Wyoming to other Arapaho, Cheyenne, Assiniboin, Gros Ventre (Atsina), Mandan, Arikara, Pawnee, Caddo, Kichai, Wichita, Kiowa, Kiowa-Apache, Comanche, Delaware (living by this time in Oklahoma), Oto, and the western Sioux, especially the Teton bands. The mechanism by which this religion spread was usually a person visiting another tribe, observing the new ceremonial dance and becoming inspired by its gospel, and returning home to urge relatives and friends to try the new faith. Leaders of these evangelists' communities would often appoint respected persons to travel to Nevada to investigate this claim of a new messiah. The delegates frequently returned as converts, testifying to the truth of the faith and firing the enthusiasm of their communities. Those who remained skeptics did not always succeed in defusing the flame of faith in others.

Never an organized church, Jack Wilson's religion thus spread by independent converts from California through Oklahoma. Not all the communities who took it up continued to practice it, when months or years passed without the hoped-for earth renewal. Much of Jack Wilson's religion has persisted, however, and has been incorporated into the regular religious life of Indian groups, especially on Oklahoma reservations. To merge into a complex of beliefs and rituals rather than be an exclusive religion was entirely in accordance with Jack Wilson's respect for traditional Indian religions, which he saw reinforced, not supplanted, by his revelations.

Though the Sioux generally dropped the Ghost Dance religion after their military defeats following their initial acceptance of the ritual, older people among the Sioux could be heard occasionally singing Ghost Dance songs in the 1930s. The last real congregation of adherents to Jack Wilson's gospel continued to worship together into the 1960s, and at least one who survived into the 1980s never abandoned the faith. There were sporadic attempts to revive the Ghost Dance religion in the 1970s, though these failed to kindle the enthusiasm met by the original proselytizers.

"Ghost Dance" is the name usually applied to Jack Wilson's religion, because the prophet foresaw the resurrection of the recently dead with the hoped-for renewal of the earth. Paiute themselves simply called their practice of the faith "dance in a circle," Shoshoni called it "everybody dragging" (speaking of people pulling others along as they circled), Comanche called it "the Father's Dance," Kiowa,

"dance with clasped hands," and Caddo, "prayer of all to the Father" or "my [Father's] children's dance." The Sioux and Arapaho did use the term "spirit [ghost] dance," and the English name seems to have come from translation of the Sioux. The last active congregation, however, referred to their religion as the New Tidings, stressing its parallel to Jesus' gospel.

To his last days in 1932, Jack Wilson served as Father to believers. He counseled them, in person and by letters, and he gave them holy red ocher paint, symbolizing life, packed into rinsed-out tomato cans (the red labels indicated the contents). With his followers, he was saddened that not enough Indians danced the new faith to create the surge of spiritual power that could have renewed the earth, but resurrection was only a hope. The heart of his religion was his creed, the knowledge that a "clean, honest life" is the only good life.

Cargo Cults

Peter M. Worsley

A cargo cult, one of the several varieties of revitalization movements, is an intentional effort on the part of the members of society to create a more satisfying culture. Characteristic of revitalization movements in Melanesia, but not restricted to that area, cargo cults function to bring scattered groups together into a wider religious and political unity. These movements are the result of widespread dissatisfaction, oppression, insecurity, and the hope for fulfillment of prophecies of good times and abundance soon to come. Exposure to the cultures and material goods of the Western world, combinations of native myth with Christian teachings of the coming of a messiah, and belief in the White man's magic—all contributed to the New Guinean's faith that the "cargo" would soon arrive, bringing with it the end of the present order and the beginning of a blissful paradise.

Peter Worsley's article depicts a movement that often was so organized and persistent as to bring government work to a halt. Cargo cult movements still occur in Melanesia, where they are often intermixed with other types of revitalization movements.

PATROLS OF THE AUSTRALIAN GOVERNMENT venturing into the "uncontrolled" central highlands of New Guinea in 1946 found the primitive people there swept up in a wave of religious excitement. Prophecy was being fulfilled: The arrival of the Whites was the sign that the end of the world was at hand. The natives proceeded to butcher all of their pigs—animals that were not only a principal source of subsistence but also symbols of social status and ritual preeminence in their culture. They killed these valued animals in expression of the belief that after three days of darkness "Great Pigs" would appear from the sky. Food, firewood, and other necessities had to be stockpiled to see the people through to the arrival of the Great Pigs. Mock wireless antennae of bamboo and rope had been erected to receive in advance the news of the millennium. Many believed that with the great event they would exchange their black skins for white ones.

This bizarre episode is by no means the single event of its kind in the murky history of the collision of European civilization with the indigenous cultures of the southwest Pacific. For more than one hundred years traders and missionaries have been reporting similar disturbances among the peoples of Melanesia, the group of Negro-inhabited islands (including New Guinea, Fiji, the Solomons, and the New Hebrides) lying between Australia and the open Pacific Ocean. Though their technologies were based largely upon stone and wood, these peoples had highly developed cultures, as measured by the standards of maritime and agricultural ingenuity, the complexity of their varied social organizations, and the elaboration of religious belief and ritual. They were nonetheless ill prepared for the shock of the encounter with the Whites, a people so radically different from themselves and so infinitely more powerful. The sudden transition from the society of the ceremonial stone ax to the society of sailing ships and now of airplanes has not been easy to make.

After four centuries of Western expansion, the densely populated central highlands of New Guinea remain one of the few regions where the people still carry on their primitive existence in complete independence of the world outside. Yet as the agents of the Australian Government penetrate into ever more remote mountain valleys, they find these backwaters of antiquity already deeply disturbed by contact with the ideas and artifacts of European civilization. For "cargo"—Pidgin English for trade goods—has long flowed along the indigenous channels of communication from the seacoast into the wilderness. With it has traveled the frightening knowledge of the white man's magical power. No small element in the white man's magic is the hopeful message sent abroad by his missionaries: the news that a Messiah will come and that the present order of Creation will end.

The people of the central highlands of New Guinea are only the latest to be gripped in the recurrent religious frenzy of the "cargo cults." However variously embellished with details from native myth the Christian belief, these cults all advance the same central theme: the world is about to end in a terrible cataclysm. Thereafter God, the ancestors, or some local culture hero will appear and inaugurate a blissful paradise on earth. Death, old age, illness, and evil will be unknown. The riches of the white man will accrue to the Melanesians.

Although the news of such a movement in one area has doubtless often inspired similar movements in other areas, the evidence indicates that these cults have arisen independently in many places as parallel responses to the same enormous social stress and strain. Among the movements best known to students of Melanesia are the "Taro Cult" of New Guinea, the "Vailala Madness" of Papua, the "Naked Cult" of Espiritu Santo, the "John Frum Movement" of the New Hebrides, and the "Tuka Cult" of the Fiji Islands.

At times the cults have been so well organized and fanatically persistent that they have brought the work of government to a standstill. The outbreaks have often taken the authorities completely by surprise and have confronted them with mass opposition of an alarming kind. In the 1930's, for example, villagers in the vicinity of Wewak, New Guinea, were stirred by a succession of "Black King" movements. The prophets announced that the Europeans would soon leave the island, abandoning their property to the natives, and urged their followers to cease paying taxes, since the government station was about to disappear into the sea in a great earthquake. To the tiny community of Whites in charge of the region, such talk was dangerous. The authorities jailed four of the prophets and exiled three others. In yet another movement, that sprang up in declared opposition to the local Christian mission, the cult leader took Satan as his god.

Troops on both sides in World War II found their arrival in Melanesia heralded as a sign of the Apocalypse. The G.I.'s who landed in the New Hebrides, moving up for the bloody fighting on Guadalcanal, found the natives furiously at work preparing airfields, roads and docks for the magic ships and planes that they believed were coming from "Rusefel" (Roosevelt), the friendly king of America.

The Japanese also encountered millenarian visionaries during their southward march to Guadalcanal. Indeed, one of the strangest minor military actions of World War II occurred in Dutch New Guinea, when Japanese forces had to be turned against the local Papuan inhabitants of the Geelvink Bay region. The Japanese had at first been received with great joy, not because their "Greater East Asia Co-Prosperity Sphere" propaganda had made any great impact upon the Papuans, but because the natives regarded them as harbingers of the new world that was dawning, the flight of the Dutch having already given the first sign. Mansren, creator of the islands and their peoples, would now return, bringing with him the ancestral dead. All this had been known, the cult leaders declared, to the crafty Dutch, who had torn out the first page of the Bible where these truths were inscribed. When Mansren returned, the existing world order would be entirely overturned. White men would turn black like Papuans, Papuans would become Whites; root crops would grow in trees, and coconuts and fruits would grow like tubers. Some of the islanders now began to draw together into large "towns"; others took Biblical names such as "Jericho" and "Galilee" for their villages. Soon they adopted military uniforms and began drilling. The Japanese, by now highly unpopular, tried to disarm and disperse the Papuans; resistance inevitably developed. The climax of this tragedy came when several canoe-loads of fanatics sailed out to attack Japanese warships, believing themselves to be invulnerable by virtue of the holy water with which they had sprinkled themselves. But the bullets of the Japanese did not turn to water, and the attackers were mowed down by machine-gun fire.

Behind this incident lay a long history. As long ago as 1857 missionaries in the Geelvink Bay region had made note of the story of Mansren. It is typical of many Melanesian myths that became confounded with Christian doctrine to form the ideological basis of the movements. The legend tells how long ago there lived an old man named Manamakeri ("he who itches"), whose body was covered with sores. Manamakeri was extremely fond of palm wine, and used to climb a huge tree every day to tap the liquid from the flowers. He soon found that someone was getting there before him and removing the liquid. Eventually he trapped the thief, who turned out to be none other than the Morning Star. In return for his freedom, the Star gave the old man a wand that would produce as much fish as he liked, a magic tree and a magic staff. If he drew in the sand and stamped his foot, the drawing would become real. Manamakeri, aged as he was, now magically impregnated a young maiden; the child of this union was a miracle-child who spoke as soon as he was born. But the maiden's parents were horrified, and banished her, the child, and the old man. The trio sailed off in a canoe created by Mansren ("The Lord"), as the old man now became known. On this journey Mansren rejuvenated himself by stepping into a fire and flaking off his scaly skin, which changed into valuables. He then sailed around Geelvink Bay, creating islands where he stopped, and peopling them with the ancestors of the present-day Papuans.

The Mansren myth is plainly a creation myth full of symbolic ideas relating to fertility and rebirth. Comparative evidence—especially the shedding of his scaly skin—confirms the suspicion that the old man is, in fact, the Snake in another guise. Psychoanalytic writers argue that the snake occupies such a prominent part in mythology the world over because it stands for the penis, another fertility symbol. This may be so, but its symbolic significance is surely more complex than this. It is the "rebirth" of the hero, whether Mansren or the Snake, that exercises such universal fascination over men's minds.

The nineteenth-century missionaries thought that the Mansren story would make the introduction of Christianity easier, since the concept of "resurrec-

tion," not to mention that of the "virgin birth" and the "second coming," was already there. By 1867, however, the first cult organized around the Mansren legend was reported.

Though such myths were widespread in Melanesia, and may have sparked occasional movements even in the pre-White era, they took on a new significance in the late nineteenth century, once the European powers had finished parceling out the Melanesian region among themselves. In many coastal areas the long history of "blackbirding"—the seizure of islanders for work on the plantations of Australia and Fiji—had built up a reservoir of hostility to Europeans. In other areas, however, the arrival of the Whites was accepted, even welcomed, for it meant access to bully beef and cigarettes, shirts and paraffin lamps, whisky and bicycles. It also meant access to the knowledge behind these material goods, for the Europeans brought missions and schools as well as cargo.

Practically the only teaching the natives received about European life came from the missions, which emphasized the central significance of religion in European society. The Melanesians already believed that man's activities—whether gardening, sailing canoes, or bearing children—needed magical assistance. Ritual without human effort was not enough. But neither was human effort on its own. This outlook was reinforced by mission teaching.

The initial enthusiasm for European rule, however, was speedily dispelled. The rapid growth of the plantation economy removed the bulk of the able-bodied men from the villages, leaving women, children, and old men to carry on as best they could. The splendid vision of the equality of all Christians began to seem a pious deception in face of the realities of the color bar, the multiplicity of rival Christian missions and the open irreligion of many Whites.

For a long time the natives accepted the European mission as the means by which the "cargo" would eventually be made available to them. But they found that acceptance of Christianity did not bring the cargo any nearer. They grew disillusioned. The story now began to be put about that it was not the Whites who made the cargo, but the dead ancestors. To people completely ignorant of factory production, this made good sense. White men did not work; they merely wrote secret signs on scraps of paper, for which they were given shiploads of goods. On the other hand, the Melanesians labored week after week for pitiful wages. Plainly the goods must be made for Melanesians somewhere, perhaps in the Land of the Dead. The Whites, who possessed the secret of the cargo, were intercepting it and keeping it from the hands of the islanders, to whom it was really consigned. In the Madang district of New Guinea, after some forty years' experience of the missions, the natives went in a body one day with a petition demanding that the cargo secret should now be revealed to them, for they had been very patient.

So strong is this belief in the existence of a "secret" that the cargo cults generally contain some ritual in imitation of the mysterious European customs which are held to be the clue to the white man's extraordinary power over goods and men. The believers sit around tables with bottles of flowers in front of them, dressed in European clothes, waiting for the cargo ship or airplane to materialize; other cultists feature magic pieces of paper and cabalistic writing. Many of them deliberately turn their backs on the past by destroying secret ritual objects, or exposing them to the gaze of uninitiated youths and women, for whom formerly even a glimpse of the sacred objects would have meant the severest penalties, even death. The belief that they were the chosen people is further reinforced by their reading of the Bible, for the lives and customs of the people in the Old Testament resemble their own lives rather than those of the Europeans. In the New Testament they find the Apocalypse, with its prophecies of destruction and resurrection, particularly attractive.

Missions that stress the imminence of the Second Coming, like those of the Seventh Day Adventists, are often accused of stimulating millenarian cults among the islanders. In reality, however, the Melanesians themselves rework the doctrines the missionaries teach them, selecting from the Bible what they themselves find particularly congenial in it. Such movements have occurred in areas where missions of quite different types have been dominant, from Roman Catholic to Seventh Day Adventist. The reasons for the emergence of these cults, of course, lie far deeper in the life-experience of the people.

The economy of most of the islands is very backward. Native agriculture produces little for the world market, and even the European plantations and mines export only a few primary products and raw materials: copra, rubber, gold. Melanesians are quite unable to understand why copra, for example, fetches thirty pounds sterling per ton one month and but five pounds a few months later. With no notion of the workings of world-commodity markets, the natives see only the sudden closing of plantations, reduced wages and unemployment, and are inclined to attribute their insecurity to the whim or evil in the nature of individual planters.

Such shocks have not been confined to the economic order. Governments, too, have come and gone, especially during the two world wars: German, Dutch, British, and French administrations melted overnight. Then came the Japanese, only to be ousted in turn largely by the previously unknown Americans. And among these Americans the Melanesians saw Negroes like themselves, living lives of luxury on equal terms with white G.I.'s. The sight of these Negroes seemed like a fulfillment of the old prophecies to many cargo cult leaders. Nor must we forget the sheer scale of this invasion. Around a million U.S. troops passed through the Admiralty Islands, completely swamping the inhabitants. It was a world of meaningless and chaotic changes, in which anything was possible. New ideas were imported and given local twists. Thus in the Loyalty Islands people expected the French Communist Party to bring the millennium. There is no real evidence, however, of any Communist influence in these movements, despite the rather hysterical belief among Solomon Island planters that the name of the local "Masinga Rule" movement was derived from the word "Marxian"! In reality the name comes from a Solomon Island tongue, and means "brotherhood."

Europeans who have witnessed outbreaks inspired by the cargo cults are usually at a loss to understand what they behold. The islanders throw away their money, break their most sacred taboos, abandon their gardens, and destroy their precious livestock; they indulge in sexual license, or, alternatively, rigidly separate men from women in huge communal establishments. Sometimes they spend days sitting gazing at the horizon for a glimpse of the long-awaited ship or airplane; sometimes they dance, pray and sing in mass congregations, becoming possessed and "speaking with tongues."

Observers have not hesitated to use such words as "madness," "mania," and "irrationality" to characterize the cults. But the cults reflect quite logical and rational attempts to make sense out of a social order that appears senseless and chaotic. Given the ignorance of the Melanesians about the wider European society, its economic organization and its highly developed technology, their reactions form a consistent and understandable pattern. They wrap up all their yearning and hope in an amalgam that combines the best counsel they can find in Christianity and their native belief. If the world is soon to end, gardening or fishing is unnecessary; everything will be provided. If the Melanesians are to be part of a much wider order, the taboos that prescribe their social conduct must now be lifted or broken in a newly prescribed way.

Of course the cargo never comes. The cults nonetheless live on. If the millennium does not arrive on schedule, then perhaps there is some failure in the magic, some error in the ritual. New breakaway groups organize around "purer" faith and ritual. The cult rarely disappears, so long as the social situation which brings it into being persists.

At this point it should be observed that cults of this general kind are not peculiar to Melanesia. Men who feel themselves oppressed and deceived have always been ready to pour their hopes and fears, their aspirations and frustrations, into dreams of a millennium to come or of a golden age to return. All parts of the world have had their counterparts of the cargo cults, from the American Indian Ghost Dance to the Communist-millenarist "reign of the saints" in Münster during the Reformation, from medieval European apocalyptic cults to African "witch-finding" movements and Chinese Buddhist heresies. In some situations men have been content to wait and pray; in others they have sought to hasten the day by using their strong right arms to do the Lord's work. And always the cults serve to bring together scattered groups, notably the peasants and urban plebeians of agrarian societies and the peoples of "stateless" societies where the cult unites separate (and often hostile) villages, clans, and tribes into a wider religio-political unity.

Once the people begin to develop secular political organizations, however, the sects tend to lose their importance as vehicles of protest. They begin to relegate the Second Coming to the distant future or to the next world. In Melanesia ordinary political bodies, trade unions and native councils are becoming the normal media through which the islanders express their aspirations. In recent years continued economic prosperity and political stability have taken some of the edge off their despair. It now seems unlikely that any major movement along cargo-cult lines will recur in areas where the transition to secular politics has been made, even if the insecurity of prewar times returned. I would predict that the embryonic nationalism represented by cargo cults is likely in future to take forms familiar in the history of other countries that have moved from subsistence agriculture to participation in the world economy.

Urban Rastas in Kingston, Jamaica

William F. Lewis

The late William F. Lewis's anthropological research and publications focused largely on religion and social movements, most recently with Rastafari culture. In this selection Professor Lewis describes in rich ethnographic detail the personalities and attributes of Nigel, Lion, and David, three urban Rastas living in Kingston, Jamaica. As Lewis describes his interviews with the three Rastas, the reader learns about Rastafarian beliefs, rituals, symbols, diet, language, and other aspects of the people he refers to as "Soul Rebels."

Many Americans think of the Rastafarians as members of a deviant subculture, knowing only the reggae music of the Rastafarian song-prophet Bob Marley, or the Rasta "dreadlocks," or perhaps the Rastafarian reputation as prodigious ganja smokers. The Rastafarian movement began in Jamaica in the early 1930s. Rastas believe that Haile Ras Tafari Selassi I of Ethiopia is their Black Messiah—the King of Kings and Lord of Lords—and that Black true believers will some day dismiss their White oppressors and be repatriated to Ethiopia, their spiritual homeland. Although the largest number of Rastas live in Jamaica, there are also followers in the United States, England, Canada, Ethiopia, and other parts of the world.

Nigel

On a sultry day in downtown Kingston a weary walker might come upon Nigel lounging on his front steps, shirtless, with a towel draped around his shoulders as he carefully dries himself after one of his periodic splash baths. That is how I first met him. A careless observer might take Nigel to be mad, a stigma with which Jamaican society labels the solitary life free from the cares of family and the demands of social responsibility. However, Nigel is affable, courteous and willing to share his wisdom with sympathetic listeners. I was one of them.

Nigel's conversations with passers-by can become serious communications. He interprets such a happy occasion as the result of a mutual consciousness that compels people to reason with him. True communication is never mere serendipity. Once a male stranger (Nigel seldom if ever converses seriously with a female) demonstrates that his interests are compatible with Nigel's, his scrutiny and suspicion change to a more relaxed and intimate tone. Then Nigel asks the visitor to remove his shoes, unburden himself of his baggage, and empty his pockets of money, tobacco, and combs, things Nigel finds polluting. He requires all to relieve themselves of these demonic influences before any can enter his mansion. I complied.

Nigel's mansion turns out to be the building that housed his formerly prosperous clothing boutique which catered to the sartorial demands of the Jamaican elite. The quarters are large, two stories high, with spacious rooms that are now bereft of furniture and decoration. Nigel's mansion is but a vestige of the glamour and prestige he enjoyed as one of the wealthiest tailors in Jamaica. The yellow clippings that hang willy-nilly from the flaking walls of the main room bear silent witness to Nigel's renunciation of both his business and family. The Jamaican media once celebrated him as a promising designer of clothes for both the wealthy and the celebrated. That was before his commitment to the principles of Rastafari.

Nigel explains his conversion to Rastafari as an odyssey, a passage that began shortly after his appendectomy operation. Then modern drugs and treatments were of no avail in restoring his energy, vitality and spirit. However, an encounter with a Rasta turned into meetings of mutual communication and disclosure. On the Rasta's advice, Nigel drank large amounts of ganja tea and smoked equally large amounts of marijuana. He recovered his health. From then on, he affiliated himself with the ways of Rastafari, and he too hallowed the herb as the healing of nations. Furthermore, he attributes the restoration and continuance of his health to his dedication to the Rasta principles of love, meditation, reasoning and ital (natural) foods of which marijuana is a part.

Nigel found peace when he embraced Rastafari. His fashion industry and family were the weapons he created to wage warfare on people. Thus, he divested himself of his career and married life.

Shortly after his conversion in 1981, Nigel began to send funds to Rastas in the rural interior. At that time, Jamaican businesses were recouping their losses suffered under the democratic socialism of the Manley government which had threatened their profits. Nigel recalls how the bank officials thought that he was donating funds to a subversive group in the interior. A popular rumor at the time was that Manley's allies had contingents ready in the country who would help Cuban communists infiltrate Jamaica. Nigel was under great suspicion. The bank refused to handle any of his transactions. The government harassed him on charges of tax evasion. His wife tried to commit him to a mental institution. Nigel muses: "Because I was becoming aware of my own identity, I had to go through this suffering. That's in the past, the price I paid. Now I am free."

Now Nigel is neither an entrepreneur nor an artist but an ascetic. He refuses to touch money, and only the free will offerings of others sustain him. His meatless diet consists only of fruits, vegetables and an occasional fish. He abhors the eating of animal meat because dead flesh will only cause sickness for the person who consumes it. Nor will he accept any fruit or vegetable whose natural appearance has been altered by any cutting, mashing or peeling. Nigel seems lanky and anorexic. However, his appearance belies his vigor and vitality which are evident in his darting about and enthusiastically engaging the visitor in philosophical discussion about the affairs of the world, the way to health and the meaning of sexuality.

An aroma of ganja smoke clings to Nigel's long, unkempt and natural dreads. This slovenliness too is deceptive because Nigel is particularly fastidious about the cleanliness of his body and he meticulously monitors its functions. This leads him to administer frequent purgatives to himself lest the accumulation of toxins within cause harm for the whole body. His frequent cleansings and purgations of the body as well as the avoidance of contact with any decaying matter, especially a dead body, are normative in Nigel's life. Were these norms violated, his spiritual and physical health would be imperiled.

Without his regimen, Nigel would be unable to find the strength to weave his philosophical reflections through his writings, his conversations and solitary moments of meditation. Esoteric writings and volumes are scattered throughout his quarters. He has amassed stacks of newspaper clippings and sundry writings whose relationship to the philosophy of Rastafari at first glance appears obscure. Nevertheless, Nigel can explain every metaphor and symbol in his literary collection and connect them to what he believes are the truths of Rastafari. Included in his assemblage of works are titles such as: "Dread Locks Judgement," "Anthropology: Races of Man," "Radical Vegetarianism," "Rasta Voice Magazine," "Economy and Business," "Women as Sex Object," and "Pan African Digest." His own essays range from glosses on Joseph Owens' *Dread* and Dennis Forsythe's *Healing of Nations* to highly idealistic writing on a new economic order. Among these pieces is correspondence from previous English and American visitors to Nigel's mansion.

Nigel's own writings have an intense and highly involuted style which gives them an arcane quality, a form somewhat reminiscent of James Joyce's stream of consciousness. Tolerance and patience are demanded of the reader who wishes to decipher Nigel's turn of phrase and novel transformation of words. Indeed, the uninitiated reader might wonder if the police are not correct in simply shrugging him off as a Rasta who has had too much ganja. His prose is obscure and agonistic, but, nevertheless, he can elicit sense from every syllable, word and line. Nigel's deftness in turning his twisted writings into an articulate message makes him a shaman and mythmaker of sorts, for his vocalizations about the revelation he bears have the rhythm, cadence and timbre of a person standing outside of the self.

. . .

The Upper Room

Nigel's "Upper Room" is on the second level of the building with two large windows opening to a view of eastern Kingston and allowing the cool breezes from the sea to circulate through the room. It is furnished with a few mats, a raggedy sleeping cot over to the side, a square table on which the herb is blessed, and shelves along the wall on which lie chillum pipes of various lengths. The chillum pipes are stored for other Rastas who might visit and join Nigel for reasoning. In his Upper Room Nigel undergoes his most intense experience with ganja and elaborates ecstatically on Rastafari. In accord with what he believes to be Rastas' tradition, he excludes women from these sessions.

When the brethren have gathered in the Upper Room, Nigel raises his arms toward the East in a grand gesture and blesses the herb with vocalizations resembling glossolalia. "Amharic," he says as an aside, "the Ethiopian language." The blessings are spontaneous and ecstatic, but on listening closely I detected a word that sounded like *mirrikat,* the Amharic word for blessing. Later Nigel mentioned that he learned some Amharic at the Ethiopian Orthodox Church in Kingston.

After the chillum is filled, and the herb is burning, Nigel is the first to draw deeply from the pipe. His chest expands as smoke fills his lungs. He exhales billows of smoke through his nostrils and mouth, and the whiffs frame his lionlike face with tendrils of plumes that seep through his long locks and beard. Through the clouds of smoke, Nigel stares at all in the room with a fierce look, regal, but cutting and penetrating. His demeanor demands a response.

"The conquering Lion of Judah shall break every chain," I acclaim.

Nigel seems pleased with this affirmation of his link with the Emperor Haile Selassie, the Lion of Judah.

Another's turn comes to partake of the chalice, and Nigel passes the pipe with a most respectful gesture. Kneeling before the next brother with his own head bowed low to the floor, his outstretched arms offer him the chillum. The brother accepts, draws from it, and proclaims, "Jah Rastafari."

The chillum moves from participant to participant, brother to brother, each honoring the other with gestures of deference but never permitting their flesh to meet. Bodily contact is assiduously avoided. Soon the participants assume unusual bodily postures. The effect is startling. Nigel takes the lead in displaying great physical agility and dexterity by twisting his body into yogalike positions. All the brethren follow suit. They throw their bodies into lionlike leaps. Nevertheless, their bodily deportments are undertaken with great concentration and awareness, for not once did their acrobatic feats threaten to harm anyone in the room.

"What is love?" asks one of the brothers.

"Love is where there are no starving people. As long as there are hungry people, hatred is in power. Caring and supporting . . ."

Their dance continues, and perhaps ten minutes passes.

"Sex is a performance, a duty."

"Women are for pickneys (babies)."

Another interval, and more of their dancing.

"Burn Babylon." Some begin chanting the familiar lyric.

"Why the police brutality and why youths beaten by Babylon? They steal because they are hungry and want to fill their bellies. No crime in taking food because you are hungry."

"Africa for the blacks, Europe for the whites, Jamaica for the Arawaks."

. . .

David and Lion

Tourists and Jamaicans alike must cross an unsteady, wooden pier in order to board the ferry that takes passengers from Kingston Harbor to the legendary Port Royal across the bay. Once celebrated as a haunt for pirates and a playground for debauchery, Port Royal now rests quietly on the bay, chastised forever, it seems, by the raging earthquake it suffered in the late seventeenth century. That cataclysm hurled much of the port into the Caribbean.

Near the ramp leading to the pier lazes David, a Rasta brother. He is attending his concession stand which is simply a large crate hoisted on a dolly for maneuverability. From the cart, David sells Red Stripe beer, D & G sodas, as well as Benson cigarettes by ones and twos, and, of course, raw sugar cane and coconut, the most popular items. A sampling from his assortment of refreshments often comes as welcome relief for the overheated traveler after the half-hour trip across the bay.

David and Lion live together in a hovel about twenty yards from their stand. The shack rests precariously on the side of the pier, supported in part by the hanging branches of a huge tree on which part of it also leans. The roof and sidings are constructed of huge pieces of cardboard and plastic sheeting. Nearby, a slipshod folding chair, unworthy of any task, clings to the pier's edge and marks out an area that serves as a reception space for guests. The sound of the rushing water against the piles, the squeaking of the rats, and the dust from the parched earth fill the place David and Lion call home with a romantic irony. They sit between two worlds, perhaps a sign of their liminality. From one viewpoint, Port Royal's outlines loom across the bay standing witness to wanton living long ago. From another angle stands the symbol of law and order, a police station, to which the Rastas pay no heed.

Lion and David eat *ital* food, a healthy low-salt, low-fat and low-cholesterol diet, that consists mainly of vegetables, plantains and the occasional red snapper, caught off the pier. At a clearing away from their hut, they prepare the food on an aluminum can cover some twenty-four inches in diameter. The fare is seasoned with hot pepper and served on tin plates. Sometimes a rat might boldly rush a dish at what appears to be an opportune moment in an effort to wrest a morsel from a distracted diner. The Rastas, however, are generous and share their food with any of their guests, human and animal alike.

When business is slow at their stand, Lion, David and other brethren hustle on the streets of Kingston, selling anything from boxed donuts to belts and tams (knitted headgear which they themselves have crafted). They are talkative entrepreneurs and quick to prevail upon a prospective customer, especially a white tourist, to purchase one of their handiworks or products.

Reasoning

Toward late afternoon on a hot July day, two brethren arrive at the pier and exchange greetings with David. David assures the visiting brethren that I, the white guest sitting near the hut, have respect and love for Rastafari. Lion emerges from below the rafters of the pier where he was resting and lends support to David's assurances that their white visitor is trustworthy.

When the group is ready, David places the Bible on the ground and marks off a few pages from which he will draw his inspiration. The spliffs are lit with a short grace: "Give thanks." At that moment, however, some youths happen on the scene, probably drawn by the whiff of ganja smoke overcoming the salty sea breezes. They ask for some herb. Lion rebukes the boys and says: "This is high reasoning, boys, and not play." They run off. The Rastas return to the matter at hand.

David mulls over the scriptural passage about the Nazarites and the proscription on the cutting of hair. "Love is the foundation of Rastafari. The covenant is the hair, the locks. This is Godly."

As a group of commuters disembarks from the ferry and hurries by the group, scarcely giving them a glance, Lion comments: "Jamaican people cannot see the truth. They have eyes, hands, feet, but don't use them properly for justice and love. They are blinded."

Rashi holds his spliff and remarks pensively: "Rastas are clever, living for truth. The weed is important. It is healing."

After reflecting a bit on the wisdom in the herb, the Rastas turn to excoriating the success of reggae musicians, a discussion that enlivens the group. Few endearing words are spent on reggae musicians who, the Rastas believe, preach the philosophy of Rastafari, give interviews to magazines, enrich themselves, but filter none of their profits into the creation of a stronger culture for the rest of the brethren.

"Look how they draw up around Nesta's place on New Hope, clean and shining. Burn reggae."

All agree.

Soon the brethren fall into a quiet, meditative mood. A few reflect in low voices on the similarity between the churches and reggae. This prompts David to take up a verse from the scriptures and freely elaborate on it. The verse is: "Let the dead bury the dead."

"The churches in Jamaica bury only dead people, and take people's money to build bigger church buildings, instead of providing work and industry for people. The Rasta never dies but has life eternal, as Christ promised. God cannot lie. To have life eternal one must follow the Rasta culture in the Bible. Rasta is a new name. It is the new Jerusalem that Isaiah promised in the prophecy."

David's words excite the group, and they all affirm the equality of people. They denounce the hypocrisy of organized religion, reggae and the government for manipulating the Bible and authority. The more their anger with society increases, so much the more does the spontaneity of the gathering quicken.

David takes the spliff from a Rasta reclining next to him. Holding it, he prays that the chalice be not a source of condemnation but a guardian of life eternal. He inhales deeply, holds the smoke within, and for almost a minute after exhalation he gazes intently on me, the white visitor sitting across from him. Then:

"Rasta is not the color of the skin. Blacks hate their fellow man, just like white man hates. Even some Rastas have words on their lips but not in their hearts."

As darkness draws closer, and fewer people queue up for the ferry, the Rastas become more vociferous.

"Living is for the Rastas. Moses and the prophets are not dead, but reign in Zion, a Kingdom that is better than the one here. I have life. I will never die but go to Zion with Ras Tafari Selassie I" [pronounced as "aye"].

Interspersed among their exultations of Selassie are monotone chantings expressing a yearning for repatriation to a land of freedom from which they have been exiled.

"Africa yes! But not the Africa of today because it is just as corrupt as Jamaica."

Silence. The spliffs are lit again, passed around and blessed. The mood changes. The brethren become serious and playful, ecstatic and earthly. Lion leads this flow of sensuousness. He rolls on the ground, smiles, laughs lightly while singing an improvisation on liberty, freedom and repatriation. He kisses the roots of a nearby tree and exclaims: "Jah Rastafari."

The others participate in his display with their own paeans on liberation and freedom. Soon they too tumble over the ground, enjoying themselves immensely, and encouraging me to "ride the vibes and feel freedom."

At dusk, bright lights illumine the decks of a British warship that had docked in the harbor earlier in the day. The sharp relief of the ship in the distance prompts Lion to remark:

"War is against Rastafari. Rastas do what is right for life and live forever. Jamaican people love war too much. I don't know why."

David pursues the thought further. "I-n-I is never listened to. We are rejected. They have no culture. They steal, kill and shoot."

Lion snuggles closer to the roots of the tree which are bulging from the parched earth. He seems to caress them.

"I-n-I Rastafari are the love in the world. We are very peaceful, loving and don't eat poisonous things, no salt, no liver, no dead animals."

Rashi adds: "We want wholeness, fullness of justice, fullness of love."

When asked to identify the source of his power, Rashi responds:

"I-n-I is the bible in the heart. The true bible is yet to be written. I-n-I moves beyond the bible. It is a word that we must move beyond. I-n-I live naturally in the fullness of divinity, don't have to go to school. Truth is in the heart. I-n-I have to learn our flesh and blood. Then everybody gets food, shelter. This is the truth."

Popes and priests irritate them. "Burn the pope. Burn the pope man. The Church is a vampire with their cars and living in the hills [an area where the elite reside]. The pope is a vampire, wants our blood. Selassie I is the head. The pope is the devil."

The light fades. More silence. The bay water slaps against the pilings. A rat tears across the planks and startles me. I jump. Lion, however, admonishes me with a reminder that the rat is only a creature.

"The barber shop is the mark of the beast. Comb and razor conquer. The wealth of Jah is with locks, in fullness of his company."

All nod in agreement. I mention that my understanding is increasing.

"Be careful with words, brother," Lion says, "overstand not understand. I people are forward people not backward."

Another interjects: "It is a brand new way of life. The language of I-n-I is forward. I-n-I people will pay no more. For five hundred years, they built Babylon on us, but they will do it no more."

. . .

Serpent-Handling as Sacrament

Mary Lee Daugherty

In this article Mary Lee Daugherty discusses serpent-handlers in West Virginia. The author, raised in the area she writes about, maintains that the handling of serpents as a religious act reflects the geographic and economic harshness of the environment in which the snake-handlers live. Professor Daugherty has been studying religious behavior and beliefs throughout Appalachia as well as West Virginia. It is a mark of her professional ability that she has been allowed by the members of several Holiness-type churches to conduct her research. Although many people in this country are appalled at the thought of religious behavior that encourages the handling of poisonous snakes and the drinking of such poisons as strychnine and lye, West Virginia's defeat of a 1966 bill that would have made serpent-handling illegal serves as an indication of the importance of religious freedom in the United States.

Reprinted from *Theology Today*, vol. 33, no. 3 (October 1976), pp. 232–43, by permission of the publisher.

And he [Jesus] said unto them, Go ye into all the world, and preach the gospel to every creature. He that believeth and is baptized shall be saved; but he that believeth not shall be damned. And these signs shall follow them that believe; In my name shall they cast out devils; they shall speak with new tongues; they shall take up serpents; and if they drink any deadly thing, it shall not hurt them; they shall lay hands on the sick, and they shall recover.

—Mark 16:15–18 (AV)

THE SERPENT-HANDLERS OF WEST VIRGINIA WERE originally simple, poor, white people who formed a group of small, independent Holiness-type churches. Serpent-handlers base their particular religious practices on the familiar passage from the "long-conclusion" of the Gospel of Mark. (They are unaware of the disputed nature of this text as the biblical scholars know it.)

The handling of serpents as a supreme act of faith reflects, as in a mirror, the danger and harshness of the environment in which most of these people have lived. The land is rugged and uncompromisingly grim. It produces little except for coal dug from the earth. Unemployment and welfare have been constant companions. The dark holes of the deep mines into which men went to work every day have maimed and killed them for years. The copperhead and rattlesnake are the most commonly found serpents in the rocky terrain. For many years mountain people have suffered terrible pain and many have died from snake bite. Small wonder that it is considered the ultimate fact of faith to reach out and take up the serpent when one is filled with the Holy Ghost. Old timers here in the mountains, before the days of modern medicine, could only explain that those who lived were somehow chosen by God's special mercy and favor.

Today serpent-handlers are experiencing, as are other West Virginians, great economic improvement. Many now live in expensive mobile homes that dot the mountain country side. They purchase and own among their possessions brand new cars and modern appliances. Many of the men now earn from twelve to eighteen thousand dollars a year, working in the revitalized mining industry. Most of the young people are now going to and graduating from high school. I know of one young man with two years of college who is very active in his church. He handles serpents and is looked upon as the one who will take over the pastor's position sometime in the future. What the effect of middle-class prosperity and higher education will be among serpent-handlers remains to be seen. It may be another generation before the effects can be adequately determined.

Knowing serpent-handlers to be biblical literalists, one might surmise that they, like other sects, have picked a certain passage of Scripture and built a whole ritual around a few cryptic verses. While this is true, I am persuaded, after years of observation, that serpent-handling holds for them the significance of a sacrament.

Tapestry paintings of the Lord's Supper hang in most of their churches. Leonardo da Vinci's *Last Supper* is the one picture I have seen over and over again in their churches and in their homes. But in West Virginia, the serpent-handlers whom I know personally do not celebrate the Lord's Supper in their worship services. It is my observation and hypothesis that the ritual of serpent-handling is their way of celebrating life, death, and resurrection. Time and again they prove to themselves that Jesus has the power to deliver them from death here and now.

Another clue to the sacramental nature of lifting up the serpents as the symbol of victory over death is to be observed at their funerals. At the request of the family of one who has died of snake bite, serpents may be handled at a funeral. Even as a Catholic priest may lift up the host at a mass for the dead, indicating belief that in the life and death of Jesus there is victory over death, so the serpent-handlers, I believe, lift up the serpent. Of course, none of this is formalized, for all is very spontaneous. But I am convinced that they celebrate their belief that "in the name of Jesus" there is power over death, and this is what the serpent-handling ritual has proved to them over and over again. This is why I believe they will

not give up this ritual because it is at the center of their Christian faith, and in West Virginia, unlike all the other States, it is not illegal.

Many handlers have been bitten numerous times, but, contrary to popular belief, few have died. Their continued life, and their sometimes deformed hands, bear witness to the fact that Jesus still has power over illness and death. Even those who have not been bitten know many who have, and the living witness is ever present in the lives of their friends. If one of the members should die, it is believed that God allowed it to happen to remind the living that the risk they take is totally real. Never have I heard any one of them say that a brother or sister who died lacked faith.

The cultural isolation of these people is still very real. Few have traveled more than a few miles from home. Little more than the Bible is ever read. Television is frowned upon; movies are seldom attended. The Bible is communicated primarily through oral tradition in the church or read at home. There is little awareness of other world religions. Even contacts with Roman Catholics and Jews are rare. Most of their lives revolve around the local church where they gather for meetings two or three times a week.

When one sees the people handling serpents in their services, the Garden of Eden story immediately comes to mind. In the Genesis story, the serpent represents evil that tempts Adam and Eve and must be conquered by their descendants. But the serpent means something far different to West Virginia mountain people; it means life over death. There is never any attempt to kill the snake in Appalachian serpent-handling services. Practitioners seldom kill snakes even in the out of doors. They let them go at the end of the summer months so that they may return to their natural environment to hibernate for the winter. They catch different snakes each spring to use in their worship services. When you ask them why, they tell you quite simply that they do not want to make any of God's creatures suffer. The serpent is always handled with both love and fear in their services, but it is never harmed or killed. Handlers may be killed from bites, but they will not kill the snake. Neither do they force the handling of serpents on any who do not wish to do so.

The snake is seldom handled in private, but usually in the community of believers during a church service. Members may encourage each other to take the risk, symbolically taking on life and testing faith. Their willingness to die for their beliefs gives to their lives a vitality of faith. Handlers usually refuse medicine or hospital treatment for snake bite. But they do go to hospital for other illnesses or if surgery is needed. In the past, they usually refused welfare. They revere and care for their elderly who have usually survived numerous snake bites. Each time they handle the serpents they struggle with life once more and survive again the forces that traditionally oppressed mountain people. The poverty, the unemployment, the yawning strip mines, death in the deep mines have all been harsh, uncontrollable forces for simple people. The handling of serpents is their way of confronting and coping with their very real fears about life and the harshness of reality as experienced in the mountains in years gone by and, for many, even today.

Yet in the face of all this, they seek to live in harmony with nature, not to destroy it or any of its creatures, even the deadly serpent. It is only with the Holy Ghost, however, that they find the sustenance to survive. They live close to the earth, surrounded by woods, streams, and sky. Most live in communities of only a few hundred people or less.

The deep longing for holiness of these Appalachian people stands out in bold relief in the serpent-handling ritual of worship. The search for holiness is dramatized in their willingness to suffer terrible pain from snake bite, or even death itself, to get the feeling of God in their lives. The support of their fellow Christians is still with them. In their experience, God may not come if you don't really pray or ask only once. The person in the group who has been bitten most often and who has suffered the most pain or sickness is usually the leader. While it is the Holy Ghost who gives the power, those who have survived snake bite do get recognition and praise for their courage and their faith from the group. They have learned to cope with their anxieties by calling upon the names of Jesus and the power which he freely offers. Support is given to each member through the laying on of hands in healing ceremonies, through group prayers, and through verbal affirmations, such as: "Help her Jesus," "Bless him, Lord," "That's right, Lord." Through group support, anxiety about life is relieved. They feel ennobled as God becomes manifest in their midst.

The person of the Holy Ghost (they prefer this to Holy Spirit) enables them not only to pick up serpents, but to speak in tongues, to preach, to testify, to cure diseases, to cast out demons, and even to drink strychnine and lye, or to use fire on their skin when the snakes are in hibernation during the winter months. In these dramatic ways, the mountain folk pursue holiness above all else. They find through their faith both meaning and encouragement. Psychological tests indicate that in many ways they are more emotionally healthy than members of mainline Protestant churches.

Having internalized my own feelings of insecurity and worthlessness for many years because I was "no count" having been born from poor white trash on one side of my family, I have in my own being a deep appreciation and understanding of the need of these people to ask God for miracles accompanied with spectacular demonstrations. Thus they are assured of their own worth, even if only to God. They have never gotten this message from the outside world. They know they have been, and many still are, the undesirable poor, the uneducated mountain folk, locked into their little pockets of poverty in a rough, hostile land. So the Holy Ghost is the great equalizer in the church meeting. One's age, sex, years of schooling are all of less value. Being filled with the Holy Ghost is the only credential one needs in this unique society.

The Holy Ghost creates a mood of openness and spontaneity in the serpent-handling service that is beautiful to behold. Even though there is not much freedom in the personal lives of these people, there is a sense of power in their church lives. Their religion does seem to heal them inwardly of aches and pains and in many instances even of major illnesses. One often sees expressions of dependence as men and women fall down before the picture of Jesus, calling aloud over and over again, "Jesus . . . Jesus . . . Jesus . . ." The simple carpenter of Nazareth is obviously a person with whom mountain people can identify. Jesus worked with his hands, and so do they; Jesus was essentially, by our standards, uneducated, and so are they; Jesus came from a small place, he lived much of his life out of doors, he went fishing, he suffered and was finally done in by the "power structure," and so have they been in the past and often are today.

As I think about the mountain women as they fall down before the picture of Jesus, I wonder what he means to them. Here is a simple man who treated women with great love and tenderness. In this sense, he is unlike some of the men they must live with. Jesus healed the bodies of women, taught them the

Bible, never told jokes about their bodies, and even forgave them their sexual sins. In the mountains, adultery is usually punished with beatings. Maybe it should not surprise us that in a State where the strip miners have raped the earth that the rape of the people has also taken place, and the rape of women is often deeply felt and experienced. Things are now changing, and for this we can be grateful.

In the serpent-handlers' churches, the Bible usually remains closed on the pulpit. Since most older members cannot read very well and have usually felt shy about their meager education, they did not read the Bible aloud in public, especially if some more educated people were present. They obviously read the Bible at home, but most remember it from stories they have heard. The Bible is the final authority for everything, even the picking up of serpents and the drinking of poison. It is all literally true, but the New Testament is read more often than the Old Testament.

In former years, their churches have given these poor and powerless people the arena in which they could act out their frustrations and powerless feelings. For a short time, while in church, they could experience being powerful when filled with the Holy Ghost. Frustrated by all the things in the outside world that they could not change, frustrated by the way the powerful people of the world were running things, they could nevertheless run their own show in their own churches. So they gathered three or four times a week, in their modest church buildings, and they stayed for three to five hours for each service. On these occasions, they can feel important, loved, and powerful. They can experience God directly.

I am always struck by the healing love that emerges at the end of each service when they all seem to love each other, embrace each other, and give each other the holy kiss. They are free from restrictions and conventions to love everyone. Sometimes I have the feeling that I get a glimpse of what the Kingdom of God will be like as we kiss each other, old and young, with or without teeth, rich and poor, educated and uneducated, male and female. So I have learned much and have been loved in turn by the serpent-handlers of West Virginia. As they leave the church and go back to their daily work, all the frustrations of the real world return, but they know they can meet again tomorrow night or in a few days. So they have faith, hope, and love, but the greatest message they have given to me is their love.

There are thousands of small Holiness churches in the rural areas of West Virginia. While four-fifths of all Protestants are members of mainstream denominations, no one knows just how many attend Holiness churches. Membership records are not considered important to these people, and although I personally know of about twenty-five serpent-handling churches, there may be others, for those in one church often do not know those in another. They laugh and make jokes about churches that give you a piece of paper as you enter the door, telling you when to pray and what to sing. They find it difficult to believe that you can "order around" the worship of the Holy Ghost on a piece of paper.

Those who make up the membership of the serpent-handling churches are often former members of other Holiness churches or are former Baptists or Methodists. In the Holiness churches, the attainment of personal holiness and being filled with the Spirit is the purpose and goal of life. Members view the secular world as evil and beyond hope. Hence they do not take part in any community activities or social programs.

Fifty-four percent of all persons in the state of West Virginia still live in communities of 1,000 people or less. Freedom of worship is the heritage of the Scotch-Irish, who settled these mountains 200 years ago. In more recent times, among Holiness groups there were no trained ministers. So oral tradition, spontaneous worship, and shared leadership are important.

Holiness church members live by a very strict personal code of morality. A large sign in the church at Jolo, W. Va., indicates that dresses must be worn below the knees, arms must be covered, no lipstick or jewelry is to be worn. No smoking, drinking, or other worldly pleasures are to be indulged in by "true believers." Some women do not cut their hair, others do not even buy chewing gum or soft drinks. For years, in the mountains, people have practiced divine healing, since medical facilities are scarce. Four counties in West Virginia still do not have a doctor, nurse, clinic, dentist, or ambulance service.

In a typical serpent-handling church service, the "true believers" usually sit on the platform of the church together. They are the members who have demonstrated that they have received the Holy Ghost. This is known to them and to others because they have manifested certain physical signs in their own bodies. If they have been bitten from snakes, as many have, and have not died, they have proved that they have the Holy Ghost. And those who have been bitten many times, and survived, are the "real saints." The "true believers" also demonstrate that they have the Holy Ghost by speaking in tongues, by the jerking of their bodies, and by their various trance-like states. They may dance for long periods of time or fall on the floor without being hurt. They may drink the "salvation cocktail," a mixture of strychnine or lye and water. They may also speak in tongues or in ecstatic utterances. Usually this is an utterance between themselves and God. But sometimes members seek to interpret the language of tongues. They lay their hands upon each other to heal hurts or even serious illnesses such as cancer. They sometimes pass their hands through fire. I have witnessed this activity and no burn effects are visible, even though a hand may remain in the flame for some time. A few years ago, they picked up hot coals from the pot bellied stoves and yet were not burned. They apparently can block out pain totally, when in a trance or deep into the Spirit of God.

One woman who attended church at Scrabble Creek, W. Va., experienced, on two occasions, the stigmata as blood came out of her hands, feet, side and forehead. This was witnessed by all present in the church. When asked about this startling experience, she said that she had prayed that God would allow people to see though her body how much Jesus suffered for them by his death and resurrection.

A local church in the rural areas may be known as "Brother So and So's" or "Sister So and So's" church to those who live nearby, but the sign over the door will usually indicate that the church belongs to Jesus. Such names as "The Jesus Church," "The Jesus Only Church," "The Jesus Saves Church," and "The Lord Jesus Christ's Church" are all common names. The churches do not belong to any denomination, and they have no written doctrines or creeds. The order of the service is spontaneous and different every night. Everyone is welcome and people travel around to each other's churches, bringing with them their musical instruments, snakes, fire equipment, poison mixtures, and other gifts.

Often the service begins with singing which may last thirty to forty-five minutes. Next, they may all pray out loud together for the Holy Ghost to fall upon them during the service. Singing, testifying, and preaching by anyone who feels God's spirit may follow. Serpents then will be handled while others are singing. It is possible that serpents will be handled two or three times in one service, but usually it is only once. Serpents are only handled when they feel God's spirit within them. After dancing ecstatically, a brother or sister will open the box and pull out a serpent. Others will follow if there are other snakes available. If only one or two serpents are present, then they may be passed around from believer to believer. Sometimes a circle may be made and the snakes passed. I have only once seen them throw snakes to each other. Children are kept far away.

There is much calling on the name of Jesus while the serpents are being handled, and once the "sacrament" is over, there is a great prayer of rejoicing and often a dance of thanksgiving that no one was hurt. If someone is bitten, there is prayer for his or her healing and great care is taken. If the person becomes too ill to stay in the church, he or she may be taken home and believers will pray for the person for days, if necessary. Even if the person does not die, and usually he or she doesn't, the person is usually very sick. Vomiting of blood and swelling are very painful. Some persons in the churches have lost the use of a finger or suffered some other deformity. But in many years of serpent-handling, I believe there are only about twenty recorded deaths.

The symbolism of the serpent is found in almost all cultures and religions, everywhere, and in all ages. It suggests the ambiguity of good and evil, sickness and health, life and death, mortality and immortality, chaos and wisdom. Because the serpent lives in the ground but is often found in trees, it conveys the notion of transcendence, a creature that lives between earth and heaven. And because it sheds its skin, it seems to know the secret of eternal life.

In the Bible, the serpent is most obviously associated with the Adam and Eve temptation (Gen. 3:1–13), but we also read of the sticks that Moses and Aaron turned into snakes (Ex. 7:8–12), and of Moses' bronze serpent standard (Num. 21:6–9). The two entwined snakes in the ancient figure of the caduceus, symbolizing sickness and health, has been widely adopted as the emblem of the medical profession. And sometimes in early Christian art, the crucifixion is represented with a serpent wound around the cross or lying at the foot of the cross (cf. John 3:14). Here again good and evil, life over death, are symbolized.

In early liturgical art, John the Evangelist was often identified with a chalice from which a serpent was departing, a reference to the legend that when he was forced to drink poison, it was drained away in the snake. Among the early Gnostics, there was a group known as Ophites who were said to worship the serpent because it brought "knowledge" to Adam and Eve and so to all humanity. They were said to free a serpent from a box and that it then entwined itself around the bread and wine of the Eucharist.

But, of course, this ancient history and symbolic lore are unknown to the mountain serpent-handlers of West Virginia, and even if they were told, they probably would not be interested. Their own tradition is rooted in their literal acceptance of what they regard as Jesus' commandment at the conclusion of Mark's Gospel. The problems of biblical textual criticism, relating to the fact that these verses on which they depend are not found in the best manuscript evidence, does not bother them. Their Bible is the English King James Version, and they know through their own experience that their faith in the healing and saving power of Jesus has been tested and proven without question. In any case, their ritual is unique in church history.

What the future holds for the serpent-handlers, no one can tell. Although the young people have tended to stay in their local communities, the temptation in the past to move out and away to find work has been very great. Now many of the young people are returning home as the mining industry offers new, high-paying jobs. And a new era of relative economic prosperity is emerging as the energy problem makes coal-mining more important for the whole Appalachian area. In the meantime, serpent-handling for many mountain people remains a Jesus-commanded "sacrament" whereby physical signs communicate spiritual reality.

New Religions and the Counter-Culture

Elizabeth Puttick

In this selection, Elizabeth Puttick examines the counter-culture of the 1960s and its role in the spawning of a spiritual awakening that swept through the Western world and led to the establishment of several new religious movements. After a brief description of the 1960s counter-culture and the various forces that led to its creation, Puttick focuses on the Human Potential Movement (HPM) and the rise and popularization of Indian gurus, notably Maharishi Mahesh Yogi, the Hare Krishna movement, Maharaji (also known as Elan Vital), and the Bhagwan Shree Rajneesh (Osho). Puttick also discusses the influence of Eastern mysticism on the counter-culture, noting that India especially has long attracted Westerners.

> *After the Second World War, Western seekers began to go on pilgrimage to India. A lone trail was blazed by Sangharakshita, but it was not until the visits of Allen Ginsberg and other Beat poets in the 1960s that the "hippie trail" began in earnest. It was a two-way traffic, accompanied and inspired by an influx of Asian teachers: gurus from India, lamas from Tibet, and Zen monks from Japan. The writings and teachings of the Asians and some of their Western followers became disseminated to a whole generation of spiritual seekers. (Puttick 1997: 15–16)*

Puttick concludes her article by observing how interesting it is that so many rebellious individualists in the counter-culture were transformed into surrendered devotees sitting at the feet of their gurus.

Reprinted from Elizabeth Puttick, *Women in New Religions: In Search of Community, Sexuality, and Spiritual Power* (New York: St. Martin's Press, 1997), by permission of St. Martin's Press, LLC.

The Counter-Culture of the 1960s

The 1960s marked the beginning of a period of rapid social change, which is transforming the world radically and fundamentally. These changes correlate with the millennialist visions of many old and new religions, but are also perceived by political leaders such as Vaclav Havel:

> There are good reasons for suggesting that the modern age has ended. Many things indicate that we are going through a transitional period, when it seems that something is on the way out and something else is painfully being born. It is as if something were crumbling, decaying and exhausting itself, while something else, still indistinct, were arising from the rubble.

This transformation of the world and of consciousness is sometimes termed a 'paradigm shift'. The causes of the shift are complex and multidimensional and can be traced back at least as far as the eighteenth-century Romantic movement. However, the explosion of rebellious creativity in the 1960s seemed both at the time and in retrospect to be a turning point. This was partly because it followed a period of particularly staid conservatism in the 1950s; partly because rather than remaining a fringe subculture it grew to have enormous impact on all aspects of society: politics, social and political activism, the arts, literature, fashion, health, gender, sexuality and spirituality. Those creating and participating in it called it the alternative society, while sociologists labelled it the counter-culture.

The counter-culture arose partly as a rebellion against the materialism and 'technocracy' of the post-war climate. An entire generation of young people—well fed and well educated—rejected their parents' goals of wealth, success and status in favour of the search for meaning and fulfilment. It was sometimes castigated by social commentators and moralists as an escapist flight into sex, drugs and rock 'n' roll—the aspect that was given the most media attention. As much as escapism, however, it was an active rejection of scientific developments and socio-political values that had been invalidated—if not annihilated—by two world wars, and most immediately by the pointless destruction of the Vietnam War. Those who looked deeper perceived it as also 'a reaction against the "disenchantment of the world", and the loss of magic, mystery, prophecy and the sacred. A search to find one's "real self" amidst the multiplicity of roles and selves we are made to act out' (Mullan 1983, 17).

The counter-culture was also a 'rebellion against reason': the arid intellectualism of Western philosophy and theology with its over-reliance on 'left-brain' thinking. Polytechnics were replaced by Polytantrics, and the 1968 Antiuniversity of London aspired to transform Western Man through such sources as Artaud, Zimmer, Gurdjieff, Reich, Marx, Gnostic, Sufi and Tantric texts, autobiographical accounts of madness and ecstatic states of consciousness—all synthesized into a 'free-wheeling succession of open-ended situations'. One of the main chroniclers of the counter-culture, Theodore Roszak, summarized this trend:

> One can discern, then, a continuum of thought and experience among the young which links together the New Left sociology of Mills, the Freudian Marxism of Herbert Marcuse, the Gestalt-therapy anarchism of Paul Goodman, the apocalyptic body mysticism of Norman Brown, the Zen-based psychotherapy of Alan Watts, and finally Timothy Leary's impenetrably occult narcissism. (1968, 64)

The Human Potential Movement

With its enthusiastic explorations of self and society, its questioning of values and overturning of conventions, the counter-culture paved the way for a spiritual revival on the broadest possible front: seeking to integrate the dualities of society and religion, psyche and soma, masculine and feminine, East and West. Since the Judaeo-Christian tradition had no developed tradition or methodology for the inner quest, the tools were provided by the relatively new science of psychology.

The Human Potential Movement (HPM) was the psycho-spiritual wing of the counter-culture. It was largely an outgrowth of humanistic psychology, which was developed by Abraham Maslow in re-

sponse to the limitations of psychoanalysis and behaviourism. Maslow's main influence on the HPM was his concept of the 'self-actualized' human being: one who is fully alive and responsive, having solved the basic survival needs and psychological problems; who has ecstatic 'peak experiences' and is therefore able to explore all the realms of human potential, including mysticism. Maslow thus paved the way for the later spiritualization of psychotherapy, although the HPM was originally more secular in its aims.

The primary goal of the HPM was to explore the realms of feelings and relationships, a taboo area in British society at the time. The militarization of two world wars had encouraged a rigidity and repression that Wilhelm Reich (1968) called 'character armour', and identified as the cause of neurosis, many psychosomatic disorders and sociopolitical problems, including fascism. Psychotherapy for the populace was integral to the socialist utopia proposed by Reich as the only effective antidote to fascism. In this austere climate the Roman virtues of discipline, duty, gravity, firmness, tenacity, hard work and frugality restrained the softer virtues and the spontaneous expression of affection. So the children of the post-war period grew up economically privileged but emotionally and spiritually deprived.

· · ·

The exploration and development of these issues and values by the HPM in the 1970s was also the precursor of the now widespread interest in personal development, the quality of relationships and emotional literacy; human values in the workplace; and the replacement of hard political causes with softer issues such as environmentalism and animal rights. Our outlook has been affected to the point where even philosophy may be interpreted in terms of the philosopher's emotional problems, as with the latest biography of Bertrand Russell. A new organization called Antidote has been set up by a group of British psychotherapists including Susie Orbach to re-engage the emotional and psychological dimensions of life with the political process, although it may have a struggle to contend with the 'stiff upper lip' attitude that still dominates the Conservative party, as expressed by the MP Nicholas Soames, grandson of Winston Churchill:

> This terrible counselling thing has grown up in Britain. Whatever you do wrong it's somebody else's fault, or your mother hit you. I think that's all

balls. It's ghastly political correctness. People need to pull themselves together. I'm not a great believer in blubbing in your tent. I do get melancholy now and again, but you go to bed, sleep well and wake up pawing the ground like a horse in the morning.

. . .

Despite the tremendous creativity and experimentation in the HPM at this time, it hit a barrier around the early 1970s. There was a widespread feeling that the full potential implied in self-actualization had not been realized: self-improvement had indeed happened, but not radical transformation. One woman, who later became a Rajneesh therapist, summarizes the mood of the time: 'By now I'd been doing groups for two years very intensively, and I began to feel there was something more. All this looking inside and emoting all these feelings, behind that was something deeper, but I had no idea how to reach it.' Many people shared this experience, and started looking for the 'something deeper' in spiritual transformation, including Eastern forms of meditation.

The Influence of Eastern Spirituality on Western Psychotherapy

The influence of Eastern mysticism on the counter-culture has been well documented. India has long exerted a magnetic attraction on Westerners. This can be traced back at least to Voltaire, who believed that 'Our religion was hidden deep in India' and 'incontestably comes to us from the brahmins' (Batchelor 1994, 252). The discovery and translation of ancient Buddhist scriptures by European scholars in the nineteenth century revealed the quality and sophistication of this religion, and led to the founding of the Buddhist Society in London in 1907 and the spread of Theravada teachings. In America the influx of Chinese and Japanese immigration during this period inspired a fascination with Zen Buddhism, leading to the foundation of many Zen monasteries. The Chinese seizure of power in Tibet in 1959 brought an influx of Tibetan lamas to the West, who set up many meditation centres. Out of these developments arose a minority but increasingly influential belief in the superiority of Eastern religion, as expressed by the renowned Indologist Conze: 'For 3000 years Asia alone has been creative of spiritual ideas and methods. The Europeans have in these matters borrowed from Asia, have adapted Asiatic ideas, and, often coarsened them' (1951, 11).

Psychologists from Jung onwards have found a natural correlation between psychology and Buddhist philosophy. Jung had been very interested in Eastern mysticism and symbolism, though his interpretations have been criticized by Indians and Westerners. Fromm and Maslow had made theoretical connections between psychoanalysis and Zen Buddhism in the 1950s, but until the 1970s psychotherapy and meditation were perceived as different, mutually exclusive paths. Fitzgerald argues that it was Alan Watts 'who constructed the intellectual bridge between the therapists and Bhagwan Shree Rajneesh' by interpreting the Eastern mystical traditions as being closer to psychotherapy than to philosophy or religion (1986, 286). He thus influenced many people to travel to India to discover meditation.

Until the 1960s, interest in Eastern religion had been largely intellectual, confined to an elite group of scholars and psychologists. However, the ground had been prepared for a more experiential, mystical approach by the American Transcendentalists, the Theosophical Society and the teachings of Krishnamurti (originally trained by the Theosophists), as well as by the visits of other Indian sages such as Vivekananda and Yogananda. After the Second World War, Western seekers began to go on pilgrimage to India. A lone trail was blazed by Sangharakshita, but it was not until the visits of Allen Ginsberg and other Beat poets in the 1960s that the 'hippie trail' began in earnest. It was a two-way traffic, accompanied and inspired by an influx of Asian teachers: gurus from India, lamas from Tibet, and Zen monks from Japan. The writings and teachings of the Asians and some of their Western followers became disseminated to a whole generation of spiritual seekers. Whether they approved, censured or simply noted, commentators agreed that the influence of Asian religions was 'one of the most striking characteristics of the counterculture'.

The Rise of Indian Gurus

The Human Potential Movement arose partly in response to widespread disillusion with on the one hand the Judaeo-Christian tradition, on the other hand scientific materialism. When it in turn failed to fulfil participants' spiritual aspirations, they were drawn to Indian gurus who offered a highly developed, ancient tradition of teachings and practices, grounded in meditation. Out of these informal gatherings of gurus and initiates arose the NRMs of the 1970s.

The first guru to popularize meditation was Maharishi Mahesh Yogi. He brought Transcendental Meditation (TM) to the West in 1958, and captured the public imagination in the 1960s when the Beatles, Mia Farrow and other celebrities visited his ashram in Rishikesh. For a small fee, people were given a mantra to be used in a simple, twice-daily, twenty-minute meditation. 'Easy is right' was the continual message, and the accompanying idea of instant enlightenment held tremendous appeal. It is claimed that millions of Westerners have learned TM over the last 30 years. The Spiritual Regeneration Movement, as it is now called, has grown into a worldwide, highly lucrative chain of organizations including meditation centres, corporate development programmes, and an International University that has conducted and motivated extensive scientific research to demonstrate and measure the benefits of meditation. Despite its popularity, most practitioners did not become involved in TM full-time. Indeed its appeal lay in its ability to be slotted into a busy working life without renouncing material comfort or retiring to a monastery. TM therefore did not take off as a religious movement on the scale of some other NRMs, but many seekers acquired their first experience of meditation through it and then moved on to other teachers.

Next on the scene was the International Society for Krishna Consciousness (ISKCON), popularly known as the Hare Krishna movement. It was founded in New York in 1966 by Swami Prabhupada, and soon reached Britain, again becoming famous via the Beatles who used Hare Krishna chants in their music. George Harrison eventually became a devotee and donated a large house which became the British headquarters, Bhaktivedanta Manor. The saffron-robed devotees were a colourful sight on street corners throughout the West, chanting the Hare Krishna mantra. Membership required an austere, traditional Hindu regime that begins at 3 a.m. with a cold shower and a schedule of rigorous devotions, and demands the renunciation of meat, alcohol, drugs and sex. This asceticism was in stark contrast to the hedonism of the counter-culture, but constituted its appeal for some members. ISKCON rejects the label NRM, seeing itself as a continuation of Vaishnava Hinduism. Its social organization has been adapted and Westernized in many ways, but it was the provision of a coherent, traditional system of doctrine and practice that attracted so many Westerners to become full-time members. These have also enabled it to survive various scandals and crises, including the death of its founder and the departure or expulsion of half the gurus initiated by Prabhupada.

The third most popular guru in the early 1970s was Maharaji, 'boy guru' of the Divine Light Mission (later known as Elan Vital) that had been founded by his father, Shri Hans Ji Maharaj. Maharaji first visited Britain in 1971, aged 13, and shortly afterwards established his headquarters in America. His devotees, called 'premies', were taught a system of self-realization called 'Knowledge'. Hundreds of thousands of followers were claimed, though numbers fell dramatically after Maharaji fell out with his mother, who denounced him, took over the movement in India, and eventually set up his brother as head of the Indian branch. As with Prabhupada and other Indian gurus who attracted Western followers, such as Muktananda and Satya Sai Baba, Maharaji offered a teaching and practice closely based on traditional Hinduism. Westerners were attracted by the exoticism, by the differences from Christianity, by the heart-centred devotionalism, and by a spiritual practice based in meditation and self-development.

The Osho Movement

The problem with the teachings of the Indian gurus was that they had no organic connection with Western spiritual and cultural traditions. This uprootedness was the main criticism made by philosophers and theologians such as Jacob Needleman (1977) and Harvey Cox (1979), although many members of NRMs claimed to feel more 'at home' in them than in their religion of birth. Still, a marriage between East and West was required. Psychology had made theoretical connections, but it was within the practical, experiential approach of psychotherapy that a living synthesis was created. Therapists of the HPM were utilizing meditation as an adjunct to 'growth' and experimenting with it in their groups, particularly at Esalen in California. The first 'growth centre' in Britain was Quaesitor, founded in London in 1970 by Paul and Patricia Lowe (later Teertha and Poonam), and it was here that these experiments were brought to fruition. At first their main focus was on psychotherapy, but as they and their clients began to meditate, a natural integration started. Clare Soloway (formerly Patricia) describes the process:

> There isn't a point where therapy ends and transformation begins; it's a continuation. We were laying the groundwork for that at that time. We were involved with meditation, because it's a process of self-awareness. We were continuously looking for the new, always looking for the next person who would come, and who could shine a light from that angle. We were on the path of searching very consciously. So there wasn't a time when anything began, we were already in that process of finding ourselves very consciously.

In 1972 the Lowes discovered Dynamic Meditation, a cathartic, neo-Reichian meditation technique, invented by an Indian guru, Bhagwan Shree Rajneesh. Patricia Lowe was 'blown out by it, very impressed. I felt it was a really powerful tool.' The rationale for this departure from static, silent meditations such as *vipassana*, was that the complexity and stress of contemporary life, with its frenzied activity and emotional repression, make it hard for Westerners to sit in meditation for long periods. As one Buddhist convert expressed it: 'I've been sitting zazen for years and I still don't like it particularly. It makes me mad. I shake, sometimes very violently' (Needleman 1977, 48). This was a problem described by some of my own respondents who had previously been Buddhists, which was resolved by the 'Dynamic': an active meditation featuring breathing, but chaotic rather than the controlled techniques of Eastern meditations. Breath is perceived as the bridge between body and soul, and the Dynamic meditation became a bridge between East and West.

Shortly after this discovery, the Lowes went to India to meet Bhagwan, and became two of his first Western disciples. His first Western disciples were drawn from hippies and seekers travelling round India, but the Lowes inspired other key HPM therapists to join. His following then grew very fast from their clientele. Wallis summarizes the phenomenon: 'Rajneesh's tantrism overlapped extensively with the principal ideological elements of Human Potential Movement, but offered something far more, a path to Enlightenment' (1986, 197). By the mid-1970s the Osho movement had become the most fashionable and fastest growing NRM in the West. . . .

Osho began his career as a professor of philosophy at Jabalpur University. In 1966, having become 'enlightened', he resigned his professorship and began travelling round India speaking to huge crowds on controversial subjects such as politics and sex. His contentiousness was part of his appeal to the rebels, drop-outs and jaded intellectuals who comprised his early following, and it is one of the aspects of his teaching that distinguishes him from other Asian gurus of the time. In 1970 he settled in Bombay, where his teachings and meditation camps started attracting Westerners to 'take sannyas'. In traditional Hinduism, sannyas is the fourth and last stage of a man's life in which the world and its pleasures are renounced. Osho gave sannyas to Westerners of all ages and both sexes, and redefined it as a life-affirmative spirituality. The initiation process involved four conditions: taking a new name, wearing orange, wearing a *mala* (a necklace of wooden beads with a locket containing Osho's photo), and doing at least one meditation daily. These conditions were not arduous, though sometimes caused difficulties with friends and family and in the workplace. The orange robes often caused sannyasins to be mistaken for Hare Krishna devotees, to the annoyance of both groups. By 1974 his following had grown to such a size that he set up his own ashram in Poona, which soon become a mecca for spiritual seekers all over the world. At the height of the movement's success in the late 1970s, there were about 250,000 sannyasins worldwide, of whom about 3000 were permanently based in Poona. As inevitably happens with successful movements, growth led to routinization, and the relaxed counter-cultural modes of the early days gave way to ever tighter organization. This phase is now referred to as 'Poona I' in distinction from 'Poona II', the return to India after the American phase.

The movement now expanded so rapidly that in 1981, after failing to find larger premises elsewhere in India, it moved to America and built a commune called Rajneeshpuram in Oregon. America has always represented a land of hope, freedom and boundless opportunity for religious communities, and since the first World Parliament of Religions at Chicago in 1893, Indian teachers have been visiting and sometimes settling in America. Rajneeshpuram became incorporated as a city and began to 'green the desert' with an assortment of agricultural and environmental projects. Great advances were made, for which the community won great admiration. However, their building projects ran up against the strict land use and planning laws of the state of Oregon. Legal battles and opposition from neighbours provoked hostility from the commune and a series of defence strategies including the stockpiling of weapons, combined with an increasingly harsh, authoritarian work regime. Rajneeshpuram collapsed in 1985 after the government brought a case with an array of charges including tax evasion, embezzlement, wire-tapping and immigration offences. Osho was deported and three of his chief administrators were arrested.

In 1986 Osho returned to Poona, where he lived uneventfully until his death in 1990. The Osho movement has quietly flourished ever since, becoming more inner-directed and less controversial. After a big drop in membership post-Rajneeshpuram, numbers are claimed to be rising again, though in Britain and America the movement is fairly quiescent.

The after-effects of Rajneeshpuran linger on, the latest episode being the trial of two former sannyasins, Sally Anne Croft and Susan Hagan, for conspiring to murder a US attorney in Oregon. The case provoked a storm of protest in Britain, partly owing to the perceived injustice of the case, which was based on the American practice of plea-bargaining, whereby their accomplices lightened their sentences by agreeing to give evidence against the two women. Since the alleged plot took place ten years ago, was never carried out, and no harm came to the intended victim, it was widely felt to be a mockery of justice. The result was a swing of public sympathy towards the women, notwithstanding the almost universal denunciations of the movement five years previously, accompanied by strong public and parliamentary support. A campaign was launched on their behalf in 1990, with the Labour leader Tony Blair and the Liberal-Democrat leader Paddy Ashdown among their defenders. However, after a four-year struggle to avoid extradition, they were finally extradited to America where they received a five-year prison sentence.

The demise of Rajneeshpuram is one incident in a history of scandals involving NRMs and their leaders—although it should be remembered that many mainstream Western religious leaders such as televangelists and Catholic priests have also fallen into disrepute. But the gurus inspired a particularly strong devotion, owing to their undoubted charisma, which was attributed by their followers to their enlightened state. As a result, many thousands of young women and men flocked to Indian ashrams, often giving up well-paid jobs, sometimes leaving behind partners and children, occasionally donating large sums of money. One of the interesting phenomena arising out of the counter-culture is the transformation of large numbers of rebellious individualists into surrendered devotees sitting at the feet of their gurus.

10

The Occult: Paths to the Unknown

The occult, from the Latin *occulere,* meaning to conceal, is a nonspecific term for things magical and mystical—a kind of esoteric knowledge available only to those initiated into the secrets of acquisition. As the authors of the following selections make clear, the study of the occult properly falls into the realm of the study of magic, witchcraft, and religion. In addition, the tremendous recent interest in the occult has made it a worthy subject for study. R. Wuthnow (1978) cites evidence that the occult has become an even more popular supernatural belief than the belief in God. The popularity of the occult serves as an index of social strain, of rebellion against tradition, and of the need for small-group reinforcement.

This chapter emphasizes occult practices in contemporary America and demonstrates that even Western groups seek wisdom and knowledge unavailable through science or established religions. The articles incorporated here will also demonstrate that occult practices in America appear to many to be more exotic in nature than the traditional religious practices of members of non-Western societies.

Most attempts at determining how believers in the occult feel about religion are met with difficulty. Some occultists see themselves as philosophers whereas others describe themselves as

Goat mask of a modern witch high priestess.

scientists or even as religious practitioners—the latter despite the usual disdain occultists have for the teachings of established religions. In regard to this point, Harriet Whitehead (1974: 561) believes the rejection by occultists of Christian theodicy does not mean a denial of Christian morality, for there is evidence that contemporary occult publications reflect a "generalized" Christian morality. What is being rejected by the occultists, according to Whitehead, is the doctrine of atonement and the belief that the unrepentant will be consigned to some sort of eternal punishment. Whitehead sums up the basis of American occultism in the following way:

> Occultism seeks to reunite the separate pieces of the intellectual, emotional, and apprehensional jig-saw puzzle by surveying and abstracting from all the traditions that address themselves to the task of *understanding* things, whether this understanding be directed at practical mastery or a passive acceptance. Occultism posits an underlying singular Truth, the search for which cannot be confined to a particular style and the content of which cannot exclude any dimension of human experience, however "irrational" it may seem. (Whitehead 1974: 587)

As is the case with all religions, occultists have developed systems of beliefs that guide true believers, but because occult practices appear exotic to most observers, they are viewed with skeptical interest and suspicion. Astrology is the most popular and accepted of the occultist traditions in the Western world. The growing popularity of witchcraft, however, and the fact that witchcraft is still well embedded in traditional beliefs in various parts of the preindustrial world, offer an opportunity for cross-cultural comparison (see Chapter 6 "Witchcraft and Sorcery").

Modern witches, according to Frank Smyth, "refer to their religion as 'wicca,' the feminine form of an Old English word, 'wicce,' meaning a witch, possibly a derivative of the verb 'wiccian,' to practice witchcraft. Wicca is a largely urban cult. . . . In common with more orthodox religions, wicca has worship as its main object, but the additional element of magic lends the cult an illicit and undoubtedly attractive aura" (Smyth 1970: 1866). Wicca has a matriarchal character, and although in most cases both men and women are referred to as witches, local organizations of witches, called covens, are made up of more women than men. Indeed, the high priestess is symbolic of the mother goddess

and not dissimilar to the Virgin Mary; the mother goddess is the principal deity of witchlore. Wicca is basically a fertility cult with its great festivals geared to the seasons (Smyth 1970: 1866). The elements of sexuality that sometimes appear as part of initiation and the symbolic or actual intercourse of members have brought Wicca into disrepute in many quarters, but the explanation that it is a fertility cult has been used as a justification for these acts. Whatever the accusations made or answers given, it has provided the media with tantalizing copy.

The popular press in this country typically portrays believers in the occult as a single group. This is an incorrect assessment. Marcello Truzzi (1974: 628–32) provides a more accurate analysis of the occult by dividing practitioners into three broad categories. At the first level are people whose involvement in the occult is minimal—who do not see themselves as occultists per se but as concerned individuals interested in explaining such strange occurrences as flying saucers, assorted land and sea monsters, and various parapsychological phenomena. Typically their activities are characterized by an absence of mysticism, supernaturalism, and antiscientific thought; in fact, scientific support for their beliefs is highly valued. On Truzzi's second level of occultism are people who seek to understand mysterious causal relationships between events—who express an interest, for example, in numerology, sun-sign astrology, and palmistry. Knowledge gained at this level is more likely to be *a*scientific or *extra*-scientific rather than *anti*-scientific. Truzzi's third level of occultism is concerned with those complex belief systems—witchcraft, Satanism, ritual magic, and other mystical traditions—that combine elements from the first two levels. Third-level believers often question or contradict scientific validation of an event or relationship and thus may see themselves as competitors to science. Truzzi concludes that although some occult believers exist in "pure form," most are a combination of all three types.

This final chapter is a departure from the preceding ones in that every article is based on American society. This is because the subject matter, the occult, constitutes a set of beliefs and practices that become distinctive only in cultures steeped in a scientific tradition of problem solving. What the scientific world regards as occult would possibly constitute a "correct" system of knowledge or of technical arts in a non-Western culture. The formulas, the spells, the paraphernalia, the reliance upon the supernatural—all aspects of the occult world— fall quite acceptably into a culture that relies on magic as a logical system of explaining events or getting something done.

There can be no doubt that from the very beginning a cloud of controversy has hung over occultism. Yet, through all the controversy its appeal has attracted scholars, scientists, and philosophers, as well as the general public. Freud at one time was fascinated by certain numerological theories but apparently discarded them as well as the entire subject of occultism. The conflict between Freud and Jung over the occult is caught in the following quotation from Jung (1961: 150):

I can still recall vividly how Freud said to me, "My dear Jung, promise me never to abandon the sexual theory. This is the most essential thing of all. You see, we must make a dogma of it, an unshakeable bulwark." He said that to me with great emotion, in the tone of a father saying, "and promise me this one thing, my dear son: that you will go to church every Sunday." In some astonishment I asked him, "A bulwark —against what?" To which he replied, "Against the black tide of mud"—and here he hesitated for a moment, then added— "of occultism."

The late Carl Sagan's article is an excellent selection to open the chapter. Sagan demonstrates that skepticism can function to confront the occult as well as New Age beliefs. In the second article, Barry Singer and Victor Benassi examine the popularity of the occult in an age of science and then speculate about the social mechanisms that may have given rise to the recent widespread interest in the occult. Next, Raymond L. M. Lee takes anthropologists to task for their failure to indicate in their writings whether they themselves believe in the paranormal events they have observed in other cultures. The final article is an account of the Heaven's Gate cult in California, its charismatic leader, Marshall Herff Applewhite, and the group's 1997 mass suicide.

Abundant information is available in anthropological and other literature that focus on the occult. For example, readers are directed to journal articles, all published in 1995, by Ellen Badone, John McCreery, Birgit Meyer, and Thomas Molnar. These are listed in the references for the introduction to this chapter.

References

Badone, Ellen
    1995 "Suspending Disbelief: An Encounter with the Occult in Brittany." *Anthropology and Humanism* 20: 9.

Jung, C. G.
    1961 *Memories, Dreams, Reflections.* New York: Vintage Books.

McCreery, John L.
    1995 "Negotiating with Demons: The Uses of Magical Language." *American Ethnologist* 22 (1): 144–64.

Meyer, Birgit
    1995 "Delivered from the Powers of Darkness: Confessions of Satanic Riches in Christian Ghana." *Africa* 65: 236.

Molnar, Thomas
    1995 "Paganism and Its Renewal." *The Intercollegiate Review* 31 (1): 28–35.

Smyth, Frank
    1970 "Modern Witchcraft." In Richard Cavendish, ed., *Man, Myth and Magic,* vol. 14, pp. 1865–70. New York: Marshall Cavendish.

Truzzi, Marcello
    1974 "Towards a Sociology of the Occult: Notes on Modern Witchcraft." In Irving I. Zaretsky and Mark P. Leone, eds., *Religious Movements in Contemporary America,* pp. 628–45. Princeton, N.J.: Princeton University Press.

Whitehead, Harriet
    1974 "Reasonably Fantastic: Some Perspectives on Scientology, Science Fiction, and Occultism." In Irving I. Zaretsky and Mark P. Leone, eds., *Religious Movements in Contemporary America,* pp. 547–87. Princeton, N.J.: Princeton University Press.

Wuthnow, R.
    1978 *Experimentation in American Religion.* Los Angeles: University of California Press.

The Burden of Skepticism

Carl Sagan

In this selection, the late Carl Sagan, a highly respected professor of astronomy and space sciences and director of the Laboratory for Planetary Studies at Cornell University, discusses the importance of skepticism. Sagan observes that humans have always clung to one or another set of belief systems, some that change quickly, some that last for thousands of years —for example, beliefs in reincarnation, channeling, UFOs, and astrology. He feels that these belief systems become popular for many unskeptical people because they address unsatisfied medical needs, spiritual needs, or various other real human needs that are for one reason or another not being met by society. Sagan's quote from the French scientist Henri Poincaré is to the point: "We also know how cruel the truth often is, and we wonder whether delusion is not more consoling."

Sagan believes that credulity—a readiness to believe even though there is slight or uncertain evidence—is rampant because skepticism challenges established institutions. And because it is the business of skepticism to be dangerous, Sagan feels there is a reluctance to teach it in schools. Ideally, he envisions a balance between two conflicting needs: skepticism and openness to new ideas. To follow blindly one of these modes of thought results in trouble. Good scientists, Sagan argues, do both: They open their minds to huge numbers of new ideas and then relentlessly criticize them.

Sagan laments the existence of a kind of Gresham's Law in popular culture, where the bad science drives out the good. He states, "Every newspaper in America has a daily astrology column. How many have even a weekly astronomy column?" Carl Sagan died in 1998.

WHAT IS SKEPTICISM? IT'S NOTHING VERY ESOteric. We encounter it every day. When we buy a used car, if we are the least bit wise we will exert some residual skeptical powers—whatever our education has left to us. You could say, "Here's an honest-looking fellow. I'll just take whatever he offers me." Or you might say, "Well, I've heard that occasionally there are small deceptions involved in the sale of a used car, perhaps inadvertent on the part of the salesperson," and then you do something. You kick the tires, you open the doors, you look under the hood. (You might go through the motions even if you don't know what is supposed to be under the hood, or you might bring a mechanically inclined friend.) You know that some skepticism is required, and you understand why. It's upsetting that you might have to disagree with the used-car salesman or ask him questions that he is reluctant to answer. There is at least a small degree of interpersonal confrontation involved in the purchase of a used car and nobody claims it is especially pleasant. But there is a good reason for it—because if you don't exercise some minimal skepticism, if you have an absolutely untrammeled credulity, there is probably some price you will have to pay later. Then you'll wish you had made a small investment of skepticism early.

Now this is not something that you have to go through four years of graduate school to understand. Everybody understands this. The trouble is, a used car is one thing but television commercials or pronouncements by presidents and party leaders are another. We are skeptical in some areas but unfortunately not in others.

For example, there is a class of aspirin commercials that reveals the competing product to have only so much of the painkilling ingredient that doctors recommend most—they don't tell you what the mysterious ingredient is—whereas *their* product has a dramatically larger amount (1.2 to 2 times more per tablet). Therefore you should buy their product. But why not just take two of the competing tablets? You're not supposed to ask. Don't apply skepticism to this issue. Don't think. Buy.

Such claims in commercial advertisements constitute small deceptions. They part us from a little money, or induce us to buy a slightly inferior product. It's not so terrible. But consider this:

I have here the program of this year's Whole Life Expo in San Francisco. Twenty thousand people attended last year's program. Here are some of the presentations: "Alternative Treatments for AIDS Patients: It will rebuild one's natural defenses and prevent immune system breakdowns—learn about the latest developments that the media has thus far ignored." It seems to me that presentation could do real harm. "How Trapped Blood Proteins Produce Pain and Suffering." "Crystals, Are They Talismans or Stones?" (I have an opinion myself.) It says, "As a crystal focuses sound and light waves for radio and television"—crystal sets are rather a long time ago—"so may it amplify spiritual vibrations for the attuned human." I'll bet very few of you are attuned. Or here's one: "Return of the Goddess, a Presentational Ritual." Another: "Synchronicity, the Recognition Experience." That one is given by "Brother Charles." Or, on the next page, "You, Saint-Germain, and Healing Through the Violet Flame." It goes on and on, with lots of ads about "opportunities"—ranging from the dubious to the spurious—that are available at the Whole Life Expo.

If you were to drop down on Earth at any time during the tenure of humans, you would find a set of popular, more or less similar, belief systems. They change, often very quickly, often on time scales of a few years. But sometimes belief systems of this sort last for many thousands of years. At least a few are always available. I think it's fair to ask why. We are *Homo sapiens*. That's the distinguishing characteristic about us, that *sapiens* part. We're supposed to be smart. So why is this stuff always with us? Well, for one thing, a great many of these belief systems address real human needs that are not being met by our society. There are unsatisfied medical needs, spiritual needs, and needs for communion with the rest of the human community. There may be more such failings in our society than in many others in human history. And so it is reasonable for people to poke around and try on for size various belief systems, to see if they help.

For example, take a fashionable fad, channeling. It has for its fundamental premise, as does spiritualism, that when we die we don't exactly disappear, that some part of us continues. That part, we are told, can reenter the bodies of human and other beings in the future, and so death loses much of its sting for us personally. What is more, we have an opportunity, if the channeling contentions are true, to make contact with loved ones who have died.

Speaking personally, I would be delighted if reincarnation were real. I lost my parents, both of them, in the past few years, and I would love to have a little conversation with them, to tell them what the kids are doing, make sure everything is all right wherever it is they are. That touches something very deep. But at the same time, precisely for that reason, I know that there are people who will try to take advantage of the vulnerabilities of the bereaved. The spiritualists and the channelers better have a compelling case.

Or take the idea that by thinking hard at geological formations you can tell where mineral or petroleum deposits are. Uri Geller makes this claim. Now if you are an executive of a mineral exploration or petroleum company, your bread and butter depend on finding the minerals or the oil; so spending trivial amounts of money, compared with what you usually spend on geological exploration, this time to find deposits psychically, sounds not so bad. You might be tempted.

Or take UFO's, the contention that beings in spaceships from other worlds are visiting us all the time. I find that a thrilling idea. It's at least a break from the ordinary. I've spent a fair amount of time in my scientific life working on the issue of the search for extraterrestrial intelligence. Think how much effort I could save if those guys are coming here. But when we recognize some emotional vulnerability regarding a claim, that is exactly where we have to make the firmest efforts at skeptical scrutiny. That is where we can be had.

Now, let's reconsider channeling. There is a woman in the State of Washington who claims to make contact with a 35,000-year-old somebody, "Ramtha"—he, by the way, speaks English very well with what sounds to me to be an Indian accent. Suppose we had Ramtha here and just suppose Ramtha is cooperative. We could ask some questions: How do we know that Ramtha lived 35,000 years ago? Who is keeping track of the intervening millennia?

How does it come to be exactly 35,000 years? That's a very round number. Thirty-five thousand plus or minus what? What were things like 35,000 years ago? What was the climate? Where on Earth did Ramtha live? (I know he speaks English with an Indian accent, but where was that?) What does Ramtha eat? (Archaeologists know something about what people ate back then.) We would have a real opportunity to find out if his claims are true. If this were really somebody from 35,000 years ago, you could learn a lot about 35,000 years ago. So, one way or another, either Ramtha really is 35,000 years old, in which case we discover something about that period—that's before the Wisconsin Ice Age, an interesting time—or he's a phony and he'll slip up. What are the indigenous languages, what is the social structure, who else does Ramtha live with—children, grandchildren—what's the life cycle, the infant mortality, what clothes does he wear, what's his life expectancy, what are the weapons, plants, and animals? Tell us. Instead, what we hear are the most banal homilies, indistinguishable from those that alleged UFO occupants tell the poor humans who claim to have been abducted by them.

Occasionally, by the way, I get a letter from someone who is in "contact" with an extraterrestrial who invites me to "ask anything." And so I have a list of questions. The extraterrestrials are very advanced, remember. So I ask things like, "Please give a short proof of Fermat's Last Theorem." Or the Goldbach Conjecture. And then I have to explain what these are, because extraterrestrials will not call it Fermat's Last Theorem, so I write out the little equation with the exponents. I never get an answer. On the other hand, if I ask something like "Should we humans be good?" I always get an answer. I think something can be deduced from this differential ability to answer questions. Anything vague they are extremely happy to respond to, but anything specific, where there is a chance to find out if they actually know anything, there is only silence.

The French scientist Henri Poincaré remarked on why credulity is rampant: "We also know how cruel the truth often is, and we wonder whether delusion is not more consoling." That's what I have tried to say with my examples. But I don't think that's the only reason credulity is rampant. Skepticism challenges established institutions. If we teach everybody, let's say high school students, the habit of being skeptical, perhaps they will not restrict their skepticism to aspirin commercials and 35,000-year-old channelers (or channelees). Maybe they'll start asking awkward questions about economic, or social, or political, or religious institutions. Then where will we be?

Skepticism is dangerous. That's exactly its function, in my view. It is the business of skepticism to be dangerous. And that's why there is a great reluctance to teach it in the schools. That's why you don't find a general fluency in skepticism in the media. On the other hand, how will we negotiate a very perilous future if we don't have the elementary intellectual tools to ask searching questions of those nominally in charge, especially in a democracy? . . .

I want to say a little more about the burden of skepticism. You can get into a habit of thought in which you enjoy making fun of all those other people who don't see things as clearly as you do. . . . We have to guard carefully against it.

It seems to me what is called for is an exquisite balance between two conflicting needs: the most skeptical scrutiny of all hypotheses that are served up to us and at the same time a great openness to new ideas. Obviously those two modes of thought are in some tension. But if you are able to exercise only one of these modes, which ever one it is, you're in deep trouble.

If you are only skeptical, then no new ideas make it through to you. You never learn anything new. You become a crotchety old person convinced that nonsense is ruling the world. (There is, of course, much data to support you.) But every now and then, maybe once in a hundred cases, a new idea turns out to be on the mark, valid and wonderful. If you are too much in the habit of being skeptical about everything, you are going to miss or resent it, and either way you will be standing in the way of understanding and progress.

On the other hand, if you are open to the point of gullibility and have not an ounce of skeptical sense in you, then you cannot distinguish the useful ideas from the worthless ones. If all ideas have equal validity then you are lost, because then, it seems to me, no ideas have any validity at all.

Some ideas are better than others. The machinery for distinguishing them is an essential tool in dealing with the world and especially in dealing with the future. And it is precisely the mix of these two modes of thought that is central to the success of science.

Really good scientists do both. On their own, talking to themselves, they churn up huge numbers of new ideas, and criticize them ruthlessly. Most of the ideas never make it to the outside world. Only the ideas that pass through a rigorous self-filtration make it out and are criticized by the rest of the scientific community. It sometimes happens that ideas that are accepted by everybody turn out to be wrong, or at least partially wrong, or at least superseded by ideas of greater generality. And, while there are of course some personal losses—emotional bonds to the idea that you yourself played a role in inventing—nevertheless the collective ethic is that every time such an idea is overthrown and replaced by something better the enterprise of science has benefited. In science it often happens that scientists say, "You know that's a really good argument; my position is mistaken," and then they actually change their minds and you never hear that old view from them again. They really do it. It doesn't happen as often as it should, because scientists are human and change is sometimes painful. But it happens every day. I cannot recall the last time something like that has happened in politics or religion. It's very rare that a senator, say, replies, "That's a good argument. I will now change my political affiliation."

. . . In the history of science there is an instructive procession of major intellectual battles that turn out, all of them, to be about how central human beings are. We could call them battles about the anti-Copernican conceit.

Here are some of the issues:

• *We are the center of the Universe. All the planets and the stars and the Sun and the Moon go around us.* (Boy, must we be something *really* special.) That was the prevailing belief—Aristarchus aside—until the time of Copernicus. A lot of people liked it because it gave them a personally unwarranted central position in the Universe. The mere fact that you were on Earth made you privileged. That felt good. Then along came the evidence that Earth was just a planet and that those other bright moving points of light were planets too. Disappointing. Even depressing. Better when we were central and unique.

• *But at least our Sun is at the center of the Universe.* No, those other stars, they're suns too, and what's more we're out in the galactic boondocks. We are nowhere near the center of the Galaxy. Very depressing.

• *Well, at least the Milky Way galaxy is at the center of the Universe.* Then a little more progress in science. We find there isn't any such thing as the center of the Universe. What's more there are a hundred billion other galaxies. Nothing special about this one. Deep gloom.

• *Well, at least we humans, we are the pinnacle of creation. We're separate. All those other creatures, plants and animals, they're lower. We're higher. We have no connection with them. Every living thing has been created separately.* Then along comes Darwin. We find an evolutionary continuum. We're closely connected to the other beasts and vegetables. What's more, the closest biological relatives to us are chimpanzees. *Those* are our close relatives—*those* guys? It's an embarrassment. Did you ever go to the zoo and watch them? Do you know what they do? Imagine in Victorian England, when Darwin produced this insight, what an awkward truth it was.

There are other important examples—privileged reference frames in physics and the unconscious mind in psychology—that I'll pass over. . . .

The search for extraterrestrial intelligence and the analysis of possible animal "language" strike at one of the last remaining pre-Copernican belief systems:

• *At least we are the most intelligent creatures in the whole Universe.* If there are no other smart guys elsewhere, even if we *are* connected to chimpanzees, even if we *are* in the boondocks of a vast and awesome universe, at least there is still something special about us. But the moment we find extraterrestrial intelligence that last bit of conceit is gone. I think some of the resistance to the idea of extraterrestrial intelligence is due to the anti-Copernican conceit. Likewise, without taking sides in the debate on whether other animals—higher primates, especially great apes—are intelligent or have language, that's clearly, on an emotional level, the same issue. If we define humans as creatures who have language and no one else has language, at least we are unique in that regard. But if it turns out that all those dirty, repugnant, laughable chimpanzees can also, with Ameslan or otherwise, communicate ideas, then what is left that is special about us? Propelling emotional predispositions on these issues are present, often unconsciously, in scientific debates. It is important to realize that scientific debates, just like pseudoscientific debates, can be awash with emotion, for these among many different reasons.

Now, let's take a closer look at the radio search for extraterrestrial intelligence. How is this different from pseudoscience? Let me give a couple of real cases. In the early sixties, the Soviets held a press conference in Moscow in which they announced that a distant radio source, called CTA-102, was varying sinusoidally, like a sine wave, with a period of about 100 days. Why did they call a press conference to announce that a distant radio source was varying? Because they thought it was an extraterrestrial civilization of immense powers. That is worth calling a press conference for. This was before even the word "quasar" existed. Today we know that CTA-102 is a quasar. We don't know very well what quasars are; and there is more than one mutually exclusive explanation for them in the scientific literature. Nevertheless, few seriously consider that a quasar, like CTA-102, is some galaxy-girdling extraterrestrial civilization, because there are a number of alternative explanations of their properties that are more or less consistent with the physical laws we know without invoking alien life. The extraterrestrial hypothesis is a hypothesis of last resort. Only if everything else fails do you reach for it.

Second example: British scientists in 1967 found a nearby bright radio source that is fluctuating on a much shorter time scale, with a period constant to ten significant figures. What was it? Their first thought was that it was something like a message being sent to us, or an interstellar navigational beacon for spacecraft that ply the spaces between the stars. They even gave it, among themselves at Cambridge University, the wry designation LGM-1—Little Green Men, LGM. However (they were wiser than the Soviets), they did not call a press conference, and it soon became clear that what we had here was what is now called a "pulsar." In fact it was the first pulsar, the Crab Nebula pulsar. Well, what's a pulsar? A pulsar is a star shrunk to the size of a city, held up as no other stars are, not by gas pressure, not by electron degeneracy, but by nuclear forces. It is in a certain sense an atomic nucleus the size of Pasadena. Now that, I maintain, is an idea at least as bizarre as an interstellar navigational beacon. The answer to what a pulsar is has to be something mighty strange. It isn't an extraterrestrial civilization, it's something else; but a something else that opens our eyes and our minds and indicates possibilities in nature that we had never guessed at.

Then there is the question of false positives. Frank Drake in his original Ozma experiment, Paul Horowitz in the META (Megachannel Extraterrestrial Assay) program sponsored by the Planetary Society, the Ohio University group and many other groups have all had anomalous signals that make

the heart palpitate. They think for a moment that they have picked up a genuine signal. In some cases we have not the foggiest idea what it was; the signals did not repeat. The next night you turn the same telescope to the same spot in the sky with the same modulation and the same frequency and bandpass, everything else the same, and you don't hear a thing. You don't publish that data. It may be a malfunction in the detection system. It may be a military AWACS plane flying by and broadcasting on frequency channels that are supposed to be reserved for radio astronomy. It may be a diathermy machine down the street. There are many possibilities. You don't immediately declare that you have found extraterrestrial intelligence because you find an anomalous signal.

And if it were repeated, would you then announce? You would not. Maybe it's a hoax. Maybe it is something you haven't been smart enough to figure out that is happening to your system. Instead, you would then call scientists at a bunch of other radio telescopes and say that at this particular spot in the sky, at this frequency and bandpass and modulation and all the rest, you seem to be getting something funny. Could they please look at it and see if they get something similar? And only if several independent observers get the same kind of information from the same spot in the sky do you think you have something. Even then you don't know that the something is extraterrestrial intelligence, but at least you could determine that it's not something on Earth. (And that it's also not something in Earth orbit; it's further away than that.) That's the first sequence of events that would be required to be sure that you actually had a signal from an extraterrestrial civilization.

Now notice that there is a certain discipline involved. Skepticism imposes a burden. You can't just go off shouting "little green men," because you are going to look mighty silly, as the Soviets did with CTA-102, when it turns out to be something quite different. A special caution is necessary when the stakes are as high as here. We are not obliged to make up our minds before the evidence is in. It's okay not to be sure.

I'm often asked the question, "Do you think there is extraterrestrial intelligence?" I give the standard arguments—there are a lot of places out there, and use the word *billions,* and so on. And then I say it would be astonishing to me if there weren't extraterrestrial intelligence, but of course there is as yet no compelling evidence for it. And then I'm asked, "Yeah, but what do you really think?" I say, "I just told you what I really think." "Yeah, but what's your gut feeling?" But I try not to think with my gut. Really, it's okay to reserve judgment until the evidence really is in.

After my article "The Fine Art of Baloney Detection" came out in *Parade* (Feb. 1, 1978), I got, as you might imagine, a lot of letters. Sixty-five million people read *Parade*. In the article I gave a long list of things that I said were "demonstrated or presumptive baloney"—thirty or forty items. Advocates of all those positions were uniformly offended, so I got lots of letters. I also gave a set of very elementary prescriptions about how to think about baloney—arguments from authority don't work, every step in the chain of evidence has to be valid, and so on. Lots of people wrote back, saying "You're absolutely right on the generalities: unfortunately that doesn't apply to my particular doctrine." For example, one letter writer said the idea that intelligent life exists outside the earth is an excellent example of baloney. He concluded, "I am as sure of this as of anything in my experience. There is no conscious life anywhere else in the Universe. Mankind thus returns to its rightful position as center of the Universe."

Another writer again agreed with all my generalities, but said that as an inveterate skeptic I have closed my mind to the truth. Most notably I have ignored the evidence for an Earth that is six thousand years old. Well, I haven't ignored it; I considered the purported evidence and *then* rejected it. There is a difference, and this is a difference, we might say, between prejudice and postjudice. Prejudice is making a judgment before you have looked at the facts. Postjudice is making a judgment afterwards. Prejudice is terrible, in the sense that you commit injustices and you make serious mistakes. Postjudice is not terrible. You can't be perfect of course; you may make mistakes also. But it is permissible to make a judgment after you have examined the evidence. In some circles it is even encouraged.

I believe that part of what propels science is the thirst for wonder. It's a very powerful emotion. All children feel it. In a first grade classroom everybody feels it; in a twelfth grade classroom almost nobody feels it, or at least acknowledges it. Something happens between first and twelfth grade, and it's not just puberty. Not only do the schools and the media not teach much skepticism, there is also little encouragement of this stirring sense of wonder. Science and pseudoscience both arouse that feeling. Poor popularizations of science establish an ecological niche for pseudoscience.

If science were explained to the average person in a way that is accessible and exciting, there would be no room for pseudoscience. But there is a kind of Gresham's Law by which in popular culture the bad science drives out the good. And for this I think we have to blame, first, the scientific community ourselves for not doing a better job of popularizing science, and, second, the media, which are in this respect almost uniformly dreadful. Every newspaper in America has a daily astrology column. How many have even a weekly astronomy column? And I believe it is also the fault of the educational system. We do not teach how to think. This is a very serious failure that may even, in a world rigged with 60,000 nuclear weapons, compromise the human future.

I maintain there is much more wonder in science than in pseudoscience. And in addition, to whatever measure this term has any meaning, science has the additional virtue, and it is not an inconsiderable one, of being true.

Occult Beliefs

Barry Singer
Victor A. Benassi

In the following article Barry Singer and Victor A. Benassi illustrate the social and scientific importance of understanding the occult; although they show these beliefs to be based on psychological and sociological rather than on rational determinants, they do not totally reject their validity. According to Singer and Benassi, media distortion, social uncertainty, and the deficiencies of human reasoning seem to be the basis of occult beliefs. They also maintain that occult phenomena are a possible index of fluctuations in religious belief or social dislocation. The article addresses the question of the origins and mechanism of the individual's occult beliefs and speculates about the social mechanisms that may have given rise to widespread involvement with the occult.

Reprinted from *American Scientist*, vol. 69, no. 1 (1981), pp. 49–55, by permission of the Scientific Research Society.

WHY IS AN UNDERSTANDING OF OCCULT BELIEFS scientifically and socially important? One reason is their current prevalence in Western societies. Occult beliefs have increased dramatically in the United States during the last two decades (Freedland 1972; Godwin 1972). Far from being a "fad," preoccupation with the occult now forms a pervasive part of our culture. Garden-variety occultisms such as astrology and ESP have swelled to historically unprecedented levels (Eliade 1976). Belief in ESP, for instance, is consistently found to be moderate or strong in 80–90 percent of our population (Gallup 1978; Polzella et al. 1975); in one survey it ranked as our most popular supernatural belief, edging out belief in God in strength and prevalence (Wuthnow 1978). Ouija boards overtook Monopoly as the nation's best-selling board game in 1967.

As indexed by audience tallies and book sales, more exotic occultisms such as spoon bending, the Bermuda Triangle, biorhythms, psychic healing, and hauntings have also increased dramatically in variety and popularity since the early 1960s. Von Dániken's book *Chariots of the Gods?*, a vivid account of ancient astronauts' bestowing their technology and spermatozoa upon human beings, has become the best-selling book of modern times. Occult beliefs are salient not only among the lay public, but also among college students, including those at some of our science-oriented campuses. The occult trend shows no signs of diminishing.

The current high level and strength of occult beliefs, which at least implicitly constitute a challenge to the validity of science and to the authority of the scientific community, may be a cause for our concern. This growing trend is also intrinsically of scientific interest as a psychological and sociological phenomenon. The psychological mechanisms involved in occult beliefs may represent more dramatic forms of some mundane pathologies of reasoning. To the extent that occult and mundane beliefs have similar determinants, the study of occult beliefs, which are at the outer limits of irrationality, may throw light on more ordinary reasoning pathologies.

From a sociological point of view, the occult phenomenon is of interest as a possible index of fluctuations in religious belief or social dislocation. Moreover, the study of occult beliefs may further our understanding of scientific belief systems as they are explicitly constructed to compensate for the cognitive shortcomings which characterize many occult beliefs. This article will address the question of the origins and mechanisms of the individual's occult beliefs, a topic which psychological research is beginning to illuminate. We will also speculate about the social mechanisms that may have given rise to the recent widespread involvement with the occult.

Let us make clear at the outset of this discussion that we do not assume the beliefs and practices termed "occult" or "paranormal" to be totally without validity. They seem rather to span a range from the objectively unsupportable at present to the demonstrably absurd. Therefore, to the extent that such beliefs are held widely and strongly, they are probably based on psychological and sociological rather than rational determinants.

A variety of methodological cautions are appropriate in this inquiry. It is likely that differing occult beliefs have different determinants. Evidence suggests, for instance, that those occult beliefs which are institutionalized and are organized around a social community of believers may serve functions similar to those of traditional religions, whereas other beliefs cluster with factors related to escapist entertainment, such as interest in fantasy and science fiction (Bainbridge 1978). Still others may be personally insignificant beliefs acquired desultorily through media misinformation. Determinants may contribute differently at various levels of strength of a particular belief. Further, it has been shown for astrology and spiritualism, for instance, that several disparate demographic populations tend to entertain these beliefs for differing reasons (Jahoda 1969; Robbins et al. 1978)

Research on occult beliefs has not reached the scope and precision necessary to address these complexities in full. A complete account of the rise in occult beliefs will have to explain the concomitant rise of such beliefs in other industrialized nations for which data are available (Jahoda 1969), and probably should also account for recent social movements which appear correlated with the occult trend, such as the development of a youth counterculture and the recent spread of pentecostal and charismatic religions through a considerable portion of the world. Social science has provided a number of plausible explanations for these social trends, but little relevant data. However, we believe we can identify at present a number of causal or contributing factors involved in occult beliefs, keeping in mind the strictures discussed above.

Media Promotion of the Occult

It is not clear how great a role promotion by the popular media played in starting the occult inflation of the early 1960s. The present treatment of the occult by the media, however, may account for much of the near universality of belief. The public is chronically exposed to films, newspaper reports, "documentaries," and books extolling occult or pseudoscientific topics, with critical coverage largely absent. Our most trusted and prestigious sources of information are no exception. When the layperson hears about New Zealand UFOs from Walter Cronkite or reads about new frontiers in psychic healing in a front-page article in the *Los Angeles Times* (1977), he has prima facie reasons for believing such phenomena valid. Such uncritical coverage may be due in part to the inherent difficulties of science reporting in a popular medium. However, media coverage of the occult may sometimes be deceptive and monetarily motivated. It is our impression that the public is not aware of the extent to which First Amendment privileges permit such practices. The public seems to trust the printed word implicitly.

Research has consistently shown that people attribute most of their occult beliefs to the popular media and/or to personal experiences (Evans 1973). In a survey of several hundred college students, we were surprised to find that "scientific media" was also listed as a source of occult beliefs—more frequently than popular media, personal experience, personal faith, or logical arguments. When the students were asked afterwards to list examples of the scientific media in question, however, not one mentioned even a single genuinely scientific source. Instead, *Reader's Digest* and the *National Enquirer* were occasionally cited as "scientific media," as were such films as *The Exorcist* and *Star Wars* (i.e., "the Force"). Television "documentaries" were also frequently mentioned, with the documentary "Chariots of the Gods?" being the single most frequently cited "scientific" source. Scientists have recently brought lawsuits against the television networks in protest of misleading occult documentaries. In response, the networks have claimed that their pro-occult coverage was formerly billed as "entertainment" rather than as a "documentary," and that the public can and does make this discrimination. Our evidence does not support these claims.

Although scientists who wish to rebut paranormal claims are sometimes denied access to the media, it also seems to be true that scientists have not extended themselves to gain media access and to issue public rebuttals. Those few scientists who do visibly protest may thus be perceived as stodgy and prejudiced isolates who have not yet climbed on the bandwagon of scientific acceptance of the occult. In addition, scientists have generally not cared to monitor or rebut occult claims issuing from their own academic institutions. Uncritical courses on occult topics are frequently found in the extension division of even our most reputable universities. In our experience the public invariably perceives the university as having then placed its stamp of approval upon the occultism, perhaps as having an entire department devoted to the topic, and understands that the extension instructor is "on the faculty."

The promotion of the occult by the popular media probably serves to heighten the general cognitive "availability" of the occult as an explanatory category in the culture. Puzzling events for which explanations might otherwise be conceived in terms of scientific phenomena or of fraud may tend to be explained as paranormal phenomena when the media bring this category so obtrusively to our attention.

Cognitive Biases and Heuristics

With occult beliefs currently so prevalent as to constitute, perhaps, part of what it means to be human, we might be justified in speculating on the basic quirks inherent in human psychological structure that support such beliefs. Current research in an area of cognitive psychology termed "cognitive biases and heuristics" has revealed deficits in human inference so universal and so stubborn that they can plausibly account for many of our errant beliefs, including occult ones. This recent spate of research, focusing on human problem-solving and judgmental processes, has resulted in an unflattering portrait of intuitive human reasoning (Nisbett and Ross 1980).

Briefly stated, the findings are that when presented with an array of data or a sequence of events in which they are instructed to discover an underlying order, subjects show strong tendencies to perceive order and causality in random arrays, to perceive a pattern or correlation which seems a priori intuitively correct even when the actual correlation in the data is counterintuitive, to jump to conclusions about the correct hypothesis, to seek and use only positive or confirmatory evidence, to construe evidence liberally as confirmatory, to fail to generate or to assess alternative hypotheses, and, having thus managed to expose themselves only to confirmatory instances, to be fallaciously confident of the validity of their judgments (Jahoda 1969; Einhorn and Hogarth 1978). In the analyzing of past events, these tendencies are exacerbated by selective memory and by failure to appreciate the pitfalls of post hoc analyses.

As an illustration of these tendencies, Wason (1960) asked subjects to try to discover a rule he had in mind for generating series of three numbers, where an example of the rule was the series "2, 4, 6." Subjects were to discover the rule by generating their own three-number series and receiving feedback on whether or not each series was an instance of the rule in question. The correct rule was "Any ascending sequence of whole numbers." Subjects typically generated sequences, such as "8, 10, 12, 14, 16, 18, etc.," repeatedly, for the duration of the experiment. They then expressed the rule as, for instance, "Even numbers increasing by two," and, having been consistently confirmed, were highly confident that this rule was the correct one.

When a judgment involves data that are probabilistic or minimally complex, people behave as if they do not possess the concept of probability, basing their estimates on a simple enumeration of positive instances rather than on the ratio of positive to negative instances. In addition, they adopt simplifying judgmental heuristics which can easily result in misconceptions (Tversky and Kahneman 1974).

Thus, an instance is judged to be a number of a larger class on the basis of whether or not it seems intuitively to "represent" that class, rather than on the basis of the known number of times the instance in fact falls either in or out of the class; or hypotheses are chosen simply on the basis of their "availability," circumstances which have made them more vivid or salient. For instance, personal experience is more potent in influencing judgments than is abstract data (Nisbett and Ross 1980). When tested in experimental situations, scientists and mathematicians as well as laypersons have displayed the above tendencies (Kahneman and Tversky 1973; Mahoney 1976).

On the whole, then, our everyday intuitions do not seem to serve us well in the understanding of probabilistic or complex patterns in our environment. Under what circumstances will such cognitive biases and limitations lead to occult beliefs? Given that through media or other influences occult ideas are highly available in the culture, and given that there is a tendency to trust intuitive rather than scientific judgments, Marks and Kammann (1979), Myers (1980), and Singer (1977) have shown how occult beliefs can easily be acquired and supported through our cognitive biases and heuristics. For instance, due to our cognitive quirks it is predictable that we will notice and be impressed by the coincidence of a dream and an external event, will overlook the disconfirming instances of failures to match our dreams with reality, and will have difficulty appreciating the concept of random occurrence as an explanation for the coincidences. Even when informed that such matches are predicted to occur occasionally on the basis of the large number of opportunities for dreams and external events to coincide by chance, we fail to appreciate intuitively the mathematics of rare events. A rare event is seen as one that seldom occurs, regardless of the number of opportunities for its occurrence. As a result of our natural tendency to misunderstand the probabilities involved in a match of dreams and reality, the hypothesis of clairvoyance is apt to be a more intuitively compelling explanation for such an occurrence than the concept of chance.

As another example of cognitive bias, an event that seems mysterious, or difficult to explain through ordinary causes, will seem to us to "represent" a mysterious cause. When an abandoned ship is found floating intact off the coast of Florida, causes such as freakish weather, geysers, or sharks are often dismissed because they seem too rare and therefore inherently unlikely. An explanation in terms of some malevolent occult force in the Bermuda Triangle, however, seems intuitively to represent or "fit" the event better. The representativeness heuristic thus fails entirely to consider the very large number of opportunities for rare but natural causes to determine the event.

In the "illusion of control," another common cognitive fallacy, a random process such as rolling of dice is perceived as under personal control to the extent that it seems to incorporate elements of skill. At Long Beach we have shown (Benassi et al. 1979) that subjects who were permitted practice sessions or active physical involvement in a dice-rolling task reported greater belief in their ability to produce psychokinesis than subjects who were instructed to "influence" the dice but were not permitted such involvement.

Experiments which have attempted to encourage disconfirmation of occult or illusory beliefs by motivating subjects to think through their judgments more carefully or by providing blatant disconfirmatory input have uniformly revealed an astonishing resistance to change of such beliefs. Marks and Kammann (1979), in attempting to reduce the impression of validity of generalized personality descriptions, provided subjects with negatively toned, highly specific, and inherently unlikely statements about their personality, but found only a slight reduction of belief in their accuracy.

In a series of experiments (Benassi and Singer 1981; Benassi et al. 1981) we arranged for an amateur magician to perform three psychic-like stunts—blindfold reading, teleportation of ashes, and mental bending of a metal rod—in front of six introductory psychology classes. Under one condition, the instructors skeptically introduced the performer as an alleged psychic, and under the other as an amateur magician. Belief was assessed through written feedback from the students to the performer. We expected to demonstrate a difference in occult belief depending on the introductory descriptions, but found instead that three-quarters of the subjects in both conditions believed strongly that the performer was psychic; more than a few, in fact, displayed an agitated conviction that the performer was an agent of Satan.

We then added a third condition in which the instructors quite emphatically repeated six different times that the performer was an amateur magician and that the students would be seeing only tricks, and not psychic phenomena. A written check attested that the students had heard and understood their instructors. This manipulation succeeded in reducing the occult belief, but only to the level where 50 percent of the class believed the performer to be psychic.

In follow-up studies with other subjects we provided neutral written descriptions of the performer and asked for an assessment of whether the performer was genuinely psychic. Again we found a majority of subjects judging that he was. We then asked whether magicians could also perform such stunts as described, and do so in identical fashion, and found near-unanimous agreement that they could; when asked how many people who performed such stunts were likely to be fakes and magicians, instead of genuine psychics, students agreed that the vast majority were likely to be tricksters and magicians. Finally, we asked students to re-estimate the likelihood that the particular performance described was in fact psychic, in light of the information they themselves had just generated. Once again the performer was judged to be psychic.

Such astonishing stubbornness of illusory and occult beliefs is typical rather than exceptional (Nisbett and Ross 1980). There may be several reasons for this intransigence. First, our intuitive reasoning errors may be like visual illusions. At some abstract level we may suspect that our perceptions are in error, but the error remains just as intuitively compelling. To the extent that we get "lost in the details" of a mental problem, as was probably the case with our subjects who watched or read about our magic act above, the problem becomes increasingly difficult to reason about abstractly. Second, to the extent that our cognitive structuring of our environment is "theory-driven," interpreted through a personal hypothesis, we may be all but blind to any evidence disconfirming our theory.

Finally, in the laboratory reasoning tasks described above, our subjects may not be strongly motivated to reason and behave at their rational best. If we had told them that they must reason accurately or be taken out and shot in the morning, they might have performed better. It may be that occult beliefs, both in the laboratory and in everyday life, surface mainly when they entail little personal cost to the believer. The following section discusses such motivational factors in occult beliefs.

Environment and Motivation

Studies in the laboratory and in naturalistic settings have indicated that, in general, superstitions (including occult beliefs) are likely to form under two conditions: environmental uncertainty (roughly conceived as the product of the unpredictability and the magnitude of an event) and low "cost" of the superstition (Jahoda 1969). The erroneous belief may thus alleviate feelings of helplessness and anxiety under uncontrollable or unpredictable circumstances, and in this sense may be functional. Superstitions seldom supplant or intrude upon rational, empirical approaches, where such approaches will serve. In his classic example, the anthropologist Malinowski (1954) described the Trobriand islanders as showing no superstitious behavior when fishing in their lagoon, where the task was routine and the returns relatively certain, but much superstitious behavior when fishing in the open sea, a more uncertain and dangerous enterprise.

As a modern example, Gmelch (1978) has recently documented the plethora of superstitions surrounding batting (a highly uncertain activity) in baseball, and the absence of superstitions in fielding, where skill and practice can virtually guarantee success. Similarly, Malinowski noted superstitious ritual in the launching of South Sea canoes and the impressive development of the science of navigating them. The islanders had done all they could empirically and rationally in developing their sailing practices, and the added superstitious behavior "cost" little and probably allayed their anxiety. Malinowski has pointed out furthermore that the supernatural and the empirical were typically emphatically compartmentalized from each other: "The body of rational knowledge and the body of magical lore are incorporated each in a different tradition, in a different social setting, and in a different type of activity" (pp. 86–87). This deliberate distinguishing of the non-rational may serve to validate, through contrast, the general validity of rational approaches.

In inspecting modern occultisms, we find that most offer an alleged ability to increase predictability and control, especially under uncertain circumstances. Thus, Tarot cards, clairvoyance, or astrology allow us to "know" the future; biorhythms and psychic healing allow us to regulate our often capricious bodies and health. It is further clear that occultisms in this category "cost" little and do not make many demands on our lives. Despite their often fervidly avowed beliefs in psychic healing, the clients of a psychic surgeon do not go to the "healer" as their first choice, but usually after all else has failed; nor do law enforcement agencies seek the aid of psychics before they have attempted traditional police methods.

Moreover, as with superstitions in South Seas cultures, the occultisms are compartmentalized. On the personal level, people seem easily able to be less than rational in their occult beliefs while being hard-headed where rational approaches are strategic. We are willing to use astrology in determining our partners for social dating, because nothing else seems to work well, but would not contemplate trusting to the stars if we were making legal and financial arrangements with these same partners. On the societal level, and particularly in America, limited and scaled involvement with the occult may be achieved through commercialization—packaging of the occult as a commodity in graduated quantities. Thus, many occult beliefs seem to be instances of superstitious or magical thought patterns. Cognitive heuristics and biases may serve as a mental substructure which leads to and rationalizes the maintenance of such beliefs, while the circumstances under which they are maintained may be defined by how dearly they cost us.

An explanation in terms of environmental determinants for the rise in occult beliefs since the early 1960s must show that, like other superstitions, occult beliefs increase as a function of environmental uncertainty, and that uncertainty has in fact increased in the last two decades. To begin with, we do have evidence that many occult beliefs are a function of shifting levels of environmental uncertainty. For example, Hyman and Vogt (1979) have shown that the practice of water dowsing was more prevalent in locations where finding water was difficult, and Sales (1973) has found that astrology beliefs increased in the United States during the years of the Depression. Lamar Keene (1976, pp. 70–71), who was once a famous and fraudulent medium, writes: "All mediums would agree. . . . Wars, depressions, personal and national disasters spell prosperity for us. The pres-

ent economic stresses in the United States are good news for mediums."

There is also evidence that environmental uncertainty in the United States and other Western countries has increased markedly since the early 1960s.

Constructing a working definition of variables such as "environmental uncertainty" at the level of a society is a decidedly complex and ambiguous task. Like the subjects in our experiments, we can find confirming evidence through post hoc analyses, depending on how assiduously we search for it and on the liberality of our interpretations. It is clear, however, that social change, which may have resulted from or given rise to feelings of uncertainty, has been marked since 1960. The past two decades have seen a decline of membership in the traditional religions in the United States and Europe, though not a decline in private religious belief; increased membership in fundamentalist, charismatic, and pentecostal religions; a proliferation of cults, paganism, and Eastern religions; a 29 percent rise in belief in the Devil; the development of a youth counterculture; disruption of traditional patterns in marriage and the family; a feminist movement; an alternative lifestyles movement and change in sexual ethics; the development of a drug culture; and the rise of a "human potential movement" (Glock and Bellah 1976; Wuthnow 1976).

These social trends overlap with the occult belief trend not only in time, but also in structural characteristics and in populations (Gallup 1976; Greeley 1975; Jahoda 1969; Johnson 1979; Wuthnow 1978). The evidence thus suggests that social trends may have caused, or may share causes with, the rise in occult beliefs. A long and unpopular war, political assassinations, and other events of the turbulent 1960s may have contributed to such trends. Other plausible determinants of these social changes include the recent increase in the youth population cohort, a long-term economic decline dating from 1965, and a devaluing of conventional meaning systems through the rising influence of social science. Thus, the prima facie case for an increase in environmental uncertainty since the early 1960s, while only partially substantiated in concrete detail, is a strong one.

Beit-Hallahmi (n.d.) has pointed out that occultisms are not the only form of magical belief that has recently increased. The National Enquirer, which has become one of the best-selling newspapers in the United States, features articles not only on UFOs and

ESP, but also on various miracle discoveries in health, dieting, cure of disease, and getting rich quickly. Whether such ideas are labelled "occult" is somewhat arbitrary, but they have similar superstitious qualities.

We have so far neglected to consider a category of occult beliefs that do make demands on believers' lives and extract heavy costs of belief. Occultisms such as Scientology, Theosophy, Satanism, and UFO cults resemble religions rather than ordinary superstitions, and there is evidence that they serve needs usually associated with religions, such as affiliation, moral direction, and an occasion for profound emotion (Bainbridge and Stark 1980). Such belief systems often demand total commitment, monetary and otherwise, from their members.

An explanation for the recent proliferation of such cults is then best couched in terms of developments in American religious practices. Stark and Bainbridge, at the University of Washington, have provided such an explanation, along with compelling documentation. A marked decline in membership in traditional religions over the past two decades has coincided with their theological retreat toward a more abstract, less personal deity, and with an orientation of these religions toward civil rights and other secular concerns, with consequently less investment in individual parishioners' needs (Bainbridge and Stark 1980; Stark and Bainbridge 1981; Glock and Bellah 1976). However, private belief in and need for the supernatural has not declined, and thus we infer that there has been a large population pool available for conversion to new, unorthodox religions, including those of the occult variety. In support of this interpretation, Bainbridge and Stark (1980) have found a negative correlation between membership in organized occult groups or reports of mystic psychic experiences, and membership in traditional religions.

In general, we do not adopt superstitions or fall prey to cognitive biases in areas where empirical approaches bear fruit and where illusory beliefs would be costly. As Sagan (1979, p. 93) observes, "A people going to war may sing over their spears in order to make them more effective. If there ever have been people who felt they could defeat an enemy in war merely by singing and who therefore dispensed with spears, we have not heard of them; they were, undoubtedly, all dispatched."

In areas where judgments under uncertainty are important, we self-consciously avoid biases and fallacies. Thus, we have institutionalized elements of the scientific method, including meticulous weighing of alternative hypotheses, into police work, criminal law, and medical diagnosis. Under conditions of uncertainty, and where the cost of illusory belief is low, however, superstitions will surface and will be maintained through the aid of our somewhat faulty cognitive apparatus. In the last two decades it has become socially permissible to entertain occult beliefs as well as many other deviant beliefs and values, and conventional meaning systems and social orders have changed rapidly, perhaps generating widespread feelings of uncertainty and occult beliefs in the process. In addition, occultisms in the form of religious cults have moved into the void created by the recent decline of traditional religions.

Deficiencies in Science Education

There remains the question of how people maintain occult beliefs in the face of contravening scientific opinion. Granted that the popular media present a distorted picture, and that dependence upon our intuitive cognitions can also result in occultisms. The public nevertheless does seem to recognize that science emphatically rejects most occultisms. The layperson usually accepts scientific opinion unquestioningly, even when it is strikingly counter to his own intuitive understandings, as in the case of the atomic structure of matter or the astronomy of the solar system. Why are occult beliefs an exception to this customary deference to scientific authority?

One general explanation rests on the observation that people seem adept at compartmentalizing incongruent beliefs. We can comfortably live with disparate scientific, religious, and common sense approaches to different beliefs, and employ the belief approach most suitable to the personal need at hand. Personal needs which support occult beliefs may include, for instance, a need to assert the validity of one's own common-sense judgment vis-à-vis scientific "authority," needs for feelings of control and predictability, and a need for affiliation with a religious community. If the need to maintain an irrational belief outweighs any cost associated with maintaining it, the fact that the belief is not rational or scientifically supportable does not usually enter the equation. If cognitive dissonance does occur in maintaining an occult belief in spite of scientific debunking, any number of simple rationalizations, such as "Scientists are prejudiced about paranormal phenomena," will serve to reduce the cognitive tension. It is thus not really inexplicable that widespread occult beliefs exist within our most scientifically advanced societies.

Nevertheless it is our impression that the occult trend cannot be attributed wholly to innate cognitive flaws and emotional needs, but that current practices in the field of science education itself facilitate the rationalizing and compartmentalizing of occult beliefs. We have examined three major aspects of this problem.

First, from elementary school through graduate training, science seldom seems to be taught as a cognitive tool, a way of reaching deeper understanding of our environment. It is taught instead as a set of facts and concepts to be acquired by the same rote methods used in other academic subjects (Godfrey 1979). Even at graduate schools, research methodology appears to be taught as a set of advanced laboratory techniques, specific to the subject matter at hand. From elementary school onward the student does not seem to learn about the validity of scientific approaches vis-à-vis his intuitive understandings, but is simply heavily socialized to accept certain counterintuitive facts—the earth is round and rotates, matter is structured atomically—as items of culturally given common sense. Science is taught in the context of a specific, often technical subject matter, such as chemistry or botany; religious claims, occult claims, everyday problems are seldom examined in the science classroom. The student is thus encouraged to compartmentalize science as a set of facts or at best a dry, technical methodology within a limited number of narrow domains, and to trust his intuitions in the larger spheres remaining. The occult is then naturally viewed as outside the domain of science, to be apprehended intuitively instead.

Second, many occult claims could be countered with even an elementary knowledge of scientific facts, but even elementary knowledge may be largely lacking. Morison (1969) has questioned whether science has in fact had any effect in raising the cognitive sophistication of the lay public above prehistoric levels, and suggested as one test asking people whether all objects fall at the same rate. We have tested hundreds of college sophomores over the past several years (Singer 1977) with the problem of estimating the duration of flight of a 4-lb and a 2-lb lead weight dropped simultaneously from the same 16-ft height. Over half the students gave different estimates for the flight durations of the two weights. Fifteen percent gave estimates in the range of 4–50 seconds, perhaps envisioning them floating down like paper airplanes. On the same test we found that over half the students did not know that water in a tipped glass remains level, and many believed that islands float in the ocean and that the moon remains fixed in the sky over them, but is only visible at night. This is not a useful armamentarium for evaluating occult claims.

Third, many students have the impression that science is entirely subjective and unable to assess or predict the validity of ideas, apparently on the basis of limited exposure to philosophers such as Polanyi, Hansen, and Kuhn. In presenting perspectives on science in our classrooms, we have perhaps overdone the critical view of the validity of our knowledge. In a series of paradoxical confusions, students attribute more empirical validity to philosophy than to science itself, and the fact that science "changes its mind" is regarded as a totally discrediting weakness. We do not read these philosophers as subscribing to the total subjectivity of science, and we do not believe they would subscribe to such a position. It would seem a service to speak more plainly and more assertively about science's track record.

One benefit of studying the mechanisms of occult beliefs is that we can thereby highlight the characteristics of science, considered as a belief process. That is, we can look at science as a cognitive system deliberately constructed to avoid or compensate for the mechanisms involved in occult beliefs. For instance, we can say that science in theory trusts data and distrusts intuition, generates alternative hypotheses, systematically attempts disconfirmation of favored hypotheses, uses mathematically calculated probabilities, and conscientiously engages in self-examination to determine whether values and motives are influencing beliefs. The question then arises whether the compensatory mechanisms of science are as comprehensive and effective as is feasible. Although the scientific enterprise is obviously successful, we have evidence that its compensatory mechanisms are not complete.

Einhorn and Hogarth (1978), Mahoney (1976), and Kahneman and Tversky (1973) have all found confirmatory cognitive biases, at a level approaching that of a layperson's, in scientists and mathematicians who were administered simple conceptual problems. Recent work in the psychology of science, particularly that of Mahoney (1976) and Mitroff (1974), has demonstrated the operation of confirmatory bias in actual scientific processes. In our own discipline, psychology, we have seen numerous cases of scientists operating in ways which seem intuitively correct to them on the basis of their personal experience, though objectively contraindicated. For example, scientifically trained clinicians continue to rely on personal interviews and clinical judgment in prediction and diagnosis of mental illness, despite twenty years of consistent evidence that simple actuarial techniques are more predictive (Dawes 1979).

Some scientists develop occult beliefs. Surveys have indicated, for example, that over half the natural and social scientists in the United States believe ESP to be established or likely (*Psychology Today* 1978; Wagner and Monnet 1979) and are either unaware of the small fraction of research psychologists who hold such a view, or convinced that their own intuitive understandings are somehow more correct than the scientific ones in this case. In addition, now as throughout the history of science there is a sprinkling of scientists, including eminent ones, who have been duped by the fraudulent practices of "psychics."

The evidence just presented raises the question of the locus of the norms of science and the mechanisms by which they are maintained. It is quite possible, for instance, that scientific rules of belief formation operate primarily at a system level. Such rules may affect scientists' cognitive behavior or public statements under particular contingencies as enforced by the scientific community, but this public attitude may not be completely internalized by the scientist as an individual. There may be tensions between the beliefs uttered by the scientist as a professional person operating within a professional community and those entertained by him as a private person who is still humanly prone to the flaws of intuition. Such tensions may substantively affect the conduct of science or the formation of scientific belief.

How should the scientific community respond to the upsurge of popular interest in the occult? The interest in occultism and pseudoscience may in fact be dangerously distracting from rational solutions to social problems and corrosive to rationality, as some scientists have feared. It seems to us, however, that occult beliefs are more symptomatic of dislocating social trends than causal of them, and that they are usually compartmentalized well enough that they do not in themselves corrupt a practical rationality, any more than does a monotheistic faith or a belief that Moses parted the Red Sea. The most serious side effect of occult beliefs may be that they are inherently discrediting of science, although the evidence does not indicate that this outcome has been realized. While recent public disaffection with science and technology is often mentioned as a stimulus to occult belief, hard evidence for such disenchantment is lacking (Marshall 1979). Further, correlational studies have more often than not found no relation between negative feelings toward science and occult beliefs (Wuthnow 1978).

The most convincing rationale for a scientific response to the occult preoccupation may simply be scientific self-integrity. The following steps seem appropriate: issuing rebuttals to fraudulent or unsubstantiated occult claims—far from being beneath our dignity, this can be considered a compelling social responsibility; increasing the availability to the media of scientific expertise on the occult; helping the public recognize which media sources speak with scientific authority and which do not; treating occult concepts in science education, including perhaps, introductory textbooks; examining policies relating to occult courses and concepts that appear in the name of a university, and relating to the selection of books and films for public school reading and science classes; and reorienting science education so that science becomes more personal, more life-oriented, and more easily apprehended as a highly useful mode of inquiry.

Amulets and Anthropology: A Paranormal Encounter with Malay Magic

Raymond L. M. Lee

In this article Raymond L. M. Lee observes that many anthropologists reject personal accounts of the paranormal because they fail to reach the standards of scientific validity. Using his personal experience with Malay magic as an example, Lee attempts to describe the emotional intensity of encounters with the paranormal, believing that is through such intense encounters that anthropology can better understand the ritual control of emotion.

The first part of the article explains why anthropologists have typically failed to indicate in their ethnographies whether they themselves believe in the paranormal events they have observed in the field, concentrating instead on the more mundane aspects of the social structure surrounding extraordinary events. However, Michael Harner's work with the Jivaro of Ecuador and Bruce Grindal's field experience with the Sisala of Ghana are briefly noted as exceptions to the rule.

The heart of the article focuses on Malay magic and Lee's personal experience with two Malay graduate students who are obsessed with the cultivation of mystical powers for practical purposes. As Lee is drawn deeper and deeper into Malayan magic, the reader will sense the conflict facing the anthropologist who endeavors to experience personally the paranormal phenomena of the culture being studied.

. . .

THERE IS A GROWING CANDIDNESS IN ANTHROPOlogical reports of fieldwork experiences. Such reports appeared occasionally since the mid-1950s, but dating approximately from the posthumous publication of Malinowski's field diaries in 1967, there has been a steady output of writings on personal reactions to varying field conditions (e.g., Freilich 1970; Golde 1970; Beteille and Madan 1975; Lawless et al. 1983). As Nash and Wintrob (1972) suggest, these writings reflect a decline in naive empiricism and recognize the surreptitious impact of personal experiences on a fieldworker's theoretical and methodological outlook. The reports comprise unpretentious and often moving accounts of various trials and tribulations in the field; some have linked personal experiences to ethical issues, but few have attempted to evaluate the effects of the experiences on the people studied and the researcher's own professional role. Rarer indeed are accounts of personal encounters with extraordinary phenomena as these phenomena relate to an understanding of the cultural system under study and the researcher's own beliefs. A few such accounts have appeared (Harner 1980; Grindal 1983) but the controversies that the works of Carlos Castaneda (1968, 1971, 1972, 1974, 1977, 1981) have created will probably prevent a flood of similar accounts. The [numbers of] anthropologists who have encountered extraordinary events in the field are, one assumes, small. Being few, they are reluctant perhaps to share their experiences in print, lest they offend the gatekeepers of the discipline or risk their reputations as scientists. Those who write do so with great trepidation. Long (1974: vii), for example, related how an eminent colleague expressed considerable anxiety over his proposed paper on parapsychology and anthropology. Grindal (personal communication,

September 1983) admitted it was with some hesitance that he wrote his paper on witnessing death divination.

Yet such accounts are highly valuable in illuminating various aspects of the subjectivity-objectivity problem in fieldwork and the accompanying ethical issues. Because paranormal encounters are highly emotional events, it is important to ask how such experiences affect the self-consciousness of the ethnographer and thereby alter his trained objectivity in conducting systematic observations. Can the experiences be harnessed to advance ethnographic knowledge and practices? As relevant as these questions are to a discipline that has become introspective of its methods of data collection, before I examine them, I will briefly consider the status of the paranormal in anthropology.

The Paranormal in Anthropology

It is probably inappropriate to say that the study of the paranormal comprises an integral aspect of anthropology. Mainstream anthropological studies of magic and witchcraft are concerned more with the social relations of such beliefs rather than their experiential aspects. While these studies provide minute details about magical practices, they avoid questions of authenticity. In fact, such questions are regarded as irrelevant, as most anthropologists perceive their task as unraveling the rules of social relationships in a particular cultural system. These works seldom indicate whether the anthropologists concerned have witnessed extraordinary events in the field and actually believe in their occurrences. A mundane focus on social structure forms an accepted language of discourse within the profession that screens out the more personal dimension of an extraordinary encounter in the field.

This professional rule was challenged in 1968 when Castaneda published an account of his initiation into Yaqui shamanism. To make his work more acceptable, Castaneda added an etic section on social structure. Readers recognize that the second section was Castaneda's forced effort to reconcile his emic approach with the etic paradigm of consensus anthropology. This book and its sequels were generally received with much cynicism and skepticism, and in the issuing debates accusations ranged from fraudulent scholarship to a lack of cultural sensitivity (see Wilk 1977; Beals 1978; De Mille 1976, 1980; Noel 1976; Murray 1979). The hostile reactions to

Castaneda's purported experiences provide ample evidence that a personal description of the paranormal threatens the scientific credibility claimed by denizens of the discipline (Maquet 1978).

The rejection of Castaneda's works by the scientific community has not prevented certain anthropologists from reporting their experiences with the paranormal. One of these reports is Michael Harner's (1980) account of his journey into the shamanic world of the Jivaro Indians of Ecuador. The Conibo Indians of Peru had introduced Harner to the hallucinogen *ayahuasca* in 1961. Three years later, he returned to Ecuador to study with Akachu, a renowned Jivaro shaman. Although his autobiographical text is not as rich as Castaneda's description, Harner highlights the problem of the formal separation of the anthropologist's subjective self from his objective, observing self. Seemingly, the paranormal experience he witnessed rendered that conventional bifurcation of roles illusory. This transformation is clearly suggested in Harner's admission that he is now a practicing shaman who seeks to disseminate his knowledge to the uninformed: "Now it seems time to help transmit some practical aspects of this ancient human legacy to those who have been cut off from it for centuries" (Harner 1980: 19).

While Harner deliberately participated in Jivaro shamanism, Bruce Grindal (1983) accidentally stumbled upon the resurrection of the dead in Sisala mortuary rituals. In a brutally frank description of his experiences in Tumu, Ghana, in 1967, Grindal records his descent into the heart of Sisala culture through a particular incident in which he witnessed the raising of a corpse by Sisala praise singers. "Stretching from the amazingly delicate fingers and mouths of the *goka*, strands of fibrous light played upon the head, fingers, and toes of the dead man. The corpse, shaken by spasms, then rose to its feet, spinning and dancing in a frenzy. As I watched, convulsions in the pit of my stomach tied not only my eyes but also my whole being into this vortex of power" (Grindal 1983: 68).

In recalling his participation in this paranormal event, Grindal notes that episodes of "great passion and mystery" possess a quality that eludes their preservation on tape or film. The very act of witnessing their occurrences necessitates such intense involvement by the observer that the question of detachment recedes beyond the pale of scientific objectivity.

In these personal reports of paranormal encounters in ethnographic fieldwork, both Harner and Grindal articulate well the common theme that phenomenological subjectivity of a paranormal experience defies the canons of objective verification. Both hold back on discussing the theoretical and ethical implications of their experiences. Similarly, two earlier attempts at bridging the gap between parapsychology and anthropology (Angoff and Barth 1974; Long 1974) also bypassed these issues in favor of discussing the application of parapsychological principles to anthropological research. If the reports by Harner and Grindal suggest a reexamination of the marginal status of the paranormal in anthropology, they also suggest it is increasingly difficult to ignore these issues or to shelve them indefinitely. Consequently, using my experiences with Malay magic as background material, I will attempt to address these theoretical and ethnical concerns.

A Note on Malay Magic

The early writings on Malay magic—as exemplified in the works of Skeat (1900), Gimlette (1915), and Winstedt (1951)—treat it largely as folkloric in content. The early ethnographers of Malay magic were mainly British colonial officers, stationed on the Malay Peninsula, who were fascinated, and perhaps even charmed, by a belief system so radically different from theirs. As folklore Malay magic was perceived as an ontological reality that existed only within Malay culture. Little in these writings suggests that the authors believed in a transcendental nature of Malay magic and that its effects could be felt beyond the confines of Malay culture and particularly in theirs. In other words, Malay magic constituted a separate reality to be empirically investigated, but it did not possess an isomorphic correspondence to the belief system of the British ethnographers. Formed in this matter, these ethnographies may be exploited to explicate abstract theoretical ideas that are relevant to Western-trained anthropologists but are quite meaningless in the world view of the Malay natives.

The construction of such theoretical knowledge, based mainly on the British colonial ethnographies, has been accomplished by Endicott (1970). He employs structural analysis to map out general abstract principles that transcend what he calls the traditional order, that order which is specific to the cultural realm of the natives. The function of his exercise is to translate, or reduce, particular categories of culture, that is, elements of Malay magic, into universal categories of logic. Such theoretical efforts do not disavow the reality of the natives' belief system but subtly insist on the subordination of that belief to an overarching logical system. Thus, the contents of Malay magic are analyzed from a distance in order to extract general principles of organization that are assumed to be applicable to magical practices in other parts of the world.

The impersonal character of such writings is not unique to Malay magic. Works on magic in Asia, the Americas, and Oceania exhibit a similar quality. As they are concerned with elucidating the tenets of a particular belief system or with building a broad data base for comparative purposes, I do not dispute the validity of these analyses. I argue that paranormal experiences with magic, however, should they occur, are relevant to anthropological considerations because they provide an important corrective to the abstractive thrust in theoretical endeavors and demonstrate that other dimensions of magic await our exploration.

A Personal Encounter with Malay Magic

In the summer of 1977, I began research on Malay spirit possession. The Malaysian mass media referred to the phenomenon as mass hysteria. This term was used to describe the manifestations of bizarre behavior that occurred frequently among Malay females in factories and schools. The drama of spirit possession (*kena hantu* or *dirasuk hantu* in Malay) is often perceived by many westernized Malaysians as a cultural anachronism that afflicts mainly uneducated villagers or individuals trapped in their superstitions. That such unseemly, primitive behavior could occur in a modern context, such as a factory or school, puzzled those unable to grasp the significance of their cultural meanings. There was much public concern about the continuous disruption of factory and school routines.

At the beginning, I relied mainly on newspaper reports for information on incidents of mass hysteria; however, I soon discovered that I was limited to a post hoc strategy of interviewing informants after the bizarre incidents had already occurred. As my method entailed painstaking patience in obtaining leads and the cooperation of bewildered witnesses, progress was slow. After the first two months, I decided to broaden my strategy to include formal discussions with Malay acquaintances on their perceptions of spirit possession and mass hysteria.

I first approached Hassan and Yusoff (pseudonyms), two Malay graduate students in sociology in their twenties whom I had known for several years, to find out what educated Malays with social science backgrounds thought about spirit possession. Although all Malays are Muslims by birth, not all can be said to be imbued with the same degree of devoutness. During my first years of acquaintance with Hassan and Yusoff, I had not gained an impression of them as pious Muslims. Unbeknownst to me, their religious attitudes had changed radically, and they were active participants in a *tarekat*, an esoteric Muslim brotherhood inspired by Sufi teachings (see al-Attas 1963).

This change, as I discovered later, resulted partly from their personal problems. Both were worried about the progress of their theses, and lack of financial support sharpened their worry. Yusoff was particularly depressed about the loss of a university fellowship because of his alleged involvement in a campus scandal. All these events occurred during an Islamic revival in the country. Hassan and Yusoff sought to alleviate their problems through fervent participation in Islamic activities. Both of them claimed that they had chosen this path to atone for their sins. Neither displayed, however, the fanaticism said to be characteristic of Islamic fundamentalism. As members of a tarekat, they were more engrossed in the mystical and magical aspects of Islam. They seemed more interested in learning arcane techniques for manipulating life-forces from their guru than in converting non-Muslims. At the time I approached them, both had practiced the mystical arts for more than a year. Yusoff had also accumulated a large collection of books on Islam and Western occultism. Although they were novices in Islamic mysticism and had been sworn to secrecy by their guru, my inquisitiveness did not threaten them. On the contrary, they eagerly sought a working relationship with me. This willingness to share their knowledge may be attributed partly to their newly found sense of power.

Initially, our conversations revolved around why women in particular were vulnerable to spirit possession. Their theories did not differ greatly from the Malay folk explanations reported by earlier ethnog-raphers, that is, women had weaker life-forces (*lemah semangat*) and therefore were more susceptible than men to attacks by roaming spirits. After several leisurely conversations on this subject, Hassan and Yusoff began to drift to topics they considered more exciting. Their discussions centered on the awe-inspiring feats by members of the tarekat brotherhood who through prescribed chants and self-discipline had developed sufficient inner strength to raise their levels of pain tolerance. It became clear to me that Hassan and Yusoff no longer sought atonement of their sins as a goal but were obsessed with the cultivation of mystical powers for practical purposes. Their obsession intrigued me. I had not entered into this relationship as a skeptic to expose their religious idiosyncrasies but with an open mind to tap the sources of their beliefs. It was this curiosity that led me to move from my inquiry on mass hysteria to a gradual involvement with their obsession.

As they steered my attention to their experiences in the tarekat, they divulged various techniques for entering other dimensions of consciousness. One concerned projecting one's consciousness outside the body during sleep—they even used the parapsychological term, out-of-body experiences. This could be accomplished, they told me, by focusing one's awareness on the critical moment of transition from wakefulness to sleep. They claimed they had mastered this technique but were still in the experimental stages of projecting their consciousness beyond the confines of their bedrooms. They also suggested how to effect subtle shifts in visual focus so as to see beyond the normal human range.

It was never clear who had taught them these techniques—their guru or someone else—but I did not probe for fear of breaching their trust in me. When they were convinced that I was not a skeptic, they offered to introduce me to a colleague who allegedly possessed powers more advanced than theirs. Their friend, Abdullah (a pseudonym), was also a social science graduate and tarekat member and a bank officer. He claimed the ability to cure headaches with his hands. I was told that in one incident he treated a fellow bank officer by literally pulling the pain out of her head and in the process caused paper clips and other metallic objects to fly off the desks. Several bank employees witnessed this event. Abdullah also could project his consciousness a considerable distance. It was alleged that on several occasions he had frightened his wife at home by projecting his astral form from his office.

When I met Abdullah, his first question to me was, "Do you have a headache?" Although he was eager to demonstrate his powers, he was reluctant to discuss their sources. As a stranger, I felt it was improper to ask him too many questions about his techniques. The meeting with Abdullah was unfruitful. Years later, I learned that he had stopped practicing the mystical arts. A practitioner of these arts is always instructed to develop and maintain sufficient powers to keep malevolent spirits at bay. Abdullah had not been able to fulfill this requisite. Abdullah's presence had attracted strange forces that disturbed his wife and family. In the end he had no choice but to terminate his mystical practices.

It was in this beguiling atmosphere that I found myself drawn deeper and deeper into Hassan's and Yusoff's obsessions. A die-hard positivist would have asked them to produce concrete proof of their claims, but I intuitively sensed that all rapport would be lost if I demanded such proof. My inquiry could only be maintained by an unqualified acceptance of their beliefs. I knew I was straying from my research goals, but I saw my association with Hassan and Yusoff as part of my effort to understand the more recondite aspects of the Malay religious world view. However, I did not request an introduction to their guru or participation in their tarekat because that would have entailed my conversion to Islam, a step I was unprepared to take. At the same time, if I did not take that critical step, the scope of my inquiry would remain limited. Hassan and Yusoff sensed my dilemma and graciously avoided pressuring me to become a Muslim. They occasionally tempted me with subtle hints about the advantages of conversion, but I was resolute in my decision to remain a non-Muslim.

Hassan and Yusoff continued to provide me with information concerning their mystical sojourns. As an outsider, I was unable to evaluate the authenticity of their claims. Acting as if they wanted to dispel doubts about their abilities, Hassan and Yusoff encouraged me vigorously to practice what they had taught me. Initially, as I was concerned about violating the rule of objectivity in fieldwork, I felt awkward getting personally involved in their mystical practices. As my association with them became more intense, however, so did my curiosity. After a month, and having only their verbal instruction, I made some attempts to imitate their practices at home. As they had not offered it, I was reluctant to request personal assistance. Since I lacked patience and the proper mode of concentration, I had no initial success. I soon discovered it was extremely difficult to maintain a state of alertness at transition between waking consciousness and sleep, and consequently, I kept failing to achieve an out-of-body experience.

Using another technique, however, I was surprised that I quickly developed an ability to shift my visual focus to see what appeared to be my own aura in the mirror. I was thrilled to be on the threshold of discovering other levels of consciousness. My friends had not lied. I became convinced that the essential requirement for further progress was the right attitude toward the paranormal.

As I continued practicing these techniques, I suddenly became aware that I was leaving behind a familiar, taken-for-granted world. My exuberance gave way to darker emotions, and I realized that, unprepared, I was venturing into other dimensions of consciousness. I became terribly frightened.

For nearly a week, I fluctuated between the ecstasy of my new experiences and the fear of the unknown. These conflicting emotions tore at my sanity, and I came to have a sense of desperation that I had never felt before. One evening I went in search of Hassan and Yusoff. I told them I was losing control of myself and I needed their guidance immediately. Hassan gave me a quizzical look, "You know," he said, "a few nights ago I had a strange dream. I dreamt that it was raining heavily outside my house and I was fast asleep. Suddenly, there was a loud knock on the door. I opened it and in the shadows stood a person pleading for help. I couldn't see his face. Then the dream ended. Now I know what that dream meant."

I did not know what to make of Hassan's interpretation of his dream. Did he possess powers of precognition? I was too confused to consider that question. Yusoff assured me that my sense of desperation was not unusual. "Many of us were like you," he emphasized. "When we were beginners, we were overcome with awe and joy. Then we became afraid of the unseen powers. But we had our guru to help us." He disappeared into the kitchen and returned with a glass of plain water. He handed me the glass and instructed me to drink the water quickly. No sooner had I drunk it than I felt a strong force penetrate my palate and in seconds reached my head. A strange warmth spread over me. I was stupefied and wondered aloud whether there was something in the drink. "There's nothing harmful in the water," Yusoff reassured me. "I didn't put anything in it. All I did was say a short prayer." I had heard of charmed water—what the Malays called *air jampi*—but until that night, its meaning had no empirical impact.

After a while I felt more at ease. It was not so much the drinking of Yusoff's air jampi that calmed me; rather, it was the company I had that night and the sympathy I received. We talked about emotions and magic, how it was impossible to practice magic without experiencing fear and later mastering it. Yusoff reiterated the importance of religion, of Islam, in establishing the psychological parameters for controlling fear. Stressing the beneficial effects of Islam on my mental well-being, he again invited me to become a Muslim. I told him this was a serious commitment that required careful consideration. He said he understood. Yusoff then gave me a bottle of air jampi and instructed me to sprinkle the water around my bedroom for protection during sleep. He also handed me a circular, metal amulet, which contained Islamic inscriptions. The amulet was attached to a black string with an intricate knot. "Before you sleep, undo the knot and tie the amulet around your neck. It will protect you throughout the night." With those final instructions, Yusoff and Hassan bade me goodnight.

At home, I felt like a scientist stripped naked of his objectivity and exposed to the powers of his subjects. I did exactly what Yusoff had told me.

Troubled by the events of the past weeks, I broke out in a sweat. I could not sleep. It was past midnight when I heard a high pitched sound, like a distant police whistle. I tossed and turned, but I could not shake off the sound. Then I realized that it was coming from the amulet, which was also emitting heat. Unlike the air jampi that I had drunk, this warmth did not spread over my body but was localized to the amulet. If the sound and the heat of the amulet were indicative of certain powers, what were they and where did they come from? I had no answers. Nor do I have now. In the early hours, I finally fell asleep. When I awoke, I removed the amulet, placed it on a table, and went into the bathroom. When I returned, I picked up the amulet and

was astonished to discover a large knot on the black string. It was the same intricate knot that I had undone last night. When I left the room, the amulet was lying with its inscribed side faced upward and the black string bunched around it. As the black string was made of smooth material, it did not get entangled. When I returned from the bathroom, the position of the amulet and string had not changed. But how did the knot get there?

Two possibilities flashed in my mind. Either someone had walked in unnoticed and cleverly knotted the string without changing its position, or some yet-to-be explained force was responsible. I had to rule out the first answer as everyone in my house had left for work. Quickly, I changed and rushed over to see Yusoff. I gave him the amulet and pointed to the knot. "The powers of the amulet are limited to a fixed number of hours. When they end, the knot returns of its own accord," Yusoff explained nonchalantly. I had no desire to probe further.

I knew that I had merely scratched the surface of a vast store of secret knowledge. The charmed water and the amulet were only an introduction to a body of beliefs and practices that now took on a different perspective for me. I could have become a Muslim, joined the tarekat, and experienced the enchantment of Malay magic, but for me the price was too high.

In Malaysia, Islam is seen as the religion of the politically dominant Malays, which demarcates them from the non-Malay populations, principally the Chinese and Indians. There are Malaysian Chinese and Indians who are Muslims by birth, but they are a minority. Those who convert to Islam often do so for political and economic reasons, and they frequently suffer ostracism from their ethnic communities. As a Malaysian Chinese, I felt that such a conversion not only implied a severance of my ethnic ties but also raised serious ethical questions concerning my motives. I weighed the consequences and found them too heavy.

After the episode with the amulet, I saw little of Hassan and Yusoff. Years later, I learned that they had become inactive in mystical practices. Hassan dropped out of school and got a job in a government department. Yusoff finished his thesis and became a government researcher. More than a year ago I ran into Yusoff. We said hello and made small talk. There was no mention of Malay magic. That belonged to the past.

Conclusion

Almost a decade has elapsed since the occurrence of those events. I have made no attempts to further understand them. The answers remain shrouded in mystery. Yet, I have not blocked them from my memory. They remain firmly etched in my mind and have indelibly changed my attitudes toward the practice of Malay magic. I can no longer treat Malay magic as merely a social and cultural practice. Its paranormal affects have an ontological basis that is not easily denied or explained away.

This does not necessarily imply that the social structural aspects of Malay magic are any less real or important than the paranormal. These two aspects are complementary. Unless we understand the sociocultural context or historical origins of particular magical chants, we are unable to grasp the relevance of their paranormal applicability. Because of the hard-nosed empiricist attitude, paranormal experiences among anthropologists are not frequent, however, and are not widely reported.

A consequence of the conventional attitude is the denial or repression of the overpowering emotions associated with the experience of paranormal events. These emotions provide important data; they are not only individually experienced but also the recipient and those around him interpret the emotions in particular ways. This interpretation of emotional states and the subsequent attempts at their management provide an important link between the phenomenology and the sociology of magic (see Winkelman 1982).

There is a qualitative difference between anthropological reports that rely on native, in-group members for information on magic and those that rely on the ethnographer's direct experience of magic. The information that local informants present may not necessarily stem from direct experiences and in fact may be many times removed from those experiences. On the other hand, an ethnographer's experience of intense emotions in paranormal encounters may provide direct glimpses into the affective core and, possibly, origins of particular magical rituals.

On the basis of my experiences, I argue that the juxtaposition of *awe* and *fear* in paranormal encounters contains such an overwhelming sensation that individuals seek its containment through the development of special ritual techniques. It is plausible that some magical rituals have evolved from highly motivated attempts to control spontaneous emotions arising from paranormal encounters. Over time, these attempts have become institutionalized into standardized ritual forms, which now conceal the emotional occurrence that gave them birth. To recover those original emotions requires a subjective approach.

There are currently no prescribed techniques on how such a subjective approach may be developed and utilized in the field. Ethnographers who encounter paranormal phenomena in the field are unprepared to deal with them. Consequently, the ethnographer's perception of certain events is unclear, and he is not alerted to the various dangers involved in his research. Anthropologists have to depend on their own resourcefulness or even seek the tutelage of traditional practitioners of magic for guidance into unchartered ethnographic realms. If anthropology is truly a science of human cultural experiences, however, then it must give unprejudiced consideration to the impact of the paranormal on people's lives. With such consideration, anthropology will have taken steps toward seeing the human side in the paranormal.

The Next Level: Heaven's Gate

Newsweek

The arrival of Comet Hale-Bopp was the sign they had been waiting for. On March 22, 1997, the first wave of suicides began. Within three days all thirty-nine members of the Heaven's Gate group near San Diego would be dead. In many ways the dynamics of the Heaven's Gate cult and its leader, Marshall Herff Applewhite, resembled various other cults that briefly flourished in recent years only to meet a tragic end: The Branch Davidians and the People's Temple of the Reverend Jim Jones come immediately to mind. One noteworthy difference between these earlier groups and Heaven's Gate is the latter's attachment to modern media and cyberspace. In addition to avidly watching Star Trek *and* The X-Files *for UFOs and other signs of "Higher Life," members combed the Internet for possible messages from other worlds. It was through the Internet that Heaven's Gate members determined a UFO was hidden somewhere in the tail of the Hale-Bopp comet.*

In this selection we learn how devotees were attracted to Heaven's Gate and how the charisma and prophecies of their leader were vital to the subordination of individual rights that ended in a mass suicide of its members (the "Next Level" refers to, in Applewhite's words, "what humans call dead"). This selection could have been placed as well alongside the Waco article in Chapter 3, "Shamans, Priests, and Prophets," due to the importance of a charismatic prophet in the founding and appeal of a millenarian group. Although there are many similarities between David Koresh's Waco group and Heaven's Gate, the differences are sufficient to merit inclusion of this selection in the book.

EXCEPT FOR THE STINK OF DEATH, EVERYTHING was neat and tidy. Police found no sign of struggle or even discomfort among the 39 corpses. Each member of the cult had followed the written instructions to "lay back and relax" after swallowing the phenobarbital-laced pudding chased with vodka. The cultists had apparently died in waves, 15 the first day, at least 15 the second and the survivors the third. Only the last two to go, a pair of women, still wore plastic bags over their heads. The rest lay quietly in their new black sneakers, under diamond-shaped purple shrouds.

There was an oddly theatrical aspect to the mass suicide near San Diego, Calif. The departed all packed overnight bags containing clothes, spiral notebooks and, for some reason, lip balm. Each of them left the earth with a five-dollar bill in their pockets, plus quarters—for what? Celestial pinball? Each wore a new pair of Nike running shoes—a play on the Nike slogan, "Just Do It"? Casual friends, who had found the cultists to be not grim but rather chipper and self-deprecating, wondered if the dead were slyly ridiculing the media storm that was sure to follow.

But only the demented mock their own demise. Quiet agonies of repression were hinted at by the coroner's finding that at least a half dozen of the men had been surgically castrated, included the cult's founder, Marshall Herff Applewhite. The members of the sect called Heaven's Gate had been taught to put aside lust and other earthly appetites and prepare for a Higher Kingdom. The men and women wore their hair close-cropped and their clothes loose and baggy, lest they show their sexuality. Their bodies were mere "containers" or "vehicles," and their occupants recoiled at the human touch. These were lost souls literally uncomfortable in their own skin, searching desperately for a home they could never find. Some had been gone so long that their families hardly missed them.

Suicide is normally the loneliest act, the ultimate alienation: There have been worse mass suicides, but probably not in America, and at Jonestown in Guyana in 1978, those who refused to drink the Kool-Aid were shot. What possessed this self-described "Next Level Crew" of 21 women and 18 men, ranging in age from 26 to 72, to go not only willingly, but apparently cheerfully? Judging from the abundant evidence—videotapes left behind, numerous written tracts and postings on the Internet—the followers of Heaven's Gate seem to have drunk from a delusional cocktail of just about every religious tradition and New Age escapist fantasy. They avidly watched old "Star Trek" episodes and "The X-Files" while cruising cyberspace looking for UFO sightings. It was from the Internet that the cult learned that a UFO was following in the slipstream of Comet Hale-Bopp. The comet's approach "is the 'marker' we've been waiting for—the time for the arrival of the space craft from the Level Above Human to take us home to 'Their World'," the cult warned in a "Red Alert" message on its World Wide Web home page.

In other ways, their chilling exit was timeless. Some experts compared Heaven's Gate to the Gnostics, early religious fanatics who felt imprisoned in their earthbound bodies. Anticipating the End Times predicted in the Book of Revelation, millennial groups have been trying to beat the rush to St. Peter's Gate for centuries. In the 16th century, whole villages of Christian "saints" self-immolated, hoping for salvation before the Fire. As the true millennium approaches in the year 2000, there will almost surely be more, and possibly more threatening, millennialists. Heaven's Gate baked luscious bourbon pound cakes and rum cakes (which they could not themselves indulge in) for their friends in the outside world. Neo-Nazis and Freemen, meanwhile, are stockpiling weapons.

The most important cause of death may have been the cult's guru. His personality has been compared to Mr. Rogers, but Herff Applewhite was a master manipulator. Indeed, the mass suicide itself may have been a bit of a con. Applewhite told his followers that he was very sick, that his body was "disintegrating," and there were rumors that he had only six months to live. Though news reports speculated that Applewhite was suffering from cancer, investigators told *Newsweek* that the autopsy shows no sign of a fatal disease.

Applewhite was driven by sexual demons. The son of a Presbyterian minister who wandered around Texas, Applewhite had been blessed with good looks and a powerful singing voice. As a music professor at the University of Alabama in the 1960s, he helped cut an album of the Crimson Tide fight song and seemed to enjoy life as a family man, with a wife and two kids. But the marriage broke up, and Applewhite left Alabama amid whispers of a homosexual affair. In that place and in that time, a homosexual would feel alienated indeed. He got a job teaching music in the late '60s at the University of St. Thomas, a small Roman Catholic school in Houston, where he produced upbeat musicals, including "Little Mary Sunshine." But college records show that Applewhite left in 1970 for "health problems of an emotional nature." Suffering from depression and shame, hearing "voices," he checked into a hospital, asking to be "cured" of his homosexual desires. He told his sister he had suffered a "near-death experience" after a heart attack, but he may actually have suffered from a drug overdose, according to Ray Hill, a radio-show host in Texas who knew Applewhite at the time. "He was kind of a Timothy Leary type," said Hill.

It was during this anguished time that he met his true life's companion, Bonnie Lu Trusdale Nettles, a nurse who dabbled in astrology and far-out religious movements. Bonnie left her husband and four children and headed for the hills with Applewhite. The relationship was apparently platonic; the two wished to shed all base desires. They had discovered that they had been infused with higher, heavenly spirits. "I'm not saying we are 'a Jesus,' it is not that beautiful, but it is almost as big," Nettles wrote her daughter, Terrie, then 20, in a letter examined by *Newsweek*. "I'm not kidding, baby, this is for real."

The pair gave each other silly nicknames—Tiddly and Wink, Guinea and Pig, Nincom and Poop, Tweedle and Dee, finally Do and Ti (mere notes in the celestial symphony)—to show that names mean nothing. But they also portentously called themselves The Two—after the two witnesses in the Book of Revelation who are slain by a beast from the depths before rising to heaven. Like Jesus Christ, Do and Ti believed they would be assassinated on earth and rise to heaven after three days in a cloud of light —a UFO.

In 1975, Do and Ti went by another set of nicknames: Bo and Peep. There were lost sheep in their flock, an assortment of hippies and dreamers and drifters who had shed their work and families to follow The Two, hoping to leave this mortal coil on a spaceship. Do was an appealing recruiter. "He had great enthusiasm, a total childlike innocence in his eyes and his bearing," said Albert Volpe, a Dallas handyman and artist who was in the cult in 1975. "Everything was very laid back. We were always in groups of two; this is how Jesus and his disciples worked." The cult members believed he was the one, a modern-day Christ.

Do asked his followers if they were ready to "walk out the door" of their lives and join him on an intergalactic voyage to a Higher Place. When the celestial transportation failed to arrive, most of his recruits slunk away, some bitterly accusing The Two of mind-control games. A raft of derisive publicity drove Do and Ti farther into the wilderness. Wandering from woodsy camps to suburban homes (sustained in part by the trust funds of wealthy followers), the small cult of fewer than 50 members who called themselves HIM (for Human Individual Metamorphosis) or the Total Overcomers Anonymous took re-education "classes" from Do and Ti. Anyone who wanted to leave was free to go. But those who stayed on at camp (called "Central") were subjected to a strict regimen. Pot and sex were outlawed. Followers had to check in with the leader every 12 minutes and sometimes wear hoods as they worked. Significantly, everyone was given a "check partner"—to guard against backsliding and independent thought. Doubters were sent to a "decontamination zone." Families were to be long forgotten.

When the trust-fund money ran out, cult members supported themselves with odd jobs and begging. Living conditions were often rustic and harsh. Tensions between cultists sometimes ran high. Applewhite had not yet resorted to castration to tame his urges. Instead, says Volpe, he had to create a "crucible effect" to stay celibate. "Bo and Peep wanted us to use our sexual tension to create the purifying heart that is necessary for spiritual enlightenment."

In 1985, Ti, who was then 57, "left her human vehicle," as Do later wrote. "To all human appear-ances, it was due to a form of liver cancer." Do was bereft; he realized that Ti "was definitely a more advanced [older] member of the Next Level." He wanted to join her—but perhaps not right away. In 1993, his cult re-emerged, now known as Heaven's Gate. It is not clear why Applewhite decided to go public. Possibly, he saw the Internet as a new vehicle that would allow him to spread the word. But he announced his return in an old-fashioned newspaper ad in *USA Today* that declared "UFO Cult Resurfaces with Final Offer." It was, the ad beckoned, "the last chance to advance beyond human." The cult talked of its philosophical bonds with other millennial groups and self-appointed messiahs, including the Branch Davidians, the Unabomber, the Freemen and the Solar Temple—a group that has conducted three mass suicides since 1994 in Europe and Canada for a death toll of 70. Heaven's Gate did not condone the methods of these groups, but Do's cult agreed on the common enemy—a corrupt world whose institutions and religions had been seized by Lucifer, or "Lucy," as Do sometimes called Satan.

Heaven's Gate was more comfortable in the cyberworld. Having mastered the Internet on its searches for UFOs and other signs of Higher Life, cult members had developed considerable computer expertise. In about 1996, Heaven's Gate started a business called Higher Source Contract Enterprises to design Web pages. With cheap rates (as low as one quarter the going rate) and up-to-date, if not terribly creative, design, Higher Source attracted clients ranging from the San Diego Polo Club to a specialty car-parts dealer called The British Masters and Keep the Faith, a Web site about Christian music. The group was given a lot of work by InterAct Entertainment Group in Los Angeles. "They were faster and more efficient than most designers," said Greg Hohertz, formerly of InterAct. The designers all went by one-name aliases—June, Steel, Nick, Rio—but "there are a lot of people with one name in Hollywood," said David Sams, owner of Keep the Faith. "We live in a land of Chers and Madonnas. Everyone in Hollywood is running around with short hair just like George Clooney. But they were very polite, and that should have tipped me off because no one in Hollywood is polite."

Heaven's Gate put on a sunny face. Al Ignato, the owner of the Rancho Car Wash at the Union 76 Station in Del Mar, washed their new-make cars for free. "They did not impress you like a Hare Krishna. They weren't on any crusade. They weren't like young Mormons," said Ignato. "There was none of that." The "nuns and sisters," as Ignato called them, even brought him a "fabulous bourbon pound cake 10 inches high."

Heaven's Gate earned enough from its business to live in a $7,000-a-month mansion rented from a down-on-his-luck Iranian businessman. The villa came with an elevator, Jacuzzi and putting green. But it was sparsely furnished from Kmart and decorated with drawings of aliens. Neighbors in ritzy Rancho Santa Fe noticed that the "monks" were all pale, in a world where a tan is part of the uniform. Heaven's Gate was also extremely secretive. The group insisted on keeping the phone in the name of the landlord and paying the rent and utilities with cash. No banks, no Social Security numbers—no contact at all with the government.

The group would rise every morning before 4 to gaze into the night sky, looking for their true home in the heavens. A simple group meal, typically of pasta, would follow. For the rest of the day, the cultists would subsist on fruit and lemonade, although several became Diet Coke addicts for the caffeine buzz they got when they worked all night designing Web pages. Clever marketer that he was, Do sent messages entitled "Time to Die for God?" to Internet newsgroups that focus on suicide (alt.suicide), depression (alt.support.depression) and substance abuse (alt.abuse.recovery). Do decreed that his new and old crew members were actually heaven-sent souls who had arrived to fight the Luciferians in "staged" spaceship crashes.

The recruiting "doubled" the size of his cult, Do wrote. But the cult was unable to sell a movie treatment about its story to Hollywood. The members became increasingly paranoid about an attack by the government. The indifference of the public at large to the cult "was the signal to us to begin our preparations to return home," said a cult communiqué on the Internet. "The weeds of humanity" had taken over earth's "garden." It was time to go to "the level above"—or "what humans call dead." Learning of a UFO "four times the size of earth" in the wake of Hale-Bopp, Heaven's Gate decided that their beloved Ti must be coming earthward to collect them.

As the comet brightened in the sky in mid-March, as Holy Week approached, the cultists got ready to shed their "earthly containers." They celebrated with a last supper of chicken pot pie and cheesecake.

The "crew" member known as Rio had a different plan. About six months ago, Rio DiAngelo, 42, left the cult to work full time for InterAct. It now appears that Rio may have been selected for a special task—to carry the group's message to the public after their suicide. Last Tuesday, DiAngelo received a Federal Express package at work. He put it aside. That night he opened the package and found two videotapes and a set of instructions.

The next morning, a shaken Rio told his boss, Nick Matzorkis, that he believed all the members from Higher Source were dead. Rio had not watched the videotape—he said he felt he knew what was on it—but he wanted to go to the house to see for himself. Matzorkis at first brushed it off; figuring that the group had "died"—and gone to Europe. But his sense of dread grew as they drove to the house, or "temple," in the hills outside San Diego. Rio went into the house; when he returned 20 minutes later, he was "white as a sheet," according to Matzorkis. "They did it," said Rio. "Did it smell?" asked Matzorkis. Rio assured him that it did. On the drive down, Rio tried to regain his composure. He remarked, "I'm surprised how well this vehicle [his body] is dealing with this." But at Matzorkis's insistence, he called the police.

Authorities believe that the entire cult has now perished, and that no one else was involved in their deaths. But they want to reserve judgment until they have a chance to download the 20 or so computers found in the house (one with a picture of Hale-Bopp shining on its screen). Late last week a science-fiction writer named Lee Shargel, who was recently befriended by Applewhite and his crew, told *Newsweek* that he had received messages saying that 13 surviving members of the cult—a "ground crew"— were traveling to some Indian ruins in the Southwestern desert to reunite with a reincarnated Applewhite, who would fly down from space to pick them up. It is impossible to know if the messages came from pranksters, real cult members—or self-appointed recruits drawn to the publicity.

Some of the Rancho Santa Fe victims died from overdoses of phenobarbital, but a fatal dose—some

50 to 100 pills—is a lot to be mushed up with apple-sauce. For most, the cause of death was apparently suffocation—from plastic bags strapped over their heads as they lay doped out by the drugs and booze. Police found about 20 white garbage bags with elastic straps carefully stacked in the trash. The killing probably began late Saturday and went on for three more days.

Police think Applewhite expired toward the end of this slow ritual, either in the second wave of 15 or the final group who died sometime Tuesday. In the videotapes, some of the cultists seem giddy. "We're looking forward to this," chirps one woman. "Beam me up!" sings another. Applewhite is more serious. "You can follow us," he intones, "but you cannot stay here and follow us." It is a measure of Apple-white's personal power, the pull of millennialism through the ages and the unsettled age we live in, that so many so readily followed.

Glossary

acculturation: Culture change occurring under conditions of close contact between two societies. The weaker group tends to acquire cultural elements of the dominant group.

age-grade: An association that includes all the members of a group who are of a certain age and sex (for example, a warrior age-grade).

age-set: A group of individuals of the same sex and age who move through some or all of the stages of an age-grade together.

ancestor worship: A religious practice involving the worship of the spirits of dead family and lineage members.

animatism: The attribution of life to inanimate objects.

animism: The belief in the existence of spiritual beings (Tylor's minimal definition of religion).

anthropomorphism: The attribution of human physical characteristics to objects not human.

anthropophagy: The consumption of human flesh (cannibalism).

associations: Organizations whose membership is based on the pursuit of special interests.

astrology: The practice of foretelling the future by studying the supposed influence of the relative positions of the moon, sun, and stars on human affairs.

avoidance rules: Regulations that define or restrict social interaction between certain relatives.

berdache: A French term for North American Indian transvestites who assume the cultural roles of women.

bokors: Haitian term for Voodoo sorcerers who administer so-called zombie powder to their intended victims.

bull-roarer: A flat board or other object that is swung at the end of a cord to produce a whirring sound; commonly used in religious ceremonies around the world.

bundu: A women's secret society among certain tribes of West Africa (also known as Sande).

cannibalism: See *anthropophagy.*

caste: An endogamus social division characterized by occupational or ritual specialization ascribed by birth.

ceremony: A formal act or set of acts established by custom as proper to a special occasion, such as a religious rite.

charisma: Personal leadership qualities that endow an individual with the ability to attract followers. Often this quality of leadership is attributed to divine intervention.

churinga: Sacred objects used by Australian aborigines in a variety of rituals.

cicatrization: Ritual and cosmetic scarification.

clan: A unilineal descent group based on a fictive ancestor.

communitarianism: A secular or religious lifestyle in which groups share beliefs and material goods; these groups are ordinarily isolated from the general population.

cosmogony: A theory or account of the creation or origin of the world.

cosmology: Theory or philosophy of the nature and principles of the universe.

couvade: Culturally prescribed behavior of a father during and after the birth of his child; for example, mimicking the mother's labor pains.

coven: An organization of witches with a membership traditionally set at thirteen.

creationism: The doctrine of divine creation. Opposed to evolutionism.

cult: An imprecise term, generally used as a pejorative to describe an often loosely organized group possessing special religious beliefs and practices.

cultural relativism: The concept that any given culture must be evaluated in terms of its own belief system.

cultural universals: Aspects of culture believed to exist in all human societies.

culture: The integrated total of learned behavior that is characteristic of members of a society.

culture trait: A single unit of learned behavior or its product.

curse: An utterance calling upon supernatural forces to send evil or misfortune to a person.

demon: A person, spirit, or thing regarded as evil.

diffusion: A process in which cultural elements of one group pass to another.

divination: The process of contacting the supernatural to find an answer to a question regarding the cause of an event or to foretell the future.

emic: Shared perceptions of phenomena and ideology by members of a society; insiders' views.

endocannibalism: The eating of the remains of kinsmen and/or members of one's own group.

ethnocentrism: A tendency to evaluate foreign beliefs and behaviors according to one's own cultural traditions.

ethnography: A detailed anthropological description of a culture.

ethnology: A comparison and analysis of the ethnographic data from various cultures.

ethnomedicine: Beliefs and practices relating to diseases of the indigenous peoples of traditional societies.

ethos: The characteristic and distinguishing attitudes of a people.

etic: An outside observer's viewpoint of a society's phenomena or ideology.

exorcism: The driving away of evil spirits by ritual.

familiar: A spirit, demon, or animal that acts as an intimate servant.

fetish: An object that is worshipped because of its supernatural power.

folklore: The traditional beliefs, legends, myths, sayings, and customs of a people.

functionalism: An analytical approach that attempts to explain cultural traits in terms of the uses they serve within a society.

Ghost Dance: A nativistic movement among several tribes of North American Indians during the late nineteenth century.

ghosts: Spirits of the dead.

glossolalia: The verbalizing of utterances that depart from normal speech, such as the phenomenon of "speaking in tongues."

god: A supernatural being with great power over humans and nature.

gynophobia: An abnormal fear of women (also spelled gynephobia).

hallucinogen: Any of a number of hallucination-producing substances, such as LSD, peyote, ebene, and marijuana.

holistic: In anthropology, the approach that emphasizes the study of a cultural and bioecological system in its entirety.

idolatry: Excessive devotion to or reverence for some person or thing.

incest taboo: The prohibition of sexual relations between close relatives as defined by society.

incubus: A male demon who seeks sexual intercourse with women in their sleep.

invocation: The act of conjuring or calling forth good or evil spirits.

legend: A folkloric category that relates an important event popularly believed to have a historical basis although not verifiable.

magic: A ritual practice believed to compel the supernatural to act in a desired way.

magic, contagious: A belief that associated objects can exert an influence on each other—for example, a spell cast using the intended victim's property.

magic, imitative: A belief that imitating a desired result will cause it to occur.

magic, sympathetic: A belief that an object can influence others that have an identity with it—for example, a bow symbolizes the intended victim.

mana: A sacred force inhabiting certain objects and people giving them extraordinary power.

mazeway: Anthony F. C. Wallace's term for an individual's cognitive map and positive and negative goals.

misogyny: The hatred of women.

monotheism: A belief that there is only one god.

mysticism: A contemplative process whereby an individual seeks union with a spiritual being or force.

myth: A sacred narrative believed to be true by the people who tell it.

necromancy: The ability to foretell the future by communicating with the dead.

neurosis: A mild psychological disorder.

New Age: A loosely used term describing a combination of spirituality and superstition, fad and farce, that supposedly helps believers gain knowledge of the unknown. Largely a North American phenomenon, the movement includes beliefs in psychic predictions, channeling, astrology, and the powers of crystals and pyramids.

oath: An appeal to a deity to witness the truth of what one says.

occult: Certain mystic arts or studies, such as magic, alchemy, and astrology.

ordeal: A ritual method to supernaturally determine guilt or innocence by subjecting the accused to a physical test.

pantheism: The belief that God is everything and everything is God; (also) the worship of all gods.

participant observation: An anthropological field technique in which the ethnographer is immersed in the day-to-day activities of the community being studied.

Peyote cult: A cult surrounding the ritual ingestion of any of a variety of mescal cactuses; commonly associated with certain Native American religious beliefs.

polytheism: See *pantheism*.

possession: A trance state in which malevolent or curative spirits enter a person's body.

primitive: A term used by anthropologists to describe a culture lacking a written language; cultures also characterized by low-level technology, small numbers, few extra-societal contacts, and homogeneity (sometimes referred to as preliterate or nonliterate cultures).

profane: Not concerned with religion or the sacred; the ordinary.

prophet: A religious leader or teacher regarded as, or claiming to be, divinely inspired who speaks for a god.

propitiation: The act or acts of gaining the favor of spirits or deities.

psychosis: A psychological disorder sufficiently damaging that it may disrupt the work or activities of a person's life.

reciprocity: A system of repayment of goods, objects, actions, and sometimes money, through which obligations are met and bonds created.

reincarnation: The belief that the soul reappears after death in another and different bodily form.

religion: A set of beliefs and practices pertaining to supernatural beings or forces.

revitalization movements: According to Anthony F. C. Wallace, a deliberate, organized, conscious effort by members of a society to construct a more satisfying culture.

rites of passage: Rituals associated with such critical changes in personal status as birth, puberty, marriage, and death.

ritual: A secular or sacred, formal, solemn act, observance, or procedure in accordance with prescribed rules or customs.

sacred: Venerated objects and actions considered holy and entitled to reverence.

sacrifice: The ritualized offering of a person, plant, or animal as propitiation or in homage to the supernatural.

sect: A small religious group with distinctive beliefs and practices that set it apart from other similar groups in the society.

secular: Not sacred or religious.

shaman: A religious specialist and healer with powers derived directly from supernatural sources.

society: A group of people sharing a common territory, language, and culture.

sorcery: The use of magical paraphernalia by an individual to harness supernatural powers ordinarily to achieve evil ends.

soul: Immortal or spiritual part of a person believed to separate from the physical body at death.

structuralism: An anthropological approach to the understanding of the deep, subconscious, unobservable structure of human realities that is believed to determine observable behavior (a leading exponent: Claude Lévi-Strauss).

succubus: A female demon who seeks sexual intercourse with men in their sleep.

supernatural: A force or existence that transcends the natural.

symbol: An object, gesture, word, or other representation to which an arbitrary shared meaning is given.

syncretism: A process of culture change in which the traits and elements of one culture are given new meanings or new functions when they are adapted by another culture—for example, the combining of Catholicism and African ancestor worship to form Voodoo.

taboo: A sacred prohibition put upon certain people, things, or acts that makes them untouchable, unmentionable, and so on (also tabu, tabou, tapu).

talisman: A sacred object worn to ensure good luck or to ward off evil. Also known as an amulet or charm.

theocracy: Rule by religious specialists.

totem: An animal, plant, or object considered related to a kin group and viewed as sacred.

trance: An altered state of consciousness induced by religious fervor, fasting, repetitive movements and rhythms, drugs, and so on.

transcendence: The condition of being separate from or beyond the material world.

Voodoo: A syncretic religion of Haiti that combines Catholicism and African ancestor worship; sometimes referred to as Tovodun or Vodun.

witchcraft: An evil power inherent in certain individuals that permits them, without the use of magical charms or other paraphernalia, to do harm or cause misfortune to others.

zombie: In Haiti, an individual believed to have been placed in a trancelike state through the administration of a psychotropic drug given secretly, thus bringing the victim under the control of another.

Bibliography

The following bibliography is a compilation of the lists of references or suggested readings that accompanied each article in its original publication. (In some cases, a list of references has been constructed from footnote citations in the original.) We have rendered the citations in as consistent a form as possible, but minor variations in form and content are inevitable because of the varied citation styles of the original publishers.

A few articles were not accompanied by references in their original publication and accordingly are not included here.

CHAPTER 1
The Anthropological Study of Religion
Religion
Clifford Geertz

REFERENCES

Bettelheim, Bruno
    1954   *Symbolic Wounds: Puberty Rites and the Envious Male.* Glencoe, Ill.: Free Press.

Campbell, Joseph
    1949   *The Hero with a Thousand Faces.* New York: Pantheon.

Devereux, George
    1951   *Reality and Dream: Psychotherapy of a Plains Indian,* New York: International Universities Press.

Eliade, Mircea
[1949] 1958 *Patterns in Comparative Religion,*
New York: Sheed and Ward.

Erikson, Erik H.
[1950] 1964 *Childhood and Society.* 2nd ed. New York: Norton.

Geertz, Clifford
1966 "Religion as a Cultural System." In Michael Banton, ed., *Anthropological Approaches to the Study of Religion.* A.S.A. Monograph No. 3. London: Tavistock Publications Limited.

Hallowell, A. Irving
1955 *Culture and Experience.* Philadelphia: University of Pennsylvania Press.

Kardiner, Abram
1945 *The Psychological Frontiers of Society.* New York: Columbia University Press.

Kluckhohn, Clyde
1944 *Navaho Witchcraft.* Harvard University. Peabody Museum of American Archaeology and Ethnology Papers, Vol. 22, no. 2. Cambridge, Mass.: The Museum.

Lang, Andrew
[1898] 1900 *The Making of Religion.* 2nd ed. New York: Longmans.

Lessa, William A., and Evon Z. Vogt, eds.
1965 *Reader in Comparative Religion: An Anthropological Approach.* 2nd ed. New York: Harper.

Lévi-Strauss, Claude
[1958] 1963 *Structural Anthropology.* New York: Basic Books.
[1962] 1966 *The Savage Mind.* University of Chicago Press.

Radcliffe-Brown, A. R.
[1952] 1961 *Structure and Function in Primitive Societies: Essays and Addresses.* Glencoe, Ill.: Free Press.

Róheim, Geza
1950 *Psychoanalysis and Anthropology: Culture, Personality and the Unconscious.* New York: International Universities Press.

Spier, Leslie
1921 *The Sun Dance of the Plains Indians: Its Development and Diffusion.* American Museum of Natural History Anthropological Papers, Vol. 16, part 7. New York: The Museum.

Whiting, John, and Irvin L. Child
1953 *Child Training and Personality: A Cross-Cultural Study.* New York: Yale University Press.

Religious Perspectives in Anthropology
Dorothy Lee

REFERENCES

Barton, R. F.
1946 *The Religion of the Ifugao.* In American Anthropological Association *Memoirs,* No. 65.

Black Elk
1932 *Black Elk Speaks. Being the Life Story of a Holy Man of the Oglala Sioux, as Told to John G. Neihardt (Flaming Rainbow).* New York: William Morrow.

Brown, Joseph Epes
1953 *The Sacred Pipe: Black Elk's Account of the Seven Rites of the Oglala Sioux.* Norman: University of Oklahoma Press.

Firth, Raymond
1940 *The Work of the Gods in Tikopia.* London: Lund, Humphries.
1950 *Primitive Polynesian Economy.* New York: Humanities Press.

Henry, Jules
1941 *Jungle People.* New York: J. J. Augustin.

Redfield, Robert, and W. Lloyd Warner
1940 "Cultural Anthropology and Modern Agriculture." In *Farmers in a Changing World,* 1940 Yearbook of Agriculture. Washington, D.C.: United States Government Printing Office.

Thompson, Laura
1946 *The Hopi Crisis: Report to Administrators.* (Mimeographed.)

Vanoverbergh, Morice
1936 *The Isneg Life Cycle.* Publication of the Catholic Anthropological Conference, Vol. 3, no. 2.

CHAPTER 2
Myth, Ritual, Symbolism, and Taboo

Genesis as Myth
Edmund R. Leach

REFERENCES

Bartsch, H. W.
1953   "Kerygma and Myth: A Theological Debate," S. P. C. K.

Groddeck, G.
1934   *The World of Man*. C. W. Daniel.

Jakobson, R., and M. Halle
1956   *Fundamentals of Language*. The Hague: Mouton.

Leach, E. R.
1961   "Lévi-Strauss in the Garden of Eden." In *Transactions of the New York Academy of Sciences*, Vol. 23, p. 4.

Lévi-Strauss, C.
1955   "The Structural Study of Myth." In T. A. Sebeok, ed., *Myth: A Symposium*. Bloomington: University of Indiana Press.

Shannon, C., and W. Weaver
1949   *The Mathematical Theory of Communication*. Champaign-Urbana: University of Illinois Press.

Betwixt and Between: The Liminal Period in *Rites de Passage*
Victor W. Turner

REFERENCES

Bettelheim, Bruno
1954   *Symbolic Wounds, Puberty Rites and the Envious Male*. New York: Free Press.

Douglas, Mary
1966   *Purity and Danger*. London: Routledge and Kegan Paul.

Elwin, Verrier
1955   *The Religion of an Indian Tribe*. London: Geoffrey Cumberlege.

Harrison, Jane
1903   *Prolegomena to the Study of Greek Religion*. London: Cambridge University Press.

Hocart, A. M.
1952   *The Life-Giving Myth*. London: Methuen and Co.

James, William
1918   *Principles of Psychology*. Vol. 1. New York: H. Holt.

Kuper, Hilda
1947   *An African Aristocracy*. London: Oxford University Press.

McCulloch, J. A.
1913   "Monsters," in *Hastings Encyclopaedia of Religion and Ethics*. Edinburgh: T. and T. Clark.

Richards, A.
1956   *Chisungu*. London: Faber and Faber.

Turner, Victor
1962   "Chihamba, the White Spirit." *Rhodes-Livingstone Papers*, No. 33. Manchester.

Warner, Lloyd
1959   *The Living and the Dead: A Study of the Symbolic Life of Americans*. New Haven, Conn.: Yale University Press

Female Circumcision in Egypt and Sudan: A Controversial Rite of Passage
Daniel Gordon

REFERENCES

Al-Hibri, Aziza, ed.
1982   *Women and Islam*. New York: Pergamon Press.

Antoun, Richard
1968   "On the Modesty of Women in Arab Muslim Villages: A Study in the Accommodation of Traditions." *American Anthropologist* 70: 671–97.

Beck, Luis, and Nikkie Keddie, eds.
1980   *Women in the Muslim World*. Cambridge, Mass.: Harvard University Press.

Boddy, Janice
  1982   "Womb as Oasis: The Symbolic Context
          of Pharaonic Circumcision in Rural
          Northern Sudan." *American Ethnologist* 9:
          682–98.

Dewhurst, Christopher, and Aida Michelson
  1964   "Infibulation Complicating Pregnancy."
          British Medical Journal 2: 1442.

El Dareer, Asma
  1982   *Women, Why Do You Weep?* London: Zed
          Press.

El Saadawi, Nawal
  1980   *The Hidden Face of Eve.* Boston: Beacon
          Press.

Hansen, Henry Harold
  1972   "Clitoridectomy: Female Circumcision
  1973   in Egypt." *Folk* 14–15: 15–26.

Hathout, H. M.
  1963   "Some Aspects of Female Circumcision."
          *Journal of Obstetrics and Gynecology of the
          British Empire* 70: 505–507.

Hosken, Fran P.
  1978   "Epidemiology of Female Genital Mutila-
          tion." *Tropical Doctor* 8: 150–56.
  1982   *The Hosken Report: Genital and Social Muti-
          lation of Females.* Lexington, Mass.:
          Women's International News Network.

Huddleston, C. E.
  1944   "Female Circumcision in the Sudan."
          Lancet 1: 626.

Kennedy, J. G.
  1970   "Circumcision and Excision in Egyptian
          Nubia." *Man* 5: 175–91.

Koso-Thomas, Olayinka
  1987   *The Circumcision of Women.* London: Zed
          Books.

Mustafa, A. Z.
  1966   "Female Circumcision and Infibulation in
          the Sudan." *Journal of Obstetrics and Gyne-
          cology of the British Commonwealth* 73:
          302–306.

Oldfield, Hayes, Rose
  1975   "Female Genital Mutilation, Fertility
          Control, Women's Roles, and the Patrilin-
          eage in Modern Sudan." *American Ethnol-
          ogist* 2: 617–33.

Rugh, Andrea
  1984   *Family in Contemporary Egypt.* Syracuse:
          Syracuse University Press.

Scotch, Norman
  1963   "Sociocultural Factors in the Epidemiol-
          ogy of Zulu Hypertension." *American
          Journal of Public Health* 53: 1205–13.

van Gennep, Arnold
  [1908] 1960   *Rites of Passage.* Chicago: Univer-
          sity of Chicago Press.

Weingrod, Alex, ed.
  1987   *Ethiopian Jews and Israel.* New Brunswick,
          N.J.: Transaction Books.

Worsley, Alan
  1938   "Infibulation and Female Circumcision."
          *Journal of Obstetrics and Gynecology of the
          British Empire* 45: 686–91.

Taboo
Mary Douglas

SUGGESTED READINGS

Douglas, Mary
  1966   *Purity and Danger.* New York: Frederick
          A. Praeger.

Steiner, Franz
  [1956] 1967   *Taboo.* London: Penguin.

You Are What You Eat: Religious Aspects of the Health Food Movement
Jill Dubisch

REFERENCES

Ehrenreich, Barbara, and Deidre English
  1979   *For Her Own Good: 150 Years of the Experts'
          Advice to Women.* Garden City, N.Y.:
          Anchor Press/Doubleday.

Geertz, Clifford
  1965   "Religion as a Cultural System." In
          Michael Banton, ed., *Anthropological
          Approaches to the Study of Religion.* A.S.A.
          Monograph No. 3. London: Tavistock
          Publications Ltd.

Hongladarom, Gail Chapman
  1976   "Health Seeking Within the Health Food

Movement." Ph.D. Dissertation: University of Washington.

Kandel, Randy F., and Gretel H. Pelto
1980 "The Health Food Movement: Social Revitalization or Alternative Health Maintenance System." In Norge W. Jerome, Randy F. Kandel, and Gretel H. Pelto, eds., *Nutritional Anthropology*. Pleasantville, N.Y.: Redgrave Publishing Co.

Kline, Monte
1978 *The Junk Food Withdrawal Manual*. Total Life, Inc.

Kottak, Conrad
1978 "McDonald's as Myth, Symbol, and Ritual." In *Anthropology: The Study of Human Diversity*. New York: Random House.

Shryock, Richard Harrison
1966 *Medicine in America: Historical Essays*. Baltimore: Johns Hopkins University Press.

Wallace, Anthony F. C.
1966 *Religion: An Anthropological View*. New York: Random House.

Body Ritual Among the Nacirema
Horace Miner

REFERENCES

Linton, Ralph
1936 *The Study of Man*. New York: D. Appleton-Century Co.

Malinowski, Bronislaw
1948 *Magic, Science, and Religion*. Glencoe: Free Press.

Murdock, George P.
1949 *Social Structure*. New York: Macmillan.

CHAPTER 3
Shamans, Priests, and Prophets
Religious Specialists
Victor W. Turner

REFERENCES

Buber, Martin
[1936] 1958 *I and Thou*. 2nd ed. New York: Scribner.

Callaway, Henry
1885 *The Religious System of the Amazulu*. Folklore Society Publication No. 15. London: Trubner.

Durkheim, Emile
[1893] 1960 *The Division of Labor in Society*. Glencoe, Ill.: Free Press.

Elwin, Verrier
1955 *The Religion of an Indian Tribe*. Bombay: Oxford University Press.

Evans-Pritchard, E. E.
[1949] 1954 *The Sanusi of Cyrenaica*. Oxford: Clarendon Press.
[1956] 1962 *Nuer Religion*. Oxford: Clarendon Press.

Firth, R. W.
1964a "Shaman." In Julius Gould and William L. Kolb, eds. *A Dictionary of the Social Sciences*, pp. 638–39. New York: Free Press.
1964b "Spirit Mediumship." In Julius Gould and W. L. Kolb, eds., *Dictionary of the Social Sciences*, p. 689. New York: Free Press.

Gelfand, Michael
1964 *Witch Doctor: Traditional Medicine Man of Rhodesia*. London: Harvill.

Herskovits, Melville J.
1938 *Dahomey: An Ancient West African Kingdom*. 2 vols. New York: Harvill.

Howells, William W.
1948 *The Heathens: Primitive Man and His Religions*. Garden City, N.Y.: Doubleday.

Knox, Ronald A.
1950 *Enthusiasm: A Chapter in the History of Religion; With Special Reference to the XVII and XVIII Centuries*. New York: Oxford University Press.

Lessa, William A., and Evon Z. Vogt, eds.
[1958] 1965 *Reader in Comparative Religion: An Anthropological Approach*. New York: Harper.

Lowie, Robert H.
1954 *Indians of the Plains*. American Museum of Natural History, Anthropological Handbook No. 1. New York: McGraw-Hill.

Nadel, Siegfried F.
 1954   *Nupe Religion.* London: Routledge.

Parrinder, Edward G.
 1954   *African Traditional Religion.* London:
     Hutchinson's University Library.

Parsons, Talcott
 1963   "Introduction." In Max Weber, *The Sociol-*
     ogy of Religion. Boston: Beacon.

Piddington, Ralph
 1950   *Introduction to Social Anthropology.* 2 vols.
     New York: Fredrick A. Praeger.

Richards, Audrey I.
 [1940] 1961   "The Political System of the Bembe
     Tribe: Northeastern Rhodesia." In Meyer
     Fortes and E. E. Evans-Pritchard, eds.,
     African Political Systems. New York: Ox-
     ford University Press.

Wach, Joachim
 1958   *The Comparative Study of Religions.* New
     York: Columbia University Press.

Weber, Max
 [1922] 1963   *The Sociology of Religion.* Boston:
     Beacon.

Worsley, P. M.
 1957a   "Millenarian Movements in Melanesia."
     Rhodes-Livingstone Journal 21: 18–31.
 1957b   *The Trumpet Shall Sound: A Study of*
     "Cargo" Cults in Melanesia. London:
     MacGibbon and Kee.

The Shaman: A Siberian Spiritualist
William Howells

REFERENCES

Bogoras, W.
 1904   "The Chuckchee." In *Memoirs of the*
 –09   *American Museum of Natural History,*
     Vol. 11.

Casanowicz, I. M.
 1924   "Shamanism of the Natives of Siberia."
     In *Smithsonian Institution Annual Report.*

Czaplicka, M. A.
 1914   *Aboriginal Siberia: A Study in Social*
     Anthropology.

Evans-Pritchard, E. E.
 1937   *Witchcraft, Oracles and Magic Among the*
     Azande. Oxford: Clarendon Press.

Field, Margaret J.
 1937   *Religion and Medicine of the Gā People.*

Handy, E. S. Craighill
 1927   "Polynesian Religion." Bernice P. Bishop
     Museum *Bulletin,* No. 34. Honolulu.

Hoernle, Winifred
 1937   In I. Schapera, ed., *The Bantu-Speaking*
     Peoples of South Africa.

Jochelson, W.
 1908   "The Koryak." *Memoirs of the American*
     Museum of Natural History, Vol. 10.
 1926   "The Yukaghir and the Yukaghirized
     Tungus." In *Memoirs of the American*
     Museum of Natural History, Vol. 13.

CHAPTER 4
The Religious Use of Drugs

Drugs
Francis Huxley

SUGGESTED READING

Lewin, Lewis L.
 1924   *Phantastica: Narcotic and Stimulating*
     Drugs. New York: Dutton.

The Peyote Way
J. S. Slotkin

REFERENCES

Slotkin, J. S.
 1952   "Menomini Peyotism." In *Transactions of*
     the American Philosophical Society XLII,
     Part 4.
 1955   "Peyotism, 1521–1891." *American Anthro-*
     pologist LVII (1955): 202–30.
 1956   *The Peyote Religion: A Study in Indian-*
     White Relations. Glencoe, Ill.: Free Press

Ritual Enemas
Peter T. Furst and Michael D. Coe

SUGGESTED READINGS

Benson, Elizabeth P.
  1972   *The Maya World*. New York: Apollo.
  1975   *Death and the Afterlife in Pre-Columbian America*. Washington, D.C.: Dumbarton Oaks.

Coe, Michael D.
  1966   *The Maya*. New York: Frederick A. Praeger.
  1975   *Classic Maya Pottery at Dumbarton Oaks*. Washington, D.C.: Dumbarton Oaks.

Furst, Peter T.
  1972   *Flesh of the Gods: The Ritual Use of Hallucinogens*. New York: Frederick A. Praeger.
  1976   *Hallucinogens and Culture*. Corte Madera, Calif.: Chandler & Sharp Publishers.
  1977   "High States in Culture-Historical Perspective." In Norman E. Zinberg, ed., *Alternate States of Consciousness*. New York: Free Press.

Thompson, J. Eric
  1970   *Maya History and Religion*. Norman: University of Oklahoma Press.

The Sound of Rushing Water
Michael Harner

SUGGESTED READINGS

Karsten, R.
  1935   "The Head-Hunters of Western Amazonas." In *Commentationes Humanarum Litteraru*. Finska Vetenskaps-Societeten 7(1). Helsingfors.

Stirling, M. W.
  1938   *Historical and Ethnographical Material on the Jivaro Indians*. U.S. Bureau of American Ethnology Bulletin 117. Washington, D.C.: Smithsonian Institution.

Up de Graff, F. W.
  1923   *Headhunters of the Amazon: Seven Years of Exploration and Adventure*. London: H. Jenkins.

Wilbert, Johannes
  1972   "Tobacco and Shamanistic Ecstasy Among the Warao Indians of Venezuela." In Peter J. Furst, ed., *Flesh of the Gods: The Ritual Use of Hallucinogens*, pp. 55–83. New York: Praeger.

Psychedelic Drugs and Religious Experience
Robert S. de Ropp

SUGGESTED READINGS

Aaronson, Bernard, and Humphry Osmond, eds.
  1970   "Effects of Psychedelics on Religion and Religious Experience." In *Psychedelics*. New York.

Alpert, Richard
  1971   *Remember: Be Here Now*. San Cristobal, N.M.

Bloom, Richard et al.
  1964   *The Politics of Ecstasy*. New York.

de Ropp, Robert S., ed.
  1976   *Drugs and the Mind*. New York.

Ebib, David, ed.
  1961   *The Drug Experience*. New York.

Efron, Daniel H., ed.
  1967   *Ethnopharmocologic Search for Psychoactive Drugs*. Washington, D.C.

Huxley, Aldous
  1954   *The Doors of Perception*. New York.

James, William
  1902   *The Varieties of Religious Experience*.

LaBarre, Weston
  1964   *The Peyote Cult*. Hamden, Conn.

Ludlow, Hugh
  1970   *The Hasheesh Eater: Being Passages from the Life of a Pythagorean*. Upper Saddle River, N.J.

Masters, R. E. L., and Jean Houston
  1966   *The Varieties of Psychedelic Experience*. New York.

Myerhoff, Barbara G.
  1974   *Peyote Hunt: The Sacred Journey of the Huichol Indians*. Ithaca, N.Y.

Pavlovna, Valentina, and R. Gordon Wasson
  1957   *Mushrooms, Russia, and History*. New York.

Wasson, Gordon, R., et al.
  1975   *Maria Sabina and Her Mazatec Mushroom Velada*. New York.

Weil, Andrew
  1972   *The Natural Mind: A New Way of Looking at Drugs and Higher Consciousness*. Boston.

CHAPTER 5
Ethnomedicine: Religion and Healing

Eyes of the *Ngangas*: Ethnomedicine and Power in Central African Republic

Arthur C. Lehmann

REFERENCES

Bahuchet, Serge
  1985   *Les Pygmées Aka et la Forêt Centrafricaine*. Paris: Bibliothèque de la Selaf.

Bibeau, Gillies
  1979   *De la maladie a la guerison. Essai d'analyse systematique de la medecine des Angbandi du Zaire*. Doctoral dissertation, Laval University.

Bichmann, Wolfgang
  1979   "Primary Health Care and Traditional Medicine—Considering the Background of Changing Health Care Concepts in Africa." *Social Science and Medicine* 13B: 175–82.

Cavalli-Sforza, L. L.
  1971   "Pygmies: An Example of Hunters Gatherers, and Genetic Consequences for Man of Domestication of Plants and Animals." In J. de Grouchy, F. Ebling, and I. Henderson, eds., *Human Genetics: Proceedings of the Fourth International Congress of Human Genetics*, pp. 79–95. Amsterdam: Excerpta Medica.

Cavalli-Sforza, L.L., ed.
  1986   *African Pygmies*. New York: Academic Press.

Feierman, Steven
  1985   "Struggles for Control: The Social Roots of Health of Healing in Modern Africa." *African Studies Review* 28: 73–147.

Green, Edward
  1980   "Roles for African Traditional Healers in Mental Health Care." *Medical Anthropology* 4(4): 490–522.

Hepburn, Sharon J.
  1988   "W. H. R. Rivers Prize Essay (1986): Western Minds, Foreign Bodies." *Medical Anthropology Quarterly* 2 (New Series): 59–74.

Hewlett, Barry S.
  1986   "Causes of Death Among Aka Pygmies of the Central African Republic." In L. L. Cavalli-Sforza, ed., *African Pygmies*, pp. 45–63. New York: Academic Press.

Janzen, John M.
  1978   *The Quest for Therapy: Medical Pluralism in Lower Zaire*. Los Angeles: University of California Press.

Lewis, I. M.
  1986   *Religion in Context: Cults and Charisma*. Cambridge: Cambridge University Press.

Motte, Elisabeth
  1980   *Les plantes chez les Pygmées Aka et les Monzombode la Lobaye*. Paris: Bibliothèque de la Selaf.

Offiong, Daniel
  1983   "Witchcraft Among the Ibibio of Nigeria." *The African Studies Review* 26(1): 107–124.

Turnbull, Colin
  1965   *Wayward Servants*. New York: Natural History Press.

Warren, Dennis M.
  1974   "Disease, Medicine, and Religion Among the Techinman-Bono of Ghana; A Study in Culture Change." Doctoral dissertation, Indiana University.

Yoder, P. Stanley
  1982   "Issues in the Study of Ethnomedical Systems in Africa." In P. Stanley Yoder, ed., *African Health and Healing Systems: Proceedings of a Symposium*, p. 120. Los Angeles: Crossroads Press, University of California.

The Psychotherapeutic Aspects of Primitive Medicine
Ari Kiev

REFERENCES

Ackerknecht, Erwin H.
1942a "Problems of Primitive Medicine." *Bulletin of the History of Medicine,* vol. 11.
1942b "Primitive Medicine and Culture Pattern." *Bulletin of the History of Medicine,* vol. 12.

Edel, May M.
1957 *The Chiga of Western Uganda.* Oxford: Oxford University Press.

Elkin, Henry
1940 "The Northern Arapaho of Wyoming." In Ralph D. Linton, ed., *Acculturation in Seven American Indian Tribes.* New York: Appleton-Century.

Frank, Jerome D.
1959 "The Dynamics of the Psychotherapeutic Relationship." *Psychiatry* 23.

Goldman, Irvin
1940 "The Alkatchoko Carrier of British Columbia." In Ralph D. Linton, ed., *Acculturation of Seven American Indian Tribes.* New York: Appleton-Century.

Harley, George W.
1941 *Native African Medicine.* Cambridge, Mass.: Harvard University Press.

Harris, Jack S.
1940 "The White Knife Shoshoni of Nevada." In Ralph D. Linton, ed., *Acculturation of Seven American Indian Tribes.* New York: Appleton-Century.

Huntingford, G.
1953 *The Nandi of Kenya.* London: Routledge and Kegan Paul.

Joffe, Natalie
1940 "The Fox of Iowa." In Ralph D. Linton, ed., *Acculturation of Seven American Indian Tribes.* New York: Appleton-Century.

Kluckhohn, Clyde, and D. Leighton
1947 *The Navaho.* Cambridge, Mass.: Harvard University Press.

Opler, Marvin K.
1940 "The Southern Ute of Colorado." In Ralph D. Linton, ed., *Acculturation of Seven American Indian Tribes.* New York: Appleton-Century.

Opler, Morris E.
1936 "Some Points of Comparison Between the Treatment of Functional Disorders by Apache Shamans and Modern Psychiatric Practice." *American Journal of Psychiatry* 92.

Radcliffe-Brown, A. R.
1948 *The Andaman Islanders.* Glencoe, Ill.: Free Press.

Radin, Paul
1957 *Primitive Religion: Its Nature and Origin.* New York: Dover Publishing.

Redlich, Frederick, and August Hollingshead
1958 *Social Class and Mental Illness.* New York: John Wiley.

Smith, Marian W.
1940 "The Puyallup of Washington." In Ralph D. Linton, ed., *Acculturation in Seven American Indian Tribes.* New York: Appleton-Century.

Warner, W. Lloyd
1958 *A Black Civilization.* New York: Harper and Bros.

A School for Medicine Men
Robert Bergman

REFERENCES

Haile, B. O. F. M.
1950 *Origin Legend of the Navaho Enemy Way.* Publications in Anthropology, no. 17. New Haven: Yale University Press.

Kluckhohn, C.
1956 "The Great Chants of the Navaho." In I. T. Sanders et al., eds., *Societies Around the World.* New York: Dryden Press.
1967 *Navajo Witchcraft.* Boston: Beacon Press.

Kluckhohn, C., and D. Leighton
1962 *The Navajo.* New York: Doubleday & Co.

Kluckhohn, C., and L. D. Wyman
1940 *An Introduction to Navaho Chant Practice with an Account of the Behaviors Observed*

in Four Chants. American Anthropological Association, *Memoirs,* no. 53. Menasha, Wis.: American Anthropological Association.

Leighton, A. H., and D. Leighton
1941   "Elements of Psychotherapy in Navajo Religion." *Psychiatry* 4: 515–23.

Pfister, O.
1932   "Instinctive Psychoanalysis Among the Navajos." *Journal of Nervous and Mental Disease* 76: 234–54.

Reichard, G. A.
1938   *Navajo Religion.* New York: Bollingen Foundation.

Sandner, D.
1970   "Navajo Medicine Men." Paper read at the 123rd Annual Meeting of the American Psychiatric Association, San Francisco, May 11–15.

Mothering and the Practice of "Balm" in Jamaica
William Wedenoja

REFERENCES

Barry, H., M. K. Bacon, and I. L. Child
1957   "A Cross-Cultural Survey of Some Sex Differences in Socialization." *Journal of Abnormal and Social Psychology* 55: 327–32.

Frank, J. D.
[1961] 1974   *Persuasion and Healing: A Comparative Study of Psychotherapy.* Rev. ed. New York: Schocken.

Halifax, J.
1979   *Shamanic Voices.* New York: E. P. Dutton.

Jones, E., and C. L. Zoppel
1979   "Personality Differences Among Blacks in Jamaica and the United States. *Journal of Cross-Cultural Psychology* 10: 435–56.

Kakar, S.
1982   *Shamans, Mystics, and Doctors: A Psychological Inquiry into India and its Healing Traditions.* Boston: Beacon Press.

Lambert, M. J., D. A. Shapiro, and A. E. Bergin
1986   "The Effectiveness of Psychotherapy." In S. L. Garfield and A. E. Bergin, eds.,

Handbook of Psychotherapy and Behavior Change. 3rd ed. New York: John Wiley.

Long, J. K.
1973   "Jamaican Medicine: Choices Between Folk Healing and Modern Medicine." Ph.D. dissertation, Department of Anthropology, University of North Carolina.

Martin, K., and B. Voorhies
1975   *Female of the Species.* New York: Columbia University Press.

Mitchell, G.
1981   *Human Sex Differences: A Primatologist's Perspective.* New York: Van Nostrand Reinhold.

Mitchell, M. F.
1980   "Class, Therapeutic Roles, and Self-Medication in Jamaica." Ph.D. dissertation, Medical Anthropology, University of California at Berkeley and San Francisco.

Mogul, K. M.
1982   "Overview: The Sex of the Therapist." *American Journal of Psychiatry* 139: 1–11.

Phillips, A. S.
1973   *Adolescence in Jamaica.* Kingston: Jamaica Publishing House.

Prince, Raymond
n.d.   *Personal communication.*

Quinn, N.
1977   "Anthropological Studies on Women's Status." *Annual Review of Anthropology* 6: 181–225. Palo Alto: Annual Reviews.

Rogers, C. R.
1957   "The Necessary and Sufficient Conditions of Therapeutic Personality Change." *Journal of Consulting Psychology* 21(2): 95–102.

Rossi, A. S.
1977   "A Biosocial Perspective on Parenting." *Daedalus* 106(2): 1–32.

Scheff, T. J.
1975   "Labelling, Emotion, and Individual Change." In T. J. Scheff, ed., *Labelling Madness,* pp. 75–89. Englewood Cliffs, N.J.: Prentice-Hall.

1979   *Catharsis in Healing, Ritual, and Drama.* Berkeley: University of California Press.

Spiro, M. E.
    1978   *Burmese Supernaturalism.* Expanded ed. Philadelphia: Institute for the Study of Human Issues Press.
    1979   *Gender and Culture: Kibbutz Women Revisited.* New York: Schocken.

Torrey, E. F.
    1972   *The Mind Game.* New York: Bantam.

Wedenoja, W.
    1988   "The Origins of Revival, a Creole Religion in Jamaica." In G. Saunders, ed., *Culture and Christianity: The Dialectics of Transformation.* Westport, Conn.: Greenwood.

Whiting, B. B., and J. M. Whiting
    1975   *Children of Six Cultures: A Psycho-Cultural Analysis.* Cambridge: Harvard University Press.

Whyte, M. K.
    1978   *The Status of Women in Preindustrial Societies.* Princeton: Princeton University Press.

The Sorcerer and His Magic
Claude Lévi-Strauss

REFERENCES

Boas, Franz
    1930   *The Religion of the Kwakiutl.* Columbia Contributions to Anthropology, Vol. X. New York.

Cannon, W. B.
    1942   "'Voodoo' Death." *American Anthropologist* 44 (New Series).

Lee, D. D.
    1941   "Some Indian Texts Dealing with the Supernatural." *Review of Religion* (May).

Lévi-Strauss, C.
    1955   *Tristes Tropiques.* Paris.

Mauss, M.
    1950   *Sociologie et Anthropologie.* Paris.

Morley, Arthur
    1956   *London Sunday Times,* Apr. 22, 1956, p. 11.

Stevenson, M. C.
    1905   *The Zuni Indians.* 23rd Annual Report of the Bureau of American Ethnology.

Washington, D.C.: Smithsonian Institution.

Folk Medical Magic and Symbolism in the West
Wayland D. Hand

REFERENCES

Anderson, John Q.
    1968   "The Magical Transfer of Disease in Texas Folk Medicine." *Western Folklore* 27: 191–99.

Bakker, Gerard
    1960   *Positive Homéopathie.* Ulm.

Black, Pauline Monette
    1935   *Nebraska Folk Cures.* University of Nebraska Studies in Language, Literature, and Criticism, No. 15. Lincoln.

Black, William George
    1883   *Folk-Medicine: A Chapter in the History of Culture.* Publications of the Folk-Lore Society, Vol. 12. London. p. 61.

Brown, Frank C.
    1952   Frank C. Brown Collection of North
    –64   Carolina Folklore. 7 vols. Durham, N.C.

Dictionnaire encyclopedique des sciences medicales.
3eme ser., 6.
    1881   9. Paris. pp. 615–18.

Fife, Austin E.
    1957   "Pioneer Mormon Remedies." *Western Folklore* 16: 153–62.

Folklore
    1913   Vol. 24, pp. 360–61.

Frazer, James George
    1911   *Golden Bough.* 3rd ed. 12 vols.
    –15   London. Vol. 1, chap. 3, pp. 52–219.

Hand, Wayland D., ed.
    1961   *Popular Beliefs and Superstitions from North*
    –64   *Carolina* (1874): 241.

Hand, Wayland D.
    1965   "The Magical Transference of Disease." *North Carolina Folklore* 13: 83–109.
    1966   "Plugging, Nailing, Wedging, and Kindred Folk Medicine Practices." In Bruce

Jackson, ed., *Folklore and Society: Essays in Honor of Benj. A. Botkin,* pp. 63–75. Hatboro, Penn.

1968a "Folk Medical Inhalants in Respiratory Disorders." *Medical History* 12: 153–63.

1968b "'Passin' Through': Folk Medical Magic and Symbolism." *Proceedings of the American Philosophical Society* 112(6): 379–402.

1971 "'The Common Cold in Utah Folk Medicine." In Thomas E. Cheney, Austin E. Fife, and Juanita Brooks, eds., *Lore of Faith and Folly,* pp. 243–50. Salt Lake City: University of Utah Press.

n.d. *Hangmen, the Gallows, and the Dead Man's Hand in American Folk Medicine.*

Handworterbuch des deutschen Aberglaubens
1927 10 vols. Berlin.
–42

Hendricks, George D.
1966 *Mirrors, Mice & Mustaches: A Sampling of Superstitions and Popular Beliefs in Texas.* Austin: University of Texas. "Paisano Books," No. 1, pp. 32–36, 51.

Journal of American Folklore
1944 Vol. 57, pp. 41 and 46.
1955 Vol. 68, p. 131.

Jungbauer, Gustav
1934 *Deutsche Volksmedizin. Ein Grundriss.* Berlin. Pp. 79–85, 89–91.

Lathrop, Amy
1961 "Pioneer Remedies from Western Kansas." *Western Folklore* 20: 1–22.

McKinney, Ida Mae
1952 "Superstitions of the Missouri Ozarks." *Tennessee Folklore Society Bulletin* 18: 107.

Mogk, Eugen
1906 *Germanische Mythologie.* Sammlung Goschen, Bd. 15, Leipzig. p. 98.

Neal, Janice C.
1955 "Grandad—Pioneer Medicine Man." *New York Folklore Quarterly* 11: 289, 291.

Notes and Queries
1903 9th Series, Vol. 12, August 15, 1903, p. 26.

Southern Folklore Quarterly
1946 Vol. 10, p. 166.

Stout, Earl J.
1936 "Folklore from Iowa." *Memoirs of the American Folklore Society* 29 (761).

Thomas, Daniel Lindsey, and Lucy Blayney Thomas
1920 *Kentucky Superstitions.* Princeton, N.J. No. 1363.

Wuttke, Adolf
1900 *Der deutsche Volksaberglaube der Gegenwart,* ed. Elard Hugo Meyer. pp. 321–22. Section 477.

CHAPTER 6
Witchcraft and Sorcery

An Anthropological Perspective on the Witchcraze

James L. Brain

REFERENCES

Bettlelheim, Bruno
1977 *The Uses of Enchantment.* New York: Random House.

Brain, James L.
1977a "Handedness in Tanzania." *Anthropos* 72: 180–92.
1977b "Sex, Incest and Death: Initiation Rites Reconsidered." *Current Anthropology* 18(2): 371–84.

Bridges, E. L.
1949 *The Uttermost Parts of the Earth.* New York: Dutton.

Browne, Thomas
1964 *Religio Medici and Other Works.* In L. C. Martin, ed. Oxford: Clarendon Press.

Chapman, Anne
1984 *Drama and Power in a Hunting Society.* Cambridge: Cambridge University Press.

Cohn, Norman
1975 *Europe's Inner Demons: An Inquiry Inspired by the Great Witch-Hunt.* New York: Basic Books.

Darst, D. H.
1979 "Witchcraft in Spain: The Testimony of Martin de Castenga's Treatise on Super-

stition and Witchcraft (1529)." *Proceedings of the American Philosophical Society* 123(5): 298–322.

Douglas, Mary
1966   *Purity and Danger.* London: Routledge and Kegan Paul.

Driberg, J. H.
1923   *The Lango.* London: T. Fisher Unwin.

Dykstra, B.
1986   *Idols of Perversity.* New York: Oxford University Press.

Dyson-Hudson, N.
1966   *Karimojong Politics.* Oxford: Clarendon Press.

Elkin, Adolphus Peter
1938   *Australian Aborigines.* Sydney: Angus and Robertson.

Fortes, Meyer
1953   "The Structure of Unilineal Descent Groups." *American Anthropologist* 55: 17–41.

Fox-Keller, E.
1983   "Feminism and Science." In E. Abel and E. K. Abel, eds., *The Signs Reader.* Chicago: University of Chicago Press.

Ginzburg, Carlo
1983   *The Night Battles: Witchcraft and Agrarian Cults in the Sixteenth and Seventeenth Centuries.* Baltimore: Johns Hopkins University Press.

Gluckman, Max
1965   *Politics, Law and Ritual in Tribal Society.* Oxford: Blackwell.

Gulliver, P.
1955   *The Family Herds.* London: Routledge and Kegan Paul.
1963   *Social Control in an African Society.* Boston: Boston University Press.

Gulliver, P., and P. H. Gulliver
1953   *The Central Nilo-Hamites.* London: International African Institute.

Huntingford, G. W. B.
1953   *The Southern Nilo-Hamites.* London: International African Institute.

Jacobs, Alan
1985   *Personal communication.*

Klaits, Joseph
1985   *Servants of Satan.* Bloomington: Indiana University Press.

Kramer, Heinrich, and Jakob Sprenger
1971   *Malleus Maleficarum.* Translated by Montague Summers. New York: Dover.

La Barre, Weston
1984   *Muelos: A Stone Age Superstition.* New York: Columbia University Press.

Lamphere, L.
1974   "Strategies, Cooperation and Conflict Among Women in Domestic Groups." In Michelle Z. Rosaldo and L. Lamphere, eds., *Women, Culture and Society,* pp. 97–112. Stanford: Stanford University Press.

Langley, Michael
1979   *The Nandi of Kenya.* New York: Saint Martin's Press.

Lawrence, J. T. D.
1957   *The Iteso.* London: Oxford University Press.

Leach, Edmund Ronald
1970   *Claude Lévi-Strauss.* Harmondsworth: Penguin Books.

Lee, Richard B.
1972   "Work Effort, Group Structure and Land Use Among Contemporary Hunter-Gatherers." In B. Ucko and R. Trimingham, eds., *Man, Settlement and Urbanism.* London: George Duckworth and Company.
1976   *Kalahari Hunter-Gatherers.* Cambridge: Harvard University Press.

Lewis, I. M.
1965   "Shaikhs and Warriors in Somaliland." In J. L. Gibbs, ed., *Peoples of Africa.* New York: Holt, Rinehart and Winston.

Mair, L.
1969   *Witchcraft.* New York: McGraw-Hill.

Marshall, L.
1962   "!Kung Bushmen Religious Beliefs." *Africa* 32(3): 221–52.

1976   *The !Kung of Nyae.* Cambridge, Mass.: Harvard University Press.

McCormack, C., and M. Strathern, eds.
1980   *Nature, Culture and Gender.* Cambridge: Cambridge University Press.

Meggitt, M. J.
1962   *Desert People.* Chicago: University of Chicago Press.

Middleton, John, and E. Winter, eds.
1963   *Witchcraft, Sorcery and Magic in East Africa.* London: Routledge and Kegan Paul.

Midelfort, H. C. Erik
1972   *Witch Hunting in Southwestern Germany.* Stanford: Stanford University Press.

Mitchell, J. C.
1965   "The Meaning of Misfortune for Urban Africans." In M. Fortes and G. Dieterlen, eds., *African Systems of Thought.* London: Oxford University Press.

Murray, Margaret
1970   *The God of the Witches.* New York: Oxford University Press. (First published by Sampson, Low, and Matson, 1931.)

Nadel, Siegfried Frederick
1952   "Witchcraft in Four African Societies: An Essay in Comparison." *American Anthropologist* 54: 18–29.

Offiong, D. A.
1985   "Witchcraft Among the Ibibio." *African Studies Review* 21(1): 107–24.

Ortner, Sherry B.
1974   "Is Female to Nature as Man Is to Culture?" In Michelle Z. Rosaldo and L. Lamphere, eds., *Woman, Culture and Society,* pp. 67–87. Stanford, Calif.: Stanford University Press.

Peristiany, J. G.
1939   *The Social Institutions of the Kipsigis.* London: George Routledge.

Robertson, E.
n.d.   *An Anchorhold of Her Own.* Knoxville: University of Tennessee Press.

Rosaldo, Michelle Z.
1974   "Introduction and Overview." In Michelle Z. Rosaldo and L. Lamphere, eds., *Woman, Culture and Society,* pp. 1–42. Stanford, Calif.: Stanford University Press.

Spencer, B., and J. Gillen
[1899] 1938   *The Native Tribes of Central Australia.* London: Macmillan.
1904   *The Northern Tribes of Central Australia.* London: Macmillan.

Stenning, D.
1959   *Savannah Nomads.* London: Oxford University Press.
1965   "The Pastoral Fulani of Northern Nigeria." In J. L. Gibbs, ed., *Peoples of Africa.* New York: Holt, Rinehart and Winston.

Thomas, Keith
1971   *Religion and the Decline of Magic.* New York: Charles Scribner's Sons.

Thomas, N. W.
1906   *The Natives of Australia.* London: Archibald Constable.

Trevor-Roper, H. R.
1969   *The European Witch-Craze of the Sixteenth and Seventeenth Centuries and Other Essays.* New York: Harper and Row.

Turnbull, C.
1961   *The Forest People.* New York: Simon and Schuster.
1968   "The Importance of Flux in Two Hunting Societies." In Richard B. Lee and I. DeVore, eds., *Man the Hunter,* pp. 132–37. Chicago, Aldine.

Wilson, M.
1951   "Witch Beliefs and Social Structure." *American Journal of Sociology* 56: 307–13.

Woodburn, J.
1968   "An Introduction to Hadza Ecology." In Richard B. Lee and I. DeVore, eds., *Man the Hunter,* pp. 49–55.
1979   "Minimal Politics: The Political Organization of the Hadza of North Tanzania." In W. A. Shack and P. S. Cohen, eds., *Leadership: A Comparative Perspective,* pp. 244–60. Oxford: Clarendon Press.

1982a "Egalitarian Societies." *Man* 17: 431–51.

1982b "Social Dimensions of Death in Four African Hunting and Gathering Societies." In Maurice Bloch and Jonathan Parry, eds., *Death and the Regeneration of Life*, pp. 187–210. Cambridge: Cambridge University Press.

Some Implications of Urban Witchcraft Beliefs

Phillips Stevens Jr.

REFERENCES

Buffalo Evening News, July 17, 1978.

Cannon, Walter B.
1942 "The Voodoo Death." *American Anthropologist* 44: 169–81.
1957 "Voodoo Death." *Psychosomatic Medicine* 19: 182–90.

Cappannari, Stephen C., Bruce Rau, Harry S. Abram, and Denton C. Buchanan
1975 "Voodoo in the General Hospital: A Case of Hexing and Regional Enteritis." *Journal of the American Medical Association* 232(9): 938–40.

Eastwell, Harry D.
1982 "Voodoo Death and the Mechanism for Dispatch of the Dying in East Arnhem, Australia." *American Anthropologist* 84(1): 5–18.

Furnham, Adrian, and Stephen Bochner
1982 "Social Difficulty in a Foreign Culture: An Empirical Analysis of Culture Shock." In Stephen Bochner, ed., *Cultures in Contact: Studies in Cross-Cultural Interaction,* pp. 161–98. Oxford: Pergamon Press.

Galvin, James A. V., and Arnold M. Ludwig
1961 "A Case of Witchcraft." *Journal of Nervous and Mental Disease* 133(2): 161–68.

Gluckman, Max
1944 "The Logic of African Science and Witchcraft: An Appreciation of Evans-Pritchard's 'Witchcraft, Oracles, and Magic Among the Azande' of the Sudan." *Rhodes-Livingstone Institute Journal* (June).

Golden, Kenneth M.
1977 "Voodoo in Africa and the United States." *American Journal of Psychiatry* 134(12): 1425–27.

Johns Hopkins Hospital
1967 "Clinical-Pathological Conference." *Johns Hopkins Medical Journal* 120: 186–99.

Leininger, Madeleine
1973 "Witchcraft Practices and Psychosocial Therapy with Urban U.S. Families." *Human Organization* 32: 73–83.

Lester, David
1972 "Voodoo Death: Some New Thoughts on an Old Phenomenon." *American Anthropologist* 74(3): 386–90.

Lewis, G. A.
1977 "Fear of Sorcery and the Problem of Death by Suggestion." In J. Blacking, ed., *The Anthropology of the Body,* pp. 111–43. London: Academic Press, ASA Monograph 15.

Lewis, Justin
1958 "The Outlook for a Devil in the Colonies." *Criminal Law Review,* pp. 661–75.

Lex, Barbara
1974 "Voodoo Death: New Thoughts on an Old Explanation." *American Anthropologist* 76(4): 818–23.

Michaelson, Mike
1972 "Can a 'Root Doctor' Actually Put a Hex On, or Is It All a Great Put-On?" *Today's Health* (March).

New Haven Register
1981 "The Brookfield Demons." Nov. 5.

New York Times
1981 "Florida Hospital Tries to Cope with Refugees." Oct. 4, p. 71.

Oberg, Kalvero
1960 "Cultural Shock: Adjustment to New Cultural Environments." *Practical Anthropology* 7: 177–82.

Pedersen, Paul, ed.
1976 *Counseling Across Cultures.* Honolulu: University Press of Hawaii.

Prince, Raymond, ed.
  1982   "Shamans and Endorphins." *Ethos* 10(4).

Raybin, James B.
  1970   "The Curse: A Study in Family Communication." *American Journal of Psychiatry* 127(5): 77–85.

Richter, Curt
  1957   "On the Phenomenon of Sudden Death in Animals and Man." *Psychosomatic Medicine* 19: 191–98.

Seelye, Hans
  1956   *The Stress of Life.* New York: McGraw-Hill.

Senter, Donovan
  1947   "Witches and Psychiatrists." *Psychiatry* 10(1): 49–56.

Snell, John E.
  1967   "Hypnosis in the Treatment of the 'Hexed' Patient." *American Journal of Psychiatry* 124(3): 67–72.

Sue, Donald W.
  1981   *Counseling the Culturally Different: Theory and Practice.* New York: John Wiley.

Times-Union, Rochester, N.Y., July 14, 1978.

Tinling, David C.
  1967   "Voodoo, Root Work, and Medicine." *Psychosomatic Medicine* 29(5): 483–90.

Tivnan, Edward
  1979   "The Voodoo that New Yorkers Do." *New York Times Magazine.* Dec. 2, pp. 181–91.

Warner, Richard
  1977   "Witchcraft and Soul Loss: Implications for Community Psychiatry." *Hospital and Community Psychiatry* 28(9): 686–90.

Williams, Glanville
  1949   "Homicide and Supernatural." *Law Quarterly Review* 65: 491–503.
  1961   *Criminal Law. The General Part.* 2nd ed. 175–76, 524. London: Stevens & Sons.

Wintrob, Ronald M.
  1973   "The Influence of Others: Witchcraft and Rootwork as Explanations of Behavior Disturbances." *Journal of Nervous and Mental Disease* 156(5): 318–26.

Sorcery and Concepts of Deviance Among the Kabana, West New Britain

Naomi M. McPherson

REFERENCES

Becker, H.
  1963   *Outsiders: Studies in the Sociology of Deviance.* New York: Free Press.

Counts, D. A., and D. R. Counts
  1976   "The Good Death in Kalisi." *Omega* 7(4):
  –77   367–73.
  1984   "People Who Act like Dogs: Adultery and Deviance in a Melanesian Community." Paper read at the conference Deviance in a Cross-Cultural Context. University of Waterloo, Waterloo, Ontario, June.

Jorgensen, D.
  1983   "The Clear and the Hidden: Person, Self,
  –84   and Suicide Among the Telefolmi of Papua New Guinea." *Omega* 14(2): 113–26.

Lawrence, P.
  1984   *The Garia: An Ethnography of a Traditional Cosmic System in Papua New Guinea.* Carlton: Melbourne University Press.

Malinowski, B.
  [1926] 1967   *Crime and Custom in Savage Society.* C. K. Ogden, ed. Totowa, N.J.: Littlefield Adams.

Scaletta, N.
  1985   "Death by Sorcery: The Social Dynamics of Dying in Bariai, West New Britain." In D. A. Counts and D. R. Counts, eds. *Aging and Its Transformations: Moving Toward Death in Pacific Societies,* pp. 223–47. ASAO Monograph Series, No. 10. Lanham, Md.: University Press of America.

Vincent, Joan
  1990   *Anthropology and Politica: Visions, Traditions, and Trends.* Tucson: University of Arizona Press.

Weiner, A.
1976   *Women of Value, Men of Renown: New Per-*
        spectives in Trobriand Exchange. Austin:
        University of Texas Press.

Zelenietz, M.
1981   "One Step Too Far: Sorcery and Social
        Control in Kilenge, West New Britain."
        Social Analysis 8: 101–18.

Voodoo Death and the Mechanism for Dispatch of the Dying in East Arnhem, Australia

Harry D. Eastwell

REFERENCES

Barber, Theodore X.
1961   "Death by Suggestion." *Psychosomatic
        Medicine* 23(2): 153–55.

Cannon, Walter B.
1942   "Voodoo Death." *American Anthropologist*
        44: 169–81.

Clune, F. J.
1973   "A Comment on Voodoo Death." *Ameri-
        can Anthropologist* 75: 312.

Ellenberger, H. K.
1965   "Ethno-psychiatrie; partie descriptive et
        clinique." In H. Ey, ed., *Encyclopedie
        medico-chirugicale: Psychiatrie.* Tome 3.

Elkin, A. P.
1977   *Aboriginal Men of High Degree.* 2nd ed.
        Brisbane: University of Queensland
        Press.

Engel, G.
1971   "Sudden and Rapid Death." *Annals of In-
        ternal Medicine* 74: 771–82.

Gelfand, M.
1957   *The Sick African: A Clinical Study.* 3rd ed.
        Capetown: Juta.

Jones, Ivor H., and David J. Horne
1972   "Diagnosis of Psychiatric Illness Among
        Tribal Aborigines." *Medical Journal of Aus-
        tralia* 1: 345–49.

Landy, David
1975   "Magical Death Reconsidered: Some Pos-
        sible Social and Cultural Correlates."

        Paper presented at the American Anthro-
        pological Association Meeting, Dec. 3,
        San Francisco.

Lester, D.
1972   "Voodoo Death: Some New Thoughts on
        an Old Phenomenon." *American Anthro-
        pologist* 74: 386–90.

Lewis, G. A.
1977   "Fear of Sorcery and the Problem of
        Death by Suggestion." In J. Blacking, ed.,
        The Anthropology of the Body. ASA Mono-
        graph 15. London: Academic Press.

Lex, Barbara W.
1974   "Voodoo Death: New Thoughts on an
        Old Explanation." *American Anthropolo-
        gist* 76: 818–23.

Reid, Janice
1979   "A Time to Live, a Time to Grieve: Pat-
        terns and Mourning Among the Yolngu
        of Australia." *Medicine and Psychiatry*
        3(4): 319–46.

Richter, C. P.
1957   "On the Phenomenon of Sudden Death in
        Animals and Men." *Psychosomatic Medi-
        cine* 19: 190–8.

Rubel, A. J.
1964   "The Epidemiology of a Folk Illness:
        Susto in Hispanic America." *Ethnology* 3:
        268–83.

Simon, A., C. C. Herbert, and R. Straus
1961   *The Physiology of the Emotions.* Springfield,
        Ill.: Charles C. Thomas.

Thompson, Donald
1939   *Report on an Expedition to Arnhem Land,
        1936–39.* Government Printer. Canberra.

Warner, W. Lloyd
1958   *A Black Civilization. A Social Study of an
        Australian Tribe.* New York: Harper &
        Row.

Yap, P. M.
1974   *Comparative Psychiatry: A Theoretical
        Framework.* Toronto: University of
        Toronto Press.

1977   "The Culture-Bound Reactive Syn-
        dromes." In D. Landy, ed., *Culture,*

Medicine and Healing: Studies in Medical Anthropology. New York: Macmillan.

Wicca, a Way of Working
Loretta Orion

REFERENCES

Farrar, Stewart
    1983   *What Witches Do. The Modern Coven Revealed.* Washington: Phoenix Publishing Co.

Lex, Barbara
    1977   "Neurobiology of Ritual Trance." In D'Aquili, Laughlin, et al., eds., *Biogenetic Structural Analysis,* pp. 117–51. New York: Columbia University Press.

CHAPTER 7
Demons, Exorcism, Divination, and Magic

Psychosocial Interpretations of Exorcism
E. Mansell Pattison

REFERENCES

Ackernecht, E. H.
    1971   *Medicine and Ethnology: Selected Essays.* Bern: Verlag Huber.

Bahr, D. M., J. Gregoric, D. I. Lopez, and A. Alvarez
    1974   *Piman Shamanism and Staying Sickness.* Tucson: University of Arizona Press.

Bandler, R., and J. Grinder
    1975   *The Structure of Magic.* Palo Alto, Calif.: Science and Behavior Books.

Baroja, J. C.
    1964   *The World of the Witches.* Chicago: University of Chicago Press.

Barrett, W.
    1958   *Irrational Man.* New York: Doubleday.

Becker, E.
    1973   *The Denial of Death.* New York: Free Press.
    1975   *Escape from Evil.* New York: Free Press.

Bourguignon, E.
    1968   "World Distribution and Patterns of Possession States." In R. Prince, ed., *Trance and Possession States.* Montreal: R. M. Bucke Society.

Bourguignon, E., ed.
    1973   *Religion: Altered States of Consciousness and Social Change.* Columbus: Ohio State University Press.

Carstairs, G. M., and R. L. Kapur
    1976   *The Great Universe of Kota: Stress, Change and Mental Disorder in an Indian Village.* Berkeley: University of California Press.

Cox R. H., ed.
    1973   *Religious Systems and Psychotherapy.* Springfield, Ill.: C. C. Thomas.

Douglas, M., ed.
    1970   *Witchcraft Confessions and Accusations.* London: Tavistock.

Ehrenwald, J., ed.
    1976   *The History of Psychotherapy. From Healing Magic to Encounter.* New York: Jason Aronson.

Eliade, M.
    1976   *Occultism, Witchcraft, and Cultural Fashions: Essays in Comparative Religions.* Chicago: University of Chicago Press.

Ellenberger, H. F.
    1970   *The Discovery of the Unconscious. The History and Evolution of Dynamic Psychiatry.* New York: Basic Books.

Fairbairn, W. R. D.
    1954   *An Object-Relations Theory of Personality.* New York: Basic Books.

Foster, G. M.
    1976   "Disease Etiologies in Non-Western Medical Systems." *American Anthropologist* 78: 773–82.

Frank, J. D.
    1973   *Persuasion and Healing. A Comparative Study of Psychotherapy.* Baltimore: Johns Hopkins University Press.

Freud, S.
    1961   "A Seventeenth-Century Demonological Neurosis" (1922). *Collected Works.* London: Hogarth.

Galdston, I.
1963   *Man's Image in Medicine and Anthropology.*
        New York: International Universities
        Press.

Glock, C. Y., and R. N. Bellah, eds.
1976   *The New Religious Consciousness.* Berkeley:
        University of California Press.

Griffith, E. H., and P. Ruiz
1976   "Cultural Factors in the Training of Psy-
        chiatric Residents in a Hispanic Urban
        Community." *Innovations* 3: 11–16.

Grotjahn, M.
1976   *The Voice of the Symbol.* New York: Mara
        Books.

Hartmann, H.
1960   *Psychoanalysis and Moral Values.* New
        York: International Universities Press.

Henderson, D. J.
1976   "Exorcism, Possession, and the Dracula
        Cult: A Synopsis of Object-Relations Psy-
        chology." *Bulletin of the Menninger Clinic*
        40: 603–28.

Jilek, W. G.
1974   *Salish Indian Mental Health and Culture
        Change.* Toronto: Holt, Rinehart &
        Winston.

Jilek-Aall, L., and W. G. Jilek
1974   "Problems in Transcultural Psychiatry."
–75   *Ethnomedizin* 3: 239–48.

Kiev, A.
1972   *Transcultural Psychiatry.* New York: Free
        Press.

Kiev, A., ed.
1964   *Magic, Faith, and Healing: Studies in Primi-
        tive Psychiatry Today.* New York: Free
        Press.

Knox, R. A.
1950   *Enthusiasm: A Chapter in the History of Re-
        ligion.* London: Oxford University Press.

Langer, S. K.
1960   *Philosophy in a New Key: A Study in the
        Symbolism of Reason, Rite, and Art.*
        Cambridge, Mass.: Harvard University
        Press.

Lebra, W. P. ed.
1976   *Cultura-Bound Syndromes, Ethnopsychiatry,
        and Alternate Therapies.* Honolulu: Univer-
        sity of Hawaii Press.

LeVine, R. A.
1973   *Culture, Behavior, and Personality.* Chicago:
        Aldine.

Lévi-Strauss, C.
1956   "Sorciers et Psychanalyse." *Courrier de
        l'Unesco* 9: 8–10.
1963   *Structural Anthropology.* New York: Basic
        Books.
1966   *The Savage Mind.* Chicago: University of
        Chicago Press.

London, P.
1964   *The Modes and Morals of Psychotherapy.*
        New York: Holt, Rinehart & Winston.

Loudon, J. B., ed.
1976   *Social Anthropology and Medicine.* New
        York: Academic Press.

Lubchansky, I., G. Egri, and I. Stokes
1970   "Puerto-Rican Spiritualists View Mental
        Illness: The Faith Healer as a Paraprofes-
        sional." *American Journal of Psychiatry* 127:
        312–21.

Margolis, J.
1966   *Psychotherapy and Morality: A Study of Two
        Concepts.* New York: Random House.

May, R.
1975   "Value, Myths, and Symbols." *American
        Journal of Psychiatry* 132: 703–6.

Neaman, J. S.
1975   *Suggestion of the Devil: The Origins of Mad-
        ness.* New York: Anchor Books.

Pande, S. K.
1968   "The Mystique of Western Psychother-
        apy: An Eastern Interpretation." *Journal
        of Nervous and Mental Disease* 146: 425–32.

Parrinder, G.
1958   *Witchcraft: European and African.* London:
        Faber & Faber.

Pattison, E. M.
1968   "Ego Morality: An Emerging Psychother-
        apeutic Concept." *Psychoanalytic Review*
        55: 187–222.

Pattison, E. M., ed.
1969   *Clinical Psychiatry and Religion.* Boston: Little, Brown.

Pattison E. M., N. A. Lapins, and H. A. Doerr
1973   "Faith Healing: A Study of Personality and Function." *Journal of Nervous and Mental Disease* 157: 397–409.

Pederson, P., W. J. Lonner, and J. G. Draguns
1976   *Counseling Across Cultures.* Honolulu: University of Hawaii Press.

Prince, R. H.
1976   "Psychotherapy as the Manipulation of Endogenous Healing Mechanisms: A Transcultural Survey." *Transcultural Psychiatric Research Review* 13: 115–33.

Pruyser, P.
1968   *A Dynamic Psychology of Religion.* New York: Harper & Row.

Rivers, W. H. R.
1924   *Medicine, Magic, and Religion.* London: Kegan Paul.

Robbins, R. H.
1959   *The Encyclopedia of Witchcraft and Demonology.* New York: Crown Publishers.

Rosen, G.
1968   *Madness in Society: Chapters in the Historical Sociology of Mental Illness.* Chicago: University of Chicago Press.

Rosenthal, B. G.
1971   *The Images of Man.* New York: Basic Books.

Russell, J. B.
1972   *Witchcraft in the Middle Ages.* Ithaca, N.Y.: Cornell University Press.

Sartre, J. P.
1959   *Existentialism and Human Emotions.* New York: Philosophical Library.

Spiro, M. E.
1965   "Religious Systems as Culturally Constituted Defense Mechanisms." In M. E. Spiro, ed., *Context and Meaning in Cultural Anthropology.* New York: Free Press.
1967   *Burmese Supernaturalism: A Study in the Explanation and Reduction in Suffering.* Englewood Cliffs, N.J.: Prentice-Hall.

Thomas, K.
1971   *Religion and the Decline of Magic: Studies in Popular Beliefs in Sixteenth and Seventeenth Century England.* London: Weidenfield and Nicholson.

Torrey, E. F.
1972   *The Mind Game/Witchdoctors and Psychiatrists.* New York: Emerson Hall.

Turner, V.
1969   *The Ritual Process.* Chicago: Aldine.

Wardwell, W. I.
1965   "Christian Science Healing." *Journal of the Scientific Study of Religion* 4: 175–81.

Wheelis, A.
1971   *The End of the Modern Age.* New York: Basic Books.

Wijesinghe, C. P., S. A. W. Dissanayake, and N. Mendis
1976   "Possession in a Semi-Urban Community in Sri Lanka." *Aust NZ Journal of Psychiatry* 10: 135–9.

Wilson, M.
1951   "Witch Beliefs and Social Structure." *American Journal of Sociology* 56: 307–13.

Zaretsky, I. I., and M. P. Leone, eds.
1974   *Religious Movements in Contemporary America.* Princeton, N.J.: Princeton University Press.

Divination

Lucy Mair

REFERENCES

Bryant, A. T.
1966   *Zulu Medicine and Medicine-Men.* Capetown.

Crawford, J. R.
1967   *Witchcraft and Sorcery in Rhodesia.* London.

Evans-Pritchard, E. E.
1950   *Witchcraft, Oracles and Magic Among the Azande.* Oxford: Clarendon Press.

Kingsley, Mary
1899   *West African Studies.* London.

Rattray, R. S.
n.d.   *Religion and Art in Ashanti.*

Turner, V. W.
1961 "Ndembu Divination: Its Symbolism and Techniques," Rhodes-Livingstone Papers No. 31, Manchester.

Rational Mastery by Man of His Surroundings
Bronislaw Malinowski

REFERENCES

Boas, F.
1910 *The Mind of Primitive Man.*

Brinton, D. G.
1899 *Religions of Primitive Peoples.*

Codrington, R. H.
1891 *The Melanesians.*

Crawley, E.
1902 *The Mystic Rose.*
1905 *The Tree of Life.*

Durkheim, E.
1912 *Les Formes elementaires de la Vie religieuse.*

Ehrenreich, P.
1910 *Die Allgemeine Mythologie.*

Frazer, J. G.
1910 *Totemism and Exogamy*, 4 vols.
1911 *The Golden Bough*, 3rd ed., in 12 vols.
–14
1913 *The Belief in Immortality and the Worship of the Dead*, 3 vols.
1919 *Folklore in the Old Testament*, 3 vols.

Goldenweiser, A. A.
1923 *Early Civilization.*

Harrison, J.
1910 *Themis.*
–12

Hastings, J.
n.d. *Encyclopedia of Religion and Ethics.*

Hobhouse, L. T.
1915 *Morals in Evolution*, 2nd ed.

Hubert, H., and M. Mauss
1909 *Melanges d'histoire des religions.*

King, I.
1910 *The Development of Religion.*

Kroeber, A. L.
1923 *Anthropology.*

Lang, A.
1889 *The Making of Religion.*
1901 *Magic and Religion.*

Lévy-Bruhl, M.
1910 *Les Fonctions mentales dans les sociétés inférieures.*

Lowie, R. H.
1920 *Primitive Society.*
1925 *Primitive Religion.*

Malinowski, B.
1915 *The Natives of Mailu.*
1916 "Baloma." *Journal of the Royal Anthropological Institute.*
1922 *Argonauts of the Western Pacific.*
1923 *Psyche.* Vols. III(2), IV(4), V(3).
–25

Marett, R. R.
1909 *The Threshold of Religion.*

McLennan, J. F.
1886 *Studies in Ancient History.*

Preuss, K. Th.
1904 *Der Ursprung der Religion und Kunst.*

Schmidt, W.
1912 *Der Ursprung der Gottesidee.*

Seligman, C. G.
1910 *The Melanesians of British New Guinea.*

Smith, W. Robertson
1889 *Lectures on the Religion of the Semites.*

Thurnwald, R.
1912 *Forschungen auf den Solominseln und Bismarckarchipel.*
1921 *Die Gemeinde der Banaro.*
1922 "Psychologie des Primitiven Menschen." In G. Kafka, ed., *Handbuch der Vergl. Psychol.*

Tylor, E. B.
1903 *Primitive Culture*, 4th ed., 2 vols.

Van Gennep, A.
1909 *Les Rites de Passage.*

Westermarck, E.
1905 *The Origin and Development of the Moral Ideas*, 2 vols.

Wundt, Wilh.
1904 *Volkerpsychologie.*

Baseball Magic
George Gmelch

REFERENCES

Malinowski, B.
1948   *Magic, Science and Religion and Other Essays.* Glencoe, Ill.: Free Press.

Mandel, Brett
1997   *Minor Player, Major Dreams.* Lincoln: University of Nebraska Press.

Skinner, B. F.
1938   *Behavior of Organisms: An Experimental Analysis.* New York: D. Appleton-Century Co.
1953   *Science and Human Behavior.* New York: Macmillan.

Stouffer, Samuel
1965   *The American Soldier.* New York: Wiley.

Thrift, Syd, and Barry Shapiro
1990   *The Game According to Syd.* New York: Simon and Schuster.

Torrez, Danielle Gagnon
1983   *High Inside: Memoirs of a Baseball Wife.* New York: Putnam.

CHAPTER 8
Ghosts, Souls, and Ancestors: Power of the Dead

Sorcerers, Ghosts, and Polluting Women: An Analysis of Religious Belief and Population Control
Shirley Lindenbaum

REFERENCES

Alland, A.
1970   *Adaptation in Cultural Evolution: An Approach to Medical Anthropology.* New York.

Berndt, R. M.
1962   *Excess and Restraint: Social Control Among a New Guinea Mountain People.* Chicago.

Brookfield, H. C., and J. White
1968   "Revolution or Evolution in the Prehistory of the New Guinea Highlands." *Ethnology* 7: 43–52.

Bulmer, R. N. H.
1965   "The Kyaka of the Western Highlands." In P. Lawrence and M. J. Meggitt, eds., *Gods, Ghosts and Men in Melanesia.* Melbourne.
1970   "Traditional Forms of Family Limitation in New Guinea." *New Guinea Research Bulletin* 42: 137–62.

Burridge, K. O. L.
1960   *Mambu: A Melanesian Millennium.* London.
1965   "Tangu, Northern Madang District." In P. Lawrence and M. J. Meggitt, eds., *Gods, Ghosts and Men in Melanesia.* Melbourne.

Douglas, M.
1966   *Purity and Danger: An Analysis of Concepts of Pollution and Taboo.* New York.
1970   *Natural Symbols: Explorations in Cosmology.* New York.

Evans-Pritchard, E. E.
1937   *Witchcraft, Oracles and Magic Among the Azande.* Oxford.

Forge, A.
1970a   "Prestige, Influence and Sorcery: A New Guinea Example." In M. Douglas, ed., *Witchcraft Confessions and Accusations.* London.
1970b   "Learning to See in New Guinea." In P. Mayer, ed., *Socialization: The Approach from Social Anthropology.* London.

Fortune, R. F.
1963   *Sorcerers of Dobu.* New York.

Gajdusek, D. C., and M. P. Alpers
1970   *Bibliography of Kuru.* Bethesda, Md.: National Institutes of Health.

Glasse, R. M.
1969   *Marriage in South Fore.* In R. M. Glasse and M. J. Meggitt, eds., *Pigs, Pearlshells, and Women.* Englewood Cliffs, N.J.

Glasse, R. M., and S. Lindenbaum
1969   "South Fore Politics." *Anthropological Forum* 2: 308–26.

Goodale, J. C., and A. Chowning
1971   "The Contaminating Woman." Paper read at the 1971 Annual Meeting of the American Anthropological Association.

Hogbin, H. I.
1958   *Social Change*. London.

Kaberry, P. M.
1940   "The Abelam Tribe, Sepik District, New
–41   Guinea." *Oceania* 11: 233–58, 345–67.

Langness, L. L.
1967   "Sexual Antagonism in the New Guinea
        Highlands: A Bena-Bena Example." *Oceania* 37: 161–77.

Lawrence, P., and M. J. Meggitt
1965   "Introduction." In P. Lawrence and M. J.
        Meggitt, eds., *Gods, Ghosts and Men in
        Melanesia*. Melbourne.

Lea, D. A. M.
1966   "Yam Growing in the Maprik Area."
        Papua and New Guinea Agricultural Journal
        18: 5–16.

Lindenbaum, S.
1971   "Sorcery and Structure in Fore Society."
        Oceania 41: 277–87.
1972   "Kuru Sorcery." In R. W. Hornabrook,
        ed., *Essays on Kuru*.

Lindenbaum, S., and R. M. Glasse
1969   "Fore Age Mates." *Oceania* 39: 165–73.

Marwick, M. G.
1967   "The Sociology of Sorcery in a Central
        African Tribe." In J. Middleton, ed.,
        Magic, Witchcraft and Curing. New
        York.

Meggitt, M. J.
1964   "Male-Female Relationships in the High-
        lands of Australian New Guinea." In J. B.
        Watson, ed., *New Guinea: The Central
        Highlands*. Special publication of *Ameri-
        can Anthropologist* 66(4), pt. 2.
1965a   *The Lineage System of the Mae-Enga of New
        Guinea*. Edinburgh.
1965b   "The Mae Enga of the Western High-
        lands." In P. Lawrence and M. J. Meggitt,
        eds., *Gods, Ghosts and Men in Melanesia*.
        Melbourne.

Newman, P. L.
1964   "Religious Belief and Ritual in a New
        Guinea Society." In J. B. Watson, ed., *New
        Guinea: The Central Highlands*. Special
        publication of *American Anthropologist*
        66(4), pt. 2.

Rappaport, R. A.
1967   "Ritual Regulation of Environmental Re-
        lations in New Guinea," *Ethnology* 6:
        17–30.
1968   *Pigs for the Ancestors: Ritual in the Ecology
        of a New Guinea People*. New Haven.

Reay, M.
1959   *The Kuma*. Melbourne.

Strathern, A. J.
1968   "Sickness and Frustration: Variations in
        Two New Guinea Highlands Societies."
        Mankind 6: 545–52.

Wagner, R.
1967   *The Curse of Souw: Principles of Daribi Clan
        Definition and Alliance*. Chicago.

Williams, F. E.
1930   *Orokaiva Society*. London.

A New Weapon Stirs Up Old Ghosts
William E. Mitchell

SUGGESTED READINGS

Lawrence, P.
1967   *Road Belong Cargo*. Humanities Press.

Lawrence, P., and M. J. Meggitt, eds.
1965   *Gods, Ghosts and Men in Melanesia*. New
        York: Oxford University Press.

Voodoo
Karen McCarthy Brown

REFERENCES

Bourguignon, Erika
1976   *Possession*. San Francisco.

Courlander, Harold
1960   *The Drum and the Hoe: Life and Lore of the
        Haitian People*. Berkeley: University of
        California Press.

Davis, Wade
1985   *The Serpent and the Rainbow*. New York.

Deren, Maya
1953   *Divine Horsemen: The Living Gods of Haiti*.
        New Paltz, N.Y. [Reprint 1983.]

Herskovits, Melville J.
1937 "African Gods and Catholic Saints in New World Negro Belief." *American Anthropologist* 39: 635–43.
1937 *Life in a Haitian Village.* New York.

Kiev, Ari
1964 "The Study of Folk Psychiatry." In Ari Kiev, ed., *Magic, Faith, and Healing.* New York.

Laguerre, Michel S.
1981 "Haitian American." In Alan Harwood, ed., *Ethnicity and Medical Care.* Cambridge, Mass.
1982 "Voodoo and Urban Life." In *Urban Life in the Caribbean: A Study of a Haitian Urban Community.* Cambridge, Mass.

Larose, Serge
1977 "The Meaning of Africa in Haitian Vodu." In I. M. Lewis, ed., *Symbols and Sentiments: Cross-Cultural Studies in Symbolism.* New York.

Leyburn, James G.
1941 *The Haitian People.* New Haven. [Revised edition 1966.]

Lowenthal, Ira P.
1978 "Ritual Performance and Religious Experience: A Service for the Gods in Southern Haiti." *Journal of Anthropological Research* 34: 392–415.

Marcelin, Milo
1949 *Mythologie voodou,* 2 vol. Port-au-Prince.
–50

Mars, Louis
1946 *La crise de possession dans le Vaudou: Essais de psychiatrie comparée.* Port-au-Prince.

Maximilien, Louis
1945 *Le vodou haïtien: Rite radas-canzo.* Port-au-Prince.

Metraux, Alfred
1959 *Voodoo in Haiti.* New York.

Simpson, George E.
1940 "The Vodun Service in Northern Haiti." *American Anthropologist* 42: 236–54.

Thompson, Robert Farris
1981 *Flash of the Spirit: African and Afro-American Art and Philosophy.* New York.

Voodoo Science
William Booth

SUGGESTED READINGS

Davis, E. W.
1983 "The Ethnobiology of the Haitian Zombi." *Journal of Ethnopharmacology* 9: 85.

Davis, W.
1988 *Passage of Darkness: The Ethnobiology of the Haitian Zombie.* Chapel Hill: University of North Carolina Press.

Yasumoto, T., and, C. Y. Kao
1986 "Tetrodotoxin and the Haitian Zombie." *Taxicon* 24(8): 747.

CHAPTER 9
Old and New Religions: The Search for Salvation

Revitalization Movements
Anthony F. C. Wallace

REFERENCES

Burridge, K.
1960 *Mambu: A Melanesian Millennium.* New York: Humanities Press.

Gerlach, L. P.
1968 "Five Factors Crucial to the Growth and Spread of a Modern Religious Movement." *Journal for the Scientific Study of Religion* 7: 23–40.

Mead, M.
1956 *New Lives for Old.* New York: Morrow.

Wallace, A. F. C.
1956a "Mazeway Resynthesis: A Bio-Cultural Theory of Religious Inspiration." Transactions of the New York Academy of Sciences 18: 626–638.
1956b "Revitalization Movements." *American Anthropologist* 58: 264–281.
1970 *The Death and Rebirth of the Seneca.* New York: Knopf.

The Ghost Dance Religion
Alice Beck Kehoe

REFERENCES

Mooney, James
[1896] 1973 *The Ghost-Dance Religion and Wounded Knee.* New York: Dover Publications, Inc. (Originally published as Part 2, *Fourteenth Annual Report 1892–93,* Bureau of Ethnology. Washington: Government Printing Office.)

Cargo Cults
Peter M. Worsley

SUGGESTED READING

Worsley, Peter
1957 *The Trumpet Shall Sound: A Study of "Cargo" Cults in Melanesia.* London: MacGibbon & Kee.

New Religions and the Counter-Culture
Elizabeth Puttick

REFERENCES

Batchelor, Stephen
1994 *The Awakening of the West: The Encounter of Buddhism and Western Culture.* London: Aquarian.

Cox, Harvey
1979 *Turning East: The Promise and Peril of the New Orientalism.* London: Allen Lane.

Fitzgerald, Frances
1986 *Cities on a Hill: A Journey Through American Subcultures.* New York: Simon and Schuster.

Mullan, Bob
1983 *Life as Laughter: Following Bhagwan Shree Rajneesh.* London: Routledge.

Reich, Wilhelm
1968 *The Function of the Orgasm.* London: Ranada.

Roszak, Theodore
1968 *The Making of a Counter Culture.* London: Faber.

Wallis, Roy
1986 "Religion as Fun? The Rajneesh Movement." In Wallis and Bruce, eds. Pp. 191–224.

CHAPTER 10
The Occult: Paths to the Unknown

The Burden of Skepticism
Carl Sagan

REFERENCE

Sagan, Carl
1987 "The Fine Art of Baloney Detection." *Parade,* Feb. 1.

Occult Beliefs
Barry Singer and Victor A. Benassi

REFERENCES

Bainbridge, W. S.
1978 "Chariots of the Gullible." *Skeptical Inquirer* 3: 33–48.

Bainbridge, W. S., and R. Stark
1980 "Superstitions: Old and New." *Skeptical Inquirer* 4: 18–32.

Beit-Hallahmi, B.
n.d. *Cults in Our Culture.* Unpublished manuscript.

Benassi, V. A., C. Reynolds, and B. Singer
1981 "Occult Belief: Seeing Is Believing." *Journal for the Scientific Study of Religion.*

Benassi, V. A., and B. Singer
1981 "Occult Belief: Seeing Is Believing." *Skeptical Inquirer.*

Benassi, V. A., P. D. Sweeney, and G. D. Drevno
1979 "Mind over Matter: Perceived Success at Psychokinesis." *Journal of Personal and Social Psychology* 37: 1377–86.

Dawes, R. M.
1979 "The Robust Beauty of Improper Lineal Models in Decision-Making." *American Psychologist* 34: 571–82.

Einhorn, H. J., and R. M. Hogarth
1978   "Persistence of the Illusion of Validity." *Psychological Review* 85: 395–416.

Eliade, M.
1976   *Occultism, Witchcraft, and Cultural Fashions.* Chicago: University of Chicago Press.

Evans, C.
1973   "Parapsychology: What the Questionnaire Showed." *New Science* 57: 209.

Freedland, N.
1972   *The Occult Explosion.* Berkeley.

Gallup Opinion Index
1976   132: 25–7.

The Gallup Poll
1978   June 15.

Glock, C. Y., and R. N. Bellah
1976   *The New Religious Consciousness.* Berkeley: University of California Press.

Gmelch, G.
1978   "Baseball Magic." *Human Nature* 1: 32–9.

Godfrey, L. R.
1979   "Science and Evolution in the Public Eye." *Skeptical Inquirer* 4: 21–33.

Godwin, J.
1972   *Occult America.* New York: Doubleday.

Greeley, A. M.
1975   *The Sociology of the Paranormal.* Sage.

Hyman, R., and E. Z. Vogt
1979   *Water Witching, U.S.A.* 2nd ed. Chicago: University of Chicago Press.

Jahoda, G.
1969   *The Psychology of Superstition.* Penguin.

Johnson, H. M., ed.
1979   *Religious Change and Continuity.* San Francisco: Jossey-Bass.

Kahneman, D., and A. Tversky
1973   "On the Psychology of Prediction." *Psychological Review* 80: 237–51.

Keene, M. L.
1976   *The Psychic Mafia.* Dell.

Los Angeles Times
1977   Dec. 25, p. 1.

Mahoney, M.
1976   *Scientist as Subject.* Ballinger.

Malinowski, B.
1954   *Magic, Science, and Religion.* New York: Doubleday.

Marks, D., and R. Kammann
1979   *The Psychology of the Psychic.* Prometheus.

Marshall, E.
1979   "Public Attitudes Toward Technological Progress." *Science* 205: 281–85.

Mitroff, I. A.
1974   *The Subjective Side of Science.* Elsevier.

Morison, R. S.
1969   "Science and Social Attitudes." *Science* 165: 150–56.

Myers, D.
1980   *The Inflated Self.* Seabury.

Nisbett, R., and L. Ross
1980   *Human Inference.* Prentice-Hall.

Polzella, D. J., R. J. Popp, and M. C. Hinsman
1975   ESP. American Psychological Association. *JSAS* 5: 1087.

Psychology Today
1978   Nov. 22. "Newsline."

Robbins, T., D. Anthony, and J. Richardson
1978   "Theory and Research on Today's 'New Religions.'" *Sociological Analysis.*

Sagan, E.
1979   "Religion and Magic." In H. M. Johnson, ed., *Religious Change and Continuity.* Jossey-Bass.

Sales, S. M.
1973   "Threat as a Factor in Authoritarianism: An Analysis of Archival Data." *Journal of Personal and Social Psychology* 28: 44–57.

Singer, B.
1977   A Course on Scientific Examinations of Paranormal Phenomena American Psychological Association. *JSAS* 7: 1404. In G. O. Abell and B. Singer, eds., *Science and the Paranormal.* Scribner's.

Stark, R., and W. S. Bainbridge
1981   *American Journal of Sociology.*

Tversky, A., and D. Kahneman
1974   "Judgement under Uncertainty: Heuristics and Biases." *Science* 185: 1124–31.

Wagner, M. H., and M. Monnet
1979 "Attitudes of College Professors Toward Extrasensory Perception." *Zetetic Scholar* 85: 7–16.

Wason, P. C.
1960 "On the Failure to Eliminate Hypotheses in a Conceptual Task." *Quarterly Journal of Experimental Psychology* 12: 129–40.

Wuthnow, R.
1976 *The Consciousness Reformation.* Berkeley: University of California Press.
1978 *Experimentation in American Religion.* Berkeley: University of California Press.

Amulets and Anthropology: A Paranormal Encounter with Malay Magic
Raymond L. M. Lee

REFERENCES

al-Attas, Syed Nagib
1963 *Some Aspects of Sufism as Understood and Practiced by Malays.* Singapore: Malaysian Sociological Research Institute.

Angoff, A. and D. Barth, eds.
1974 *Parapsychology and Anthropology.* New York: Parapsychology Foundation.

Beals, Ralph L.
1978 "Sonoran Fantasy or Coming of Age." *American Anthropologist* 80: 355–56.

Beteille, Andre, and T. N. Madan, eds.
1975 *Encounter and Experience: Personal Accounts of Fieldwork.* Delhi: Vikas.

Castaneda, Carlos
1968 *The Teachings of Don Juan: A Yaqui Way of Knowledge.* Berkeley: University of California Press.
1971 *A Separate Reality: Further Conversations with Don Juan.* New York: Simon and Schuster.
1972 *Journey to Ixtlan.* New York: Simon and Schuster.
1974 *Tales of Power.* New York: Simon and Schuster.
1977 *The Second Ring of Power.* New York: Simon and Schuster.

1981 *The Eagle's Gift.* New York: Simon and Schuster.

De Mille, Richard
1976 *Castaneda's Journey.* Santa Barbara: Capra Press.
1980 *The Don Juan Papers.* Santa Barbara: Ross-Erickson.

Endicott, Kirk M.
1970 *An Analysis of Malay Magic.* Oxford: Clarendon Press.

Freilich, Morris, ed.
1970 *Marginal Natives: Anthropologists at Work.* New York: Harper and Row.

Gimlette, John D.
1915 *Malay Poisons and Charm Cures.* London: Oxford University Press.

Golde, Peggy, ed.
1970 *Women in the Field.* Chicago: Aldine.

Grindal, Bruce
1983 "Into the Heart of Sisala Experience." *Journal of Anthropological Research* 39: 60–80.

Harner, Michael
1980 *The Way of the Shaman.* New York: Harper and Row.

Lawless, Robert, Vinson H. Sutlive Jr., and Mario D. Zamora, eds.
1983 *Fieldwork: The Human Experience.* New York: Gordon and Breach.

Long, Joseph K., ed.
1974 *Extrasensory Ecology.* Metuchen, N.J.: Scarecrow Press.

Malinowski, Bronislaw
1967 *A Diary in the Strict Sense of the Word.* New York: Harcourt Brace.

Maquet, Jacques
1978 "Castaneda: Warrior or Scholar?" *American Anthropologist* 80: 362–63.

Murray, Stephen O.
1979 "The Scientific Reception of Castaneda." *Contemporary Sociology* 8: 189–96.

Nash, Dennison, and Ronald Wintrob
1972 "The Emergence of Self-Consciousness in Ethnography." *Current Anthropology* 13: 527–42.

Noel, Daniel, ed.
    1976   *Seeing Castaneda.* New York: Putnam.

Skeat, William Walter
    1900   *Malay Magic.* London: Macmillan.

Wilk, Stan
    1977   "Castaneda: Coming of Age in Sonora."
            American Anthropologist 79: 87–89.

Winkleman, Michael
    1982   "Magic: A Theoretical Reassessment."
            Current Anthropology 23: 37–44.

Winstedt, Richard O.
    1951   *The Malay Magician.* London: Routledge
            and Kegan Paul.

Index